Forecasting Urban Travel

For Nani Boyce and Stephanie Williams
and in memory of Gale Strauss

Forecasting Urban Travel

Past, Present and Future

David Boyce

University of Illinois at Chicago and Northwestern University, USA

Huw Williams

Cardiff University, UK

Cheltenham, UK • Northampton, MA, USA

Published by
Edward Elgar Publishing Limited
The Lypiatts
15 Lansdown Road
Cheltenham
Glos GL50 2JA
UK

Edward Elgar Publishing, Inc.
William Pratt House
9 Dewey Court
Northampton
Massachusetts 01060
USA

Paperback edition 2016

A catalogue record for this book
is available from the British Library

Library of Congress Control Number: 2014950742

This book is available electronically in the **Elgar**online
Social and Political Science subject collection
DOI 10.4337/9781784713591

ISBN 978 1 84844 960 2 (cased)
ISBN 978 1 78471 359 1 (eBook)
ISBN 978 1 78471 360 7 (paperback)

Typeset by Servis Filmsetting Ltd, Stockport, Cheshire

Printed on FSC-certified paper

Printed and bound in Great Britain by
Marston Book Services Ltd, Oxfordshire

Contents

About the authors

David Boyce majored in civil engineering at Northwestern University, and then earned a Ph.D. in regional science at the University of Pennsylvania. He also received the Master of City Planning degree from Penn. From 1966 to 1977 at Penn, he taught courses in regional science and transportation planning, and conducted research on urban transportation and land use planning programs. He then moved to the University of Illinois, at the Urbana-Champaign campus from 1977 to 1988, and at the Chicago campus from 1988 to 2003. His teaching and research concerned the integration and solution of urban models of travel demand and network equilibrium as well as activity location, among many topics. He served the Regional Science Association International in several roles since 1968. He was Co-Editor of *Environment and Planning* A and Associate Editor of *Transportation Science*, as well as a member of several journal editorial boards in regional science and transportation. He is now Professor Emeritus of Transportation and Regional Science at the University of Illinois at Chicago and Adjunct Professor of Civil and Environmental Engineering at Northwestern University.

Huw Williams graduated in physics and received his Doctorate in theoretical physics from Oxford University. He also obtained a Masters degree in operational research from Lancaster University and a Diploma in economics from the Open University. Between 1972 and 1986 he held various research positions at the Institute for Transport Studies and the School of Geography at Leeds University where his main interests were in modelling transportation and urban systems. In 1986 he moved to the School of City and Regional Planning at Cardiff University where he taught and researched in transportation and spatial systems analysis until 2008. He has published widely on the theory and application of transportation models, public transport systems, transportation investment appraisal and spatial models of various sectors. He has served as Short Notes Editor for *Transportation Research*, and was a member of the editorial advisory boards of *Transportation Research Part B, Civil Engineering Systems* and *International Planning Studies*. He is now Emeritus Professor of Transport and Spatial Analysis at Cardiff University.

Preface

We can trace the origins of this book to the start of a personal friendship and professional collaboration of over 40 years when we first exchanged views at the Institute for Transport Studies, University of Leeds, in 1973 about the similarities and differences between US and UK transportation studies. At that time one of us (DB) was on leave from the University of Pennsylvania, the other (HW) was at the very start of his academic career in transportation. Much more recently we started to write about the developments in these countries (Boyce and Williams, 2005). What began as a comparative interest gradually broadened into a study of the evolution of ideas in the field of urban travel forecasting. The advent of retirement has allowed us to rethink and develop this project, which has proved stimulating, frustrating and almost overwhelmingly challenging.

From very modest beginnings in Detroit and Chicago in the 1950s, interest in travel behaviour and forecasting has expanded into a world-wide activity of deep relevance to students and academics in a variety of disciplines, and to transportation planning professionals in all cities of the world. Some choose to study travel behaviour through sheer interest, while others have a more direct and urgent involvement in employing forecasting models to confront and anticipate the challenges of what is collectively understood as the urban transportation problem. The theories and models adopted to understand and forecast travel behaviour and the transportation planning framework within which they are set continue to have a profound influence on the way our cities function and how they develop.

This field is one of the finest examples of multi-disciplinary research and practice, where over the years ideas and methods derived from the natural and engineering sciences have both vied with and combined with those from a range of social sciences to guide the practice of planners and the decisions of public officials. Throughout the past six decades, the contributions from a wide range of disciplines can be clearly identified. The application of urban travel forecasting is computationally and data intensive, much of the relevant literature is technical, and a good deal is expressed mathematically, often conveying the impression of solidity, reliability and logical rigour. But there are many views on the adequacy of the techniques, methods and theories which support travel forecasting, and this has always been the case. We shall encounter a wide variety of viewpoints in the course of this book.

While many texts, reports and review papers cover different periods in the development of the subject, with different degrees of detail, we know of no unified account of the evolution of the field that is both sufficiently detailed and widely accessible. To write a history of these times is a daunting challenge, which we have attempted with very limited recourse to mathematics, but also without oversimplifying the essential ideas at the heart of the subject. We hope this book will interest academics, transportation planning professionals and concerned citizens, of whom many take an interest in planning decisions heavily reliant on travel forecasts. Above all we hope that it will serve the needs of students at the undergraduate, master's and doctoral levels in transportation engineering, operations research, economics, regional science, geography, environmental studies and transportation planning, as a prelude to more detailed study. We emphasise that this is not a text on 'how to do' travel forecasting, but we see it complementing standard texts as part of a course of study. Nor will any new travel forecasts be found here, although we report on many that have been made in the past. We hope to convey our fascination for the application of technical procedures within the social sphere, the ideas that underpin them, and why we believe it all ultimately matters greatly to the quality of life in cities throughout the world.

The field is fortunate to have benefited from the efforts of several remarkable people. We salute their contributions in grappling with undoubtedly one of society's most challenging and urgent problems – that of urban transportation. We have written to several of them, some of whom are long retired, to get a sense of the context and spirit of the times in which they worked, the way they viewed relevant problems and the innovations they proposed. Sometimes their views have been expressive and presented with such clarity that we have, with their permission, used their words directly. This exchange of views has been crucial in helping us to understand the origins and background of ideas and innovations, particularly where these might have differed from more standard historical accounts.

We have benefited greatly from the comments on these developments, and our account of them, from numerous individuals, in particular Staffan Algers, Richard Allsop, Kay Axhausen, John Bates, Martin Beckmann, Alan Black, Peter Bonsall, John Bowman, Michael Bruton, Walter Buhr, Richard Carr, Michael Clarke, Robert Cochrane, Denvil Coombe, Roger Creighton, Peter Davidson, Robert Dial, Birgit Dugge, Ronald Eash, Marcial Echenique, Paul Emmerson, Sven Erlander, Suzanne Evans,

James Fennessy, Michael Florian, Tony Fowkes, Marc Gaudry, David Hensher, Irving Hoch, Alan Horowitz, Sergio Jara-Diaz, Peter Jones, Niels Jorgensen, Frank Koppelman, Shin Lee, David Levinson, P.O. Lindberg, Jordan Louviere, Lars-Gören Mattsson, Anthony May, Chris McDonald, John McDonald, Daniel McFadden, Bartlett McGuire, Eric Miller, Anna Nagurney, Hugh Neffendorf, Yu (Marco) Nie, Klaus Nökel, Dimitris Papaglou, Michael Patriksson, Neil Paulley, Andrew Plummer, David Quarmby, John Rose, Werner Rothengatter, Roberto Sarmiento, Joseph Schofer, Simon Shepherd, David Simmonds, Howard Slavin, Kenneth Small, Frank Southworth, Frank Spielberg, Peter Stopher, Art Trager, Dirck Van Vliet, Tom Van Vuren, Michael Wegener, Edward Weiner, Kermit Wies, Ian Williams, Luis Willumsen, Sir Alan Wilson and John Wootton, and many others whose names have slipped from our memories.

Hillel Bar-Gera, Chandra Bhat, Elisabetta Cherchi, Andrew Daly, Frederick Ducca, Peter Mackie, Juan de Dios Ortúzar, Martin Richards, Martyn Senior and Maya Tatineni provided detailed comments on several chapters, for which we are especially grateful. We thank them all most warmly. They do not necessarily agree with all opinions expressed here. As ever, we remain responsible for any mistakes or omissions.

We thank the University of Illinois at Chicago for the use of the plagiarism-checking software system iThenticate, which we applied to confirm that all sources were properly cited. Our editors at Edward Elgar have been most supportive and have greatly facilitated the completion of our book. We wish to thank our colleagues and friends, too numerous to mention, and especially our wives, to whom this work is dedicated, as well as our extended families, for their interest and constant encouragement in completing this endeavour.

We would finally like to acknowledge the intellectual contributions of Professors Martin Beckmann and Sir Alan Wilson to this field and thank them warmly for their personal encouragement.

David Boyce
Evanston, Illinois, USA

Huw Williams
Cardiff, UK
June 2014

1. Introduction

1.1 BACKGROUND AND PURPOSE

Over 60 years ago, urban transportation was first subjected to systematic investigation, perhaps appropriately, in Detroit. The Detroit area study became the forerunner of transportation planning studies conducted in most large cities and countless other urban areas throughout the world. At the heart of this process were forecasts of personal travel and goods movement for evaluating alternative plans and policies. Significant planning decisions concerning transportation infrastructure investment and travel demand management policies, as well as major land use changes, have relied on the methods, techniques and ideas that emerged in this field over these six decades.

The aim of this book is to describe the major developments in urban travel forecasting models and methods of analysis that were first established in the US and Canada in the 1950s and 1960s, transferred to the UK and other countries, and then extensively advanced and refined through research and practice. We trace the major technical and theoretical developments, with periodic hints of revolution, and their selective absorption into planning practice. We consider the 'drivers of innovation' over the years, in particular: (a) the increasing range of transportation policies considered; (b) the widening evaluation frameworks; (c) the means of analysing data; (d) burgeoning computing power; and (e) the role of simple intellectual curiosity.

From travel forecasting's roots in operations research, transportation engineering and urban planning, we explore the widening perspectives of various academic traditions. In particular, contributions from economics, psychology, geography and regional science have provided insights and improved representations of the travel and location behaviour of individuals, households and firms as a basis for urban travel forecasts. We also discuss the different policies and projects that attempted to influence that behaviour and how their impacts were analysed.

As participants in our field of study, we are all extremely fortunate. Each of us comes to the subject of urban travel with different views and expectations. Each of us is a participant in the systems we study, often with strong views about the travel behaviour of ourselves and others, how the transportation system should perform, or how its shortcomings should be addressed. How we construct a framework to identify and address urban transportation problems matters greatly to the lives of citizens, whether they reside in the urban areas of the highly industrialised world or the rapidly developing cities of Asia, Latin America and Africa.

From meagre beginnings, research and applications in this field expanded to such an extent that vast published and unpublished materials have accumulated over the past 60 years. The synthesis and presentation of this material presented a daunting challenge for selection and emphasis. We approached the task of describing and interpreting the historical record by identifying what we saw as important 'themes' in the development of urban travel forecasting models and methods of analysis. As will become apparent, we adopted a sympathetic view of innovations and considered them against the background of approaches existing at the time. We resisted the temptation to compare the past unfavourably with the present. Indeed, there is little reason to believe that current approaches will seem particularly enlightened or sophisticated when assessed a few decades from now.

1.2   NATURE OF MODELS AND FORECASTS

Before introducing the themes and the questions they raise, a few words on the nature of travel forecasting models may be helpful. The questions faced by the pioneers of the field can be summarised as follows:

1.   What will be the pattern of flows in the transportation networks in 20 or 30 years under changes in population, car ownership and decentralisation of land uses?
2.   What will happen in the future if specific changes are made to the transportation networks?

Faced with scant historical data on the use of urban transportation systems, as well as rapidly rising levels of car ownership, early urban transportation studies performed 'base-year' surveys of (a) personal travel by individuals and households, and (b) goods movement by firms and other organisations. Using these 'cross-sectional' data, analysts fitted empirical relationships between the demand for travel and what were identified as its determining factors in the survey year.[1]

Their objective was to apply these relationships in forecasting future travel or assessing changes in travel resulting from proposed policies or projects. In this approach forecasting travel involves: (a) attempting to understand the nature, extent and cause of variations in travel behaviour among different population groups, including variations over geographic space, as a basis for assessing changes under policies and projects; and (b) making statements about the future, conditional on assumptions about improvements in transportation facilities and services.

Travel demand is expressed in terms of demographic, social, economic and activity location (land use) variables, together with monetary costs (fares, parking charges, fuel purchases, etc.) and level-of-service variables (e.g., travel time along a road or a public transport line, waiting and transfer times), collectively referred to as the 'generalised costs of travel'. We often refer to these quantities simply as 'costs', with the understanding that they embody several components, each with different units: time, money and so on.

Generally, the amount of travel is observed to decrease in response to increasing generalised costs. In turn, travel costs usually increase with the amount of travel, and are also dependent on the capacities and regulations governing movements in networks. Travel and its costs, and the functions relating them, therefore, are simplified representations of reality, embodying our understanding of these relationships.

We emphasise, in agreement with leading scholars, that travel forecasting is not directly concerned with determining transportation supply, such as the configuration and capacities of a road system, the network of bus services or pricing arrangements for a toll road, with its connotations of an agent actively managing the capacity of services and network regulations.[2] Therefore we avoid reference to what is sometimes referred to as a 'supply function' in discussing the mutual interdependencies between travel demand and the various costs and levels-of-service on the transportation networks. Travel forecasting is often used indirectly in conjunction with an evaluation framework as a basis for the design of transportation systems and the supply of services that they provide; we shall refer to this design process only occasionally.

Let us summarise these two sets of relations as follows:

1. A demand function: travel demand depends on a set of external factors and generalised costs. The external, sometimes called 'exogenous', factors, such as demographic and land use characteristics, are outside the immediate influence of planners, but may change over time.
2. A cost function: generalised costs on network links depend on link flows for given capacities and regulations.

These deceptively simple relations, expressed in mathematical form, conceal a great deal of complexity in the representation of the real world and are subject to a number of important extensions. One of the most interesting and complex is that the land use system itself is dependent on the transportation system and will in general be influenced by changes in the costs of travel. To incorporate this mutual interdependency between the land use and transportation systems leads us into the development of what are called integrated land use – transportation models. We shall have much to say about these at various stages of our story.

The numerical solution of these interdependent travel demand and cost functions under specified conditions and assumptions to prepare a forecast typically requires the determination of the values of millions of variables, usually by some iterative procedure. This solution determines the equilibrium flows and costs over (a) the transportation networks and (b) the associated personal travel or goods movement between different locations by various modes. This problem has proven to be as fascinating as it is challenging, and is of the utmost practical importance.

Forecasting has the popular connotation of projection over time, much as a weather forecast indicates the likelihood of rainfall at some future time. Although forecasting travel at some future point(s) in time, perhaps a few years or even decades ahead, is certainly part of our story, this book is also centrally concerned with forecasting the impact of plans and policies. The possibility of such forecasts rests on the expression of policies and projects in terms of changes in the variables (e.g., the times and costs of travel) that influence behaviour. Models have evolved considerably to embrace the following planning contexts expressed at various levels of spatial detail:

1. alternative arrangements of activity locations (land use);
2. investments in new roads and capacity expansion of existing roads;
3. investments in public transport systems, as well as changes to levels-of-service and fares;
4. traffic management, such as one-way street systems and allocation of lanes to particular users;
5. demand management, such as parking restrictions and road user charges;
6. applications of computer and information systems to operate and control transportation systems more intelligently.

In this book we are largely concerned with forecasting the response to plans and policies belonging to categories 1–5 at future points in time. We do not focus on operational issues, such as setting or adaptive control of signals.

From a technical point of view, forecasting and/or the analysis of policies require:

1. a 'base-year analysis' establishing analytical relationships between the travel demand and cost functions, and their respective sets of variables, from data obtained for that year and possibly for earlier years;
2. a 'reference state' analysis to determine the future levels of certain variables, such as land use, population, car ownership and employment;
3. impact analyses of policies or plans through their representation as measurable changes in prices and levels-of-service;
4. evaluation of changes from the reference state arising from the policies or plans.

1.3 THEMES IN MODEL DEVELOPMENT AND APPLICATION

From our present vantage point, we looked back and identified certain themes that proved relevant to developing models, to understanding the differences among them and in charting their progression to the present states of theory and practice. The themes with which we are concerned relate to: (a) the changing contexts of models development; (b) the ways in which demand and cost functions were specified, their parameters estimated, the mathematical relations solved, and travel forecasts obtained; and (c) our views on the validity of the whole enterprise. Many of the following themes are strongly intertwined and presented as such in the different eras considered. We describe them here for emphasis and clarity.

The first theme is the role of institutions in developing, sponsoring or promoting models. While academics and practitioners, separately or in combination, were often the 'drivers of innovation', a variety of institutions had a major impact on the funding, development, promotion or ratification of models. We refer to institutions in the broadest sense, ranging from national and local governments and, more particularly, public agencies charged with responsibilities for transportation systems, to research institutions, expert committees and funding agencies, whose pronouncements were particularly influential in the promotion of key ideas and sometimes set the agenda for model improvements. Legislatures sometimes also made pronouncements on appropriate model forms or modelling practices. We describe ways that institutions influenced or attempted to standardise the process of modelling, promote innovations, and disseminate material relating to models.

The second theme is planning contexts of the development and application of models. For 60 years forecasting models served an important role in transportation planning for the purpose of evaluation and informing choices among alternative plans and policies. This book does not concern the urban transportation planning process or how it changed over the years. It is sometimes necessary, however, to identify the role of models and technical methods within this process and how the objectives and evaluation framework were influential in determining the nature of models, the information that was sought and the precision of solutions required.

At the outset of the urban transportation planning field in the 1950s, travel and traffic forecasts were often provided in the context of a formal transportation study with a well-defined scope and duration. The terms of reference for such studies changed greatly over the years, with major implications for the development and application of models. Three aspects are particularly important: (a) the particular purposes or role for which model(s) were assembled; (b) the range of policies, projects or plans to which models were applied; and (c) the information required by evaluation frameworks for identifying problems and assessing the relative merits of alternative policies or plans for ameliorating these problems. We describe many innovations over the years to improve the design of forecasting models themselves and make them, in the modern jargon, 'fit for purpose'.

The third theme is the role and relevance of theory. The behaviour of land use – transportation systems is the outcome of many decisions by governments and by millions of behavioural units – individuals, households and firms – constituting the urban or regional systems of interest. Information about the behaviour of distinct groups of individuals or firms, perhaps identified by a zoning system and/or socio-economic characteristics, under conditions of change is necessary for the forecasting and evaluation processes.

The models we portray which seek to describe, explain and forecast system behaviour are simplified theoretical statements, invariably expressed mathematically, governing the relationship among many key variables of interest. What concerns us as we move through six decades of model applications is the successive conceptual frameworks and specific theoretical constructs for organising our assumptions about the current and future behaviour of personal travel and goods movement. Whether old theories or assumptions are discarded, or continue to stand alongside the new, is a matter of considerable interest in judging the theoretical maturity of the field and the requirements of practice.

Much has been written about the nature of mathematical models in the social sciences, and in economics in particular; and the similarities and differences between model developments in the natural sciences are often noted. We do not pursue these general issues here, but note a few key features that will accompany our discussion. At the heart of model development is the process of simplification. As Paul Samuelson [1915–2009] reminded us long ago:[3]

> Even if we had more and better data, it would still be necessary – as in every science – to *simplify*, to *abstract* from the infinite mass of detail. . . . All analysis involves abstraction. It is always necessary to *idealise*, to omit detail, to set up simple hypotheses and patterns by which the facts can be related, to set up the right questions before going out to look at the world as it is. Every theory whether in the physical or biological or social sciences, distorts reality in that it over-simplifies. But if it is a good theory, what is omitted is outweighed by the beam of illumination and understanding that is thrown over the diverse empirical data. . . . But recall again this important point. . . . how we *perceive* the observed facts depends on the theoretical spectacles we wear (Samuelson, 1970, 8–9, italics from the original text).

We encountered several conceptual frameworks which differ in the nature of the explanations they offer about travel behaviour, some having different implications for forecasting, evaluation of projects and formulation of policies. Some theories of urban travel will, in Richard Lipsey's words, 'allow us to comprehend reality in new and different ways' (Lipsey, 1989).[4]

The fourth theme is data requirements. Urban travel forecasting models are traditionally extremely heavy users of data relating to land use and transportation networks and services, the travel of persons and the movement of goods. Early transportation studies were characterised by very large household surveys. Over time important innovations occurred in the way that data were acquired, and used in establishing and testing hypotheses and in forecasting travel behaviour. As our story unfolds, we depict issues bearing on the relationship between models and data.

The fifth theme is solution of models. The outputs of forecasting models may be conditioned by the evaluation framework adopted in a transportation study. Typically these outputs include travel demands, vehicle flows on network links, and user costs associated with a given equilibrium state. The differences in these quantities between the equilibrium states associated with a specific plan or project are usually required. The necessity to determine such differences, which are often small, imposes a level of precision on the solution of equilibrium states associated with the forecasting model. Whatever are the merits or demerits of a particular model, some requirements on its solution are usually implied to secure sufficiently precise information. At various points in the historical development of the field, theoreticians and practitioners confronted important technical questions about the efficiency, precision and computational burden involved in solving equilibrium models. Specifically, three questions are relevant: (a) Do solutions actually exist for the demand and cost functions specified? (b) What are the mathematical means for determining these solutions? (c) Are the solutions determined to the precision required for the comparisons sought?

The sixth theme is validation and performance of models. How theoreticians and practitioners have developed criteria for accepting particular models for their intended purposes will emerge as an important theme of our discussion. In turn these criteria will be influential in determining the accuracy of forecasts. Forecasting travel one, five, ten or 20 years into the future poses special problems and may involve a multitude of potential errors. These may arise from a number of sources, such as: (a) our understanding of the demand and cost relationships; (b) the forecasting assumptions for variables such as land use and population, which represent the future state of the city or region; (c) errors in data; and (d) human error. In our discussions of developments and innovation, we shall be concerned with the framework for assessing the validity of models and how models performed in relation to outcomes.

The seventh theme is practical compromises in model development. Some models and methods that we describe are much more complex than others, in both the representation of behaviour and the resulting system of equations. Throughout the last 60 years, more sophisticated models were generally presumed to be more accurate, and therefore preferred over more simplified ones. Yet, with some exceptions which we describe, complex models are apparently not widely sought after or used by planners. We can anticipate some of the reasons, so we wish to alert readers new to the field that to judge a model or method solely on the basis of its technical or behavioural sophistication would be to miss an important point. Planners often find themselves in that awkward position of having to make and justify their decisions on the basis of limited data, uncertain knowledge and limited resources, particularly money, manpower and time (Shepherd et al, 2006a). Only if this point is appreciated can we hope to understand the gap that has emerged between the cutting edge of theory and the world of planning practice.

As already noted, an essential feature of travel modelling for the purpose of forecasting is simplification. In the complex systems of equations that represent the behaviour of personal and goods vehicle flows in the land use and transportation systems, what simplifications are justified? What are the implications of alternative assumptions for forecasts and policy decisions which rest on them? These are questions that lie at the heart of applications of travel forecasting models.

1.4 SCOPE OF OUR WORK

The contexts of urban travel forecasting are now very wide-ranging, and include: (a) projects undertaken for private companies, as well as those proposed and financed by public agencies; (b) various spatial environments from massive, densely populated urban areas or conurbations with rich travel options to relatively small towns in extensive rural hinterlands; (c) strategic considerations as well as specific scheme-based impact studies; (d) the initial sifting of alternative plans through to testing final detailed designs; (e) area-wide, corridor-based and specific local applications; (f) the investigation of the long-range impact of large, expensive projects as well as the short- and medium-term appraisal of much more modest schemes; (g) those projects for which the knowledge base of traveller behaviour is reasonably secure or, at least, largely uncontested, and those for which there may be very little available evidence. In this book we exploit the common features of many travel forecasting models used with the cross-sectional approach, rather than consider each of these cases individually. We did, however, set some limits on the scope of our discussion based on model types, policies and spatial contexts:

1. Application to world cities. Although the approaches that we describe had their genesis in the cities of North America and Western Europe, they were over the years applied with relatively minor modifications to the large majority of major cities and urban areas in the world. In some contexts, particularly on the periphery of some cities in the developing world, data collection and model building are highly problematic. Discussion of these cases is outside the scope of this book.
2. Operational applications. We generally exclude operational issues, such as those relating to traffic control systems, although on occasion we do refer to some models used for such purposes.
3. Policy and project evaluation and design. We are almost exclusively concerned with what are sometimes referred to as 'positive' issues – investigations of 'how the world works' and how people do behave under given conditions, rather than 'normative' issues of how people should behave and the means by which they may be induced so to do. We consider the policies and plans to be given rather than address either how they are formed or normative issues relating to the formulation of 'optimal' plans for the supply of transportation facilities and services. As noted in section 1.2, when used in conjunction with an evaluation framework, these forecasting models are widely used in the design of policies and projects.

1.5   LIMITATIONS OF OUR APPROACH

This book is about the evolution, influence and application of ideas in urban travel forecasting over 60 years. Although we fervently hope that it will add to an understanding of the subject, we do not view our work to be a definitive history of the subject. Any history is conditioned by the personal experience, knowledge, interpretation and social context of its authors, and we are even more aware of this fact now than we were at the outset. Just as we did not always accept certain early accounts in their entirety, others may judge ours as incomplete or subject to qualification. It will be for them to fill in the gaps, amend a viewpoint here and there and perhaps correct some bias. We are aware that our account, particularly its breadth and the depth in particular areas, has been influenced by several factors, which imposed limitations on our approach. We mention the following:

1. In assessing and synthesising material from thousands of articles published in our field, and the large number of transportation studies conducted over this period, we attempted to identify the main forms of model development, bring out the key ideas, and give credit to their originators. In synthesising this vast range of material, the possibility of omissions or inaccuracies is always present. Our own research experience has been confined to only a part of what is now an extremely broad and deep subject covering several academic traditions including mathematics, engineering, operations research, psychology, economics, geography, regional science and urban planning. We do not claim to have delved into all sub-specialities let alone possess expert knowledge in each. Others from different backgrounds or research experience would without doubt identify different themes for their discussion and emphasis. To partly compensate for this situation, we have sought the views of many experts, and in several places we point the reader to specialist texts and manuals where more details can be found. In an extensive and rapidly developing field we hope to have achieved sufficient perspective to identify the main issues, themes and developments; however, omissions are inevitable and we invite comments where these are considered significant.
2. In most cases, identification of innovations and their originators presents few problems. In the case of the significance of innovations, we sometimes resorted to existing papers, texts or reviews, sought the insight of experts, and drew on our own experience. Where attribution of ideas was in doubt, we returned to the historical record, reread relevant articles, consulted colleagues and relevant experts in the field,

and then came to a personal view. In some cases we were informed through correspondence that standard accounts are inaccurate, and we revised or revisited these. It is unlikely that we found them all.

3. While it is relatively straightforward to consult the international literature and conference reports to assess the contributions of academics and consultants, access to transportation study reports, particularly those subject to commercial confidentiality, is more problematic. New models with catchy acronyms emerge regularly, although few are highly innovative. While we are confident that our views are broadly representative of practice, we were unable to scrutinise the full range of applications. Important innovations arising in practical studies quickly tend to find their way into the international literature and, in turn, are disseminated back into future practice. In various discussions and correspondence, we were directed to unpublished work that is often of great interest and significance. Sometimes that work was published in less visible journals and perhaps covered later in more popular or widely disseminated accounts, and the original work is forgotten, as was pointed out to us on a number of occasions. We imply no malpractice here. Sometimes it just happens.

4. Even in a largely technical subject, the history as seen through North American eyes is rather different from that seen through European eyes; we tried to blend our two perspectives. Furthermore, we are well aware that reporting of innovations in this field is overwhelmingly in the English language, and through historical circumstances and by sheer weight of research capacity over the years this in turn is US dominated. Even less likely would be a knowledge of the French, German, Russian, Spanish, Japanese or Chinese experience both then and today. We were not able to do justice to many articles published in other languages or papers that were not presented at international conferences or published in the international literature. We had some help with important work published in other languages, especially German, French and Spanish, but this dilemma remains a major challenge for our field at a time when the research output of Asian countries is expanding rapidly.

5. Finally, since our intention is to present ideas to a wide audience, recording developments in one of the most highly analytical fields of public policy analysis poses particular challenges in how to deal with its formal language – mathematics. Often both the language and the techniques (such as calculus and statistical analysis) are central to the expression and solution of theoretical and technical problems. As both authors have mathematical backgrounds, we know well how their use in a highly technical field has been vital to establishing

logically coherent arguments and contributing to knowledge – even if it sometimes failed to achieve the level of knowledge creation and precision sometimes claimed. But the benefits of formal developments are often exaggerated when it comes to the discussion of principles and ideas, particularly when issues in the real world are 'staring us in the face'.

We therefore adopted a dual approach: the main text is free of mathematical analysis. However, where we felt that it would contribute significantly to the discussion, we added mathematical endnotes. References to specialised discussion are also included. Others will judge whether this approach has been successful. Even with the substitution of words for symbols, many parts of the discussion may prove difficult to newcomers. As noted in the Preface, we feel that it will be appropriate to read this book in conjunction with a technical textbook on travel forecasting and a formal course in order to augment the discussion and fill in the gaps.

1.6 NAVIGATING THE TERMINOLOGY AND ACRONYMS

Experienced readers of American and British transportation literature are well aware of differences in terminology between these two major branches of the English language. A few words of explanation may be helpful. We adopted British spelling throughout, except in quotations, where the original spelling is retained. The noun 'transportation' is mainly used in American English, whereas 'transport' is the preferred noun in British English. We agreed to use 'transportation' in this book, except in proper titles and quotations. In British English, 'public transport' is the noun used to refer to public transportation systems and services. In American English, 'transit', 'mass transit' and 'public transit' are all used. We decided to use 'public transport' to refer to these systems in all countries.

In the UK and some other places, the term 'transport model' is a convenient shorthand used to refer to travel forecasting methodology. We do not use this term here, except occasionally in the UK context, in order to avoid possible confusion for readers unacquainted with it.

In an effort to be concise and improve the flow of the text, we introduced a number of commonly used acronyms. Although they are defined when introduced, an overview and some explanation may be warranted.

Throughout the book, we abbreviate the United States of America (US) and the United Kingdom (UK). Names of governmental agencies at the national level are always preceded by these initials. The US Department of Transportation (US DoT) was created in 1967. Prior to that event, the federal highway agency, the Bureau of Public Roads (BPR), resided in the US Department of Commerce (US DoC). At some point shortly after the establishment of US DoT, BPR was transferred and renamed the Federal Highway Administration (FHWA), the acronym 'FHA' having already been used to designate the Federal Housing Agency. In 1964 responsibility for public transport was assigned to the newly created US Department of Housing and Urban Development (US HUD). Subsequently, this responsibility was transferred to US DoT, where the agency responsible for public transport was named the Urban Mass Transportation Administration (UMTA). Finally, in 1970 the US Environmental Protection Agency (US EPA) was established. In a few cases 'DoT' is also used to designate a state department of transportation.

The UK Ministry of Transport (UK MoT) was established in 1919, and continued in some form until 1970.[5] At that time transportation matters were transferred to the newly formed UK Department of the Environment (UK DoE). From 1976 to 1995, the UK Department of Transport (UK DoT) by and large had responsibility for transport problems. Following several name changes during 1997–2001, the UK Department for Transport (UK DfT) was created.

Cross-references are inserted at many places to connect one topic to a related discussion in another section. Often these cross-references state only the word 'section' followed by the section number. Transition and connecting phrases are omitted in the interest of brevity.

Finally, for historical interest, we give the birth and death dates of deceased contributors to our field and related fields. Living contributors are not so designated. In the Notes, we also cite Wikipedia web pages of many individuals for whom such pages have been posted. We have inevitably missed some, and others may be added in the future, so we ask readers to refer to Wikipedia for more information about contributors to our field.

1.7 CONTENTS OF THE BOOK

Writing about our field would be considerably easier had it developed from a single point in a generally agreed direction to an identifiable, unambiguous and unchallenged 'state of the art' where the world of practice harmonises neatly with that of theory. But that was not to be. The field developed in a rather complex way with theoretical advances intertwined with practical developments, the latter first moving ahead of, but later lagging behind, the former. The 'mainstream' of practice has also revealed significant variations over time, among various countries and in different planning contexts. This situation has prompted many questions about the distinct alternatives available for travel forecasting at any particular time and their relative merits for different applications.

We consider this rather irregular and sometimes disjointed evolution of theory and practice by developing a broadly chronological account of overlapping periods, where significant 'break-points' were suggested by either innovation in methods or policy development. Some have suggested that these correspond to changing paradigms, when one set of ideas and world view for interpreting issues is, by power of explanation or force of relevance to planning problems addressed, traded for another. (We shall later argue that this represents an oversimplified view of the realities of planning practice over the years.) We sometimes follow particular ideas up to the present day. We also backtrack to pick up various themes and, on occasion, to address what we consider to be missed opportunities where alternatives to the 'mainstream' appeared and only much later were seen to be of considerable value to forecasting practice.

In Chapter 2 we chart the rise of the field and the establishment of what became variously described as the traditional, conventional, classical, four-step or sequential approach to travel forecasting. This account is confined to developments in the US, and Canada, where the challenge of the motor age was first confronted with a 'systems approach'. This review takes us up to the early 1970s when political and economic imperatives (e.g., the grass-roots freeway revolts in the US and the first oil crisis) led to more emphasis on transportation system management and public transport.

During this period the 'systems approach' to transportation planning was exported to other countries, such as the UK, which also took up the challenge in the early 1960s of planning for mass motorisation. Chapter 3 addresses the transfer and application of the techniques and the innovations in travel forecasting that occurred up until the early 1970s, in part owing to their adaptation to local requirements. Departing from a largely common approach being applied in the US, we describe significant innovations in forecasting models, which led to major changes in the way that forecasts were prepared.

We then turn to a discussion of what some called the 'disaggregate behavioural' revolution, which emerged in the early 1970s. We describe a theoretical approach, with its roots in the statistical study of modal choice a decade earlier, based on the rational choices of individuals over discrete sets of alternatives, such as the choice between several transportation modes. Within this framework we show how the motivation and actions of decision makers (individuals and households) in a wide range of urban travel situations was described, explained and forecast, based on assumptions of economic rationality. This micro-behavioural approach, founded on what became known as the random utility maximising theory of discrete choice, provided an appealing and enduring approach to travel forecasting. Gradually it established itself as a practical alternative, and a complement to the traditional forecasting approach in urban transportation. It also enabled a theoretical reinterpretation and reformulation of the traditional four-step procedure.

In view of the extent and importance of this micro-behavioural approach, we present it in two chapters. Chapter 4 concerns those theoretical and practical innovations that occurred in a short but formative period in the early 1970s. These were largely associated with the theory and application of a particular model form, the multinomial logit model, but also included important early research on the relationship between the basic structure of models and hypotheses about travel-related decisions. Chapter 5 introduces a large number of innovations in model specification, parameter estimation and applications. In particular, Chapter 5 describes how theoretical arguments led to the development of new models and methods for analysis and forecasting of travel behaviour, which allowed a number of problems with conventional models to be addressed.

The micro-behavioural approach was greatly enriched in the late 1970s and 1980s by examining the wider context of individual and household decision making and impact of transportation policy at the micro-level. This development began an era of 'behavioural realism' in which many assumptions of the past were scrutinised and refined. By representing the demand for travel as derived from the need to conduct activities separated in space and time, activity-travel models offered an innovative approach. With their inherent emphases on constraints and interdependencies among trips and household members, they were initially presented as a distinct alternative and a possible rival to both the traditional and the micro-economic approach. Now they may be seen as part of a grand behavioural synthesis, their practical contribution being expressed first through the development of 'tour-based' forecasting models in the early 1980s and, subsequently, to 'schedule-based' analysis of travel behaviour in time and space. This framework and the models that evolved from it are the subject of Chapter 6.

In Chapter 7 we reflect on what we see as a missed opportunity. In the mid-1950s, concurrent with the origins of the traditional approach, an intellectually demanding book appeared (Beckmann et al, 1956) that proposed a conceptual framework, which might have been used to interpret and address some of the technical and theoretical problems confronting travel forecasting. We examine the contrasts between the traditional approach to specifying and solving the sequential procedure and what later became known as the combined model approach. We offer some views of why the latter was not recognised for 20 years and discuss its significance.

In Chapters 8 and 9, we consider the world of practice in more detail. Taking the US and UK as important examples, we examine developments of the traditional trip-based travel forecasting models as well as more advanced approaches. In addition, we record the innovations and practical application of models which incorporate the interdependency between the land use and transportation systems and goods movement. While drawing on the legacy of earlier times, we focus on the last two decades. In the early 1990s in the US, new legislation had profound implications for the specification and solution of travel forecasting models, as well as launching a major attempt to reform the way that travel forecasts were made. Important innovations also occurred in the UK in this period; however, here the emphasis was on the adaptation of traditional methods to address a broader range of policies.

From its beginnings in the early 1950s, urban transportation planning generally, and travel forecasting in particular, was closely associated with the development and use of digital computers. In Chapter 10 we take a step back and trace the history of these ambitious efforts from the early mainframe applications on through to the current use of personal computers, and associated developments in travel forecasting software. In particular, we note how changes in computing power had profound implications for the specification and solution of these models. We also trace the evolution of the principal software systems for urban travel forecasting.

In Chapters 11 and 12 we draw our story to a conclusion. In the former we consider the achievements and current challenges and offer some views on the future prospects for the field. Drawing on our themes we summarise the major developments in the theory, methods and practice of urban travel forecasting over a period of 60 years and reflect on the innovations that occurred to provide more satisfactory ways of undertaking existing tasks, to answer critical concerns and to address new requirements. We consider the longevity of the traditional approach, the hitherto limited application of alternatives, and the multiple 'states of the art' which characterise contemporary practice. We consider some views on current challenges faced and, without being prescriptive, discuss some questions and issues which might guide the future development of the field. In Chapter 12 we return to the context of urban travel forecasting and ask how innovative ideas emerged. Finally, we offer comments for those approaching urban travel forecasting as a field of study for the first time.

We are about to take the reader back to a time quite different from the modern age, not only in the nature and scale of the problems faced and the approaches to their resolution but also in the technology of analysis and what is sometimes referred to as the 'culture of research' in our field. In 1950 many countries were still recovering from the Second World War. The transistor had only recently been invented (1947), while the advent of the laser was a decade in the future (1958). Computers were extremely primitive by modern standards and practically unavailable for civilian use. The inventions of the now ubiquitous internet and World Wide Web[6] were decades away. The problems of dealing with large amounts of data from surveys of urban transportation were enormous. Indeed, many of the mathematical, statistical and data analysis tools that are now taken for granted were then being invented.

In those early days there was no 'culture of research' in our field. Transportation was not an academic discipline. There were no research institutes devoted to its development, few conferences devoted to the subject, minimal published material, no dedicated journals to serve the advances in the subject, and no automated way to conduct searches of what little literature was available. The modern age is as different and in some aspects unimaginable to those of 1950 as the world will be in perhaps 30 years for the citizen of today.

We are now ready to tell our story.

NOTES

1. For a definition of cross-sectional data, see en.wikipedia.org/wiki/Cross-sectional_data (accessed 9 May 2014).
2. Beckmann et al (1956, xiii–xiv, 59); Manheim (1979, 29–30); Florian and Gaudry (1980, 1–5); Sheffi (1985, 6–8).
3. en.wikipedia.org/wiki/Paul_Samuelson (accessed 25 December 2013).
4. en.wikipedia.org/wiki/Richard_Lipsey (accessed 25 December 2013).
5. en.wikipedia.org/wiki/Ministry_of_Transport_United_Kingdom (accessed 25 December 2013).
6. en.wikipedia.org/wiki/World_Wide_Web (accessed 10 January 2014).

2. Emergence of the traditional approach

2.1 INTRODUCTION

To understand the emergence of urban transportation planning in the US, try to imagine the situation in large urban areas such as Chicago in the early 1950s, a prosperous period following the Second World War. Their populations had increased substantially through in-migration from rural areas, especially from the south, as well as from abroad. Moreover, within metropolitan areas, out-migration to the suburbs was increasing.

In response to increased use of cars, and trucks for deliveries and goods movement, expressway plans proposed for the Chicago area in the 1930s were being implemented. For example, a six-lane, 13-mile expressway connecting north-west Chicago to its northern suburbs opened to traffic in 1951. Four radial expressways centred on Chicago's central area were planned, but construction funding was not available. A circumferential tollway with radial extensions into the outer suburbs was being planned. In contrast, following the peak ridership achieved in 1946, bus, streetcar and subway-elevated ridership had steadily declined.[1] Similar conditions were found in Detroit, Los Angeles and Philadelphia.

Profound changes were occurring in the planning of urban transportation systems in the US in response to these socio-economic trends and advances in urban freeway design. This chapter explores these developments from the viewpoint of the pioneering transportation studies in the Detroit, Chicago and Philadelphia areas, and the efforts of the federal (national) highway and transit agencies. These efforts were remarkable for their originality and ambitious objectives. Some succeeded in creating and applying novel travel forecasting methods; others had grand visions, but failed to achieve them. Coincident with and essential to these efforts were new computational capabilities, the first mainframe computers, unprecedented in memory and speed. Although tiny from today's perspective, these facilities, and the programs created for their use, enabled a huge advance in implementing new methods.

Following a short background statement (section 2.2), the innovations and contributions of the Detroit and Chicago area transportation studies are examined (sections 2.3, 2.4). Next, the activities of the Bureau of Public Roads of the US Department of Commerce (section 2.5) and the US Department of Housing and Urban Development (section 2.6) are described. Finally, efforts to extend the early urban transportation planning studies to the consideration of land use are chronicled (section 2.7). These sections consider the development of travel forecasting from the early 1950s to the late 1960s. Terminology of this period is used, for example 'trip table' rather than 'trip matrix'. A brief conclusion completes the chapter (section 2.8).

2.2 IMPETUS FOR URBAN TRANSPORTATION STUDIES

Urban and rural highway studies followed innovations in car technology early in the twentieth century. Likewise, studies of privately owned and operated urban and inter-urban electric railways provided the basis for their regulation. Reviews of these early studies lie outside the scope of this book. Two developments, however, are noteworthy.

The first was the early planning for an interregional highway system, later known as the National System of Interstate and Defense Highways. These efforts began in the late 1930s and resumed near the end of the Second World War, with the passage of the Federal-Aid Highway Act of 1944, designating the system, and the Federal-Aid Highway Act of 1956, funding its construction with user taxes (Weiner, 1997, Chapter 3).

The second was the initiation of urban origin–destination studies, also known as home interview traffic studies. Such studies continued sporadically through to the 1930s (Heightchew, 1979).[2] Following the resumption of origin–destination studies after the Second World War, more ambitious programmes were organised, first in Detroit and then in Chicago, known as 'urban transportation studies'.

2.3 DETROIT METROPOLITAN AREA TRAFFIC STUDY

2.3.1 Overview and Objectives

In 1953 highway agencies in the Detroit, Michigan area embarked upon an origin–destination study and the preparation of a long-range plan for highways. J. Douglas Carroll, Jr. [1917–1986] was appointed study director. Following graduation from Dartmouth College, and service in the US

Navy during the Second World War, Carroll earned the third Ph.D. in city and regional planning awarded by Harvard University in 1950. From 1948 to 1953, he was resident director of the University of Michigan Social Science Research Project in Flint, Michigan. Based on his analyses of urban travel and traffic, Carroll explored hypotheses related to the separation of residences and workplaces, and urban spatial patterns (Carroll, 1949, 1952).

In contrast to earlier origin–destination studies, the Detroit Metropolitan Area Traffic Study (DMATS) embarked on the preparation of a long-range plan for urban highways based on surveys, analyses and forecasts of future traffic. Its purpose was 'to insure effective functioning of the movement' of persons and vehicles 'by thoroughly understanding the nature of the movement and then by devising the most effective highway plan to serve it' (DMATS, 1955, 13). The principles of the study stated that 'a valid road network plan must':

1. Derive from a thorough knowledge of travel that is taking place today, its component parts, and the factors that contribute to it, limit it, and modify it.
2. Conform to and encourage the land development planned for the area.
3. Serve the *future* traffic demand.
4. While being consistent with the above principles and realistic in terms of travel trends, be economically feasible (DMATS, 1955, 13).

DMATS issued two reports (DMATS, 1955, 1956) describing its multi-step travel forecasting procedures. One difference between later studies and DMATS was its focus on expressway network planning to the near exclusion of public transport.

2.3.2   Forecasting Traffic Patterns and Testing the Plan

DMATS proceeded with data collection as follows. First, a home interview study was conducted in 1953 for the study area, including interviews at external stations for sampling travel in and out of the area. The home interview study obtained data on dwelling types, the number, age and occupation of residents aged five or over, and the number of cars owned. For each resident, a trip record over a 24-hour period was obtained: for each trip, the time and place of origin; the time and place of destination; the mode of travel; and the purpose. For stable residential areas, 4 per cent of households were interviewed; for outlying suburbs undergoing active growth, the interview rate was increased to 10 per cent (DMATS, 1955, 19, 21). Over 39 000 home interviews were completed, as well as interviews of 7200 trucks and taxis.

Second, trip rates were determined for five land use types by distance from the centre and density. Third, travel volumes between pairs of traffic zones in relation to travel distance were compiled. The findings showed that 'the travel volumes between any pair of zones would be proportional to the product of the number of trips terminating at each zone and inversely proportional to the "friction of travel" between those zones' (DMATS, 1956, 29). Fourth, maps of vehicular traffic desire lines were prepared showing the density of travel, as shown in Figure 2.1.

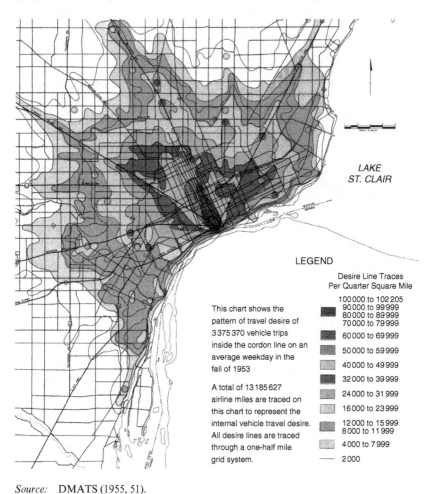

Source: DMATS (1955, 51).

Figure 2.1 Desire line density chart of internal vehicle trips in the Detroit area

The analyses performed were described in detail in the two-volume report. Although the actual procedure followed is not entirely evident, the following points seem clear:

1. All analyses and forecasts were prepared for a typical 24-hour weekday; peak period traffic was hardly mentioned.
2. Although public transport usage was inventoried, and was significant (15 per cent of all person trips), no forecasts were prepared of its use.
3. Trips were classified by nine purposes defined by activity and land use at the destination.
4. Trip rates (person trips per land area, or per floor area in the case of the central area) were then computed in terms of arrivals at destinations by purpose.
5. Departure rates from residential land uses were determined in relation to the means of four variables computed for 16 relatively homogeneous residential areas by relative income level, number of cars owned, distance from city centre and residential density.
6. A 'predictive formula' describing the relationship between zonal trip interchanges and the number of departing and arriving trips, and a function of the separation of the zones, was fitted (DMATS, 1955, 92–93). However, this relationship was not used in the travel forecasting procedure; instead, a growth factor procedure was applied to the survey trip table, which was an extension of the method of Fratar (1954).[3]
7. Much emphasis was placed on desire line density analysis. A technique of McLachlan (1949) accumulated the density of trips whose airline route traversed areas of one-quarter square mile. Extensive maps showing contours of these densities were prepared to visually inspect the travel patterns.

The findings of these studies were applied in preparing the 1980 expressway plan. Forecasts of population and employment for 1980 were made for the study area. Land use inventories and existing land use plans for the City of Detroit and the Detroit suburban area were used to devise a forecast by traffic zone of the extent of development in 1980. This forecast in terms of land area, or in the case of the central area by floor area, was the basis for preparing a forecast of future daily person trips.

Based on the analysis of survey traffic volumes, a modified growth factor method was devised, which included factors at both the origin and the destination of the trip (DMATS, 1956, 28–30). Suburban zones largely vacant in 1953 had their zero interchanges increased to provide the basis for a realistic 1980 forecast. External local travel and through travel were forecast separately. The forecast was validated by a thorough comparison with the 1953 survey.

Prior to DMATS, origin–destination studies generally concluded with the preparation of maps of desire lines of future travel patterns. Forecasts of the diversion of arterial traffic to a proposed expressway began to be performed in the late 1940s in the design of the first urban expressways, such as in California, Texas and Detroit. M. Earl Campbell [1902–1979] stated:

> The estimated allocation of traffic to a proposed highway facility is commonly termed 'traffic assignment.' The estimated allocation may indicate annual average daily traffic volumes, periodic directional movements, and composition by types. . . . The assignment of traffic to a proposed facility involves an estimation of volumes of the following components . . . : (1) traffic diverted from alternate routes; (2) traffic created by the new facility . . . ; (3) traffic resulting from intensified land use . . . ; (4) traffic increase due to growth in . . . use of vehicles (Campbell, 1952, iii).

The methods of traffic assignment described by Campbell were limited to assessing the impact of a new facility on an arterial corridor, and relied on relationships between the proportion of traffic diverted to the facility and the ratio of travel times, or distances, over expressway and arterial routes. DMATS advanced these methods by considering both savings in travel time and additional travel distance required to utilise a new expressway. Such methods were applied on an area-wide basis, evidently for the first time. The discussion of the traffic assignment procedure suggests the authors understood the complexity of their task. They knew the difference between 'the theoretical total demand for expressway service' and 'the actual flows of traffic that would obtain if the expressway network were in place' (DMATS, 1956, 86). They also considered that travel speeds on expressways would fall as volumes increased towards capacity, and that:

> With each additional increment of traffic, congestion naturally worsens. Under actual conditions, as congestion developed on one route drivers would tend to seek alternate travel paths [routes]. Thus, actual flows probably represent a condition where the capacities and comparative 'friction' of all possible routes of travel must be considered. This involves the knowledge of the number and capacity of all surface routes as well as of express routes (DMATS, 1956, 86).[4]

DMATS succeeded in making traffic assignments of the 1953 origin–destination traffic volumes to the existing road network and of the 1980 forecasted volumes to an expressway plan consisting of 46 miles of existing and committed expressways and 164 miles of proposed expressways. The assignments did not include volumes on arterial routes; rather the proportion of each zone-to-zone volume assigned to expressways was tabulated by expressway route. The plan was then revised twice, and a final expressway plan devised. The ratio of the benefit of the improvement to its cost was computed for each section of the expressway network.

Finally, DMATS appears to be the first study to combine an 'origin–destination study' with an 'areawide traffic assignment', resulting in a forecast of an origin–destination traffic pattern for a metropolitan area on a network of proposed expressways. Because of the joining of these two methods, the new concept of an 'urban transportation study' was born. Weiner (1997, 29) stated: 'DMATS put together all the elements of an urban transportation study for the first time.'

2.3.3 Computational Aspects

DMATS was remarkable in many methodological respects, including its application of computational methods of the early 1950s. In 1949, the IBM 407 accounting machine was the last and best of the electromechanical accounting machines. The IBM 407 read a deck of 80-column punch cards on an integrated card reader, accumulated totals, subtotals, or other simple statistics in counters made of gears, and printed the results on an integrated 132-column line printer.[5] Speed of operation was 100 to 150 cards per minute. As with all IBM punch-card equipment, except the key punch and sorter, a control panel was wired to specify: what card columns to read, what to do with them, and how to format the report. Although the IBM 407 was really just a big adding machine, creative use could be made of the control program. The machines were large and heavy, as shown in Figure 2.2(a).[6]

Factoring of the 1953 zonal interchange volumes was performed iteratively for the 254 zones plus ten external stations along the study area boundary. Of the 70 000 possible interchanges, 34 574 movements were represented in the 1953 survey data, plus added interchanges for six suburban zones with insufficient trips recorded in the survey. These movements were multiplied by origin zone factors and destination zone factors.

> The process adjusted all travel volumes from the inventoried system and thereby created a new system of movements more consistent with the predicted trip totals at each terminal zone or station group. The new traffic pattern thus obtained did not, however, meet the condition of having the predicted number of trips terminating at each zone or station group. . . . Therefore, the process was repeated using the newly predicted traffic pattern as the new point of departure. This complete repetition . . . is known as an 'iteration.' In actual practice, five complete calculations or iterations were made before the trip totals at each terminal point . . . closely approximated the totals predicted at each of these zones or station groups (DMATS, 1956, 31).

(a)

(b +)

Source: da Cruz, Columbia University Computing History, www.columbia.edu/cu/
computinghistory/.

Figure 2.2   (a) IBM 407 accounting machine (b) IBM 704 computer

Such a procedure was later called 'balancing the trip table'. Balancing a trip table of nearly 35 000 interchanges in five iterations on a tabulator surely required considerable ingenuity.

Likewise, a detailed procedure employing punch cards and accounting machines was developed for the preparation of desire line density charts (DMATS, 1955, 105–107) and the traffic assignment procedure (DMATS, 1956, 129–131). The assignment procedure consisted of three steps:

1. measuring the distance of the shortest route of travel via city streets for a pair of zones;
2. measuring the distance for a route using expressways for the same zone pair, including separate measurements of distances from the zone centres to the expressway ramps and the distance along the expressways, so that separate speed ratios could be applied to each;
3. calculating speed and distance ratios, and determining the efficient allocation of zonal interchanges to expressways.

Measurements were performed manually, but punch cards were used to record intermediate steps to automate the procedure partially.

2.3.4 Lessons from the Detroit Area Study

The final report of DMATS provided extensive details on procedures and empirical analyses, but no overall description of the travel forecasting procedure. Fortunately, Douglas Carroll provided these insights in what may be the first diagram of the sequential travel forecasting procedure, shown as Figure 2.3. The diagram articulates the innovations and advances of DMATS summarised below:

1. Travel forecasting is based on an 'inventory of daily movements of persons and vehicles', a 'record of land activities by location' and 'a detailed inventory of transport networks'.
2. 'The relationships of these surveys are examined and quantified. People in a particular land use setting . . . have particular travel needs. Travelers must move through the utility network. People with requirements represent positive potentials; land use sites to which people may go represent negative potentials; and people and vehicles moving through the network to equalize these potentials react to the network resistances and create flows.'
3. 'The economic activity of the community is examined and population change potentials are equated with expected future economic growth.' A forecast of population, economic activity and land use is prepared.

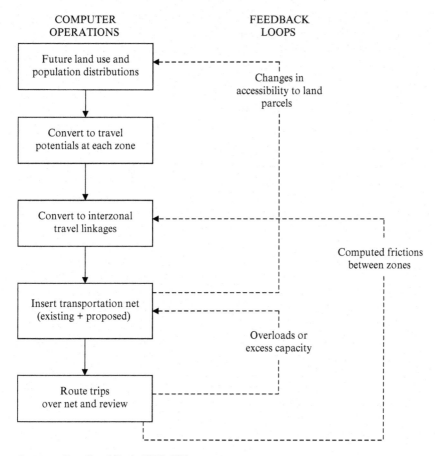

COMPUTER
OPERATIONS

FEEDBACK
LOOPS

Future land use and
population distributions

Changes in
accessibility to land
parcels

Convert to travel
potentials at each zone

Convert to interzonal
travel linkages

Computed frictions
between zones

Insert transportation net
(existing + proposed)

Overloads or
excess capacity

Route trips
over net and review

Source: Carroll and Bevis (1957, 187).

Figure 2.3 Urban travel forecasting procedure

'These gross estimates of future size are then translated into specific land uses which are distributed throughout the area.'

4. 'Based on future land use and population distribution, new travel estimates are inferred.'

5. 'These estimated travelers are forced to flow through a newly designed transport network. Gradually a plan suited to the future growth is tested and refined.'

6. 'These results are then related back to the initial assumption of growth. Land uses, and population distributions are reviewed in the light of an anticipated new transportation network. If changes result,

the process is repeated. This process is logical but difficult when it is
realized that balance and equilibrium are required at successive points
and for the entire model. Any change in any part of the metropolitan
area will disturb this equilibrium with consequent reaction toward a
new equilibrium' (Carroll and Bevis, 1957, 185–186, excerpts are in
quotes).

Figure 2.3 'shows that travel is inferred from land use, and trips are
forced to flow through a proposed network. The return arrows or loops
show that the results at successive steps feed back information that will
modify and repeat until a satisfactory solution is achieved. At present,
feed back is not automatic. . . . It is, however, certain that in the future
estimating and plan testing will become increasingly automatic' (Carroll
and Bevis, 1957, 186–187).

Figure 2.3 and the above statement describe clearly the vision of
Douglas Carroll and colleagues for urban travel forecasting. They understood that travel was related to urban activities and their locations, called
land use. They understood that interzonal interactions must be consistent
with travel times and distances. Moreover, they understood that interzonal
travel must be routed over road networks, which had capacity limitations
that affected travel times and costs. They used the terms 'balance and equilibrium' to describe interactions of land use and transportation networks
in reality, and adjustments of each system to the other. They described the
process of feedback of information as achieving a 'satisfactory solution'.
Carroll (1955) had earlier described a model of spatial interaction, which
he tested with data on toll telephone calls.

Douglas Carroll did not consider the contribution of public transport
in the Detroit study, perhaps because of institutional constraints. Also
absent were a concern and means of relating travel forecasts to the timing
of travel during the day; instead, 24-hour forecasts were prepared. Trip
frequencies by origin and destination and by purpose, however, were
explored in detail. Finally, the handling of large masses of data with
punch-card technology, and manipulating it to achieve credible results, is
truly remarkable.

Within a month of the presentation of the above paper, Douglas
Carroll and Roger Creighton (1957) presented a somewhat more refined
version of their thinking for the Chicago study. Among these statements,
one finds the following quoted points concerning the estimation of zonal
interchanges:

1. Zonal interchanges may be a function of opportunities for interchange
    between two zones;

2. Zonal interchange may be a function of competing opportunities;
3. Zonal interchange may be an inverse function of some combination of distance, speed, cost and/or convenience that, for lack of a better term, may be called 'travel resistance;'
4. Zonal interchange may be a function of demand, as expressed by the willingness or need to travel (Carroll and Creighton, 1957, 4).

They elaborated on these ideas as follows:

Travel resistance between zones, which must be known or estimated in order to predict zonal interchange, is a function of mode of travel, whether automobile, bus, train, or rapid transit. . . . Since travel resistances differ by mode, then zonal interchanges will also be a function of the modes which are available to serve any pair or group of zones. . . . the most logical place to study modal distribution is at the point where traffic is assigned, because it is there that flows on routes must immediately affect each other and it is there that the individual considers the use of competing modes to take him from origin to destination. Knowledge gained in the assignment problem must then be fed back into the zonal interchange problem to make any necessary changes in assumed modal travel resistances.

Feedbacks during the estimating process are essential for reasonable solutions. One of the most important is the effect which traffic flow has on zonal interchange. If the method of estimating zonal interchange predicts so many trips between two zones that the speed of travel is reduced, then the amount of travel between the two will decline and other zones, now relatively more advantageously located with respect to one another, may increase travel linkages until a status of equilibrium is achieved consistent with the new routes and the travel demands (Carroll and Creighton, 1957, 5).

Flowcharts accompanying the text illustrated the authors' concept of feedback. This brief paper shows that the leadership of the Chicago study had a clear vision of their task.[7]

Before turning to the Chicago study itself, we draw attention to Carroll's use of the term 'travel resistance', and related terms from that period. Brian Martin, Frederick Memmott and A. J. Bone, in their extensive review of travel forecasting methods, also used the term 'travel resistance'. Perhaps they were influenced by Carroll and Creighton (1957), which is Reference No. 40 in Martin et al (1961, B-2).

Other papers of that period, however, used a different term, 'travel impedance'. The earliest known use of 'impedance' is in a glossary by Lee Mertz:

impedance may be some average value for travel time. It may be distance if minimum distance routes are desired or it may be a combination of the two. It is generally agreed, however, that travel time alone will not give balanced assignments inasmuch as there are many other factors besides travel time that influence the motorist in route selection. Travel time is probably the strongest single factor, however, and thus furnishes a good point of beginning for defining link impedances (Mertz, 1961, 96).

In a slightly earlier paper with a similar glossary, Mertz (1960b, 29) had included only travel time and distance. Walter W. Mosher, Jr., at the Institute of Transportation and Traffic Engineering at the University of California at Los Angeles, published a scholarly paper on a capacity restraint assignment algorithm. In a detailed glossary, he wrote:

> Link Impedance – A value assigned to each link of the network. This impedance may be some average value of travel time, it may be distance if minimum distance routes are desired, it may be cost for use of the link, or it may be any other parameter or combination of parameters so desired (Mosher, 1963, 70).

'Impedance' was used without definition in an early Bureau of Public Roads report on the trip distribution problem. In defining travel time factors, the authors stated: 'These factors are a measure of the impedance to interzonal travel due to the spatial separation between zones' (US DoC, 1963a, III-4). In its report on trip distribution programs, Peat, Marwick, Livingston & Co. (1967, 30) stated: 'the contents of the skim trees supplied by the user could reflect some other measures of impedance than time alone'. This report was issued as US DoT (1969a), with the same quote appearing on page 30.

In the same year, Alan Wilson (1967, 254) wrote in his classic paper on spatial interaction models (section 3.5.1): 'impedance between i and j, which may be measured as actual distance, as travel time, as cost, or more effectively as some weighted combination of such factors sometimes referred to as a generalized cost'. The indices i and j refer to origin and destination zones. In later publications, 'impedance' fell out of use in favour of 'generalised cost'.

2.4   CHICAGO AREA TRANSPORTATION STUDY

2.4.1   Overview and Objectives

Douglas Carroll agreed to accept the challenge of leading an even more ambitious study of the Chicago area in 1955. He recruited Roger Creighton, also a city planning graduate of Harvard University's School of Design, to be assistant director for research and planning. Moving with Carroll to Chicago were Wilson Campbell [1925–2007], a transportation engineer, and John Hamburg [1928–2000], an urban sociologist.[8]An early description indicated the study was to last three years, with a budget of $2.35 million. The home interview survey, truck–taxi survey and other inventories of land use and transportation facilities were initiated in 1956. Nearly 50 000 home interviews, 7000 truck interviews and 73 000 roadside vehicle interviews were completed.

Although DMATS established the general concept and approach to urban transportation studies, the Chicago Area Transportation Study (CATS) devised and tested several innovative travel forecasting models. Some were successful and set the research agenda for several years. Others were less useful, and are long since forgotten. As with DMATS, data processing was a key component, as travel forecasting moved from electromechanical accounting machines to the first generation of mainframe computers.

The purpose and objectives of the study were stated as:

> The task of the study is to analyze the present travel behavior, to forecast what the future requirements of the metropolitan region will be and, on the basis of this information, to devise a long range plan for needed highways and for mass transportation facilities. ... In summary, the Study has two goals – first, to prepare a transportation plan and second, to provide the basic understanding and facts needed for continuing review and appraisal of the plan by responsible public officials. The plan to be purposeful and to represent the needs of the people, must have an objective. Stated formally, this is to maximize the ease of travel within the urban region, subject to the constraints of limited income, related effects on land use and development patterns, and a most probable estimate of future size and character of the region (CATS, 1959, 1–2).

The study was extensively documented and widely disseminated as an example of how to perform an urban transportation study. Its three-volume report, *Survey Findings, Data Projections* and *Transportation Plan*, became an *ad hoc* textbook (CATS, 1959, 1960, 1962). For those requiring more details, an extensive set of working papers and manuals was produced, together with a serial publication, *C.A.T.S. Research News*. Within a decade of the completion of the study, Roger Creighton (1970) described the philosophy, concepts and techniques employed in the Chicago area study in *Urban Transportation Planning*.

The study design strongly reflects the methods of DMATS with regard to developing relationships between land use and travel activities (trip generation), prediction of future interchanges of travel between zones (trip distribution), and choice of routes in a congested road network (traffic assignment). Although public transport systems were mentioned, the study description focused on planning for roads. A brief description of the electrical accounting machines and a 'medium-speed, magnetic-tape, electronic computer' conveyed the strong orientation of the study towards data processing and computation. A plan to build a cathode ray tube device, later dubbed the Cartographatron, for displaying desire lines of travel and related data was also described.

Not found in this early description are several technical innovations of the study listed below. In addition, the study innovated with regard to regional economic and demographic forecasts (Hoch, 1959). The three-volume study report is relatively non-technical. In presenting the key technical innovations, such as the opportunities model and traffic assignment, the exposition was more detailed and analytical. CATS followed the basic DMATS outline, but embarked upon several major innovations. Regarding travel forecasts, these innovations included:

1. forecasts of land use and the associated trip origins, destinations and car ownership patterns in the absence of a land use plan; all forecasts were prepared for a typical 24-hour weekday in 1980;
2. allocation of trip origins to modes and destinations to modes;
3. formulation and application of the intervening opportunities model for car trip distribution;
4. formulation of a tree-by-tree assignment method for car traffic assignment;
5. integration of the trip distribution and traffic assignment models into a single solution procedure.

2.4.2   Land Use, Trip Generation and Mode Split

Unlike DMATS, there was no land use plan for the Chicago area to serve as the basis for forecasting future travel. Therefore, the study made a detailed forecast of future land use for 1980 as a basis for forecasting person trip origins and destinations. An inventory of developed land was compiled for 1956. Land requirements for total development by land use type in 1980 were determined from a regional forecast, and allocated to undeveloped land with decreasing densities from the region's centre. Land unsuitable for urban development, as well as open space, was removed beforehand. The land use allocation procedure was detailed and empirical, and controlled by development density and concepts of competition for the use of land. Six types of developed land were allocated to 582 analysis zones defined on a square mile grid and covering 1237 square miles.

Based on the forecast of 1980 land uses, and trip rates by land use type derived for 1956, a preliminary forecast of 1980 weekday person trips was prepared. Next, an independent forecast of weekday person trips per household was derived from forecasts of zonal residential density (ratio of dwelling units to residential land use) and zonal car ownership per dwelling unit, averages that vary substantially by zonal location. The latter forecast based on households, being substantially higher than the land use-based forecast, was adopted as the controlling forecast of daily trips internal to the study area. These trips were then allocated to the six land use types and distributed to zones. In summary, total weekday travel in the region was based on car ownership and residential density at the zonal level, and distributed to zones based on the land use forecast. External trips to and from the study area were forecast, amounting to nearly one-quarter of internal trips. Truck trips were forecast by land use type.

Having established the number of trips originating and terminating in each zone by land use type at the origin and destination, a portion of all trips was allocated to two types of public transport: trips beginning or ending in the central area, and local trips. For public transport trips to/ from the central area, the opposite trip ends were allocated to outlying areas according to the distance relationship observed in 1956 travel and the land use forecast. The number of public transport trips arriving at the central area per day in 1980 was assumed to equal the number estimated for 1956.

Local public transport trips were determined as a proportion of total person trips at the origin and destination based on the observed use of public transport in 1956. In the case of trips from or to home, car owner-ship rates were considered in this allocation. For the Chicago study area, the number of local public transport trips was forecast to be 2 per cent higher in 1980 than in 1956, which was considered to be optimistic in view of substantial decreases in bus travel since 1945. The modal split allocation method devised by CATS sparked considerable discussion. The method was criticised for insufficiently accounting for the time and monetary cost of travel by public transport as compared with car (Stopher and Meyburg, 1975, 188; section 2.5.4).

2.4.3 Trip Distribution

CATS departed substantially from DMATS with regard to forecasting interzonal travel. DMATS had both applied the growth factor method and experimented with the gravity model. The new approach adopted by CATS was one of several important contributions of Morton Schneider [1928–1993], who had studied physics at the University of Chicago (Black, 1990, 35). Papers by Schneider (1959, 1960) provide insights into his enig-matic personality; he was clearly talented and able to exploit the early mainframe computers.

Morton Schneider's contribution to trip distribution was the 'inter-vening opportunities model' (CATS, 1960, 81–86, 111).[9] The attraction of Schneider's model was its simplicity and elegance. The model rested on two basic assumptions: trips prefer to remain as short as possible; a destination opportunity has a fixed probability of being accepted, if considered. The first assumption was the basis for ordering the destination opportunities for a given origin from nearest to farthest based on travel time or generalised cost. Since the probability of acceptance of each opportunity is small, the originating trips are distributed over the entire range of destinations, the extent of their dispersion being determined by a fixed probability. One should realise there was great scepticism at that time concerning the gravity model, which was regarded as an empirical regularity without theoretical basis, an attitude that changed substantially over the next ten years (section 3.5).

Schneider (1960, 136) discussed two shortcomings of his model: first, since trips are distributed independently by origin, the total number of trips arriving at destinations from all origins does not sum to the total destinations; second, there is a 'distinct difficulty in obtaining parameters for future or unknown situations'. The first shortcoming was also attributed to early gravity models (section 2.5.3). As became clearer by the late 1960s, trip tables can be 'balanced' to sum to specified numbers of destinations as well as origins (Wilson, 1967; section 3.5). That this aspect was not understood in the late 1950s may be partly attributed to computers being too small to perform such balancing calculations readily. Schneider's point about estimating parameter values for the future, of course, is a shortcoming of all such models.

The intervening opportunities model was applied separately to car and public transport trip origins and destinations, as allocated by the modal split procedure. For these applications, trips were divided into three classes: short residential, long residential and non-residential (Pyers, 1966, 74; Ruiter, 1967, 3). Trips in the two residential classes began at home and ended at work or other non-residential destinations. Short residential trips were effectively trips that ended within the zone of origin. Non-residential trips began at work and other activities, and ended at home, with distinctions made for central area versus non-central area locations of both origins and destinations. How trips were allocated into short and long residential was not described. The probability of an opportunity being accepted was different for each class, and effectively calibrated with an assumed trip length frequency distribution.

The study carefully analysed the empirical frequency distribution of car driver trip lengths as a basis for calibrating the model. Hence, the model was seen as a means for distributing trips with respect to an exogenously determined forecast of vehicle-miles of travel (VMT), as contrasted with forecasting total VMT. Travel time was the basis for ordering destination opportunities, although travel distance, time and costs were also considered (CATS, 1960, 83). No terminology such as travel resistance, impedance or generalised cost was used.

The intervening opportunities model garnered considerable support during the 1960s. Its theoretical basis was attractive to academics, and its operational features were considered positively by practitioners; Martin et al (1961, 150) offered a contemporary account of its advantages over the gravity model: its basic assumption is closer to the basic reasons for interzonal travel; the model is, computationally convenient, independent of zonal or regional boundaries, and requires no special adjustments to fit the model to data. Comparisons showed better accuracy and reliability than for the gravity model. Its disadvantages were described as: loss of simplicity and ease of application by inexperienced personnel, cost of obtaining necessary input data and difficulty of determining parameter values.

Kevin Heanue and Clyde Pyers (1966, 36) concluded on the basis of calibration studies that the opportunities model and gravity model had 'about equal reliability and utility in simulating the 1948 and 1955 trip distribution for Washington, DC'. The model was incorporated into the computer package of the Bureau of Public Roads (BPR) (section 2.5.3). Except for its use by CATS to 2000, however, the intervening opportunities model generally fell into disuse after the 1960s.

2.4.4 Traffic Assignment

The coincidence of three essential factors brought about the major advance of CATS over DMATS with regard to traffic assignment: (a) solution of the shortest route problem (Moore, 1957); (b) availability of first generation mainframe computers; (c) the insights and computing skills of Morton Schneider. Edward Moore [1925–2003] was a mathematician working at Bell Laboratories in the 1950s.[10] He devised a label-correcting algorithm, in which 'labels' are initially assigned to each node, and then corrected such that each label gives the shortest distance from the origin to the node when the tree is complete. Whiting and Hillier (1960) proposed a label-setting algorithm; these labels denote the shortest distance from the origin, but are determined in order from the origin.[11] The novel procedure implemented for road and transit assignment was described in CATS (1960, 104–110).

Douglas Carroll and his team, like their counterparts at BPR, approached traffic assignment as a somewhat mechanical procedure for placing origin–destination flows on to links of a road network. Evidently, they were unaware of the concept of user equilibrium described by Wardrop (1952), and they were not aware that Beckmann et al (1956) had formulated an aggregate demand model and user-equilibrium flows in a road network (section 7.3.2).[12] Abraham Charnes, however, had independently formulated a fixed demand user-equilibrium model, and worked with CATS on solving a test problem (Charnes and Cooper, 1961).[13]However, like others of that period, he was unsuccessful in devising a practical solution algorithm (see section 7.3.4 for biographical details about Charnes).

Creighton (1970, 248–254) described these developments as 'the story of a breakthrough'; additional details were given by Carroll (1959). As Carroll recognised that a capability to finding shortest routes through a network was crucial to moving traffic assignment from a cumbersome hand accounting procedure to a computer-based method, a contract was given to Armour Research Foundation, an independent research institute in Chicago. The researchers identified the shortest route algorithm of Moore (1957), and began applying it to a small test problem. Based on Armour's investigation, Schneider wrote a computer program capable of solving such problems for CATS's 582-zone, 2500-link road network.

Later, Schneider and Carroll recognised that link capacities needed to be taken into account in the calculation of shortest routes, leading to the creation of the so-called capacity restraint method to modify the results to take account of congestion. Solving the shortest route problem was only the first of three tools needed to find the route and link flows such that, for each origin–destination (O-D) pair, the flows were on routes of equal and minimal travel costs, as Wardrop (1952) had stated in his first criterion. Also required was a way to load the O-D flows on to the network, which Schneider devised, and a way to average successive assignments in order to move towards the desired equilibrium.

From the description of the traffic assignment procedure in CATS (1960, 104–110), one may grasp how the trip distribution and assignment problem was solved in an integrated manner:

1. for each origin zone, find shortest route travel times from each origin zone to all destination zones, assuming zero-volume link travel times;
2. use these shortest route travel times to order the destination opportunities from nearest to farthest;
3. apply the intervening opportunities model to compute the origin–destination flows from that origin to each destination;
4. load these flows on to the links of the subnetwork constituting each shortest route.

Following the completion of this procedure for all origin zones, and storing the origin–destination trip table determined by this process, perform a second capacity restraint assignment as follows:

1. choose an origin zone at random;
2. update link travel times based on route and link flows assigned so far;
3. solve the shortest route problem for that origin;
4. allocate the flow for each O-D pair previously found to the shortest routes emanating from that origin, and return to step 1; continue until all origin zones are processed.

The travel time function for performing step 2, updating the link travel time, was not given in the CATS final report. The procedure was to multiply the zero-volume link travel time by a factor of 2 raised to the power of the volume-to-capacity ratio.[14] The source of this function is unknown, but presumably it was specified by Schneider. The function differs substantially from the BPR function (section 2.5.5). For example, if volume equals capacity, the zero-volume time is doubled, whereas for the BPR function it is increased by 15 per cent.

This assignment procedure was later dubbed 'tree-by-tree incremental assignment', since each shortest route tree was loaded on to the network after the link times were updated. The procedure was solved twice for each origin zone, once to compute the trip table, and a second time to perform the congested assignment. In contrast, in iterative assignment and another form of incremental assignment, the set of shortest route trees was solved several times (sections 2.5.5, 2.5.6). Hence, the tree-by-tree assignment procedure was considered to provide a reasonable approximation to the solution of the congested assignment problem. Only one route was used for each origin–destination zone pair in this solution, in contrast to the general situation of possibly many used routes at equilibrium. Since heavily loaded links were avoided, the flows were spread over alternative links, perhaps in a rough approximation of a user-equilibrium solution. Just how rough was not determined, since it was unknown at that time how to assess the quality of an assignment in terms of user equilibrium (section 7.4.2.4).

The travel forecasting procedure devised by CATS considered the 24-hour weekday as a single period. That is, travel for all purposes during the 24 hours was assigned to the road network. The daily road capacities during those 24 hours were based on the percentage of daily volume occurring in the highest one-hour period, which was 11 per cent. To account for the fact that 60 per cent of the flow occurred in the peak direction, the percentage was adjusted to 13.2 per cent. Hence, daily capacity was set equal to hourly capacity divided by 0.132 (Haikalis and Joseph, 1961, 45).

In reality, of course, traffic is not distributed uniformly over the 24-hour day. Therefore, a procedure was developed for reducing the estimated total travel delay according to the empirically observed relationship between the hourly rank of the traffic flow and the proportion of daily traffic during that hour. To our knowledge, this procedure is unique, and was not applied in subsequent studies. Using a rank–size relationship, 'the integration of each hour's expected delay over that hour's fraction of the daily flow provided a weighted average daily delay' (Haikalis and Joseph, 1961, 48).

At the time of its implementation in the late 1950s, the combined trip distribution and traffic assignment procedure implemented by Schneider was a very substantial advance. An O-D trip table could be computed and assigned to represent a congested network with the computation of short-est route trees equal in number to twice the number of zones. As compared with the highly cumbersome procedure used by DMATS just a few years earlier, now several alternative roadway plans could be evaluated.

2.4.5 Computational Aspects

The Chicago study coincided with the availability of first generation main-frame computers, in particular the IBM 704. The IBM 704 computer was the first mass-produced computer with core memory and floating point arithmetic, shown in Figure 2.2(b).[15] The IBM 704 installation available to CATS was in Cincinnati, Ohio. To solve the intervening opportunities and traffic assignment models, Morton Schneider travelled to Cincinnati and worked through the weekend, debugging and running his programs. When the program finally worked after months of effort, he related that one unused word of memory remained.[16]

According to Carroll (1959), an assignment to the arterial and express-way network required about 11 hours, 4 hours for the zero-flow assignment and 7 hours for the capacity restraint assignment (CATS, 1960, 108). The inputs consisted of 5225 data cards representing the existing network and 630 cards representing zonal trip origins and destinations. Computation of one copy, consisting of the shortest routes from one origin, calculation and assignment of trips, and loading of trips on to links, required about one minute and computing costs of $10. Carroll estimated that to perform these calculations by hand would require five person-weeks and cost $450.

A second technological innovation of CATS was the invention and application of the Cartographatron. Its development also marked the end of the transition from origin–destination surveys portrayed as desire lines to forecasting of travel on road and transit networks. DMATS began that transition with the use of electromechanical accounting machines to assign origin–destination flows to a road network. CATS completed the transi-tion with the heuristic solution of the trip distribution and assignment problem. The development of the Cartographatron was a parallel effort.

Douglas Carroll was a visionary planner; 'he firmly believed in the rational planning process and thought that planning should be made as scientific as possible' (Black, 1990, 28). Carroll understood the potential of the human eye and brain to process and analyse information. Perhaps based on the new technology of that day, black-and-white television, he imagined that data representing trips could be displayed on a cathode ray tube and captured on film for analysis and representation of observed and desired travel patterns. Such a display was the essence of the Cartographatron, which displayed trips recorded on magnetic tape as streaks of light on a tube to be captured on film. Photographs produced by the device graced the covers of the three volumes of the CATS reports; the device was described in Carroll and Jones (1960). Figure 2.4 shows an example of a map produced with the Cartographatron.

According to Carroll, the Cartographatron performed its intended tasks well and inexpensively. The results extensively illustrated the CATS reports, perhaps adding to their credibility. In the end, these photos lacked the specificity of the computed vehicle-hours and vehicle-miles of travel for road network alternative plans based on the newly developed traffic assignment method. Roger Creighton later remarked: 'the Cartographatron was a brilliant success. No longer were we slaves to the notion that all travel goes to the central business district. . . . Travel turned out to be much more evenly spread, more scattered in direction. . . . the complexity was enormous; our ignorance had been very great' (Creighton, 1970, 36).

Perhaps the views of these pioneers should be accepted at face value. However, CATS was the only transportation study to use the device.[17] Maybe once these lessons were learned they did not need to be repeated elsewhere. Moreover, the Cartographatron was not used to analyse the forecasts of travel for 1980, but was restricted only to the analysis of the 1956 origin–destination survey. The device was remarkable in its time, but its usefulness was limited, as abilities to analyse and forecast the effects of travel on road network congestion rapidly improved. One may also wonder whether Carroll had higher aspirations for this machine. Irving Hoch recalled that the original hope for the Cartographatron was to develop recommendations for locations of expressways, including estimates of roadway usage.[18]

2.4.6 Lessons from the Chicago Area Study

For summarising the advances contributed by CATS, a contemporary review such as was provided by Carroll and Bevis (1957) is unavailable. Creighton (1970) gave a general policy assessment of strengths

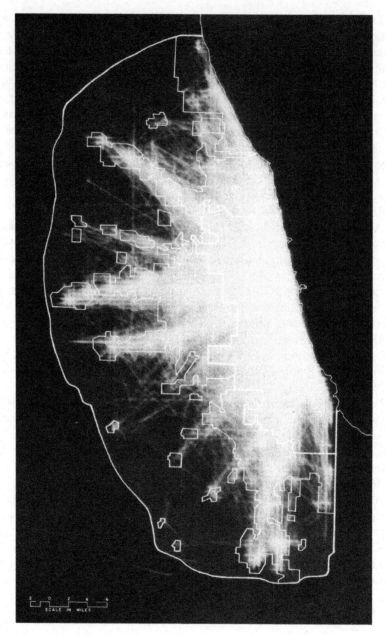

Source: CATS (1959, 46).

Figure 2.4   Desire lines of internal person trips in the Chicago area

and weaknesses, but no detailed technical critique. Martin et al (1961) recorded the state of practice, but did not offer a critical assessment. The advances of CATS may be summarised as follows:

1. A land use forecast was prepared based on detailed inventories and past trends.
2. Detailed trip rates by land use and zonal location were prepared and used to make forecasts of total travel based on residential density and car ownership.
3. Procedures for allocating portions of trip origins and destinations to transit were devised, taking into account the important role of the central area in determining mode choice.
4. A new method for distributing three classes of trips from origins to destinations by mode was formulated from simple propositions, implemented and tested.
5. A new traffic assignment method based on shortest routes was devised and implemented successfully.
6. The trip distribution and assignment methods were implemented on a mainframe computer, and combined to solve these two steps logically into a single procedure.

The shortcomings of CATS from the perspective of the early 1960s included the following:

1. CATS was criticised by planners for not being based on a land use plan; however, an effort based on land use – transportation alternatives followed in the mid-1960s (Boyce et al, 1970) (section 2.7.3).
2. Despite its success in improving the theoretical basis for modelling origin–destination travel, the study did not contribute to an understanding of the theory of traffic assignment; the mathematical formulation of the traffic assignment method, which is related to the method utilised by CATS, was evidently not appreciated (Beckmann et al, 1956; Charnes and Cooper, 1961; see also section 7.3).
3. CATS, as well as others, continued to approach the travel forecasting problem in terms of the 24-hour weekday, rather than the congested peak period; to the authors' knowledge, the implications of this approach in terms of forecast error were never fully explored.

Alan Black (1990) described the conceptual approach from a planning theory perspective, and added insightful details about the attitudes and working conditions of the staff. Many technical papers were published

during the study period. John McDonald (1988) provided a useful retrospective of the 1980 forecasts.

The contribution of the completed study to urban travel forecasting practice, and theory, was immense and unprecedented. A prototype
procedure with extensive documentation was now available for others to
follow. The use of first generation mainframe computers was successfully
demonstrated. Drawing on the experience of the Detroit and Chicago area
studies, as well as the efforts of the Bureau of Public Roads, the urban
transportation planning process could be transferred to large urban areas
throughout the country, as mandated by the 1962 Federal-Aid Highway
Act (Weiner, 1997, 37–38).

Before turning to other developments of travel forecasting methods,
we briefly consider the fate of the 1980 Chicago area plan. The Chicago
study devised an expressway spacing formula and an economic evaluation method to guide the design of the road network.[19] The spacing
formula provided a systematic framework for generating alternative plans
of increasing density of facilities, to which the travel forecasting models
could be applied to gauge their performance in terms of vehicle-miles
and vehicle-hours of travel as well as system travel time, operating costs
and accident costs. CATS prepared, tested, evaluated and presented six
expressway plans. The evaluation of the roadway plan concluded that an
extensive system of expressways was efficient and desirable (Haikalis and
Joseph, 1961). Perhaps discouraged by the complexity of the method, later
transportation studies did not explore this approach further (Creighton,
1970, 283, footnote 3).[20]

In the final analysis, the plan did not win the support of local and state
elected officials. A discussion between Douglas Carroll and Richard J.
Daley [1902–1976], the powerful mayor of the City of Chicago from 1955
until his death, was reported in the *Chicago Sun-Times*, following the
release of Volume 3 (CATS, 1962). In proposing the 1980 plan, Carroll
stated to the press:

> We have too much traffic to handle on the streets. . . . Our proposal is . . . a
> carefully designed and spaced system of freeways which leave the surface and
> go underneath or above the ground. With this kind of system we can function
> very effectively, leaving little islands of local residential areas and drawing the
> bulk traffic off to these heavy-duty systems that will carry it below or above-
> ground. And thus we will provide a workable network of roads and streets.

According to *Sun-Times* reporter Donald Schwartz:

> one of Carroll's main premises is that the city will thin out, being reduced in
> time to an area of density resembling a suburb. Carroll contends that this is

because of personal choice – a desire to live in areas of reduced density. Others say that all-out catering to the auto, through expressway building, would force the change. But wherever the truth lies, Carroll foresees a steady dispersal of the city (Schwartz, 1962, 1).

Only one expressway (I-355) recommended by the 1980 plan was constructed within the CATS study area in addition to those facilities whose locations were specified in the existing and committed system of 1955.[21] Although Mayor Daley supported the construction of the Crosstown Expressway, even that basic link in the committed system of expressways did not come to fruition. In 1962 when the plan was released, the northwest and west sides of Chicago had been a construction zone for the past six years. Residents were distraught with the dirt, noise and disruption of expressway construction.

With the benefit of 20–20 hindsight, one wonders what Carroll and his staff were thinking in proposing a grid of expressways with a three-mile spacing, enclosing 'islands of local residential areas' in the City of Chicago. But then an urban expressway system of the scale being proposed had never been experienced by anyone up to that time.

2.5   BUREAU OF PUBLIC ROADS

2.5.1   Overview

Development of travel forecasting methods and associated computer programs was initiated by the Bureau of Public Roads, a long-standing unit of the US Department of Commerce (US DoC), based on the experience with the Detroit and Chicago area studies, and other pioneering efforts in Puerto Rico and Washington, DC.[22] BPR initiated the development of computer programs for factoring survey-based trip tables and solving gravity-type trip distribution models and traffic assignment models, when electronic computers became available for civilian use (Brokke, 1969, 32).

Glenn Brokke [1912–1992] and W. Lee Mertz [1920–1993][23] initiated tests of the Fratar and Detroit area methods for factoring a survey trip table for a future forecast year with an IBM 705 computer (Brokke and Mertz, 1958). Somewhat later, programs for calibrating and testing a gravity model were written for the IBM 704 and later modified for the IBM 7090/94 (US DoC, 1963a, ii). Programming for a 'battery' of assignment programs for the IBM 704 was initiated in 1958 under contract with the General Electric Computer Department, Phoenix, Arizona (Mertz, 1960b, 1961). 'This project produced a battery of high-speed computer programs that would assign nondirectional interzonal traffic movements', including options of using diversion curves or all-or-nothing assignment based on the shortest route algorithm of Moore (1957) (US DoC, 1964, I-3). These programs were extended to permit directional assignments as well as turn penalties and prohibitions. Following the transition to second generation machines, BPR incorporated its major programs into a library of programs.

These two manuals (US DoC, 1963a, 1964) sought to provide computer programs needed 'to complete the analytical phase of a comprehensive transportation planning study' (US DoC, 1963a, ii).[24] No overall statement of objectives for the BPR travel forecasting procedure, however, was described in these manuals. In the following sections, the models and methods that make up the four-step or sequential travel forecasting procedure are reviewed. The dates of the reports and manuals indicate the order of their development, which differ from their description here.

Section 2.5.8 reviews early studies of urban goods movement undertaken by three transportation studies; subsequent studies are considered in section 8.6.

2.5.2 Trip Generation

In early transportation studies in the US, procedures were devised to forecast the number of trips leaving or entering a zone according to the following definitions:

1. the number of trips 'produced' by a zone, or 'trip productions', was defined as the trips originating at and returning to the zone;
2. the number of trips 'attracted' by a zone, or 'trip attractions', was defined as the trips arriving at and departing from a zone.

Both productions and attractions were related by statistical methods to total values or averages of selected zonal characteristics. For trip productions, these variables were typically the number of persons or households, number of cars owned by households and number of employed residents; zonal averages were also used, such as the number of workers per household, mean household income or number of cars per household. Trip attractions were related to floor area, land area or employment in various activity classes (retail, manufacturing, etc.) at the non-home end of the trips (US DoC, 1963a, III-2) (section 8.4.2).[25] In subsequent studies, trips were categorised as home-based and non-home-based. Home-based trips were further divided into classes by purpose: work, shop, school and other. Documentation of these procedures was found only in early transportation study reports, as there was no BPR manual on trip generation before 1967.

By the early 1960s, academic research and some transportation studies found substantial variations in the rate of trip making among individual households, which were not captured by these zone-based methods. Using data from two home interview studies, Paul Shuldiner identified the most significant variables associated with trip making of individual households as household size, income, and car ownership (Oi and Shuldiner, 1962; Shuldiner, 1962). His research also explored which statistical methods were appropriate for the analysis of such data, concluding that cross-classification methods based on household types were superior to linear regression, which requires assumptions of linearity and continuity of variables, as well as normality of errors, for hypothesis testing. The use of dummy variables to represent classification variables, however, provides another way to combine elements of the regression and cross-classification approaches.

Forecasting the explanatory variables on which to base travel rates of households posed new challenges, since each variable would need to be forecast for the target year of the study. Forecasting household size and car ownership was a significant challenge. Progress in implementing the household-based category analysis, drawing on the research of Shuldiner, was also being made in the UK (Wootton and Pick, 1967) (section 3.3.1).

Guidelines for Trip Generation Analysis (US DoT, 1967) and Fleet and Robertson (1968) built upon and incorporated the experience from urban transportation studies. Trip Generation Analysis (US DoT, 1975) provided more specific guidance. Concerning the definition of trip categories and trip generation modelling procedures in the early transportation studies, Stopher and Meyburg noted:

> production and attraction and origin and destination are not synonymous. Briefly, it can be summarized as follows: For a home-based trip, the zone of production is the home end of the trip; while the zone of attraction is the non-home end of the trip. Thus, a trip from home to work and a trip from work to home will both have a production end which is home and an attraction end which is work. For non-home-based trips, the production end is the origin and the attraction end is the destination (Stopher and Meyburg, 1975, 64).

2.5.3 Trip Distribution

Following the tradition of the earliest urban transportation studies, a future trip table for a study area was estimated by adjusting the sampled table from the survey year to conform to future origin and destination totals. An early approach to this adjustment was proposed by Fratar

(1954). Subsequently, additional adjustments were proposed using the newly available electronic computers. Computer programs prepared by the Bureau of Public Roads for adjustment of survey trip tables were not included in BPR's first trip distribution manual (US DoC, 1963a), but were later included in Peat, Marwick, Livingston & Co. (1967, 3–14) and US DoT (1969a, 3–14). Concurrently with Fratar's proposal, Alan Voorhees (1955) and Douglas Carroll (1949, 1952, 1955) were exploring the application of the gravity model in forecasting interzonal urban travel. These early studies led to applications by Voorhees (1958), Voorhees and Morris (1959) and Hansen (1962).

US DoC (1963a, sections I, II) reviews the theory and history of the gravity model, plus a brief description of the intervening opportunities model (Schneider, 1959), as well as the competing opportunities model (Tomazinis, 1962), and proceeds to a description of the model implemented in BPR computer programs. The implementation was highly empirical, incorporating 'travel time factors', based on the shortest route travel time, and specific zone-to-zone adjustment factors, known as 'K-factors'. The BPR gravity model stated that the number of two-way trips produced in an origin zone and attracted to a destination zone, also known as the number of trip interchanges, is directly proportional to:

1. the number of trips produced by the origin zone, or two-way trip productions;
2. the number of trips attracted to the destination zone;
3. 'an empirically derived travel-time factor, which expresses the average areawide effect of spatial separation on trip interchange between zones which are a given travel time apart', also known as 'friction factors';
4. 'a specific zone-to-zone adjustment factor to allow for the incorporation of the effect on travel patterns of defined social or economic linkages not otherwise accounted for in the gravity model formulation', also known as K-factors;
5. a denominator term equal to the sum over all destination zones of the product of the number of trip attractions, the travel time factor and the adjustment factor.[26]

The denominator term ensured that the sum of the trips from an origin zone to all destination zones equals the origin zone productions. The converse that the sum of the trips to a destination zone over all origins equalled the destination zone attractions was not satisfied by the function. This lack of agreement between the trip sums to a destination zone and the zonal trip attractions was addressed later in the report (US DoC, 1963a, IV-37–39), as noted next.

An automated adjustment procedure was described as follows: 'the program adjusts each zonal attraction factor by the ratio of the trip attraction factor to the gravity model results', that is, the sum of the trip interchanges over all origin zones. Three iterations of this adjustment procedure were recommended. No interpretation of the adjusted trip attraction factors was offered, but the description of this procedure as part of the calibration, or fitting of the function to data, suggests that these adjusted attraction factors were considered to have been 'calibrated'. These adjustments are equivalent to the imposition of a destination constraint such that the sum of trips to a destination zone from all origins equals the destination zone attractions (section 3.5.1). Unlike the case of the doubly-constrained procedure, the effect of adjusting the attractions in order to invoke the attraction constraints is implicit.

The calibration of the travel time or friction factors was based upon the frequency distribution of trip lengths. A separate empirical, decreasing function of interzonal travel times was determined for each trip purpose by adjusting an initial guess by the ratio of the observed proportion of trips of a given length to the proportion computed from the model. After a trial function was calculated, the attraction factors were updated before the predicted trip length frequency distribution was compared with the observed distribution. Finally, zone-to-zone adjustment factors (K-factors) were specified by trip purpose and mode to account for poorly fitting results. The report describes in detail how such factors should be specified.

Although Carroll and Voorhees investigated the empirical values of the negative power of travel time, in the calibration section of the report only empirical factors were presented. Generally, the report is clearly and precisely presented, especially computational details related to computer programs for the IBM 7090. Statistical tests were reported for a small urban area, Sioux Falls, South Dakota. A procedure for converting two-way trips to one-way trips for use in traffic assignment was described (US DoC, 1963a, VI-1–5). A final section described assumptions necessary to use the model and associated programs for forecasting. The authors of the report noted: 'travel-time factors, as developed from present data, are used for the future time period. Very limited evidence leads to the conclusion that this is a reasonable assumption to make. However, much research work is required on this point before the assumption can be accepted without reservation' (US DoC, 1963a, VI-4).

2.5.4   Modal Split

The report Modal Split documented the procedures used in nine urban
transportation studies between 1955 and 1966 for estimating the proportion of future urban travel by public transport (US DoC, 1966). Early
transportation studies, such as Chicago and Pittsburgh, implemented
'trip-end' modal split procedures (section 2.4.2). Car ownership, residential density and distance from the central area were the principal explanatory variables. Later, transportation studies for Erie, Puget Sound and
Southeastern Wisconsin introduced level-of-service variables at each
origin zone to represent the effect of differences in accessibility by car and
public transport to other destinations. Diversion curves related the mode
share from an origin zone to the ratio of accessibility by car to accessibility
by public transport (Hutchinson, 1974, Chapter 3; Stopher and Meyburg,
1975, sections 3.7, 9.5).

   Alternatives to the trip-end modal split procedure were proposed in the
early 1960s for two reasons. First, the trip-end procedures proved to be
insensitive to changes in public transport service, which was attributed
to the 'gross accessibility measures used' (Stopher and Meyburg, 1975,
188). Second, federal funding for public transport improvements at that
time required an appraisal of changes in transit levels-of-service between
specific locations. Hence, alternative methods for modal split analysis
were designed to improve the responsiveness of the models to proposed
improvements in public transport systems.

   By having the modal split step follow the distribution stage, known
as trip-interchange modal split models, modal choice could be directly
related to the modal travel times and costs for each pair of zones. In contrast to trip-end models, which tended to emphasise the identification of
captive users of public transport, the trip-interchange structure emphasised choices facing travellers between pairs of zones.

   Hill and von Cube (1963) prepared modal split studies for Washington,
Toronto and Philadelphia, which 'represents the first major attempt to
hypothesize the decision process that may underlie modal split and to
incorporate this process into a predictive model' (Stopher and Meyburg,
1975, 189). Their procedure expressed the modal split between car and
public transport for zonal interchange in terms of:

1.   relative overall travel time of the modes expressed as a ratio;
2.   relative overall travel cost of the modes expressed as a ratio with four
     levels;
3.   relative out-of-vehicle time of the modes expressed as a ratio with four
     levels;

4. income of the worker with five levels;
5. trip purpose – work or non-work.

Based on these variables, 80 diversion curves were specified for work trips. Data were analysed both separately and in combination for samples from Washington, Toronto and Philadelphia to assess transferability and extend the variable ranges.

While a rigorous behavioural basis for the location of modal split in the travel forecasting procedure, either before or after trip distribution, was not established during this period, the justification for different structures seemed to reflect travel decisions. The language of choice and the conditionality of decisions slipped into the discussion. Those researching the individual models, and particularly modal split, were often conscious of the broader context of their investigations and the behavioural ambiguities of the structure. In a paper summarising the findings of DoC (1966), Edward Weiner wrote: 'the most actively debated issue in modal split is whether an urban area should use a trip-end or trip-interchange model' (Weiner, 1969, 25).

2.5.5 Traffic Assignment

Well before BPR released its manual, transportation planners had agreed that link capacities needed to be considered in the assignment of traffic to a road network. The earlier reliance on unconstrained assignments, called 'all-or-nothing assignment', was not practical. The Traffic Assignment Manual documented 'in detail the complete process of traffic assignment, as it was then defined' (US DoC, 1964, i). As with the gravity model manual, the presentation is detailed and precise, including useful historical background: 'Traffic assignment may be defined as the process of allocating a given set of trip interchanges to a specific transportation system' (US DoC, 1964, I-1). In the manual one finds little discussion of 'route choice'; rather, assignment was viewed as a mechanical procedure for placing trips on to the network. Chapter V – Theory, however, did state: 'it is assumed that the vehicle operator desires to use the "easiest" route between his origin and destination' (US DoC, 1964, V-1).

A method of assignment that considers link capacity was described in the 1964 manual as 'iterative capacity restraint'. This method consisted of performing a sequence of all-or-nothing assignments in which the link travel speeds were updated after each all-or-nothing assignment of the trip table. Iterative capacity restraint assignment was described in more detail in Chapter V. What has became known as the BPR volume-delay or link performance function was stated there, relating 'travel time at the assigned

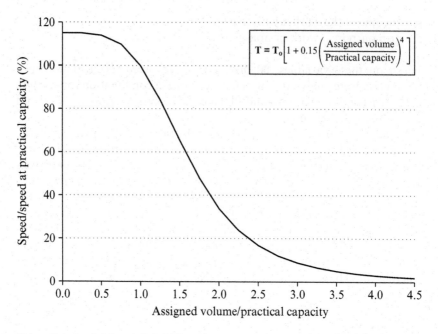

Speed/speed at practical capacity (%)

$$T = T_o\left[1 + 0.15\left(\frac{\text{Assigned volume}}{\text{Practical capacity}}\right)^4\right]$$

Assigned volume/practical capacity

Note: Speed = link length/T (miles/hour).

Source: US DoC (1964, V-20).

Figure 2.5   Relative link speed versus ratio of assigned link volume to practical capacity

volume' to a 'base travel time' defined to be the travel time at practical capacity times the factor 0.87, which is the reciprocal of 1.15. Therefore, if the assigned volume equalled the link's practical capacity, the travel time function equalled the base travel time. The basis for the parameter value was not described. Hence, as it was originally defined, the BPR function was related to the travel time at practical capacity, and not to zero-volume, or free-flow, travel time. Practical capacity was defined as the maximum flow that can be achieved at a specified level-of-service.[27] As shown in Figure 2.5, the BPR function is expressed as the ratio of the speed at the assigned volume to the speed at practical capacity; its property that travel time increases without limit as volume increases was not stated.

Following the completion of an all-or-nothing assignment of the entire trip table, the link 'parameters' were adjusted, and a second all-or-nothing assignment was performed. The parameter adjustment was to the link speed, not to the link travel time. Moreover, to 'moderate the full effect of the change' a speed for the next iteration was obtained by averaging the new speed and the former speed, thereby eliminating 'large oscillations of loads on links from one iteration to the next. . . . This process may be continued for as many iterations as desired. However, experience showed that after four iterations the accuracy of the assignments does not improve appreciably' (US DoC, 1964, V-21). The term 'link loads' was sometimes used to refer to link volumes. A subsequent manual reported that 'reasonable assignments are obtained by using the average of four loadings' (US DoT, 1973a, 36).

One forgotten aspect of these early trip distribution and traffic assignment methods is that most calculations were performed in integer arithmetic. Trips, link volumes, capacities and speeds were all integers. If averaging was performed, the result was rounded or truncated to an integer, further restricting the ability of the procedure to converge to a stable solution.

2.5.6 Alternative Traffic Assignment Methods

The iterative capacity restraint method of traffic assignment implemented by BPR was one way of solving this problem during the 1960s. Robert Smock (1962, 1963) proposed a different way of averaging link volumes from a sequence of all-or-nothing assignments for the continuing Detroit area study. Following an initial all-or-nothing assignment to shortest routes based on free-flow link travel times, and a second assignment to shortest routes based on the travel times corresponding to the link volumes from the first assignment, he averaged the link volumes from these two assignments with equal weights (0.5/0.5). After the travel times were updated for the averaged volumes, a third all-or-nothing assignment was performed. This third assignment was averaged together with the previously averaged results. Precisely how the volumes were averaged is unclear (Smock, 1963, 15).[28] If each all-or-nothing assignment had equal weight in the final averaged result, then Smock's procedure would correspond to the method of successive averages (MSA). Michael Patriksson (1994, 23) stated that Smock may have been unknowingly responsible 'for what is probably the first adaptation of a convergent traffic assignment algorithm'. Smock used the term 'convergence' to describe the behaviour of his method, as is now common (see sections 7.4.2.4 and 7.4.3.2).[29]

Traffic Research Corporation implemented a method incorporating the trip distribution and assignment models in a complex cyclic process (Irwin and von Cube, 1962). The assignment method consisted of all-or-nothing assignments of an updated trip table to shortest routes. No averaging of link volumes is apparent from their paper.

For CATS, Morton Schneider had implemented and applied a type of incremental assignment, later termed quantal loading (Patriksson, 1994, 21) (section 2.4.4). Brian Martin proposed another 'incremental assignment' method (Martin and Manheim, 1965). Martin may have been the first to use that term; however, his method bore only a general resemblance to later usage.

A different incremental assignment procedure was implemented in the assignment programs offered by the Control Data Corporation (CDC) (1965) in its Transportation Planning System for the Control Data 3600 Computer or TRANPLAN (section 10.3.2). In this method, the trip table was divided into several increments, possibly but not necessarily of the same proportion of the entire table. The first increment was assigned to shortest routes defined on free-flow travel times. The assigned volumes on each link were then scaled up to represent the full volume, as if the entire trip table had been assigned. New shortest routes were computed for these volumes, and the second increment assigned to them. Next, the link volumes from the two increments were combined according to the proportion of each increment, and again the volumes were scaled up to represent the entire trip table, the link times were updated, and new shortest routes were re-computed. This procedure was repeated until all increments were assigned and averaged together. Although this procedure was described in US DoT (1973a, 38) and in CDC (1965, 147), these descriptions differed from the typical descriptions of 'incremental loading' (Van Vliet, 1976, 146; Ortúzar and Willumsen, 2011, 369) in which a sequence of increments of the trip table were assigned with the link volumes, travel times and shortest routes being updated after each increment.

CDC's averaging of volumes according to their proportions, and the scaling of those volumes to the full trip table, may correspond to the method of successive averages described above, and therefore may also be a convergent assignment method. The originator of this scaling procedure is unknown. Presumably, the rescaling of the link volumes was intuitively more plausible than using the partially assigned volumes directly in the volume-delay function. No tests of this variant of incremental assignment have been found, and seem unlikely to have been performed, since no meaningful measures for assessing the quality of an assignment were known at that time (section 7.4.2.4).

As noted in section 2.5.5, traffic assignment computations were performed in integer arithmetic. Therefore, in devising the increments, the values of each increment had to be determined so that the sum over all increments would equal the integer values in the original trip table. In assigning a large trip table even in the 1960s, a typical origin–destination flow was a single digit number, and possibly one vehicle per day. In this case, the cells with values equal to one were typically assigned in the middle increment.[30]

Drawing upon his experience with the development of computer programs for transit network problems in the late 1960s, as described in sections 2.6 and 10.3, Robert Dial (1971) proposed a method for more widely distributing origin–destination flows over multiple routes using an exponential function of fixed route travel times.[31] Dial was initially motivated by a desire to provide a better method than all-or-nothing assignment to fixed travel time routes, and not by the shortcomings of the capacity restraint assignment method. His STOCH method was sometimes used by practitioners, however, as an alternative to the iterative capacity restraint method. Later, STOCH was understood to be a stochastic network loading method, given fixed link costs, in the same sense that all-or-nothing assignment is a deterministic loading method of a trip table to shortest fixed cost routes (Patriksson, 1994, 148). Dial's method depended upon a definition of 'efficient' routes. One example of an efficient route is a route that does not backtrack: 'As it progresses from node to node it always gets further from the origin and closer to the destination' (Dial, 1971, 89).

2.5.7 Application and Experience

BPR offered no advice concerning the solution of the sequence of models described in the four manuals issued between 1963 and 1967. In Urban Transportation Planning, General Information (US DoT, 1972a, I-5), these models were described together for the first time, and their relationship was depicted diagrammatically in Figure I-2, reproduced as Figure 2.6. Modal split was not shown in this figure. Solving the trip distribution and traffic assignment steps with feedback was not addressed in the report. 'Feedback' is denoted in the figure, but in the context of land use – transportation network interaction, and not travel forecasting.

As the agency charged with oversight of road planning, design standards and road financing, BPR was at the forefront of the development of urban travel forecasting methods, and the use of mainframe computers. The staff charged with these responsibilities acquired their skills on the job to prepare for this rapidly developing field. Highway engineers and mathematics majors were thrust into model development and the programming of the latest mainframe computers. They eagerly applied research findings, such as Moore's algorithm for finding shortest routes through a network, although they were unschooled in the optimisation methods that advanced rapidly from the late 1940s (section 7.2.2). They did their best to apply common sense and experience gained on the job.

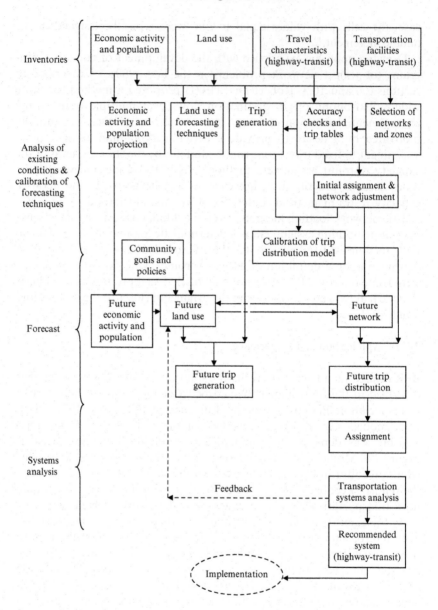

Source: Redrawn from US DoT (1972a, I-5).

Figure 2.6   Elements of the urban travel forecasting process

The principal accomplishments of this era pertaining to travel forecasting may be summarised as follows:

1. Using data from the Washington, DC area home interview surveys, trip distribution models for 1948 and 1955 were implemented on an IBM mainframe.
2. Road traffic assignment methods were implemented on a mainframe based on the shortest route method. Procedures for solving a capacity restraint method were experimental. Empirical travel time-volume functions, later known as volume-delay functions, were devised based on little data, but continue in use to this day.
3. Over a period of years, computer programs, later called 'packages' or 'batteries', for solving trip distribution and traffic assignment models were developed, documented and distributed to urban transportation studies and computer service bureaus. These programs became the mainstay of urban travel forecasting methods during the 1960s.
4. Procedures for trip generation and modal split were also reviewed and documented in support of urban transportation studies.

2.5.8 Urban Goods Movement

BPR reports of this period did not consider truck traffic. Early urban transportation studies did survey truck use, and analysis was performed with these data. These early studies are briefly described here. For developments from 1970 onwards, see section 8.6.

The Detroit and Chicago studies each inventoried truck movements. Assignment of future truck traffic was not described in the final report of the Detroit study. The Chicago study explored the relation of truck originations and terminations to land use. Origin–destination flows of trucks were forecast and assigned in the 1980 plan evaluations (CATS, 1960, 48).

Magne Helvig (1964), a graduate student at the University of Chicago, performed a study of Chicago's external truck movements with data from the Chicago Area Transportation Study. Helvig investigated the relationship between the number of trucks entering the Chicago study area in relation to the size of the shipment origin (population, employment) and distance. He estimated the parameter value of a simple gravity model defined on a power function of distance at three geographic scales: states; counties in the four states surrounding the Chicago study area; and municipalities in the larger Chicago region. This study is probably the first detailed application of the gravity model to interregional truck flows in a metropolitan area. Helvig's study followed the completion of the 1980 transportation plan for the Chicago area.[32]

Donald Hill (1965b) proposed a 'truck interactance' model based on the gravity hypothesis for implementation in the Toronto, Canada region. Hill hypothesised that interzonal truck flows were proportional to the number of truck trips originating and terminating at zones and to the negative exponential function of the interzonal travel time or distance, giving no reason for using the negative exponential function and no references except Helvig (1964). Although the use of the negative exponential function in such a model was not typical, Hill offered no explanation for its choice.[33] Hill estimated his model with Toronto data, and determined parameter values of the exponential function for three classes of trucks. His study is probably the first implementation of a spatial interaction model of truck flows.

The first transportation study to undertake a comprehensive inventory of freight movements was the Tri-State Transportation Commission for the New York region (Wood, 1967; Wood and Leighton, 1969). Extensive inventories were performed for trucking, but no forecasts were prepared by 1970.

2.6   URBAN MASS TRANSIT PLANNING PROJECT

The urban transportation studies initiated in the 1950s were strongly orientated towards planning for road systems. The Detroit area travel forecasts ignored public transport altogether. Travel forecasting for public transport was later added to the original study design at CATS. The impetus for urban transportation planning, after all, was the planning of urban sections of the National System of Interstate and Defense Highways. Even so, the Federal-Aid Highway Act of 1962 required that the planning process be comprehensive. BPR defined and interpreted section 134 of the 1962 Act as follows:

> The comprehensive character of the planning process requires that the economic, population, and land use elements be included; that estimates be made of the future demands for all modes of transportation both public and private for persons and goods; that terminal and transfer facilities and traffic control systems be included in the inventories and analyses; and, that the entire area within which the forces of development are interrelated and which is expected to be urbanised within the forecast period be included (US DoC, 1963b).

Responsibility for planning of urban public transit systems was assigned to the US Department of Housing and Urban Development (US HUD) by the Urban Mass Transportation Act of 1964, as amended in 1966 (Weiner, 1997, Chapters 4, 5). The 1966 amendments provided for a technical studies programme, including federal assistance for planning, engineering and designing of urban public transit projects.

Charles Graves, a HUD land use planner from the Puget Sound Regional Transportation Study, Seattle, proposed the development of a program battery for public transport systems planning comparable to BPR's highway program battery. Since HUD had no technical staff to develop such a capability, a contract for the Urban Mass Transit Planning Project was awarded to Alan M. Voorhees and Associates for development of computer programs for modal split, transit assignment and related functions.

Walter Hansen headed the HUD project; Richard Bunyan and Robert Dial[34] were the initial programming staff. Bunyan prepared a process diagram, mimicking BPR's highway package, which consisted of seven modules (Dial and Bunyan, 1968): 'network description; transit path builder; O-D travel times; modal split model calibration; modal split model application; load trip table; and report generator'. Several of these programs, especially the transit path builder and the modal split model, were highly innovative for that time (US HUD, 1966, 1967, 1968). Independently, John Wootton was developing similar methods for analysing public transport networks in the UK; see sections 3.6.1 and 10.3.1.[35]

The HUD transit battery provided computer programs for modal split forecasting and transit network planning that were compatible with the BPR highway program battery. These in turn became the basis for the Urban Transportation Planning System (UTPS) developed during the 1970s (section 10.3.3).

The US Department of Transportation (US DoT) was established in 1966. In 1968, an agreement between US DoT and US HUD established the Urban Mass Transportation Administration (UMTA) and transferred responsibility for many public transport programmes to US DoT. After that time, further responsibility for development of travel forecasting computer programs became the joint responsibility of the Urban Mass Transportation Administration and the Federal Highway Administration.

2.7   LAND USE – TRANSPORTATION STUDIES

2.7.1   Overview

The successes of the Detroit and Chicago area studies, as well as BPR and US HUD, in creating models and computer programs for travel forecasting stimulated other large metropolitan areas to initiate studies. Moreover, some metropolitan areas were forming regional planning commissions or councils with broader scopes than transportation planning, including land use, sewer and water utilities, open space, housing and employment.

Urban planners argued that transportation planning should not be undertaken in isolation, without coordinated planning for urban activities (land use) to be served by the new highway and public transport systems. As financial support for land use planning activities became available from federal, state and local governments, several land use – transportation studies were proposed.

One of the first, and most ambitious, was for the south-east Pennsylvania – south-west New Jersey region centred on Philadelphia. The proposal was written by Robert Mitchell [1906–1993], formerly director of city planning of the City of Philadelphia, and the first chair of the Department of City and Regional Planning at the University of Pennsylvania. Mitchell had co-authored an early study of land use and traffic with Chester Rapkin [1918–2001] (Mitchell and Rapkin, 1954). The Penn Jersey Transportation Study (PJTS) resulting from Mitchell's proposal is examined in section 2.7.2.

Influenced by the PJTS proposal, other large metropolitan areas proposed metropolitan land use and transportation planning programmes, based on the belief that:

1. land use arrangements different from recent development trends could be more efficiently served by balanced transportation systems that included new public transport services as well as new freeway systems;
2. transportation systems were an important lever for obtaining a more desirable physical pattern of metropolitan development through the relationship of the type and density of urban activities to the level of transportation facilities and services available.

BPR contracted for a review of these new studies by two junior faculty at the University of Pennsylvania, David Boyce and Norman Day [1933–2002]. Their 1969 report *Metropolitan Plan Evaluation Methodology*, later published as *Metropolitan Plan Making* (Boyce et al, 1970), provided detailed descriptions of these studies for seven urban regions.[36]

A young urban economist at the Pittsburgh Regional Study, Ira Lowry, formulated a prototype model of urban activity location, which influenced research on land use models in the US and the UK. Other researchers built upon Lowry's 'Model of Metropolis', spawning new research on urban land use models (section 2.7.4). Douglass Lee's (1973) 'Requiem for Large-Scale Models' quelled interest in land use models for several years (sections 2.7.5, 8.5).

2.7.2 Penn Jersey Transportation Study

The Detroit and Chicago area studies were respectively based on a land use plan and a forecast of land use activities for the target year. The Penn Jersey Transportation Study proceeded differently, in a way considered revolutionary at the time. As stated in the study's Prospectus:

> It is intended not only that the recommended transportation system should provide convenience and economy of travel, but also that its influence on the development of the area should tend toward facilitating a desired pattern of regional development. Stress is to be laid on the design and analysis of alternative patterns both of possible transportation systems and of the future regional development likely to be associated with each system. The workable alternatives are to be evaluated so that a reasonable choice can be made from among them (PJTS, 1959, 2).

The proposed approach, first described by Robert Mitchell, is paraphrased as follows:

1. 'A dynamic metropolitan growth model needs to be constructed, expressing the relationships among the components and influences of the future area distribution of population, jobs, and land uses', based in part upon 'the amount, nature and location of transportation facilities and services. . . . Using the metropolitan growth model, a first projection is made of the distribution of population and jobs by major classes of industry based on the assumption of the past rate of improvement in transportation services.'
2. 'With the first land use projection as a basis', alternative transportation schemes for highways and transit should be prepared, 'giving varying weight to highways and transit'.
3. The distribution of population and jobs should be forecast for each transportation alternative, holding constant other factors. In this manner, 'several sets of internally consistent land use and transportation alternatives for comparison' should be prepared.
4. A travel forecasting 'model should be applied to the various transportation plans to determine their feasibility with respect to the capacities of critical transportation facilities. It may be found, for example, that the "maximum highway – minimum transit" plan would not be sufficient to carry expected volumes of traffic. . . . Readjustment of the plan and reassignment of traffic . . . should be repeated until a balance is attained' (Mitchell, 1959, 19–20).

The PJTS Prospectus, paraphrased below, described the application of Mitchell's approach:

1. A traffic model based upon land use variables, and consisting of trip generation, trip distribution and assignment, is first described, based upon the current state of practice.
2. A regional growth model 'identifying and analysing those factors and relationships in the physical, social and economic structure of the region which determine the growth and change in regional land development' is then described. 'Sets of mathematical relationships . . . which reflect in simplified form the relationships between land development and the key factors determining growth and change' will be developed. 'The influence of transportation on non-transportation factors in establishing land development patterns will be particularly important.'
3. The regional growth model will be applied 'to produce a range of alternative patterns of future regional transportation and land development. . . . Each alternative must be realizable in a practical sense, but different from the others in some important aspect. . . . Alternative transportation systems, emphasizing different modes of travel, locational patterns or construction priorities, will be taken as the starting point for investigating possible patterns of regional growth.'
4. 'Each regional alternative pattern, and its related transportation system', will be evaluated with regard to a range of effects. 'One of the alternative generalized transportation systems, possibly with modifications, will be selected as the basis for proceeding' to elaborate 'a single transportation plan and program' for the region (PJTS, 1959, 12–16).

The Prospectus and budget for a three-year study were adopted in December 1959, and the submission of the final report was scheduled for September 1962. The cost of the study was $2.9 million, of which $1.8 million was budgeted for data collection, coding and processing. PJTS evolved into the Delaware Valley Regional Planning Commission (DVRPC) in 1964. The principal developments related to land development models were the following.

The first description of the regional growth model (RGM) was issued in April 1961. Vladimir Almendinger, a PJTS staff member and an innovative systems analyst, gave a broad outline of the model. Britton Harris [1915–2005], on leave from the University of Pennsylvania, was cited as the 'intellectual progenitor and moving spirit of the model'. The RGM was described as an attempt:

to simulate the aggregate locational and trip-making behavior over time of a population of decision-making units within an intra-regional setting made up of: (1) a spatial distribution of land use and activities, (2) a transportation system, and (3) a market for land and space. The heart of the model is the allocation procedure . . . [for] the distribution of residential activity in a metropolitan region (Almendinger, 1961, 8).

Almendinger described a detailed stochastic simulation method for residential locators, location-serving industries and 'footloose' industries, and their land requirements, which he proposed to apply to a region sub-divided into 162 districts. His brief description ends with a flowchart depicting how the method would be solved.

During the summer of 1960 at the University of Pennsylvania, John Herbert, a Ph.D. student in city planning, and Benjamin Stevens [1929–1997], an assistant professor of regional science, formulated a residential location model as a linear programming problem (section 7.2.2). By formulating the model with this method, they were not seeking to optimise the location of households. Rather, they sought to emulate a spatial market clearing process for the housing sector using the concept of households offering competing bids for residential locations (Herbert and Stevens, 1960).[37]

The proposal of Herbert and Stevens led Britton Harris to embark upon a search for fast methods for solving large-scale linear programming problems, which occupied him during his ensuing academic career at the University of Pennsylvania. Harris also sought to conceptualise and design models for location of retail trade and services. Generally, Harris was not inclined to publish his research. However, in 1961 he did offer a relatively detailed description of the proposed regional growth model. In the following, Harris used the term 'iteration' to refer to a five-year time period, sometimes described as a recursion by others:

> The model is a simulation model, and will detail the growth of the metropolitan area in five-year increments. By this means, it is anticipated that we will be able to deal with nonlinearities and time-lags. At the same time, we substantially reduce the number of variables, since locators at any iteration will react not with each other but only with the pre-existing distribution of population and activity.
>
> The model will contain behavioral parameters and functional relations for groups . . . of households and firms. The membership by population classes defined by manifest variables such as age and income in these groups will be probabilistically defined. The transition over time from one household or business state to another will be similarly defined, and the propensity to move in any given iterations, similarly. . . .
>
> The allocation of locators to land areas at any particular iteration we hope to accomplish by a linear-programming technique. This will probably involve four

operations: the supply of land, and the take-up of land and housing by industry and commerce, by home-renters, and by home-buyers. These four markets will interact within and between iterations by way of the rents generated in the linear-programming models. The effects of these interactions will be changes in the state: locating the locators, and assigning to land various fixed improvements, alterations, or redevelopments.

A transportation system is an integral part of the model. It establishes accessibility measures that in part determine the behavior of locators. One output of the model is a set of transportation flows, expenditures, and facility loadings.

Inputs to the model include increments of population and economic activity for the period of the iteration, and changes in policy variables or technological relations. The most important of the last group is changes in the transportation systems, which will presumably have marked effects on the behavior of locators and thus on future patterns of development and on the use of the transport system itself (Harris, 1961, 715–716).

In 'Linear Programming and the Projection of Land Uses', Harris (1963) expounded on extensions of the Herbert–Stevens model, and offered an illustrative example. However, he did not describe further implementation progress. Shortly thereafter, work on the RGM ended. By the end of 1964, an activities allocation model (AAM) had replaced the RGM. The AAM consisted of seven major submodels: residential location; manufacturing location; non-manufacturing location; and four space consumption models, one for each of these sectors plus one for street area. David Seidman explained:

> Our thinking then turned to an alternative type of model which did not attempt to explain locational or land use behavior in economic terms at the household or firm level, but simply described this behavior in an aggregated manner sufficiently accurately that we could use these descriptions to project the locational tendencies of activities in the future. These descriptions are still mathematical models, but they have a form similar to that of a multiple regression; that is, they define the location of an activity as a function of a number of variables which specify the characteristics of each subarea (Seidman, 1964, 2).

Development of the AAM continued to the mid-1960s. An initial set of assumptions concerning transportation policies consisted of six alternative sets of transportation plan inputs. In the testing of the 1985 plan, six combinations of policies were used: two alternative levels of freeway plans in combination with two alternative levels of public transport plans, together with varying assumptions concerning fares and parking fees. In the results, the largest variation in land use output was about 5 per cent, which was produced by a 30 per cent variation in accessibility among the plan alternatives; only a 10 per cent difference in accessibility was found between the two extreme highway and public transport alternatives (DVRPC, 1967, 26–30; Boyce et al, 1970, 69, 420–424).

DVRPC's *1985 Regional Transportation Plan* candidly summarised the conclusions of ten years of effort:

> Earlier efforts to determine the relationship of regional transportation systems and alternative land use plans provided DVRPC with some important insights. Essentially, there is no defined single optimal regional plan. It has been observed that most land use activities locate in space to satisfy human needs rather than conforming to specified spatial patterns. Past experiments in simulating the interaction between land use and transportation with varying transportation systems, varying transportation capital investments and varying transportation policies have been rather ineffective in appreciably altering land use patterns. In contrast, it is known that when different combinations of highway and transit test plans are input to the traffic simulation models, significant changes or variations in travel by mode may be indicated (DVRPC, 1969, 43).

Seidman (1969) completed a detailed report documenting his efforts to implement a forecasting model suitable for bringing the original land use and transportation alternatives concept of the Penn Jersey Transportation Study to a successful conclusion. Further efforts to develop land use and transportation alternatives for the Delaware Valley Region ended.

2.7.3   Consideration of Land Use – Transportation Alternatives

The attempt to implement an innovative land use and transportation planning programme for the Philadelphia region represented a break from the approach of Douglas Carroll and his associates in Detroit, Chicago and Pittsburgh. During the early 1960s, metropolitan planning agencies were formed in several major US metropolitan areas. Criticism of the emphasis on road networks in the Detroit and Chicago transportation studies stimulated the exploration of a range of modal combinations, as well as land use arrangements for a future target year. The examination of alternative comprehensive land use and transportation alternatives had become a common approach to analysing and evaluating urban transportation problems for large metropolitan areas by the mid-1960s. Whether or not mathematical land use models were applied, several transportation planning studies, sometimes in conjunction with the regional land use planning agency, began to explore the interdependencies between the transportation and land use systems. An extensive review of land use models by Irwin (1965) offered an indication of the extent and variety of models implemented.

One attempt to relate the effect of the transportation system to urban development was made by the Traffic Research Corporation with its EMPIRIC model developed for the Boston Regional Planning Project in eastern Massachusetts (Boyce et al, 1970, 197–221). Changes in population and employment were allocated to zones by a set of simultaneous regression equations using accessibilities by car and public transport to various land uses. Other independent variables included existing activity distributions and quality of water and sewer services (Hill, 1965a; Hill et al, 1965). The population differences among the four alternatives forecast for 1990 were compared with the change in population from 1963 to 1990 (Boyce et al, 1970, 69–72). Outside the area developed by 1963, the relative differences among the alternatives were extremely small. Hence, like the Penn Jersey case, the Boston model was unable to forecast differences in land use patterns, given different transportation system assumptions.

During the same period, the Regional Planning Council serving the Baltimore, Maryland area pursued a land use planning activity based on a retail market potential model (Boyce et al, 1970, 147–195). Unlike other programmes described here, this effort was not part of an urban transportation study. The programme did successfully employ a market potential model to explore alternative patterns of future retail growth in the Baltimore area (Hansen, 1959; Lakshmanan and Hansen, 1965). The land use alternatives elaborated with the use of this model were substantially different, but still relatively similar as compared with the forecast change in population over the 20-year planning period (Boyce et al, 1970, 72–73).

Other US metropolitan areas (Chicago, Minneapolis – St Paul, Minnesota and Milwaukee, Wisconsin) constructed land use and transportation alternatives using conventional (non-model) allocation techniques. These programmes succeeded in elaborating and evaluating plans that led to the selection or recommendation of a preferred land use and transportation plan (Boyce et al, 1970, 74–78). The methods employed were based on arrangements of land use exhibiting a singular organising principle for the physical structure of the region called 'plan-form' concepts. These arrangements related to the design of alternative plans, as well as the expected density of development, current or expected zoning regulations, holding capacity of vacant or agricultural land, and expected timing of its development. The methods applied were often labour-intensive and time consuming, but the results were generally considered meaningful and worthwhile.

The broad conclusions of Boyce et al provided a sombre termination to this period of excitement and anticipation of a new era of metropolitan planning:

1. Many of the methods for preparing alternatives that had been envisaged for these programs were substantially more difficult to implement than expected. This conclusion applies both to the computer models of urban

development, and to the refinement of plan-form concepts for preparing alternatives.

2. The land use and transportation alternatives prepared were much less different than expected, given the variation in the number and range of policies and the assumptions examined. This conclusion applies both to differences in land use patterns forecast for alternative transportation policies, and to differences in transportation systems requirements forecast for different land use patterns. . . .

3. The subsequent evaluation of alternative plans was much less successful than expected in terms of providing an adequate basis for decisions. This was partly attributable to the difficulties and delays in preparing alternatives, and the consequent shortage of time for evaluation, and partly a result of the reluctance to attach significance to the minor variations that emerged (Boyce et al, 1970, 4, 7).

At a more general level, the premise that a land use pattern and associated transportation systems could be found that were in some sense optimal for a region's future development was not supported by the experiences of these programmes.

2.7.4   Lowry's 'Model of Metropolis'

Of the urban land use models developed during the 1960s, one became the best known by far, a prototype model offered by Ira (Jack) Lowry (1964). Lowry completed a Ph.D. in economics at the University of California, Berkeley in 1959. He then joined the Economic Study of the Pittsburgh Region, a three-year effort of the Pittsburgh Regional Planning Association. His research was undertaken as part of a regional economic study, and not as a component of a land use – transportation study. In 1963, Lowry joined the RAND Corporation, where he completed his report on the model's development in 1964. Subsequently, he contributed to the discussion of land use models (Lowry, 1965, 1968).

The Lowry model was formulated on a two-sector representation of employment, basic and retail: basic employment was exogenously allocated to zones; retail employment included not only retail trade and services, but also local government and schools. The location of residential population was based on the location of total employment according to a gravity or spatial interaction model. A second gravity model located retail activity according to the distribution of population and total employment. Through a set of economic multipliers, and with due regard for physical constraints on development, the interdependencies among exogenous regional employment and regional population totals, and their spatial distribution to discrete zones, were solved through an iterative scheme, leading to what was characterised as an 'instant metropolis'.

The simplicity of the mechanisms at the heart of the model and the relative ease of its implementation led to additional research and some applications, especially in the San Francisco Bay Area. Refinements included a time-oriented metropolitan model and a projective land use model (Goldner, 1971; Goldner et al, 1972). Putman (1975) reviewed this research, as well as describing his own model implementation efforts that evolved from it.

Generalisations of the Lowry model took many forms, including:

1. an increased disaggregation (stratification) of the population sector;
2. explicit consideration of the supply side and decisions affecting the allocation of stock;
3. relaxation of the comparative static status of the model to take account of incremental (quasi-dynamic) change over time;
4. more sophisticated representation of spatial interaction behaviour.

Further academic research on allocation and locator decisions in competitive housing and land markets drew on the bid-rent concepts of Herbert and Stevens (1960). Examples include Ingram et al (1972), Anas (1973) and Wilson (1974, Chapter 10).

2.7.5   Lee's 'Requiem for Large-Scale Models'

In 1973 Douglass Lee was an assistant professor in the Department of City and Regional Planning at the University of California, Berkeley. Following completion of his Ph.D. thesis on land use models at Cornell University in 1968, Lee continued his interest in urban land use models, as well as engaging in empirically oriented research on the impact of large-scale rail transit investment. His article 'Requiem for Large-Scale Models' (D. B. Lee, Jr., 1973), in the *Journal of the American Institute of Planners*, was an attack on land use models and their developers, initiated in the past 15 years.

By the time the article appeared, nearly all urban model implementation efforts in the US had ceased. In this sense, Lee's use of the term 'requiem' was appropriate. Nevertheless, his article caused an uproar among the proponents of urban activity models. The article was seen as a polemic, an aggressive attack on or refutation of the opinions or principles of another.

Lee summarised his conclusions in three points:

1. In general, none of the goals held out for large-scale models have been achieved, and there is little reason to expect anything different in the future.

2. For each objective offered as a reason for building a model, there is either a better way of achieving the objective (more information at less cost) or a better objective (a more socially useful question to ask).
3. Methods for long-range planning – whether they are called comprehensive planning, large-scale systems simulation or something else – need to change drastically if planners expect to have any influence on the long run (Lee, 1973, 163).

From the perspective of this book, some of Lee's concerns are no longer relevant, in view of the enormous increases in computing, data handling and geographic data analysis capabilities now available to urban modellers. Nevertheless, his views remain worthy of consideration. A retrospective on Lee's Requiem was published in 1994; the introduction by Richard Klosterman (1994) and the papers by Michael Batty (1994), Britton Harris (1994), Douglass Lee (1994) and Michael Wegener (1994) are relevant to Lee's original article.

2.8   CONCLUSION

Urban transportation planning, and specifically urban travel forecasting, was definitely 'where the action was' for young transportation engineers and planners entering the field in the 1960s. The problems were challenging, from both a research and a policy perspective. Opportunities for innovation were ample, and agency directors were receptive. By applying the new computer technology of the day, as well as recent mathematical advances, new findings could be anticipated.

Considering the time schedules for these studies, staff members were clearly under great pressure to produce results. Shortcuts were necessary. Judgements had to be made based on incomplete analyses. Some efforts were probably doomed to fail from the outset. Even so, much knowledge and experience was gained from this period, laying a foundation for future activities by both practitioners and academic researchers. US practice matured during the 1970s, as the new computer programs emerging from US DoT became available (section 10.3). Academic research offered new developments during the 1970s, after rediscovering a fundamental contribution of the mid-1950s, recognised by neither practitioners nor researchers for nearly 15 years (section 7.3).

NOTES

1. Daily surface weekday ridership was 45 rides per 100 persons in the City of Chicago, one-half of the post-war peak ridership (Chicago Area Transportation Study, 1960, 124).
2. The first procedural manual for conducting such studies was issued in 1944, revised as US DoC (1954), and updated and reissued as US DoT (1973b).
3. Fratar's growth factor method adjusts an observed trip table constructed from a home interview survey to a forecast trip table corresponding to independent forecasts of origin and destination (row and column) totals. In contrast, in a gravity model forecast, the number of trips from origin to destination is proportional to the row and column totals, and inversely proportional to a function of travel time. Section 2.5.3 offers more details about the gravity model. See also Brokke and Mertz (1958, 78) and Mertz (1960a, 24–25).
4. This discussion reflects a level of understanding similar to that found in Wardrop's more succinct description 'that traffic will settle down into an equilibrium situation in which no driver can reduce his journey time by choosing a new route' (Wardrop, 1952, 345). At this same time, fundamental research on this problem was under way at the Cowles Commission for Research in Economics located at the University of Chicago, which led to the publication of Beckmann et al (1956), as described in section 7.3.
5. The standard punch card, invented by Herman Hollerith [1860–1929], was first used for vital statistics tabulation by the New York City Board of Health and by several states. After this trial use, punch cards were adopted for use in the 1890 census. After Hollerith had perfected his first series of electromechanical punch-card machines, including a punch, a tabulating machine to accumulate statistics from the information punched on cards, and a sorting machine, he founded the Tabulating Machine Corporation. As with more recent 'high-tech start-ups', the company had a somewhat rocky start until an experienced manager, Thomas Watson, took over. One of Watson's moves was to rename the company International Business Machines (IBM). en.wikipedia.org/wiki/Herman_Hollerith (accessed 18 February 2014).
6. www.columbia.edu/cu/computinghistory/ (accessed 26 January 2013).
7. W.L. Mertz (1961, 100) described the use of feedback between trip distribution by gravity model and assignment by the Traffic Research Corporation; for an anecdotal description of his experience, see www.fhwa.dot.gov/infrastructure/memories.cfm (accessed 17 February 2014). Martin Wohl [1930–2009] published an insightful paper on the principles of the travel forecasting procedure with feedback, and its relationship to travel demand, link capacity and travel time on a link (Wohl, 1963).
8. Guide to the John R. Hamburg Transportation Papers, 1956–1992, sca.gmu.edu/finding_aids/hamburg.html (accessed 17 February 2014).
9. According to Bruce Hutchinson (1974), Schneider's intervening opportunities model was a modification of the hypothesis of Samuel Stouffer [1900–1960] (1940), although Schneider apparently never so stated.
10. en.wikipedia.org/wiki/Edward_F._Moore (accessed 28 March 2014).
11. The study of the properties of shortest route algorithms is a subfield in network optimisation. Gallo and Pallottino (1984) made a detailed study of these algorithms.
12. Roger Creighton, personal communication with David Boyce in 2005.
13. Robert Dial, personal communication with David Boyce.
14. The CATS congested travel time function is stated in Muranyi (1963, 20):

$$t_l(V_l) = t_l^o \cdot 2^{(V_l/C_l)}$$

where $t_l(V_l)$ = congested travel time on link l at volume V_l
t_l^o = travel time on link l at zero volume
V_l = volume on link l
C_l = design capacity of link l

15. From 1955 to 1960, 140 units of the IBM 704 were sold. The IBM 700 series were binary computers, as opposed to decimal, vacuum-tube logic computers with 32 000 words

of 36-bit length. The IBM 709 succeeded the 704, adding overlapped input/output, indirect addressing, and decimal instructions. The IBM 7090 was a 709 with transistor, rather than vacuum-tube, logic. The 7040 and 7094 were scaled-down and scaled-up variations of the 7090. www.columbia.edu/cu/computinghistory/701.html (accessed 25 March 2014). The 36-bit 700 and 7000 series were IBM's scientific computers from 1952 until the introduction of the 32-bit System 360 in 1964. en.wikipedia.org/wiki/IBM_704 (accessed 18 February 2014).

16. Recollection of David Boyce of a discussion with Morton Schneider about 1962.

17. The CATS staff performed a transportation study for the Pittsburgh area using the same methods as developed in Chicago. The Cartographatron was also used to prepare images for the Pittsburgh region.

18. Comments by Irving Hoch to David Boyce, 2006.

19. Creighton et al (1959, 1960) described the derivation of the expressway spacing formula. CATS (1962, 39–42) described the application of the method; also see Appendix to CATS (1962, 121–123). Boyce (2007a) reviewed the expressway spacing formula and economic analyses of the expressway plans.

20. A hypothetical study by Levinson and Roberts (1965) compared grid and radial free-ways systems, and showed small advantages for grid layouts. Peter Steenbrink (1974a, 1974b) applied a heuristic network design procedure to the Netherlands.

21. Additional details were treated by Scheff (1977). Garrison and Levinson (2006, Chapter 14) discussed the problems faced in locating urban segments of the Interstate System.

22. The detailed history of the Bureau of Public Roads and the Federal Highway Administration are found at www.fhwa.dot.gov/highwayhistory/history_fhwa.cfm (accessed 19 February 2014).

23. Lee Mertz wrote a memoir about his early experiences with travel forecasting models and learning to write computer programs for the new IBM mainframe computers; www.fhwa.dot.gov/infrastructure/memories.cfm. A biography of W.L. Mertz is at www.fhwa.dot.gov/infrastructure/mertz.cfm. Guide to the William L. Mertz trans-portation collection, 1955–1990, sca.gmu.edu/finding_aids/mertz.html (accessed 17 February 2014).

24. Several additional manuals were issued during the 1970s; of these, the most useful from a historical viewpoint is Urban Transportation Planning, General Information (US DoT, 1972a).

25. The concepts of trip production and attraction originated with BPR's early efforts to implement the gravity model as a trip distribution model, and related to two-way travel between an origin and a destination.

26. The gravity model described in US DoC (1963a) may be stated in slightly simplified form as follows:

$$T_{ij} = \frac{P_i \cdot A_j \cdot F_{ij} \cdot K_{ij}}{\sum_{k=1}^{n} A_k \cdot F_{ik} \cdot K_{ik}}$$

where T_{ij} = trip interchange between zone i and zone j
P_i = trip production of zone i
A_j = trip attraction of zone j
F_{ij} = travel time factor for zone pair ij
K_{ij} = zone-to-zone adjustment factor for zone pair ij
n = number of zones

The denominator term ensures that $\sum_{j=1}^{n} T_{ij} = P_i$ for each origin zone. The adjustment procedure for the values of A_j ensures approximately that $\sum_{i=1}^{n} T_{ij} = A_j$ for each desti-nation zone. If these two equations are considered to be constraints on the matrix (T_{ij}), then it may be said to be 'doubly-constrained'. Section 3.5 provides further details.

27. The originally stated form of the BPR volume-delay function is as follows:

$$T = T_0 \left[1 + 0.15 \left(\frac{V}{C} \right)^4 \right]$$

where T = travel time at which the assigned volume can travel on the link
     T_0 = base travel time at zero volume = travel time at practical capacity × 0.87
     V = assigned volume
     C = practical capacity

Practical capacity was defined in the 1950 *Highway Capacity Manual* as 'the maximum number of vehicles that can pass a given point on a roadway or in a designated lane during one hour without the traffic density being so great as to cause unreasonable delay, hazard, or restriction to the drivers' freedom to maneuver under the prevailing roadway and traffic conditions' (US DoC, 1950, 7). Furthermore, the Manual stated: 'The maximum practical capacity of multilane freeways in urban areas, when access and egress facilities are not a factor, is 1,500 passenger cars per lane per hour in the direction of the heavier flow. At this volume . . . the average speed of all vehicles will be 30 to 35 miles per hour' (US DoC, 1950, 47). In highway capacity manuals subsequently issued by the Transportation Research Board, the concept of practical capacity was replaced by the 'level-of-service', which in turn is related to the maximum flow and density.

28. Smock wrote: 'For the third pass the same procedure is followed, and such passes can be repeated, dividing interzonal volumes over more and more paths, until capacity-adjusted speeds, on the average, come to approximate typical speeds.'

29. Smock devised his volume-delay function based on 'mathematical logic and trial-and-error experimentation':

$$T_i = T_0 \exp\left(\frac{V_i}{C} - 1\right)$$

where T_i = travel time on a link at i iteration n
     T_0 = 'original (typical) travel time on the link', by which he clearly meant the time when volume equals capacity
     V_i = averaged assigned volumes from all preceding iterations
     C = link capacity
     $\exp(x)$ = the exponential function, 2.71828, raised to the power x

Smock's function evaluated at zero link flow yields a value of $0.37T_0$, which is substantially less than the value of $0.87T_0$ yielded by the BPR function.

30. Comments by James Fennessy to David Boyce in 2013; Fennessy was an early user of CDC TRANPLAN, and a developer of subsequent versions of this software (section 10.5.1.1).

31. For biographical details of Robert Dial, see sections 10.3.1 and 10.3.3.

32. The expanding literature on gravity, potential and spatial interaction models was synthesised by Walter Isard (1960), *Methods of Regional Analysis*, in Chapter 11 with 51 references. Although much of Isard's treatment concerned interregional flows of population as well as freight, the concepts are general. Helvig cited several of Isard's papers and books, but he did not include a reference to Isard's *Methods*.

33. Wilson (1967) is generally credited with the introduction of the negative exponential function into trip distribution models of person travel.

34. Based on an interview with Robert Dial in November 2003, and extensive notes he provided in August 2007, and subsequently.

35. Interviews of John Wootton by Huw Williams.

36. The publication of *Metropolitan Plan Making* resulted from the dedicated efforts of Chris McDonald.

37. William Wheaton (1974) revisited the Herbert–Stevens model, discussed some of its shortcomings, and proposed an alternative formulation and solution method.

3. Early developments in the UK

3.1 INTRODUCTION

In the late 1950s, after a post-war economic boom, London and other Western European cities were starting to encounter the growing impact of the motor age that many US and Canadian cities experienced over a decade earlier. The problems were manifest in a variety of ways, as described by Gerard Drake, director of the first London Traffic Study:

> acute and growing traffic congestion; central area parking shortages; increased incidence of road traffic accidents; decreasing patronage of bus and tram services; financial difficulties for the railways, even though suburban commuter services are overcrowded; the need for restrictions on the individual's use of his private vehicle to improve traffic flow and promote safety in the interest of the general public; and last, but certainly not least, mounting pressures for greatly increased capital expenditures for the construction of new highways and the modernization of existing main roads (Drake, 1963, 81).

In response to these growing concerns, the UK minister of transport, Ernest Marples [1907–1978], who had already endorsed an inter-urban motorway programme, introduced three activities concurrently: (a) he formed the London Traffic Management Unit; (b) he initiated major studies of traffic in London and Glasgow; and (c) he asked a senior civil servant, Colin Buchanan [1907–2001],[1] to look into problems arising from the car (Wootton, 2004).

Fifty years later, it is hard to imagine the apprehension and sense of urgency at the start of the 1960s with which British planners approached these problems and the prospect of mass motorisation. Rereading the report *Traffic in Towns* (Buchanan, 1963), one perhaps gets a flavour of those times and also the dilemmas faced presently by many cities of the developing world that are experiencing rapid rises in personal income and car ownership. The team of traffic engineers and town planners assembled by Buchanan was charged with investigating the long-term consequences for mobility and the urban environment of car ownership and use suggested by trends evident at that time.

In their report to the minister, the Steering Group addressed the challenge and potential consequence of 'the impending motor age' in words of Churchillian gravity:

It is impossible to spend any time on the study of the future of traffic in towns
... without being at once appalled by the magnitude of the emergency that is
coming upon us and inspired by the challenge that it presents. There is another
source of fascination. We are nourishing at immense cost a monster of great
potential destructiveness. And yet we love him dearly. Regarded in its collec-
tive aspect as 'the traffic problem' the motor car is clearly a menace which can
spoil our civilisation. But translated into terms of the particular vehicle that
stands in our garage (or more often nowadays, is parked outside our door, or
someone else's door), we regard it as one of our most treasured possessions or
dearest ambitions, an immense convenience, an expander of the dimensions of
life, an instrument of emancipation, a symbol of the modern age (Report of the
Steering Group to the UK Minister of Transport, preface to Buchanan, 1963,
para 55).

For inspiration Britain had already started to look westwards and was
quick to embrace the new systems approach to transportation planning
and the methods of travel forecasting under development. Visitors to the
US who were charged with witnessing these new developments embodied
in the transportation studies were clearly impressed by what they saw and
returned to convert the doubters:

As far as motor traffic is concerned, predictions about the increase in vehicle
ownership and the effect on traffic flows have not been conspicuously accurate in the past, and this has created doubts in many people's minds whether
it is really possible to predict changes in the pattern and scale of movement
in a complex urban community. Such doubts are fermented by the general
lack of understanding about how and why movement is generated and what
dictates the choice of method. If movements were completely random and
irregular no amount of study would be of any use, but research in the United
States in the last decade shows beyond doubt that urban movement is remarkably orderly, that motivation is basically rational and predictable, and that
definable relationships exist between any given pattern of land uses and the
character and amount of traffic that is generated (Buchanan and Crow, 1963,
37).

These authors saw the scientific study of movement and its relationship
to urban development as not only desirable but inevitably leading to the
'deployment of transportation studies on the American pattern but refined
and adapted to the smaller and more intimate scale of our own conditions'
(Buchanan and Crow, 1963, 37).

Soon after the Buchanan Report was published, the inauguration
of further transportation studies took place. These were to become
major instruments of the UK Ministry of Transport (and after 1970
the Department of the Environment) in policy development and local
decisions on capital investment and the balance between public transport
and the car. This chapter charts the transfer, adaptation and the main

theoretical and practical innovations in urban travel forecasting in UK transportation studies up until the early 1970s.

In section 3.2 we record the establishment of such transportation studies in the UK and the means by which, primarily through US consultants, the torch was passed, resulting in strong similarities in the approach to urban transportation analysis in the US and the UK. We note, as part of this legacy, the main variants of the conventional zone-based multi-stage[2] travel forecasting models applied in the early to mid-1960s.

In section 3.3, we describe a successful attempt to account for greater variability in travel behaviour 'within zones', rather than solely 'between zones', by adopting household classes as the units for analysis at the generation stage. The resulting household-based category analysis approach introduced by Wootton and Pick (1967) had major implications for both trip generation models and car ownership forecasting in UK studies.

Initially, as if on a parallel track, the multivariate statistical models based on modal choice observations of individual travellers, stemming from Stanley Warner's [1928–1992] pioneering research (Warner, 1962), appeared to offer an alternative to the mainstream in both the US and the UK. The derivation of information on the way people were considered to trade off travel time and money costs in their modal choices was however to be of great significance for the analysis and forecasting of travel, and the evaluation of transportation schemes. In the mid- to late 1960s we witness the emergence of the variously termed 'disutility' or 'generalised cost' concept derived from the studies of modal choice, and its adoption in conventional forecasting practice. In section 3.4 we describe these developments and the absorption of generalised costs into UK travel forecasting models in the late 1960s.

One of the most trenchant criticisms of models and methods of the early 1960s was the absence of a unifying theoretical approach to guide the formation of travel relationships and establish their validity in the forecasting process. This omission was most evident in the wide use of empirically derived functions: 'friction factors', 'diversion curves' and 'look-up' tables in the distribution, modal split and assignment models. In section 3.5, we describe the gradual emergence of analytic forms for the relationship between travel demand and its determinants, and particularly the wide use of the multinomial logit (MNL) share model. We discuss the introduction of a new approach by Alan Wilson, the 'entropy maximising method', to the interpretation of statistical variability or dispersion in travel patterns, and the theoretical and practical synthesis it provided, particularly in forecasting the modal split and the distribution of trips. Because Wilson offered an important new perspective on many of the problems confronting transportation analysts and urban and regional researchers, we discuss his contributions in some detail.

As in the US, the 1960s was a period of considerable refinement in the analysis, assignment and forecasting of flows in both highway and public transport networks. Two aspects received particular attention in the former:

1. the use of capacity restraint methods for achieving consistency between route selection and level-of-service provided by the highway system;
2. the incorporation of what were variously described as probabilistic or stochastic models of route selection.

In addition, a more realistic representation of the behaviour of passengers in public transport networks was partly a consequence of a greater emphasis on this mode in the formation of UK transportation plans. These advances are addressed in section 3.6.

In section 3.7 we discuss three aspects of UK practice in the late 1960s and early 1970s and note some important differences in the structure and form of the models adopted. Firstly, we describe the travel forecasting model applied in the SELNEC (South East Lancashire North East Cheshire) Transportation Study, which anticipated important subsequent developments, and must be regarded as one of the most technically advanced models anywhere at that time. Secondly, we discuss the variation in the overall specification of models together with their justification, particularly in relation to the position of modal split in the overall structure, and the means by which the multiple stages were joined together. Finally, we comment on the notion of validity accompanying the construction and testing of the travel forecasting models in this period and the results of a major study on their predictive accuracy.

In section 3.8, we examine the expanding scope of economic evaluation, and the relationship between the models developed for travel forecasting, and the performance measures adopted for project evaluation. In particular, some intriguing theoretical developments in the construction of economic measures of user benefit accompanying project appraisal are noted, which were later to be of great significance.

In section 3.9, the final section, we comment on the problems solved, outstanding challenges and changing attitudes towards traditional travel forecasting procedures. Throughout, we note some of the similarities and differences between the practices adopted in the US and the UK.

3.2 METHODS INHERITED FROM THE US AND EARLIER STUDIES

3.2.1 Establishment of Land Use – Transportation Studies in the UK

Prior to the adoption of a comprehensive US-style systems approach in the UK, there was already a suggestion of what was to come. In the late 1950s, the UK Ministry of Transport started to encourage local authorities in the conurbations to co-operate in the production of long-term highway plans for their areas and, for this purpose, to adopt the US practices of surveying traffic patterns, particularly origin–destination movements, and analysing them with computers (Starkie, 1973; Bruton, 1975). There is some debate as to the first 'comprehensive analysis of the movement of people and goods in a single large urban area', although 'Leicester and the County of London vie for the claim to have been first to place stress on the quantified approach' (Starkie, 1973, 328). The first major conurbation traffic studies, however, were undertaken in London and Glasgow. Begun in 1961–62, the London Traffic Survey was primarily concerned with establishing land use and traffic data for a base year of 1961 and forecasting traffic on highway networks for 1971 and 1981 (Freeman, Fox, Wilbur Smith and Associates, 1966).[3]

At the turn of the decade when these studies were in their early stages, there was a growing appreciation of the relationship between urban development and transportation planning that was emerging from early studies in the US (Starkie, 1973). This led, as noted in section 3.1, to the appointment of Colin Buchanan to lead a team to investigate the long-term consequences for the urban environment of traffic growth and potential road construction. The Buchanan Report, *Traffic in Towns* (Buchanan, 1963), was destined to have a major guiding influence on urban transportation planning in the UK. Following publication of the report, a joint circular was produced by the UK ministers of transport and housing and local government in January 1964, endorsing the report's findings and emphasising the need for local authorities to undertake land use – transportation studies 'to achieve a co-ordinated approach to land-use and transport planning' (Bruton, 1975, 20).

The first study was the West Midlands Transportation Study, begun in 1964; those in the other conurbations and larger urban areas soon followed: Greater Glasgow (1964), Teesside (1965), Belfast (1965), SELNEC (1965), Merseyside (1966), West Yorkshire (1967) and Tyneside (1967) (see Spence, 1968 and Starkie, 1973, 332 for the timing, duration and organisation of the first generation of UK transportation studies in the conurbations and larger free-standing towns). The UK Ministry of Transport was active in encouraging these studies, making a contribution to their technical direction and sharing the costs with the local authorities involved.

These 'comprehensive' studies were meant to contribute to decisions on the future highway and public transport networks in a study area. As in the US, central to their execution were:

1. surveys of the use of land and the movement of people and goods in an area;
2. projections of car ownership, population, employment and other land uses;
3. on the basis of computer models, the derivation of travel and traffic forecasts for networks envisaged for some future year(s).

3.2.2 Transfer of Expertise and Technology in the Early 1960s

The earliest conurbation studies in the UK, such as those in London and Glasgow, were carried out by consortia involving teams of British and American consultants. 'The formation of these teams ensured that the experience gained in the urban land use – transportation studies carried out in America in the 1950s was transferred to British practice' (Wootton, 2004, 274). As described in an early textbook, 'This knowledge of the traffic forecasting model was an essential first step in developing fresh methods designed more specifically to answer the particular problem of obtaining the best return from the limited funds available for investment in urban and rural transport infrastructure' (Lane et al, 1971, 205).

John Wootton (M.Eng., University of California Berkeley, 1963) was one of a handful of British transportation engineers who undertook graduate work in the US and returned to the UK to distinguished careers in transportation consultancy, senior transportation planning and management, and academia (others were Brian Martin, M.S., MIT and Tony Ridley, Ph.D., University of California Berkeley). Wootton joined Wilbur Smith and Associates in London in 1962 to work on the London Traffic Survey. As one of the few people with analytic experience at that time, he recalled being drawn inexorably to traffic modelling.[4] Echoing the earlier comments of Chapter 2, Wootton recalled how the analysis of transportation survey data and computers grew up together:

> in 1962, when the analysis of the London and Glasgow Survey data began, computers were so new that there were only two computers in Britain (IBM 7090's) powerful and large enough for completing the task. . . . Happy hours were spent during the middle of many nights watching magnetic tapes turn and lights flash until the results produced by the computer programmes were printed (Wootton, 2004, 276).

These initial studies were limited in scope and drew on the earlier experience in Detroit and Chicago for their methodology (Lane et al, 1971; Starkie, 1973; Bruton, 1975). Even so, they provided formidable challenges for the collection and analysis of data. The surveys were processed and analysed with specially written computer programs, while those for implementing the traffic models were acquired from the US. In the case of Freeman, Fox and Wilbur Smith, Wootton recalls: 'Initially, we used the BPR suite of programs but Wilburs bought a CDC 3300 for which we had to write new programs.'[5] This development resulted in the Transport Analysis Programs (TAP), written by Wootton and his colleagues, allowing innovative methods and models developed in the UK to be incorporated in an evolutionary way in the second half of the 1960s.

Certainly, in those early days access to computing services was influential on what could be achieved. As Martin Richards, who joined the London Traffic Management Unit direct from his civil engineering degree at University College London, later recalled:

> access to computing and the limited software available on a bureau basis influenced much of what was done. I recall, when working on the Worcester Transport Study of the mid 1960s, we would send run specifications to English Electric Computers (later to become BARIC) by British Rail's Red Star, and collect the output many days later, also sent Red Star. What we could do was limited by their software as well as the time taken to complete a run, including checking for input/keying errors and re-runs.[6]

With reference to data, he added:

> much of the modelling depended on data collected specifically for the studies, and there was a steep learning curve as skills in survey design and execution developed as well as survey processing and analysis software. Sampling, interview process, dealing with missing data, geo-coding were among the areas on which real progress was made.

3.2.3 Methods for Forecasting Travel in the Early Transportation Studies

3.2.3.1 Available methods

In Chapter 2 we outlined in some detail the general approaches to transportation planning and travel forecasting in early US studies. These studies were reviewed for a British audience by Davinroy et al (1963), and later for the field generally by Hutchinson (1974) and Stopher and Meyburg (1975). We review briefly the situation in the early 1960s as a basis for considering future innovations.

In the early days of the 1960s, prior to any standardisation of the methods around a broadly common multi-stage approach, there were almost as many ways of preparing forecasts as there were studies. One example is the relationship between trips generated at the zonal level and land use characteristics, where expansion factors and regression models were applied in various forms (Davinroy et al, 1963). At the distribution stage, growth factor methods devised by Fratar and Furness were applied, as well as intervening opportunity and gravity models to determine the effect of changes in travel times on the distribution patterns. At the assignment stage, the diversion curve approach was giving way to a computer-based 'all-or-nothing' allocation of origin–destination (O-D) flows to shortest routes. Capacity restraint methods relating travel times to congestion on individual links were at a very early stage of development.

Methods for analysing public transport systems were rudimentary both with respect to determining modal choice and in the network representation and assignments. In the early 1960s modal split models were still in their infancy; there was a widespread view that 'at the present time this phase is probably the most inadequate of those comprising traffic analysis' (Davinroy et al, 1963, 371). The earliest travel forecasting models were appropriately described as three-stage models; studies giving serious consideration to forecasting modal split were based on zonal averages of socio-economic variables, such as car ownership and income, at the trip ends, which Starkie (1973) identified as one of the more unsuitable transfers of US methods to a UK setting. Because of a failure to identify level-of-service (the times and costs of travel on the modes) as a determining factor of modal choice, such models would indicate an inexorably declining share of public transport as real levels of income and car ownership rose, irrespective of policy to improve the public transport system. As David Starkie remarked:

> This was the situation in general terms when the concept of the North American urban transportation study was first introduced in this country and it was therefore out of step with British circumstances, where the overwhelming proportion of conurbation journeys was made by public transport and out of phase with the views and attitudes then germinating amongst those who determined transport policy (Starkie, 1973, 371).

There were attempts in the early 1960s to introduce zonal accessibility variables, both in US studies (for example, in the studies for Puget Sound, Erie and south-eastern Wisconsin)[7] and in Britain (in the studies for Glasgow, Leicester and London). These approaches were viewed as being rather crude, however, and lacking in sensitivity to level-of-service variables to appropriately inform policy. Later in this chapter we comment further on this issue.

In the early 1960s, modal split models of the 'trip-interchange' variety, which treated modal opportunities as a travel market, had only recently been formulated. The pioneering contributions of Traffic Research Corporation (TRC) on post-distribution modal split models (Hill and von Cube, 1963) were absorbed into UK practice in the Merseyside Area Land-Use/Transportation Study (MALTS) and West Yorkshire Transportation Study undertaken by the Traffic Research Corporation (1969a, 1969b), as well as adopted in the London Transportation Study (LTS III) (Tressider et al, 1968). In these studies the distribution and modal share models were expressed in terms of empirically derived functions based on modal travel times.

Interestingly, Davinroy et al (1963) emphasised the interdependency of the models in the overall procedure, and the need for some feedback mechanism to achieve consistency in travel times throughout. They remarked:

> Today the trend is towards a systems approach. This implies a consideration of each step as part of the whole process and not as one of three separate steps. As yet the techniques which have been developed have not been able to consider the complete process. For this reason, separate methods have been described here. Yet it is important to emphasize the interdependence of each phase. This interdependence is not one way. Not only does assignment depend on generation and distribution, but there must also be a 'feedback' of data from the assignment phase to the earlier phases. . . . Up to the present no great progress has been made in the feedback of data. There have been some elementary attempts, but largely because of the complexities which are introduced, they have not been extensive. There has been use of iterative techniques in order to achieve convergence of the distribution and assignment phases (Davinroy et al, 1963, 371).

There is little evidence that feedback was undertaken in any systematic way in the earliest UK studies, but by the late 1960s there was both recognition of its importance and some rudimentary attempts to achieve consistent solutions. An example of the implementation of feedback is described in section 3.7.

3.2.3.2 Treatment of land use

Although the studies were termed land use – transportation studies, there was little attempt in the UK to reflect the effect of transportation on land use other than in a general descriptive way (Starkie, 1973; Bruton, 1975). Moreover, compared to the US, where land use models were being used to allocate population and employment in several land use – transportation studies, Bruton commented:

In Britain ... with its long history of comparatively strong land-use controls, the approach to forecasting of future land-use distribution and characteristics has been somewhat different. Indeed, with notable and recent exceptions, such as the Teesside study, it could be argued that in Britain no real attempt has been made to forecast, on a systematic and comprehensive basis, estimates of the future land-use characteristics and distribution. Rather, *ad hoc* estimates of land-use distribution tend to be produced, based on generalized and rather crude predictions of population and employment (Bruton, 1975, 35).

To our knowledge no UK transportation study in the 1960s utilised land use forecasts derived from urban models. However, a great deal of research, development and application to regional growth based on the Lowry model occurred in the UK in the 1960s, particularly in a structure planning context (Wilson, 1971, 1973a; Batty, 1972). In section 3.5 and more extensively in Chapter 9, we discuss the development of land use models and particularly the evolution of integrated land use – transportation models in Britain.

Furthermore, very few transportation studies carried out systematic testing of alternative land use plans (Dalvi and Martin, 1973). Unlike several studies in the US where land use – transportation alternatives were analysed (Boyce et al, 1970), in the UK the time and resources involved in drawing up the latter almost invariably resulted in a single land use arrangement with the possibility of some minor sensitivity analysis about that plan.

3.3 FROM ZONES TO HOUSEHOLDS AT THE TRIP GENERATION STAGE

3.3.1 Household-Based Category Analysis for Trip Generation

The early methods of trip generation based on zonal regression equations, while sometimes identifying key determining variables and giving impressive goodness-of-fit statistics, were often to be found wanting. Problems of multicollinearity and the dangers of ecological fallacy were ever present (Stopher and Meyburg, 1975; Ortúzar and Willumsen, 2011). The lack of causality and stability of parameters, when transferred to different areas and zoning systems, made them an unpromising basis for forecasting.

The early studies of Oi and Shuldiner (1962) in the US (section 2.5.2) drew attention to the potential of trip generation approaches based on the household as the unit of analysis. By directly addressing and accounting for the variation of travel between household classes or categories rather than the zone, this new approach offered the potential for greater behavioural content and stability in forecasting. Loss of information accompanying aggregation of trips and explanatory variables to the zonal level prior to model specification was avoided. Indeed, it was later shown that zone-based models captured a relatively small proportion of the variation of travel among households in an urban area (Fleet and Robertson, 1968). These realisations led to 'household-based category analysis' models in the UK (Wootton and Pick, 1967) and 'cross-classified household models' later in the US (US DoT, 1972a, 1975). In the following we use the UK terminology as expressed in the mid-1960s by its originators John Wootton and Gerald Pick at Freeman, Fox and Wilbur Smith.

In this disaggregated formulation the number of trips generated in a zone could be expressed in terms of the number of households in different household categories multiplied by the average trip rates for those categories. Summation over the contributions from the various categories would then generate zonal trip production totals. Under the assumption that trip rates for various household categories and other external factors would remain stable, the burden of forecasting was passed to determining the number of households in the different categories within each zone for the future year(s).

In applying the approach, Wootton and Pick were concerned with four different questions:

1. What combination of household characteristics should be taken to define the categories?
2. Did these combinations allow statistically reliable trip rates to be established?
3. How were the distributions of households over household groups to be forecast?
4. Was the approach transferable to other study areas?

These choices implied a trade-off between the number of categories to be included to account for significant variation between households, on the one hand, and the requirement for reliable estimates of the mean trip rates to be established, particularly in those categories with relatively few observations, on the other. This approach prompted the search for relatively homogeneous household categories with low intra- and high inter-category variations in trip rates. They first successfully addressed these issues in the London Traffic Survey and, more fully, in the West Midlands Study (Wootton and Pick, 1967).

John Wootton recalled these early efforts:

Attempts to predict trip ends using multiple linear regression analysis were proving to be poor and there was the added need of predicting future levels of car ownership at a zonal level. The moment of inspiration came when I linked some illustrations I had seen in a paper while at Berkeley in 1962/3 to probability theory. The paper, by Paul Shuldiner illustrated the number of journeys made by families with no car and those with a car. I suddenly realised that using probability theory it should be possible to determine the number of families with no car, one car, two cars, etc. using probability distributions and a few independent variables. One could then tabulate the home interview data in a corresponding structure and estimate the number of trips made.[8]

Wootton and Pick tested various household categories in terms of combinations of income, car ownership and household structure variables and also formulated different probability distributions to estimate the numbers of households in each:

> Once we could classify the number of families by car ownership estimating the trips generated was a fairly straightforward process. Income proved to be important not only in determining the probability of owning a car but also in the level of trip making. The other important variable was the number of people in the family. We spent some time exploring different ways of representing family structures (size, age and children were important), eventually settling on a Poisson distribution to determine the number of people in a family and a binomial to determine the number of children. A strong influence on the choice of categories was the need to maintain reasonable sample sizes. Less important, but relevant, was where a family lived. It was clear that a family was more likely to own a car if they lived in a suburb than if they lived in a city centre, but we could not determine the precise factors involved. We decided to use residential density as a proxy for the location effects.[9]

In the West Midlands Transportation Study, mean trip rates were established for 108 household categories, which were combinations of various levels associated with three variables: (a) car ownership (0, 1, 2+); (b) household income (six levels); and (c) household structure (six levels relating to household size and number of workers) (Wootton and Pick, 1967). This categorisation provided a template for many other UK transportation studies.[10] To test the stability and transferability of their approach, Wootton and Pick investigated the variation in household trip rates in both London and the West Midlands and the extent to which different levels of public transport accessibility would be significant.

Their studies on London and Birmingham, including a back-casting exercise, suggested that trip generation rates by both car and public transport were reasonably transferable over space and time. They noted: 'it is encouraging to find families in the same category behave in a similar manner in both areas', adding that the trip rates were relatively insensitive to accessibility indices. 'These indices suggest that the effects of changes in levels of public transport service are less important than the household characteristics' (Wootton and Pick, 1967, 141, 150).

Trip attraction models could be developed on the same basis, in which land use categories were defined, based on standard industrial classes, and trip rates established for each. In the West Midlands and typical applications that followed, eight categories were applied.[11] In the UK, household-based category or cross-classification analysis made a dramatic impact on the trip generation procedures applied in practice from the late 1960s onwards. At least in the larger studies, zone-based regression models for trip production quickly fell from grace, although zone-based regression analyses were often retained to forecast trip attractions.

In the late 1960s and early 1970s various practical and theoretical developments of the category analysis technique took place (Pick and Gill, 1970). From a methodological viewpoint, the approach was quickly recognised to be a form of regression analysis incorporating dummy variables, the dependent variable being the number of trips made by a household and the independent variables recording the presence or absence of a household in the various categories (for example, Douglas and Lewis, 1970, 1971; Douglas, 1973). Analysis of variance techniques were also applied to identify the significance of individual variables and the structure of dependency between the variables over which categories were defined (Dale, 1973, 1977).

In the West Midlands model, the number of trips generated per day in each household category was further disaggregated by purpose (work, business, education, shopping, social and non-home-based) and by mode (car drivers or motorcyclists, public transport passengers and others, mostly car passengers), and became a fairly widely used method of travel forecasting for those studies that performed modal split prior to the distribution of trips.

3.3.2 Developments in Car Ownership Forecasting

Early forecasts of car ownership in the UK were made on the basis of past trends and comparisons with conditions in the US. 'Thus in the London Transportation Study (1966) it was assumed that car-ownership in London in 1981 would be similar to levels already achieved in metropolitan Boston, Philadelphia and New York' (Lane et al, 1971, 162).[12]

Along similar lines, John Tanner's influential studies at the UK Road Research Laboratory used a time series approach (Tanner, 1965) involving the estimation of the parameters of a logistical curve, expressing the number of vehicles per person as a function of time. This curve was assumed to reflect that the market penetration of cars would rise, slowly at first, then grow at a fairly constant rate and eventually approach a 'saturation rate', S. The initial model contained three parameters, α, β and S, the saturation rate.[13] Forecasts were particularly sensitive to the value of the saturation rate, which was estimated by Tanner on the basis of linear regressions and assumptions relating the rate of growth of car ownership to the actual levels of that variable. Data from the UK and the US were used for this purpose; for a good exposition of this approach, see Ortúzar and Willumsen (2011, section 15.3). Tanner revised his forecasts in 1965, 1974 and 1977, and included more explanatory variables: income per capita, residential density and the cost of motoring.

By the late 1960s, there was discomfort among some car ownership forecasters with the use of trend extrapolation techniques, which were considered to contain too many assumptions and to be of limited practical use at the local level (e.g., Button et al, 1982; Whelan, 2007). As described above, in the early 1960s, in contrast to adopting the aggregate time series approach, Wootton and Pick were exploring the possibility of using cross-sectional data to relate car ownership to household income as a basis for deriving forecasts of both car ownership and the generation of trips. From functions expressing the conditional probabilities of car ownership against income and knowledge of the distribution of household income across a population, the numbers of households with 0, 1 and 2+ cars were established. Forecasts could then be made by estimating the number of households in each income group in future periods.

Using data from the West Midlands, Wootton and Pick derived the set of conditional probabilities of car ownership against household income relative to the price of cars. They noted that 'evidence has also been gained that these relationships remain remarkably stable from one area to another, even between countries' (Wootton and Pick, 1967, 144), and assumed these forms would remain stable over time while the distribution of income would change. To test the validity of the technique, they estimated car ownership in the West Midlands over the period 1953–65 using the historical variation in car prices, and obtained 'good agreement with actual car ownership' (Wootton and Pick, 1967, 148).

Over the period to the early 1970s several variants of the above approach were developed in the UK characterised by differences in the functional forms and number and type of explanatory variables. Button et al (1982) gave a full discussion and critique of the various approaches to car ownership forecasting and their application in the UK; for a more recent perspective, see Whelan (2007, section 2).

3.4 DRAWING FROM MICRO-STUDIES: THE 'GENERALISED COST' OF TRAVEL

3.4.1 Introduction

The impression is often given that the approach to travel forecasting based on 'micro' or 'disaggregate' models, specified and estimated at the level of the individual, made little impact on the conventional travel forecasting methods of the 1960s. There is some truth in this assertion, but it is more relevant to the US than to the UK. Certainly, during this period, there was no systematic attempt to derive network flows or travel demand by aggregating model results obtained at the individual level. However, there are three reasons why we consider here in a preliminary manner the micro-level or disaggregate approach to modal choice, pioneered by Stanley Warner in his study of Chicago commuters (Warner, 1962):

1. Studies at the micro-level established the concept of 'generalised cost', which was absorbed directly into conventional aggregate multi-stage demand models in the late 1960s in the UK.
2. During this period, the generalised cost concept provided a bridge between the travel forecasting procedure and the economic evaluation of transportation projects, and attained a standard form.
3. As early as the mid-1960s, the micro-approach was being referenced in powerful critiques of the conventional styles of analysis.

We shall have much to say about this class of models in Chapter 4 and, in particular, the marriage of theoretical perspectives based on micro-economics with greater statistical sophistication of dealing with data on individuals. Here we briefly record the background to selected studies of modal choice conducted in the 1960s, and how a standard form of 'generalised cost', or 'disutility', emerged in the UK, to be widely applied in subsequent travel forecasting models.

3.4.2 Disaggregate Modal Choice Models: Research of Warner and Quarmby

Early disaggregate studies of modal choice were not primarily directed at forecasting, but at understanding, and in some cases measuring the trade-off individuals were assumed to make between travel time and money cost (interpreted as the 'value of time'), and more generally determining the range of measurable factors influential in modal choice. In this respect the studies of Warner (1962), Moses and Williamson (1963), Lisco (1967) and Lave (1969) in the US, and of Beesley (1965), Quarmby (1967) and Stopher (1969) in the UK, were particularly significant. Reichman and Stopher (1971) and Stopher and Meyburg (1975) provided a detailed review of these studies. Investigations in the late 1960s and early 1970s at the Local Government Operational Research Unit (LGORU) of modelling choice between modes for the journey to work, drawing on the research of Warner, Beesley and Quarmby, are also noteworthy (Gapper and Rolfe, 1968; Rogers et al, 1970; Davies and Rogers, 1973).[14] For a fuller discussion of early UK work on demand analysis and the value of time, see Daly (2013).

Rereading Stanley Warner's Ph.D. thesis, *Stochastic Choice of Mode in Urban Travel: A Study in Binary Choice*, undertaken at Northwestern University (Warner, 1962), one cannot help being struck by how utterly different it was compared with practical transportation study procedures in use at that time. Here was a study of choice between competing travel options based on the trip characteristics and socio-economic attributes of the individuals concerned. Warner's model of modal selection was specified in probabilistic terms, economic in flavour, with concern for elasticities, and with detailed regard for parameter estimation within a multivariate statistical framework.

Warner's main objective was to determine how modal choice was influenced by the travel times and costs of various modes, as well as demographic and socio-economic variables of the travellers, such as income, age and sex. He used data on trips to the Chicago central business district (CBD) from an outer suburban area of Chicago in multiple regression and discriminant analyses to predict the probability of an individual selecting a particular mode in binary choice contexts (car and urban rail transit; car and suburban train; and suburban train and urban rail transit) for work and non-work trips. From the parameter estimates, the significance of different factors in individual choice was determined and the associated demand elasticities derived. In the probabilistic model derived by Warner for modal choice between train and car, the logarithm of the cost ratios for the two modes, and the logarithm of the time ratios were taken as part of the discriminant function to allocate individuals to the modes.

As Stopher and Meyburg later noted: 'Following this work, whose significance was not recognised for some time, there appears to have been something of a hiatus in disaggregate, mode-choice work until a number of pioneering efforts were published in the period 1967 through 1969' (Stopher and Meyburg, 1975, 300).

Included in the reviews by Reichman and Stopher (1971) and Stopher and Meyburg (1975, Chapter 16) was research undertaken in the mid-1960s by David Quarmby, which was particularly important for the way that cost and level-of-service variables were incorporated in aggregate travel forecasting models in the UK. Moreover, it was central to the methodology applied in the UK for the economic evaluation of transportation projects (section 3.8).

David Quarmby graduated from the University of Cambridge in 1962 with a degree in engineering and economics, an unusual combination in those days. He moved to the University of Leeds, where after a one-year post-graduate course in management he started his professional life as a lecturer in operational research and subsequently in transport economics. In contrast to that of Stanley Warner, the study undertaken by Quarmby for his Ph.D. thesis, 'Factors Affecting Modal Choice for the Journey to Work', and reported in Quarmby (1967), was conducted against a background of considerable practical development of aggregate 'trip-interchange' modal split models. By the mid-1960s, the 'trip-end' modal split models were gradually being replaced in the larger US transportation studies by trip-interchange models, applied after the distribution of trips in the overall four-step sequence. The innovative modal split model developed by Hill and von Cube (1963) of Traffic Research Corporation of Toronto was, according to Quarmby (1967, 277), 'undoubtedly the best available for predicting travel within urban areas for aggregated groups of zones, and it is based on reasonable hypotheses of behaviour'. However, Quarmby was critical of the zonal basis of the TRC approach, noting that modal choice was found to be fairly sensitive to level-of-service ratios, and:

one would expect as much variation of travel time ratios, service ratios and perhaps cost ratios among individual observations *within* one zone as among the mean values of these variables *between different* pairs of zones. This is recognised by TRC and is one of the strongest arguments against attempting to use diversion curves and zonal analysis for predicting the use of public transport for particular routes or corridors, or for investigating policy changes on a 'micro' basis (Quarmby, 1967, 276).

He warned of the problems of adopting aggregate zone-based approaches, including the dangers of ecological fallacies and relationships that would lack true behavioural correlations and temporal validity.

In the theoretical foundations of Quarmby's study, there was a close relationship between the assumed economic motivation of individuals and the multivariate statistical analysis. Here, Quarmby drew on the discriminant analysis approach adopted by Warner (1962) and the insights obtained from a simpler graphical approach used by Beesley (1965) to determine the trade-off between time differences and cost differences. He summarised the relationship between the underpinning notion of utilities and choice and the statistical technique in the following terms:

We have thus derived, from first principles, a discriminant analysis solution: from basic notions of disutility and choice advancing to the simple misclassification criterion used by Beesley, and subsequently to a form using total population characteristics, in a way that is both behaviourally and intuitively valid. The relative disutility function becomes what is known as the discriminator or discriminant function (Quarmby, 1967, 304).

In deciding which independent variables to test, he drew on the results of both Warner and TRC.

Data for Quarmby's study of modal choice for the journey to work to the Leeds CBD were drawn from a firm-based survey, yielding 542 observations for commuters who had a choice between car and bus, and 97 between car and train. The following seven factors formed the basis for the initial data analysis: (a) relative overall travel time; (b) relative excess (walking, waiting and transfer) travel time; (c) relative cost; (d) income; (e) car demand ratio (the ratio of the number of driving licences to the number of cars in the household); (f) use of car for work; and (g) ownership of the car by the firm. Quarmby found differences in relative times and costs, as determinants of modal choice, reflected in statistical goodness-of-fit measures, to be consistently better measures than ratios or logarithms. He drew the following conclusion:

> travel time difference, excess travel time difference, cost difference, and the possibility of use of the car at work are all important in influencing modal choice; income is an insignificant factor most probably because of the very small cost differences between modes . . . as also manifested by a small difference between mean incomes for both sets of mode users. It was also found that walking and waiting times are worth between two and three times in-vehicle times; that an average value of time on both modes lies between about . . . 21 percent and 25 percent of wage rates (or, leaving out two significant factors, about one third of wage rates, corresponding closely with Beesley's results) (Quarmby, 1967, 297).

While the initial motivation for Quarmby's study was the need to understand what factors affected the choices people were making, he related: 'Discovering that I had also thereby elicited a value of time was a fascinating and unexpected by-product!'[15] Quarmby left the University of Leeds in October 1966 to join the Mathematical Advisory Unit (MAU) in the Economic Planning Directorate of the UK Ministry of Transport, then under Alan Wilson's leadership. There he played a crucial role in the development of the evaluation methodology for land use and transportation schemes.

Although mode selection in the multivariate statistical studies of Warner, Quarmby and others was sometimes cast in different functional forms and employed different techniques for parameter estimation, they

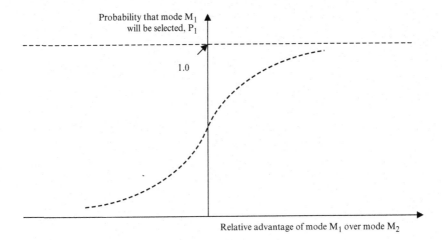

Figure 3.1   Probability of mode selection as a function of relative
                  advantage

gave rise to rather similar ogive-shaped curves; see Figure 3.1. These
curves expressed the probability of an individual selecting, or being allocated to, a given alternative (mode) in terms of the relative advantage
of one mode in relation to the other. This relative advantage was often
reduced to a linear function of the difference between the modal attributes
or some transformation of them. We postpone to section 4.2 further discussion of the theory for generating such curves and the subtle differences
between their functional forms.

3.4.3   Emergence of the Concept of 'Generalised Cost' of Travel

In conventional travel forecasting models the term 'impedance' was
often reserved for describing the inhibiting character of travel time and
geographical separation; as discussed in section 2.3.4, this term was
used in the international literature mainly in the early 1960s. Interzonal
centroid-to-centroid car travel time was often taken as a single measure
of impedance, especially for spatial interaction models (trip distribution).
The above studies on modal choice, however, postulated the disutility of
travel to be a (typically linear) function of various attributes assumed to be
influential in individual mode choice. From the late 1960s in the UK, the
terms 'disutility' and 'generalised cost' were increasingly treated almost
interchangeably to describe this linear expression. These terms began to
replace 'impedance' in network and spatial interaction models.

Following Quarmby's findings, the disutility or generalised cost of travel in money units was understood in the UK to represent a linear combination of travel attributes, as follows:

$$\text{generalised cost} = \alpha_1 \times \text{travel time} + \alpha_2 \text{ excess time} + \text{money cost}$$

The parameters α_1 and α_2 were, respectively, often referred to as the behavioural values of travel time and excess (walking, waiting and any transfer) time. These values varied by income, by trip purpose and over time, and were adapted from Quarmby's original study.

As a 'rule-of-thumb', excess times were regarded as approximately twice as onerous as in-vehicle time. This factor was usually taken to imply that people were prepared on average to pay double (or more) the amount to reduce excess times by one unit compared with a similar reduction of in-vehicle time. In this regard, the quantitative challenge of improving the relative position of public transport in relation to the car, and thus bringing about significant modal switching 'through the carrot' – improving times on the public transport system (average vehicle speed, frequencies and spatial coverage) or reducing fares – against the proverbial 'stick' of parking and other restraint policies, became much clearer.

By substituting the interzonal (centroid-to-centroid) values of the travel attributes into the generalised cost formula, and applying the relative weights derived by Quarmby, the 'average' interzonal generalised costs by each mode could be obtained. In the UK, the stage was set for the introduction of generalised cost, with its flexibility in the representation of transportation policies, into the mainstream of conventional travel forecasting practice. According to David Quarmby, who actually referred to 'disutilities' in his 1967 study, the term 'generalised cost' was coined by Alan Wilson at the Mathematical Advisory Unit.[16] It is to a discussion of his contributions that we now turn.

3.5 THE ENTROPY MAXIMISING APPROACH TO TRAVEL MODELLING

3.5.1 Wilson's Early Work and Its Impact

In 1967 an extraordinary paper was published in the first volume of the new journal *Transportation Research*, which became one of the most cited papers in the history of urban transportation and regional science. Its author was a University of Cambridge-trained mathematician who, after a period in the theoretical physics section of the Rutherford Nuclear

Laboratories, had converted to the social sciences by joining the Institute of Economics and Statistics at the University of Oxford in 1966. There, Alan Wilson[17] joined a team led by Christopher Foster,[18] who with Michael Beesley had recently published a seminal paper on cost–benefit analysis applied to the proposed addition of the Victoria Line to the London Underground system (Foster and Beesley, 1963).

Foster and his colleagues were interested in the impact of such major transportation investments on land use. In that new research environment, Wilson began his research on travel behaviour and the interrelationship between transportation and land use. Reviewing US transportation and urban development models of that period, Wilson was struck by what he later described as 'fudge factors' introduced to make the spatial interaction models consistent with outputs from the generation stage. Being familiar with the principles of statistical physics, he immediately saw a correspondence between the partition functions of the statistical mechanics of gases and the 'balancing factors' used for the distribution of trips in standard models of that time.[19]

Wilson's insight was to interpret the spatial interaction pattern, hitherto viewed in terms of a gravitational analogy, as the most likely arrangement of trips between origin and destination zones that was consistent with the total trips produced by, and attracted to, each zone, and with the total generalised cost of travel of the trip distribution pattern observed in survey data. Although the initial derivation of the 'doubly-constrained' spatial interaction model for the journey to work drew on the analogy from statistical physics, Wilson showed how such models were compatible with different interpretations, drawing on ideas from information theory and Bayesian statistics (Wilson, 1970), and later described the procedure as 'a statistical average of the behaviour of individuals making trips' (Wilson, 1973a, 288).

In Wilson's approach, travel and location models were derived by determining the most likely pattern of trips (or trip proportions) that maximised an entropy function that expressed the number of possible ways that travel could occur, subject to a set of constraints reflecting the information independently available to the analyst.[20] In this constrained maximisation problem, the 'balancing factors' of the standard gravity trip distribution models were introduced naturally through Lagrange multipliers accompanying each constraint, ensuring that the distribution pattern was consistent with the 'trip-end constraints' determined from the trip generation models. These balancing factors bore a strong (reciprocal) resemblance to accessibility measures and were often interpreted as such.[21] The empirically derived 'deterrence function' of conventional distribution models emerged in this approach as a specific form, a negative exponential function of the generalised cost, with an associated parameter λ_D.[22]

In a synthesis of existing spatial interaction models, what Wilson described as a 'family of models' could be generated by maximising the entropy associated with the distribution of trips, subject to various constraints to be satisfied by the trip pattern. Thus, 'doubly-constrained' (sometimes termed 'production–attraction-constrained') journey-to-work distribution models were characterised by independent estimates of the trips generated by workers and attracted to employment opportunities in the various zones obtained from the generation model.[23] 'Singly-constrained' (sometimes referred to as 'production-constrained' or 'attraction-constrained') models pertaining, for example, to shopping and residential choice contexts required the distribution pattern to be consistent with information available at only one end, either the origin or the destination, of the trip. What was both interesting and significant was the expression of such location models as multinomial logit forms, with an added zone-dependent multiplier, or balancing factor, for the journey-to-work model. Later, we will say more about these particular forms and how the demand for travel varied with the generalised cost of alternative travel options.

Although Wilson's 1967 paper is mainly noted for its development of a new approach to the derivation of the gravity model from entropy maximising principles, it introduced several significant contributions, which are often overlooked, as follows:

1. reinterpretation of spatial interaction/location models within a probabilistic (entropy maximising) framework;
2. derivation of a family of spatial interaction/location models of multinomial logit form that included all existing types;
3. the introduction of new multi-modal, multi-person-type models of practical importance, in particular a 'joint distribution modal split' model, which we denote **D-M**, of multinomial logit form;
4. establishment of the concept of generalised cost in zone-based spatial interaction (distribution) and modal split models;
5. identification of 'composite impedance' measures for the distribution of trips in terms of the modal costs;
6. synthesis of the gravity and intervening opportunity models;
7. introduction of accessibility measures consistent with the models used for the distribution of trips.

In introducing the concept of generalised cost in the multi-modal distribution model, Wilson referred to the work of Quarmby, also in the Mathematical Advisory Unit, in these terms:

It should be remarked that the modal split formula ... is identical in form to that derived from a statistical approach to modal split using discriminant analysis (Quarmby, 1967). There could be a complete identification if the generalised cost c could be identified with the discriminant function used by the statisticians. If such an identification can be made, then discriminant analysis would provide a method for determining the generalised costs (Wilson, 1967).

Thus, Wilson took the disutility/generalised cost concept, which in Quarmby's formulation was used to express hypotheses relating to individual behaviour, and embedded it directly into the forecasting procedures for groups travelling between zones. In section 3.7 we discuss its introduction into the forecasting model adopted in the SELNEC Transportation Study, where, as a first approximation, the relative weightings on the travel attributes derived from Quarmby's micro-approach were retained in the calibration of the model.

3.5.2 Wilson's Synthesis: Multinomial Logit Share Models

Wilson (1969, 1970) provided a unified way of viewing the statistical dispersion that could be 'observed' in personal location and travel choices accompanying trip distribution, modal split and route split patterns between different zones. With suitable market stratification, he showed that the respective models could all be expressed as proportions or shares of a travel market associated with different locations, modes and routes, respectively, and were of multinomial logit form. These could be derived by maximising an appropriately defined entropy function, subject to any relevant constraints. This formulation resulted in the most likely probability distributions consistent with information available to the analyst.

In this way, the distribution of trips among various locations (d) and their share among various modes (m) and among various routes (r) could be described, analysed and predicted through multinomial logit expressions,[24] with corresponding parameters λ_D, λ_M and λ_R, and a suitably constructed generalised cost as the explanatory variable mediating the effect of transportation policies.[25] In this framework the dispersion or spread in trip patterns was interpreted in entropy maximising terms.

3.5.3 Linking the Stages Together: Towards Hierarchical Logit Models

Having derived distribution/location **D**, modal split **M** and route split **R** models, the latter implicit in the assignment model **A**, each of similar analytic form, within the entropy maximising framework, Wilson (1967, 1969, 1970) considered in detail how they could be linked together. With his eye firmly on the conventional multi-stage travel forecasting models, he explored different ways of linking distribution and modal split models, representing the demand for combinations of destinations and modes. He generated different travel forecasting models, which we refer to as a joint form **D-M** and a sequential form **D/M**. The latter, which corresponded to the conventional **G/D/M/A** arrangement of stages, involved the construction of interzonal costs for the distribution model **D** as an 'average' over, or composite of, interzonal modal costs. Here **G** refers to trip generation and **A** to trip assignment; see section 3.7.1. As Wilson noted: 'The question of determining the form of composite impedance or cost, which is a question of long standing in the construction of transport-demand models, turns out to be very important in an analysis of alternative modal split models' (Wilson, 1970, 27).

Similarly, for models that combined modes and routes, corresponding to the sequential arrangement **M/A**, composite modal costs needed to be specified as an 'average' over the costs associated with potentially several routes or services used by travellers in the corresponding modal networks between any origin–destination pair. He argued that these 'composite impedances' or 'composite costs' that linked together the different stages in the sequential models could not be arbitrary. He proposed at each stage several candidates, the appropriate composite cost in principle being governed by the way that travellers perceived their opportunities, and in practice it would be determined through empirical investigation (Wilson, 1970, 29–33).

Here we see a rather detailed discussion of the use of similar analytic models of a particular form, the multinomial logit model, arranged either 'jointly' or 'hierarchically' to represent the demand over combinations of destinations, modes and routes and linked together through composite costs. Specific models would be determined by the values of the parameters λ_D, λ_M and λ_R and the form of the composite costs selected. Furthermore, Wilson was well aware that, in special cases when the parameters λ_D and λ_M were equal, and the composite cost took a particular form, which later became known as a 'logsum', a sequential arrangement of models **D/M** would transform mathematically into a joint model **D-M** of multinomial logit form, in which different combinations of destination and mode were treated on the same footing.

To the authors' knowledge, Wilson's formulation, and the application described in section 3.7, were the first time that travel forecasting was expressed in terms of a 'hierarchy' of multinomial logit models, linked together by composite cost functions that expressed the interdependency between the stages and transmitted the effect of policies. For reasons that emerge later, these rather theoretical ideas on alternative model structures turned out to have particular significance. We consider them further in section 3.7 and in Chapters 4 and 5.

3.5.4 Parameter Interpretation, Properties, Computation and Forecasts

Within the formulation of the models from entropy maximisation principles, the parameter λ had a specific, although unenlightening, interpretation relating the marginal change in the entropy function at its optimal value to the marginal change in the total cost of travel. Within the resulting multinomial model, the parameter λ also has a functional interpretation and properties that determine the dispersion or spread in the pattern of travel predicted by the model and, in the distribution model in particular, the form of the trip length distribution. It also governed the variously described 'sensitivity', 'response' or 'elasticity' properties of travel demand to changes in the generalised costs. In these travel forecasting models, therefore, the parameter λ was the link between modelling the variability or spread in aggregate behaviour at the cross-section and determining the response to transportation policies mediated through the generalised costs. We refer to λ as a cost sensitivity or response parameter in the relevant model (Wilson, 1970, Chapter 2). In any practical application, the parameter λ would be determined from travel data in a way described later in this section and in section 3.7.

In general terms it was the limiting property of entropy maximising models, corresponding to $(\lambda \rightarrow \infty)$, that led Wilson to interpret his approach to modelling as injecting some 'sub-optimality' in travel or locational behaviour about the 'optimal' or 'lowest cost state'. Specifically, if this limit $(\lambda \rightarrow \infty)$ was applied to the 'singly-constrained' spatial interaction (location) models, all trips from a given zone were distributed (or allocated) to the nearest (least cost) destination. Similarly, in a mode (M) or route (R) selection context, when the parameters λ_M and λ_R of the corresponding MNL model increased without limit, the mode or route option(s) with the minimum generalised cost was selected by all in the relevant market segment. In the 'doubly-constrained' trip distribution model, used in modelling the journey to work, the trip pattern for the $\lambda_D \rightarrow \infty$ limit tended towards (one of) the solution(s) of the 'transportation problem of linear programming', which was studied by Evans (1973a) in this context. Related applications of this linear programming formulation have been studied in relation to:

1. logistics models for individual firms;
2. modelling the spatial flow patterns of relatively homogeneous commodity groups;

3. distribution models for personal travel forecasting;
4. generalisations of the Herbert–Stevens model of competitive housing markets (Herbert and Stevens, 1960; Senior and Wilson, 1974).

Entropy maximising models were thus considered by Wilson to be generalisations of these limiting forms and would therefore almost inevitably allow a better fit to relevant data sets than the corresponding limiting forms.

In practical applications of the journey-to-work trip distribution and location models, the numerical values of the model parameters and, in particular, the parameter λ_D were determined as part of the calibration process that involved reconciling the predicted travel pattern with its various constraints, including the requirement that the predicted mean generalised cost of travel be equated with the observed mean generalised cost in the survey data. Much research was conducted in the late 1960s and early 1970s in order to devise efficient methods for this purpose (Hyman, 1969; Evans, 1971; Batty and Mackie, 1972).

In a forecasting context, the parameter λ_D was implicitly assumed to remain constant over time, and the distribution pattern (or modal/route shares) would adjust to any future changes in the exogenous variables such as the land use arrangement, and the user costs arising from transportation policies or projects. Wilson viewed this assumption of constant λ_D as but one hypothesis and explored the consequence of alternatives: for example, (a) that the total travel cost remained constant; or (b) the product of λ_D and the total travel cost was constant in forecasting. Hyman and Wilson (1969) showed that the distribution pattern was indeed sensitive to the hypothesis selected.

Wilson (1973b) took this analysis a stage further, arguing that, if the total travel cost could be independently estimated, a means of determining the parameter λ would be directly available, making the parameter λ endogenous (or internal) to the model. In generalising this argument, Wilson (1973b; 1974, 162) envisaged travel relationships being determined in a multi-level scheme based on the utility tree concept of Strotz (1957), in which an individual's travel was described and modelled at various levels of resolution or aggregation, interpreted here as a 'commodity hierarchy'. More specifically, the hierarchy was expressed in terms of: (a) the amount of travel consumed; (b) the distribution of travel among trip purposes; (c) the distribution of travel among destinations for each purpose; and (d) the distribution of travel among modes. Wilson saw this approach as a way of fruitfully combining economic models with entropy maximising procedures at appropriate levels of the 'commodity' hierarchy. As he put it: 'what has been suggested here is that there is an aggregation level at which economic theory and utility maximising should be helpful (and best) and another, finer level at which entropy maximising remains the most useful procedure' (Wilson, 1973a, 295).

3.5.5   Wider Contributions of the Entropy Maximising Approach

In less than five years after the publication of his 1967 paper, Wilson produced innovative model applications in several study areas, including: travel forecasting, commodity flows, location and land use, problems of missing information, and general urban systems theory. These were assembled in a research monograph, *Entropy in Urban and Regional Modelling* (Wilson, 1970), which became a classic text in theoretical geography and regional science. Some further developments, particularly those relating to the foundations of general urban models, were included in a subsequent text (Wilson, 1974).

The gravity analogue was traditionally used to describe the interaction of activities in space in terms of the attractive influence of 'mass effects' and the deterrence effects of increasing transportation distance, times or costs. The entropy maximising approach introduced a probabilistic basis for that interaction. At the heart of model development was the determination of the most likely arrangement for the relevant person trip or commodity flow matrix elements (for example, interzonal flows), which was consistent with a set of constraints appropriate to the problem at hand. These might include some or all of:

1. logical interdependencies between matrix elements;
2. consistency with any independent information available to the analyst;
3. requirement that the predicted travel costs are equated with those observed;
4. non-negativity conditions on trips or flows.

His contributions to land use, commodity flow and general urban models would later prove to be particularly significant. What Wilson and other researchers did was to take relatively simple, but incompatible, urban development and multi-stage travel forecasting models and provide not only greater realism in their founding assumptions but also a synthesis in which the demand for travel was derived from urban and regional location decisions (Wilson, 1974, Chapter 11). In this way significant progress was made on the conceptual framework for integrating land use and transportation models. Inevitably this generality was achieved at the expense of additional complexity; the development and implementation of such models would prove to be a protracted process. In Chapters 8 and 9, we consider in much greater detail the integrated models that were taking shape at the end of this period.

3.5.6 Some Reactions to the Approach

As an approach to model building, the entropy maximising method had a wide and enduring role in urban and regional research generally, and in transportation planning practice in the UK in particular (see Wilson, 2010, for recent developments, interpretations and research agenda). It was not however uncontroversial, encouraging the full range of emotions, from the great enthusiasm with which it was initially greeted to outright hostility. The name alone engendered suspicion among those who were uncomfortable with analogies drawn from the natural sciences, drawing comments along the lines of 'people are not particles'. As Wilson observed, the approach 'ran into trouble with the Marxists later in the 1970s'.[26]

The approach was seldom accepted, and sometimes summarily dismissed, by those who saw the constructive derivation of travel demand functions from behavioural principles as necessary for a convincing forecasting approach for a social system. It was becoming clear that spatial interaction, modal split and related models could be derived from the economic principles of utility maximisation that began to provide a competing paradigm from the late 1960s (for example, Neidercorn and Bechdolt, 1969; Quandt, 1970; Golob and Beckmann, 1971; Beckmann and Golob, 1972). Wilson was equally sceptical about the strict and restrictive optimising assumptions underpinning standard utility maximising models, particularly in a locational context where dispersion, the statistical spread of trips (for example, from a given origin zone), could arise from many sources in historical, economic and social contexts. Nor, as we noted above, did he believe that the entropy maximising approach was necessarily incompatible with micro-economic foundations, which he argued could happily co-exist at different levels of resolution of a system under study. In later reflections, Wilson saw entropy maximisation as a general approach to model building with a range of interpretations, and in his view: 'Entropy maximising methods can be used to derive robust most-probable state models of large population systems. . . . It is worth emphasising that although this idea was introduced as one borrowed from physics, it in no way relies on this analogy' (Wilson, 2000, 63).

We note the remark of Stopher and Meyburg (1975, 251) writing at the end of the period considered in this chapter: 'one may perhaps question the importance of the controversy between utility-maximization and entropy maximization approaches to the gravity model. Indeed, it appears from the literature that proponents of each approach can muster as many arguments against the other approach as for their own.'

Jumping ahead in our story we shall see developments in, and alternative interpretations of, the entropy maximising method, as in the 'minimum information adding' approach of Snickars and Weibull (1977). In a further development, Erlander (1977) interpreted the entropy function directly as a measure of dispersion or spread in the travel pattern. He then noted that equivalent trip distribution models could be derived by determining the pattern of trips that minimised overall travel costs consistent with any constraints, including the requirement that the predicted and observed spread of trips, interpreted through an entropy function, be equated. Erlander's approach exchanged the entropy objective function and cost constraint in the optimisation problem used to derive the distribution model (section 7.4.4.3).

We shall meet these issues again and will later reflect on a wider range of theories and methods for building comparable models in land use and transportation systems. The implementation of the entropy maximising models of distribution and modal split in UK transportation studies is considered further in section 3.7.

3.6 NETWORK ANALYSIS AND ASSIGNMENT

3.6.1 Developments in Public Transport Network Representation and Assignment

In the early 1960s, if they were constructed at all, public transport networks were conceived on the same basis as highway networks. This representation implied a level of connectivity qualitatively different from that associated with the fixed routes, interchanges and timetables that characterised real systems. By the mid-1960s major improvements had been made to the representation of public transport systems in independent initiatives in the UK and US. In the UK, the modern line-based representation of networks was pioneered by Freeman, Fox, Wilbur Smith and Associates (1967). John Wootton recalled 'poring over maps of railway lines and bus routes plus timetables and wondering how we could realistically represent these services'.[27] His efforts resulted in the TRANSITNET suite of programs (Wootton, 1967; Tressider et al, 1968).

The new approach accounted appropriately for: (a) the detailed structure of different services; (b) their boarding and alighting points; (c) the relationship between average waiting times and service headways; and (d) the interchange between different services. Within the new representation, information appropriate to route (service) choices could then be made available, with public transport travel times between origin and destination zones suitably expressed as the sum of access, wait, in-vehicle, transfer and egress times.[28] Interchange time penalties could be added to reflect the aversion of passengers to changing services. In turn this information could be used to determine the share of trips by each mode (Tressider et al, 1968). Similar developments occurred independently in the US under contracts with US HUD (Dial, 1967; Dial and Bunyan, 1968) (sections 2.6 and 10.3.1).

Usually assignments were based on minimum time or generalised cost with simple distance-dependent fare functions. At the assignment stage, passengers were loaded on to a single route between an origin and destination, or split equally between routes (services) of equal time or generalised cost. Later, multi-route algorithms were used to share interzonal travel demand for public transport among groups of services (section 3.6.3). During this period there was little attempt to incorporate formally the effect of vehicle loadings on waiting, boarding and in-vehicle times, although adjustment by inspection would often accompany unrealistic service levels and load factors.

3.6.2   Improved Methods for Road Capacity Restraint Assignment

In the early years of experimenting with capacity restraint methods, several alternative formulations for the time-volume or speed-flow curves were proposed that were to a greater or lesser degree informed by traffic flow theory. In the UK these were typically of a piecewise linear form for different road types with some non-linearities introduced in the flow regime above capacity. Commenting on these level-of-service functions applied in this era, Marcus Wigan (1977, 136) noted: 'The basic choice between speed flow functions is a three stage series of straight and curved lines, and an exponential or power law function.' The latter included the fourth power function recommended for use by the US DoT (1972a), as discussed in sections 2.5.5 and 2.5.6. In the UK, curves recommended by the UK Department of the Environment, Advice Note 1A, were commonly used (Wigan, 1977). Their basic form is shown in Figure 3.2. The free-flow speed, free-flow limit and speed at capacity were specific to the road type.

As in the US, a great amount of experimentation was evident on capacity restraint methods in the 1960s and early 1970s (for example, Almond, 1965; Steel, 1965; Van Vliet, 1973, 1976, 1977; Wigan, 1977). In the incremental method, the number of increments was varied, as well as the proportions applied in successive allocations of the trip matrix. In the iterative method,

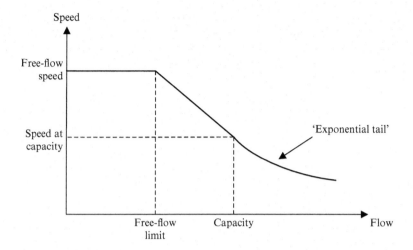

Source: UK DoE (1971) Advice note 1A.

Figure 3.2 Speed-flow curves widely applied in UK transportation studies after 1970

different proportions were applied to weight successive solutions. As an early example, the traffic assignment procedure employed by the SELNEC Transportation Study (1971, 31) employed three iterations of a 'serial loading technique' that corresponds to the method of successive averages, in which the link volumes from each iteration received equal weight; section 7.4.3.2 provides a definition of the method. See also section 2.5.6.

In view of the limited computing resources available, solutions were often limited to three or four increments or iterations. Study teams needed to strike a balance between the number of increments or iterations and the precision to which equilibrium states were considered to be determined. Until the mid-1970s, the nature of convergence and quality of the solutions, and their dependence on the way iterations or increments were applied, were not well understood. For this reason, it was always the convention to apply the same procedures to seek convergence in different networks for consistent comparisons in evaluation. It became clearer by the early 1970s that some of these heuristic methods did not converge to the equilibrium solution (Van Vliet, 1977), as examined in more detail in sections 7.2.1, 7.4.2.4 and 2.5.6.

Many transportation study teams found that assigning the future car trip matrices to networks in the peak period, particularly in the 'do-nothing' situation, resulted in severe overload of some and often many links. This result posed a significant dilemma for both the acceptability of the assignment itself and the lack of consistency between the supposedly equilibrium link flows and the level-of-service throughout both the network and the model as a whole. Much lip service was paid in transportation studies of this period to the search for this consistency, and there is some evidence in later studies of the application of 'feedback' of modified travel times from the capacity restraint assignment stage to the modal and distribution stages, although this was typically done on an *ad hoc* basis with no formal measures of convergence offered.

3.6.3 Multi-Route Selection Methods

The above assignment methods were based, for any given flow pattern, on a single numerical value for the travel time (or cost) accompanying each link in the network. Each traveller was assumed to face the same set of times (or costs) of travel along each link. In capacity restraint assignments, the existence of multiple route selection between any pair of zones was considered to be a consequence of the decline of level-of-service (increased travel times) associated with increasing congestion, and was characterised by equal route times, as required by Wardrop's first principle (Wardrop, 1952). However, it was a matter of empirical observation that multi-routeing occurred and could be extensive, even in relatively uncongested networks (Lane et al, 1971).

As noted in Chapter 2, in the late 1960s various attempts were made to introduce the consequences of imperfect information, the effect of zone sizes and the effect of non-measured factors on route choices. Two approaches in particular, developed respectively in the UK and the US by Burrell (1969) and Dial (1971), led to practical and enduring route selection and associated trip assignment models. Their methods differed according to the procedure for generating acceptable alternative routes between each zone pair (or pairs of nodes) and the rules for allocating portions of the interzonal flow to each. Here we describe Burrell's approach that was applied in several UK transportation studies from the late 1960s as a means of introducing probabilistic elements into the link level-of-service and route selection.

In order to reflect variation in behaviour over the relevant population confronted by a route choice, the assumption that link times were perceived equally by all travellers was relaxed. The detailed nature of the assignment was determined by the probability distributions selected for the journey times on the different links, as well as the number of times these were sampled for route building from each trip origin. In Burrell's original approach, the distributions of link times took a rectangular form, in which times could take one of eight values. The standard deviation was set at typically 20 per cent of the actual link time. To economise on computing time, the times on each network link were sampled once for each trip origin and shortest route trees built accordingly. The trips from each origin were then assigned on an all-or-nothing basis. The possibility of drawing several link time samples prior to building a number of shortest route trees from each origin centroid and assigning portions of the trip matrix to the network was well recognised as the basis for a stochastic model of route choice (Lane et al, 1971), although the additional computing times did not encourage use of this approach.

Burrell's procedure was quite effective at spreading trips over competing routes or services in highway and public transport networks, and was applied on its own, and in conjunction with capacity restraint methods in highway networks. We examine the approaches of Burrell and Dial further in section 7.4.3.1.

3.7 STATE OF PRACTICE AROUND 1970

3.7.1 Overview

Towards the end of the 1960s and in the early 1970s, travel forecasting models were being applied in the UK in several different contexts, including the formulation of structure plans and new town development plans, as well as conventional land use – transportation studies undertaken in the conurbations, cities and large towns. For various reasons, including academic review, general audit purposes, and learning from the experiences of the past, the methods of travel forecasting adopted during this period later came under particular scrutiny and comparative analysis (for example, UK House of Commons, 1972; Starkie, 1973; Senior and Williams, 1977; Mackinder and Evans, 1981).

Mackinder and Evans (1981) provided a summary of the forecasting models or approaches applied in 45 UK studies completed before 1971, as shown in Table 3.1. Although the table does not indicate the progression of modelling practices over time, we can assume that, in the major studies conducted in the late 1960s, household-based category analysis was becoming the dominant method at the trip generation stage, gravity or entropy-based models were used for trip distribution, and road traffic was assigned with capacity restraint for the peak period. Modal split models were applied about equally in pre-distribution and post-distribution forms (we shall use the notation **G/M/D/A** and **G/D/M/A** to describe these respective arrangements of the generation, distribution,

Forecasting urban travel

Table 3.1   Summary of techniques applied in UK travel forecasting models up to 1971

Stage of model	Modelling technique	Studies using technique (%)
Trip generation model	Zonal growth factors	29
	Zonal regression analysis	17
	Category analysis	54
Trip distribution model	Gravity model*	63
	Intervening opportunities	2
	Furness iteration	35
Modal split model	Highway only	40
	Trip-end modal split	30
	Post-distribution modal split	30
Assignment model	All-or-nothing	59
	Multi-routeing	8
	Capacity restraint	33

Note: * This includes entropy maximising models.

Source: Mackinder and Evans (1981, Figure 1).

modal split and assignment stages within the overall model), with the gradual move to the latter form being one of the most significant modelling developments.

In this section we summarise the state of UK travel forecasting practice in this period, highlighting the innovations applied in the SELNEC study centred on the city of Manchester (Wilson et al, 1969). Some significant and more general points on the overall structure of UK models are then discussed; in particular, we refer to those attempts to apply closer relationships between the various stages in each of the **G/M/D/A** and **G/D/M/A** forms. We conclude the section with a discussion of the validation of models and their predictive accuracy derived from comparison of forecasts to actual outcomes in a design or target forecast year. Sometimes the latter is referred to as 'out-turn' data.

3.7.2   Travel Forecasting Models Adopted in the SELNEC Transportation Study

In terms of forecasting methodology, the study was distinguished by its incorporation of most of the important advances in travel forecasting proposed and applied in the UK up to the late 1960s (Wilson et al, 1969; SELNEC Transportation Study, 1971, 1972). In outline the forecasting approach had the conventional four-stage **G/D/M/A** structure, inelastic at its trip ends. The computational organisation of the programs was 'loosely based on the TAP package developed by Freeman, Fox, Wilbur Smith and Associates (1967)', with 'major innovations . . . introduced . . . in relation to trip distribution and modal split, and in the use of generalised cost concepts to replace travel time' (Wilson et al, 1969, 337–338). The overall model included:

1. household-based category analysis for the trip generation stage, in a form very similar to that introduced by Wootton and Pick (1967);
2. the modern line-based public transport programs (TRANSITNET) introduced in the third phase of the London Transportation Study (Wootton, 1967; Tressider et al, 1968);
3. capacity restraint road assignments; and
4. 'feedback' of level-of-service variables to the distribution and modal split stages to seek consistency among demand and cost variables.

Goods vehicle forecasting assumed its usual 'poor-relation role' in the overall model with the application of growth factors.

The study had the direct involvement of the Mathematical Advisory Unit of the UK Department of the Environment, headed by Alan Wilson, which enabled his theoretical developments on the modal split and distribution stages based on generalised costs to make a rapid and smooth transition into practice. A unified approach was adopted in which generalised costs quantified the relative importance of time and money components in the distribution, modal split and assignment stages, with a distinction made between in-vehicle and out-of-vehicle (walking and waiting) time components. The study thus represented a watershed between those forecasting procedures founded on empirically derived diversion curves for modal split and deterrence functions for trip distribution, and analytic forms based on the multinomial logit model in the **D** and **M** stages ordered hierarchically. A summary of the travel forecasting procedures adopted in the SELNEC study is given in Table 3.2.

The SELNEC Transportation Study was not only a major investigation for a large conurbation. In implementing innovative travel forecasting models in the distribution and modal split stages, it was a research application representing work in progress. Several subsequent studies in the UK applied very similar modal split (binary logit) and distribution (singly- and doubly-constrained entropy maximising) models, perhaps with differences in their market segmentation, composite cost structures and methods of parameter estimation. Some studies retained empirical deterrence functions at the distribution stage, but applications of interzonal-based binary

Table 3.2   Characteristics of the SELNEC travel forecasting models

	Procedure/categories	Comments
Survey	Standard household survey of 3% of the population of 2.5 million by WS Atkins.	Base year – 1966. Forecast year – 1984.
Spatial resolution	362 zones, 6000-plus links in the highway network.	
Journey purposes	Home-based work (HBW), school, home-based other (HBO). Non-home-based (NHB).	
Temporal resolution	Peak, 24 hours.	
Transportation variables	Generalised costs used in assignment, modal split and distribution models.	Costs defined differently in modal split and distribution models (see below).
Model structure for passenger journey forecasting	G/D/M/A.	Growth factors used for commercial vehicles and external trips.
Generation model	Category analysis based on six household structure classes, six income classes and three car ownership classes.	108 household categories used for trip generation; eight activity categories used for trip attractions; insensitive to transportation level-of-service variables.
Distribution model	Doubly-constrained entropy maximising/ multinomial logit.	Car owner, non-car owner stratification.
Interface between **D** and **M** composite costs	'Logsum' for car owners – see text.	Distribution parameter λ_D used in 'logsum' formula; parking charge and modal penalty removed from generalised cost.
Modal split model	Binary logit model based on interzonal generalised costs. Value-of-time parameters obtained from disaggregate studies of modal choice. Split between bus and rail determined at the assignment stage.	Stratified by two person types (car owners, non-car owners). Generalised cost with parking charges and modal penalty included.

Table 3.2 (continued)

	Procedure/categories	Comments
Assignment (highway) model	Wardrop equilibrium based on minimum generalised cost routeings.	Iterative loading with averaging used in capacity restraint approach.
Assignment (public transport) model	Minimum cost routeing in line-based public transport system.	TRANSITNET model used for public transport.
'Feedback' sought for internal consistency of the model?	Yes, to distribution and modal split models.	No formal convergence criterion used.

Sources: Derived from Wilson et al (1969); SELNEC Transportation Study (1971, 1972).

logit share models for determining modal split between car and public transport became common.

The entropy maximising approach did not make an impression on travel forecasting practice in the US, where other methods were available through FHWA computer programs, publications and procedures, and subsequently the Urban Transportation Planning System (UTPS). In the UK however it was increasingly adopted, and entropy maximising entered the travel forecasting lexicon, implying models interpreted in terms of most probable trip patterns at the aggregate (interzonal) level. Distribution and modal split models were analytic functions of the multinomial logit form, and transportation policies were mediated through generalised and composite costs.

It was not for improving 'goodness-of-fit' that entropy maximising models began to make an inroad in the UK into the position held by the BPR gravity model and modal split diversion curves in the US. Rather, the approach was seen to have stronger conceptual foundations than the gravity analogue for trip distribution. In the modal split context, the approach was supported by the analytic forms appearing in concurrent studies at the micro-level. As we noted in section 3.4, it also harmonised with the economic evaluation of schemes based on the generalised cost concept.

3.7.3   Variations in Model Structures

3.7.3.1   The rationale for alternative structures

We wish to make a number of comments about the overall travel forecasting model structures and describe some similarities and apparent differences between the approaches applied in the UK and the US. These issues will later emerge to be of great theoretical and practical interest. As noted in Chapter 2, by the late 1960s the position of the modal split model in the overall ordering of the stages, and the choice between the sequential four-stage orders, **G/M/D/A** and **G/D/M/A**, was a topic of considerable importance and some contention (Weiner, 1969; Starkie, 1973). As we shall see later, it remains a subject of debate to this day.

The increasing choice of the **G/D/M/A** form in major studies undertaken after the mid-1960s was one of the most significant developments in model specification (Starkie, 1973). In the theoretical literature (for example, Wilson, 1967, 1969), we also saw the development of a 'simultaneous' structure (**G/D-M/A**) with the distribution and modal split models specified together. This arrangement did not appear in any major UK transportation study until the early 1970s, however, when it was adopted in Coventry and in the Greater London Transportation Study (Coventry City Council, 1973; Havers and Van Vliet, 1974; Senior and Williams, 1977).

Since the mid-1960s, the sequential arrangement of the modelling 'stages' was often tacitly assumed to reflect an underlying decision process of travellers over the various 'dimensions' of choice (for example, Quarmby, 1967; Starkie, 1973). Thus, the commonly applied **G/D/M/A** structure was associated with a decision sequence in which an individual, after deciding to make a trip (reflected by a frequency choice **f**), was considered to select the destination **d**; then the mode of travel **m** was selected conditional on the destination; and finally the route or public transport service **r** was selected conditional on the selected mode. Symbolically, we represent this sequential decision process as $f \Rightarrow d \Rightarrow m \Rightarrow r$. Each successive decision was considered to be conditional on the previous decision. However, there was no clear rationale or empirical evidence for selecting one particular ordering ($f \Rightarrow d \Rightarrow m \Rightarrow r$) over another ($f \Rightarrow m \Rightarrow d \Rightarrow r$).

In the case of the journey to work it was sometimes argued that the selection of residence and/or workplace would precede the choice of mode, justifying a **G/D/M/A** structure, while for discretionary travel it was sometimes suggested that the reverse might be true, supporting a **G/M/D/A** structure. More often than not, a common structure was adopted for all journey purposes. Towards the end of the period considered in this chapter, the 'simultaneous' structure **G/D-M/A**, although rarely found in major studies, was justified as a result of an assumed greater interdependency between the destination and mode decisions with the destination and mode 'selected together' (symbolically f⇒d⇔m⇒r). This conclusion may well have been inspired by US research conducted in the early 1970s, described in detail in section 4.4. The structures and their assumed decision sequences are shown in Figure 3.3.

There were also other considerations in selecting an appropriate model structure, notably: (a) practical convenience; (b) representation

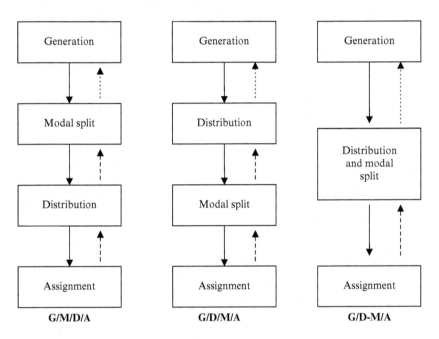

Assumed underlying decision sequence

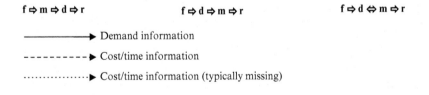

f ⇒ m ⇒ d ⇒ r   **f ⇒ d ⇒ m ⇒ r**   **f ⇒ d ⇔ m ⇒ r**

⟶▶ Demand information

- - - - - - - - -▶ Cost/time information

··················▶ Cost/time information (typically missing)

Note: For notation, see text.

Figure 3.3   *Alternative model structures and information flows for travel forecasting and the assumed conditional dependency on the underlying trip decision process*

of captivity to a mode; and (c) the assumed responsiveness of demand to proposed public transport schemes (Hutchinson, 1974; Stopher and Meyburg, 1975). With regard to broad usage of the different model structures applied internationally in this period, Bruce Hutchinson noted:

> In transport studies performed to date in medium- and smaller-sized cities, trip end modal split models have normally been used. . . . The basic assumption of the trip-end-type models is that transport patronage is relatively insensitive to the service characteristics of the transport modes. Modal patronages are determined principally by the socioeconomic characteristics of the trip makers. Transport studies performed in larger urban areas, where the public-transport system is well developed, or where significant improvements in the public transport system are contemplated, have usually employed trip-interchange modal split models (Hutchinson, 1974, 55–56).

To sum up, the structure of the forecasting procedure, and specifically the position of the modal split stage within it, was at various times justified in the US, Canada and the UK by: (a) practical considerations; (b) variables assumed to influence modal demand; (c) the relative sensitivity of modal split to level-of-service and socio-economic determinants; (d) the prominence of public transport schemes in current transportation systems and in policies to be tested; and (e) the assumed nature of the travel choice process. In fact, no data, surveys or analyses were offered in support of the last view.

3.7.3.2 Joining the stages together

The problem of structural ambiguity and choice of model specification, which form to select from the options **G/M/D/A** and **G/D/M/A**, did not end there. For each sequential ordering, **M/D** and **D/M**, how were explicit links to be made between the modal split and distribution models to reflect the influence of level-of-service variables within the different stages? In the former this ordering established at the zonal level the differential effect on modal split of accessibilities to different destinations by the two main modes, car and public transport. In the latter they reflected at the interzonal level, as in the SELNEC study, the differential effect of modal opportunities and their levels-of-service on the distribution pattern.

As noted, in those early studies in the US that adopted a **G/M/D/A** structure, if the issue was considered at all, the commonly interpreted accessibility variables derived from the denominator of the gravity trip distribution model were used for the purpose, the ratio of the accessibilities by car and public transport being a popular choice of variable (US DoC, 1966; Hutchinson, 1974; Stopher and Meyburg, 1975). A similar example could be found in some UK studies, such as in Glasgow (Scott Wilson Kirkpatrick & Partners, 1969).

For the more popular **G/D/M/A** structure, a corresponding problem arose. By the mid-1960s a common method for determining the composite interzonal time for each zonal pair in the gravity model was simply to take the minimum time across modes, which was almost invariably that of the highway mode. This procedure had the advantage of not requiring detailed information about the predicted modal share and was easily generated from the network analysis routines. A review of US practice relevant to this period observed: 'the travel impedance factors are typically based only on car travel. . . . The full range of travel time and cost factors for all relevant modes of transportation is very seldom included in the impedance factor' (Domencich and McFadden, 1975, 19). But there were clear problems with this approach, as those authors pointed out. Changes in the travel time or cost for those who selected an improved public transport mode might not be reflected in changes to the distribution pattern.

In the UK there appears to have been considerably more experimentation with different combinations of modal level-of-service variables to insert into the distribution model. In their survey of 25 British transportation studies conducted over the period 1962–73, Senior and Williams (1977) found eight possible methods of combining modal information for distributing trips in the **G/D/M/A** structure. As in the US, the minimum cost or travel time or generalised cost was widely applied, but various combinations of modal travel times or generalised costs were also implemented, including: (a) weighting by modal proportions; (b) geometric weighting; and (c) the 'logsum' measure adopted in the SELNEC study.

There was also the problem of representing the effect of level-of-service variables on the demand for travel at the generation stage in both the **G/M** and **G/D** structures. By far the most common approach was to assume that the demand for travel from a given zone was insensitive to transportation variables. In those few attempts to make the zonal demand for travel elastic with respect to the times and cost of travel, variously defined accessibility variables derived from the distribution model (or a proxy variable denoting distance from the city centre) were incorporated. In terms of additional explanatory power, these attempts were generally not very successful. However, we would emphasise that the dependence of trips generated by a zone on accessibility variables was almost invariably absent throughout this period, a source of considerable criticism of the standard forecasting approach. Indeed, Starkie (1973, 367) commented: 'It is with regard to making the sum total of travel sensitive to the conditions of travel that least progress has been made.'

With the exception of Wilson's formulations (section 3.5.3), questions of appropriate linkages between stages of the travel forecasting model were not formulated rigorously nor were the procedures informed by theory.

For reasons that will emerge later, however, there were many attempts to link the stages in a way that would pass level-of-service variables from one stage to the other to reflect interdependency between them. However, the way that the models were usually calibrated and applied from the 'top down' (e.g., in the order $G \rightarrow D \rightarrow M \rightarrow A$) posed real problems for both specification and implementation. Therefore, modellers often resorted to simplified structural relationships.

The impression from several transportation study reports of this period is that these structural issues, the ordering and interfacing of the individual steps or stages, were considered to be technical problems to be solved at the discretion of the study team. They did not appear to have been endowed with great conceptual or numerical significance. The lack of a theoretical framework also reinforced the view that the travel forecasting procedure was a set of four (or three if modal split was omitted) somewhat independent stages or 'submodels' strung together in a rather *ad hoc* way. Not only were there conceptual issues to be resolved here; these specification choices had significant practical implications for the organisation, calibration and equilibration of the overall model.[29] Moreover, they were the crucial means by which the effects of policies were to be transmitted throughout the solution procedure and thereby influence the broad pattern of travel. We take up these issues in Chapters 4 and 5, where their full significance is considered further.

3.7.4 Validation and Predictive Performance of the Models

Except when time series data or before-and-after studies were used to assess the stability of parameters such as trip rates (Wootton and Pick, 1967; Downes and Gyenes, 1976), model validity during this period was almost exclusively assessed by the ability of models to provide close correspondence between the predicted and observed patterns of travel in the base year. This correspondence was assessed in the various stages of the model through 'goodness-of-fit' statistics, with additional checks made on factors such as screen-line crossings and so on that depended on the output of the forecasting model as a whole. Usually a large amount of 'fine-tuning', adjustment of network coding and small changes to the specifications was required before the model was deemed satisfactory. Analysts often found themselves in the predicament of adopting a relatively parsimonious specification and accepting modest 'fit statistics' for travel demand patterns (interzonal movements, modal proportions and network flow patterns), or including additional parameters to improve the goodness-of-fit. This approach was sometimes seen as investing in additional accuracy in the base year at the expense of incurring added problems of parameter forecasting over time; the default solution was usually to assume the constancy of such parameters.

The calibration process for a large urban travel forecasting model of several hundred zones and several thousand network links was an extensive and computationally costly task. The succession of model calibration, adjustment of specification, network checking and adjustment and any recalibration, all in the context of developing forecasts for multiple trip purposes, multiple users competing on the networks and (possibly) multiple time periods, made the attempt to secure a well-fitting model for the base year nothing less than monumental. Few studies attempted additional iterations of the model sequence between demand and assignment in order to obtain consistency with the generalised cost of travel. An attempt to achieve greater consistency was considered a luxury to be treated in a very cursory fashion or not at all.

The most exacting assessments of the validity of models adopted in this period were those very few *ex post* comparisons of model predictions with data collected for the year of forecast, sometimes referred to as 'out-turn data'. Mackinder and Evans (1981) of the Local Government Operational Research Unit assessed the predictive accuracy of a wide range of UK land use – transportation models, following a small investigation of five transportation studies in the US (Institute of Transportation Engineers, 1980). Data were obtained from 44 UK transportation studies conducted during 1962–71 that fell into three categories: (a) urban studies; (b) conurbation studies and land use – transportation studies, including county structure plans; and (c) new town master plans.

The UK study sought to assess the extent and implications of the various errors and uncertainties associated with forecasts, including: (a) data errors; (b) misspecification errors; (c) errors in the forecasting of exogenous variables such as land use, socio-economic and transportation system variables; and (d) human errors. Because these were related to the actual forecasting date, 15–20 years from the base year, they were particularly influenced by errors in model specification and exogenous variables such as population, employment and car ownership. The findings of Mackinder and Evans (1981) involved the forecasting performance against out-turn results for 12 demographic, socio-economic, modal demand and screen-line crossing variables. Ominously, the authors came to the following conclusions:

Nearly all of the forecast items considered were overestimated. On average, population was overestimated by 10%, car ownership and household income by 20%, and highway and public transport trips by 30 to 35%. Traffic flows across highway screenlines were overestimated by an average of 13%. An assumption of zero change in the input parameters would not have produced markedly greater forecast errors in any of the items and in many the average errors would have been considerably less. There was no evidence that the more recent transport studies or those that used more sophisticated modelling techniques (up to 1971) performed better than the others. Although the highway trip forecasts were dominated by the errors in the planning variables, there is evidence that the models used for forecasting public transport trips contained errors of specification (Mackinder and Evans, 1981, 1).

They also noted that errors in forecasts for public transport trips, amounting to an overestimate of 42 per cent, arose both from errors in exogenous factors and from model misspecification. They added, significantly: 'anecdotal evidence obtained during the feasibility stages of the project and certain of the analyses described in this report lead to the conclusion that optimistic planning forecasts and insufficient checking procedures were the most important factors in reducing the overall accuracy of the forecast' (Mackinder and Evans, 1981, 26).

We return in section 5.2, and later in section 9.5 and Chapter 11, to various aspects of goodness-of-fit and the notions of validity adopted in many urban travel forecasting models, particularly those relating to the specification of the models and their ability to generate logically consistent forecasts accompanying policy tests.

3.8   TRAVEL FORECASTS AND THE EVALUATION FRAMEWORK

3.8.1   The Widening Evaluation Framework

In the early 1960s the relationship between the travel forecasting procedures and the evaluation framework was rudimentary. It was dominated by operational considerations and measures of the cost and effectiveness of modifying (highway) networks to accommodate future patterns of demand. With the greater appreciation of urban transportation problems, a richer set of objectives emerged by the end of the decade and with them a growing concern for: (a) economic efficiency; (b) the distribution of benefits over space and social groups; and (c) the environmental impact of plans (Lane et al, 1971; Dalvi and Martin, 1973; Prestwood-Smith, 1977). These objectives stimulated research into the relationship between road and public transport network flows, levels-of-service, and the wider impacts of schemes; investigations of energy and environmental effects were developing rapidly.[30] However, in practice, the impacts of increased traffic flows and transportation infrastructure on noise, pollution, pedestrian delay, community severance effects and visual intrusion were assessed in a rather cursory way and conditioned by the quality of the information that could be provided by the forecasting procedures.

Towards the end of the 1960s, measures of economic efficiency attained an increasingly important role in the evaluation process. In particular, the money value of travel time savings that dominated the 'quantified' measures of benefits derived from transportation plans and projects exerted considerable influence. We comment here on specific aspects of the relationship between travel behaviour and user benefit measures, which was destined to have important consequences for conceptualising user benefits, and on the structuring of travel demand models themselves.

3.8.2 Economic Measures: Equilibrium States and User Benefit Assessment

Whether a project was worthwhile or not was almost invariably assessed through a social cost–benefit analysis (SCBA) framework that was applied with varying degrees of sophistication. For determining the economic benefits, the assumed equilibrium measures of travel demand and user (generalised) costs were 'passed on' from the 'bottom' of the multi-stage travel forecasting procedure to the evaluation stage, where the language of the transportation planner and traffic engineer changed abruptly into the language of the applied transport economist. The travel forecasts were used to assess the consequences of 'doing something', in the form of various transportation schemes, in relation to the do-nothing or 'reference' situation. The alternatives were sometimes designated the 'with' and 'without' schemes. The latter was often the consequence of literally 'doing nothing' or including previously committed facilities and, very occasionally, some management or restraint measure (Dalvi and Martin, 1973; Starkie, 1973). UK studies in the mid- and late 1960s into the monetary expression of travel time savings, formulated through disutilities or generalised costs and incorporated into user benefit measures, were central to this analysis (Quarmby, 1967; Harrison and Quarmby, 1969; McIntosh and Quarmby, 1972).

During the 1960s, in urban and regional land use – transportation studies in the UK, there emerged subtle differences between methods for determining the total user benefits accruing from projects, according to what allowance was made for the response of travellers to changes in user costs. Some early studies assumed that, apart from route switching, the change in demand attributed to transportation schemes would be sufficiently small to be safely neglected, and thus evaluation was conducted under a 'fixed demand' or 'fixed trip matrix' calculation based on changes in route times and costs determined at the assignment stage (Neuberger, 1971). The number of trips between a pair of zones was multiplied by the change in user costs, incorporating the value of travel time saved among other cost-related measures, and then summed over all zone pairs.

Later UK studies, specifically those that followed the cost–benefit evaluation method applied in phase III of the London Transportation Study (LTS III) (Tressider et al, 1968), sought to accommodate the effect on interzonal demand of user cost changes by adopting the change in consumer surplus as a measure of benefit. An *ad hoc* extension of the Marshallian consumer surplus measure, which became known as the Rule-of-a-Half (RoH), was proposed during LTS III (Tressider et al, 1968; Lane et al, 1971).[31] Its origin is attributed to Tim Powell and his colleagues at Freeman, Fox, Wilbur Smith and Associates (Wootton, 2004, 278). This approach for estimating the perceived user benefits derived from a scheme, which became standard practice, involved multiplying the change in generalised cost for each O-D pair and each mode of travel, by the average number of trips for that O-D pair by mode, made in the 'with' and 'without' schemes. These contributions were then summed over all zone pairs and modes to give a total perceived user benefit. In this analysis it was assumed that the change in user costs would be sufficiently small that any curvature of the demand function could be safely ignored and, furthermore, that income effects would be negligible (Neuberger, 1971; Williams, 1976; Jara-Diaz, 2007). This RoH measure,[32] a key link between the forecasting process and the economic assessment, was often applied to different trip purposes and modal splits and sometimes subject to sensitivity tests with respect to variation in the value-of-time parameters (Dalvi and Martin, 1973). To this day, it remains the most widely applied measure of user benefit accruing from transportation schemes. Jara-Diaz (2007) offered an extended discussion of the approach and its theoretical basis.

3.8.3 Neuberger's Analysis of User Benefits

Henry Neuberger [1943–1998] derived some intriguing results that would later turn out to be of considerable theoretical and practical significance for both demand analysis and the evaluation of land use – transportation plans. In Neuberger (1971) he considered three alternative approaches of increasing sophistication for calculating the user benefits arising from land use and transportation projects (see also Wilson and Kirwan, 1969). These methods entailed different assumptions and approximations for treating the forecast of traveller responses to those projects, the first two having already been noted above. They may be summarised as follows.

Method I simply ignores the demand response, apart from route switching; the user benefit is derived from the reduction in perceived user cost for each zone pair. Method II is based on the Rule-of-a-Half as a marginal approximation to the change in the Marshallian consumer surplus measure. Method III is a generalisation of the Marshallian measure due to Hotelling (1938); it consists of the (path) integral of demand with respect to user cost between the initial and final generalised cost states.[33]

Method III was of particular interest to Neuberger. It sought to accommodate the mutual changes of demand and all interzonal user costs arising from a modification to the transportation networks, and took explicit account of the curvature of the demand function between the initial and final equilibrium cost states. The technical details underpinning the approach need not concern us here other than to note that Hotelling's generalised consumer surplus measure is defined unambiguously only if certain 'integrability conditions' are satisfied by the demand function (Hotelling, 1938; Neuberger, 1971). These conditions express a form of 'cross-symmetry' in the responses of any two different groups of travellers under a change in the generalised costs of travel of the alternative group.[34]

By good fortune (was it a coincidence?), these mathematical conditions were satisfied for demand models expressed in multinomial logit form, which were increasingly applied in the UK by the late 1960s for determining both the distribution of trips and their modal split. Furthermore, for the MNL function the required consumer surplus measure could be calculated exactly. Therefore, in principle, it was not necessary to invoke a linear approximation to the demand curve underlying the RoH. From the MNL distribution model, the user benefits associated with each zone could be expressed in terms of the number of trips generated in that zone multiplied by the change in the natural logarithm of the denominator of the MNL model evaluated in the 'after' and 'before' states. What was of immediate interest about this rather esoteric procedure was that the denominator was commonly interpreted as an accessibility measure to all opportunities from that zone.[35]

This result showed that the measures of economic user benefit for such models of MNL form could be derived from either:

1. the trip pattern and generalised costs in the do-something and do-nothing states, approximated by the RoH, and summed over all origin–destination zone pairs in the study area (Method II);
2. the trips generated *in each zone* and the change in (the logarithm of) the accessibility measure computed in the do-something and do-nothing states, summed over all trip origin zones in the study area (Method III).

Neuberger extended the application of Method III to situations where both the land use and transportation costs were subject to change. The change in consumer surplus again resulted in expressions involving terms previously interpreted as accessibility measures (Neuberger, 1971, 68).

Thus, in the context of the spatial interaction share models of MNL form, Method III could be used to generate more precise measures of user benefit, accounting for the curvature of the demand function. For typical projects, the difference between Method II and III estimates of user benefit was in the range of 2–5 per cent (Neuberger, 1971; Williams and Senior, 1977). For transportation projects that resulted in modest changes in user costs, the RoH measure turned out to be a satisfactory approximation. For larger changes in user costs, associated with such projects as estuary crossings or completely new land use and transportation opportunities, however, Method II could result in significant inaccuracies, or be invalid. In these cases, and for demand models of multinomial logit form, recourse to Method III was available.

However, as Neuberger recognised, a far more important conceptual issue emerged:

> it shows the relation between economic evaluation on the one hand and the notions of accessibility and comfort and convenience on the other: hitherto these have usually been regarded as completely unrelated. . . . There is a close connection between economic analysis and the measurement of accessibility, and that the two do not need to be assessed separately (Neuberger, 1971, 64, 66).

Accessibility measures and benefits could thus be closely integrated with the standard user benefit analysis.

The full significance of these results was not apparent in the early 1970s. Moreover, it was unclear whether they could be extended to more complex travel forecasting models such as the **G/D/M/A** forms being used in practice. Indeed, it seemed unlikely, since the conventional demand functions did not satisfy the technical symmetry conditions noted above for the consumer surplus measure to be unique, except in very special cases. But it raised the question: how could the travel demand relations used in practical transportation studies, involving generation, distribution, modal split and assignment models, be formulated so as to allow an extension of Neuberger's result? If this could be achieved, it would forge a closer integration between the models used to forecast the response of travellers to changes in the transportation networks and land use arrangements, on the one hand, and the economic measures of welfare change associated with that response and interpreted in terms of accessibilities, on the other. This issue will later take centre stage in our story.

3.9 CONCLUSION

By the mid-1960s, the systematic study of urban transportation and methods of travel forecasting had been successfully transferred from the US and Canada and incorporated into the UK transportation planning process. Within a period of a few years, considerable experience in their application had been gained and local innovations were evident. While still recognisably the outgrowth of the earlier studies in Detroit, Chicago, Toronto and other metropolitan areas, major practical developments in the UK resulted in a proliferation of models and methods reflecting an evolution of objectives, information requirements and state of the art in travel forecasting. The resulting variation of methods is important for our story. It was not only against widely applied forms, but also against the leading edge of practice, that progress could be assessed and against which subsequent competitors would need to be compared. As becomes clearer in later chapters, such assessments were seldom performed.

There was significant progress in addressing some of the problems of urban travel forecasting of the early 1960s; it is easy to discount this achievement in the light of what was to come. Much of that advance was common to the UK and US:

1. improved representation of passenger behaviour in public transport systems and its application in the assignment of demand to services;
2. modal split models that were more sensitive to travel time and cost variables;
3. refinements in the modelling of congestion in road networks;
4. a limited practical incorporation of 'feedback', to seek consistency between the demand for travel and the level-of-service variables entering different parts of the forecasting procedure.

Other innovations appear to have been more fully developed in the UK. By the end of the 1960s, advanced urban travel forecasting models contained some or all of the following:

1. model specifications that addressed the greater degree of the variability of travel behaviour within zones, particularly through household-based category analysis at the generation stage;
2. establishment of travel demand models formulated in terms of generalised costs that began to reflect behavioural discrimination and choice, and provided a succinct means of representing transportation policies;

3. a new theory of statistical dispersion in travel patterns, the entropy maximising approach, that enabled a synthesis of the distribution and modal split stages based on share models of multinomial logit form;

4. composite cost formulations of varying sophistication that allowed an interdependency between the different stages of the model to be established, and the effects of policies represented by changes in generalised costs, to be transmitted through the assignment, modal split and distribution stages of the travel forecasting process;

5. a closer integration between demand analysis and the method for calculating economic user benefits founded on generalised costs and the Rule-of-a-Half consumer surplus measure.

The leading edge of practice in the early 1970s was perhaps best described as a 'hybrid' approach that drew on 'disaggregate' concepts and methods, household-based category analysis for trip generation, and generalised costs derived from the modal choices of individual travellers, grafted on to the conventional zone-based approach. By introducing new concepts and procedures within all stages of the forecasting procedure, these efforts were seen by many as a strengthening process.

At this point it is important to mention the collaborative and collegiate nature of several of the advances made in travel forecasting and economic evaluation in the period 1966–70, in particular the pivotal role played by the Mathematical Advisory Unit at the [UK] Ministry of Transport, headed by Alan Wilson from 1965 to 1968. As David Quarmby, who joined the MAU in 1966, noted:

> It was an incredibly fertile period; the academic publications tend to be in the name of one or two individuals, and certainly Alan Wilson's own personal contribution was enormous, but you only have to see the huge range of really innovative output in the form of MAU notes to realise that this was a group of individuals who working with economists like Henry Neuberger elsewhere in the Economic Planning Directorate was pushing back the frontier on several fronts. I think this phenomenon and this period is quite unique in the annals of Whitehall; and it is a testament to Christopher Foster's vision, his leadership and ability to persuade senior civil servants and Ministers that it all mattered.[36]

John Wootton also attested to the collaborative nature of this key period, recalling: 'with Alan Wilson at the Ministry of Transport we were constantly bouncing ideas and papers off one another'.[37] Although we have emphasized advances in the larger transportation studies, particularly those which had a research focus, it is important to note that the MAU was also influential in the work undertaken in the smaller cities and towns. [38]

However, there were also many examples of transportation studies that incorporated few of the above innovations, which caught the eye of critics. Also, in relation to growing requirements overall progress was being made rather slowly and against a moving target. The transportation planning framework was evolving, and what was emerging was a lengthening list of objectives, a wider range of policies, and evaluation frameworks that required greater precision in the information sought. Furthermore, there were growing expectations for the speed and cost with which data could be gathered and travel forecasting procedures could be implemented.

In both the US and the UK, at the start of this era there was considerable sympathy, even enthusiasm, for the application of mathematical models in travel forecasting and transportation policy analysis. By the early 1970s, in spite of the achievements made, the conventional methods were beginning to take a battering, as we noted in section 2.7. The role and purpose of the forecasts within the planning framework, the theoretical foundations of the models, the practical procedures for generating appropriate information for the evaluation of projects and policies, and the 'policy sensitivity' of the models were all subject to attack. Prior criticism was revisited and expressed more forcefully, confidently and systematically.

The charge of 'policy insensitivity' was of central importance and now tended to imply one or more of the following criticisms (Charles River Associates, 1972; UK House of Commons, 1972; Ben-Akiva, 1973; Starkie, 1973; Wachs, 1973):

1. The models failed in some or all parts of the forecasting process to reflect the full range of changes in price and level-of-service variables deemed to represent the policies.
2. The models embodied a limited range of behavioural responses to policies. While the more advanced models, through generalised and composite costs and feedback, could reflect the effect of policies through route, mode and destination switching, progress in representing the influence of policies on timing of travel, car occupancy, trip frequency, car ownership and land use arrangements was very limited or non-existent.
3. With their limited market segmentation, the models lacked, particularly in post-distribution modal split models, the variation of socio-economic conditions to fully represent limited choice and captivity to either public transport or car.
4. The models, specified and estimated at the zonal level and for long daily time periods, lacked spatial and temporal precision, particularly in their ability to address the subtleties of fare policies and

parking charges, or the consequences of new and improved public transport facilities.

5. Only motorised modes were treated in any detail; and representation, let alone policies towards walking and cycling, were treated either crudely or not at all.
6. Emphasis was often on peak hour problems and policy impacts on associated journey-to-work movements. Progress in modelling the effect of projects and policies on other types of journeys, such as those for business and goods movement, was considerably slower.
7. The models were often deemed too spatially aggregated to produce useful information pertaining to groups distinguished by socio-economic characteristics and location.

There were also important unresolved questions relating to the specification of the travel forecasting model as a whole:

1. What overall structure should be adopted and why?
2. Were the relevant alternatives confined to the **G/D/M/A, G/M/D/A** and **G/D-M/A** forms?
3. How were the underlying decision processes of travellers for different trip purposes reflected in the model forms?
4. How should the different stages be linked together so that policies would influence the several aspects of behaviour represented by the model?
5. To what extent did all this matter?

These were questions that remained in the air in the late 1960s and early 1970s.

Travel forecasting models were increasingly seen by many in the planning community as a whole, sometimes by their users, and certainly by their critics, as monolithic black boxes. Expensive in resources, the models appeared incapable of delivering in a timely manner the sort of detailed economic, social and environmental indicators increasingly required by planning agencies (Lee, 1973; Starkie, 1973; Wachs, 1973; Bruton, 1975). Frequently, too much time was devoted to developing the model and not enough time to exhaustive testing of alternative policy options. According to Bruton (1975, 21), the transportation planning process was 'too concerned with the technical problems associated with traffic estimation and network planning, and too little concerned with the transport needs of the community at large'.

Public opposition to road construction schemes on a grand scale was growing. Energy conservation, air quality, noise abatement, road safety and the accessibility provision of particular groups were beginning to emerge as important considerations among the criteria by which transportation schemes and policies would be judged. In the US, the UK and many other countries, the initial strong emphasis of urban transportation planning on road network development had moved on to address public transport investments and even restraint schemes. However, most transportation budgets were still dominated by highway schemes, often assembled from plans compiled years, even decades, earlier, in order to ameliorate congestion and cater for increased mobility for current and future car users.

Then, suddenly the world changed. The first oil shock occurred in late 1973, with its profound economic consequences that gave rise to a period of austerity and of cut-backs in transportation budgets in many industrialised countries including the US and the UK. The era of ambitious large-scale capital projects gave way to one where greater emphasis was placed on public transport initiatives, transportation systems management and a range of shorter-term measures, including various parking instruments and restraint mechanisms, and car pooling incentives in the US. The conventional forecasting methods, developed in both the US and the UK, were not particularly well suited for the policies contemplated in this new era (Ben-Akiva, 1973; Brand and Manheim, 1973; Domencich and McFadden, 1975). Marvin Manheim [1937–2000] commented on the continued relevance of the traditional four-step approach, or the urban transportation model system (UTMS), as he preferred to call it:

> The UTMS was a major accomplishment for its time. The profession and the governmental transportation agencies (federal, state and local) must recognise that the UTMS is no longer satisfactory; it is neither relevant to the practical issues that must be addressed in the urban transportation studies of today . . . nor acceptable when viewed from a theoretical perspective. The UTMS should be neither completely discarded nor allowed to remain unchanged as the basic working tool of urban transportation analysis. A new generation of transportation analysis tools is required. Development of new systems should build on the several directions of current research, as well as the practical experience gained from the UTMS. The recommendation is that we begin by asking not whether but how (Manheim, 1973, 35).

How this challenge was taken up is the subject of the next two chapters.

NOTES

1. en.wikipedia.org/wiki/Colin_Buchanan_(town_planner) (accessed 4 November 2013).
2. In the early days of the 1960s the 'multi-step' terminology, employed in the US, was in

common use in the UK. Increasingly, the term 'multi-stage' was adopted in the UK. In this chapter 'multi-step' and 'multi-stage' are used interchangeably.

3. The first London Traffic Survey began as a roads-only study; some 30 000 households were selected for the home interviews. As John Wootton recalled (personal communication with Huw Williams, 2010), 'It was Gerry Drake, the Director of the study, who persuaded London County Council/Greater London Council and Ministry of Transport to expand the work to include public transport and a further 10 000+ households were added. This also provided one of the incentives for the later development of the public transport assignment procedure.'

4. John Wootton, personal communication with Huw Williams, 2010.

5. John Wootton, personal communication with Huw Williams, 2010.

6. Martin Richards, personal communication with Huw Williams, 2013.

7. See Stopher and Meyburg (1975, Chapter 9) for an extended review.

8. John Wootton, personal communication with Huw Williams, 2010.

9. John Wootton, personal communication with Huw Williams, 2010.

10. More details on the form and estimation of the distributions for determining the future distributions of households over the categories can be found in the paper by Wootton and Pick (1967, 143–148) and in the textbooks by Wilson (1974, 136–140) and Ortúzar and Willumsen (2011, section 4.3).

11. The categories employed by Wootton and Pick were related to aggregations of standard industrial classes for seven of the categories and residential land use for the eighth. The number of trip attractions to a given zone was then written as the sum over the contributions from the different categories. This involved multiplying the intensity of activity in the different categories in each zone by the corresponding rate at which trips were attracted per unit of activity. For further details see Wootton and Pick (1967, 152) and Wilson (1974, 140).

12. For the London Transportation Study (1966), see Freeman, Fox, Wilbur Smith and Associates (1966).

13. Early forms of the logistical model adopted by Tanner for car ownership forecasting related the number of cars per capita CO_t to time t as follows:

$$CO_t = \frac{S}{1 + \beta\exp(-\alpha St)}$$

in which S (the saturation level), and α and β are parameters to be determined. For a discussion of the estimation of these parameters, and subsequent modifications to the basic model form, see Tanner (1965) and Button et al (1982).

14. The authors are grateful to Andrew Daly for discussion of the LGORU studies.

15. David Quarmby, personal communication with Huw Williams, 2011.

16. David Quarmby, personal communication with Huw Williams, 2008.

17. en.wikipedia.org/wiki/Alan_Wilson_(academic) (accessed 5 June 2014).

18. en.wikipedia.org/wiki/Christopher_Foster_(economist) (accessed 5 June 2014).

19. Alan Wilson, personal communication with Huw Williams, 2007.

20. The entropy of a physical system is an expression of the disorder arising from the different ways its state can occur. In this social system it relates to the number of possible ways in which a trip pattern could arise from different arrangements of the trips. This is also related to the statistical dispersion in the trip data.

21. In the doubly-constrained form the balancing factors accompanying the origin and destination constraints were explicit and treated on an equal footing, although one or the other set of constraints could be used to make one set of balancing factors explicit, as in the BPR manuals.

22. In Wilson's writing this parameter was usually given the symbol β. For reasons that will become clear we shall use the symbol λ_D when discussing the distribution model.

23. Wilson's 'doubly-constrained' model, widely used to forecast the spatial distribution of work trip journeys, is derived by determining the non-negative trip pattern $\{T_{ij}\}$ which maximises the entropy function σ, subject to the independent constraints reflecting

information available to the analyst. These include the requirement that the trips generated by, and attracted to, any zone are equal to the values derived from the generation model, and the requirement that the predicted trip cost is equal to that observed in the data:

$$\max \sigma = -\sum_{ij} T_{ij} \ln T_{ij}$$

$$\sum_j T_{ij} = O_i \text{ for all } i$$

$$\sum_i T_{ij} = D_j \text{ for all } j$$

$$\sum_{ij} T_{ij} c_{ij} = C$$

$T_{ij} \geq 0$ for all i and j.

Here O_i is the number of trips generated by the activity in zone i and D_j is the number of trips attracted to the activity in zone j. In the journey-to-work model these are related to the population and employment in the respective zones. The solution to this constrained optimisation problem is given by:

$$T_{ij} = a_i b_j O_i D_j \exp(-\lambda_D c_{ij})$$

in which the balancing factors, on substitution, are given by:

$$a_i = \left[\sum_j b_j D_j \exp(-\lambda_D c_{ij}) \right]^{-1}$$

$$b_j = \left[\sum_i a_i O_i \exp(-\lambda_D c_{ij}) \right]^{-1}$$

The model may also be written in the form:

$$T_{ij} = O_i \frac{b_j D_j \exp(-\lambda_D c_{ij})}{\sum_j b_j D_j \exp(-\lambda_D c_{ij})}$$

24. Thus, the distribution or location, modal share and route split share models considered by Wilson take the following multinomial logit share forms:

$$p_{ij} = \frac{A_j \exp(-\lambda_D c_{ij})}{\sum_{j \in J} A_j \exp(-\lambda_D c_{ij})}; \quad p_m = \frac{\exp(-\lambda_M c_m)}{\sum_{m \in M} \exp(-\lambda_M c_m)}; \quad p_r = \frac{\exp(-\lambda_R c_r)}{\sum_{r \in R} \exp(-\lambda_R c_r)}.$$

with $j \in J$ denoting an alternative j in a set of destinations J available from location i; $m \in M$ a mode m in the set of modes M available, and $r \in R$ a route r in a set of routes or services available between an arbitrary origin–destination pair. A_j is here a measure of attraction of zone j. In general, the set M is dependent on person type (such as those with a car available and those without). The parameters λ_D, λ_M and λ_R determine both the dispersion (spread) of the trips over the various options and the response of the respective distribution, modal and route shares to changes in the relevant costs.

25. Although most of Wilson's model development with destination, mode and route alternatives was based on the negative exponential function, as in notes 23 and 24, he argued that the functional form describing the variation of demand with the travel attributes (e.g., under increasing spatial separation) would actually be determined by the way in which people perceived travel costs and that this might depend on the length of the trip. Thus, if generalised costs, or their components, were perceived logarithmically instead of linearly, the negative exponential terms would be transformed into power functions (see, for example, Wilson, 1970, 34–35). This allowed a link to be established with the

class of abstract mode models applied in the mid-1960s, as, for example, in the model of Quandt and Baumol (1966).

26. Alan Wilson, personal communication with Huw Williams, 2007.
27. John Wootton, personal communication with Huw Williams, 2010.
28. This sum could be weighted to reflect the different importance of components in the generalised cost between the origin and destination.
29. Here, equilibration is interpreted as a method for seeking consistency of level-of-service (travel times and costs) throughout the demand model.
30. In the UK other key studies, such as the Roskill Commission into the siting of the third London airport and the Greater London Development Plan Inquiry, also were important drivers for the development in methods of environmental assessment.
31. en.wikipedia.org/wiki/Economic_surplus (accessed 11 March 2014).
32. If the trip and generalised cost matrix elements for the zone pair (i, j) and mode m are written T_{ijm} and c_{ijm} and the superscripts 1 and 2 denote their computation in the initial (do-nothing or reference) and final (do-something) equilibrium states, the user benefit UB, which is given by the change in consumer surplus, is approximated by the Rule-of-a-Half (RoH):

$$UB = \frac{1}{2} \sum_m \sum_{ij} ((T_{ijm}^{(1)} + T_{ijm}^{(2)}) (c_{ijm}^{(1)} - c_{ijm}^{(2)}))$$

33. If $D_\xi(c_1 \ldots c_\xi \ldots c_N)$ represents the demand for a travel-related option A_ξ out of a set of N alternatives $(A_1 \ldots A_\xi \ldots A_N)$, the generalised costs of which are given by $(c_1 \ldots c_\xi \ldots c_N)$, the change in generalised consumer surplus is given by:

$$\Delta CS = - \sum_\xi \int_Q D_\xi(c_1 \ldots c_\xi \ldots c_N) \, dc_\xi$$

in which Q is the path of integration between the initial and final cost states $c^{(1)} = (c_1^{(1)} \ldots c_\xi^{(1)} \ldots c_N^{(1)})$ and $c^{(2)} = (c_1^{(2)} \ldots c_\xi^{(2)} \ldots c_N^{(2)})$, respectively (Neuberger, 1971). It was later shown by Williams (1976) that the Rule-of-a-Half measure of user benefit:

$$\Delta CS \cong \frac{1}{2} \sum_\xi ((D_\xi^{(1)} + D_\xi^{(2)}) (c_\xi^{(1)} - c_\xi^{(2)}))$$

can be generated within the Method III framework by taking a linear path of integration and applying a first order approximation for the expansion of the demand function between the initial and final cost states. For a more extensive discussion of the assumptions and developments of this approach, see Jara-Diaz (2007).

34. Broadly, this symmetry condition requires that the change in demand D_ξ for a particular option A_ξ under a marginal change in the cost c_ψ of a substitute A_ψ is equal to the change in the demand D_ψ for A_ψ under a marginal change in the cost of c_ξ of A_ξ. More formally, the generalised surplus change is unambiguously defined only when the following symmetry or integrability conditions hold:

$$\frac{\partial D_\xi}{\partial c_\psi} = \frac{\partial D_\psi}{\partial c_\xi} \text{ for all } A_\xi, A_\psi.$$

35. For a demand function of the form:

$$T_{ij} = O_i \frac{A_j \exp(-\lambda_D c_{ij})}{\sum_j A_j \exp(-\lambda_D c_{ij})}$$

in which A_j is here a measure of the attraction of zone j, the measure of user benefit accompanying a change in the user costs from $c^{(1)}$ to $c^{(2)}$ is given (Neuberger, 1971) by:

$$\Delta CS = \sum_i O_i(B_i^{(2)} - B_i^{(1)}) \text{ in which } B_i = \frac{1}{\lambda_D} \ln\left(\sum_j A_j \exp(-\lambda_D c_{ij})\right)$$

or

$$\Delta CS = \frac{1}{\lambda_D}\sum_i O_i \ln\left(\frac{\sum_j A_j \exp(-\lambda_D c_{ij}^{(2)})}{\sum_j A_j \exp(-\lambda_D c_{ij}^{(1)})}\right)$$

where ln (x) again denotes the natural logarithm of x.

36. David Quarmby, personal communication to Huw Williams, 2011.
37. John Wootton, personal communication to Huw Williams, 2008.
38. An example of this involvement was the development of the software program COMPACT, which the UK MoT encouraged some studies to use. Furthermore, UK MoT officials, such as Roy Spence, A.E. Fieldhouse and Gordon Wells, used their involvement in studies for the cross-fertilisation of methods and ideas and learning from successes and failures (Martin Richards, personal communication with Huw Williams, 2013).

4. Travel forecasting based on discrete choice models, I

4.1 INTRODUCTION

The early 1970s was the beginning of a golden age for travel demand analysis and forecasting. Progress made in the following two decades still has major theoretical and practical relevance today. Innovations were achieved in all phases of model development and application: survey design and sampling methods, model specification, parameter estimation, validation, aggregation, and forecasting, policy analysis and evaluation. The framework established in this period also allowed traditional methods to be subjected to detailed scrutiny, which had quite unforeseen consequences for the validity of travel forecasting models based on the four-step approach. For the purposes of our review, we divide this material into two parts. In this chapter we consider advances in the short but formative period 1970–76, ending with several practical applications of the new forecasting methods in the US (Spear, 1977). This period is largely associated with the emergence of a behavioural approach at the individual level, based on the economic analysis of choice between travel-related alternatives, and the formulation and application of the multinomial logit (MNL) model. These investigations were mainly associated with modal choice; however, increasingly complex choices were considered. Advances following this initial period are reviewed in Chapter 5.

At the conclusions to Chapters 2 and 3, we noted the rising criticism of traditional travel forecasting methods which was directed at their theoretical and statistical deficiencies, their limitations in the representation of behaviour and the effects of policies, and their lack of precision in generating information of relevance to the evaluation of policies and projects. By the early 1970s, in many parts of the industrialised world and in particular in the US and the UK, emphasis was changing from long-range highway dominated planning towards transportation system management (TSM) and public transport investment, requiring analyses of greater precision and more sensitive to the behaviour of individuals. The Williamsburg conference in 1972 (Brand and Manheim, 1973) gave impetus to a new approach to travel forecasting conceived in terms of individual motivation and choice, which held the promise of greater data efficiency, improved policy sensitivity, and more relevant information for economic and social evaluation (Stopher and Lisco, 1970; Charles River Associates, CRA, 1972; Ben-Akiva, 1973; McFadden, 1973). A challenge was laid down that offered a new approach for a new era. The whiff of revolution was in the air.

As is always the case with revolutions – if this was to be one – its roots were to be found in earlier times. Our story returns to the 1960s in the US when the 'disaggregate behavioural approach' to the analysis of travel demand, introduced at the start of that decade, was taking shape, particularly in the context of academic research into modal choice and the value of time (Reichman and Stopher, 1971). The term was intended to signify a break with the past in two respects. Rather than specify and calibrate models for groups of passengers, such as those travelling between zones, 'disaggregation' implied an attempt to capture greater statistical variability in trip making and its determining factors, and avoid information loss and potential bias accompanying the grouping of data prior to model specification and parameter estimation. Probabilistic models would be specified at the micro-level and their parameters estimated from data pertaining to individuals or households. Although not emphasised in the earliest studies, it would later become more explicit how summation over the probable behaviour of individuals would provide the required aggregate travel demand information.

The case against specifying travel demand models at the level of the zone and calibrating them with grouped zonal data had been growing steadily through the 1960s (Oi and Shuldiner, 1962; Quarmby, 1967; Wootton and Pick, 1967; Fleet and Robertson, 1968; Stopher and Lisco, 1970; de Neufville and Stafford, 1971; Reichman and Stopher, 1971; CRA, 1972). In relation to modal split models, specified and calibrated at the zonal level, Reichman and Stopher were to remark:

> these second generation models are all aggregate models and have drawbacks in that they can neither be transferred geographically nor readily subdivided; they are extremely sensitive to zoning; and the measurements of trip distances, particularly for short trips, are inaccurate because of the aggregation under which all trips are designated as originating or terminating at a point, the centroid of a zone (Reichman and Stopher, 1971, 92–93).

In retrospect, perhaps the term 'disaggregate' was an unfortunate descriptor for an approach based on data pertaining to individuals and households. 'Micro-approach' might have been preferable, because different components of traditional models were also applied in a stratified or disaggregated form. Several household types were identified at the trip generation stage, and trip matrices were usually stratified by car owner-ship classes and, occasionally, by person type (e.g., blue collar/white collar workers). However, for the purposes of trip generation, distribution, modal split and assignment in the US, traditional travel demand variables and data were aggregated to the 'zonal' level prior to model formulation, typically with a very coarse socio-economic segmentation.

The term 'behavioural' indicated a response to the common criticism that traditional urban travel forecasting was essentially a curve-fitting exercise or based on analogues from the natural sciences, and lacking a theoretical approach underpinning the choices made by individuals and households. Only if demand forecasts were based on explicit behavioural hypotheses at the level of the fundamental decision-making unit, it was increasingly argued, could there be any hope or expectation for the trans-ferability of models to different geographical settings and forecasting sta-bility over time. Although economic concepts of utility underpinned some of the research applied in the 1960s, the detailed link between the statisti-cal analysis of individual data and the derivation of probabilistic modal choice models based on behavioural hypotheses was still rather tenuous and subject to different interpretations (Domencich and McFadden, 1975).

By the mid-1960s travel behaviour was also being investigated, and operational models of the choices associated with the generation, dis-tribution and modal split behaviour established within an aggregate (zone-based) econometric framework. A number of travel demand models were constructed which, to some extent, anticipated the reformulation of consumer demand theory by Lancaster (1966), in which demand was expressed in terms of the characteristics of goods or services from which utility was derived. Specified in terms of the attributes of the alternatives, these models had been applied successfully but predominantly within an inter-urban travel context (Kraft, 1963; Quandt and Baumol, 1966; McLynn et al, 1967). Urban applications were confined to isolated cases (Domencich et al, 1968; Plourde, 1968), although the general approach and detailed specifications established a point of comparison with the tra-ditional four-step procedure. But these economic foundations were typi-cally based on the actions of 'representative' consumers for whom utility functions were expressed. This approach did not harmonise well with the data on individual choices, which disaggregate probabilistic models applied in the 1960s were originally designed to address (McFadden, 2000b, 2001).

Could an alternative approach to acquiring the sort of information relevant for transportation planners be developed based on the summa-tion (aggregation) of information derived from theoretically convincing behavioural models constructed at the micro-level? Over the next decade many people were to contribute to the development of such an approach. Outstanding among these was the US economist Daniel McFadden, and we shall have much to say about his work in this and the following chapter.

The origins of the initial impetus for the practical application of the discrete choice approach based on the random distributions of cost or utility remain a matter of some discussion. Andrew Daly (2013) has drawn attention to the initial progress on demand analysis and value of time made in the UK (section 3.4), and particularly the influence of Michael Beesley, prior to major initiatives in the US in the 1970s, following the early research of McFadden. Almost certainly the initial analysis of a travel choice situation with random distributions of costs was that of Claude Abraham in the late 1950s (Gaudry and Quinet, 2011), with a seminal publication in 1961, as noted in section 4.2 (see also notes 1 and 12).

If a micro-behavioural approach was to be developed, major issues needed to be confronted. Throughout the 1960s the analysis of individual travel behaviour was confined to the treatment of binary choice, and almost invariably the selection of one of two alternative modes for the journey to work.[1] But the aspirations accompanying the 'disaggregate behavioural' approach implied a new style of modelling that addressed the travel forecasting problem from first principles. What was missing was the formulation and implementation of probabilistic choice models that could be applied to an arbitrary number of alternatives (be they modes, destinations, time periods, routes, etc.) and to combinations of such choice 'dimensions'. The aggregation process would then need to be confronted to generate the urban trip and flow patterns on networks and information required in the policy analysis and evaluation stages of the transportation planning process. Only if these challenges were met could an alternative to the traditional four-step travel forecasting procedure be established.

This chapter gives an account of the early developments of the theory and practice of disaggregate modelling based on the analysis of discrete choices conceived within an economic framework. The first half of the 1970s is particularly noted for the application in studies of the MNL model specified at the micro-level and estimated from data derived from a sample of individuals. But far more was achieved. The groundwork laid in this period has had major implications for travel forecasting to this day. Important theoretical issues relating to the structure of models appeared right at the start. We therefore chart our way through difficult territory in which theoretical innovations interweave with important practical advances. We forgo a strictly chronological account to address the innovations involving the simple MNL model prior to examining the more complex forms relating to model structures derived from it.

The formulation of the discrete choice approach, in which individuals were considered to select one of a set of alternatives according to the maximisation of utility, was the theoretical basis upon which behavioural travel modelling progressed into and beyond the 1970s. In section 4.2 we consider this early conceptual development and the formulation of discrete travel choice models based on random utility maximisation (RUM) with the MNL model as an important special case.

As Spear (1977) noted, in about 1970 transportation planning practitioners in the US began to become aware of the new disaggregate behavioural techniques and their potential for use in urban travel forecasting. In section 4.3 we describe the uptake of the new approach, recording early applications of disaggregate travel forecasting models, and particularly those of travel choice forecasting based on the MNL model applied to more than two modes.

In section 4.4 we consider the development of more complex models that combined different choice dimensions, such as frequency, destination, trip timing and mode. For an explicit theory of model structures derived within a discrete choice framework and its empirical development in an urban context we turn to the pioneering study of Charles River Associates (CRA, 1972) and the subsequent work of Ben-Akiva (1973, 1974), which were to attain particular importance and influence. Judged from later times neither study is completely unproblematic, and we later pinpoint issues of concern; but both have great merit in three respects: (a) in providing alternative behavioural hypotheses governing the structure of demand models involving complex travel choices they anticipated important future developments; (b) they greatly extended the scope of disaggregate model applications; and (c) the research agenda emerging from these studies would guide the field and eventually establish the disaggregate behavioural approach as an intellectually coherent and practically viable alternative to traditional methods. Because the contributions were of such importance, we shall describe these and related studies in detail.

By the early 1970s the merits of a discrete choice approach based on distributed utilities or generalised costs had been independently recognised by several researchers. In section 4.5 we describe some early innovative European applications and theoretical investigations, particularly relating to model structures, which were later to have considerable significance.

While great strides were made in the early years of the 1970s to develop individual choice models for a range of practical situations, a new set of problems was to emerge. In section 4.6 we summarise the difficulties pertaining to both disaggregate and traditional aggregate models encountered in the mid-1970s, together with some views expressed at that time on the possible way ahead. An assessment of the contribution of the discrete choice models applied at the micro-level in this period concludes the chapter.

4.2 DISCRETE TRAVEL CHOICE MODELS: EARLY THEORETICAL PERSPECTIVES

4.2.1 Rise of the Behavioural Approach

In Chapter 3 we introduced the disaggregate studies of modal choice conducted in the 1960s, the purpose of which was to identify and quantify the influence of the factors involved in the selection of one mode over another (Stopher and Lisco, 1970; Reichman and Stopher, 1971). This approach established a functional relationship between the probability $P_j(\mathbf{x})$ that an individual would select or be associated with one or other of two modes A_j, $j = 1,2$ and a set of measured attributes $\mathbf{x}$ of the individual and the alternatives. The models embodied hypotheses suggesting how certain attributes might influence the choice probabilities and were sometimes expressed explicitly in terms of utilities or disutilities.

Various statistical techniques were applied in the formulation and estimation of these multivariate statistical models: discriminant analysis by Warner (1962), Quarmby (1967) and McGillivray (1970); and probit analysis by Lisco (1967) and Lave (1969). Parameters of logit models were estimated by Warner (1962) and Stopher (1969).

Reichman and Stopher summarised the probabilistic models in the following terms:

> the stochastic model of modal choice may be considered as a translation of the theoretical elements of decision-making into operational terms. . . . This probability is assigned on the basis of the consideration of user and system characteristics, and this procedure is most consistent with modern theories of human discrimination and choice (Bock and Jones, 1968; Luce, 1959). These theories state that every human decision is, in essence, probabilistic (Reichman and Stopher, 1971, 94).

What was not always clear in these early models was the extent to which an individual was considered to be consistent in the way choices were made, and in what sense the probability of choice reflected uncertainties of the individual confronted by that choice and/or that of the modeller. After all, the latter was an unprivileged observer of the process of choice, having only limited information and measurements from a survey of the individual characteristics and a few attributes of the alternatives. The means of extending such models to the choice among multiple alternatives was also not fully apparent.

Where attempts were made in the late 1960s to establish a specific theoretical link between individual behaviour and the probability of selecting a given alternative, particularly where the formulation of models involved more than two alternatives, it was often to mathematical psychology, and in particular the work of Duncan Luce [1925–2012], that researchers turned.[2] In the psychological perspective an individual, when repeatedly confronted with a set of choices under the same conditions, was considered to select an alternative with a given probability.

We note the historical significance of the axiomatic approach to probabilistic choice models of Luce (1959). In any discussion of the foundations of choice models to more than two alternatives, the 'independence of irrelevant alternatives' (IIA) axiom[3] assumes particular importance. The axiom, which in this context may be regarded as a postulate or assumption, required the ratio of the probabilities P_j/P_i of an individual selecting the alternatives A_j and A_i from a choice set A of N alternatives $A = \{A_1. \ldots A_N\}$ to be independent of the presence or absence of any other alternative in that choice set. Luce showed as a consequence of the IIA condition that the probability of selecting an alternative P_j could be written in proportion to the psychologists' concept of 'strict utility', a function of the attributes of the alternative and the individual (Luce, 1959; Luce and Suppes, 1965). McFadden (1968, 1973), Domencich and McFadden (1975, 69) and Stopher and Meyburg (1975, 275–278) give a full discussion of the strict utility model and the derivation of the MNL model from the IIA axiom.

Another basis for the establishment of probabilistic choice models was one in which individuals were considered to select an option from distributions of the utilities of alternatives. This approach has a long pedigree; a time-line dating back to the work of Thurstone [1887–1955] (1927) is given by McFadden (2000b).[4] The contribution of Jacob Marschak [1898–1977] (1960) is of central importance.[5] He explored the implications of the IIA axiom and demonstrated that the resultant choice model was consistent with utility maximisation (a good discussion of this early work is provided by Kenneth Train, 2009). Marschak established what we now refer to as probabilistic choice models based on random utility maximisation: the probability P_j that alternative A_j is selected is equal to the probability that an individual draws a utility from a distribution associated with A_j which is greater than the utilities drawn from the distributions of all other alternatives. The relationship between the distribution of utilities and different choice probabilities is considered later in this section.

This formulation of the choice model as a maximisation problem involving distributed utilities was to prove both attractive and powerful in both theoretical and practical studies on travel behaviour. Although the large majority of early work on RUM models in transportation was done in the context of modal choice, the earliest examples of the approach can be found in random cost models of route choice. Gaudry and Quinet (2011) have traced the approach back to work by French engineers in the late 1950s and particularly to research by Claude Abraham (see note 12). For an authoritative discussion of this and earlier unpublished French work, see Gaudry and Quinet (2011, 10).

For his fundamental contributions to establishing the economic foundations and providing a unified approach to general discrete choice models on the basis of random utility theory it is to the work of Daniel McFadden[6] that we now turn.

4.2.2 McFadden's Early Research on Economic Models of Discrete Choice

In McFadden (2000a, 2000b, 2001), he reflected on his progression from an undergraduate physics major to doctoral studies in behavioural science and economics at the University of Minnesota, his early interests in discrete choice analysis, and the influence of mathematical psychologists, notably Thurstone, Marschak and Luce. McFadden recalled the way, in the mid-1960s when he first started thinking about problems of discrete choice, in which economists approached such problems by adapting the traditional methods of demand analysis, where the quantity of a product consumed is a continuous variable, through the device of a 'representative consumer' who exhibited 'fractional consumption rates'. This adaptation of the standard marginal analysis approach, he noted, was not plausible in cases when the decision maker's alternatives are qualitative or 'lumpy' and data on individual choices were expressed in terms of the selection of one item from a set of distinct alternatives (McFadden, 1973, 106):

> I observed that in a population with heterogeneous tastes self interest would lead some to one discrete choice and others to a different one. The attributes of the different alternatives, such as their costs, would determine a tipping point in the distribution of tastes where people would switch from one alternative to another. Thus, the same reasoning that led to the indifference curves and substitution effects found in economics text books would, in a world of discrete alternatives and distribution of tastes, lead to probabilities of choice that depend on economic variables and the attributes of each option in a predictable way (McFadden, 2002, 4).

Although his active interest in discrete choice analysis applied to travel behaviour came through a project in 1970–71 (CRA, 1972) (section 4.4), it was work on a problem in transportation that proved to be a useful precursor to that study. McFadden recounted his formulation of an econometric version of the Luce model for the analysis of data on the highway routeing choices of the California DoT. Drawing on the work of Thurstone, Marschak and Luce, he expressed the utilities associated with different routeing options in terms of a set of measured attributes, including the cost of construction, route length and areas of parkland and open space taken. He then recalled commencing the task of developing software for the estimation of what he then called the conditional logit model: 'I set about writing a computer program to produce maximum likelihood estimates for this model, a difficult exercise in the early days of FORTRAN when linear algebra and optimization routines had to be written from scratch. The program was finally finished in 1967' (McFadden, 2000b, 3).

This work was initially described in McFadden (1968) and in a fuller account several years later. In the hands of McFadden (1973) the theoretical foundation of travel behaviour forecasting based on discrete choices was to take a different direction from that developed by the mathematical psychologists, one consistent with the tenets of consumer economics. This would preserve the notion of a rational decision maker who would make the same choice if repeatedly confronted with a set of choices under the same conditions. As he later expressed:

> the assumption that a single subject will draw independent utility functions in repeated choice settings and then proceed to maximize them is formally equivalent to a model in which the experimenter draws individuals randomly from a population with differing, but fixed, utility functions, and offers each a single choice; the latter model is consistent with the classical postulates of economic rationality (McFadden, 1976a, 365).

In this interpretation, it is hypothesised that an individual selects the option that conveys maximum satisfaction, or utility, and the notion of probability 'reflects the effect of individual idiosyncrasies in tastes or unobserved attributes for alternatives' (Domencich and McFadden, 1975, 52). Here, the limits of knowledge of the modeller become central to the description and explanation of the travel behaviour of an individual who is always assumed to act rationally in the situation in which he finds him- or herself (McFadden, 1973, 1976a; Manski, 1977).

To discuss historical developments and prepare for later innovations, we draw on the above references to sketch the formulation of choice models based on random utility maximisation.

4.2.3 Probabilistic Choice Models Based on Random Utility Maximisation

As noted, the RUM approach to the development of probabilistic choice models is consistent with both psychological and economic viewpoints. 'The fundamental difference between the psychologist's approach and the economist's approach is that the economist postulates individuals as being deterministic utility-maximisers, while the psychologist asserts that individuals make probabilistic choices based on utility assessment' (Stopher and Meyburg, 1975, 278).

In the economic approach to disaggregate modelling the imperfect knowledge of the modeller played a crucial role in explaining why utility maximising individuals with the same observable characteristics and facing the same choice situation might make different selections. The problem of generating aggregate information is then decomposed into the two distinct processes:

1. derivation of the probabilistic choice model on the basis of utility maximising behaviour to account for variations of individual behaviour due to unobserved features and unmeasured attributes of those *within* each market segment (those with the same **x**);
2. an aggregation process, which summed up the contributions to any required aggregate information from each travel-related choice arising from the variation between market segments (those with different measured attributes **x**).

Because of the limits of knowledge of the modeller, the utility that an arbitrary individual derives from selecting an alternative is considered by the modeller to be a random variable; it has been convenient to express this utility as the sum of a representative or systematic component common to all individuals in the market segment (those with the same **x**), and a random term, often referred to as a residual error term. That is:

Utility, $U(x)$ = Representative Value, $V(x)$ + Error Term, $E(x)$

The error term is usually attributed to one or more of the following: the variation in tastes over the population; the contribution of unobserved or unmeasured attributes; the use of proxy variables; and any measurement errors (McFadden, 1973; Manski, 1977; Ben-Akiva and Lerman, 1985). Both the representative utility and the residual error term will in general vary with **x**, the measured socio-economic attributes of the individual and attributes of the alternatives.

Under the assumption of utility maximisation, the modeller assigns to an individual q, drawn randomly from the market segment with the same $\mathbf{x}$, a probability P_{jq} of selecting any alternative A_j in the choice set A. P_{jq} is equal to the probability that the utility U_{jq} is greater than the utilities of all other alternatives.[7] An operational discrete choice model based on RUM is now formed from assumptions about:

1. the dependence of the representative utility $V_j(\mathbf{x}, \phi)$ derived from any alternative A_j on the set of attribute values $\mathbf{x}$;
2. the distribution of the unobserved components of utility for the N alternatives, $F(E) = F(E_1 \ldots E_j \ldots E_N, \theta)$

in which the sets of parameters ϕ, θ characterise the representative utility and the joint distribution of errors, respectively.

Although different approaches were adopted for expressing the variation of the representative component of utility with the set of attributes $\mathbf{x}$, by far the most common approach in early studies of travel behaviour was simply to treat all relevant attributes, such as in-vehicle times, out-of-vehicle times and money costs, on the same footing. The representative utility was then typically expressed in terms of a weighted sum of the attributes, in so-called compensatory utility functions, which allowed in principle the 'good' features of an alternative to compensate for what might be considered its 'bad' characteristics. The weights in this expression, sometimes referred to as the taste parameters, reflected the partial or unit contribution of each attribute to the overall utility derived from an alternative.[8] In addition to their simple form, these linear-in-parameters utility functions allowed contact to be made with the disaggregate modal choice models applied in the 1960s and provided a *post-hoc* rationalisation for their form (McFadden, 1976b; McFadden and Train, 1978).[9]

These assumptions established the relationship between the probability of selecting any alternative $P_j(\mathbf{x})$ in terms of the set of characteristics $\mathbf{x}$ of the individual and those of the attributes of the alternatives, together with the sets of parameters ϕ, θ.[10]

The selection of the joint distribution of the utilities $F(E_1 \ldots E_j \ldots E_N)$ was historically governed by the need to strike a balance between the formulation of choice models which were based on reasonable behavioural hypotheses, on the one hand, and the practical computational requirements for solving the model and estimating its parameters, on the other (McFadden, 1973). Various simplifications were adopted to render workable models, and a considerable part of the history of discrete choice modelling concerns the justification for successive generalisations of this function $F(E_1 \ldots E_j \ldots E_N)$ and the consequent computational challenge for estimating the parameters of the choice model. In the early 1970s assumptions were made more for mathematical convenience than for behavioural sophistication, as well as for achieving a touchstone with prior disaggregate choice models.

4.2.4 Random Parameter and Invariant Random Utility Maximisation Models

A distinction that would later become important in classifying different models was based on the assumed nature of the variation (randomness) underpinning choices and how it was incorporated into the utility function (McFadden, 1973). In so-called random parameter models, the random nature of the utilities was attributed explicitly to variation in the tastes over the population, reflected in the distribution of the parameters in the representative utility function or generalised cost. This assumption allowed the trade-off between times and costs associated with the different alternatives to vary over the population. Some early studies on the value of travel time invoked this model of choice with differing degrees of formality as an explanation for modal choice decisions.

In terms of its subsequent influence, the most important random parameter model developed in the 1960s was that by Richard Quandt. Quandt (1968) discussed the formulation and estimation of a modal choice model in which individuals selected either air or car between several Californian cities on the basis of minimising a disutility function involving the trade-off between travel time and travel cost attributes. The parameters of the utility function, of power function form, were considered to be exponentially distributed, reflecting differences in taste in the choice making population.[11]

Later in this and the following chapter we have more to say about random parameter models, but now we concentrate on invariant random utility maximising (IRUM) models, which have dominated practical applications up to the present. In IRUM models the random utilities for the different alternatives are expressed in the form:

Utility, U_j = Representative Utility, V_j + Random Residual, ε_j

in which the utility residual or error terms ε_j subsume all unobserved factors and errors in measurement. Further, they are assumed to be independent of the value of the representative or systematic component V_j. As a judicious choice for the distributions of the residuals led to well-established choice model formulations (CRA, 1972; McFadden, 1973), their popularity was effectively guaranteed.

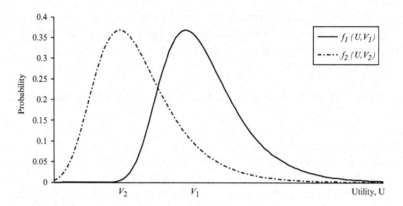

Figure 4.1   Utility distributions for choice between two alternatives

Not surprisingly, in early discrete choice models based on random utility concepts, the most convenient assumptions were made for the form of the representative utilities and the distributions of the random residual error terms (CRA, 1972). As noted, the linear-in-parameters compensatory model was almost invariably taken for the former. In the case of both binary choice and subsequent extension to an arbitrary number of alternatives, the distributions for the error terms for the different alternatives were assumed to be identical and independent. In the conceptual development of choice models, this so-called IID assumption of 'identical and independent distributions' for the random utilities $(U_1. \dots U_j. \dots U_N)$ was of utmost importance; for many applications it seemed both plausible and mathematically convenient.

In Figure 4.1 we illustrate the RUM approach to discrete choice between two alternatives A_1, A_2. Here, each individual's choice is assumed to be the result of a random draw from the two distributions $f(U_1, V_1)$ and $f(U_2, V_2)$ with respresentative utilities, V_1 and V_2. Alternative A_j which offers the maximum utility, $\max(U_1, U_2)$, is selected. For independent random utility distributions there is non-zero probability of selecting the option from the distribution with the lower mean, shown in Figure 4.1 as V_2, in the region in which the probability distributions 'overlap'. We note here a trap awaiting early researchers, which had important implications for the formulation of complex demand models and the evaluation of transportation plans: the quantities V_1 and V_2 are not the mean utilities actually *achieved* from utility maximising individuals selecting the alternatives A_1 and A_2, respectively, because some of those individuals whose utilities contribute to the distribution $f(U_j, V_j)$

of alternative A_j, say $j = 1$, are destined not to select it (sections 4.5 and 5.2.1.2).

Although the selection of normal distributions for the random utility variables had an obvious conceptual appeal, its application to two or more choice alternatives carried with it an increasingly onerous numerical task as the number of attributes and alternatives increased. For this reason there were relatively few applications of the binary or multinomial probit model to the analysis of travel choices (Abraham, 1961;[12] Lisco, 1967; Lave, 1969; Golob and Beckmann, 1971; Spear, 1977). For both binary choice and particularly the generalisation of discrete choice models applied to multiple alternatives, the extreme value or Weibull distribution, similar in shape to the normal distribution but slightly skewed, was of particular interest.[13]

The Weibull distribution has a number of fascinating properties. Most notably the distribution of the maximum value (U_{MAX}) of identical and independent distributed (IID) Weibull variables ($U_1 . ...U_N$), with corresponding ($V_1 . ...V_N$) but common standard deviation s, is itself Weibull distributed with the same standard deviation s and a mean equal, up to a constant term, to the logarithm of the denominator of the MNL choice probabilities (Cochrane, 1975; Domencich and McFadden, 1975). The latter is often referred to as the 'logsum'.[14] This invariance or stability property under maximisation led Domencich and McFadden to comment: 'In our problem, where maximization of utility is the critical operation, this stability property of the Weibull distribution makes it a natural distribution with which to work, just as the normal distribution is natural for problems involving addition of random variables' (Domencich and McFadden, 1975, 61).

Adoption of IID Weibull distributions for the distribution of utilities for the N alternatives within the above RUM framework leads directly to the MNL model for the choice probabilities.[15] The resultant choice model had great attraction from two perspectives: 'this model is computationally tractable and in many applications corresponds to a plausible stochastic specification. It is virtually the only multinomial choice model known to date satisfying both these criteria' (Domencich and McFadden, 1975, 61).

Although slightly skewed, the IID Weibull distribution results in the closed form MNL model, the numerical predictions from which are similar to those derived from IID normal distributions (the probit model). Because the probit model requires numerical methods for its solution, and for the other reasons mentioned above, the MNL model was to have a charmed future.

Towards the end of a long and productive academic life, Waloddi Weibull [1887–1979][16] learned that the probability distribution that bore his name was being used in the derivation of the MNL model and was having wide application in travel forecasting. The venerable professor chuckled and pointed out that, although related, it should be attributed to the Gumbel Type I extreme value distribution.[17] To this day many, including the second author, have referred to the Weibull function when discussing the derivation of the MNL model. From this point onwards, we refer more appropriately to the Gumbel Type I distribution or, for short, the Gumbel distribution.[18]

After several years of study, Daniel McFadden (1973) set out the theoretical foundations of discrete choice modelling based on RUM, together with the properties, statistical estimation and early applications of the MNL model, including his collaboration with Thomas Domencich (CRA, 1972). The paper outlines:

> a general procedure for formulating econometric models of population choice behavior from distributions of individual decision rules. A concrete case with useful empirical properties, conditional logit analysis, is developed in detail. The relevance of these methods to economic analysis can be indicated by a list of the consumer choice problems to which conditional logit analysis has been applied: choice of college attended, choice of occupation, labour force participation, choice of geographical location and migration, choice of number of children, housing choice, choice of number and brand of automobiles owned, choice of shopping travel mode and destination (McFadden, 1973, 106).

McFadden also spelt out central tasks which would occupy theoreticians to this day: (a) identifying the relationship between specific distributions of utilities and econometrically useful choice probabilities that result from utility maximisation; and (b) the identification of the classes of choice models that are consistent with random utility maximization (McFadden, 1973, 108).

This reference, more than any other, provided a concise statement of the new behavioural approach to travel choice analysis combining a plausible theoretical framework with a rigorous statistical estimation method. It was this formidable combination that gradually established the discrete choice approach based on RUM as the dominant theoretical and practical approach to travel forecasting at the micro-level. Although a wider range of choice models was discussed in this period (sections 5.3 and 5.4), including the general multinomial normal form (McFadden, 1973) and the elimination-by-aspects model of Amos Tversky [1937–1996] (1972), the main empirical tool of the disaggregate behavioural approach was the MNL model.

McFadden (1973) was followed by McFadden (1974, 1976a) in setting out the foundations of travel demand analysis from a disaggregate behavioural perspective, outlining theoretical and practical problems, and discussing wider economic applications and outstanding issues of that time. Amemiya (1975) offered a further discussion of the development and estimation of multivariate statistical models of qualitative choice from this era. By the mid-1970s the theoretical basis for, and applications of, econometric analysis to a range of discrete choice problems was becoming well established.

4.3   APPLICATIONS OF NEW TRAVEL DEMAND FORECASTING TECHNIQUES IN THE US

Returning to the early 1970s, we now consider the early applications in the US of the MNL model to more than two alternatives. Much of the commentary in this section draws on a report by Bruce Spear (1977) for US DoT describing several early applications of the disaggregate behavioural approach. These studies were conducted by consultants with a substantial commitment to research, sometimes in conjunction with state and large metropolitan planning organisations.

Spear organised his discussion around three general areas in which 'individual choice models' (his descriptor) had been applied: (a) as elements in the traditional transportation planning process; (b) in the evaluation of transportation system management policies, such as those directed at public transport fares, fuel prices and parking charges, as well as car pool preferential policies; and (c) for demand forecasting for new transportation systems and major service improvements. All applications involved modal choice either on its own or, infrequently, in combination with other individual and household decisions. We first consider the contexts and motivation for the new approach, before examining methodological aspects relating to specification and estimation of the choice models, aggregation issues, and validation and some evidence relating to the performance of such models.

4.3.1   Contexts and Motivation for Adopting the New Approach

In the early 1970s there was some unease about the conceptual and theoretical deficiencies of the dominant four-step approach to travel forecasting. On the whole, however, this was confined to academic debates. The concerns of practice were largely its efficiency and the resources required for the forecasting process, and the precision and timeliness of the information generated. The resources required to collect the data, the expense of solving traditional models, and the insensitivity of the latter to transportation system management (TSM) policy variables were often cited in critiques of traditional methods. In transportation planning practice there was (probably) widespread agreement with the view that:

> while the traditional travel demand forecasting process is reasonably effective in long range planning, it is quite inefficient in evaluating short range, TSM type policies. There are several reasons for this. First, the data needed to drive the models in the traditional process are both costly and time consuming to collect. Secondly, the models themselves are expensive to run, making it impractical to evaluate more than one or two alternatives. Finally, most of the models are insensitive to changes of the magnitude associated with TSM policies. Because of these problems, some planners have turned to individual choice models for evaluating TSM policies (Spear, 1977, 67).

In this regard Spear expressed the view: 'Clearly, the greatest assets of individual choice models are their relatively small data requirements, their consistency with theories of individual choice behavior, and the ease with which policy variables can be included in the linear utility expression' (Spear, 1977, 17).

The possibility of geographical transferability of these models also offered planning agencies the opportunity for adapting existing calibrated models from other metropolitan areas with little additional data.

4.3.2   Specification and Estimation of the Discrete Choice Models

4.3.2.1   Application of the multinomial logit model
Another spur to the implementation of the disaggregate behavioural approach related to the unsatisfactory specification of traditional demand models in which car occupancy factors were inserted between the modal split step and the assignment step. Spear suggested this practice had 'resulted more from the inability of early mode split models to handle more than two modes at one time than from any attempt to reflect human behavior' (Spear, 1977, 23).

Expressing car occupancy as the outcome of a choice process, and specifically combining modal choice and car occupancy into a single choice, not only made the forecasting approach more sensitive to policies being proposed to encourage transfer from the drive-alone option, but also was considered to be more behaviourally realistic.

Traditional binary modal choice models, which aggregated modal opportunities into two main groupings, car and public transport, were extended to the exploration of multi-modal choice as represented by the MNL model. These were formulated with linear utility functions, whose parameters were estimated by the maximum likelihood method, for which programs were becoming more widely available, later through the Urban Transportation Planning System (US DoT, 1976).

The study undertaken for the San Diego County Planning Organization by the consultants Peat, Marwick, Mitchell & Co. (1972) was one of the first applications of individual choice models for a transportation planning agency. Three factors were influential in their decision to apply the approach: (a) the low usage of public transport trips in San Diego would have made traditional trip factoring statistically unreliable; (b) the desire to specify a combined modal split and car occupancy model; and (c) the experience gained with a very early example of a multiple choice MNL model in a study of airport access by Rassam et al (1971). In the application for San Diego, the model was applied to the journey to work with the choice of car driver, car passenger and public transport passenger, as represented by the MNL model choice set illustrated in Figure 4.2(a).

In the first half of the 1970s individual choice models were applied in a variety of settings, including a range of TSM initiatives, applications of initial design and preliminary feasibility studies, and detailed impact and evaluative studies in access and new mode investigations. The latter included studies of: modal access to and egress from parking facilities at commuter rail stations; new commuter rail stations; a community feeder bus service; various combinations of dial-a-ride subscription bus and fixed route bus services; and the feasibility of alternative light rail and express bus systems. Examples of the mode choice sets applied in conjunction with the MNL model drawn from these studies are also shown in Figure 4.2. Various forms of market segmentation were adopted, including standard home-based work (HBW), non-home-based (NHB) and other home-based (OHB) purposes, in some cases further sub-divided or limited to a subset of journeys.

4.3.2.2 Variables, parameters and model estimation

The prospect of developing statistically reliable models on the basis of a few hundred observations was a considerable attraction of the new approach, making it particularly suitable for evaluation of TSM policies. Socio-economic and mode choice data were obtained from individual trip records derived from home interview surveys, while level-of-service variables were derived from perceived, reported or measured values of the attributes for the accepted and one or more rejected alternatives (Stopher and Meyburg, 1975; Spear, 1977). A commonly applied approach was to use, particularly for non-selected alternatives, zone-to-zone travel times and costs, derived from the shortest route searches for the network model, in place of the point-to-point values associated with individual journeys (McFadden, 2000b).

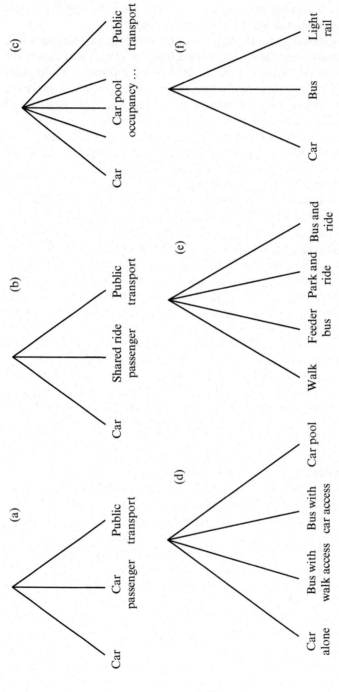

Source: Derived from Spear (1977) and review by the authors.

Figure 4.2   Examples of modal choice sets applied in conjunction with the multinomial logit (MNL) model in early US studies

Spear also noted examples of the use of data derived from attitudinal surveys to 'enhance the information derived from the choice models' and, in particular, cited studies conducted by the New York State DoT. He added:

> Attitudinal data can also be used to create variables for such attributes as comfort, convenience, or reliability where objective data is difficult or impossible to obtain. And they can be used to define market segments based on attitudes or perceptions of transportation service. These and other potential applications of attitudinal research are just beginning to be recognised by transportation planners (Spear, 1977, 141–142).

Early studies of modal choice investigations involving attitudinal variables may be found in the work of Hartgen and Tanner (1971), Hartgen (1974), Stopher et al (1974), Hensher et al (1975) and Spear (1976). Wider reflections on the use of attitudinal measurement and psychometric techniques in such studies are summarised in the book by Stopher and Meyburg (1975, 312).

Models specified with linear utility functions, in which time, cost and any other factors were weighted with coefficients, were widely adopted in MNL specifications. The acceptability of the resultant parameter estimates, typically derived from a maximum likelihood criterion, was subjected to several additional statistical and 'behavioural' checks, using overall likelihood ratios, success tables and statistical significance, as well as the requirements that the signs of parameters be in accord with expectations and their numerical values be broadly consistent with the range of estimates achieved in similar studies elsewhere. Because these coefficients represented the relative importance of the included attributes in decisions and the response to changes in attribute values induced by policies, their values and associated demand elasticities were widely reported. They were particularly useful for the rapid analysis of system management policies and in the design of changes to transportation systems.

4.3.3 Aggregation Issues

In the early days of disaggregate modelling, the main focus of development was 'on improved understanding of travel choice behavior', as Koppelman and Ben-Akiva (1977, 165) noted. Later work was directed towards using disaggregate models in the analysis of practical planning issues. For these, the aggregation problem needed to be confronted directly. Summing individual contributions to travel-related alternatives over distributions of socio-economic and level-of-service variables or spatial groups associated with the zonal system to generate required aggregate output information, while in principle straightforward to state, constituted a significant practical challenge. By the time Spear had completed his survey, various aggregation methods and their potential accuracy and bias in different contexts had been studied by, among others, Talvitie (1973), Domencich and McFadden (1975), McFadden and Reid (1975) and Koppelman (1975, 1976).

The approach used most commonly in early urban applications became known as the 'naïve method'. It involved substitution of the mean values of explanatory variables in the estimated individual choice probabilities to represent the choice probabilities for the group concerned. For non-linear models this procedure gives rise to biased estimates of group behaviour. From the early 1970s, aggregation procedures of varying sophistication were formulated to attempt to correct for such bias. For applications with zonal-level variables, Talvitie (1973) proposed a formulation to derive estimates of choice frequencies for interzonal trips based on zonal means and estimates of within-zone variances of the explanatory variables (Spear, 1977, 86).

The most extensive numerical analysis of the aggregation process was undertaken by Frank Koppelman (1975, 1976). Koppelman graduated from MIT (BS, Civil Engineering) and Harvard (MBA), later returning to MIT for his Ph.D. (Civil Engineering), for which he undertook a comprehensive analysis of the aggregation process involving discrete choice models, including the development of taxonomy of methods. He proposed five practical approaches for integrating or summing the contributions to a final demand measure from individuals with different socio-economic and level-of-service variables and the choice sets available to them. These procedures were based on information that was either commonly available in current forecasting studies or could be developed with little additional effort. The selection of an appropriate procedure from those available was determined by several factors, including input data availability, accuracy requirements, and the outputs and required level of detail of the forecasts. Koppelman (1976) and Koppelman and Ben-Akiva (1977) reported on numerical studies of the bias that may arise under inappropriate aggregation over population segments.

As more applications were undertaken, the two approaches that were used most often in practical studies were those based on market segmentation and sample enumeration as defined in Koppelman's taxonomy. Market segmentation involved the division of the population into relatively homogeneous groups with respect to the socio-economic and level-of-service variables; then, the average values of the independent variables were substituted for each market segment. For the sample enumeration method, currently in widespread use, the disaggregate model was applied separately to each member of a sample of households or individuals; the sample was then expanded to be representative of the whole population. Spear (1977, 105) concluded: 'the random sample explicit enumeration procedure seems best suited for those studies involving short range area wide policy evaluation in an area which has travel choice data from a recent population based travel survey'.

4.3.4 Model Validation and Evidence

As noted in Chapter 3, there was no established tradition for assessing the validity of forecasts derived from aggregate models beyond requiring a 'good fit' of predictions against observed travel patterns, major flows and screen-line crossings, and obtaining 'sensible' signs and magnitudes for model coefficients. In the disaggregate cross-sectional approach, param- eter significance and goodness-of-fit were also necessary conditions for assessing an adequate model; the latter could be applied both before and after the aggregation process.

Increasingly, it was recognised that goodness-of-fit was an insufficient test for the validation of models for the purpose of policy testing, particularly if the applications (e.g., modifications to a transit system) exhibited significant differences from conditions in the base year. From this period the notion of validity in travel forecasting based on probabilistic choice models, founded as they were on behavioural assumptions, became closely associated with the possibility of geographical transferability of model forms and their estimated parameter values. As a hypothesis this was not uncontroversial, as there was little theoretical basis to assert that disaggregation itself was adequate to ensure geographic or temporal transferability, other than that some causes of non-transferability arising from the use of aggregate data were eliminated (Koppelman, 1975; Koppelman and Wilmot, 1982).[19]

Nevertheless, models applied in one urban area, if constructed on sound behavioural principles, it was suggested, would be a good representa- tion of travel behaviour in another, or at least would require only minor adjustment of their parameters with a small sample derived from the new study area. Different methods of transferring and updating disaggregate modal choice models were considered by Atherton and Ben-Akiva (1976). This approach to model development was in stark contrast to the practice of calibrating traditional aggregate model forms which lacked a sound behavioural basis and contained parameters reflecting the zoning systems. Sometimes transferability of probabilistic choice models with little or no parameter adjustment was asserted *a priori*, allowing the wholesale lifting of models from one geographical context to another, a practice represented in Spear's review.

The most exacting test of the validity of disaggregate behavioural models was to compare forecasts with observed outcome measurements in well-designed before-and-after studies. The most prominent and well-documented example of such a study in the early 1970s was undertaken by Daniel McFadden and colleagues at the University of California, Berkeley. This research sought to refine urban travel demand forecasting models and to investigate potential applications of disaggregate models in demand forecasting for new modes and short-range policy analysis. The completion of the Bay Area Rapid Transit (BART) system in the San Francisco Bay Area provided 'a natural experiment that would give this modelling framework an acid test' (McFadden, 2002, 3). For this short-term forecasting test an MNL model was applied with choice sets in the forms shown in Figure 4.3. In the collection of data, scrupulous concern was given to the accuracy of the level-of-service and access variables. McFadden later recalled:

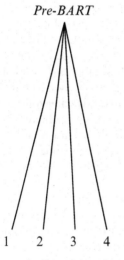

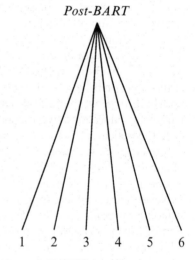

1. Car, drive alone   5. BART, bus access
2. Bus, walk access   6. BART, car access
3. Bus, car access
4. Car pool

Source: Based on McFadden (2000b).

Figure 4.3   *Choice sets used in conjunction with the MNL model in the before-and-after study of the introduction of BART*

The critical experiment came when our pre-BART forecasts from 1972 data, adjusted for actual 1975 travel times and costs, were compared with the observed BART mode shares in 1975. . . . The predictions . . . are made by summing over the representative sample the estimated choice probabilities for each alternative, with the new BART modes added to the list of alternatives in the MNL formula. . . . Coefficients of alternative-specific variables and interactions for the new BART alternatives were assumed to be identical to the corresponding coefficients for the existing bus variables. . . . The model forecast a total BART share of 6.4 per cent in 1975, closer to the actual share of 6.2 per cent that might reasonably have been expected given the sizes of standard errors. The model under-predicted the Auto Alone mode, and substantially over-predicted transit share, 21.3% versus 18.4% (McFadden, 2000b, 8).

The Berkeley team's forecasts for BART were considerably better than achieved by the official forecast in 1973, which foresaw that BART would carry about 15 per cent of all work trips (McFadden, 2002, 5). McFadden recognised that good fortune was on their side: 'We were lucky to be so accurate, given the standard errors of our forecasts, but even discounting luck, our study provided strong evidence that disaggregate RUM-based models could out-perform conventional methods. Our procedures were also more sensitive to the operational policy decisions facing transportation planners' (McFadden, 2001, 355). The validation test and detailed analysis of the discrepancies in this application of the MNL model were recorded by Train (1978).

4.4 TOWARDS A DISCRETE CHOICE THEORY OF TRAVEL DEMAND MODEL STRUCTURES

4.4.1 Prior Influential Work

Having examined some applications of MNL models in the US in the early 1970s, we next consider another major theoretical challenge noted in section 4.1: extending the modelling capabilities to address combinations of choice dimensions, such as frequency, destination and mode of travel at the disaggregate level. The key early research on this problem was undertaken by McFadden and Domencich (CRA, 1972) and Ben-Akiva (1973, 1974).

To understand their motivation, it is helpful to refer to prior influential work, notably the development of aggregate econometric models in the US in the mid-1960s, and to the backdrop provided by the traditional travel forecasting models, which were not endowed with a coherent behavioural basis. In this respect we recall that the traditional aggregate zone-based models were viewed as *reflecting* a sequential decision-making process over the various choices, whether in **G/D/M/A** or **G/M/D/A** form, as described in section 3.7. The nature of this link between model structure and decision process over frequency, destination, mode and route alternatives, however, was vague and lacked a first principles derivation. As we saw in Chapters 2 and 3, the justification of the ordering of the four steps and the interrelationships among them were subject to different interpretations and variations in practice.

A major source of weakness of such traditional forms was their failure to represent consistently the influence of price and level-of-service variables throughout the model (CRA, 1972; Manheim, 1973). One of the consequences of the sequential procedure was that research on the demand models in the 1960s and early 1970s became rather specialised; academics and practitioners often spent many years of their professional lives investigating the intricacies of individual steps, which were then assembled in a rather *ad hoc* way.

The aggregate econometric models of the late 1960s, largely associated with intercity travel forecasting, sought to represent choices over several dimensions, including frequency, destination and mode. They were initially viewed as a generalisation of the gravity model to allow the travel market as a whole to be sensitive to changes in transportation characteristics. The common approach developed in these models was the simultaneous treatment of generation, distribution and modal split (Stopher and Meyburg, 1975, Chapter 15). In an influential review of passenger travel demand models, Kraft and Wohl (1967) contrasted such economically motivated models with traditional forms:

> It is of crucial importance to note that this type of model, one that incorporates both direct elasticities and cross-elasticities, differs in structure from the so-called 'gravity model' (and others most often used in traffic forecasting processes) in at least two significant ways. First, the use of demand relations and cross-relations permits *both* the total amount of tripmaking and the split among modes (for example) to be altered as the trip price or travel time for any mode is changed; this differs considerably from the more usual 'trip generation, trip distribution, modal split and route assignment procedures' which hold the amount of trip making constant and vary only the 'split' of trips among attraction zones, modes and routes. Second, with demand models of the sort proposed (in form at least), trip maker decisions about whether to take a trip, where to take it, and by what mode and route to take it are treated as simultaneous and interrelated decisions, rather than dealt with as sequential, separate and unrelated decisions faced by tripmakers (Kraft and Wohl, 1967, 211).

To emphasise the point, they reaffirm: 'Tripmaking decisions are made simultaneously rather than sequentially' (Kraft and Wohl, 1967, 212).

The extension of the disaggregate approach beyond modal choice to complex decisions was not contemplated in detail before the late 1960s. Peter Stopher and Thomas Lisco (1970) discussed the application of extended disaggregate behavioural models to urban travel forecasting, offering numerous insights and proposing the application of a hierarchy of logit models within a disaggregate framework. Although limited in its theoretical scope, their paper was one of the first to indicate how the traditional approach to demand forecasting could be moulded to be more consistent with a behavioural formulation at the micro-level.

4.4.2   A Pioneering Study of Model Structure

Because this chapter is not structured chronologically, there is a danger that we will fail to convey the full contribution and sense of ambition of the study by Charles River Associates for FHWA (CRA, 1972), later revised and published as Domencich and McFadden (1975). To obtain a sense of what was attempted and achieved we quote from the report's summary:

> This study has developed, and successfully tested in limited applications, a new methodology for designing and calibrating disaggregated, policy oriented behavioral models of urban travel demand. By travel *demand*, we mean not simply the choice of mode but rather the entire set of decisions faced by the traveller – the choices of mode, destination, time of day of travel and trip frequency. With the approach developed in this study, the entire demand function is policy sensitive. Thus, both the number of trips and the percentage splits between competing modes, destinations and times of day are responsive to changes in the transportation system (CRA, 1972, 1–1).

According to McFadden (2000b, 1), the founding ideas for the original model were based on the research of MIT economists Peter Diamond and Robert Hall. McFadden noted:

> From the economic principles of consumer demand, they developed a behavioral travel demand model that emphasized separable utility and multi-stage budgeting, so that the complex dimensions of trip generation, timing, destination, and mode choice could be broken into manageable segments, with 'inclusive values' tying the segments together in a coherent utility-maximization framework. In the style of the times, they developed this theory for a representative utility-maximizing consumer, and were then faced with the problem of putting the model together with data on individual trips from trip diaries (McFadden, 2000b, 2).

McFadden recalled being asked to implement this model after coming to MIT in 1970 (McFadden, 2000b). It was the theoretical development and practical implementation of the Diamond–Hall framework to accommodate data on individual choices that broke new ground in travel behaviour modelling, and econometrics more generally.

At the heart of the behavioural representation, individuals were considered to engage in several decisions – where to live and work, how many vehicles to own, how to travel to work, how often, where, when and how to shop, and so on – in terms of discrete choices over the options available. To simplify the process of choice, it was assumed that the utility function governing choices had an additive, separable structure, which allowed the demand function to be factored into component decisions, as illustrated in Figure 4.4(a), 'in a way that enables the separate decisions to be modelled separately but tied back together into a conceptually satisfying demand function' (CRA, 1972, 1–4).

Individuals were first considered to exercise a choice of work and residential location, then vehicle ownership and then the shopping journey. The tree structure for the shopping trip shown in Figure 4.4(b) reflects the decomposition of the underlying choice process into a decision 'sequence', although it was stressed that each individual was seeking the maximum utility option over the alternative choice combinations of frequency (f), location (d), time period (τ) and mode (m). The model thus represented a process of optimal choice within a decision hierarchy composed of several levels, corresponding to these individual choice dimensions.

With regard to the information flows accompanying the process of arriving at a decision, the authors noted:

> At each decision level, choice can be viewed as being made conditional on fixed preceding decisions and optimal succeeding decisions. For example, destination choice is made conditional on fixed decisions on location, vehicle ownership, and trip frequency, with time-of-day of travel and mode assumed to be chosen for each alternative destination to be the most desirable. The solid arrows in the diagram represent the decision sequence while the broken arrows represent the flows of information on optimal values of succeeding choices which enter the decision process at any level (Domencich and McFadden, 1975, 43–44).

This representation permitted the probability $P(f, d, \tau, m)$ of selecting a given combination of frequency (f), destination (d), time of day (τ) and mode (m) for the shopping trip to be expressed as the product of marginal and conditional probability distributions: $P(f)$, $P(d|f)$, $P(\tau|d, f)$ and $P(m|d, f, \tau)$, here taken as MNL models in which level-of-service variables in the different models were linked through the underpinning assumption of utility maximising behaviour by 'inclusive prices'.

At the lowest level of the tree, choices were determined by the times and costs on the different modes in an 'index of desirability' or 'inclusive price of travel', or what we referred to in section 4.2 as a disutility function

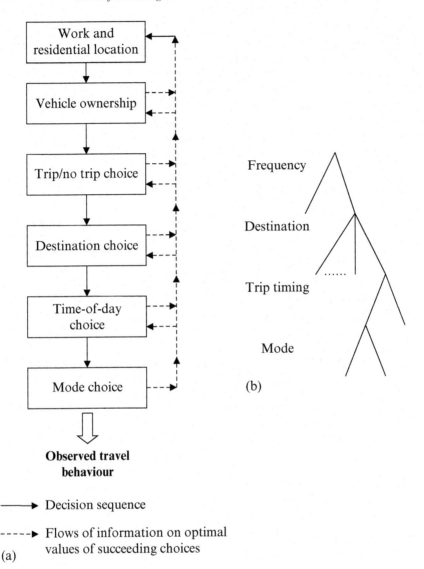

Source: (a) Based on Domencich and McFadden (1975, Figure 3.2); (b) based on Domencich and McFadden (1975, Chapter 3).

Figure 4.4   (a) Observed travel behaviour arising from multiple discrete choices (b) Decision tree for the shopping demand model

or generalised cost. This information is then transmitted to decisions at higher levels of the tree through further inclusive price functions, in earlier chapters referred to as composite utilities or composite costs. The form of these inclusive prices at a particular level of the tree was taken to be equal to the generalised prices for the various choices at the next lower level weighted by the conditional probability of that choice.[20] Interestingly, in the context of destination choices, Domencich and McFadden (1975, 175) saw the inclusive price as having a role to play in the definition of accessibilities which 'would be useful in land use planning, in shopping center location studies, and in urban development analysis'.

We note, for later reference, an observation by the authors:

> It is instructive to compare the decision structure outlined above with conventional modal split and trip generation and distribution models. One may depict such models on the figure above with the trip–no trip choice corresponding to trip generation, and the destination choice corresponding to trip distribution. In this sense, conventional models are compatible with the utility maximization structure we have outlined. However, the information on succeeding decisions implicit in the conventional models is often either inconsistent with a theory of individual utility maximization or corresponds to an implausible utility structure (Domencich and McFadden, 1975, 44).

In the actual implementation of the framework, the multiple choices were decomposed into a modal choice model for travel to work and a demand model for shopping trips. The empirical estimation of the linked hierarchy of MNL models for the latter proceeded from the bottom of the tree (mode) to the top or apex (frequency). Through the transference of information from one level of the tree to the next, the effect of policy variables was expressed explicitly and consistently throughout the model. Data on individual trip decisions from the Pittsburgh home interview survey were adopted for the study, and alternative transportation and socio-economic variables were explored in model specification and parameter estimation.

Working with samples of 115 observations for work trips and 140 observations for shopping trips, the researchers viewed the statistical results as 'extremely encouraging' (CRA, 1972, 1–5). Although in this study the methodology was stressed rather than empirical findings, the authors noted the following interesting result regarding the sensitivity of the various shopping choices to changes in policy variables: 'time of day, destination, and trip frequency decisions are far more responsive to changes in relative travel times and costs than are modal choice decisions' (Domencich and McFadden, 1975, 180).

Apart from its innovative applications to choice contexts other than mode, CRA (1972) demonstrated in theory and application how a 'sequential' decomposition of a probabilistic choice model was consistent with a utility maximising decision process in which decisions over combinations of alternatives were considered 'jointly'. Here, the inclusive values play a key role of information transfer between separate choice dimensions to preserve the notion of an optimal decision maker. There was a 'significant flaw' in the analysis (McFadden, 2000b, 5), relating to this transfer of information between the different choice models within the hierarchy (see section 5.2), and subsequent research would suggest that different orderings of the component choices might have been justified. Nevertheless, in our view, for the sheer number of influential ideas presented, this pioneering project represents the single most important research contribution to disaggregate travel behavioural analysis based on the economics of discrete choices. We shall encounter the full implications of this analysis in Chapter 5.

4.4.3   An Alternative Approach to Model Structure

Moshe Ben-Akiva has been responsible for some of the most significant and innovative applications of disaggregate travel forecasting models, and we shall refer to a number of them in this and subsequent chapters. A graduate of the Technion – Israel Institute of Technology, Ben-Akiva came to MIT for graduate study in the late 1960s. Research for his Ph.D. thesis, described here, represented a further development of, and alternative to, the analysis of CRA. While both studies were conceived within the discrete choice framework based on random utility theory, they expounded different approaches to the behavioural theory of model structures involving combinations of choice dimensions.

According to Ben-Akiva, his research was inspired by two developments:

The first was the recognition that the representation of the trip decision as a sequential process is not completely realistic. It has been argued (Kraft and Wohl, 1967) that the trip decision should be modeled simultaneously with no artificial decomposition into sequential stages. Attempts to develop simultaneous models followed the conventional approach of aggregate demand analysis, in which the quantity demanded is taken as a continuous variable (Domencich et al, 1968; Kraft, 1963; Plourde, 1968; Quandt and Baumol, 1966). The second development was the introduction of disaggregate probabilistic demand models that relied on a more realistic theory of choice among qualitative trip alternatives. However, all the disaggregate models that were developed could be used either for a single stage of the UTMS (Reichman and Stopher, 1971) or, more recently, for all the stages, but again with the assumption of a recursive structure (CRA, 1972) (Ben-Akiva, 1974, 26–27).

Rejecting the conditional dependency inherent in the recursive[21] model structure selected by CRA (1972), in which the traveller was assumed to decompose his or her decision into several linked stages, as unrealistic, Ben-Akiva strove to capture the complexity and interdependence of the decision process over multiple dimensions and, in particular, the destination and mode of shopping trips. In addressing the question of how the characteristics of modes serving different destinations were to be reflected in the choice of destination, and vice versa, he adopted a 'symmetric' model structure in which the different choice dimensions were treated on the same footing. This structure contrasted with CRA's 'asymmetric' approach in which one particular 'hierarchy' of the choices was favoured, as reflected by the structure of the utility function, with the ordering imposed *a priori*. The symmetric treatment harmonised with Ben-Akiva's view that there was a close correspondence between the analytic structure of the model and the nature of the joint decision process underpinning it, as follows: 'simultaneous and recursive structures represent simultaneous and sequential decision-making processes. Theoretical reasoning indicates that the simultaneous structure is more sensible. Moreover, if a sequence assumption is accepted, there are several conceivable sequences, and generally there are no a priori reasons to justify a selection among them' (Ben-Akiva, 1974, 26). What this study set out to do was to show that a simultaneous structure, although complex when combining different choice dimensions with many accompanying explanatory variables, was operationally feasible, and he chose the multinomial logit model for the investigation.

More generally, as a basis for treating the interdependency between the many location and travel-related choices facing individuals and households over the short, medium and longer term, Ben-Akiva (1973) hypothesised that these would be grouped according to the frequency with which the decisions were taken and the potential speed of response to changes in the transportation system. Two groups of choices were distinguished: (a) 'mobility choices', consisting of employment and residential location, housing type, car ownership and journey-to-work modal choice decisions, were considered to be made infrequently; (b) 'travel-related choices' for non-work trips, consisting of frequency, destination, mode, time of day and route, were made frequently, perhaps every day, and assumed to respond rapidly to changes in transportation variables. He then hypothesised that:

1. mobility and travel choices were made 'hierarchically', the latter conditional on the former;
2. within each group of decisions, the choices were highly interdependent and should be modelled as a joint decision process.

The shopping trip was the main subject of empirical study. Although advocating the simultaneous structure provided by the MNL model applied to combinations of destination and mode, Ben-Akiva also considered what he referred to as alternative recursive models (which, he argued, corresponded to alternative behavioural assumptions) in order to identify and evaluate significant differences between the two model forms. By analogy with the notation adopted in Chapter 3 we shall refer to these simultaneous and recursive structures at the disaggregate level by *D-M* and *D/M*, *M/D*, respectively. For the destination and modal choices associated with shopping trips he thus considered the following:

1. *D-M*: a multinomial logit model for the probability of choosing each alternative (d, m) out of a choice set containing combinations of destination and mode;
2. two sequential or recursive structures, expressible as the product of marginal and conditional probability distributions, which we shall label, symbolically, *D/M*: $P\{d\}P\{m|d\}$ and *M/D*: $P\{m\}P\{d|m\}$, respectively.

The recursive structures, which were similar in their general conception to the CRA model, were expressed as a hierarchy of marginal and conditional probability models, as illustrated in Figure 4.5, with MNL models applied at each stage of the hierarchy. The solid arrows in the diagrams indicate the conditionality assumed, while the dashed arrows indicate the transmission of information, via compositional rules, from the lower to the upper level of the tree, as in the CRA study.

For each of the structures *D/M* and *M/D*, three different 'composition rules' for combining the attributes of travel times and costs from the MNL model at the 'lower level' for entry as an inclusive value at the 'upper level' were examined. Ben-Akiva (1974, 34) referred to these as:

1. 'weighted prices', in which the level-of-service variables were weighted by the conditional probability, for example that of selecting a mode given the destination choice, in the $P\{d\}P\{m|d\}$ structure;
2. 'weighted generalised prices' (equivalent to the CRA procedure of inclusive prices, described above);
3. 'log of the denominator', the natural logarithm of the denominator of the MNL model expressing conditional choice, for example the log of the denominator of $P\{m|d\}$ in the structure $P\{d\}P\{m|d\}$. Later this expression was referred to as the 'logsum', and we shall use this expression below.

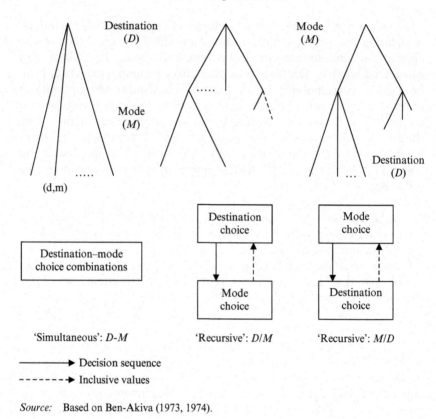

'Simultaneous': *D-M*   'Recursive': *D/M*   'Recursive': *M/D*

⟶ Decision sequence

------ ➤ Inclusive values

Source: Based on Ben-Akiva (1973, 1974).

Figure 4.5   Three probabilistic choice model structures with their corresponding decision trees

In all, seven alternative models were specified: one *D-M* structure; three *D/M* structures; and three *M/D* models, based on the three composition rules.

Ben-Akiva noted that if the coefficient, say θ, of the 'logsum' variable in the 'higher-level' choice, destination choice in the *D/M* structure, turned out to be equal to unity (or statistically not significantly different from unity), the whole sequential model structure 'collapsed' into an MNL model form extending over the combination of destination–modal choice alternatives. In other words, Ben-Akiva formulated and made operational a choice model structure, in which MNL models were arranged in a hierarchy with a 'logsum' link, which contained the extended MNL model, over destination and mode combinations, as a special case. This formulation would turn out to be of great theoretical and practical interest.[22]

The sample used for estimation of the various models consisted of 123 household home–shop–home round trips selected randomly from a home interview survey from the northern corridor of metropolitan Washington, DC. Ben-Akiva showed that five of the seven alternative models specified gave reasonable coefficient estimates, as determined by maximum likelihood. He remarked:

> As expected, the empirical evidence does not show which of the alternative structures, one simultaneous and two recursive, is more likely to be correct. All the models gave reasonable coefficient estimates. Furthermore, all the models gave essentially equal goodness of fit: $\rho^2 = 0.25$. The simultaneous model includes seven coefficients, whereas the recursive models included eight. This implies that the simultaneous model has a slight edge in this category, but it is certainly not a conclusive difference (Ben-Akiva, 1974, 39).

However, Ben-Akiva was able to demonstrate an important result: the estimated parameters, the resultant elasticities and therefore the sensitivity to policy variables of alternative models which passed standard goodness-of-fit tests for micro-models vary considerably with the model structure selected. With regard to the wider development of the models, he concluded: 'The empirical evidence taken together with the theoretical assumptions of a simultaneous structure and the advantages of disaggregate models suggests that future efforts in travel demand modeling should be in the direction of simultaneous disaggregate probabilistic models' (Ben-Akiva, 1974, 40).

4.4.4 Related Studies

The research agenda suggested by the hierarchical framework of mobility and travel choice groups, and the application of the MNL to jointly determined choices within each group, was subject to extensive development. The findings of Ben-Akiva's Ph.D. thesis were extended by Adler and Ben-Akiva (1975) to incorporate the frequency of shopping journeys in a joint structure based on the MNL model applied to frequency, destination and modal alternatives.

The first joint disaggregate model for a subset of mobility choices, namely car ownership CO of the household and mode to work M of its primary worker, applied in the form CO-M, was that of Steven Lerman, the MNL model adopted for this purpose. It was argued that 'car ownership and mode to work are closely related and therefore to model them as jointly determined is most appropriate' (Lerman and Ben-Akiva, 1975, 35). Further research by Lerman (1976) on choices in the 'mobility bundle' argued that household location decisions were closely related to other choices of housing, car ownership and mode to work, and as such were jointly determined. The application of the joint choice MNL model 'eliminat[ed] the need for an arbitrary set of assumptions about a sequence of choices. . . . Each potential location–housing–automobile ownership–mode of work combination is a distinct alternative' (Lerman, 1976, 6).

The study by Ben-Akiva and Atherton (1977) made a number of contributions to the methodological development of the field, and was distinguished in its treatment of:

1. A substantial application of the disaggregate approach to test various policies to promote car pooling, and disincentives to drive-alone options, as a basis for reduction in traffic congestion and energy consumption, and improving air quality. These policies included: employer-based car pool matching and promotion; preferential parking measures; preferential traffic control; and fuel price increases.
2. A micro-level specification of interrelated individual decisions within households.
3. A clear discussion of the aggregation of behaviour by sample enumeration (section 4.3).
4. An early example of the application of the MNL model in pivot-point or incremental form in which the probability of selecting an alternative under a change in the attribute values is expressed in terms of the base probabilities and the utility differences associated with each alternative before and after the change.
5. The validation of forecasts on the basis of a before-and-after study.

To our knowledge this was the first example of a model which addressed 'micro-level interdependency' directly; in this case, it allowed the effect of choice of mode for the journey to work by the primary worker of a household to impact directly on the car availability of other household workers. The MNL model was applied in the four separate contexts:

1. joint car ownership, work mode choice model for the household's primary worker;
2. work trip mode choice for the household's secondary workers;
3. car ownership model for households without workers;
4. joint frequency–destination–mode choice model for non-work trips.

4.5   SOME EARLY EUROPEAN STUDIES

During the second half of the 1960s and early years of the 1970s several important disaggregate studies of modal choice and the value of time were conducted by researchers in Europe and, as noted in section 3.4, particularly the UK. The following studies, selected for their relevance to the application of the disaggregate approach and the theory of model structures, illustrate how the discrete choice RUM approach was transferred from the US to the Netherlands and also adapted and independently developed in the UK from earlier ideas.

In 1970 documentation of discrete choice models based on random utility maximisation was very sparse, and confined to a small number of articles, such as those of Quandt (1968, 1970) and Golob and Beckmann (1971). Prior to the release of CRA (1972), Brand and Manheim (1973) and particularly McFadden (1973), a broad academic reference did not exist.

4.5.1   Transfer of the Approach to the Netherlands

A study by Buro Goudappel en Coffeng in association with Cambridge Systematics in 1973–74 is an example of the way that ideas were transferred through collaborations of US and European researchers, just as the traditional travel forecasting procedure had been transferred from the US to the UK a decade earlier. The project methodology drew extensively on research conducted at MIT at the time and in particular that of Ben-Akiva. Its development was testimony to the openness of the Dutch government to the import of ideas from abroad and was possible because the Dutch ministry had funded a major household interview survey designed as a demonstration project.[23]

The objective of the project, conducted in the Eindhoven region of the Netherlands, was to 'further the development of behavioural urban travel models, and in particular to implement the methods of disaggregate and simultaneous probabilistic travel demand models in a Dutch context' (Richards and Ben-Akiva, 1975, 7). The study focused on choices for two trip purposes: choice of mode for home-to-work trips; and joint choice of destination and mode for shopping trips. For the journey to work, an MNL model was constructed in which the modes included car, bus, train, bicycle and moped, appropriate to the Dutch context. The study 'demonstrated that multinomial logit is a practical tool in the development of multi-modal models' (Richards and Ben-Akiva, 1975, 115). For the shopping trip, the joint choice of destination and mode was also represented by the multinomial logit model.

Interestingly, this is one of the few studies on the disaggregate approach in this period that makes detailed reference to UK work and specifically to generalised cost formulations in what the authors refer to as Wilson-type models[24] (Richards and Ben-Akiva, 1975, Chapter 7). In relation to the specification and application of choice models at the micro-level and, in particular, the adoption of the MNL model, the authors concluded:

> Using disaggregate data and the multinomial logit model it is possible to esti-
> mate a destination- and mode-choice model essentially comparable with that
> of the origin constrained Wilson-type distribution/modal split model, but with
> many fewer observations. . . . As with the mode choice model, the ability to
> include socio-economic variables in the utility function adds considerably to
> the potential power of disaggregate modelling using multinomial logit. Thus
> the disaggregate conditional and disaggregate simultaneous models estimated
> using the multinomial logit model offer major improvements over most con-
> ventional urban transportation modelling procedures, even those based on the
> Wilson model (Richards and Ben-Akiva, 1975, 138).

In relation to the efficiency in the use of data the study team eloquently expressed the case for disaggregate modelling and the relative advantages over the traditional aggregate approach:

> The advantages are two-fold. First, with the same range of variables, the
> various coefficients can be estimated more readily, with fewer observations and
> probably with a greater degree of reliability; thus they offer a potential saving
> in either time or cost, or both. Secondly, they offer the opportunity to include
> more variables, and thus, for a similar cost, to develop models with more com-
> plete specifications, and therefore, better models (Richards and Ben-Akiva,
> 1975, 138).

The book that followed the study (Richards and Ben-Akiva, 1975) was, along with that of Domencich and McFadden (1975), among the earliest accessible introductions to practical applications for those new to this area of research.

4.5.2   A Mode–Route Freight Model Developed for the Channel Tunnel Study

Although our review focuses mainly on urban transportation systems, in view of the generic nature of the modelling process and some common assumptions made for longer distance travel, we include an innovative study for the economic assessment of the proposed Channel Tunnel linking Britain with France undertaken by Coopers and Lybrand Associates (1973) during the period 1972–73. Separate hierarchical models were developed for passengers and freight transportation. The discussion here refers to the freight model.[25]

The study was unusual in that data were available from a specially commissioned freight survey of unitised trade between regions of the UK and continental Europe, which allowed a disaggregate approach to be used for model estimation and forecasting. For the large majority of unitised shipments, two modes were available: lift-on/lift-off containers; and roll-on/roll-off heavy goods vehicles (HGVs), some carrying containers and some with fixed covered trailers. For each origin–destination pair, two or three routes were identified for each pair of ports.

Choices of mode and route for commodities depended on many factors: (a) characteristics of the consignment itself; (b) characteristics of the freight forwarders and manufacturers; and (c) transportation service attributes such as freight charges and transit time. The model eventually selected was a nested or hierarchical probit model for choices among route and mode combinations in which the choice of route was conditional on the choice of mode. The modal choice adopted for a shipment, between roll-on/roll-off HGVs and lift-on/lift-off containerisation, was of binary probit form; the choice of route (ferry services) was determined by a least generalised cost model with normally distributed costs, represented by a multinomial probit model. The approach was proposed by Tony Flowerdew and developed further by Robert Cochrane and colleagues (Coopers and Lybrand Associates, 1973, 80).

In the probabilistic route choice model, the sources of variation in generalised costs were: (a) terminal costs in relation to the relative location of shipper or receiver and the ports; (b) charge rates and discounts; and (c) the value of time. The probability that a given route would be selected, expressed as a multiple integral over the joint distribution of costs, was equal to the probability that the generalised cost on the route was less than that on any other. Maximum likelihood estimates of the parameters of the probit model were computed by numerical integration.

The commodity characteristics and service available by each mode were known to be important determinants of mode choice. The binary probit model was formulated in terms of minimisation over normally distributed generalised costs, establishing a methodological consistency between route and mode selection. Various methods were considered for expressing the modal generalised costs in terms of the various route generalised costs available to each mode. The one selected 'was computationally the simplest yet provided much the best fit to the data. For each origin–destination pair, the characteristics of the best routes on average observed for the two modes were used for all comparisons' (Coopers and Lybrand Associates, 1973, 88).

Almost as an aside, the consultants note what later became an important issue in the development of linked multi-stage demand models:

> There is in fact an interesting theoretical justification for this approach in the methodology of the route model. A statistical expression for the distribution of generalised cost on the optimal route of a set can be developed. This will, of course, in general have a *lower mean* than any of the individual route costs, and a slightly different distribution. The route which is on average the best will however normally provide a reasonable approximation to it (Coopers and Lybrand Associates, 1973, 88, emphasis added in italics).

As applied to forecasting, the Channel Tunnel was added to the routes available to the two modes. For the lift-on/lift-off container component, re-marshalled block container trains ran through the tunnel, since demand was too low for dedicated trains from origins to destinations at that time; for the roll-on/roll-off vehicles, a rail ferry link through the tunnel was included. An estimate of the diversion of traffic to the tunnel was determined for this new arrangement.

4.5.3   Random Utility Models of Destination Choice

Robert Cochrane's derivation of spatial interaction models of the gravity type from random utility theory is noteworthy for several reasons (Cochrane, 1975). Although an economic basis for the gravity model appeared earlier in the literature (Neidercorn and Bechdolt, 1969; Neuberger, 1971), here was an approach based on random utility theory which better reflected the discrete choices involved.[26] His paper made three important contributions in the present context: (a) an economic derivation of the family of zone-based spatial interaction (gravity) models proposed earlier by Wilson (1967); (b) derivation of compatible measures of the net benefit associated with the spatial choices, reproducing the results of Neuberger (1971); and (c) constructive suggestions for linking generation, distribution and modal split models.

By the early 1970s Wilson's entropy maximising formulation of the gravity model provided a practical basis for forecasting trip interactions between the zones of cities and regions, and was becoming the dominant form applied in UK transportation studies. The theoretical basis for that model, however, was not appealing to those who sought some constructive behavioural explanation for trip making and destination choice. In Cochrane's derivation, offered as an alternative to Wilson's approach, aggregation of the spatial decisions made in a zoned system was a key part of deriving the probabilistic choice model. The central assumption was that 'the probability that a particular trip maker from one zone will travel to a second zone is the probability that a trip to that zone offers a surplus (or net benefit) greater than that of a trip to any other zone' (Cochrane, 1975, 38).

The essence of the argument involved the decomposition of the problem to determine: (a) the distribution of consumer surplus (utility minus generalised cost) over the opportunities *within* zones to obtain the distribution of utility of the best trip associated with a journey to each zone; and (b) the resultant choice of the destination zone according to the maximum surplus offered by each zone.

Referring to point (a), a crucial and innovative aspect of Cochrane's argument was the observation that, as a result of the maximisation process, it would be the form of the (net) utility curves in the upper tails of their distributions that would be the essential determinant of the probabilities of choice. No specific functional forms for the utility distributions were given, other than that the behaviour in the tails was assumed to decline in an approximately exponential fashion. This choice was not arbitrary, but ensured that two axiomatic requirements, noted below, could be met. The distribution of maximum surplus over the opportunities within each zone was then determined under the two further assumptions about the number of opportunities: that it was large, and that it was proportional to a measure of zonal attraction (such as floor space). Drawing on the classic work of Gumbel (1958), Cochrane showed that the probability density function for the surplus of the 'best trip' to any zone approximated to a Gumbel Type I extreme value distribution, a result which held for a wide range of utility distributions, including Gaussian, log normal, logistic and Gumbel forms. The distribution of maximum surplus within each zone was thus expressed in terms of the number of opportunities and therefore the attraction of the zone.

The second stage of the argument, that of determining the probability that a particular zone was selected, led directly to the 'singly-constrained gravity model'. Through the addition of zonal costs, which were assumed to reflect a bidding process that reconciled the number of trips to different zones with the number of opportunities available, the doubly-constrained spatial interaction model was also derived.

Because an intrinsic part of the calculation involved the determination of the distribution of consumer surplus over the zonal system, it was a straightforward process to find the mean and total surplus attained in the choice process, and the change arising from a modification to the trip costs between two situations accompanying the introduction of a transportation project. In this way Cochrane showed the social benefit to have the same 'logsum' form as in Neuberger (1971).

Cochrane also considered the integration of the three aspects of a trip, corresponding to a combined generation, distribution and modal split model. As in Quandt (1968), the generation of trips was made sensitive to the generalised cost by assuming a threshold; a trip would only be made when the utility of doing so exceeded the generalised cost, reflected in the limits of integration over the distribution of net utilities. In this way a combined generation–distribution model was found in which the total interzonal demand was sensitive to the travel cost.

To integrate the distribution model with the modal split model, Cochrane drew on the model of MacNicholas and Collins (1971). They had considered a random parameter model in which modal choice was determined on the basis of the minimum generalised cost specified in terms of travel time and money cost, with a value of travel time normally distributed over the choice making population. Cochrane suggested using the mean of the distribution of minimum cost as the basis for integrating the two models, noting:

> In order to determine the likely choice of destination, we can use the distribu-
> tion of trip costs for the modes actually chosen . . . and consider the two modes
> as being a single mode with this probabilistic distribution of cost. The mean
> cost for this combined mode is in fact *lower* than the mean cost for each mode
> separately. Averaging trip costs across modes would give a very biased estimate
> of the combined mean trip cost. A much better (but still biased) estimate would
> be the lower mean cost of the two (Cochrane, 1975, 44, emphasis added in
> italics).

This approach to integration of the two choices within a combined hier-archical model reflected Cochrane's contributions to the mode–route problem for the Channel Tunnel.

We also note here the independent contribution of Jean-Gerard Koenig, who studied the destination choice problem within a random utility approach and derived a similar 'logsum' expression for the relationship between average utility received in the choice process and commonly used measures of accessibility. Koenig's results were distributed in French in 1974, but were probably part of his 1972 doctoral thesis. A fuller description of this study and, in particular, the role of random utility measures of accessibility in planning and welfare measurement was given in Koenig (1975).

4.5.4   A 'General Theory of Travel Demand'

Finally, we draw attention to a rarely cited, but historically important, contribution by A.J. Harris and John Tanner (1974) of the UK Transport and Road Research Laboratory. The study was highly technical, but had important practical implications. Its full significance was certainly not widely recognised at that time. The study offers great insights, addressing major theoretical problems and anticipating important key developments in the field. The research of Quandt (1968, 1970) and Neuberger (1971) appeared to be particularly influential in the development of their approach.

Their analysis sought to establish the properties of probabilistic choice models within the framework of random utility theory in which the variation in utilities was distributed over a population in different ways. The paper set out:

> a general theory from which a variety of models can be derived by making different assumptions about the statistical distributions of parameters which vary from one person to another and which give rise to observable differences in trip making behaviour. . . . The basic model assumes that there are observable variables representing times, money costs etc. which are common to all people. Each potential trip has a personal generalised cost which is a linear function of the observable variables; the coefficients of this function, which represent terminal costs, values of time etc. have a distribution over the population of potential trips. By integrating over regions of this distribution one obtains trip demand functions which are functions of the observable variables only (Harris and Tanner, 1974, 1).

A central part of their investigation concerned the relationship between such random utility models and consumer surplus measures, defined as the mean value of the distribution of maximum net benefit achieved in the choice process. A primary motivation of the work was to place methods of demand analysis and evaluation measures derived from generalised costs on a rigorous footing. Although most of the paper was directed at the problem of modal choice, the analysis had far wider implications, and related to any discrete choice modelling context in which that option with the highest value of benefit minus cost was selected. Following Quandt, a cut-off in the distribution of net benefit was introduced, where generalised cost exceeds benefit, to represent the condition in which a trip would not be made.

Although the paper was for the most part concerned with a general mathematical analysis, important special cases were taken to illustrate the power of their approach. Of particular interest and importance for future developments was their analysis of discrete choice models generated by distributions in which the (dis-)utility associated with any alternative was written as the sum of a term common to all in the relevant choice making population and a random error term. The authors referred to this as 'the personal difference case', which can also be termed a *translational invariant* case in which the random term in the utility function is independent of the average or representative value. They also considered what they referred to as 'the personal multiplier case'. For its wide relevance to urban transportation modelling we shall restrict our discussion to the former case.[27]

The authors addressed two questions:

1. For an arbitrary distribution of utilities satisfying the personal difference case, what is the resulting demand function and corresponding consumer surplus measure derived from the utility maximising process? And its converse:
2. For a demand function generated by the random utility function of translational invariant form, what is the distribution of utilities that gives rise to it?

Harris and Tanner (1974) established general expressions for the demand function and the consumer surplus measure associated with the choice process, and then showed for the 'personal difference case' that the demand function could be derived directly from the consumer surplus function by the mathematical process of differentiation. As an immediate consequence of this result, they established that the demand function was characterised by integrability or symmetry conditions (Hotelling, 1938), which we considered in section 3.8.3. They argued that demand functions satisfying such symmetry conditions were consistent with generalised cost formulations. They then reversed the process and derived an expression for the density function for the utility distribution that would generate an arbitrary demand model consistent with the translational invariant utility functions.

What was the practical relevance of this approach and how would specific models, consistent with these technical conditions, be generated? Because the demand models could be derived from consumer surplus (*CS*) functions, they argued that suitable forms for *CS* could be sought to generate demand models that were consistent with a personal difference generalised cost formulation. As the authors put it:

> By taking different arbitrary forms for the function *CS* we can get a variety of expressions for the T_i [the demand function]. It is clear that the function *CS* is not completely arbitrary; it must satisfy certain conditions. . . . In the personal difference case, for example, these probably reduce to the condition that the implied probability distribution must never be negative (Harris and Tanner, 1974, 13).

They then illustrated their argument by selecting expressions for the consumer surplus measures that generated demand models of MNL and other related forms such as singly-constrained spatial interaction models. These models were generalised to incorporate net utility thresholds to render the generation of trips sensitive to changes in generalised costs.

For the purpose of what followed, we summarise their major contributions as follows:

1. integration of the process of choice model formulation and the derivation of economic (consumer surplus) measures appropriate to welfare assessment and their relationship in the case of particular forms of utility function;
2. development of a strategy for generating choice models by selecting suitable consumer surplus functions and forming the demand function consistent with the theory by differentiation;
3. demonstration of this integration in the formulation of commonly applied models, such as the MNL model and its associated consumer surplus measure of 'logsum' form.

The authors concluded their paper in this way:

> The fact that a paper dealing with such a fundamental aspect of transport models needed to be written is a reflection of the youth of the subject. In the past 10 or 15 years, our understanding of the interaction between land use, transport facilities, costs, trips, flows, speeds and so forth have developed enormously, and so has our capacity to process the relevant data. But there is still no consensus about how models should be constructed (Harris and Tanner, 1974, 15).

But how was this theory to be applied in the more complex choice contexts typical of practical transportation studies? We address this question in Chapter 5.

4.6   SOME CHALLENGES IN MULTI-MODAL AND MULTI-DIMENSIONAL CHOICE MODELLING

4.6.1   Problem of Similar Alternatives and the IIA Property

4.6.1.1   Mixed blessing of the IIA property

As the review of Spear (1977) and other studies confirmed, applications of the MNL model in travel forecasting, particularly to problems involving multi-modal choice, resulted from its relatively simple structure, modest data requirements and growing availability of parameter estimation software. The simplicity of its structure had important practical implications, which had long been recognised as characteristic of simple share models. McFadden later referred to the mixed blessing of its independence of irrelevant alternatives property (section 4.2):

> The IIA property is a blessing and a curse for share models. It has two advantageous implications which make it extremely useful in practical planning. First, it implies that model calibration can be carried out by studying conditional choice in a small subset of the full set of alternatives. Thus, the dimension of the calibration data set can be reduced substantially, particularly when the full set of alternatives is large. Further, data for the omitted alternatives need not be collected, leading to economy in data collection and the possibility of improved detail on the examined alternatives. . . . A second, and related advantage that IIA has for a share model is that it allows quick analysis of the effects of introducing new alternatives. . . . The IIA property implies that the relative odds among the old alternatives are unchanged when the new alternative is introduced (McFadden, 1976b, 49–50).

However, the MNL model was starting to be used with impunity, even though the potential drawbacks of its structure and associated elasticity properties were becoming increasingly well known. McFadden had earlier warned:

> The primary limitation of the model is that the independence of irrelevant alternatives axiom is implausible for alternative sets containing choices that are close substitutes. . . . Application of the model should be limited to situations where the alternatives can plausibly be assumed to be distinct and weighed independently in the eyes of each decision-maker (McFadden, 1973, 113).

The consequences of applying the MNL model in a multiple choice context, where two of the alternatives were considered by individuals to be very similar, had long been recognised (Debreu, 1960). In transportation applications, this concept was illustrated in a binary choice setting between car and bus as the notorious 'red bus – blue bus' problem, when a particular alternative is artificially partitioned into two, according to a superficial attribute, colour, which (presumably) would have negligible effect on demand. The subsequent application of a three-mode MNL model for choice among car, red bus and blue bus clearly yields implausible results (Mayberry, 1970; McFadden, 1973).

This conundrum, which represents an extreme case of similarity between a subset of options, could be readily resolved in practice by specifying a choice model in hierarchical form with successive binary choice models used to divide the relevant market between car and bus, and then divide the latter share between the two coloured bus modes. But, in more realistic practical applications, how was the problem of similarity among alternatives to be treated? What constituted a distinct alternative? Would the MNL model prove satisfactory in most applications? More generally, could the potential limitations arising from the failure of the IIA property of the MNL model in different mode choice situations be empirically detected and suitable adjustments applied?

4.6.1.2 Avoiding the IIA property: hierarchical structures in multi-modal choice

Over the wide experience gained in traditional aggregate (zone-based) demand models and the growing applications of disaggregate methods, two possible ways of forecasting within a multi-modal system between car and two public transport modes, such as bus and rail (PT1 and PT2) had been formulated and applied. These are represented by the hierarchical approach in Figure 4.6(a) and the MNL model approach extended over three modes in Figure 4.6(b). In the former, which is not subject to the IIA property, the public transport option (PT) was effectively treated as a 'composite' mode, requiring the specification of appropriate level-of-service attributes in the main mode selection between car and the composite PT mode. Different composition formulations were proposed, including the 'maximum method', in which the attributes of the public transport submode with maximum probability were assigned to the composite PT mode, and in US terminology the 'cascade method', in which attributes of the different alternatives were weighted by their choice

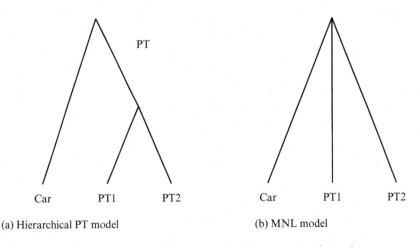

(a) Hierarchical PT model   (b) MNL model

Figure 4.6   Alternative model structures for representing choice between car and two public transport modes (PT1 and PT2)

probabilities (McFadden, 1974). But, according to Spear, 'None of these approaches have proved to be satisfactory because none of them attacks the cause of the IIA issue – the fact that there is no place in the share model formulation where the relative similarity or competitiveness of alternatives can be defined' (Spear, 1977, 146).

4.6.1.3   Diagnostic tests for the failure of the IIA property

A more general issue of key relevance to practice emerged. If the MNL model had a downside in a multi-modal choice setting, in what circumstances could its advantages of ease of application outweigh its potential disadvantages? Was the IIA property acceptable in the majority of practical studies, and to what extent was its potential failure important in relation to other problems of model misspecification or data quality? A study by Charles River Associates (1976) addressed these problems and provided diagnostic tests for the failure of the IIA property in the application of the MNL model to modal choice (McFadden et al, 1977b). They described a 'typology of failures of the IIA property', identifying six possible reasons with their origins in the nature of the 'unobserved' components of the utility functions that determined choice over the discrete alternatives. 'As a rule, the violations may be traced to the MNL assumption that the unobserved utility component (the ε_i) is independent across alternatives and independent of the observed attributes' (McFadden et al, 1977b).

The diagnostic tests for the IIA property were based on a generalisation of the MNL model referred to as the 'universal logit' model, introduced by McFadden, and an interesting structure in its own right. Although not in general consistent with the random utility maximisation hypothesis, the universal logit model provided the basis for a statistical exploration of the failure from the IIA property. Its formulation 'takes advantage of the fact that every choice model with positive probabilities can be written in apparent MNL form except that the scale function of alternative i will depend on attributes of other alternatives' (McFadden et al, 1977b).

At that time the significance of the IIA property in practice was unclear in relation to the practical problems associated with assembling appropriate and accurate data (Train, 1978). McFadden remarked:

> practicing planners should accept MNL as a working model, concentrate on expanding data sources for calibration, market segmentation, and variable specification, and test the IIA assumption during each application. The practicing planner should avoid 'miracle cures' for the IIA restriction, and examine carefully whether proposed solutions have a sound behavioral foundation or establish a germane or sensible mathematical proposition (McFadden, 1976b, 55).

4.6.2   Structure of More General Urban Travel Forecasting Models

The work of CRA (1972), Ben-Akiva (1973, 1974), Ben-Akiva and Koppelman (1974) and the related studies described above offered a first principles attack on the problem of deriving a behavioural basis for structuring travel demand models that had been around for many years, at least since the issue of 'where to put modal split' in the traditional multi-step model had emerged in the early 1960s. These authors proposed different hypotheses for the appropriate relationship between the structure of models and the (assumed) underlying decision process. However, no definitive solution to the treatment of travel-related choices had emerged, whether a hierarchy of MNL models should be applied to the different choices or a single MNL model should be applied to the combined set of choices.

Among some researchers it appeared that the simultaneous structure based on the MNL model had considerable appeal and was starting to be applied in studies at both the aggregate (zone-based) and disaggregate levels. Ben-Akiva and others had made an important point: in a problem of joint selection between combinations of choice alternatives, such as destination and mode, why should one ordering of choices be preferred to another? The appeal was both intuitive and practical. There was something inherently satisfying about representing a problem in which alternatives were treated jointly with a symmetric model structure, in this case the MNL model, which favoured neither choice dimension. This offered the practical benefit of avoiding the ambiguity of what particular ordering to choose. But what about the IIA property of the MNL model? Would this property cause problems in practice? Were the choices consisting of combinations of location and mode perceived to be sufficiently distinct to justify the use of such a model?

The relationship between the structure of the demand model and the nature of the decision process in different choice contexts continued to attract comment throughout the period (Brand, 1973; Liou and Talvitie, 1974; Stopher and Meyburg, 1975). With regard to the application of behavioural models across the whole range of choice situations of relevance to urban travel forecasting, Stopher and Meyburg remarked: 'On balance, it must be concluded that the evidence for simultaneous or recursive, sequential models is inconclusive as yet and may depend upon the specific modelling situation, and the specification problems of the models' (Stopher and Meyburg, 1975, 305–306).

4.7 CONCLUSION

Within a brief period in the early 1970s, significant advances were made in the theoretical development and practical application of the disaggregate behavioural approach to travel demand founded on discrete choice theory. These advances built on, and provided a *post-hoc* rationalisation for, the studies of binary modal choice of the 1960s. Most applications were still associated with the choice of mode for its relevance to peak period flows and potential policy and project development. Relative to traditional forecasting methods of that time, the new approach offered greater sophistication in the representation of individual and household behaviour, data efficiency, and applicability at any level of aggregation, as well as the prospect of (approximate) transferability in space, with the suggestion that forecasts would be more reliable.

With the increasing availability of software for the maximum likelihood estimation of its parameters, the MNL model was becoming more widely applied: (a) in more elaborate modal choice applications; (b) to a wide variety of other decision contexts; and (c) as a component of more complex multi-dimensional models.[28] Many theoretical and technical issues accompanying specification, parameter estimation, transferability, validation and aggregation were studied in depth, together with applications to substantive planning problems involving transportation infrastructure projects and system management. Substantial progress was also made in a first principles approach to the structuring of travel demand models based on discrete choice theory.

By 1976 the problems of similarity in mode choice selection and of ambiguity in structuring more complex demand models appeared somewhat distinct and still to be resolved in practice: the former, a consequence of assumptions about the random components of utility accompanying different alternatives; and the latter, somehow related to the nature of the decision process and the utility functions determining preferences over alternative choices, for which different solutions had been proposed. It appeared that corresponding problems of specification were also present in the application of conventional aggregate travel forecasting models.

At that time it appeared that the general multinomial normal model (section 4.2) might have a significant role to play in choice modelling and, in particular, resolving 'similarity issues' in multi-modal choice. Indeed, in addressing unresolved problems in the mid-1970s, McFadden expressed the opinion:

> There is a pressing need for development of practical models for selection probabilities which do not have the independence of irrelevant alternatives

property. . . . It would be particularly useful to achieve a computational break-through on the multinomial normal model. . . . An alternative approach which may yield practical functional forms for applications is to seek more general axioms characterizing classes of selection probabilities. One such construction is the *elimination by aspects* model of Tversky (1972) (McFadden, 1976a, 381, 370).

On the distinction between aggregate and disaggregate models, McFadden (1976b) commented:

> They differ primarily in degree. Disaggregation carries . . . market segmen-tation to the extreme; it emphasizes the regularity of individual choice behavior. . . . Aggregate and disaggregate models differ significantly in the number and form of explanatory variables, consistency across different aspects of travel behaviour, calibration methods, and forecasting technique. These dif-ferences are, however, primarily technical, the result of historical development and the practical limitations of data compilation and computation. Behind every good aggregate model is a disaggregate model, and vice versa. The dis-covery of empirically valid regularities which simplify and extend forecasting methodology and the relaxation of empirically invalid restrictions should be the goal of every transportation analyst. From this point of view, disaggregate behavioural forecasting is a natural evolution of traditional aggregate demand analysis (McFadden, 1976b, 8).

In retrospect, the disaggregate approach based on random utility theory clearly encouraged a range of sentiments among researchers and practitioners. From the literature one senses a true spirit of optimism among its pioneers. Here was an approach based on what were consid-ered sound behavioural foundations that addressed some of the perennial problems of traditional practice, and appeared up to the challenge of the times. Moreover, in practice a barrier was breached in the application of complex choice models; those coming after would be able to improve on the approach and be less daunted by practical challenges.

The number of active researchers in disaggregate modelling remained relatively small, but was growing in various university departments, some consultancies and some government agencies. By the mid-1970s the new thinking had been exported from the US, and was becoming increas-ingly applied in research and some applications in Canada, Europe and Australia. The development and transfer of ideas require inspirational people with intellectual energy and powers of persuasion. In this regard Marvin Manheim [1937–2000] was a key figure in the introduction of the disaggregate behavioural approach, not only in persuading people to work in the area, but also in founding the consultancy Cambridge Systematics. His collaboration with Moshe Ben-Akiva was particularly productive in this regard, especially in transferring the approach to the Netherlands. Moreover, the random utility approach to behavioural modelling was being independently developed for local requirements and interests, as illustrated by the innovative British studies noted. As Stopher and Meyburg stated, by the mid-1970s it was 'widely held by researchers that this approach has the greatest likelihood of providing the basis for a totally new and more policy-responsive travel-forecasting procedure' (Stopher and Meyburg, 1975, 273).

Among the broad community of urban policy analysts and transportation practitioners, however, feelings at this time appear to have been rather mixed. Although the theory and techniques were becoming increasingly widely known, whether they were accompanied by wide acceptance is debatable. Indeed, notwithstanding the advances claimed, some (perhaps many) practitioners at the time considered the approach rather naïve and impractical relative to tested aggregate methods.[29] After all, the approach had yet to be fully tested on the traditional application grounds of urban travel forecasting models. In this regard, many eyes were on the Metropolitan Transportation Commission (MTC) of the San Francisco Bay Area; unsatisfied with its existing travel demand model system, MTC was implementing the new approach to address the prospects for a wide range of long-run and short-run plans and policies. Spear remarked:

> The MTC project is clearly at the forefront of applications of individual choice models. Both researchers and planners alike are watching this project closely to see whether the resulting travel demand forecasts are more reliable or can be obtained more efficiently than with traditional models. Its outcome should go a long way towards determining the ultimate role of individual choice models in transportation planning (Spear, 1977, 31–32).

We recount the outcome of these developments in the next chapter.

NOTES

1. The earliest study of route choice from a choice theoretic perspective is that by Abraham (1961). See also Thomas and Thompson (1971) and the references cited therein.
2. en.wikipedia.org/wiki/R._Duncan_Luce (accessed 28 December 2013).
3. The IIA axiom is sometimes referred to as the independence *from* irrelevant alternatives axiom.
4. en.wikipedia.org/wiki/Louis_Leon_Thurstone (accessed 6 March 2014).
5. en.wikipedia.org/wiki/Jacob_Marschak (accessed 6 March 2014).
6. en.wikipedia.org/wiki/Daniel_McFadden (accessed 2 January 2014).
7. The probability that an arbitrary individual q will select an alternative A_j from a set of alternatives $A = (A_1 . . . A_j . . . A_N)$ will be written P_{jq}. In general the choice set will vary within the population, and we shall denote $A(q) \in A$ as the set of alternatives from A that are available to the individual q. From the modeller's perspective, the probability that a utility maximising individual q will select A_j is given by:

$P_{jq} = \text{Prob} (U_{jq} \geq U_{iq} \text{ for all } A_i \in A(q))$

In terms of the representative utilities and residual errors the choice probability becomes:

$P_{jq} = \text{Prob} (V_{jq} + E_{jq} \geq V_{iq} + E_{iq} \text{ for all } A_i \in A(q)).$

8. The compensatory linear-in-parameters utility function is written as follows:

$$V_{jq} = \sum_k \theta_{kjq} h (x_{kjq})$$

where $h(.)$ is a function of the measured attributes x_{jkq}. The parameters θ_{kjq} will, in general, vary over the alternatives (j), the attributes (k) and the individuals (q). In the common 'fixed coefficients' model, the parameters θ_{kjq} are common across individuals, while in 'random coefficients' or 'random parameters' models the parameters $\theta = (\theta_{kjq})$ will vary over individuals. In the linear-in-parameters–linear-in-attributes form (this is not unduly restrictive), with the parameter set θ independent of the individual:

$$V_{jq} = \sum_{k=1}^{K} \theta_{wjk} x_{jkq},$$

which in vector notation is abbreviated as

$$V_{jq} = \theta_j \cdot x_{jq}.$$

In the practical implementation of the MNL, the utility function may be expressed in several ways. For a full discussion of utility forms, see McFadden (1976b) and the texts: Hensher and Johnson (1981), Ben-Akiva and Lerman (1985), Hensher et al (2005), Koppelman and Bhat (2006) and Ortúzar and Willumsen (2011, Chapters 7, 8).

9. Two different strategies were applied to suggest different functional forms for the utility functions. The utility-theoretic approach based on goods–leisure trade-off models of individual budgeting, in which the representative utilities V emerge as indirect utility functions, was first considered by McFadden (1976b) and McFadden and Train (1978). For a discussion of an alternative approach that identified the functional form that gives the best fit to the data see Gaudry and Wills (1978), Jara-Diaz (2007) and Ortúzar and Willumsen (2011).

10. Dropping the individual label q, the probability that an arbitrary individual will select A_j is given in terms of the joint probability density function of the residuals $F(E_1 \ldots E_N)$ as follows:

$$P_j = \int_{R(j)} F(E_1 \ldots \ldots E_N) dE_1 \ldots dE_N,$$

in which the region of integration $R(j)$ is defined by:

$R(j): U_j \geq U_i$ or $E_i \leq E_j + (V_j - V_i)$ for all $A_i \in A$.

11. In Quandt's model, the selection probabilities for each mode were determined by identifying the combination of parameters which minimised disutility (a process of integrating over the parameter distributions) with a cut-off introduced to reflect the hypothesis that a trip would not be made if the disutility exceeded that threshold. In this way, a generation effect, in which the total journeys were made sensitive to the transportation service characteristics, was built into the modal split model. The determination of the selection probabilities for this model required numerical solution.

12. Gaudry and Quinet (2011) have discussed the seminal work of French engineers in the late 1950s and in particular the work of Abraham (1961), who derived choice models for two and three routes, in which the link generalised costs were distributed according to a variety of assumptions, including normal and rectangular forms. Various probabilistic choice models were derived including the probit, which were seen as a justification of the then current use of the 'log logit' forms. The complexity arising from the existence of a common link in the three-route case was also considered.

13. The difference between this distribution and the normal curve is portrayed in several texts, for example Domencich and McFadden (1975, 62) and Koppelman and Bhat (2006, 27).

14. For the MNL model written in the form:

$$P_j = \frac{\exp(\lambda V_j)}{\sum_{A_i \in A} \exp(\lambda V_i)}$$

the 'logsum' is given by:

$$\text{'logsum'} = \frac{1}{\lambda}\left(\ln \sum_{A_i \in A} \exp(\lambda V_i) \right),$$

or

$$\text{'logsum'} = \left(\ln \sum_{A_i \in A} \exp(V_i) \right)$$

if the model is standardised such that $\lambda = 1$.

15. The formulation of the MNL model from distributed utilities was first established by Marschak (1960), adopting a 'nonconstructive proof' (McFadden, 1973, 111), and was strengthened by E. Holman and A. Marley (cited by Luce and Suppes, 1965). 'McFadden (1968, 1973) completed the analysis by showing the converse: that the logit formula for the choice probabilities necessarily implies that unobserved utility is distributed extreme value' (Train, 2009).

16. en.wikipedia.org/wiki/Waloddi_Weibull (accessed 29 December 2013).

17. We are grateful to Jorgen Weibull for this anecdote about his grandfather.

18. The Gumbel Type I extreme value distribution is written as follows:

$$f(U_j, V_j) = f(U_j - V_j) \equiv f(\varepsilon_j)$$

with $f(\varepsilon_j) = \lambda \exp(-\lambda\varepsilon_j) \cdot \exp(-\exp(-\lambda\varepsilon_j))$, and cumulative distribution given by the double exponential form:

$$F(\varepsilon_j) = \exp(-\exp(-\lambda\varepsilon_j))$$

The mean of the random variable U_j is given by $V_j + \gamma/\lambda$ where γ is Euler's constant $= 0.577$, and the variance of U_j is given by $\pi^2/6\lambda^2$. The derivation of the MNL model from the IID Gumbel distributions is relatively straightforward; details may be found in McFadden (1973) and Domencich and McFadden (1975); see also Stopher and Meyburg (1975) and Ben-Akiva and Lerman (1985).

19. The authors are grateful to Frank Koppelman for discussion on this point.

20. The form of the shopping model adopted by CRA (1972) was as follows: the probability of selecting a given combination of frequency, destination, timing and mode $P(f, d, \tau, m)$ was written:

$$P(f, d, \tau, m) = P(f)P(d|f)\,P(\tau|d, f)\,P(m|\tau, d, f)$$

in which f, d, τ and m denote choices relating to: frequency (one trip per day versus no trip), destination (ranging from three to five for each observation), time of day of travel (both legs in the off-peak versus one leg in the off-peak and one leg in the peak) and mode (car driver versus transit rider with walk access), respectively. Linear probability and logit models were applied and many variable combinations were tested.

21. When applied to model structure, Ben-Akiva used the term 'recursive' to correspond to a sequential decision-making process. In the general literature the term 'sequential' is also used to describe the structure of a model.

22. For example, in a context involving destination and mode with a utility function of the form:

$$V(d, m) = V_d + V_{dm}$$

the MNL model with probabilities P_{dm} can be written:

$$P_{dm} = \frac{\exp(V_d + V_{dm})}{\displaystyle\sum_{d \in D\; m \in M} \exp(V_d + V_{dm})} = \frac{\exp(V_d + \theta V_d^*)}{\displaystyle\sum_{d \in D} \exp(V_d + \theta V_d^*)} \frac{\exp(V_{dm})}{\displaystyle\sum_{m \in M} \exp(V_{dm})}$$

with $\theta = 1$ and $V_d^* = \ln \displaystyle\sum_{m \in M} \exp(V_{dm})$.

23. Martin Richards, personal communication to Huw Williams, 2013.

24. Wilson (1967, 1970) proposed many models according to different contexts and assumptions. Here Richards and Ben-Akiva (1975) are referring to his 'joint distribution modal split model'.

25. Robert Cochrane, personal communication to Huw Williams, 2011, stated that the passenger demand model, developed by John Pendlebury, was of hierarchical logit form with generalised cost in power function form.

26. Cochrane's paper was submitted to the *Journal of Transport Economics and Policy* in 1972. It had a protracted journey through the review process, and its publication was delayed until 1975, partly because of the difficulty of selecting suitable reviewers (Robert Cochrane, personal communication to Huw Williams, 2010).

27. Interestingly, the personal multiplier case has recently received attention by Fosgerau and Bierlaire (2009), who report improvements in 'goodness-of-fit' compared with the more usual error structures.

28. There are many specialist texts and manuals that discuss the specification, estimation and application of the MNL model: see, for example, Ben-Akiva and Lerman (1985), Hensher et al (2005) and Ortúzar and Willumsen (2011), as well as the excellent Self Instructing Course by Koppelman and Bhat (2006, Chapters 4–7) for more details.

29. Peter Stopher, personal communication to Huw Williams, 2009.

5. Travel forecasting based on discrete choice models, II

5.1 INTRODUCTION

Great strides were made in the early 1970s to develop an approach to urban travel forecasting that involved summing up (aggregating) the probable behaviour of individuals derived from models specified and estimated at the micro-level. For such models, the discrete choice random utility maximising (RUM) framework provided the theoretical and practical foundations for multi-modal forecasting and for exploring the relationship between the structure of models and hypotheses relating to the trip decision process. In this chapter we recount further theoretical and practical developments of this approach. We arrange this material in two parts: sections 5.2 to 5.6 recount developments in the period from the mid-1970s to the mid-1980s, while section 5.7 provides a guide to more recent advances.

The reasons for this partition are as follows. The first period contains a large amount of innovative material, which found its way fairly quickly into applied studies and remains of great practical relevance today. However, a very substantial volume of research on discrete choice travel-related modelling based on random utility theory has been conducted since the mid-1980s and disseminated in journals, conferences and texts. Although it is too early to say which models and methods will become widely absorbed into routine travel forecasting practice, this work proved to be conceptually appealing, technically demanding and (therefore) irresistible to exponents of quantitative research. This divide in the mid-1980s is also rather convenient for introducing what some have described as a new behavioural paradigm based on the human activity approach, considered in Chapter 6, which began to make a major impression on how travel behaviour was viewed and analysed. Those who seek to preserve a broadly chronological progression between chapters might find it convenient to skip section 5.7 on first reading.

Let us return now to the mid-1970s when the multinomial logit (MNL) model had become the dominant instrument of practical analysis within the disaggregate modelling approach to travel forecasting. In section 4.6.1

we saw how the ease of application of the MNL model was offset by a set of potential problems that were also encountered with some conventional aggregate models. We also noted that by the mid-1970s the selection of the order of individual choice models within model hierarchies, the means of interfacing or 'linking' them, and indeed whether that structure should be abandoned in favour of an approach consisting of a single MNL model extended over several choice dimensions were all outstanding issues requiring further research.

In seeking to relax the restrictive properties of the MNL model, researchers had been aware since the early 1970s (McFadden, 1973) of the need to balance the generality attributed to the joint distribution of utility variables over the different alternatives with the practical consequences for the solution of the model and estimation of its parameters. From the mid-1970s two approaches would be adopted to achieve practical extensions to the family of random utility models. The first, the direct approach, involved specifying explicit distributions for the random components of the utilities of alternatives that reflected credible behavioural assumptions. With careful selection these might be amenable to analytic resolution of the choice model and result in closed form expressions for the probabilities of choice. Otherwise, a direct numerical attack would be required in order to solve the mathematical problem (the multiple integral) that determined the choice probabilities. The second approach to generating choice models was through the establishment of general mathematical conditions to be satisfied by the model, which rendered it consistent with the hypothesis of random utility maximisation, and to seek suitable model forms that offered behavioural realism while being amenable to practical implementation (McFadden, 1973, 1976b; Harris and Tanner, 1974). In this chapter we shall encounter both of these approaches.

By the early 1970s the construction of travel demand models by linking together MNL models in a sequence or hierarchy had appeared in various studies both at the aggregate zone-based level (Wilson, 1969, 1970; Wilson et al, 1969; Manheim, 1973) and in discrete choice models applied at the micro-level (see section 4.1 for a discussion of the term) (Stopher and Lisco, 1970; Charles River Associates, CRA, 1972; Ben-Akiva, 1973, 1974). In such models travel markets (associated with different modes, destinations, etc.) were successively partitioned according to MNL shares in aggregate forms or through the product of MNL probabilities in discrete choice models applied at the micro-level.

For more than one MNL model arranged hierarchically it would turn out that the 'logsum', the logarithm of the denominator of the MNL model at a lower level, would be a particularly suitable choice of variable for the linkage to the MNL at the next higher level. To our knowledge the first application of a correctly specified 'logsum' linkage within a hierarchical arrangement of MNL models was by Ben-Akiva (1973, 1974), as described in section 4.4.3. The full theoretical significance of this linkage, as Ortúzar (2001) remarked, was not however fully resolved until the mid-1970s. Indeed, it is interesting to note that by the early 1970s a 'logsum' expression was making an appearance in travel demand modelling in different ways and, from a historical perspective, it is important to note the distinction between them. The 'logsum', or an equivalent analytical form,[1] appeared in three different contexts:

1. structural decomposition of the MNL model applied to two or more dimensions, such as destination and mode (Wilson, 1967, 1970; Ben-Akiva, 1973, 1974; Manheim, 1973);
2. generalised consumer surplus measures derived for spatial interaction models of MNL form (Wilson and Kirwan, 1969; Neuberger, 1971) (section 3.8);
3. expected maximum utility (or expected minimum generalised cost) measures for discrete choice problems involving Gumbel distributed utility (or generalised cost) variables (Harris and Tanner, 1974; Cochrane, 1975; Domencich and McFadden, 1975; Koenig, 1975) (sections 4.2, 4.5).

The first was a purely mathematical consequence of the properties of the MNL share model applied to different subsets of the alternative choices; the second and third were theoretical consequences of the economic analysis of travel choice at the aggregate and micro-levels, respectively, arising from particular forms for the utility functions used to generate the MNL demand model. In the early 1970s the connection between these different interpretations was not apparent.

The search for a practical generalisation of the MNL model, consistent with random utility maximisation (RUM), that was not subject to the independence of irrelevant alternatives (IIA) property led to the derivation of the nested logit (NL) model by Williams (1977a) and Daly and Zachary (1978), and a wider class of choice models by McFadden (1978), which contained the NL model as an important special case. Because the NL model and its special case, the MNL model, have dominated practical applications of discrete choice methods in urban travel forecasting to this day, we give an extended description of the contexts within which these studies took place.

In section 5.2 we discuss alternative approaches to the derivation, interpretation and application of the variously described structured logit, tree logit, hierarchical logit and nested logit model of Williams and that of

Daly and Zachary. These British researchers first became aware of their independent work on the NL model in December 1975, prior to presentations at conferences in Leeds and the 1976 annual meeting of the Planning and Transport Research and Computation Co. (PTRC), respectively. In section 5.3 we turn to the theoretical highpoint of the discrete choice random utility maximising approach in this period with an account of McFadden's research on the generalised extreme value (GEV) model (McFadden, 1978, 1981).

Concurrent with efforts in the early 1970s to achieve manageable closed form generalisations of the MNL model were direct numerical approaches to solve a range of individual choice models within the discrete choice random utility framework. In particular, an efficient solution of the multinomial probit (MNP) model that would address both general patterns of similarity among alternatives and taste variation over a population was keenly sought. In section 5.4 we consider these numerical approaches, and in particular the early use of the microsimulation technique and some of the wider contexts within which it was applied.

We return in section 5.5 from the broader theoretical development of the behavioural approach based on discrete choice theory to consider progress on the practical challenge of adapting the new disaggregate style of travel forecasting to the short-run and longer-term policy requirements of a metropolitan planning organisation. We describe the first successful attempts, achieved initially in the US and subsequently in the Netherlands, to apply behaviourally sophisticated models as practical alternatives to conventional methods. These efforts constituted the highpoint of what is sometimes referred to as the 'trip-based' approach to travel forecasting.

One of the most significant developments in the history of our field was the introduction of experimental methods for the examination of attitudes, preferences and choices as a basis for travel forecasting. In section 5.6 we discuss the emergence of 'stated preference' methods out of the fields of mathematical psychology and marketing, and their gradual acceptance by the travel forecasting community in the first half of the 1980s.

In section 5.7 we turn to the second part of the chapter and describe those developments of the discrete choice random utility maximising approach that have occurred since the mid-1980s, only a few of which have as yet found routine application in urban travel forecasting. All are, nevertheless, of great significance in the conceptual development of the field, currently widely applied in research, and an essential means by which the assumptions underpinning more widely used models are scrutinised.

An assessment of the contribution of the behavioural approach to travel forecasting based on discrete choice random utility models concludes the chapter.

5.2   CHOICE BETWEEN SIMILAR ALTERNATIVES: THE NESTED LOGIT (NL) MODEL

5.2.1   Derivation and Application of the NL Model: Research by Williams and Senior

In late 1973 Huw Williams was working at the Institute for Transport Studies at the University of Leeds on a set of problems that, at the outset, appeared to him to have little or no connection. Having completed a review of the travel demand models adopted in 25 British transportation studies (see section 3.7.3), Williams was seeking to understand a number of aspects:

1. justifications for the different ordering of the steps in the traditional forecasting structure and the means by which they were inter-linked;
2. different ways models were specified for multi-modal systems and, in particular, for 'pure mode' and 'mixed mode' problems;
3. means by which the demand models were 'interfaced with' the evaluation stage to compute measures of user benefits derived from projects and policies.

To address these problems Williams turned to the discrete choice approach and, in particular, to the random utility formulation proposed by CRA (1972) and Ben-Akiva (1973, 1974).

5.2.1.1   Tree representations, patterns of similarity and the NL model

Williams argued that the conditions required for the MNL model to be applied, that of 'distinctness of the alternatives', and mathematically expressed by the independence of the random utility variables, would in general be violated for many applications involving both multiple modes and complex combinations of choice dimensions, and for the same reasons. He suggested that the issue of similarity between the alternative choices and the correlation of their utilities was at the heart of model specification for both applications, and rejected the view that the MNL form would in general prove to be appropriate for practical analysis in these cases.

Drawing on the findings in CRA (1972), Williams explored the formation of random utility models in terms of the transmission of information required for individuals to make optimal choices over a set of alternatives (either a set of modes, or more complex multi-dimensional cases involving combinations of frequency, location, mode and route) endowed with utility functions of additive separable forms. As discussed in section 4.4, these forms allowed the decision process to be conveniently represented as choices in tree-like structures in which conditional utility maximising decisions were made at the different nodes N and at different levels L of the tree.

Williams argued that the structure of the tree reflected the pattern of similarity among the different alternative choices and that correlation between the utilities of those alternatives occurred because of the presence of random components of utility on the various branches above the 'lowest' choice, which would be common to a subset of the choices. He proposed that the distinctions between alternative ordering of choices underpinning travel forecasting models and, in particular, the structures $F/D/M/R$, $F/M/D/R$ and $F/D - M/R$, shown in Figure 5.1, could be interpreted as representing different assumptions about the distinct patterns of similarity among the choice combinations of frequency (F), destination (D), mode (M) and route (R). In all cases, individuals were considered to make rational choices according to utility maximisation, and the structure of the demand model would reflect *a priori* assumptions about the pattern of correlation among the utilities of the different alternatives in the set of choices available.

In a similar fashion, in the case of multiple modes and mixed modes, the tree structures shown in Figures 5.2 and 5.3, respectively, represented choice between alternatives whose associated utility functions contain a common (random) utility component among subsets of choices. For the three modes, car, train and bus, the existence of this random component of utility, common to the public transport modes, as shown in Figure 5.2, reflects a pattern of correlation and similarity which required their inclusion within a composite public transport 'nest' within the tree. For the case of mixed modes involving park and ride Williams hypothesised that the location of parking with respect to the origin and destination of the trip would determine the extent of any common component of utility, and therefore of any similarity, between the park-and-ride option and an alternative mode (car or public transport). This would then determine the form of hierarchy adopted, as shown in Figure 5.3.

As in the analysis of CRA (1972), individuals could be thought of as making conditional decisions at each node N over the relevant set of alternatives within such tree structures (within an overall utility maximising framework). The solution for the probability of choice of any combined alternative thus involved solving the problem as if individuals were making decisions progressively, at each node seeking their maximum utility option from the available set of subsequent choices, and progressing upwards through the tree to achieve an optimal (utility maximising) solution.

In order to generate the MNL probabilities for the conditional

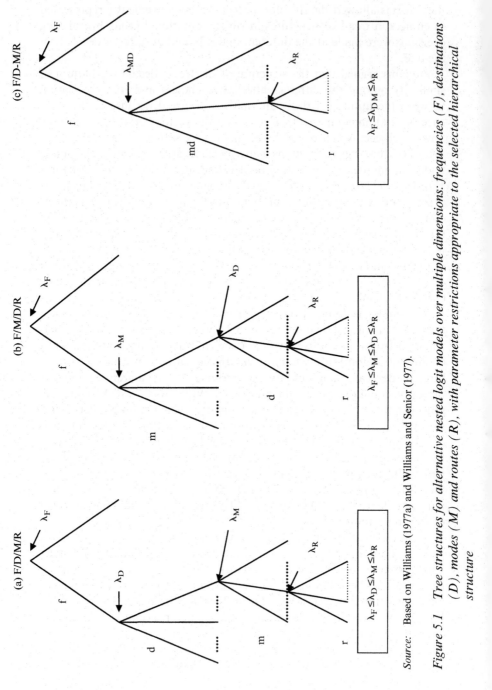

Source: Based on Williams (1977a) and Williams and Senior (1977).

Figure 5.1 Tree structures for alternative nested logit models over multiple dimensions: frequencies (F), destinations (D), modes (M) and routes (R), with parameter restrictions appropriate to the selected hierarchical structure

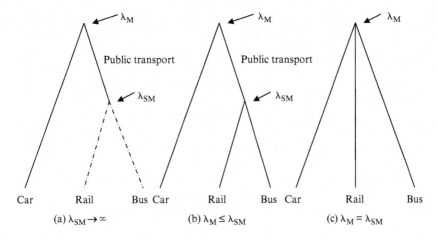

Source: Adapted from Williams (1977a, 1977b).

Figure 5.2   Tree structures for nested logit and multinomial logit models for choice between car, rail and bus

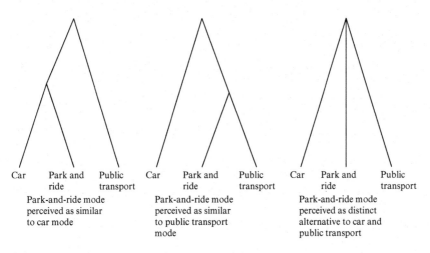

Source: Adapted from Williams (1977b).

Figure 5.3   Alternative nested logit and multinomial logit model structures for mixed mode forecasting

probabilities at each node and at every level of the tree, Williams made the assumption that the utilities at the nodes were Gumbel distributed with standard deviation that was common to all alternatives at the same level of the tree. At any node and at every level, the probability of selecting an option in the relevant set of choices would be represented by an MNL model, with a characteristic response parameter λ_L, common to all nodes at that level L. The probability of an individual selecting a given combination of frequency, location, mode and route was then described as a product of MNL models with associated parameter values $\lambda_B \ldots \lambda_L \ldots \lambda_T$ for the various levels L from the bottom (B) to the top (T), or apex, of the tree.

5.2.1.2 Nature of composite utilities or costs

With regard to the nature of the variously described 'composite utility', 'composite cost' or 'combination rule', CRA (1972) had already done most of the hard work; however, 'inclusive values using linear averaging formulas brought over from the theory of separable preferences for a representative consumer' (McFadden, 2000b, 5) had resulted in an inappropriate form. Williams argued that within the random utility framework the mean of the distribution of maximum utility $F_{MAX}(U)$ over the set of choices at any node was responsible for transmitting information about optimal choices 'further down' the tree to its higher levels.[2] For Gumbel distributed variables, responsible for generating the MNL models at each level of the tree, expressions for the expected maximum utilities, and hence the composite cost functions, were given by the 'logsums' over the appropriate choice set. Williams provided these expressions for the different levels to derive random utility models corresponding to the three tree structures in Figure 5.1. Similarly, in the multiple mode context the mean of the distribution of the maximum utility, the 'logsum' (in this case, the natural logarithm of the denominator of the bus–rail binary logit choice model in Figure 5.2), would be used to represent the composite utility (disutility) associated with choice over the public transport 'nest'.

In exploring the properties of the composite utilities or costs, Williams (1977a, 1977b) also sought to explain why the widely adopted form, the mean of the representative utilities (or generalised costs) of the different choice alternatives weighted by their probabilities of selection, was unsuitable for use as an 'average measure' for transmitting information to different levels in structuring demand models. This question led him to consider the distribution of utilities over 'selected choices', and he gave some attention to what is now referred to as the distinction between the 'offered' and 'achieved' or 'received' utilities.[3] This distinction had also been noted by Cochrane (1975), as discussed in section 4.5.3. Williams showed that the expected value of the distribution of maximum utility could also be

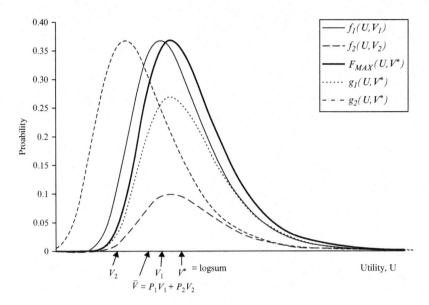

Source: Original diagram by the authors.

Figure 5.4   *The five Gumbel utility distributions associated with a binary logit choice model*

expressed as the weighted sum of the average *achieved* utilities for the different alternatives rather than the mean *offered* utilities, the $V_1 \ldots V_j \ldots V_N$. What he was not aware of at that time was that for Gumbel distributions, which underpin the MNL model, these distinctions have a particularly interesting form and important consequence for the mean utilities achieved by individuals: the mean achieved utility for those selecting *any* alternative has the same value – the 'logsum'. The distinctions between the offered and achieved utility distributions, their mean values and the weighted mean are illustrated in the case of binary choice in Figure 5.4.[4]

5.2.1.3   Condition to be satisfied by the demand function: parameter inequalities

In previous applications, in which MNL models had been arranged in a sequence or hierarchy, no restrictions had been placed on the response parameters at the different levels. Williams deduced that the parameters λ_L, which determined the sensitivity of behavioural responses at different levels L of a tree to changes in the generalised and composite costs, would be subject to a set of inequality constraints. In the random utility approach, he argued, these restrictions arose as a consequence of the variance of the utility distributions accompanying the choices at each level *increasing* under progression 'up the tree'. Using the properties of the Gumbel distribution (section 4.2.4):

1. that the parameter λ at any level is inversely proportional to the common standard deviation of the utility distributions at that level; and
2. that the maximum of a set of Gumbel distributed variables with a common standard deviation is itself Gumbel distributed with the same standard deviation,

Williams deduced that the parameters λ of the MNL models associated with different levels should not increase under progression towards the apex of the tree. For consistency with rational behaviour, he argued that the model should be subject to the inequality condition

$\lambda_B \geq \ldots \geq \lambda_L \geq \ldots \geq \lambda_T$, concluding the following:

1. Ordering of choices within the tree must progress from the most responsive (at the bottom of the tree) to the least responsive (at the top, or apex, of the tree).
2. Any estimated model structure inconsistent with the inequality conditions would be an invalid representation of behaviour in an empirical application of the model.
3. Different orderings could be subject to empirical test and the inequality conditions used as the basis for eliminating an inappropriate model structure(s) (Williams, 1977a; Williams and Senior, 1977).

5.2.1.4   MNL and NL models as special cases of a more general model

The relationship between the λ parameters at different adjacent levels of a tree, say λ_L and λ_{L+1}, allowed a set of special cases to be established when the correlation between the random components of utility for different alternatives tended to zero. In this case, the two levels of the hierarchy of MNL models 'collapsed' to an extended MNL form. This result established, as expected, the MNL model as a special case of the NL model when the similarity among alternative choices vanished, and the alternatives were then judged to be distinct. For the NL models displayed in Figure 5.1(a)–(c) the form $F/D - M/R$ could be written as a special case of both the $F/D/M/R$ and $F/M/D/R$ forms when the response parameters λ_D and λ_M were equal. Similarly, in the multi-modal model represented in Figures 5.2 and 5.3, the NL form 'collapsed' to the three-way MNL model when the main modal choice and submode choice parameters were equal,

$\lambda_{MM} = \lambda_{SM}$, and only then would the MNL model be an appropriate representation of choice among the three modal alternatives. Extension to the mixed mode case followed in a similar way.

Inherent in NL models, Williams noted, was a hierarchy reflecting an asymmetry in the chosen form of the random utility function. This function and the resultant ordering had to be provided *a priori*, and different possible orderings (*D/M* and *M/D*) were available according to the assumed pattern of similarity among the alternative choices. This observation raised a fundamental question: what was the structure of the model, consistent with random utility maximisation, that treated the different choice dimensions, such as destination and mode, on the same footing, and for which the random components of the utility function over destination and mode were symmetric?[5] It could not, in general, be the MNL model because of the presence of similarities and correlation in both dimensions of choice. Different combinations of destination and mode alternatives could be similar on some of their locational characteristics and on the basis of some of their modal characteristics.

Williams (1977a) sought a closed form random utility model for the case of choice among destination–mode combinations that embodied these more complex patterns of similarity. He called this a cross-correlated logit (CCL) model, *D*M*, and noted its 'collapse' into different NL structures and ultimately the MNL model in different special cases. His proposal for such a model was not however consistent with utility maximisation, although later he and his colleague Juan de Dios Ortúzar solved a random utility model with a similar correlation pattern by Monte Carlo simulation (Williams and Ortúzar, 1982).

5.2.1.5   The NL model, expected maximum utility measures and social welfare analysis

The derivation of 'logsum' consumer surplus measures for discrete choice models of MNL form is sometimes attributed to Williams (1977a); however, from our discussion in section 4.5 prior findings of Harris and Tanner (1974), Cochrane (1975) and Koenig (1975) should be acknowledged in this regard. In order to explore the more general relationship between welfare (user benefit) measures and probabilistic choice models, Williams examined the properties of expected maximum utility (*EMU*) measures for the case described in section 4.2 as 'translational invariant' utility distributions. For such forms the expected maximum utility measures would yield the probability of choice for different alternatives on differentiation, and that the probabilistic choice model satisfied the Hotelling symmetry conditions (Harris and Tanner, 1974; Williams, 1977a).

In the case of the NL model, Williams derived an expression for the expected maximum utility (*EMU*) accompanying choice over the complete choice set, and showed this quantity could be easily extracted at the highest node (the apex) of the decision tree. This result was in the form of a generalised 'logsum' expression. He also presented exact *EMU* results for hierarchical arrangements involving multi-modal choice (Williams, 1977a, 1977b) and argued that these measures could be used in user benefit calculations accompanying changes arising from projects and policies. He saw these measures as a generalisation within the discrete choice RUM framework of the results of Neuberger (1971).

With his University of Leeds colleague Martyn Senior, Williams demonstrated how such generalised 'logsum' measures could be used in conjunction with travel demand models of NL form to check the accuracy of the Rule-of-a-Half (RoH) measure in user benefit calculations, and to replace it if necessary, where large changes in user costs were involved. As Neuberger had done they also reinterpreted the RoH mobility benefits, derived from changes in user costs, in terms of changes in commonly adopted measures of accessibility. They further generalised this interpretation in a case study to evaluate different land use and transportation plans for the West Yorkshire region, and established the spatial distributions of benefits arising from a set of highway, public transport and demand restraint policies (Williams and Senior, 1977, 1978).

In the discrete choice theory of travel demand models developed at the micro-level, therefore, relationships emerged among variously expressed consumer surplus measures, expected maximum utilities, composite costs and commonly adopted measures of accessibility (Harris and Tanner, 1974; Cochrane, 1975; Domencich and McFadden, 1975; Koenig, 1975; Williams, 1977a; Williams and Senior, 1978). With regard to the latter, Ben-Akiva and Lerman (1979) argued that the concept of accessibility could be *defined* in terms of the expected value of the distribution of maximum utility accompanying random utility choice processes, thereby providing an economic (discrete choice) interpretation for what was often presented as a purely empirical concept. From this time on, the expected value of maximum utility linkage for the NL model, the 'logsum', was often described in the US as an 'accessibility measure'.

For a full historical review, technical discussion and further application of the 'logsum' expression, we refer the interested reader to de Jong et al (2007b).

5.2.1.6 Reformulating and applying conventional four-stage models in NL form

While the above results were derived in the context of individual choice at the micro-level, it was natural to enquire what practical implications they have for hierarchical models specified at the aggregate (zonal) level and, in particular, the four-stage procedure to forecasting travel. Did the new behavioural models based on random utility theory provide the 'knock-out blow' that some had predicted, or could conventional procedures profit by drawing on the innovations of the period, much as they had done in the past? What were the numerical consequences of reformulating traditional four-stage travel forecasting models in NL forms and apply-ing them to policy analysis? In a study inspired by Ben-Akiva's earlier findings for disaggregate structures (Ben-Akiva, 1973, 1974), described in section 4.4, Senior and Williams examined the implications of applying a range of nested and 'simultaneous' distribution–modal split models in the form **G/D/M/A**, **G/M/D/A** and **G/D-M/A** for the Leeds–West Yorkshire study area. As in Ben-Akiva's study, several compositional rules or com-posite cost functions were taken to interface the distribution **D** and modal split **M** models, including suitably specified 'logsum' measures. However, in addition, the λ response parameters accompanying the various MNL model stages were examined to check whether their estimated values were consistent with the inequality conditions for an appropriate ordering of the stages in the overall demand model structures (Senior and Williams, 1977; Williams and Senior, 1977).

Primarily as a result of Wilson's research (Wilson, 1969; Wilson et al, 1969), by the end of the 1960s many urban travel demand models in the UK (in contrast to those applied in the US) were already in a form having strong similarities to the NL model, albeit with inappropriate composite costs (section 3.7.2). As was common in applications of that period, the generation (or choice of trip frequency) model was taken to be insensitive to level-of-service variables, corresponding to an MNL form with $\lambda_F = 0$. For user-equilibrium assignments in which all travellers, facing determin-istic costs with no variation, sought their least generalised cost (or travel time) routes, the route choice model corresponded to an MNL form with $\lambda_R \to \infty$. The consistency of the overall demand model structure with the parameter inequalities was thus determined by the relative size of the dis-tribution and modal choice parameters λ_D and λ_M. Specifically, for the ordering **G/D/M/A** to be an acceptable representation of rational behav-ioural response, the empirically determined parameters were required to satisfy the condition $\lambda_D \leq \lambda_M$. Similarly, for the structure **G/M/D/A** to be acceptable required the corresponding parameters, which we distinguish by an asterisk, to obey the inequality $\lambda_M^* \leq \lambda_D^*$.

Different calibrated journey-to-work models were used to generate a range of travel forecasts and evaluation measures for four different policies: (a) an extensive highway scheme; (b) a free-fare public transport policy; (c) a parking charge policy; and (d) the exclusion of cars from a central Leeds zone.[6] These policies ranged in extent from marginal adjustments to very significant changes in the generalised cost of travel, and from local to spatially extensive impacts. Among the conclusions drawn were the following:

1. A variety of **G/D/M/A** and **G/M/D/A** model specifications could perform quite adequately on standard 'goodness-of-fit' criteria in the base year and yet generate very different demand responses and evaluation measures in policy tests.
2. Some of the results from the policy tests derived from the **G/D/M/A** demand model structure appeared to be counter-intuitive. The direct and cross-elasticities with respect to generalised modal costs of the calibrated models appeared to be of the wrong sign.[7]

In the mid-1970s the last observation was quite unexpected; the problem had not been noted in any previous urban transportation study where traditional forecasting models had been applied, either because the problem was absent or because the implications were not recognised. The diagnosis of this problem was traced to violation of the parameter restrictions required for a valid **G/D/M/A** model specification; the relative size of the estimated modal and destination choice response parameters λ_M and λ_D was inconsistent with the form of the nested structure selected. Williams and Senior (1977) referred to this as a 'parameter size anomaly'. In fact, they were not able to specify a **G/D/M/A** structure that satisfied the requirement $\lambda_D \leq \lambda_M$. Furthermore, they found that the ratio of these estimated parameters in their study on Leeds–West Yorkshire was similar in size to those found in several other UK studies that had applied MNL models hierarchically; they noted the general implications of this result:

> In every transportation study which has adopted analytic functions in the **G/D/M/A** structure, the peak-hour work trip parameters violate the condition $\lambda_D < \lambda_M$. Typically, the ratio λ_D/λ_M is of the order of 2–3, as in the present study.[8] . . . The **G/D/M/A** models, which have been widely adopted in transport studies, have all been subject to the parameter size anomaly which can have serious implications for [testing] localised policies or the local impact of a strategic policy. . . . The fundamental problem we face here is one of reconciling the *calibrated* model with the behavioural requirements of the model structure (Williams and Senior, 1977, 466, 469).

In contrast, when the NL structure **G/M/D/A**, with mode 'above' the distribution model in the hierarchy, was applied with the same Leeds–West Yorkshire database, the ratio of the estimated parameters λ_M^*/λ_D^* was equal to 0.3, a value compatible with the parameter inequality $\lambda_M^* \leq \lambda_D^*$ appropriate to that demand model structure.[9]

Williams and Senior (1977) drew these further conclusions with regard to zone-based applications:

1. Traditional zone-based travel forecasting models, suitably stratified and reformulated as NL structures, could be endowed with a behavioural interpretation if the appropriate parameter inequalities were satisfied.
2. Appropriate structures would possibly vary with person type, trip purpose and the structure of the activity system.
3. Standard 'goodness-of-fit' criteria were not sufficient to ensure acceptable travel demand forecasts; the process of validating models widely used in urban transportation studies urgently required extension to include scrutiny of their response (elasticity) properties to eliminate the possibility of perverse results.

We take up these issues in Chapter 9.

5.2.2   An Alternative Approach to the NL Model: Research by Daly and Zachary

5.2.2.1   Context of the study

An alternative approach to the development of the NL model was presented by Andrew Daly and Stan Zachary working at the UK Local Government Operational Research Unit (LGORU). These researchers, mathematics graduates from Oxford and Cambridge universities, respectively, were at the forefront of introducing discrete choice modelling based on random utility theory into the UK and were heavily involved in value-of-time and disaggregate modelling in the early 1970s (Daly and Zachary, 1975; Dalvi and Daly, 1976; Daly, 2013).

As part of its investigations in urban transportation studies, LGORU had developed a bus transport system model, TRANSEPT, which was applied in the Coventry Transportation Study in the early 1970s based on a sophisticated analysis of alternative choices available to individuals. It sought to refine the TRANSEPT suite of programs by extending an existing demand model to include choice among car, walk and various bus options travelling along different routes between origin–destination pairs. Daly and Zachary (1978) made several important contributions, including: (a) the introduction of a fully specified NL model; (b) demonstration of its consistency with the RUM hypothesis; and (c) its application in the Huddersfield Urban Bus Study.

The authors first clearly identified the source of the problem arising from the application of the MNL representation for a problem involving a combination of modes and routes, where the similarity among subsets of the options (multiple routes for the public transport mode) leads to pronounced differences in the cross-elasticities of demand between the different alternatives. Because other bus options by alternative routes between the same origin and destination would be considered much closer substitutes to a particular bus-route combination than the car mode, the MNL model was an unpromising candidate for modelling the whole set of alternative choices. The authors expressed the problem in terms of the variance of the utility *differences* associated with the various mode–route alternatives: 'In a mode-plus-route choice situation . . . the variance in the relative evaluation of two bus routes (with mean utilities fixed) is very much less than that in the evaluation of either route relative to the car choice' (Daly and Zachary, 1978, 343). They then derived and applied to this situation a more flexible and practical choice model, free of the IIA property, with a more general pattern of cross-elasticities among the alternatives.

5.2.2.2 Translational invariant RUM models: Harris–Zachary conditions on the probabilistic choice model

Building on the results of Harris and Tanner (1974), Zachary (1976) derived five conditions that were necessary and sufficient for a probabilistic choice model $P_j(V_1 \ldots V_j \ldots V_N)$ derived from random utility maximisation to be underpinned by translational invariant utility functions (section 4.2). We refer to these five conditions as the Harris–Zachary (H-Z) conditions.[10] They are recorded in Daly and Zachary (1978).

Among these technical conditions can be found the 'Hotelling condition' and the 'sign change' condition, the former referring to the symmetry properties of the choice model, and the latter requiring that the derivatives of the probability of an alternative being chosen P_j with respect to the utilities V_k of the other alternatives change sign in a particular way. With regard to these two conditions, the authors noted, the former 'may be regarded as the essential condition that the P_j's are compatible with each other', while the latter requires 'the implied probability density function [of the random components of utility] to be non-negative' (Daly and Zachary, 1978, 339).

5.2.2.3 The nested logit model and the estimation of its parameters

In seeking to extend the MNL model, Daly and Zachary envisaged choice within a tree structure, shown in Figure 5.5(a), in which some alternatives, arranged within subsets or nests, $s = 1 \ldots S$, were deemed more similar

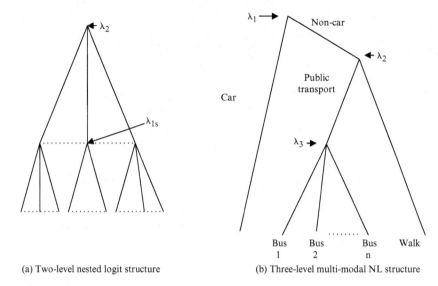

(a) Two-level nested logit structure   (b) Three-level multi-modal NL structure

Source: Based on Daly and Zachary (1978).

Figure 5.5   Alternative nested logit structures for multi-modal forecasting

than others. They demonstrated that the NL model with a 'logsum' link
and parameters λ_2 and λ_{1s}, $s = 1 \ldots S$ at the different levels of the tree
satisfied the H-Z conditions, and thus represented a valid choice model
derivable from translational invariant utility functions, if and only if
the parameters satisfied the inequalities $\lambda_2 \leq \lambda_{1s}$ for all nests. Daly and
Zachary (1978) further generalised this model to an arbitrary number of
levels and noted the collapse of the structure to an extended MNL model
when the λ parameters at adjacent levels were equal.

   The authors went on to consider the estimation of the model by
maximum likelihood through a sequential procedure similar to that
applied by CRA (1972) and Ben-Akiva (1974), estimating the parameters
of the MNL model(s) at one level of the hierarchy, starting at the lowest
level, transferring the results through the 'logsum' variables to the next
level, and then estimating the parameters of the MNL model(s) at the
higher level. They contrasted this method, termed a heuristic estimation
procedure, with that of a simultaneous procedure that determined the
best estimates of the model's parameters, referred to as the 'true values'.
The authors observed: 'There is no doubt . . . that the true maximum-
likelihood estimates are to be preferred' (Daly and Zachary, 1978, 351).
They also emphasised the necessity 'to remove spurious degrees of

freedom from the model' (Daly and Zachary, 1978, 348) in the process of estimation, the implications of which are noted below.

5.2.2.4   Application of the nested logit model to a mode–route choice problem

In the Huddersfield Urban Bus Study, the researchers developed a three-level tree, shown in Figure 5.5(b), to represent fully the choice for a journey between car, bus by four routes, and walk. The nesting reflected the assumed similarity among the options and the corresponding differences in the cross-elasticities between the different modes and mode–route combinations. Successively, they hypothesised that the choice among the alternative bus routes represented the closest substitutes for a particular bus journey, then the choice between bus and walking, and finally the choice between the bus–walk combination and car. Corresponding to these three levels were the three parameters λ_3, λ_2 and λ_1, respectively, and for consistency with the requirements for random utility maximisation the model was subject to the inequality condition $\lambda_1 \leq \lambda_2 \leq \lambda_3$.

To remove spurious degrees of freedom in the estimation of the model parameters, Daly and Zachary recast the model in terms of the ratio of the λ parameters at different levels in the hierarchy through the parameters $\Theta_1 = \lambda_1/\lambda_2$ and $\Theta_2 = \lambda_2/\lambda_3$. The authors noted:

> $\Theta_1 = \lambda_1/\lambda_2$ and $\Theta_2 = \lambda_2/\lambda_3$ are the ratios of the standard deviations of utility differences at the different levels in the hierarchy. These Θ parameters can be used as tests of the significance of the generalisation of the model, since the simple multiple logit model results if $\lambda_1 = \lambda_2 = \lambda_3$, i.e., if $\Theta_1 = 1$ and $\Theta_2 = 1$. A significant divergence of Θ to a value less than 1 thus indicates a significant improvement in the modelling from the simple multiple logit (Daly and Zachary, 1978, 353).

The model was estimated through the maximum likelihood method, both implemented sequentially (heuristically) from the lowest to the upper nest, and through optimal (full information maximum likelihood) estimation. With regard to the specification of the model in relation to its special case, the MNL, referred to as 'the simple model', and the two alternative methods for estimation, they remarked: 'Broadly, these results show that the generalised model gives a significant improvement over the simple model, but there is little difference between the heuristic and optimal calibrations of the generalised model. The values of Θ_1 are significantly different from 1 at the 0.1 percent level' (Daly and Zachary, 1978, 354).

The authors reflected on the implications of making policy judgements from the results of applications of restricted models, such as the simple MNL model, when in fact the data are more suitably represented by the NL model. They also commented on the effectiveness of policies that encouraged bus transport or sought to restrain the private car, which would depend crucially on the nature of close and distant substitutes. They noted the problems arising from seeking evidence from oversimplified models of the trip decision process.

Andrew Daly went on to write extensively on the NL model (e.g., Daly, 1987) and to develop the program ALOGIT for its estimation. He remains one of the pre-eminent contributors to the theory and application of discrete choice random utility models; we note some of his further contributions in sections 5.7 and 9.5. We now consider how the results of Williams and of Daly and Zachary were developed further.

5.3 WIDENING THE FRAMEWORK: FURTHER RESEARCH BY DANIEL McFADDEN

Although Daniel McFadden made several significant contributions to other areas of economic analysis, 'his development of theory and methods for analysing discrete choice' was central to his recognition by the Nobel Committee (Royal Swedish Academy of Sciences, 2000). At the heart of this body of work were three papers (McFadden, 1973, 1978, 1981). The first, as we have noted in Chapter 4, provided the theoretical and statistical foundations for application of discrete choice random utility models, and in particular the MNL model. The 1978 paper is best known for the introduction of the generalised extreme value family of models, which contains the NL and MNL models as special cases. His substantial 1981 chapter was a review, development and synthesis. It explored a range of problems: (a) the detailed conditions under which probabilistic choice models were consistent with the RUM hypothesis; (b) the relationships between the theory and methods of the discrete choice RUM approach and classical consumer theory, particularly in relation to welfare analysis; (c) the connection between seemingly different classes of model; and (d) a numerical comparison of alternative NL models for mode choice and procedures for their estimation. We comment on the 1978 and 1981 contributions.

5.3.1 The Generalised Extreme Value Family of Models

Although McFadden's 1978 paper, first presented at a conference in Sweden in 1977,[11] considered discrete choice within a housing or residential location context, it is most noted for its presentation of a class of models which 'allows a general pattern of dependence among the unobserved attributes of alternatives and yields an analytically closed form for the choice probabilities' (McFadden, 1978, 80). The paper became one of the most cited in the history of transportation research and econometric modelling generally. While Daly and Zachary (1978) showed that the NL model was under certain circumstances a suitable choice model by appealing to the Harris–Zachary conditions, McFadden went one step further. He derived a general class of choice models, expressed in a particular mathematical form, consistent with the RUM hypothesis derived from translational invariant utility functions. This formulation was to be of great theoretical interest and practical relevance.

Just as the MNL model could be derived from the assumption that the unobserved random variables $(\varepsilon_1 \ldots \varepsilon_j \ldots \varepsilon_N)$ in the utility specification were distributed according to identical and independent univariate extreme value (Gumbel Type I) functions, McFadden established a set of models in which the choice probabilities were derived when the random error terms $(\varepsilon_1 \ldots \varepsilon_j \ldots \varepsilon_N)$ were jointly distributed according to a generalised extreme value distribution, characterised by a functional form $G\{\varepsilon_1 \ldots \varepsilon_N\}$.[12] He showed, through what was to become known as the GEV theorem, that this function had to be endowed with several requirements to generate a model consistent with the RUM hypothesis. If these conditions were satisfied the choice probabilities could then be expressed in terms of the function G (and its derivatives). Further, he showed that *log* G was equal (up to a constant term) to the mean expected utility (*EMU*) achieved in the choice process and that the probabilities of choice P_j could be derived simply from *EMU* by differentiation.[13] Through suitable selection of the G function, or *EMU*, individual choice models could be generated that exhibited different patterns of correlation among the unobserved attributes and degrees of similarity among the alternatives.

A central result of McFadden (1978) was the identification and generation of the MNL and NL models as members of the GEV family.[14] In the latter case this involved partitioning groups of alternatives into mutually exclusive groups or 'nests' across a series of levels of a tree structure and associating 'similarity' parameters σ_k for the alternatives within the different nests, $k = 1 \ldots K$. A choice model of NL form was derived and conditions for consistency with random utility maximisation established, which required the parameters be confined to the unit interval $0 \leq \sigma_k < 1$. The coefficients of inclusive value variables ('logsums') associated with the individual nests, identified as $1 - \sigma_k$, allowed the special case, the MNL model, to be retrieved when the similarity parameter σ_k equals zero. A value of this parameter significantly different from zero could then be used to test for the existence of a significant degree of similarity among members of a nest, and as a justification for adopting the NL in preference to the MNL model.

Although the NL, and its special case, the MNL, models were destined to remain the most widely adopted and durable forms for practical applications, the GEV formulation opened up the possibility of deriving further closed form choice models, consistent with the RUM hypothesis, which are both practical and based on behaviourally plausible specifications. However, it was unclear in the early 1980s how such practical forms, which satisfied the requirements on the *G* function, should be generated. Kenneth Train, a long time Berkeley colleague and collaborator of McFadden, later remarked on the properties that *G* was to satisfy:

> There is little economic intuition to motivate these properties. . . . The lack of intuition behind the properties is a blessing and a curse. The disadvantage is that the researcher has little guidance on how to specify a *G* that provides a model that meets the needs of his research. The advantage is that the purely mathematical approach allows the researcher to generate models that he might not have developed while relying only on his economic intuition (Train, 2009, 93–94).

In section 5.7 we note further specific GEV models and developments in generating practical forms.

5.3.2   Applications of the Nested Logit Model

As part of his discussions of the GEV family and NL model, McFadden (1978) undertook a theoretical analysis of residential choice involving problems of similarity and aggregation, in which neighbourhood effects introduced similarities among the alternative dwelling choices, which could be captured within the NL framework. This contribution allowed comparison with prior studies of housing choice, including those of Lerman (1976) and Quigley (1976).

In his 1981 paper, McFadden returned to a mode choice context to discuss alternative formulations of models for multi-modal choice, noting the potential complexity in applying the NL model to a set of choices in which different alternatives were grouped in various subsets. He took the example of four modes (car alone, bus, rapid transit and car pool) in the San Francisco Bay Area to explore the pattern of similarity among the alternatives, and the theoretical consistency and numerical differences among predictions from seven possible preference tree structures, as compared with the MNL model representing choice between the four alternatives. Sequential estimates of the parameters were derived from a sample of 616 commuters revealing parameter values (such as value of time) quite sensitive to specification. These results were compared with full information maximum likelihood (FIML) estimates of the parameters for a subset of the models.

With regard to the application of the NL model to the multi-modal context, sometimes designated the nested multinomial logit (NMNL), and alternative estimation methods (sequential and FIML approaches), McFadden remarked: 'The application . . . suggests that these models can provide significantly better fits than the MNL models. Sequential estimation of the NMNL model is practical even for relatively large and complex trees, while the FIML method is practical for problems of moderate size' (McFadden, 1981, 248).

5.3.3 Relationship between Different Classes of Models

In the historical development of transportation models, an important issue of interest to both theoreticians and practitioners has been the establishment of taxonomy for the many different models. Classification permits similarities and differences in theoretical foundations, mathematical structure and detailed specification to be made explicit, and can be adopted to reveal the numerical consequences from the use of alternative forms. In this regard McFadden (1981) made a number of interesting observations on what he called Thurstonian forms (multinomial probit models, considered below), Lucian forms (including the MNL and GEV models) and Tverskian forms (e.g., the elimination-by-aspects model).

In section 4.2 we briefly mentioned discrete choice models within the framework of mathematical psychology and noted one particular model, the elimination-by-aspects (EBA) model of Amos Tversky (1972), which was once seen as a possible alternative to the MNL model, as it avoided the IIA property which was proving to be the MNL model's Achilles heel. The EBA model was an especially interesting concept that identified alternative choices in terms of the presence or absence of a collection of features or aspects. Individuals were considered to approach the choice process in terms of a hierarchical ranking of the aspects or attributes of the alternatives and the successive elimination of alternatives which do not have the required aspect. (Preferences are described here as lexicographic over the aspects.)

McFadden (1981) examined the mathematical structure of the GEV and EBA models and drew a correspondence between them by expressing the probabilities of choice in terms of individuals making transitions between subsets of the alternatives. In the late 1970s there was considerable speculation by Tversky, McFadden and others about the properties of, and numerical correspondence between, the GEV and EBA models, which 'permit very general patterns of similarities among alternatives' (McFadden, 1981, 230). This similarity between the models arose through the structure of the correlation among random residuals in the former model; in the latter it was due to the presence of an aspect unique to a subset of alternatives. Of particular interest in this discussion were the similarities between the NL (referred to here as a tree extreme value or TEV) model, and a special case of the EBA model known as the hierarchical elimination-by-aspects (HEBA) model, proposed by Tversky and Sattath (1979), in which a subset of alternatives sharing aspects formed what they described as a preference tree structure. To examine the similarity, McFadden compared the choice probabilities derived from the TEV, HEBA and a suitably specified multinomial probit model (see section 5.4) in a range of numerical tests, concluding for models with the same parameter degrees of freedom:

> The most striking feature [of the test results] is the closeness of the multinomial probabilities predicted by HEBA, TEV and MNP. . . . We conclude that, at least for simple preference trees . . . these models are for all practical purposes indistinguishable. . . . [T]he MNP, HEBA and TEV functional forms, when restricted to the same number of parameters, permit closely comparable fits to data generated by various patterns of similarities (McFadden, 1981, 236, 248).

He thus showed that particular members of the GEV and EBA families of models, although having their basis in different theoretical approaches, nevertheless exhibited deep structural similarities and would under certain conditions result in very similar numerical values for the choice probabilities (see also Batley and Daly, 2006). McFadden (1981) drew a more general and important practical point from this analysis: 'Practical experience suggests that functional forms that allow similar patterns of inter-alternative substitution will give comparable fits to existing economic data sets.'

5.3.4 Discrete Choice Analysis and Economic Welfare Assessment

One theme of the previous and present sections has been the establishment of an intimate relationship between discrete choice models based on random utility theory as predictors of behavioural response, on the one hand, and welfare (consumer surplus) measures which accompany their derivation, on the other. The latter are useful for the evaluation of transportation policies and projects. The relationships for the NL model (Williams, 1977a, 1977b) were discussed above and, as noted, McFadden (1978) extended these results to the GEV family by showing that *EMU*, the expected value of the distribution of maximum utility over the choice set, was equal (up to a constant) to the logarithm of the generating function G.[15]

McFadden (1981) placed this analysis within the wider context of micro-economic welfare analysis by establishing the conditions under which the RUM framework would generate acceptable measures of social surplus. In particular, he introduced and explored the properties of a class of 'additive income random utility maximisation' (AIRUM) models. As McFadden later succinctly put it, when (indirect) utility functions are linear in income, so that the marginal utility of income is constant, and in the case of translational invariant forms:

> choice behaviour . . . can be described in terms of a 'representative' consumer whose utility is the expected utility function and whose choice probabilities are given by derivatives of this function using Roy's Identity. This is convenient both for the derivation of choice probabilities and for applications of travel demand models where willingness-to-pay (WTP) for social policies such as transportation system improvements is needed. In economic terms, this is a case where Marshallian and Hicksian demand functions coincide and social aggregation of preferences is possible (McFadden, 2000b, 14).

McFadden (1981) and Small and Rosen (1981), who also gave consideration to the relationship between discrete choice models based on RUM and welfare economics, established rigorous theoretical and practical foundations for adopting measures such as the 'logsum' and its extensions to evaluate the benefits from projects and policies. This work has resulted in a fruitful line of research for determining the welfare implications of behaviour derived from more general RUM-based probabilistic choice models, including those displaying taste variation and non-linear income effects. See McFadden (1997), Train (1998), Herriges and Kling (1999), Cherchi et al (2004), de Jong et al (2007b), Jara-Diaz (2007) and Small and Verhoef (2007) for more details.

Although there were further significant developments involving the GEV framework, which we consider in section 5.7, McFadden's justly acclaimed 1978 and 1981 papers represent a theoretical highpoint of the discrete choice approach based on RUM and set within a wider bound the issues on model structure and economic welfare analysis considered by CRA (1972), Ben-Akiva (1974), Harris and Tanner (1974), Cochrane (1975), Domencich and McFadden (1975), Koenig (1975), Williams (1977a), Daly and Zachary (1978), Williams and Senior (1978) and Ben-Akiva and Lerman (1979). His two papers also provided clues on how to address choice situations characterised by more complex patterns of similarity among the alternatives. But there was a pause in the extraction of more general practical models from the family, and in some respects these papers represent the end of an era, one of considerable mathematical elegance in generating a wide class of closed form models. From now on we are going to witness a bit of numerical brute force to pay for further refinements in the specification of choice models based on RUM. We return to the mid-1970s to pick up the story.

5.4   USE OF NUMERICAL SOLUTION METHODS: MICROSIMULATION

5.4.1   Use of Numerical Methods in the Disaggregate Modelling Process

From the mid-1970s the use of numerical methods for solving particular mathematical problems (typically problems of multiple integration) became increasingly common in implementing the micro-approach based on discrete choice random utility theory, as less restrictive behavioural assumptions were sought and adopted. In particular, microsimulation, hitherto widely encountered in numerical resolution of stochastic models in operations research, econometrics and traffic modelling, entered the travel forecasting lexicon in this period. Although it was often taken to mean different things, sometimes implying a static or dynamic character, 'microsimulation' meant a range of techniques and approaches to modelling in which samples of individual agents (persons, households and firms) were used for the solution and aggregation of a system of equations representing the likely behaviour of such agents. The Monte Carlo method, which uses random numbers in the process of integration, was widely applied in this context.

In this section we outline the increasing use of microsimulation methods for the solution and implementation of models for which analytic resolution was not possible. These were to become increasingly relevant as more sophisticated and complex models of behaviour were adopted. They include the following three contexts: (a) the simulation of discrete choice models based on the random utility approach and, particularly, for the solution of the multinomial probit model; (b) the aggregation process in conjunction with micro-behavioural models, including the formation and use of synthetic samples; and (c) more general applications representing a range of urban market processes, particularly in stratified housing, labour and travel-related markets.

5.4.2   Simulation of Choices: Multinomial Probit and Other RUM Models

The NL model addressed one limitation of the MNL model, that of catering for the similarity of different alternatives in the choice process and avoiding the restrictive IIA property. However, the MNL model, the NL model and the GEV family more generally were subject to the restriction arising from the 'homogeneity of tastes'. With such models, incorporation of taste variation required explicit market segmentation and the specification of separate taste parameters for each segment. Concurrent with the investigations on the NL model, there were attempts to address problems of both similarity among a subset of the alternatives and taste variation over the population by adopting the multinomial normal or probit (MNP) model.[16]

In the MNP model both the taste parameters of the representative utility and the random error terms in the utility function were considered to be normally distributed with arbitrary variance–covariance matrices. In this way the taste parameters could be varied over the population and complex patterns of similarity among the alternative choices introduced. The price of this additional flexibility was, for any set of parameter values, the numerical challenge of solving an $N-1$ dimensional integral for a choice process involving N alternatives. Unless a more efficient approach or suitable approximations became available, parameter estimation would thus require this multiple integral to be embedded within an iterative procedure in order to derive optimal values for the parameters.

The interest associated with the MNP specification was so intense that in the mid-1970s, at MIT alone, there were three teams of researchers seeking efficient numerical procedures for its estimation and application. Albright et al (1977), Daganzo et al (1977) and Hausman and Wise (1978) explored different numerical approximations and applications. In the present context two approaches to the computational feasibility of the MNP model are of particular interest:

1. adoption of the Clark approximation (Clark, 1961; Daganzo et al, 1977);
2. a numerical simulation approach (Albright et al, 1977; Lerman and Manski, 1981).

The first was based on the repeated application of an approximation (for the distribution of the maximum of two jointly normal distributed variables) suggested by Clark (1961), which Daganzo et al (1977) applied to the MNP, considerably simplifying the numerical integration problem. The numerical simulation approach to the choice process involved drawing random variables from normal distributions to represent the utilities of the alternatives for each member in a sample of 'individuals'. Each 'individual' was then allocated to the alternative which offered the maximum utility. As the number of trials increased, the simulated choice frequency converged to the choice probability (Albright et al, 1977, 15). In the estimation of the model parameters, the probability of choosing an alternative in the likelihood function was replaced by the relevant approximation derived from simulation and acquired the label of maximum simulated likelihood (Lerman and Manski, 1981).

In the mid-1970s the application of the MNP model with the simulation method required approximately 100 times the computing (CPU) time of the Clark method to achieve similar precision. However, in respect of the attractions of the simulation approach, Albright et al (1977) remarked:

> it can be used to generate choice probabilities associated with any random utility model, not just multinomial probit ones. . . . [O]ne need only substitute a random number generator for the desired distribution in place of the normal generator we are using. . . . The potential drawback of the simulation approach is that the CPU times required to achieve acceptable accuracy in the probability calculations may be too large to make the method practical (Albright et al, 1977, 17–18).

An empirical case study compared the MNL with different MNP specifications in a mode choice context, and explored the consequences of adopting MNL estimates of the parameters as useful starting values for MNP estimation.

In this period the solution of discrete choice models by numerical methods, and in particular Monte Carlo methods, became more widely applied and served an important research role to test particular approximations. More generally, simulation was adopted to examine the consequences of alternative decision models and error structures compared with simpler assumptions. As in the above MNP study, misspecification tests of the MNL model, and the assumptions used in its derivation, were often of central interest. For example, Langdon (1976) examined the consequences of assuming different variances associated with the distribution of modal utilities in a modal choice context.

Ortúzar (1979) and Williams and Ortúzar (1982) used Monte Carlo simulation to examine a range of specifications for the choice process, including: (a) alternative utility structures displaying similarity among alternatives; (b) alternative decision rules, including elimination strategies, as an alternative to compensatory selection mechanisms; (c) limited information and 'satisficing' behaviour (see section 6.2.2); (d) the distribution of choice sets within a population; and (e) the implications of habit in modelling response. Using data from Washington, DC, they examined how the application of different models could result in comparable goodness-of-fit statistics and yet generate significantly different responses to policies.

A further contribution of McFadden clarified the statistical theory of estimating discrete choice models using simulation methods. As an alternative to the method of maximum simulated likelihood in which the probability of choosing an alternative in the likelihood function was replaced by the relevant approximation, McFadden (1989) and McFadden and Ruud (1994) adapted the generalised method of moments through what became known as the 'method of simulated moments'. Although more widely applicable, parameter estimation for the MNP model was of particular interest. This approach avoided the complexity of multiple integrals for the response probabilities by adopting estimators obtained by Monte Carlo simulation, and was computationally tractable even for models with many choice alternatives.

5.4.3 Generation of Synthetic Samples for Aggregation and Forecasting

One of the first times we encounter the term 'microsimulation' in travel demand analysis is in the process of aggregation for generating estimates of aggregate shares from probabilities of choice derived from samples. We saw in section 4.3.3 how various approaches to this summation or integration process were effected (Koppelman, 1976; Ben-Akiva and Atherton, 1977; Koppelman and Ben-Akiva, 1977). We noted in that section how sample enumeration proved to be highly convenient for short-range forecasting when the original sample was representative of that for the forecasting situation. When conditions change so that the sample is no longer representative of the required population in a forecasting context:

> The sample enumeration is approximated for long range prediction or when a prior sample does not exist by a Monte Carlo integration procedure which we refer to as the *pseudo-sample enumeration procedure*. In this procedure a pseudo sample is synthesized by taking random drawings from the expected future distribution of independent variables (Koppelman and Ben-Akiva, 1977, 161).

The production of large synthetic samples for use in transportation and urban research, particularly in conjunction with discrete choice models, dates from the mid-1970s. The research of McFadden et al (1977a) on SYNSAM, part of the travel demand forecasting project at Berkeley, became an important precursor to later applications in which samples from synthetic populations were formed which drew information from several different sources. The procedure was used:

> for generating a synthetic representative sample of households for an urban area for any specified date. . . . In addition to residence and work locations, data for each household comprises a subset of the socioeconomic variables

tabulated in the Public Use Sample (PUS) of the 1970 Census. . . . A principal feature of the SYNSAM procedure is the use of Iterative Proportional Fitting (IPF) to construct and update the contingency table for zone of residence and for a selected set of household characteristics, starting from the various marginal tabulations on census tapes and other sources. . . . The other principal step is to actually construct the synthetic sample by random sampling, once the contingency tables for socioeconomic characteristics have been computed (McFadden et al, 1977a, 2, 3).

In the San Francisco Bay Area application, a synthetic sample of 12 000 households was generated for the year 1976.

While the generation of synthetic samples in the above case was motivated by problems of aggregation and forecasting with disaggregate travel-related choice models, the creation of synthetic samples by Wilson and Pownall (1976) at the University of Leeds was motivated by a wider set of geographical problems. They saw microsimulation based on synthetic spatial databases as a means of studying micro-level interdependencies, avoiding the processing of large, very sparse (trip) matrices, incorporating complex patterns of interdependency arising from the choices and constraints of individuals within a household context, and for dealing with distributional issues in highly heterogeneous populations.

This study was a forerunner of major initiatives in the School of Geography and the Institute for Transport Studies at the University of Leeds into the use of the microsimulation approach, and the use of synthetic spatial databases, for policy analysis in a range of geographical settings, including housing, the labour market, transportation, health care, and retail systems. Such was the interest in the approach that around 1980 four groups of researchers were working on microsimulation methods in transportation and geographical problems (Bonsall, 1980, 1982; Clarke et al, 1981; Williams, 1981; Mackett, 1985; Clarke and Holm, 1987; Birkin and Clarke, 1988).

The generation of synthetic samples, either by augmenting the characteristics of existing samples with additional information, or developed wholly from secondary sources, became increasingly important in travel behaviour research. Used in conjunction with discrete models of choice processes, the approach was later to become a key component of many travel and transportation planning models.

5.4.4 Microsimulation Models of Individual Choice and Market Processes

By the second half of the 1970s microsimulation involving samples drawn from parametric and non-parametric distributions became more widely recognised as a strategy for aggregating micro-models derived from choice processes (see Koppelman and Ben-Akiva, 1977; Watanatada and Ben-Akiva, 1979). Building on the earlier results on synthetic samples, and disaggregate choice models, the ground was laid for the development and solution of more intricate models of behaviour and the explicit consideration of urban 'market processes'. These models involved the interplay between the demand for and supply of services in housing, labour, land and travel-related markets, as the basis for forecasting and policy analysis. This approach involved linking up individuals or households with supply units (households with houses, individuals with jobs, etc.) in a market-clearing process achieved computationally through 'matching lists' according to prior probability relations or explicit behavioural models that simulated the actions of consumers and suppliers.

One of the first large-scale applications of microsimulation in this context, which had interesting technical and substantive aspects, was begun in the late 1970s by Peter Bonsall at the Institute for Transport Studies, University of Leeds (Bonsall, 1980, 1982). Bonsall independently saw the potential of an approach to travel demand forecasting based on sampling from synthetic populations and processing 'individuals' according to the outcome of random draws from choice models. The context of the application was the representation of the behaviour of individuals and assessing the performance of organised car sharing programmes in West Yorkshire. Prior to this application, the complexity of the choice process that would lead to successful matches between potential users of such schemes had received little attention (Bonsall, 1980). Bonsall created a synthetic sample of 180 000 individuals, and through calibrated choice models he simulated the decisions to: (a) join an organised car sharing programme; and (b) undertake a pooling arrangement with potential partners. For the latter, a mutual evaluation of utilities and constraints determined what arrangements would come to fruition. The model was used to assess the performance of alternative organisational environments for car pooling and investigated the effects of major policy variables, including changes in public transport fares, fuel price and parking incentives for those who car-shared. Bonsall noted the inherent attractions and potential of the microsimulation approach in travel demand analysis for the more realistic assessment of the choice environment of individuals, noting that 'it is only recently that decreasing computer costs made microsimulation a viable branch of travel demand modelling' (Bonsall, 1980, 12).

In another early example of microsimulation, Kreibich (1979) examined the interdependence between car availability, travel and locational behaviour under time budget constraints. According to Axhausen and Herz (1989, 317), Kreibich first proposed the simulation of activity chains using Monte Carlo methods as early as 1972 in a German publication. We discuss activity-based travel demand models in Chapter 6.

The origins of large-scale dynamic microsimulation models in transportation and regional science, which assumed considerable importance in the 1990s and beyond, can be found in the fields of operations research and econometrics in the mid-1950s. Of particular importance were the studies of Guy Orcutt and his collaborators at the University of Minnesota (Orcutt et al, 1961, 1976). The essence of their approach involved the evolution of an initial representative sample of individuals and households from a base year through transitions induced by a range of deterministic and stochastic processes, the latter implemented through Monte Carlo methods. These included a range of demographic events and transitions in the labour market and the implications for the accumulation of income and wealth.

Complex dynamic simulation models in urban spatial contexts stem from the early 1980s. These sought to capture the interdependencies between demographic and economic processes and events in the housing, labour and transportation markets. Early examples include: the Dortmund housing model (Wegener, 1985), which was a forerunner of Michael Wegener's land use – transportation model (section 8.5.2); and MASTER (Micro-Analytical Simulation of Transportation, Employment and Residence), by Roger Mackett (1985). A further well-known microsimulation housing market model constructed and applied in this period was the Harvard Urban Development Simulation (HUDS) model developed in the early 1980s by Kain and Apgar (1985).

Subsequently, we encounter several references to the microsimulation approach both in comparative static and in fully dynamic settings. The motivation to develop such models in preference to some simplified version stemmed from the complexity and interdependence among (choice) processes governing the behaviour of individuals, households and firms, as well as the distributional impact of policies over highly heterogeneous populations.

5.5 URBAN TRAVEL FORECASTING WITH DISAGGREGATE MODELS AND METHODS

5.5.1 Introduction

Let us return once again to the mid-1970s to discuss progress in the practical development of disaggregate models as the basis for travel forecasting in urban areas. In this section we describe a range of applications that began to address missing requirements of urban transportation planning agencies (metropolitan planning organisations, MPOs, in the US), specifically the development of urban travel forecasting procedures to serve not only traditional longer-term concerns of infrastructure planning but also shorter-term policies associated with transportation systems management (TSM). We consider first the landmark study conducted for the Metropolitan Transportation Commission (MTC) in the San Francisco Bay Area, in which the innovations of the previous five years were integrated into a travel forecasting system. The MTC study was important for three reasons: (a) it provided the first real comparison with the traditional four-step procedure; (b) it served as a template for the wider dissemination of the approach for urban applications; and (c) it acted as a stepping stone to further important theoretical and practical developments. The present description is based on Ruiter and Ben-Akiva (1978) and Hague Consulting Group (1997).

Through Cambridge Systematics, a similar disaggregate modelling approach was applied in the Netherlands, the SIGMO study of the Amsterdam metropolitan area (Ben-Akiva et al, 1978). The innovative work undertaken by Cambridge Systematics, first in San Francisco and later in the Netherlands by Cambridge Systematics Europe, which became the Hague Consulting Group (HCG), could claim to be the most advanced trip-based model forecasting system in the world at that time. We first describe the MTC model and then various Dutch applications from the late 1970s and early 1980s.

5.5.2   Disaggregate Models for the San Francisco MTC

The MTC model, based on disaggregate concepts, arose from the dissatisfaction of local transportation planners with the traditional forecasting approach 'because of deficiencies in their ability to represent existing travel or to provide reasonable future estimates' (Ruiter and Ben-Akiva, 1978, 122). In the mid-1970s, a Travel Model Development project was set up by MTC in which it was decided to make a 'quantum jump in the state of the art of travel forecasting' (Kollo and Purvis, 1989, quoted in HCG, 1997, 16) by basing a new model system as far as possible on disaggregate concepts. For this purpose a team of consultants consisting of Comsis Corporation, Cambridge Systematics, and Barton-Aschman Associates was commissioned. A requirement of the model development was its estimation with data normally available to a metropolitan planning organisation.

To address the policy analysis requirements of the MTC, two computerised model application procedures were developed: (a) a regional network analysis (RNA) system, which was to be compatible with traditional matrix manipulation and assignment procedures; and (b) a short-range generalised policy (SRGP) analysis system based on random-sample forecasting. The former was described as 'similar to but more sophisticated than the conventional trip generation–trip distribution–modal split methodology' (Ruiter and Ben-Akiva, 1978, 126). Through a set of models, specified and estimated at the micro-level, 11 24-hour person trip matrices classified by mode and purpose were generated. These trip matrices were then used to generate 24-hour and peak hour highway and public transport assignments. The SRGP procedure was designed to produce information on broadly defined transportation policy options appropriate to short and medium time frames, including the derivation of elasticities relating to fuel price, travel time, fare level, parking charges, access times for transit, and so on.

The MTC model system involved what the authors refer to as a 'hierarchy of conditional dependency' (Ruiter and Ben-Akiva, 1978). Following earlier results (Ben-Akiva, 1973; Ben-Akiva and Atherton, 1977), choices were grouped into a three-step choice hierarchy:

1. urban development decisions (location of jobs, location of housing types);
2. mobility decisions (made infrequently): number of workers, workplace location, residential location, housing type, car ownership and mode to work;
3. travel decisions (non-work trips) (short-run decisions which are made almost daily): frequency, destination, mode, route and time of day.

The projective land use model (PLUM) was adopted for the purpose of forecasting future land use, employment location, residential location, housing-type choices and socio-economic characteristics (section 2.7.4).

Mobility decisions of households with and without workers were handled separately, and travel decisions were divided into two groups. Primary and secondary workers in a household were distinguished. As in traditional practice, home-based (HB) and non-home-based (NHB) trips were dealt with separately, simplifying the representation of trip chains. The home-based other (HBO) purpose was predicted according to all non-work home-based travel decisions. There was also an indirect provision for non-work travel to affect mobility decisions.

We shall not describe in detail the model specification, which is one of considerable behavioural sophistication, or its estimation (see Ruiter and Ben-Akiva, 1978, 122–126), but note two issues:

1. An NL model was applied to represent the two-way dependency according to the assumed choice hierarchy, with wide application of 'logsum' variables to record the expected maximum utility accompanying choices at lower levels of a hierarchy.
2. Incorporation of 'intra-household, inter-person dependencies' was one of the most striking features of this application, as discussed in the earlier example in Chapter 4 (Ben-Akiva and Atherton, 1977; HCG, 1997, 16). This formulation involved the interdependence among household members and among trips for different purposes, the home-based work (HBW) mode choice decision directly affecting the car availability measure in the HBO models.

With regard to the relative efficiency of estimating aggregate and disaggregate models, the authors observed:

> In terms of types of data required, the aggregate and disaggregate approaches are identical. The key difference for disaggregate systems arises from the significant reduction in sample size required to yield statistically significant parameters. . . . A complete disaggregate model system can be estimated with data from as few as 1000 households (Ruiter and Ben-Akiva, 1978, 126).

As a result of this increased efficiency in the estimation techniques, more variables could be included in the model system, thereby increasing the sensitivity of travel forecasts to changes in the urban environment and in government policies.

For the short-range SRGP system, only a subset of the models representing short-range choices of the full MTC system were included. For aggregation, random-sample enumeration was adopted (section 4.3.3); all the relevant choice models were applied to each household in turn, and the results accumulated and presented for different groups, including household income classes. The processing was based on the sample of surveyed households, which was then expanded to be representative of the whole population. Applications were limited to general policy issues, such as the determination of price elasticities.

The regional network analysis (RNA) model system used only data that were readily available at zonal level, thus omitting income and most other socio-economic data. For the network application, 'Aggregation is performed by market segmentation by using average socio-economic values for each of three income groups initially, followed by segmentation based on auto-ownership after the prediction of auto-ownership in the mobility blocks' (Ruiter and Ben-Akiva, 1978, 126). In application, this zonal model performed in a similar way to traditional travel forecasting models. Matrices of trips among all pairs of zones for each of the modes were forecast, and car driver trips were assigned to the highway network using all-or-nothing or capacity restraint assignment techniques.

Ruiter and Ben-Akiva (1978) gave an extended discussion of the comparison between the specification, estimation and validation of the disaggregate model system with that for a conventional aggregate system. For the MTC example the authors remarked:

> The only disadvantage that exists in the use of this approach relative to conventional aggregate models is the increased complexity of the system. Due to improved behavioural representation, more models are estimated; they are closely inter-connected; and they are not yet well understood by practitioners. The cost of a full zone aggregate application of a disaggregate model system is marginally higher than its aggregate counter-part, but this cost differential is not a significant issue since the major costs of both types of systems are network skimming and assigning (Ruiter and Ben-Akiva, 1978, 127).

The authors concluded:

> Work undertaken to date has shown that this modeling approach is feasible, that careful estimation and testing are necessary during the model development phase, that extensive training is necessary to familiarize planners with the new approach and, of course, that the resulting model systems are sufficiently improved over the conventional system they replace to warrant the investment in training and model development (Ruiter and Ben-Akiva, 1978, 127).

See Kollo and Purvis (1989) and HCG (1997) for subsequent developments of the MTC forecasting model.

5.5.3   Application of Disaggregate Models in the Netherlands (1977–85)

The similarities and differences between the MTC model applied to the San Francisco Bay Area and the SIGMO model applied to the Amsterdam metropolitan area were described by Ben-Akiva et al (1978). The broad template established in the MTC study, that of dual model development, was applied to: (a) address longer-term network developments requiring assignments derived from trips aggregated within a zoned system; and (b) provide broader short-term system-wide transportation policy applications based on sample enumeration methods. There were also some differences between the MTC and SIGMO applications arising from: (a) urban transportation environments requiring much greater concern for cycling and walking trips in Amsterdam; (b) data and software availability; and (c) planning priorities (Ben-Akiva et al, 1978).

During the period 1977–85 much innovative research was undertaken in the Netherlands by Cambridge Systematics Europe (which became the Hague Consulting Group in 1985), some of which is described in an unpublished paper (HCG, 1985). We note briefly some of the novel features of: (a) the South Wing (Zuidvleugel) study (1977–81); (b) the transferability study (1981–84); and (c) the national model.

5.5.3.1 South Wing (Zuidvleugel) study
The South Wing study, based on the cities of Rotterdam and The Hague, was the first full-scale regional study based on disaggregate techniques. A dual model template, similar to that described above, was adopted for similar reasons. The zonal system used only data that were available at the zonal level, again omitting income and most other socio-economic data. The shorter-term system-wide model adopted a fully disaggregate approach employing the full richness of the data collected in the home interview survey (Daly and van Zwam, 1981).

The model systems set up were unusually comprehensive, with travel modelled separately for eight purposes. We begin to see in a major study a progression of methodology in which travel was represented in terms of 'tours' – complete journeys from home. The motivation for the latter, which we consider in much greater detail in Chapter 6, was 'to ensure consistency of mode choice and timing for the entire tour, and to improve the travel frequency (trip generation) models by relating travel more strongly to its main objective: an activity away from home' (HCG, 1985, 2). In the Zuidvleugel study, tours were explicitly modelled as simple round trips using the definition of a 'primary destination' (HCG, 1985).

5.5.3.2 Transferability study
The motivation for conducting studies on the transferability of disaggregate methods from one area to another was not only to check basic assumptions about the similarity and differences of individual choice behaviour, but also to reduce the cost of implementing models. Building on the earlier US findings on model transferability (Atherton and Ben-Akiva, 1976; Ben-Akiva, 1981), HCG (1985, 4) addressed the question of 'how much of the understanding of behaviour derived in one area is transferable to the other area'. By what was termed a 'scaling approach', a set of scaling factors was introduced into the choice models, each factor multiplying part of the generalised cost function of each mode and destination. As well as introducing and testing refined methods of transferring models, the approach successfully transferred models from those developed for the South Wing study to a region that included the city of Utrecht.

A further methodological advance of this study was the estimation of a set of disaggregate models from the use of data derived from: (a) households; and (b) 'en-route' surveys taken on roads and railways crossing screen-lines. These techniques offered substantial scope for cost savings in many applications (HCG, 1985, 4).

In parallel to research in the Netherlands, developments in urban modelling also occurred in France, notably in Paris, Grenoble and Nantes, where the emphasis was on cost effectiveness of the disaggregate analysis approach. Models developed in a Grenoble study were transferred to Nantes using the scaling technique developed in the Netherlands. In both cities the issues were similar: the estimation of demand elasticities for a range of policy measures; and, in both cities, forecasts arising from the proposed installation of tramway systems.

5.5.3.3   Dutch national model

Although it is outside our specific urban focus, we mention the application of disaggregate methods in developing a Dutch national model for its methodological interest. This study was intended to produce forecasts of traffic flows on the major road and rail networks for planning up to 2010 (Daly and Gunn, 1986). The approach exploited models applied in the transferability study as well as adopting artificial sampling and incremental (pivot-point) methods. We note the wide use of sample enumeration methods and the adoption of synthetic sampling methods for forecasting. The latter was achieved through re-weighting an existing sample so that it met a series of specified marginal totals. For the national model, a sample was extracted from the national travel survey for 1983 and weighting factors calculated for the 345 zones of the national model system so that the sample met the known characteristics (age/sex distribution, household size, employment rates) of each zone. For forecasting, the socio-economic developments implied by different scenarios were expressed in terms of changes to the marginal distributions, and the weighting factors recalculated.

5.6   DEVELOPMENTS IN THE ANALYSIS OF PREFERENCES AND CHOICES

5.6.1   Introduction to Two Major Innovations

For the implementation and estimation of the discrete choice random utility approach to modelling, established in the early 1970s, a standard approach was adopted based on revealed preference (RP) data sets. The socio-economic characteristics of a sample of individuals, typically based on the household or workplace, were taken along with information on their accepted and rejected option(s) (or a sample drawn from the latter), including measured or reported network data. The maximum likelihood method was used to estimate the value of parameters of a typically linear-in-parameters utility function (McFadden, 1973, 2000b; Ben-Akiva and Lerman, 1985).

Although this was standard practice, widely and routinely applied in studies of modal choice by the late 1970s, the potential problems of the approach were evident to most of its exponents. These concerned one or more of the following: (a) paucity of information derived from random samples that related to the use of infrequently chosen options; (b) multicollinearity between the various travel-related variables, such as travel times and costs attributed to individual journeys; (c) difficulty of identifying the 'traders' necessary to obtain reliable estimates of the choice model parameters; (d) dominance of certain attributes that masked the contribution of other variables relevant to policy action (such as the service characteristics, comfort, safety, etc.); and (e) difficulty of imputing behaviour in situations with new options, such as when modes based on new technology were involved, or when the future mix of attributes was very different from that governing current behaviour (Louviere and Hensher, 1982; Sheldon and Steer, 1982; Hensher, 1994; Ortúzar and Willumsen, 2011). A major virtue of the approach, however, was that it was deemed to reflect the actual preferences of respondents 'in the field'.

Two major innovations occurred in the exploration of preferences and estimation of parameters of discrete choice models in the late 1970s and early 1980s. The first involved different strategies for collecting samples, which in particular addressed the problem of dealing with infrequently selected options, when 'it was recognised that travel data could often be collected efficiently from on-board, screen-line or destination surveys. These have the advantage of concentrating observations on modes, locations, and times that are of particular interest for behaviour and policy. In addition they offer cost advantages over general home surveys' (McFadden, 2000b, 25).

Theoreticians turned their attention to the implications for sampling strategy and parameter estimation derived from data collected according to different criteria, specifically in the form of: random samples; 'exogenous samples', where the basis for stratification was according to the characteristics of the individual; 'endogenous samples', where the samples were based on the choices made; and combinations thereof (Manski and Lerman, 1977; Lerman and Manski, 1979; Cosslett, 1981; Manski and McFadden, 1981). From the late 1970s it would also become increasingly common to estimate the parameters of discrete choice models with samples derived from combined data sources, as noted in relation to the Dutch studies described in section 5.5.3.

In response to some of the difficulties encountered with this revealed preference approach, the other major development of this period was the introduction and refinement of a set of techniques that became collectively known as stated preference (SP) methods.

5.6.2   Development and Acceptance of Stated Preference Methods

For accounts of the early historical development of the stated preference techniques in transportation, the papers by Fowkes (1998), Hensher (1994) and Rose and Bliemer (2013), and the texts by Louviere et al (2000) and Ortúzar and Willumsen (2011), as well as communication with the above authors, were very helpful in preparing this section.

5.6.2.1   Advantages and disadvantages of the SP approach

Stated preference methods are effectively sophisticated variants on the practice of asking people to express their views and preferences over hypothetical combinations of attributes associated with alternative choices. Here, in conjunction with suitably specified models and carefully designed experiments, involving the ranking and rating of, and choice between, options endowed with different combinations of travel-related attributes, analysts were able to tease out the attitudes, preferences and trade-offs that people were considered to make in their decisions. The utility models employed for the analysis of SP data were similar to those adopted in traditional discrete choice RP studies and were typically of a linear-in-parameters compensatory form. More formal discussion of the various approaches adopted in practice can be found in Bates (1988), Hensher et al (1988), Kroes and Sheldon (1988), Louviere (1988), Pearmain and Kroes (1990) and Hensher (1994).

The advantages of the SP approach were effectively the converse of the disadvantages of the RP approach. Here, the nature of the experiments could be efficiently designed to focus directly on the trade-off between relevant attributes; they could place emphasis on precisely those attributes normally dominated in the choice process; they could remove correlation among the attributes; they could give prominence to variables subject to policy action; and, importantly, they could be applied in situations involving new options, as in the case of new modes, or where policies or projects implied large adjustments from currently experienced attribute values. Additionally, because each individual in an SP experiment would normally generate several observations, a relatively large amount of data could be obtained at reasonable cost.

A further advantage derived from the multiple responses by each individual was that the experimental method could be applied relatively efficiently to investigate how the form of utility functions, including non-linear and interaction terms among the attributes, and their associated parameters, varied among individuals (Lerman and Louviere, 1978). However, as noted, in practice the approach was applied, almost exclusively, with linear-in-parameters additive utility functions with fixed parameters over any market segment.

All these suggested advantages did not come without a potential downside, whether the preferences, attitudes and choices made in an experimental situation would be a good predictor of behaviour 'in the field'. Certainly, this concern was a rather large potential problem, and accounting for it would become a major challenge both to theoreticians and to practitioners over the years. Furthermore, while SP data would (eventually) be accepted as a good way to estimate the relative values of attributes in a utility function, for travel forecasting it would be necessary to combine SP and RP data.

5.6.2.2 Origins and early developments of SP methods in transportation

Although the origins of what we now refer to as stated preference methods date back to the 1930s and 1940s,[17] much of the early development of the stated preference approach occurred in the US in the field of theoretical and experimental psychology in the 1960s and subsequently in market research studies conducted in the 1970s. Such studies were often referred to as conjoint analysis or conjoint measurement, and were centred on the way that individuals were considered to value the various attributes (the utility weightings) constituting alternatives in a choice process. In the case of market research studies the primary objects of study were the attitudes towards and preferences between different products or services characterised by combinations of attributes as a basis of forecasting and product design (Luce and Tukey, 1964; Tversky, 1967; Green and Rao, 1971).

Applications in the field of transportation began to appear in the early 1970s (Hoinville and Johnson, 1971; Davidson, 1973; Louviere et al, 1973; Johnson, 1974; Hensher and Louviere, 1979). Several important investigations in that period were undertaken by Louviere et al (1973) and Louviere (1979a, 1979b). Jordan Louviere, one of the pioneers of the conjoint analysis approach both within transportation applications and in more general marketing and environmental studies, obtained his Ph.D. from the University of Iowa in 1973 and has remained one of the central contributors to stated preference analysis in these fields for nearly four decades. His collaboration over the years with David Hensher has proved to be particularly productive and influential; important early joint contributions, noted below, are Louviere and Hensher (1982, 1983).

While early applications were predominantly US-based they were increasingly applied in Europe and Australia. According to Wardman, 'the early transportation applications in the UK were undertaken by transport consultancy agencies . . . while in the US their use was encouraged by public bodies such as the New York [State] Department of Transportation' (Wardman, 1987, cited in Fowkes, 1998, 3).

These early applications were almost invariably associated with modal choices and were in the form of the ranking and rating of different attribute combinations (Hensher, 1994; Fowkes, 1998). Such analyses of SP data did not make use of discrete choice theory – more *ad hoc* techniques (like MONANOVA) were used, especially in market research. Arguably, it was the contribution of transportation modellers, who were already adept at formulating and implementing logit models and interpreting their results, that put the analysis of SP data on a firmer footing. The findings of Chapman and Staelin (1982) and Beggs et al (1981) further allowed ranking data to be analysed by discrete choice methods.

A further variant of the stated preference approach was the so-called 'transfer price' method in which information was elicited on the change in an attribute that would leave the respondent indifferent between two options, such as modes characterised by different attribute values, or lead to a definite change between two alternatives. Such an approach was also referred to as contingent valuation and focused on the measurement of utility differences. An early example of the approach was that of Lee and Dalvi (1969) in their research on the value of time, where travel time and out-of-pocket costs were the relevant attributes influencing choice. Bonsall (1983) and Gunn (1984) commented on the strengths and weaknesses of the approach, and its wider application in conjunction with choice experiments. The method currently has few advocates in travel behaviour research because of it being dominated by other forms of stated preference analysis. However, it is still widely applied in contingency valuation studies in environmental economics.

5.6.2.3   Towards the wider acceptance of the SP approach

The rather slow uptake of the SP approach in transportation in the 1970s is sometimes attributed to the suspicion held by many transportation analysts, and particularly economists, towards an approach to measuring preferences based on hypothetical data rather than actual behaviour. According to David Hensher (1994), who contributed widely to the theory and application of the SP approach, two things gave rise to the change in this situation after 1983. These were: (a) the wider availability of computer software to calibrate reasonably large disaggregate choice models; and (b) an experimental approach based not on the ranking or rating of options but on a stated choice formulation in which individuals were asked to choose between combinations of attributes in particular contexts. This method allowed the estimation of similar discrete choice models applied in conjunction with RP data and hence the direct prediction of market share (Louviere and Hensher, 1982, 1983; Louviere and Woodworth, 1983; Hensher, 1994). In Hensher's words:

> The introduction of stated choice modelling using the set of established discrete choice modelling tools routinely applied with revealed preference data widened the interest in SP-methods. For the first time travel researchers could see the benefit of stated-preference data in enhancing their travel choice methods. This I would argue was *the* major watershed which after 10 years has resulted in widespread acceptance of SP methods in practice in transportation (Hensher, 1994, 108).

Jordan Louviere, David Hensher and Joffre Swait (2000) later wrote the standard text on stated choice methods.

In the UK the stated preference approach was given a considerable boost and a stamp of official approval in a major programme of research on the value of time which began in 1980. The official value attached to travel time savings had been subject to periodical updating, but there had been no fundamental reassessment since David Quarmby's work well over a decade earlier. As Mackie et al (2003) later reflected, one of the key reasons for considering the SP approach was that since 'the non-working time values were derived predominantly from commuting evidence in towns . . . it would be very difficult, and expensive, to find suitable locations where genuine choices could be "revealed" and the statistical data properties necessary for successful estimation of the value of travel time savings guaranteed' (Mackie et al, 2003, 3).

The adopted programme of studies involved SP and RP investigations in different mode and route choice contexts and was undertaken in the early 1980s by a consortium consisting of: the MVA Consultancy; the Institute for Transport Studies, University of Leeds; and the Transport Studies Unit, University of Oxford. Their final report was published as MVA et al (1987), with key findings presented in 1986 (Bates and Roberts, 1986; Bradley et al, 1986; Fowkes, 1986). Wardman (1988) suggested that this study played a major part in convincing the doubters of the merits of the stated preference approach, at least in the UK.

By the mid-1980s an increasing number of papers had begun to appear in conference proceedings and in international journals on the theory, practicalities and applications of the SP approach in transportation. A special issue of the *Journal of Transport Economics and Policy*, edited by John Bates (1988), contains several papers covering key findings, several different aspects of the design of experiments, their realism and the potential sources of bias in responses.

By the late 1980s the SP approach was being applied to a wide range of application areas in transportation, including:

> Evaluating passenger priorities for the various characteristics of public transport systems, with a special emphasis on qualitative factors (marketing audits); estimating demand elasticities for various service attributes, including fare, frequency and journey time; developing market share analysis and forecasts for transport operators and for managers of airports and coach termini; undertaking route choice studies (for example, for cars and bicycles); researching and developing new products for transport operators; conducting planning studies for government bodies (Kroes and Sheldon, 1988, 21).

While the importance of travel cost and time(s) in determining choices, and the value of time were often the focus of attention for their relevance both to forecasting and to evaluation, attributes such as comfort, convenience and reliability became more widely studied within this framework and their influence subject to detailed quantification. From the mid-1980s there was also a considerable expansion of applications of SP studies for determining the relative importance of attributes in determining choice in situations other than that of mode and route. These included a variety of destination choice and consumer preference studies relating to studies of the housing market and residential location and to destination choice for retail services.

These developments were not confined to personal travel. The approach also began to be applied in the freight sector to examine the valuation of the attributes influential in the mode choice of freight shippers. The SP approach was considered to be particularly suited to the study of freight demand because it avoided problems of commercial confidentiality (which would be present in an RP approach) and was an appropriate means of exploring the effects of new technologies in the industry (see Fowkes and Tweddle, 1988; Fowkes et al, 1991). Additionally, relevant markets were often dominated by a small number of firms or organisations, which made it both difficult to collect large quantities of RP data and possible to cover a large proportion of the market with an SP approach.

The rapid improvement of the processing power of portable PCs meant that face-to-face interviews could now be done efficiently and the combination of attributes associated with alternatives 'customised' to situations close to the respondents' current experience. In a further development, stated preference designs were established in which attribute combinations appearing later in an interview could be 'adapted' to responses recorded earlier (Bradley et al, 1987), although the potential for introducing bias in the results was later noted (Bradley and Daly, 1993).

Although there remained considerable scepticism among some

transportation analysts, by the end of the decade the SP approach and methodology were becoming established and an increasingly accepted part of the behavioural investigation of travel, transportation policy and project design. Careful design of the experiments was crucial to generate reliable results, and SP became quite a specialist task, for whose implementation key personnel and small consultancies arose.

5.6.3 Comparing and Combining the Results from RP and SP Approaches

With the proliferation of SP studies in the 1980s, a number of questions arose, some of which were long-standing and the result of widespread applications in market research. Were the RP and SP approaches measuring the same preferences? How did the results of SP compare with actual behaviour? How did the results derived from similarly specified models estimated from RP and SP data sets compare? How could the results derived from similar choice models, whose parameters were estimated from RP and SP data sets, be combined to exploit the benefits from and partly compensate for the deficiencies of each?

The validation of SP results against market observations and the results derived from similarly specified models estimated from RP data sets took two basic forms: (a) comparison of predicted choices and market shares with current observations; and (b) comparison between the (ratio of) parameters of linear compensatory models (Hensher, 1994). With regard to the latter, a direct comparison between the coefficients (e.g., of times and costs) themselves was not possible, because such coefficients were unique only up to a scale transformation. However, it was possible to make comparison between the ratios of coefficients, since the scale factor then cancelled out. Because of its wide relevance to forecasting and evaluation, in particular, the implied value-of-time comparisons derived from revealed and stated preferences were of particular interest (Louviere et al, 1980; Kocur et al, 1982; Bates and Roberts, 1986; Bates, 1988; Wardman, 1988, 1998).

While the comparison of the value of time obtained from RP and SP data sets gave some reassurance of the validity, or at least the acceptability, of the latter approach, towards the end of the 1980s we begin to see a further question being addressed: could RP and SP data sets be combined within a common discrete choice framework? Although discrete choice models such as the MNL model were applicable to both RP and SP data sets, the 'definition of the observed and unobserved influences on the choice outcome however varies' (Hensher, 1994, 120). It was not therefore possible simply to pool the different sources of data. Could, however, the utility scales be adjusted to reflect the differences with which choices were perceived and responses made in the two different contexts? That was the challenge which began to be addressed in the late 1980s. David Hensher commented:

> The mixing of sources of data however is not a matter of 'naïve' pooling. It requires careful consideration of the unit of the (indirect) utility scale. For example, the utility scale in an MNL model is inversely related to the variance of the unobserved influences, summarised as the random error term; hence the parameter estimates of two identical indirect utility specifications obtained from two data sources with different variances will necessarily differ in magnitude, even if the choice process that generated the indirect utilities is identical (Hensher, 1994, 113).

One solution to recognising and accommodating this variance difference, originally proposed by Morikawa (1989), was to 'scale the variance of the unobserved effects associated with the SP data so that the equality of variances across the RP and SP components of a pooled model is reinstated' (Hensher, 1994, 120–121). Different methods were proposed, based on sequential and simultaneous approaches for the estimation of the choice model parameters and the factor scaling the different variances (Ben-Akiva and Morikawa, 1990; Ben-Akiva et al, 1994; Swait et al, 1994; Daly and Rohr, 1998).

One approach, which proved to be popular in practice, was proposed by Bradley and Daly (1991). This accommodated the differential variance across the RP and SP data within a single empirical model by exploiting the NL framework as a means of identifying the rescaling parameter. They showed that this could be achieved with available NL model software by setting up an artificial tree structure with twice as many alternatives as there were in reality. Half of these were labelled SP alternatives and half RP alternatives. This method came to be known as the 'Nested Logit trick' (Louviere et al, 2000).

Although the stated preference method was seen as enjoying the distinct advantage of generating multiple observations from each individual, this advantage came with a potential downside – the possibility of correlation among the observations of each individual. This problem was usually ignored in practice and, if considered at all, correction factors were sought to address the possible upward bias in the t-ratios associated with the parameter estimates. The first attempt to correct the potential bias accompanying the latter issue was made by Louviere and Woodworth (1983). More recently, in the 1990s, it was addressed by re-sampling methods of statistical inference, such as the bootstrap and jackknife techniques (see Ortúzar and Willumsen, 2011). In section 5.7.4 we comment further on these and other issues relating to the combination of different data sources and the problem of correlation within a common discrete choice framework.

By the early 1990s the SP approach was becoming widely recognised as a powerful addition to the methodology of preference analysis. As Ampt et al remarked: 'In the 1990s when transport planners and policy makers want to know something about the probable effects of a change to the transport system, it is very likely that they would call for a stated preference study' (Ampt et al, 1995, 73). These views were partly the result of the versatility of the SP approach and some reassuring evidence coming from the comparing and combining of RP and SP results that were steadily accumulating.

5.6.4   A Note on the Design of Stated Preference Experiments

It is not our intention to discuss in detail the standard approaches to the design and application of stated preference experiments, specifically the systematic way in which researchers select attributes and their levels, identify alternative choices, and present such choices to the individual. Together with the determination of an appropriate sample size, this process is subject to the twin requirements that the parameters of the selected model can be estimated with the necessary precision, and the experiment is manageable for the respondents. Such topics receive comprehensive coverage in standard texts (e.g., Louviere et al, 2000, Chapters 4, 5; Hensher et al, 2005; Ortúzar and Willumsen, 2011, section 3.3.4, Chapter 8). However, we do wish to comment briefly on certain developments in the design and implementation of stated choice experiments.

Traditionally, so-called orthogonal designs, in which attribute combinations are varied independently of each other, were applied in order to eliminate correlation between attributes and the different choices, while minimising the variances (and covariances) of the parameter estimates. Because of the explosive number of combinations arising when the number of attribute levels is increased, in typical applications a fraction of the attribute combinations in the full set of choices is then used. The standard approach based on such fractional factorial designs is discussed in the above texts.

Since the late 1980s a number of researchers working in a transportation context, and elsewhere in market research, have begun to question the optimality of designs 'still most frequently based on assumptions rooted in standard linear regression theory' (Watson et al, 1996). Although orthogonal designs remain to this day the most widely used design type, there has been increasing interest in different notions of efficiency and optimality in non-orthogonal designs for estimating the parameters of non-linear models such as the MNL model.

Only relatively recently has a unified design theory been developed that allows the assumptions defining the different approaches for constructing SP experimental designs to be compared. Much of this research in the transportation field was undertaken at the University of Sydney. Excellent reviews and explanations of the different strategies of experimental design for stated choice experiments have been given by John Rose and Michiel Bliemer (2008, 2009, 2013), which contain several examples of transportation applications published since 2000; see also Street and Burgess (2007). This literature discusses the arguments for using 'optimal' or 'efficient' designs instead of orthogonal constructs for non-linear models.

5.7 FURTHER DEVELOPMENTS IN DISCRETE CHOICE ANALYSIS: A SHORT GUIDE TO THE TERRITORY

5.7.1 Overview of More Recent Developments

Theoretical and practical developments in the discrete choice random utility approach over the last 25 years have been extensive. Some see the 1990s as heralding a second golden age in view of the range of more flexible models available and the greater efficiency in their estimation. Many contributed to this development, which resulted in wide application of increasingly sophisticated econometric models in transportation and such fields as market research/consumer behaviour, health, energy and environmental economics. Travel-related choices were examined in ever greater depth, and the journey timing decision emerged as a major research area for its relevance to current policy impact (e.g., time-dependent pricing) and appraisal studies (e.g., Ben-Akiva and Bierlaire, 1999; Small, 2012). From this wide array of subject matter, we have selected a few topics for further discussion on the basis of their theoretical and technical importance and topicality in research studies. While many advances have yet to find routine application in applied travel forecasting, they are essential ingredients in many research papers, and relevant to the assessment of widely applied models and methods.

Although many of these advances are mired in technical details their motivation is straightforward enough and, within any new development, one or more of the following can be detected:

1. incorporation of a wider range of attributes influential in choice between discrete alternatives;

2. derivation of willingness-to-pay (WTP) measures accompanying a range of economic and environmental factors;
3. relaxation of some of the restrictions on existing models in order to provide more general and flexible demand model structures;
4. establishment of closer links between economic and psychological aspects of choice processes;
5. search for efficiencies in the numerical solution of models and parameter estimation.

Within most of the following, there is often a trade-off to be made between the greater generality and conceptual appeal of certain theoretical and methodological advances, on the one hand, and their practical implications – the complexity, interpretation and computational challenges – involved in model implementation, on the other. This tension often proves to be context- or application-dependent and makes the practical decisions involving the application of advanced models or methods a non-trivial one, a feature usually emphasised by researchers. For this reason such developments are often seen as 'add-ons' to, rather than substitutes for, discrete choice analysis based on well-tried methods or models. In applied research the MNL or NL models are therefore widely used as the first line of attack in any proposal to investigate and apply generalisations.

5.7.2 Responses to and Willingness to Pay for Changes in Attributes

For the application of cost–benefit analysis, there has long been an interest in deriving money values attached to changes in a range of environmental and economic factors based on willingness to pay, and specifically where impacts involve changes in congestion, safety, noise, pollution, visual intrusion and amenity. Over the last two decades there has been an upsurge in their estimation from discrete choice models, particularly since stated preference methods became an accepted and widely adopted method for collecting data and analysing preferences. See McFadden (1997) and Ortúzar and Willumsen (2011) for discussions of basic theoretical issues.

In suitably designed SP experiments, individuals are invited to make choices between bundles of attributes, often including travel time and other journey and environmental attributes, in route, mode, residential choice and journey timing situations (e.g., Bennett and Blamey, 2001; Ortúzar and Rizzi, 2007; Ortúzar and Willumsen, 2011). Often such responses have been compared or combined with results derived from revealed preference data sets.

The valuation of travel time (VoT) savings still holds a special affection among travel forecasters and transportation economists not only for its own intrinsic interest and relevance for understanding travel behaviour and the appraisal (*ex ante* evaluation) of schemes, but also because it often acts as a 'gold standard' against which the willingness to pay for changes in other attributes is assessed. Over the last 25 years there have been concerted attempts to apply increasingly sophisticated techniques to measure heterogeneity in the VoT both between and within segments of different urban and inter-urban travel markets (e.g., Ben-Akiva et al, 1993; Mackie et al, 2003; Hess et al, 2005; Small et al, 2005; Fosgerau, 2006; Small, 2012).

A major area for research in recent years has been on the effect of uncertainty arising from the variability in travel time on choices of both mode and trip timing in order to establish responses to and willingness to pay for changes in journey time reliability, as an expression of this uncertainty. Such efforts have generally employed models of scheduling choice that incorporate departure time changes in response to the expected costs accompanying the variability in travel time. The work of Kenneth Small over many years has been very influential in the development of such models; see, in particular, Small (1982), Noland and Small (1995), Brownstone and Small (2005) and Small et al (2005). In the context of the travel timing decisions of the commuting journey, Small (1982, 471) introduced the concept of schedule delay (SD) as the 'difference between the chosen time of arrival . . . and the official work start time'. As he remarked:

> schedule delay is an attribute of a given scheduling choice *s* which measures the deviation inherent in that choice between actual and 'standard' arrival time. Arriving early (SD < 0) is likely to involve some time wasted, or at least less productively used, and thereby decreases utility. Arriving late (SD > 0) has, for most workers, more severe repercussions. It is the tradeoff between scheduling considerations, as represented by the variable *SD*, and travel time *t* which is crucial for studying the impact of scheduling behavior on congestion (Small, 1982, 471).

To reflect the variability in travel time and the uncertainty that it engenders, individuals are assumed to select that option which maximises expected utility, a function that incorporates, along with travel time, some measures of schedule delay accompanying both early and late arrival at the destination. In the case of public transport systems, the analysis is adapted to accommodate fixed timetables (e.g., UK DfT, 2009b).

In addition to the references cited above, we refer the interested reader to several excellent commentaries, reviews of the theoretical frameworks, and meta-studies of the empirical evidence relating to reliability.[18] Small

(2012) has offered a fine overview of what is known and not known in relation to the value of time and the value of reliability.

5.7.3   Developments in Closed Form RUM Models within the GEV Family

Since its inception in 1978, the nature and properties of the GEV family of choice models (McFadden, 1978) have been subjected to forensic scrutiny by researchers in and well beyond the transportation field. The GEV family comprises a veritable treasure chest awaiting useful models to be identified from particular patterns of similarity (correlation between the utility residuals of the alternatives) and credible behavioural hypotheses. However, the number of practical structures, beyond the NL model, that have emerged has been rather small and slow in coming. This result has been attributed both to the difficulty of establishing the means by which practical models should be constructed and shown to meet specific requirements of the GEV family, and to the availability of suitable software to estimate the resultant models.

While the NL model allows patterns of similarity and 'differential cross-substitution' between alternatives, these are subject to the restriction that alternative choices belong to no more than one nest. Catering for more complex patterns of similarity in realistic choice situations, in which one or more alternatives have features similar to those of alternatives in different subsets, was one of the principal motivations for identifying further practical GEV models, along with the attraction of dealing with closed form expressions. As Daly and Bierlaire (2006, 287) remarked, 'some suggestions for cross-nesting in GEV models are implicit in McFadden (1978, 1981)'.

By the time of the review of closed form models by Koppelman and Sethi (2000) a wide range of structures had been proposed, some from the GEV family, which differed in the nature of similarities among alternatives and the ease of practical implementation (e.g., Small, 1987; Vovsha, 1997; Koppelman and Wen, 2000; Wen and Koppelman, 2001). These included generalisations of the MNL and NL structures, and what was termed the cross-nested logit (CNL) model identified and applied by Vovsha (1997).

The practical motivation for Peter Vovsha's research was the examination of choice between the various modes in typical urban transportation systems (here, the application was of modal choice in Tel Aviv, Israel), including car, public transport (bus, suburban rail, light rail and subway), and various combinations in mixed mode possibilities. In the presence of the latter the NL model was found to have limitations as an analysis tool. The CNL model, which took into account the cross-similarities between different pure and combined modes, was shown by Vovsha to be a member of the GEV family. The properties of the model have been studied in some detail by Bierlaire (2006).

Further developments allowed the generalisation of existing models and provided the basis for identifying other practical choice model structures consistent with the conditions required by the GEV family. These included the recursive nested extreme value (RNEV) model of Andrew Daly (2001), which is a generalisation of the CNL model, based on a 'multiple layering' of nests. The network-GEV model formulation of Daly and Bierlaire (2006), entirely equivalent to the RNEV model, provides the theoretical basis and intuitive method for formulating GEV models, which they argue captures the potentially complex forms of correlation to be found in practice. The network representation, introduced by Michel Bierlaire (2002), allowed 'an easy way of generating new GEV models without the need of complicated proofs'. The technique 'requires only a network structure capturing the underlying correlation of the choice situation under consideration. If the network complies with some simple conditions, we show how to build an associated model' (Daly and Bierlaire, 2006, 285).

In McFadden (1978, 1981), we saw how probabilistic choice models of GEV form could be derived from the expected maximum utility (*EMU*) achieved in the choice process through the mathematical process of differentiation. The *EMU* may be seen as a choice probability generating function for the model. In recent theoretical work, Fosgerau et al (2013) returned to the central problem of determining the necessary and sufficient conditions that need to be satisfied for a probabilistic choice model to be consistent with RUM. They showed for additive random utility models that 'a multinomial choice probability vector is consistent with RUM if and only if it is the gradient of a choice probability generating function . . . with specified properties that can be checked in applications' (Fosgerau et al, 2013, 2).

The conditions required for the generation of models in this way are described in detail. As a special case they consider random utility models based on multivariate extreme value distributions, and review existing methods and propose extensions for constructing generating functions for applications. Further, they show that the choice probabilities for any additive random utility model may be approximated by a cross-nested logit model.

5.7.4 Developments in Open Form Models: the MMNL Model

While the search over the last two decades for further closed form travel choice models based on the GEV framework has been productive and is ongoing, research devoted to this approach has been surpassed by the interest in numerical solution procedures to derive more general and flexible choice models.

Relaxation of the assumptions underpinning the derivation of the MNL model, and in particular the identical and independent (IID) assumptions associated with the distributions of random residuals, was one focus of attention. Chandra Bhat (1995) formulated the heteroscedastic extreme value (HEV) model, in which the error terms for the alternatives are of Gumbel form with variances that are allowed to be different across all alternatives. The resultant model requires only a one-dimensional integration for its solution.

In his book on simulation approaches to choice modelling, in our view outstanding in its clarity and pedagogic value, Kenneth Train (2009, 1–2), writing in the early 2000s, described the progress in the way researchers 'think about, specify and estimate their models' as a quantum leap, freeing up researchers to examine more realistic and varied choice situations. Most of the development in numerical approaches was associated with different representations of the mixed multinomial logit (MMNL) model, the provenance of which has been discussed by several authors (McFadden and Train, 2000; Train, 2009; Ortúzar and Willumsen, 2011). There appears to be agreement that its origins may be found in results on random parameters models in the late 1970s (Cardell and Reddy, 1977; Boyd and Mellman, 1980; Cardell and Dunbar, 1980). Its more recent theoretical expression and investigation in different forms date from the early 1990s, and can be attributed to Ben-Akiva et al (1993), Ben-Akiva and Bolduc (1996), Bhat (1998), Brownstone and Train (1998), Train (1998), McFadden and Train (2000) and Ben-Akiva et al (2001). Exploration and development of the model continue.

At the heart of the MMNL family of models is the specification of a random utility function for an alternative which, for the purpose of exposition here, we shall write in 'error components' form (Ben-Akiva and Bolduc, 1996; Brownstone and Train, 1998; Train, 2009), as the sum of a representative value, dependent on measured attributes, and two random components, the first of which we denote RC and the second, a Gumbel distributed error term:

$$\text{Utility} = \text{Representative Value} + \text{Random Component, } RC$$
$$+ \text{Gumbel Error Term}$$

In the usual way, the probability of choosing a given alternative according to the maximum utility criterion involves integration over distributions of relevant variables or parameters.

The detailed form and interpretation of the model is determined by the source and nature of the stochastic variation. The identical and independently distributed Gumbel term over the different alternatives would, in the absence of the first random component, *RC*, result in MNL choice probabilities, which thereby provides the touchstone for any embellishment of the model arising from a non-zero random term, *RC*. The analyst selects and interprets the structure of the distribution *RC* to reflect the variation of the underlying preferences thought to represent the problem at hand. Through suitable selection of the random error terms over individuals, alternatives and responses, different features may be represented which successively relax the restrictive assumptions underpinning the MNL model. In particular, the MMNL model can accommodate the following:

1. distributions of tastes over the population;
2. correlation among utility residuals for different alternatives (thereby introducing different patterns of similarity and cross-substitution among alternatives);
3. correlation among different observations for the same individual in SP experiments;
4. correlation among utilities over time (when panel data are used).

Good discussions of these various contexts of application may be found in Bhat (2000, 2007), UK DfT (2006e) and Ortúzar and Willumsen (2011).

The 'error components' expression for the MMNL model may be readily transformed to the entirely equivalent random parameters logit (RPL) or logit kernel form. The latter designation is sometimes reserved for the case in which the *RC* term is normally distributed with a general covariance structure, in which case 'logit kernel is a discrete choice model that has both probit like disturbances as well as iid Gumbel variation a la MNL. The result is an intuitive, practical and powerful model that combines the flexibility of probit with the tractability of logit' (Ben-Akiva et al, 2001, 1).

In random parameter forms the MMNL model is expressed in terms of an MNL model in which the parameters of the representative utilities are considered to vary over the population with a distribution, referred to as the mixing density function or simply the mixing distribution, which accounts for the model's name.[19] It can be shown that, by judicious choice of the mixing distribution, in all practical cases 'any discrete choice model derived from random utility maximisation has choice probabilities that can be approximated as closely as one pleases by a MMNL model' (McFadden and Train, 2000, 447). In that regard there has been much interest and numerical experimentation to examine the extent and practicality of using the MMNL model to approximate the results of multinomial probit (MNP) specifications (see Ben-Akiva and Bolduc, 1996; Ben-Akiva et al, 1997; and Munizaga and Alvarez-Daziano, 2005).

Different forms for the mixing distribution have been used in practical studies for describing the variation of the taste parameters in the representative utility function in the embedded MNL model, and the results derived from the model are reportedly quite sensitive to this selection (Fosgerau and Bierlaire, 2007). Normal, log normal, triangular and discrete distributions have been found to be popular forms, the parameters of which become part of the set to be estimated (McFadden and Train, 2000; Greene and Hensher, 2003; Hensher and Greene, 2003; Train, 2009).

As noted above, the selection of a particular form for the MMNL model, in error components or random parameters logit form, is motivated by the heterogeneity in the above utility function that it is intended to capture. The random parameters model form is particularly suited to the analysis of taste variation within the choice making population. By the supplying of a covariance matrix of the distributed parameters, the propensity for the observations of any particular individual to be correlated can be accommodated and examined (Revelt and Train, 1998). The error components form is suited to modelling the patterns of similarity among the choice alternatives, including 'cross-nested' patterns of correlation. Because it allows the variance of the utility to vary with different responses it can also be further exploited for the merging and mixing of RP and SP data sets (see Bhat and Castelar, 2002; UK DfT, 2006e; Hensher et al, 2008).

Practical estimation of the model is usually carried out by the 'maximum simulated likelihood' (MSL) method. By the late 1990s computational power was so much greater than in the 1970s that approaches to the numerical integration of discrete choice models could be made with more impunity. However, the estimation of the MMNL model by simulation still remained a considerable numerical challenge, and much experimentation has been performed on the selection of number sequences for the efficient solution of the model. At the time of writing, quasi-Monte Carlo-based (QMC) methods (Bhat, 2001, 2003; Train, 2009) are becoming increasingly widely used for estimating mixed logit and other open form choice models. A further contribution by Bhat (2011) is the maximum approximate composite marginal likelihood (MACML) approach, which is reported to be much more computationally efficient in its estimation of multinomial probit choice models than the simulation-based (MSL-based) QMC approach.

While the MMNL model allows different approaches to be integrated within the same conceptual framework, its practical adoption is advocated only for 'trained analysts' (UK DfT, 2006e) and for its adoption to be undertaken in conjunction with standard methods and models, such as the MNL and NL forms.[20] Although this class of models has been explored for nearly two decades, exponents of the MMNL model tend to assert that this is only the beginning, and conference proceedings devoted to discrete choice analysis attest to its wide interest for research applications (Hess and Daly, 2013).

Perhaps too, after this period of intensive research and application, as more has become known of its strengths so too are its potential weaknesses appearing in the form of: identification problems (specification of the model with an appropriate number of parameters which can be determined) (Walker, 2002; Chiou and Walker, 2007); the possibility of confusion over the effects represented and interpretational problems arising in estimated models; and the possibility of obtaining very similar fits but radically different response predictions with small changes in specification. In the absence of data of sufficient quality the very flexibility of the mixed logit model may also prove its Achilles heel. For a discussion of these wide-ranging issues see Walker (2002), Cherchi and Ortúzar (2008, 2010) and Ortúzar and Willumsen (2011).

5.7.5　Hybrid Choice Models: Discrete Choice Models with Latent Constructs

Over the last 15 or so years there have been many embellishments to the error structures and the representative components of the utility functions for discrete choice analysis and, for practical settings, there is some debate as to where the main research effort should lie in refining these different components. One of the most significant developments has been the introduction of the hybrid choice (HC) framework, which 'integrates many types of discrete choice modeling methods, draws on different types of data, and allows for flexible disturbances and explicit modeling of latent psychological explanatory variables, heterogeneity and latent segmentation' (Ben-Akiva et al, 2002a, 164).

The marriage of discrete choice models with what are referred to as 'latent variable models' has arisen in response to two rather distinct developments: firstly, the need, expressed increasingly since the early 1980s (Koppelman and Hauser, 1979; McFadden, 1986, 2000b; Ben-Akiva et al, 1997, 1999, 2002b, 2012; Walker, 2001; Walker and Ben-Akiva, 2002) to forge a closer relationship between economic and psychological representations and provide an insight into the deeper motivation for the process underpinning travel-related decisions; and, secondly, the advances, witnessed throughout the social sciences since the 1980s, of more general statistical models which incorporate latent variables, variables that cannot be measured directly but can be inferred from relationships with other observable and measurable variables.[21]

After the ascendancy in the 1970s of the micro-economic representation of travel demand cast within a discrete choice RUM framework, the concern given in practical modelling to the cognitive process and such factors as attitudes, perceptions and personality traits was limited until the 1990s. To some extent this occurred because the primary motivation for developing economic models was often to produce predictive models by emphasising 'the systematic, invariant features of choice behaviour that can be used for forecasting' (Ben-Akiva et al, 2002a, 164), while the prime concern from a psychological perspective was the deeper understanding of the cognitive process underpinning behaviour and decisions, rather than forecasting.

It is beyond the scope of the present review to discuss the detailed differences between the psychological and economic perspectives on the choice process (Ben-Akiva et al, 1999, 2002a, 2002b, 2012; McFadden, 2000b; Cherchi, 2012). Some of this discussion has focused on the nature and limits of rationality, and we shall say more about this in Chapters 6 and 11. One way in which the different perspectives on travel and related choice processes were (partly) bridged was introducing psychometric factors through latent variables (McFadden, 1986, 2000b; Morikawa and Sasaki, 1998; Walker, 2001; Walker and Ben-Akiva, 2002; Raveau et al, 2010; Bhat and Dubey, 2013). The core motivation for such developments was the conviction that 'the incorporation of psychological factors leads to a more behaviourally realistic representation of the choice process, and consequently better explanatory power' (Ben-Akiva et al, 2002b). Latent class models, obtained when (some of) the variables are categorical, have been used to identify segments of the market which exhibit similar taste parameters, choice sets, or means by which decisions are made (Ben-Akiva et al, 1997, 2002b; Greene and Hensher, 2003).

The means of embedding latent variables into discrete choice models comprises two steps:

1. specification of the latent variables in terms of objective variables;
2. specification of the discrete choice model in terms of measured and latent variables.

There is now a sizeable literature on the estimation of this integrated process: (a) in terms of the sequential and simultaneous estimation of these relations; and (b) in relation to the estimator itself (e.g., classical maximum likelihood, Bayesian). In the sequential estimation of the model, the latent variables are first estimated and then incorporated along with the contribution of other measured variables into the choice model. With modern software it is also possible to perform the simultaneous estimation in which the two processes are combined. For a technical discussion of choice models incorporating latent variables, alternative methods for their estimation and several examples from the transportation field, interested readers are referred to Ben-Akiva et al (1999, 2002a, 2002b), Walker (2001), Bolduc and Alvarez-Daziano (2010), Ortúzar and Willumsen (2011, 288–291), Cherchi (2012) and Bhat and Dubey (2013).

Progress in this field has been frequently reviewed and research agendas offered in multi-author contributions to *Marketing Letters* (Ben-Akiva et al, 1997, 1999, 2002a, 2012; de Palma et al, 2008), and we shall have more to say about extensions to standard models of discrete choice in section 11.3.

5.8 CONCLUSION

Within the period from 1970 to the mid-1980s, the discrete choice approach based on random utility maximisation made a profound contribution to the quantitative study of traveller behaviour. It brought to fruition the earlier promise of a theoretically coherent and practically viable approach to travel forecasting that addressed some of the shortcomings of the traditional four-step approach, and was beginning to cater for the transportation planning information requirements of the time.

In the early 1970s the MNL model became the mainstay of practical analysis. The model was applied to an ever wider range of contexts with revealed preference (RP) data sets and, increasingly, using approaches based on stated preference (SP) information. By the end of the period, the nested or hierarchical logit model was serving in applications and research studies as a practical compromise between generality of structure and computational ease (Sobel, 1980; Train, 1980; Hensher and Johnson, 1981; Ortúzar, 1983; Ben-Akiva and Lerman, 1985). The NL model addressed a large range of problems involving similarity among subsets of alternatives, including multi-modal applications and those derived from more complex choice processes. A rigorous theory of model structure based on rational choice behaviour had emerged, and the selection between alternative hierarchical structures could now be subject to empirical test in which different orderings would be screened for consistency with theoretical requirements. The analytic and theoretical characteristics and practical implementation of the NL model have now been extensively studied (e.g., Daly, 1987; Carrasco and Ortúzar, 2002; Koppelman and Bhat, 2006; Ortúzar and Willumsen, 2011, 240–248).

After the initial major funded programmes of the 1970s in the US were completed, progress in the research and development of the micro-behavioural approach based on discrete choice theory was mixed. In the US several of the early researchers moved to modelling in the energy, telecommunications, health care and environment sectors (McFadden, 2000b). But the seeds had been sown, and the basic approach was becoming more widely applied in practical planning applications, particularly in the US, Canada, Europe and Australia, but still mostly confined to modal choice problems. As we have seen, the template for serving the traditional requirements of transportation planning agencies was established, and the experience in the San Francisco Bay Area with the MTC model, and developments in Europe, particularly the Netherlands, provided 'a clear demonstration that disaggregate models could be applied for the various requirements of mainline work' (HCG, 1985). Several advantages over traditional methods were claimed, with improved behavioural sophistication, issues of transferability, policy sensitivity, data efficiency and cost savings emphasised throughout.

The approach provided the basis for reinterpreting a wide range of spatial interaction models, which somewhat earlier had been addressed within the entropy maximisation and constrained optimisation frameworks. We begin to see the random utility approach applied to destination choice, in MNL or NL form at the individual level, or at the zonal level, adopted as the preferred theoretical means for addressing location and travel behaviour modelling. Destination choice models were embedded within equilibrium and quasi-dynamic models of urban housing, labour and land markets, where prices were adjusted to bring about market clearing in the short or longer term. These advances led to a unification of 'the currently separate but logically connected sub-disciplines of urban economics, transportation planning and urban modeling' (Anas, 1982, xi). Integrated land use and transportation models were formulated or reformulated with a random utility discrete choice basis (Coelho and Williams, 1978; Williams and Senior, 1978; Wilson et al, 1981; Anas, 1982, 1983, 1984; Mattsson, 1987; de la Barra, 1989; Martinez, 1992). We shall meet their practical development and application in Chapters 8 and 9. Applications of the theoretical framework to normative studies of land use (Wilson et al, 1981) and location of public services (Leonardi and Tadei, 1984) were also developed in the early 1980s. Discrete choice theory also served as a framework for the discussion of product diversity and consumer choice in economic markets (Anderson et al, 1992).

What implications did these developments have for the traditional methods of travel forecasting founded on an aggregate (zone-based) multi-stage approach? Ironically, the new disaggregate behavioural approach, which was meant to produce a clear alternative to the traditional methodology, served in a sense to bring them closer together. With the conceptual limitations of the MNL model much more evident, and the formulation of the NL generalisation, the theoretical differences emphasised at the start of the 1970s were to some extend reduced. By reformulation and reinterpretation of the demand function in terms of the NL model, the multi-stage approach was reinvented in behavioural clothes applied at aggregate level. But this came with unexpected consequences. The necessary validation checks revealed that, in the frequently applied **G/D/M/A** structure, with typical market stratification, the parameter values might well be inconsistent with the 'post-distribution modal split' form selected, yielding the possibility of perverse travel forecasts when subject to policy tests. 'Goodness-of-fit' was an insufficient basis for assessing the validity of a model; it was necessary also to check the response properties of models to ensure that their implied elasticities were of the correct sign, a topic to which we return in Chapters 9 and 11.

In the broader historical context there was a further irony here. With regard to the ordering of steps within the overall models, was opinion in the field about to come full circle? We noted in Chapter 3 that in the early 1960s the modal split model was placed 'above' the distribution model in the organisation of the stages. Then, in the mid-1960s, in order to achieve a more sensitive modal response to changes in the level-of-service variables (accompanying the introduction of improved transit systems), the modal split model was moved from above to below the distribution stage. Would it now be appropriate to move it back to a **G/M/D/A** form precisely because the modal response relative to the destination response was less than had been thought? We delay further discussion of this issue until Chapters 8 and 9, where we consider more recent research and current practice in both the US and the UK.

In the early to mid-1970s details of the new micro-behavioural approach to travel forecasting were largely confined to specialised articles in the academic literature and to the books by Domencich and McFadden (1975) and Richards and Ben-Akiva (1975), and texts by Hutchinson (1974) and Stopher and Meyburg (1975). A decade later, additional specialist texts on the econometrics of discrete choice applied to problems in transportation, housing and urban systems had appeared (e.g., Hensher and Johnson, 1981; Anas, 1982; Ben-Akiva and Lerman, 1985; Train, 1986; Börsch-Supan, 1987), and several conferences were held at which papers on discrete choice models were well represented (Stopher and Meyburg, 1976; Hensher and Stopher, 1979; Stopher et al, 1981). The virtues of the new approach to forecasting were becoming more widely proclaimed.

If the disaggregate behavioural approach based on discrete choice random utility theory had all the advantages claimed, then why did it not make a greater and more rapid impression on transportation planning practice? Ominously, the new theoretical and application issues were not well understood by practitioners and, in retrospect, a divide was opening up between the 'cognoscenti' in university departments and research consultancies on the one hand and many transportation planning professionals on the other. Indeed, Hartgen (1983) expressed the view:

> Although newer methods offer significant advantages over conventional methods, criticism of newer methods is widespread. Most practitioners view them as excessively mathematical and/or theoretical, cumbersome and jargon-bound, poorly packaged and disseminated, difficult to understand in lay terms, of uncertain precision and accuracy, and of questionable relevance to the practicing profession. Few real-world tests have been made of the value of many procedures, and thus their increasing usefulness over existing or more traditional techniques is not clear (Hartgen, 1983, 3).

From this period we continue to see the parallel development and application of the approaches based on disaggregate behavioural models and traditional aggregate travel forecasting styles, cast in multi-stage forms that were either in or began to resemble the NL structures.

The theoretical micro-behavioural approach based on discrete choice random utility theory was itself not without criticism. With regard to the advances attributed to it in this period, there was yet a further irony. The behavioural basis of the travel forecasting models, and the set of assumptions that they embodied, generally regarded a virtue in relation to the 'non-behavioural' traditional style, made the econometric approach itself vulnerable to attack from more realistic and intricate models of individual and household behaviour. These will be the subject of our next chapter. We shall comment further in Chapter 11 on the more recent developments of the discrete choice utility approach, considered in section 5.7.

NOTES

1. For example, in Wilson's paper, the composite cost over modal alternatives c_n was expressed in the form:

    $$\exp(-\lambda c_n) = \sum_{k \in H(n)} \exp(-\lambda c_k)$$

    where the summation is over all modes k available to households $H(n)$ of type n. This is equivalent to:

    $$c_n = -\frac{1}{\lambda} \ln \sum_{k \in H(n)} \exp(-\lambda c_k).$$

As we noted in Chapter 3, for the implementation of the 'logsum' in the hierarchical SELNEC model (Wilson et al, 1969), the parameter of the distribution model λ_D rather than λ_M was used.

2. The resolution of the IIA problem by forming a choice hierarchy and selecting the 'best' option at the lower choice level, as expressed by the mean of the distribution of maximum utilities (or distribution of minimum costs), is apparent in the work of Cochrane (1975), as described in section 4.5, and Domencich and McFadden (1975).

3. Consider a choice process involving N alternatives in which the random utilities $U_j, j = 1 \ldots N$ are distributed according to IID functions $f(U_j, V_j), j = 1 \ldots N$. We shall refer to these as the distributions of 'offered' utilities. The distribution of the utility U_j for alternative A_j, conditional on the option A_j being selected $g_j(U_j, X_j)$, is referred to as the distribution of 'achieved' or 'received' utility. From this definition, and the behaviour of utility maximising individuals:

$g_j(U_j, X_j) = f(U_j, V_j) \times$ Probability that the utilities of all other alternatives are $\leq U_j$

4. For IID 'offered' utility distributions $f(U_j, V_j), j = 1 \ldots N$, of Gumbel form, the distributions of achieved utilities $g_j(U_j, X_j), j = 1 \ldots N$ are also *all* of similar Gumbel form, with common standard deviation σ, and $X_1 \ldots X_N$ all equal to V^*. It may be shown that:

$g_j(U_j, X_j) = P_j \times f(U_j, V^*), j = 1 \ldots N,$

in which $V^* =$ logsum + constant). The area under the achieved distribution $g_j(U_j, X_j)$ is equal to the probability of choice, P_j. It would be some years before the significance of this 'self-replicating' property of the Gumbel distribution was recognised in the literature (Strauss, 1979; Robertson and Strauss, 1981; Anas and Feng, 1988; Johnston, 1988). The authors are grateful to Lars-Göran Mattsson for pointing us to the relevant literature. For further discussions of invariance conditions for more general random utility models, see Lindberg et al (1995) and Mattsson et al (2014).

5. For example, in the notation adopted in the text, the utility function has the following form:

$U(d, m) = U_d + U_m + U_{dm} = V_d + V_m + V_{dm} + \varepsilon_d + \varepsilon_m + \varepsilon_{dm}$

in which, for example, V_d varies over destinations but not modes, V_m varies over modes but not destinations, and V_{dm} varies over both (see Williams 1977a, 319, for further details).

6. As was UK practice at the time, generalised costs were formed from standardised value-of-time parameters, and the λ parameters and any modal penalties were estimated by maximum likelihood.

7. An increase (decrease) in generalised cost of a travel-related alternative would decrease (increase) the demand for a substitute.

8. We have changed the designation of the parameters β and λ in the original quote to allow consistency with the convention selected in this chapter, that is: $\beta \Rightarrow \lambda_D, \lambda \Rightarrow \lambda_M$

9. Because of a relatively coarse socio-economic segmentation and aggregation problems in a zone-based system, Williams and Senior (1977, 466–468) were very doubtful that the estimated λ values in the MNL-type distribution and modal split models would adequately represent response parameters. They proposed various reasons for bias and the perverse results, and considered the possibility of distinguishing between, or decoupling, the 'dispersion' characteristics from the 'response' properties of the model. In order to implement this they adopted an incremental formulation in which the 'dispersion' and 'response' characteristics were represented by separate parameters. They then conducted a sensitivity analysis on the response parameters consistent with the required inequality for the G/D/M/A structure.

10. We are grateful to Andrew Daly for discussion on the originators of these conditions.

11. The paper was actually presented, as well as discussed, by Tony Smith, University of Pennsylvania.

12. The function $F(\varepsilon_1. \ldots \varepsilon_N) = \exp(-G(\exp(-\varepsilon_1). \ldots \ldots \exp(-\varepsilon_N)))$ is a multivariate extreme value distribution when the function G satisfies the conditions in note 13; see McFadden (1978, 80–81).

13. We take the following notation and presentation from Train (2009). Writing $G = G(y_1. \ldots y_j. \ldots y_N)$, in which $y_j = \exp(V_j)$, McFadden (1978) established that, if G satisfies the following conditions:

   (1) $G \geq 0$ for all positive values of y_j for $j = 1 \ldots N$
   (2) G is homogeneous function of degree 1 (later generalised by Ben-Akiva and Francois)
   (3) $G \to \infty$ as $y_j \to \infty$ for any alternative j
   (4) The cross-partial derivatives change sign in the following manner:

   $$G_i = \frac{\partial G}{\partial y_i} \geq 0 \text{ for all } i; \; G_{ij} = \frac{\partial G_i}{\partial y_j} \leq 0 \text{ for all } j \neq i; \; G_{ijk} = \frac{\partial G_{ij}}{\partial y_k} \geq 0$$

   for all distinct i, j, k and so on for higher order cross-partial derivatives, then:

   $$P_j = \frac{y_j G_j}{G}$$

   defines a choice model consistent with utility maximisation.

14. McFadden (1978) showed that the G function:

   $$G(y_1 \ldots y_j \ldots y_N) = \sum_{j=1 \ldots N} y_j$$

   yields the MNL model. By partitioning the alternatives $j = 1 \ldots N$ into K nests, labelled $B_1 \ldots B_k \ldots B_K$ and introducing the coefficients a_k and parameters σ_k, $k = 1 \ldots K$, the function given by:

   $$G(y_1 \ldots y_j \ldots y_N) = \sum_{k=1 \ldots K} a_k \left(\sum_{j \in B_k} y_j^{\frac{1}{1-\sigma_k}} \right)^{1-\sigma_k} \text{ with } a_k > 0, 0 \leq \sigma_k < 1, k = 1 \ldots K$$

   may be shown to satisfy the conditions required for the model to be consistent with RUM, and the nested logit model can be shown to be a special case of the above (McFadden, 1978, 83 et seq.). This form can be further generalised to represent nesting to a number of levels to yield a broader class of functions (McFadden, 1981, 226 et seq.).

15. For members of the GEV family resulting from the generating function G, the expected value of the distribution of maximum utility, *EMU*, is given:

   $$EMU(V_1 \ldots V_j \ldots V_N) = \log_e G(\exp(V_1), \ldots \exp(V_j), \ldots \exp(V_N)) + \gamma$$

   where Euler's constant, $\gamma = 0.577$. In terms of the *EMU*, the probabilities of choice are given by:

   $$P_j = \frac{\partial EMU}{\partial V_j}, \; j = 1 \ldots N.$$

16. A full discussion of the MNP model, its estimation and its application can be found in Daganzo (1979).

17. We are grateful for useful discussion with John Rose in November 2013.

18. Further details may be found in the following papers and reports: Bates et al (2001), Noland and Polak (2002), de Jong et al (2004), Batley (2007), UK DfT (2009b), Fosgerau and Karlstrom (2010), Li et al (2010) and Carrion and Levinson (2012).

19. The MMNL model may be considered to be made up from a combination of MNL

models in which the vectors of parameters θ in the utility function $V_j(\theta)$ are distributed over the population with a 'mixing' density function $m(\theta)$. Writing:

$$MNL_{jq}(\theta) = \frac{\exp(V_{jq}(\theta))}{\sum_i \exp(V_{iq}(\theta))}$$

the MMNL choice probabilities become:

$$P_{jq} = \int MNL_{jq}(\theta)m(\theta)d(\theta).$$

20. For further discussion of the theoretical and practical applications, see de Jong et al (2003), Hensher and Greene (2003) and Hess et al (2005, 2007), and the texts by Train (2009) and Ortúzar and Willumsen (2011).

21. In travel behaviour research, there are many influential factors that do not have an obvious measurement scale or are intrinsically subjective (for an overview, see Ortúzar and Willumsen, 2011, 265–266). Because of the prominence of qualitative variables, such as comfort, convenience, reliability, safety, security or environmental quality associated with alternatives, as well as the importance of attitudes, opinions and the perceptions of individuals in a variety of travel choice situations, it is not surprising that such latent constructs have impacted this area of research and discrete choice modelling.

6. Activity-based travel analysis and forecasting

6.1 INTRODUCTION

6.1.1 The Micro-Economic Approach to Travel Forecasting under Fire

By the early 1980s the potential of discrete choice travel forecasting models based on random utility theory was increasingly widely recognised and had achieved considerable support within the academic community. The move towards explicit behavioural foundations at the micro-level was seen by many to represent significant progress. The achievements noted in Chapters 4 and 5 appeared to be capable of addressing the problems of the past, as well as contemporary requirements. Here was a set of models consistent with economic theory which offered the language and authority of that tradition. The discrete choice random utility framework provided a 'first principles' approach to the construction of travel forecasting models as well as providing the basis for reinterpreting and refining the forecasting structures of old. The acceptance among practitioners was limited, however; where applied, the 'disaggregate behavioural' approach, with a few honourable exceptions noted in Chapters 4 and 5, was still confined to the study of policies and planning contexts for which modal switching was considered the sole or dominant behavioural response.

While there was some acknowledgement that improvements had been made over the traditional four-stage approach, the micro-econometric approach based on discrete choices did not command universal appeal. The idea of an autonomous, highly discriminating individual, endowed with perfect (or, more realistically, very good) information on simple trip alternatives and attributes, and considered to make travel-related decisions on the basis of trading off a few attributes (typically including time and cost components) to maximise satisfaction, was to a number of critics an unpromising starting point for the causal analysis of travel and behavioural response to policies.

In an analysis of the theoretical basis for both the traditional methods and contemporary applications of the disaggregate approach based on discrete choice random utility theory, Ian Heggie (1978a) made the following points in a measured critique:

> It is clear that recent developments in disaggregate behavioural modelling have not led to the break-through that was originally hoped. They are at least more behavioural than the usual transportation models, but they still do not give wholly realistic results and do not obviously replicate the way in which people actually behave (Heggie, 1978a, 124).

To Ian Heggie and Peter Jones, the inconsistencies that were starting to be revealed in empirical investigations were the result of the application of models, both traditional and individual choice forms, outside their appropriate 'domain of validity' for which their inherent simplifications were justified. They expressed the view:

> The all-embracing generality which they sought – and often claimed . . . always proved elusive. This paper . . . argues that current techniques, whether multistage transportation models, disaggregate behavioural ones, or simple econometric models, have limited applicability and are only appropriate within a relatively narrow domain. Outside this domain, behaviour is complicated by the incidence of linkages – spatial, temporal and inter-personal – and incomplete knowledge (Heggie and Jones, 1978, 119–120).

Overall then, in a number of important respects, existing behavioural models founded on discrete choice random utility theory appeared inconsistent with the accumulating evidence on the response of individuals and households to transportation policies and certainly seen by some academics, who aspired to a behavioural explanation of travel, as a straitjacket on progress. Later, on the same theme, Peter Jones and his University of Oxford colleagues observed: 'This work drew heavily on theoretical developments in economics and psychology, but often with little recourse to surveys of how people actually make travel decisions. Indeed, it has, at times, concentrated more on elegant mathematical structures rather than on attempting to replicate the travel decision processes themselves' (Jones et al, 1983, 5). With regard to traditional practice it was as if the behavioural interpretation, based on individual trip choices over frequency, location, mode and route, had acquired among travel modellers a reality of its own, divorced from empirical evidence. It was time to look at behaviour in the real world (Heggie, 1978a, 1978b).

There was also a critical concern for the research methodology, language and style of analysis accompanying the study of travel behaviour. By the 1980s there was even the hint of a backlash against the austere mathematical style of the previous decade, which some social scientists saw as developing a stranglehold on the subject. In relation to the developing study of travel within the context of individual and household activities, Phil Goodwin expressed a view that one can now imagine struck a chord with many:

> One of the most welcome features of the seminars, conferences and discussions of this stream of work has been its tendency to use the language and categories of ordinary life – graphs and tables are about men, women, children, babies, grandmothers. . . . Some discussion must be at a higher level of abstraction or mathematical detail, but in a much less intimidating context to the non-specialist than has often been the case with other schools of work (Goodwin, 1983, 472).

Over the next few years every assumption inherent in that generation of behavioural models based on the discrete choice random utility approach would be subject to critical scrutiny as this alternative perspective, based on an explicit demand for travel within the context of household activity demand and participation, vied for recognition. To the contributions of the economist and psychologist were to be added those of the geographer, regional scientist and sociologist. In a sentiment that echoed the audacious question posed a decade earlier by Torsten Hägerstrand (1970) in 'What about People in Regional Science?', Ian Heggie (1978b) saw the research agenda in terms of 'Putting Behaviour into Behavioural Models of Travel Choice'.

In Europe, where the activity approach first started to flourish, the concern was certainly not just about travel forecasting, but also about casting the discipline of transportation planning at a more human scale less dominated by the car. The time had come to acknowledge fully the role of transportation in society and recognise and cater for the diversity of behaviour and the travel needs of all citizens as they went about their daily lives. The objective was to re-emphasise the concerns of those commentators writing in the late 1960s and 1970s about the biases present in the traditional transportation planning process, with reference to policy formation, impact assessment and evaluation (Hillman et al, 1973, 1976; Starkie, 1973; Wachs, 1973; Bruton, 1975; Langdon and Mitchell, 1978).

A large number of people from various disciplines contributed to this theoretical and practical development. During the period examined in this chapter, the field lost two of its most distinguished younger members, Eric Pas [1948–1997] and Ryuichi Kitamura [1949–2009].

6.1.2 The Activity Approach to Travel Analysis: A New Behavioural Paradigm?

The study of travel within the context of individual and household activities was well under way by the end of the 1970s. Although dating back to the early years of the twentieth century, as discussed at length in Parkes and Thrift (1975) and the excellent trilogy by Carlstein et al (1978), its modern development and focus on travel are usually attributed to work in the 1960s and early 1970s and, in particular, that of Torsten Hägerstrand [1916–2004] (1970)[1] and F. Stuart Chapin, Jr. (1974). Chapin emphasised the role of activities in meeting a variety of human needs, whereas Hägerstrand, working in a geographic tradition, sought to examine the role of constraints, particularly those expressed in space and time and in a household context, in determining individual opportunities and shaping individual and household choices (Fox, 1995).

Was this then a further 'new approach' or merely an elaboration of the existing paradigm for understanding and forecasting travel behaviour? After all, the discrete choice approach based on utility maximisation was a framework that lent itself to considerable generalisation in terms of improved market segmentation, extended choice sets and alternative decision mechanisms. Additionally, it could well be claimed that some of the features of this further 'new approach', such as the study and incorporation of trip chaining and intra-household dependencies, were already on the research agenda in the mid-1970s (Ruiter and Ben-Akiva, 1978; Adler and Ben-Akiva, 1979). Moreover, the simplification of trip tours and the distinct features of travel behaviour of different life cycle groups were explicitly recognised in the discrete choice literature in the early 1970s, by for example CRA (1972, Appendix).

There is no sharp distinction between these two eras. Chronologically, there was considerable overlap between the application of the human activity approach to travel behaviour and the discrete choice random utility framework described in the last two chapters. Some of the critiques of the latter were already anticipated, and started to be addressed in the design of models. That said, by the early 1980s large differences in the study of travel behaviour were becoming evident. A relatively short period separates publication of two outstanding texts, the outcome of major research studies that in many ways set the tone for their respective era: Domencich and McFadden (1975), *Urban Travel Demand: A Behavioral Analysis*, and Jones et al (1983), *Understanding Travel Behaviour*, from the University of Oxford's Transport Studies Unit. Both discuss travel from a behavioural perspective, yet were utterly different in their scope, description and explanation of travel, their methods of investigation and their motivation.

In the new lexicon that was emerging, 'activities', 'tours', 'constraints', 'needs', 'roles', 'interdependencies', 'scheduling', 'time use', 'adaptation', 'lifestyles', 'habits', 'satisficing' and 'empirical inductive research style' would become much more prevalent in the description, analysis and explanation of travel behaviour. In the eloquent words of Ryuichi Kitamura:

> In terms of the nature of the forces that drove its development, the activity analysis field is fundamentally different from the area of disaggregate choice analysis. The thrust for the latter development was improved statistical efficiency, economy in data collection, and versatile policy application. The development was strongly methodological and application orientated. Indeed, the product, the multinomial logit (MNL) model, is easy to understand, inexpensive to estimate, and usually offers sensible results (see, e.g. Horowitz, 1985). The activity-based approach was initiated with almost entirely reversed emphases. Its data collection was based on 'in-depth' interviews, which are by no means economical and large samples are practically impossible to obtain. Prediction was least emphasized. Instead 'understanding' was the initial main focus; rather than statistically quantifying relationships among objectively defined household and personal attributes, network level-of-service and land use variables, activity analysis sought to reveal why such relations existed (Kitamura, 1988, 26–27).

While the initial stimulus to the development of travel demand analysis based on the activity approach can be traced to critical assessment of both traditional models and the emerging behavioural style in the US in the early years of the 1970s (Jones et al, 1983), the first formal recognition of this new stream of work was at the Third International Conference on Behavioural Travel Modelling in 1977 (Carpenter and Jones, 1983, x). If the Williamsburg conference in 1972 (Brand and Manheim, 1973) proved to be a major stimulus to further development of discrete choice random utility models, it is generally agreed that the Oxford conference in 1981 served a similar role for the analysis of travel behaviour based on the activity approach (Carpenter and Jones, 1983; Kitamura, 1988).

Although transportation systems and demand management policies were becoming more widely considered in some countries, it is worth emphasising at this stage that the traditional concerns for urban land use and infrastructure planning did not simply go away. By the 1980s highway planning in urban areas of the heavily industrialised world was significantly less emphasised than in previous decades. However, public transport investments, sometimes of grandiose proportions, were often present in urban transportation plans. And both land use change and large-scale infrastructure investments were prevalent in many developing countries, in particular those that were experiencing rapid economic growth in the 1980s. The requirements on travel forecasting professionals throughout the world were getting greater, more diverse and much more challenging.

A word of caution may be appropriate at this point. Those encountering activity-travel models for the first time could be forgiven for assuming that all travel forecasting models that were described as 'activity-based' had a great deal in common. In fact, there can be very great differences between them, which have major implications for the required data, knowledge of behaviour, practical expertise and computer resources involved in model specification, implementation and solution. To avoid inappropriate comparisons when we describe selected models later, we note here some major factors that condition their development and determine differences: (a) scope of the model (e.g., whether policy responses are required in a base year or some years into the future); (b) particular behavioural responses to a policy or project that are considered relevant over the time frame chosen; (c) extent to which decision processes are explicitly modelled and validated; (d) whether interactions between household members are introduced explicitly; (e) aggregation, classification or categorisation assumptions made in model specification and variable definition; (f) the range of policies the models are meant to address (e.g., infrastructure planning and/or demand management, technological innovation); and (g) information generated by the model. We hope to bring out some of these distinctions in the chapter.

6.1.3   Contents of the Chapter

In this chapter we consider advances in the understanding of travel behaviour and the contribution to operational travel forecasting models founded on the human activity approach from the late 1970s until the present. The evolution towards operational models is now usually seen as a transition from 'trip-based' models to 'tour-based' models to full-day 'activity scheduling' models, and this progression is reflected in the structure of the chapter.

In section 6.2 we consider in more detail the nature of the critique of the travel forecasting approaches in the late 1970s and early 1980s, directed at both the traditional multi-stage models and the dominant behavioural style based on discrete choice utility theory. In section 6.3 we describe the evolution of travel demand models when the unit of analysis is the trip tour. Advances in tour modelling in both the traditional 'aggregate' style and the micro-economic discrete choice framework based on random utility theory are presented.

As a prelude to discussing different activity-based demand models, we describe in section 6.4 selected daily activity scheduling models presented in the 1980s and early 1990s. We then introduce in section 6.5 two very different approaches in theory and method to the development of activity-based travel forecasting models towards operational status. We discuss, in turn, an econometric model for Portland, Oregon, which built on an earlier prototype for Boston (Bowman, 1995; Bowman et al, 1999) and then the application of an entirely different model called the activity model simulator (AMOS) to Washington, DC, by Resource Decision Consultants (RDC, 1995; Pendyala et al, 1998). Both started to address the operational requirements of urban transportation planning agencies.

In section 6.6 we draw on contemporary materials to summarise the main developments in activity-based travel demand forecasting over the last 15 years, which saw significant applications and practical developments, particularly in the US, Europe and Japan. An assessment of the contribution of the activity approach to the analysis and forecasting of travel concludes the chapter.

6.2   A CRITIQUE OF TRAVEL FORECASTING MODELS OF THE EARLY 1980s

6.2.1   Two Targets for Critics

By the early 1980s the disaggregate behavioural approach based on discrete choice random utility models had, with the possible exception of its application to modal choice, yet to make a significant impression on travel forecasting practice, for which the traditional four-stage approach remained the mainstay. The two approaches stood alongside each other: the former starting to dominate the conceptualisation of travel and theoretical analysis of travel behaviour, with limited applications; the latter serving the traditional requirements of urban transportation planning agencies. In this period critics of travel forecasting procedures had two rather large targets, and they could and did take aim at both.

For as long as the traditional four-stage model was in wide use in practice, it would be the object for critical judgement and promotion of alternatives. This was definitely the case in the 1980s – and to some extent remains the case today. It was time for the aggregate approach based on the four-stage model to be subject to another round of pummelling. Prior criticisms, perhaps advanced one or two decades earlier, were revisited with a modern twist arising from changes in study objectives, policy emphases and information requirements. In addition, its lack of behavioural foundations was often and increasingly scorned. The assumptions of the disaggregate behavioural approach, conceived in terms of the discrete choice random utility framework as then applied, were also to be subject to negative critical evaluation according to their behavioural realism. Against this background, the activity approach to travel analysis and forecasting made its appearance.

The critique of travel forecasting models in this period and the foundations of the activity approach have been widely reviewed over the years (Kutter, 1973; Jones, 1977, 1979b; Heggie, 1978a, 1978b; Heggie and Jones, 1978; Brög and Erl, 1983; Recker et al, 1986; Kitamura, 1988; Gärling et al, 1994; RDC, 1995; Rossi and Shiftan, 1997; Ben-Akiva and Bowman, 1998; Bhat and Koppelman, 1999a; McNally, 2000a, 2000b; Donnelly et al, 2010; Pinjari and Bhat, 2011). In this section we elaborate on our earlier comments by summarising some of the critical issues and common themes that emerged from this literature.

6.2.2 A Critique of Prior Models on the Basis of 'Behavioural Realism'

6.2.2.1 Travel as a derived demand and its implications

In traditional zone-based models the trip (almost invariably by motorised modes) was the basic unit of analysis in terms of which a demand was expressed. Purpose categories, typically classified as home-based work (HBW), other home-based (OHB) and non-home-based (NHB), or some further disaggregation (home-based shopping or education, etc.) reflected the nature and rationale for the trip. Often the disaggregate approach dealt with simple return trips on home-based tours.

In the activity approach, travel as expressed through the trip or journey became secondary, a consequence of the demand to partake in particular activities away from the home.[2] This shift from an emphasis on the trip to one on activities was not only theoretically appropriate but necessary, it was argued, in order to strengthen the behavioural basis for the model of trip generation (Kutter, 1973; Jones, 1977; Allaman et al, 1982; van der Hoorn, 1983) and address issues such as the possible substitution of in-home activities for out-of-home activities (involving travel). This revision would later become important for assessing the impact of technological developments where undertaking an activity previously involving a journey away from home might be accomplished through modern technology in a domestic setting, as in teleworking, e-shopping and so on (e.g., Salomon, 1986; Mokhtarian, 1990; Ben-Akiva et al, 1996; Golob, 2001).

6.2.2.2 Activities and the structure of journeys: from trips to tours to a daily schedule

The trip-purpose categorisation into HBW, OHB and NHB, which allowed different types of trip to be treated independently, might in the early development of the subject have been seen as a master-stroke for the simplification of models. Increasingly, however, it was seen as not only unrealistic, limited in its ability to relate NHB trips to relevant household characteristics, but potentially the cause of an upward bias in forecasting the response to policies aimed at modal transfer. Many journeys were not simply composed of outward and return legs associated with a single purpose, but often involved complex arrangements of trip legs in tours with intermediate stops to undertake, possibly with other people, different activities separated in space and time.

The need to expand the existing behavioural framework came from both within and outside the existing travel demand forecasting community. In the late 1970s Thomas Adler and Moshe Ben-Akiva commented: 'Existing models have the shortcoming of not representing the inter-dependencies among trip links in trip chains with multiple non-home stops. . . . The results indicate the need for expanding the scope of existing travel fore-casting models to explicit considerations of trip chaining behavior' (Adler and Ben-Akiva, 1979, 243).

Two problems arose with the decomposition of household-based tours into independent trips. The first was a consequence of the treatment of mode choice as successive independent decisions which failed to respect modal continuity on a tour (or, more strictly, a set of transfers between 'compatible' modes within a tour, as we describe later in the chapter). The second implication of the independence assumption was the failure to rep-resent temporal interdependencies, specifically the potential implications that any changes to the conditions affecting the activity or the trip leg undertaken in one period might have for activities and associated travel at other times in the day.

This was of fundamental theoretical relevance and could radically change assumptions about the rationale for particular behaviour. For instance, was the explanation for modal choice for the journey to work to be found in the relative values of a few modal attributes associated with a single independent trip, or in the interrelated requirements to conduct different activities at different times of the day, possibly involving other household members? Furthermore, would the effect of policies be con-fined to changes involving trip(s) undertaken in one time period alone or involve a complex substitution between different tour types within the whole pattern of daily activities? In response to a policy or project, would two simple home-based tours conducted at different times of the day be substituted for one complex tour involving multiple activities with accompanying travel (Jones et al, 1983; Bowman, 1995; Ben-Akiva and Bowman, 1998)?

6.2.2.3   Role of constraints in determining feasible choices

Prior behavioural investigations had considered in principle the effects of constraints on the set of opportunities available to a person or household, and the choice sets in the discrete choice methodology were often stated in very general terms. However, they were usually applied in relatively simple and limited terms. Constraints were confined to income, time availability in a broad sense and, perhaps, car availability. It was hard to deny that in the 1970s the greater emphasis of the behavioural approach was usually on preference structures and models of choice between discrete alternatives, with less consideration given to the nature and formation of the set of choices available to different people – or segments of the market.

In the activity approach the treatment of constraints and their limits to possible courses of action were to become central features. Hägerstrand (1970, 17) classified constraints in three forms:

1. capability constraints (which might involve the requirements of particular needs such as those associated with sleeping, eating, etc., and those that limited spatial opportunities owing to the technological characteristics of available modes);
2. coupling or interdependency constraints (such as those requiring different family members to meet at particular locations and times);
3. authority or institutional constraints (such as those that limited temporal access to shops, work, etc.).

Major themes of Hägerstrand's research were the role of time in human activities and the consequences of constraints for performing different activities at different locations and times, which he illustrated through the concept of the 'space-time prism' (Hägerstrand, 1970; Jones et al, 1983). The prism, defined over regions of space and time, effectively placed bounds on the locations at which activities of given duration could be performed when accessed by any particular mode. This concept also placed bounds on the time available to participate in an activity at a particular location arising from the time involved in travelling to and from that location. A person's daily experience could now be charted as a 'path' in space and time in which the possibilities to perform activities were subject to a range of spatial and temporal constraints determined, in part, by such prisms (Hägerstrand, 1970; Lenntorp, 1976, 1978; Burnett and Hanson, 1979, 1982; Burnett and Thrift, 1979; Jones, 1979b). In later research such prisms would become central features in determining available feasible scheduling arrangements for different activities performed by individuals throughout the day.

In some cases, it was argued, the range of constraints on individual action was so extensive that they limited the very many possibilities to relatively few feasible options, possibly only one in the short term (Jones et al, 1983). However, although possible action was often heavily constrained, paradoxically, with the increased 'degrees of freedom' available in temporal and inter-personal contexts, individuals were potentially more adaptable than suggested by the limited responses embodied in existing travel demand models. Individuals and the households in which they resided were often highly inventive in offsetting or accommodating the effect of policies, and this was well confirmed empirically. In studies in the city of Oxford, for example, Heggie (1978a) found that individuals and households could consolidate choices in different tour arrangements and/ or reassign tasks among household members, in addition to the standard responses involving frequency, destination and mode of travel. As he observed:

> Perhaps the most dramatic examples of adaptability were identified in the study of the possible effects of car restraint. At least 12 different types of adaptation were identified. Most related to non work journeys and ranged from the consolidation of journeys (apparently the most frequent response), through the choice of alternative local destinations (usually reached on foot), to diversion to out-of-town shopping centres. Some of the adaptations were quite elaborate and involved quite complex substitutions. For example, some people go to enormous trouble to find ways around selective car restraint, others will reassign family tasks so that one parent can be released to perform the activity at another time, in another place, using a different mode (Heggie, 1978a, 113).

Individual decisions associated with particular journeys were now conceived within combinations of activities within tours, or trip chains, of varying complexity and extended to the pattern of activities over the whole day. In this regard, the extent to which the spatial and temporal aspects of some activities were relatively fixed while others were relatively flexible was recognised as an important determinant of behaviour and response to policy (Cullen and Godson, 1975; Heggie, 1978a; Jones et al, 1983). The implications for the 'chaining' of activities and trips were recognised and widely studied in the mid- to late 1970s (Hensher, 1976; Hanson, 1979; and later Thill and Thomas, 1987).

6.2.2.4 Models of the decision-making process
The travel decision process itself was increasingly the subject of study involving not only what choices people made out of those available, but fundamentally how and why they were selected. Social science perspectives and qualitative research methods began to be more fully deployed and further developed in travel-related research (Jones et al, 1983; Pickup

and Town, 1983; Kitamura, 1988). In addition to the quantitative analysis of travel diary data, unstructured in-depth interviews and the use of focus groups were increasingly applied – with the tape recorder becoming the indispensable tool – for the ultimate purpose of hypothesis generation and theory building (Jones et al, 1983).

The nature of the decision process underpinning common discrete choice random utility models came in for particular criticism with the paradigm of the 'economic man', often summarily dismissed as patently unrealistic. There was growing evidence that choice processes were characterised by decision strategies involving household evolution and dynamics, and search strategies involving limited and uncertain information, risk and complex choice sets and that were even – for that most studied of choices, modal split – subject to habit formation and inertia (Banister, 1978; Heggie, 1978a; Jones et al, 1983) for which the cross-sectional modelling approach was not particularly well suited. As RDC would later comment:

> the information individuals have is partial and incomplete; the number of items individuals can incorporate into their cognitive systems is limited; their perceptive ability to discriminate between stimuli is limited; the outcome of a decision is usually highly uncertain; and individuals' decisions may not be internally coherent and consistently rational. Moreover, there is evidence that behavioural inertia is prevalent, and that individuals tend to resist behavioural changes. Our travel behaviour is probably not in the state of equilibrium which the paradigm of optimisation assumes (Goodwin et al, 1987) (RDC, 1995, section 4.1, 2–3).

Indeed, it was argued (e.g., Gärling et al, 1994) that the very complexity of choices rendered utility maximisation an untenable assumption and warranted the search for alternative models of the decision process to the standard discrete choice approach based on micro-economic theory. In this quest the 'principles of bounded rationality' and 'the satisficing approach' (Simon, 1957), in which the capability and inclination to seek information in highly complex decision contexts were considered limited, became an attractive alternative to the optimisation of utility. Here, an option would be selected if it was considered 'good enough' according to some threshold of satisfaction.

6.2.2.5   Interdependencies between individuals within households
As we noted, the importance of the life cycle in determining significant variation in activity and travel behaviour was already recognised in the early 1970s, for example by Domencich and McFadden (1975, 193), although its full significance in policy analysis was not clarified until the activity approach was more fully developed (Heggie and Jones, 1978;

Allaman et al, 1982; Goodwin, 1983; Jones et al, 1983; Pas, 1984). In relation to the traffic restraint studies in the city of Oxford, Heggie and Jones remarked: 'This study also demonstrated the importance of stage in the family life cycle as the basis of grouping household responses, since it affects both needs and roles (and hence the mix of trip purposes) as well as constraints on, and opportunities for, adaptation' (Heggie and Jones, 1978, 121). Of particular interest were the presence and influence of children on the travel relationships of households and for the transportation planning process more generally. In Phil Goodwin's judgement:

> the single most important 'discovery' of activity work to date has been the importance of children – not, primarily, because of their own trips (which though important in a social framework tend to be relatively few and simple) but because the very fact of children in a household imposes highly complex and binding constraints on the activities and travel patterns of all other members of the household. . . . [T]his simple and well known fact of family life has been almost entirely ignored in generations of transport plans. . . . The other major findings in this field have related to what is sometimes described as the role of women, but is more accurately seen as being about the relationships between men and women, in a social context. . . . [E]mpirical work still shows how dominating are the traditional roles and constraints of home, children and kitchen (Goodwin, 1983; 472–473).

Decisions were often made within a household context in which interdependencies and interactions were crucial elements of the outcome. Although some progress was made to incorporate intra-household linkages (section 5.5), disaggregate models almost invariably reflected this interrelationship inadequately when considering travel and activity participation. This was not limited simply to who had access to the family car for a particular journey but also the people involved, location, timing, mode, and tour on which the shopping activity would be achieved (Algers et al, 1996).

6.3 OPERATIONAL TOUR-BASED TRAVEL DEMAND FORECASTING MODELS

6.3.1 Introduction

Recasting travel behaviour within an activity framework stimulated an enormous amount of empirical and theoretical research in the late 1970s and early 1980s, which was followed by extensive reviews in journals, edited books and contributions at international conferences. The subject matter was diverse and ranged over such topics as: (a) data acquisition and analysis; (b) activity participation and time use; (c) scheduling in time and space; (d) effect of spatio-temporal, inter-personal and other constraints; (e) household structure and roles; (f) adaptation and other dynamical aspects; (g) variability of activities and travel within and between days of the week; (h) policy applications; (i) activity models; and (j) methodological developments (e.g., Damm and Lerman, 1981; Carpenter and Jones, 1983; Damm, 1983; Golob and Golob, 1983; Jones et al, 1983; Kitamura, 1988). These early initiatives provided a more sophisticated view of travel behaviour which would slowly but progressively make an impression on travel demand analysis. The first stage of this development started with rejoining trips into tours and exploring the nature of travel within a chain of activities and the likely responses to policies.

Travel demand forecasting models that were based on tours were first developed in continental Europe in the late 1970s and early 1980s. By the middle of the 1990s they were applied in several places in Europe and the US (Daly et al, 1983; Axhausen and Herz, 1989; Gunn et al, 1989; Cascetta et al, 1993; Algers et al, 1996; Fellendorf et al, 1997; Hague Consulting Group, HCG, 1997; Rossi and Shiftan, 1997). In this section we describe two tour-based models, developed respectively in Germany and Sweden.

It is interesting to note the rather different approach to the refinement of the four-stage model in German travel forecasting practice in the late 1960s. Kay Axhausen and Raymond Herz indicate that, in contrast to the efforts evident in the US and UK to base developments around the discrete choice random utility models, in Germany 'Research concentrated on . . . rethinking the trip generation stage within the transportation planning process, which was approached by simulating activity chains' (Axhausen and Herz, 1989, 316). What they described as 'the German approach' to modelling activity chains, along with prior related work in Germany, was outlined in their paper.

The first application represents a relatively straightforward extension of the traditional multi-stage method and was part of a forecasting approach that replaced the first three modules of conventional models in a move from a trip-based to a tour- (chain-)based methodology. The second relates to an application of the disaggregate discrete choice random utility approach to the city of Stockholm. This model incorporated a variety of substitution possibilities (responses to policy variables) and interactions within the household that were not found in traditional models.

6.3.2 Modifications to the Multi-Step Approach: VISEM

The travel forecasting approach based on activity chains and applied in the PTV's VISEM, with relatively few refinements, remains part of their urban and regional travel forecasting system (section 10.5.1.6). By the mid-1990s this software was being applied in many German and other European cities, ranging in population from 0.3 to 2.4 million (Fellendorf et al, 1997).

VISEM was used to estimate and forecast mode-specific traffic volumes 'in a more realistic manner than presently done using conventional four step models' (Fellendorf et al, 1997, 55) and to address the continuity issues arising from linking journeys into activity or trip chains. The application of VISEM involved identification of: (a) relatively homogeneous groups of people in terms of the pattern of activities undertaken; and (b) the relationship between the trip characteristics to the chains of activities for each of the different group categories. The model system developed in the late 1980s included a set of modules that performed the following functions:

1. generation of daily mobility patterns derived from activity chains;
2. derivation of trip chains from mobility patterns and a gravity model to allocate activities to specific destination zones;
3. application of logit mode choice models in order to associate specific modes with the trip chains.

The output of VISEM was a set of mode-specific origin–destination (O-D) matrices by time of day. We briefly summarise each of the above procedures in turn.

The behavioural information underpinning the model was derived from both national and local data sources. The former consisted of the German nationwide travel surveys of activity-based travel diaries, which were undertaken in 1976, 1982 and 1989. The sample size of about 20 000 households in 1989 consisted of 40 000 persons who made 120 000 trips. This information was used as the basis for identifying person categories with distinct patterns of travel behaviour, the local household survey with a minimum sample size of about 500 households providing trip details for one specific day.

The person categories were characterised by similar within-group and significantly different between-group travel behaviour. Their number was determined for each zone in a study area. The resultant groups were segmented by employment or education characteristics and car availability: (a) employees with car available; (b) employees without car available; (c) non-employees with car available; (d) non-employees without car available; (e) apprentices; (f) students in high school; and (g) pupils, 10–19 years.

In VISEM the traditional trip generation model was replaced by a model that records the number of activity chains, according to their relative occurrence among about 300 different chains in the national database. The chains were in the form HXH, HOXH and HXOH, where H represents the home, X represents the job, shopping, school and so on, and O represents other activity. As the authors noted: 'Even if VISEM does not limit chain length, computation time is the main reason to drop chains of exceeding length and low probability' (Fellendorf et al, 1997, 56). The model then associated a probability (proportion) of each person category with different chains of activities on an average day, and then applied factors to determine the temporal distribution of activities during the day.

The conversion of activity chains to trip chains was effected by means of a gravity-type distribution model that determined the destination zones of trips according to their spatial separation (as measured by distance, travel time or generalised cost) and the sensitivity of each activity to separation. The attractiveness of any zone for the performance of an activity was, in turn, derived from 'structural quantities determined from land use studies' such as number of jobs, retail floor space and student enrolment. For each activity and trip group, the spatial dependence was determined by the parameters of the deterrence function. From the allocation of destinations the gravity-type submodel generated the trips associated with each activity chain, resulting in a trip matrix and the total number of trip chains.

A modal split model of MNL form then allocated the trip chains with specified origin and destination zones to the relevant modes according to the socio-economic characteristics of the population group and modal attributes. Generalised costs were determined for five modes: walk, bicycle, car driver, car passenger and public transport:

> To ensure continuity/compatibility of mode selection along an activity chain available modes of transport are sub-divided into exchangeable (usually foot, car passenger, public transport) and non-exchangeable ones (car, bike). For the first trip of the trip chain the LOGIT model is applied and one of the available modes chosen on the basis of generalised cost of travel (Fellendorf et al, 1997, 65).

The mode-specific O-D matrices were then assigned to relevant network scenarios. In this particular model the specification allowed transportation policies to influence modal and destination choice within chains but contained no substitution mechanism between different chain types or time of day of travel. Further development of VISEM is described on the PTV Group's website and in Chapter 10.

6.3.3   A Discrete Choice Tour-Based Approach: The Stockholm Model

The following application by transportation planning agencies in the city of Stockholm in conjunction with Hague Consulting Group (HCG) was distinguished in a number of respects, but primarily in its treatment of household interactions within a tour-based representation (Algers et al, 1996). The Stockholm Integrated Model System (SIMS) built on the tradition established in the MTC and SIGMO models (Ben-Akiva et al, 1978; Ruiter and Ben-Akiva, 1978) in which increasingly sophisticated discrete choice models based on nested logit structures were applied to individual choice within a household decision-making unit. The interdependence and relative sensitivity of different behavioural responses to travel cost and level-of-service policy variables were the outcome of a hierarchical model structure and the expected utility measures embedded within it. For the latter the 'logsum' variable was widely used. The nature of the model and the behavioural aspects to be represented were determined by its requirement to address both land use and transportation infrastructure planning over a 20-year period, as well as shorter- and medium-term demand management policies, such as area licensing.

For a description of the model and its application we draw on Algers et al (1996), HCG (1997) and Algers and Eliasson (2006). In this brief description we focus on the range of response mechanisms and interdependencies not present in the traditional four-stage approach, examples of which include:

> a shift of car use between the different members of the household, which might be the effect of an area licensing scheme. Another example might be a shopping trip, which can be assigned by the household to other household members as a consequence of a price or trip time change, affecting accessibility for different household members. A third example would be to substitute a home based trip by a second destination on the work trip between work and home. A change of travel times or costs may make it relatively easier to carry out shopping on the way home than as a home based trip (Algers et al, 1996, 346).

The household behaviour was subject to a set of constraints such as limits to walking distance, and expense in relation to household income and activities requiring too much time.

Of particular interest in this application are the work tour and shopping tour models shown in Figure 6.1. By construction, the former was conditional on mobility and lifestyle decisions, including car ownership, and in turn conditioned other activity and travel decisions. The complete model system recognised ten travel purposes. The choice model structure is that for a household with two working members, and shopping

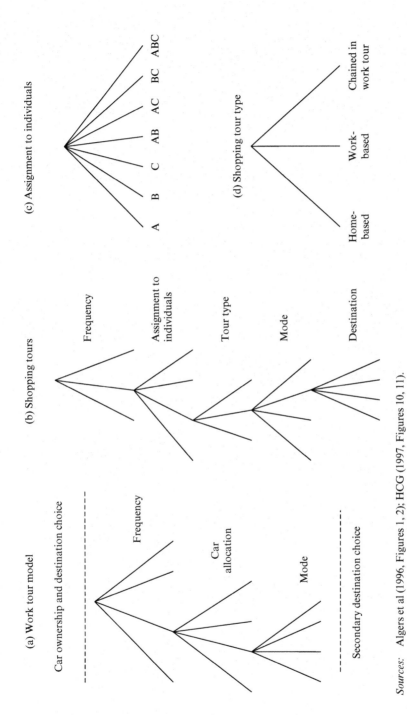

Sources: Algers et al (1996, Figures 1, 2); HCG (1997, Figures 10, 11).

Figure 6.1 Choice model structures in the Stockholm Integrated Model System (SIMS)

allocations involving three members. Where practicable in such extensive hierarchical representations, the researchers undertook simultaneous (full-information maximum-likelihood) estimation of parameters, or otherwise estimation occurred sequentially, and 'logsums' passed between different sets of choices from the 'bottom up'. Revealed preference data were used throughout, and estimation of the hierarchical logit models was performed with ALOGIT software (Daly, 1987).

As Figure 6.1(a) shows, at the 'top' of the work trip hierarchy was the joint car ownership and workplace location decision; this was followed by the joint choice model for work trip frequency, car allocation and mode of travel; and at the 'bottom' was the choice of secondary destination (see below). Each of these three sub-structures was estimated separately with interconnecting 'logsum' variables passing upwards through the different structures to convey cost and level-of-service policy variables.

The work decision conditions the household shopping tours model, which involves the five-level hierarchy shown in Figure 6.1(b). This structure is composed of models that determined: (a) frequency of travel, determining the number of trips per household per day; (b) allocation of the activity to individuals; (c) trip type (home-based tour, work-based tour or a work trip detour); and (d) destination and mode, which are modelled for home-based tours, and destination only for work-based and secondary destination trips. The allocation of the household shopping trips to individuals within a multi-worker household including A (a worker), B (a worker) and C (other household members aged 12 or above) then involved the possibilities A, B, C, AB, AC, BC, ABC, as shown in Figure 6.1(c). Specification of model variables was dependent on the nature of the grouping involved.

Through level-of-service variables directly, and 'logsum' variables indirectly, changes in the transportation system could influence the location and mode of shopping journey, the tour type, the assignment to individuals, and the frequency itself. A new finding in the Stockholm study was that:

> the accessibility of different trip types has an influence on the choice of trip type, and that the accessibility of different combinations of the household members has an influence on the allocation of the shopping trip in the household. . . . [I]t seems that the estimated model has proved that there is an allocation process in the household and that accessibility (and thus transportation) has an important role in this process (Algers et al, 1996, 354).

Forecasts of the development of household structure and other relevant socio-economic variables used in conjunction with the choice models were made by 'prototypical sampling', which was applied in a number of previous studies by HCG, including the Dutch national model (Gunn et al, 1989) (section 5.5). It was necessary for the travel demand forecasting system to be able to produce matrices on a zonal basis in order to assign trip matrices to the different networks with the software system EMME/2.

This micro-econometric model applied in a major conurbation may be considered the state of the art of practical disaggregate choice modelling in the mid-1990s. It incorporated many of the key patterns of substitution and interactions thought to be relevant to the planning and policy contexts. Although a wider set of possible schedule and timing decisions was recognised as possible, this behaviourally complex model was taken as a practical compromise, 'while not imposing too great computational requirements either in estimation or in application' (Algers et al, 1996, 348). Algers and Eliasson (2006) described the further development of the model within a microsimulation framework.

6.4 ACTIVITY SCHEDULING MODELS: NEGOTIATING THE ACRONYMS

6.4.1 Introduction

In the remainder of this chapter we encounter several references to the modelling of activity schedules – the order, duration, location and timing of a set of activities over a daily period – and their implications for travel and mode selection for an individual and possibly other household members. This typically involved gathering, recording or modelling information on one or more of the following:

1. pattern and time use associated with different (combinations of) activities and relating these to socio-economic and other variables of individuals and/or households;
2. feasible alternatives to a given schedule in order to identify possible substitutes to current arrangements in a changed environment;
3. behavioural adjustments of individuals and/or households to different policies on the basis of particular decision rules, both in the base and in future years.

Feasible alternative schedules are defined as those that satisfied relevant sets of constraints or behavioural rules. These might include simple logical constraints influencing activity and travel behaviour, such as some or all of the following (Jones et al, 1983; Recker et al, 1986; RDC, 1995; Pendyala et al, 1998):

1. continuity constraints associated with timing and location of activities and accompanying trips;
2. minimum time periods allocated to basic psychological needs, such as sleep and preparing meals;
3. institutional constraints relating to the location and time at which certain activities may be performed;
4. constraints relating to the availability and operational characteristics of particular modes, as well as modal continuity conditions on trip tours.

Other rules relate to more specific assumptions about roles, responsibility of individuals and priorities for different household members. We refer briefly to some of the early notable activity scheduling approaches which emerged in the 1980s and early 1990s. Fuller discussions are available in Axhausen and Gärling (1992) and Gärling et al (1994, Figure 2, 360), as well as more recent reviews (Bhat and Koppelman, 1999a; Timmermans et al, 2002; Algers et al, 2005; Pinjari and Bhat, 2011).

6.4.2 Household Activity-Travel Simulator

Although the household activity-travel simulator (HATS) did not constitute a formal mathematical model or computational algorithm representing behaviour, rather than a framework for representing and discussing behaviour, it was one of the most interesting early applications of the activity approach to travel analysis (Jones, 1979a; Jones et al, 1983). Based on a physical representation on a display board of the spatial and temporal aspects of activity and travel patterns for each individual within a household setting over an 18- or 24-hour day, HATS allowed: (a) representation of current activity-travel behaviour; (b) investigation of its rationale; and (c) stated intentions relating to the short-term adjustments of household activity schedules to a range of policies. What rescheduling and other response possibilities occurred were the result of human search and choice (by the interviewees) under the watchful eye and encouragement of an interviewer. It was the experience with HATS that led Peter Jones and his colleagues to conclude:

> in practice the constraints, linkages, personal household and social requirements, and habits, serve to reduce the millions of possible combinations to a small, tractable number (sometimes, even, only one) which *can* be handled by ordinary processes of thought and decision taking. In this sense, the constraints may paradoxically be acting not only as limitations on behaviour, but as aids which allow behavioural decisions to be made at all (Jones et al, 1983, 195).

The challenge to develop a computational representation soon progressed to a computer-aided information gathering and analysis system that was widely used for demonstration projects and applications in the UK and Australia (Jones, 1985; Jones et al, 1989).

6.4.3 PESASP and CARLA

Two early programs that were designed to exhaustively explore possible alternatives to current schedule arrangements under changed conditions were PESASP (Lenntorp, 1976, 1978) and CARLA (Clarke, 1980; Jones et al, 1983). PESASP (program evaluating the set of alternative sample paths), developed by Bo Lenntorp at Lund University, was designed for the analysis of possible combinations of activities in time and space. Essentially, it investigated how individuals were able to perform activities in different constraint environments, and was described by Lenntorp as follows:

> The PESASP simulation model maps the set of alternative ways in which a particular activity programme can possibly be carried out. The number and kinds of these activities are a function of the *combined* qualities of the individual and the environment. The individual has to make choices which fall within the set of possible alternatives, although the model does not pre-determine which choices will be made. A person's behaviour is controlled both by the structure of the existing environment and by individual preferences of which the latter are less known (Lenntorp, 1978, 179).

CARLA (combinatorial algorithm for rescheduling lists of activities) was a program for generating all feasible activity-destination patterns and accompanying travel arrangements as a result of changes in external conditions arising from a policy measure (Clarke, 1980; Jones et al, 1983). The input required by the algorithm for a sample of individuals was a list of the activities to be scheduled, their durations and the times of day between which each was allowed to take place. The output produced was a list of all feasible permutations of those activities. Unlike PESASP it identified the likely response by evaluating schedules 'according to least disruption from the current arrangement', which is 'a measure of the dissimilarity between that arrangement and the observed activity schedule' (Jones et al, 1983, 203). The process was repeated for 149 people in a survey in Oxfordshire.

Clarke undertook a series of experiments, summarised in Jones et al (1983, Chapters 11–12), which illustrated the dependence on the algorithmic performance and computer resources on such factors as the nature of constraints and classifications in recording such features as the width of time bands, the number of activities, and so on. He noted the balance to be achieved between computational efficiency of searching for the number of possible feasible arrangements on the one hand and the detail to which the problem was specified and the danger of rejecting behaviourally sound schedules on the other.

6.4.4 STARCHILD

Drawing on and synthesising several earlier ideas on the individual and household decision process and activity scheduling models, Will Recker et al (1986) introduced STARCHILD (simulation of travel/activity responses to complex household interactive logistic decisions). This effort contributed to the theoretical and conceptual analysis of the activity programme and existed as a prototype research model. The model attempted to explain behaviour at the household level and did so by constructing daily activity patterns. It comprised five modules, representing choices within a constrained environment (Recker et al, 1986):

1. generation of a set of activity programmes corresponding to each household member from an analysis of household interactions;
2. generation of feasible activity programmes for each household member;
3. reduction of feasible programmes to a distinct pattern set;
4. specification of the choice set formation model;
5. application of an activity pattern choice model.

The means by which individuals, faced with a complex and potentially very large choice set, adopted decision strategies which reduced the number of distinct feasible activity patterns to manageable proportions was given particular attention. The authors noted:

> This set formation process restricts the number of available options; yet that number, in general will be quite large – a consequence that is problematic from both operational and behavioural points of view. Furthermore, there is no guarantee that the resulting feasible activity patterns are perceived by the individuals as distinct options. Certain activity patterns, because of their similarity along a number of dimensions, may be perceived by the individual as being indistinguishable and therefore not treated as separate alternatives. It is hypothesized that a classification reduction process operates on the opportunity set in such a manner that distinct elements are produced. Various decision rules may be applied before or after the classification process, further narrowing the set of alternatives (Recker et al, 1986, 311).

The authors proposed the use of pattern classification techniques as a basis for identifying 'representative activity patterns', which were homogeneous groups of distinct patterns. In the multi-criteria world within which choices were considered to be made, simplification was further achieved through identification of so-called 'non-inferior patterns'. By the fifth module the choice was between feasible, non-inferior and distinct representative patterns. Although the MNL model was adopted to determine the probability that an activity pattern would be selected on the basis of utility maximising behaviour, the authors emphasised that any compensatory or non-compensatory choice model could be adopted for this purpose.

In summary, within a multi-criteria framework individuals, acting in a household context, were considered to select an optimal distinct sequence of activities, in terms of their durations, locations and modes, in order to maximise the total utility of the activities.

6.4.5 SCHEDULER, SMASH and AMOS

The three programs SCHEDULER (Gärling et al, 1994), SMASH (simulation model of activity scheduling heuristics) (Ettema et al, 1993) and AMOS (activity mobility simulator) (RDC, 1995; Kitamura et al, 1996; Kitamura and Fujii, 1998; Pendyala et al, 1998) share some common characteristics involving heuristic 'sub-optimal' decision-making processes. They adopted a set of heuristic rules and procedures in searching for an activity schedule and for this reason were referred to as rule-based, computational processes, and sometimes hybrid simulation models (Ben-Akiva and Bowman, 1998; Timmermans et al, 2002). Unlike some of the models described above that exhaustively determined the feasible arrangements from which one alternative may be selected on the basis of one or more criteria, in these models scheduling arrangements that satisfy the large number of constraints are successively generated. From these, 'sub-optimal' decisions may be made during the process, a decision to terminate or continue the search process being made on the basis of a set of evaluation criteria. These models usually involved an intricate algorithmic structure in which a set of rules reflects constraints and priorities, as, for example, illustrated in RDC (1995, section 5.3) and in Pendyala et al (1998, Figure 3).

The similarities and differences between these programs were discussed, for example, by Axhausen and Gärling (1992), Timmermans et al (2002, 183–184) and more recently Pinjari and Bhat (2011). We describe AMOS in more detail in the next section.

6.5 ACTIVITY-BASED TRAVEL DEMAND FORECASTING: TOWARDS OPERATIONAL MODELS

6.5.1 Towards 'a New Generation of Travel Demand Models'

In a rallying call that signalled the start of the Travel Model Improvement Program (TMIP) (section 8.3.1), Martin Wachs, chair of the TMIP Review Board (1993–96), spoke of the need to develop 'a new generation of travel demand models'. He expressed a view that resonated with many:

> Most practicing transportation planners employ travel demand models which were developed over thirty years ago. . . . Yet, with the exception of greatly improved modal choice models, the stepwise approach to travel demand modeling in wide application today looks quite similar to the modeling package of the late sixties and early seventies. We have undergone a revolution in computing capabilities and geographical information systems are increasingly being applied to transportation planning data sets, but the state of practice in transportation planning consists of an obsolete approach to modelling which has been marginally updated and adapted by clever technicians but which has not been fundamentally rethought from the ground up (Wachs, 1996, 213).

With the short-term intention of seeking to establish incremental progress in urban travel forecasting, TMIP had the long-term goal of 'fundamentally revolutionizing the state of practice in transportation modelling' (Wachs, 1996, 213). As in the early 1970s the 'old regime' consisting of the widely applied four-step aggregate model once again served as the comparator for alternative innovative proposals.

In an effort to improve the urban travel forecasting process, the Federal Highway Administration awarded small research grants in 1992 for initial designs of alternative approaches. Teams from the following organisations participated: Resource Decision Consultants; Caliper Corporation; MIT; and Louisiana Transportation Research Center (LTRC). Each submitted a proposal for the development of an appropriate model system. Bruce Spear, much as he did in reviewing progress on individual choice models in the mid-1970s, summarised the different approaches. In so doing he sought to: 'identify common themes suggested by several of the research teams, to point out what appear to be critical elements missing from some approaches, and to combine the best aspects of the four approaches into a research plan for improving the current generation of travel demand models' (Spear, 1996, 215).

Several features were common to the different initiatives. In particular, the activity approach was a prominent feature of the proposals. As Bruce Spear remarked:

Three of the four reports (RDC, MIT and LTRC) explicitly recommend that the current 'trip-based' model framework be replaced by an 'activity-based' framework in which the demand for travel is derived from the more basic demand to engage in various activities. . . . While each of the reports suggest a slightly different approach to modeling activity behavior, all of them rely heavily on the use of constraint parameters to reduce the number of choice options to a manageable size (Spear, 1996, 229–231).

In this section we describe the further development of two of these initiatives and how they were to be refined, partly under TMIP funding, towards operational status in Portland, Oregon and Washington, DC.

6.5.2 Two Contrasting Approaches to Activity-Travel Modelling

Because of their significance as operational models we describe some aspects of two innovative studies which exemplify very different approaches to activity-travel modelling. Each started to address some of the travel forecasting requirements of transportation planning agencies. We make no attempt to compare them in detail for, as in the two applications described in section 6.3, they were designed for different ends and, more specifically, to generate different outputs. Both served as points of comparison for later developments and both give fascinating insights into the difficulties involved in forging a path towards operational activity-based forecasting models.

Although described as activity-travel models there were rather few similarities between them. In the case of the Portland model the econometric discrete choice approach was adopted for the synthesis of the whole activity schedule (the pattern and timing of individual activities and travel) over a 24-hour period as a basis for determining significant explanatory variables and establishing elasticities for policy analysis and forecasting. Additionally, it generated trip matrices for network assignment.

In the case of the Washington model, designed around the heuristic search process model in AMOS (section 6.4.5), the response of a sample of individuals to a range of policy measures was directly estimated. This effectively involved determining short-term adjustments to the activity schedules of the base-year sample, using stated preferences or intentions derived from a specially implemented survey. In the econometric approach the familiar utility maximising rationale was used as a basis for determining choices and structuring analytic demand relations; in the Washington model a 'satisficing' approach to individual action was implemented as part of the search for feasible alternatives to current behaviour under a modified policy environment.

There were, however, some common features of the approaches. Both were designed to draw on databases available to typical metropolitan planning organisations (MPOs), consisting of trip diaries of individuals and households, and land use and network data. Both also drew on stated preference or intentions survey data, these being central to the implementation of the Washington model. The following description of the Portland model is derived from the papers and reports by Ben-Akiva et al (1996), HCG (1997), Ben-Akiva and Bowman (1998) and Bowman and Ben-Akiva (2001) and, in particular, the paper by Bowman et al (1999). For the Washington prototype of AMOS, we refer to Kitamura and Fujii (1998) and Pendyala et al (1998), but mainly to the extensive documentation by RDC (1995).

6.5.3   An Econometric Activity-Travel Approach: The Portland Model

The Portland model was derived from a proposal in 1994 by Ben-Akiva et al (1996), which was subsequently developed as a prototype for the Boston metropolitan area (Bowman, 1995; Bowman and Ben-Akiva, 2001). It employed the familiar econometric methods of discrete choice analysis, and constituted according to its developers 'the third step in the evolution of disaggregate econometric model systems towards an activity basis' (Bowman et al, 1999, 172). The application was funded under the FHWA's TMIP initiative with Cambridge Systematics, and by a project entitled Portland Traffic Relief Options Study (PTROS) funded jointly by the FHWA, the State of Oregon and Portland Metro. The prime objective was to incorporate activity-based methods into econometric travel demand model systems, and the effort was described by the study team as:

> an important improvement over trip and tour-based models in use today. It provides a more advanced activity-based representation of travel behavior in an operational general purpose metropolitan travel forecasting model system, including the ability to capture changes in activity participation, trip chaining, inter-tour and at-home vs on-tour trade-offs, as well as changes in timing, mode and destination (Bowman et al, 1999, 183).

6.5.3.1   Overall model structure
By building up a daily activity pattern, the Portland model and the earlier application in Boston were designed to address two weaknesses of the tour-based approaches. The choice of daily activity patterns which 'overarches and ties together tour decisions' (Ben-Akiva and Bowman, 1998, 41) and the introduction of schedule and timing decisions directly introduced a richer pattern of cross-substitution (responses to policies) within the model. It introduced: firstly, the possibility of substituting out-of-home activities involving travel for in-home activities; and,

secondly, the possibility of substitution between complex tour patterns (e.g., exchanging a single extended tour involving multiple activities for two separate tours at different times of the day, or vice versa).

The method drew heavily on previous disaggregate model systems developed at MIT and by Cambridge Systematics based on a hierarchy of decisions, and reflecting their conditional dependency (lower-level choices were dependent on decisions at a higher level) while incorporating interdependencies through linking 'logsum' variables representing the mean expected utility of a lower-level choice. Again, the nested logit model provided the analytic framework within which this conditionality and interdependency were expressed.

6.5.3.2 The activity-travel model system and its individual components

The structure of the travel forecasting model, shown in Figure 6.2, was arranged in a hierarchy of five modules. The choice of daily activity pattern, expressed as a combination of tours undertaken over a 24-hour period, involved a choice over combinations of primary activity, primary tour type, and the number and purpose of secondary tours. For each tour the destination, time of day and mode were modelled. The probability of a particular day activity schedule was thus formulated by Bowman et al (1999, 172–173) as the product of a 'marginal pattern probability and a conditional tours probability . . . given the choice of pattern', as described below. MNL models were applied to the various choices with the tour utilities; in this way the network level-of-service variables influenced the choice of activity pattern through 'logsum' variables.

In all, 114 possible household activity pattern choices were identified, consisting of the number, purpose and trip chain types of all tours undertaken during the day. The primary tours were identified by various tour types accompanying primary activities performed either at home or away from home ('on tour'). Three classes of primary activity were defined: subsistence (work or school), maintenance (shopping, personal business, etc.) and discretionary (social, recreational, etc.). For the primary activity undertaken away from home various tour types were identified in the form of the relatively common 'there and back' structures HXH, and more complex arrangements, such as HOXH, HXOH or HOXOH, where X represents a primary activity type, and O represents a secondary stop of undetermined purpose.

Once the daily activity pattern was determined, time-of-day models determined the sequencing and duration of these tours and the out-of-home activities that formed them. Five different daily time periods were distinguished, each consisting of several hours:

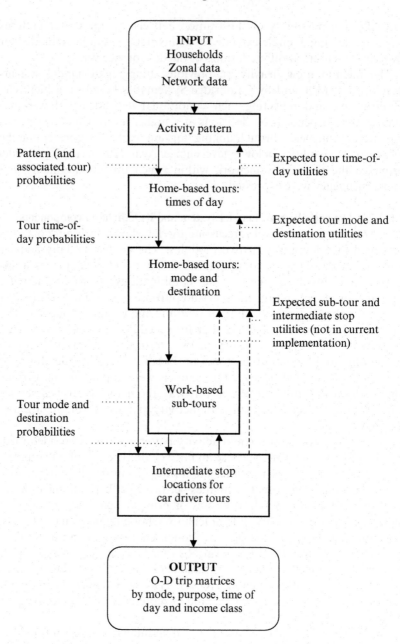

Source: Bowman et al (1999, Figure 3).

Figure 6.2   Structure of the Portland Activity Schedule Model System

1. For each tour, the time-of-day model in MNL form predicted the combination of departure time from home, and departure time from the primary activity; in all 15 departure time combinations were identified.
2. Time-of-day models were separately developed for work or school tours, maintenance tours and discretionary purpose tours.

The independent variables consisted of various person and household variables and also 'logsums' from the lower-level mode or destination choice models. Tour purpose and tour type were also used as variables.

The developers of the model noted particular difficulties dealing with the time-of-day dimension and the problem of resolution of the schedule, requiring a compromise between the need to capture variation in behaviour and the practicality of dealing with the immense number of possible combinations of activity sequences when fine categorisation of the continuous time variable is involved. The specific choice of time intervals thus represented a compromise in distinguishing major time periods in the day.

Once the activity schedule (pattern and tour type(s) and timing) was determined, the model system predicted the primary mode and destination for each tour. It determined the probability that each zone would be the primary tour destination and that each of nine possible modes would be the main mode of the tour; household and personal data as well as network distance time and cost data were used as variables.

Synthetic populations were used for implementing the model for each forecast year or demographic scenario. The application of the above choice models for the day pattern model and the home-based tour models, in conjunction with the synthetic population, predicted activity schedule probabilities for each person, which were then aggregated into a set of 'half tour matrices' for assignment to the relevant networks.

Bowman et al (1999) described a range of tests on the model and assessment of the aggregate effects of complex substitution effects – part of the *raison d'être* for developing the model, arising from a range of travel demand management-related measures, including a time differentiated toll policy. The authors reported satisfactory and logically consistent results.

6.5.4 AMOS: The Washington Prototype

6.5.4.1 An overview of context and policies
The Washington prototype of AMOS was described in pioneering terms:

This project represents the first implementation of a full-fledged activity-based model system for transportation planning and policy analysis. . . .

The development of AMOS and its implementation in the Washington DC metropolitan area ... represents a significant step forward in transportation planning and policy analysis. The development is especially significant considering the importance of travel demand management in the current planning contexts set forth by the Clean Air Act Amendments and Intermodal Surface Transportation Efficiency Act (RDC, 1995, section 1, 4).

The project in Washington, DC was jointly sponsored as part of TMIP by FHWA and US EPA. The sponsors' intention was to 'investigate and develop the idea of activity-based forecasting in an applied setting' (RDC, 1995, 1). The model was developed specifically to address six short-term travel demand management (TDM) measures, including congestion charging, parking pricing and employer supplied commuter vouchers, and to improve pedestrian facilities, the policies being described in terms of their influence on out-of-pocket costs, travel times, modal attributes and individual constraints. In addition to the trip diary data derived from a 1994 household travel survey and other land use and network data normally available to a metropolitan planning organisation, a specially commissioned survey of the stated preference responses to the proposed policies was collected from over 650 commuters.

6.5.4.2 The overall model structure and its components

The five components at the heart of AMOS are shown in the boxes with bold borders in Figure 6.3. The intricacies of the many different aspects of the overall model belie a basic simplicity: each individual trip record in a base sample was examined and an initial response to a proposed policy identified. The wider ramifications of this response for the activity-travel pattern were then sought and, on the basis of an evaluation criterion and stopping rule, any additional responses to the initial stimulus determined. Because of the unfamiliarity of the concepts, we shall describe three of these components in a little more detail, with further details available in the project report (RDC, 1995) and subsequent academic papers (Kitamura and Fujii, 1998; Pendyala et al, 1998). The first and fifth modules were responsible for checking the integrity of the input data and providing a range of summary statistics, respectively.

The TDM response option generator created what was termed the 'basic response' of an individual to a TDM policy. This was achieved by applying a model whose parameters were estimated from revealed and stated preference data obtained from the AMOS surveys (RDC, 1995). The model was used to determine the probability that an individual would respond to any policy in one of the following ways:

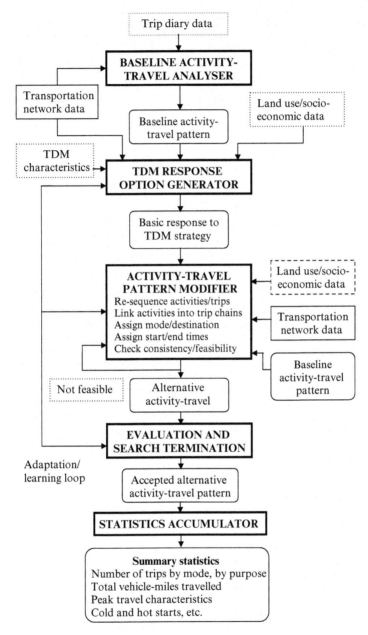

Source: Redrawn from RDC (1995) Figure 4.1.

Figure 6.3 AMOS model structure

1. no change in travel behaviour;
2. change of departure time for work trip;
3. change of mode:
    (a) switch work trip mode to transit;
    (b) switch work trip mode to car/van pool;
    (c) switch work trip mode to bicycle;
    (d) switch work trip mode to walk;
4. work at home.

On the basis of these probabilities, a specific response was selected by means of Monte Carlo methods.

The activity-travel pattern modifier is the most intricate component of the overall model and goes to the heart of the implementation of the constraint-based action of the individual. For any basic response (such as modal switching) output from the TDM response option generator a set of alternative feasible activity-travel options were identified for the individual concerned. The possible ramifications of the basic response included: (a) re-sequencing of activities; (b) linking of activities into trip chains; (c) modifications to the mode or destination; (d) retiming of trips. These possible responses were the result of a 'complex algorithm that can re-sequence and re-schedule activities, break and make chains, and change travel modes and activity locations' (RDC, 1995, section 5, 5). A much more detailed description is available in RDC (1995, Figure 5.4) and Pendyala et al (1998, 758–762).

Attributes of trips in the new activity-travel patterns generated by the algorithm were determined by using a series of models. For example, destination (location) choice was determined by gravity-type trip distribution models, and MNL models were incorporated to determine modal choice, the modal constraints determining the choice sets available for each trip. Trip departure times were also determined within the rule-based algorithm, recognising any temporal constraints. The output of the module was a modified activity-travel pattern which was feasible in terms of the set of rule-based constraints.

The evaluation module and acceptance routines provided, respectively, a utility assessment of a modified activity schedule and a decision whether it would be accepted on the basis of a 'human adaptation and learning model incorporating a set of search termination rules'. The evaluation module implemented in AMOS was based on the utility that an individual derived from the time and money spent on various activities and the 'quality' of time spent on each activity (RDC, 1995, Appendix D; Pendyala et al, 1998). The total utility of the series of activities pursued during the day was expressed as the sum of the utilities of the respective activities. The decision model 'incorporates a search termination procedure that allows an individual to adopt a sub-optimal activity-travel pattern so long as it satisfies his or her activity needs' (Pendyala et al, 1998, 762).

The summary statistics generated by the model included: (a) number of trips by mode and purpose; (b) total vehicle-miles travelled; (c) peak travel characteristics; and (d) information on cold and hot starts and fuel consumption. An extensive discussion of the implementation, policy design and simulation runs from the Washington prototype of AMOS was given in RDC (1995, Chapters 6, 7).

6.5.5　Some Comments on the Two Applications and Their Approaches

Both the models described above involved considerable compromises in specification and implementation of the conceptual frameworks initially set out. This was work in progress, and the documentation of the prototypes for both Boston and Portland (Bowman et al, 1999; Bowman and Ben-Akiva, 2001) and that for Washington (RDC, 1995) was exemplary in its discussion of the limitations which always characterise pioneering work (see also Rossi and Shiftan, 1997; Algers et al, 2005). It was the intention that the assumptions, approximations and compromises would become the foci for a sustained research and development programme that future applications would also need to address. The authors of the Portland model concluded their work with the assessment:

> The day activity schedule model, as implemented in Portland, retains some weaknesses . . . including incompleteness, coarse schedule resolution, and misspecification of utility functions, model structure and availability. . . . Many of the weaknesses described above arise primarily from technology limits and incomplete knowledge of the decision process, which can both be dealt with as the model is used in policy studies and enhanced through further research and development (Bowman et al, 1999, 182–183).

AMOS was designed to be different from conventional forecasting model systems in a number of respects, reflecting what the authors described as 'multiple paradigm changes' (RDC, 1995, section 4.1). Several limitations of the Washington application were acknowledged and emphasised as points of research. These included:

1. extensions to incorporate household interactions;
2. activity substitution and its effect on time spent in and out of the home;
3. incorporation of weekly variability;

4. ability to model changes in behaviour for non-commuters in response to transportation policy.

In the version of AMOS reported, there was no attempt to perform network assignments or achieve self-consistent zone-to-zone travel times.

What was clear was the very different views at that time on the state of the art and how activity-travel forecasting models, in the various different application contexts, might or should develop. Whatever their limitations, in our view these models provided the necessary implementation breakthrough – practical activity-based model systems were developed, key issues were identified, research agenda were established and, again, others who followed would be less intimidated by the practical challenges involved.

In the several years since their respective claims began to be discussed there was much comment in the literature about the distinctions and relative merits of the econometric and rule-based hybrid simulation models of the activity schedule. Moshe Ben-Akiva and John Bowman remarked:

> Although both approaches represent a two-stage decision protocol of choice set generation followed sequentially or iteratively by the choice itself, econometric models focus, on the one hand, on the complex representation of a utility-based multi-dimensional choice. Hybrid simulations, on the other hand, focus most of their attention on choice set generation, employing a complex search heuristic that yields a very small choice set. A simple choice model is used to represent the choice from this set, frequently with iteration occurring between choice set generation and choice (Ben-Akiva and Bowman, 1998, 35).

6.6 MORE RECENT DEVELOPMENTS IN ACTIVITY-BASED TRAVEL DEMAND FORECASTING

What was a highly fragmented field encompassing various hypotheses, methods and empirical studies at the start of the 1980s had, within a decade, attained mainstream status in the travel research community and was gathering momentum (Kitamura, 1988; Jones et al, 1990; Gärling et al, 1998b). Among this community there was the definite feel of moving towards the next generation of travel forecasting methods based on activity-travel concepts, although, as the above examples showed, there were several problems to be addressed and very different views about the appropriate means for representing and forecasting behaviour (RDC, 1995; Kitamura et al, 1997a; Bowman et al, 1999).

There seemed to be some agreement that in this venture the treatment of time and time use would attain centre stage (Kitamura et al, 1997a, 1997c;

Pas and Harvey, 1997; Pas, 1998; Bhat and Koppelman, 1999a, 1999b). As Pinjari and Bhat (2011, 19) later noted, 'the appropriate treatment of the time dimension of activity-travel behaviour is perhaps the most important prerequisite to accurately forecasting activity-travel patterns'. Since that formative and productive period in the mid-1990s there has been further extensive research and development work on activity-based models within the academic community and research-oriented consultancies and institutions. Our intention here is briefly to survey some of these major developments. Fortunately the field is well served by excellent and accessible reviews and application reports.[3] Here we provide a brief overview of developments, and readers can seek further details in the papers cited in note 3 and the additional references below.

By far the largest part of the effort devoted to model development has been to understand and reproduce base-year activity-travel patterns and model the likely response to fairly traditional policy instruments relating to investment and particularly demand management measures. Additionally, since the mid-1980s there has been a burgeoning literature on the impact of advanced communications technology on travel-related behaviour, for which the activity framework proved to be highly suitable. Within this literature the substitution between and complementarity of travel and telecommunications have been recurrent themes (Salomon, 1986; Mokhtarian, 1990, 1991, 2002; Pendyala et al, 1991; Golob and Regan, 2001; Golob, 2001; Mokhtarian and Salomon, 2002).

While the differences between activity-based travel demand models often reflected particular requirements of policy, information sought, data availability, and so on, the distinctions made in the 1980s between an econometric discrete choice style, exemplified by the Portland application considered above, and computational process or 'rule-based' models have persisted. These distinctions however narrowed and in some cases merged, as exponents of both sought to incorporate more realistic choice sets and decision models in representing individual and household activity-travel behaviour. As Bowman noted, 'Within the consulting world, there have been an increasing number of model systems implemented primarily for practical use. These have been hybrid model systems, relying on econometric models that are integrated in a simulation framework using a blend of econometric principles and rule-based assumptions' (Bowman, 2009, 61).

In the new wave of applications and laboratory studies following the mid-1990s the application of microsimulation techniques, based on the processing of synthetic populations endowed with multiple and complex interdependencies between the attributes of 'individuals' and 'households', became more common (McNally, 1997; Kitamura et al, 2000; Miller et al,

2004; Balmer et al, 2008). Joan Walker (2005, 3) noted that 'most state of the art travel demand models now employ microsimulation', and that is more likely to be the case today.

The major challenges for the behavioural approach to travel demand forecasting remained those of catering for: the diversity of households and individuals' characteristics and the wide variety of spatial, temporal and inter-personal constraints to which they were subject; the huge number of potential substitutes for particular activity-travel behaviour, many of which would exhibit close similarity; the construction of realistic decision models whose parameters could be estimated and predictions validated; the allocation to networks and the achievement of consistency in level-of-service variables; and the problems of data availability and knowledge to support the development of such models. In all of this the issue of model design was central – what forms of simplification and/or approximations were necessary and justified to make models operational in particular policy testing and information contexts?

After its initial application, the Portland model in the form described in the last section was discontinued, but its legacy lives on in several of the activity-based travel demand model applications in the US. John Bowman (2009) produced a valuable review of the recent US metropolitan and regional applications of the micro-econometric approach. In particular, he drew attention to the similarities and differences between those models applied in Portland, San Francisco, Sacramento, Denver, Seattle, New York, Columbus, Atlanta and the San Francisco Bay Area.

In their overview of utility maximisation-based econometric models Pinjari and Bhat (2011) also included two models developed in the research community, namely CEMDAP (comprehensive econometric microsimulator for daily activity-travel patterns), developed for Dallas, Texas (Bhat et al, 2004; Pinjari and Bhat, 2011), also discussed by Bowman (2009), and FAMOS (Florida activity mobility simulator) (Pendyala et al, 2005).

Among the similarities of US applications, Bowman (2009) drew attention to: (a) representation of an entire day of activities and travel for each member of a synthetic population within a microsimulation framework; (b) adoption of an integrated system of econometric models; and (c) inclusion of traditional traffic and public transport assignment components. A rather common form of hierarchy of the levels in the integrated econometric model systems is shown in Figure 6.4 (Bowman, 2009, 315).

Within this broad similarity, with some models being directly developed from others, the differences are relatively small, although significant. The main differences relate to the following classification and specification issues (Bowman, 2009, 315–318):

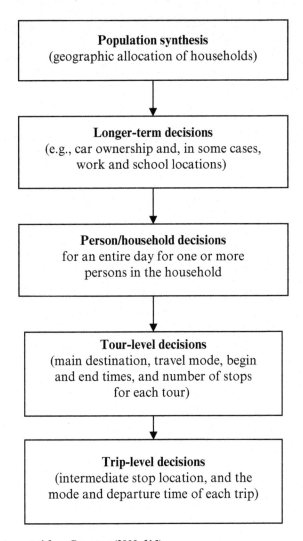

Source: Interpreted from Bowman (2009, 315).

*Figure 6.4   Common form of decision hierarchy applied in several
practical activity-based models*

1.   spatial resolution (assignment zones and sub-zones/parcels);
2.   time periods, out-of-home journey purposes;
3.   treatment of household interactions (and the nature of day patterns,
     and the extent to which they explicitly link across household members);

4. level at which intermediate stop purposes and frequencies are modelled;
5. structure of models in relation to the interdependency between mode, destination and tour time of day;
6. accessibility variables incorporated in the above for linking choices.

Further practical details and commentary of these models may be found in Vovsha et al (2005), Vovsha and Bradley (2006), Davidson et al (2007), Bradley et al (2009), Donnelly et al (2010) and Pinjari and Bhat (2011).

CEMDAP, developed by Chandra Bhat and colleagues, is similar to the model systems described above: 'the activity-travel patterns in CEMDAP are represented in a hierarchy of pattern-level attributes, tour-level attributes, and stop-level attributes. The difference, however, is that the attributes in CEMDAP characterize a continuous time activity-travel pattern built within the space-time constraints imposed by work and school activities' (Pinjari and Bhat, 2011, 8).

In recent applications of CEMDAP to Los Angeles, developed partly to evaluate the effects of policies on gaseous emissions, a household-level pattern model jointly predicted all combinations of purpose participation by accompaniment (Bhat et al, 2013). The multiple discrete-continuous extreme value (MDCEV) model (Bhat, 2005; Bhat and Eluru, 2010) allowed participation and time investment in multiple alternatives to be modelled simultaneously.

While work on AMOS was not continued in the form applied in Washington, DC (RDC, 1995), some of the key ideas in AMOS and PCATS (prism constrained activity-travel simulator), presented in Kitamura and Fujii (1998), would later find expression in other micro-simulation models of activity-travel behaviour (Kitamura et al, 2000), and notably in FAMOS (Pendyala et al, 2005). FAMOS may be regarded as a hybrid model, in the sense described by Bowman (2009), and is similar to CEMDAP in the explicit representation of space-time constraints, and the continuous time nature of the modelling system.

6.6.1 Advances in Rule-Based Computational Process Models

In the early 1990s Axhausen and Gärling expressed the view that:

> several basic problems are related to the process of activity scheduling. In fact the details of this process, how information on the environment and the trans-portation system is acquired and used, how utilities or priorities are assigned to activities, and which heuristics and decision rules are used, are largely unknown (Axhausen and Gärling, 1992, 335).

By 2000, alternatives to the utility maximising framework which attempted to mimic the way individuals solve problems were much discussed in the activity-travel literature (Gärling et al, 1994; RDC, 1995; Ettema and Timmermans, 1997; Gärling et al, 1998b; Kitamura and Fujii, 1998; Pendyala et al, 1998; Svenson, 1998). Few examples were applied in metropolitan planning practice, however.

One interesting development of a computational process model (CPM)-based activity modelling system came along with one of the more exotic acronyms, ALBATROSS (a learning-based transportation-oriented simulation system) (Arentze and Timmermans, 2004), developed at Eindhoven University. Other related activity-travel programs developed in the Netherlands, including AMADEUS, MASTIC and RAMBLAS, have been reviewed by Buliung and Kanaroglou (2007).

A further noteworthy rule-based scheduling microsimulation model of activity-travel over a 24-hour period, TASHA (Toronto area scheduling model for household agents), has been developed by Eric Miller, Matthew Roorda and colleagues at the University of Toronto (Miller and Roorda, 2003; Roorda et al, 2008).

Despite significant research and development over the last 20 years, substantial challenges continue to be posed by the intricacies of the decision process in a complex choice environment. These have commanded lengthy reviews and special issues of journals, and good surveys of the challenges ahead may be found in Buliung and Kanaroglou (2007), Davidson et al (2007) and Pinjari and Bhat (2011). The following topics have been subject to vigorous research over the last decade, and contributions frequently appear in the literature on activity-travel behaviour: (a) the perception of space and time, cognitive learning, habitual travel, information acquisition, adaptation and dynamics; (b) the interaction of individual daily activity-travel within household decisions, joint decisions and conflict resolution, and the data to support their study; (c) wider interactions and social networks; and (d) the detailed ordering of multiple decisions within a hierarchical framework.

As the development of activity-travel models became more refined in spatial and temporal detail, their scope also extended to related aspects of systems behaviour. Over the last two decades much effort has been devoted to the construction of activity-travel/traffic microsimulation models which are based on increasingly complex and realistic representations of behaviour, and response to changes, in network conditions. These were in part stimulated by the requirement to output more detailed energy and environmental information and, more particularly, the surge in interest in policies of demand management and intelligent transportation systems. There have been major initiatives to match the precision of

activity-travel behaviour on the demand side with corresponding developments on the supply side requiring improved network representations, for
which microsimulation served as a suitable representational and solution
framework. Prominent examples are TRANSIMS (Nagel et al, 1999) and
MATSim (Balmer et al, 2008) (section 8.4.1).

There were also calls for more integrated models of the land use –
transportation system (Pinjari and Bhat, 2011) in which the activity-travel
system is more highly developed than in traditional model forms. The
microsimulation land use – transportation models developed by Waddell
et al (2003) (UrbanSim), Salvini and Miller (2005) (ILUTE) and Pendyala
et al (2012) contain the activity-travel framework to varying degrees of
detail.

The great increase in computer power and more versatile languages
again contributed to this development. Some of these initiatives, which
incorporate the activity approach in different degrees, are discussed in
more detail in Chapter 8.

6.7 CONCLUSION

It took a decade from Warner's pioneering study in the early 1960s for
the disaggregate approach to start to make a significant impression on the
practice of travel demand forecasting, and several more years before the
discrete choice approach based on random utility theory was offered as
an alternative to the traditional aggregate methods based on the four-step
procedure. In a similar way, while the conceptual aspects of the activity
approach were relatively quickly absorbed by the travel research community, two decades would pass before the activity scheduling models would
emerge from academia in operational applications, and a further decade
before they started to make a significant though still a relatively small
impact on mainline travel forecasting and transportation planning. In the
process, elements of transportation geography were fused with those of
micro-economics and psychology, and the amalgam, merged with network
models of varying description, found a home in many civil or transportation engineering departments and some research-oriented consultancies.

Since the second half of the 1990s three styles of travel forecasting
model existed side by side at various stages of refinement and development: (a) traditional trip-based approaches founded on the multi-step
framework, which by now incorporated 'disaggregate' features, particularly in its treatment of trip generation and modal split; (b) tour-based
approaches, whether conceived at the micro-level or as an adaptation of the zone-based multi-step approach; and (c) activity scheduling

approaches, which treated the pattern of activities and travel over the whole day as the unit of analysis. Within each, a range of models became available, based on different approximations, technical refinements and alternative behavioural hypotheses.

The original critique and research agenda set out at the start of the 'activity era' were broadly stated in terms of the nature of the personal and household choices that were made, the constraints to which they were subject, and the representation of the decision process itself. There was much progress in addressing the first two of these, rather less so the third, where reliance on a utility maximising decision criterion holds sway in most practical models. What emerged was a set of sophisticated urban travel forecasting models, based on assumptions large and small, capable of addressing policies as diverse as infrastructure and land use development, and demand and traffic management instruments of various descriptions. For some applications, such as technological and 'smart' policy instruments, development is still at a relatively early stage. While there was doubtless much impressive work on the implementation of operational models, the lack of a consensus on their specification, and the range of specific research issues noted above, indicates that there is still much to be done, and this is widely acknowledged. We return to consider the contribution and further research issues of activity-based models in Chapters 8, 9 and 11.

NOTES

1. en.wikipedia.org/wiki/Torsten_Hägerstrand (accessed 4 March 2014).
2. It is worth noting that the derived nature of demand was also a feature of the standard discrete choice approach where, for example, in trip destination models the benefit derived from undertaking an activity at a particular location would be offset against the generalised cost of travel. Critics often argued however that this merely paid 'lip service' to activity participation in a more fundamental process by which trips were generated by individuals in order to fulfil their daily needs (Jones, 1977).
3. For our task, in addition to those papers cited in the text, we have found the following to be particularly useful: Bhat and Koppelman (1993, 1999a), Ettema and Timmermans (1997), Gärling et al (1998a, 1998b), McNally (2000a, 2000b), Wen and Koppelman (2000), Bowman and Ben-Akiva (2001), Recker (2001), Timmermans et al (2002), Algers et al (2005), Bhat and Pendyala (2005), Timmermans (2005), Vovsha et al (2005), Arentze and Timmermans (2007), Axhausen (2007), Buliung and Kanaroglou (2007), Davidson et al (2007), Bowman (2009), Timmermans and Zhang (2009), Donnelly et al (2010) and Pinjari and Bhat (2011).

7. Transportation network equilibrium

7.1 INTRODUCTION[1]

Building on the experiences of the Detroit, Chicago and Penn Jersey transportation studies, the sequential travel forecasting procedure was adopted by several North American metropolitan areas by 1970 and transferred to large conurbations in the UK (Chapters 2–3). Unrelated to these early studies, major advances in mathematics and mathematical economics occurred during the post-war period, some evolving from wartime applications of mathematics and statistics in the US and UK. Efforts to apply mathematics and economics to solve defence mobilisation problems led the US Department of the Air Force to investigate project planning methods and to establish the RAND Corporation.[2] Fields called 'operations research' in the US and 'operational research' in the UK emerged from these activities.

These pioneering efforts laid the foundations for a new field of mathematics concerned with efficiency and equilibria of physical and economic systems, which exists today as mathematical programming and optimisation, and was formerly known as 'activity analysis'. Research to understand the properties of these new constructs, and to apply them to problems of national defence, challenged mathematicians and mathematical economists.

The objective of this chapter is to trace developments emerging from these new fields, which led to major contributions to travel forecasting. Today, the cumulative effects of these lines of research are found in research monographs and edited volumes that appeared from the 1970s, listed here in order of publication: Potts and Oliver (1972); Hutchinson (1974); Steenbrink (1974b); Florian (1976); Newell (1980); Florian (1984a); Sheffi (1985); Erlander and Stewart (1990); Nagurney (1993); de la Barra (1994); Patriksson (1994); Florian and Hearn (1995, 1999); Oppenheim (1995); Sen and Smith (1995); Bell and Iida (1997); Bell (1998); Hall (1999); Gendreau and Marcotte (2002); Patriksson and Labbé (2002); Yang and Huang (2005); Marcotte and Patriksson (2007); Cascetta (2009); and Erlander (2010).

The chapter begins with a statement of the assumptions underlying network equilibrium models with variable demand in section 7.2.1. Although similar to those found in Chapters 4 and 5, some are restated here so that this chapter is self-contained. Section 7.2.2 offers an overview of the mathematics of optimisation and equilibria that forms the basis for the chapter. Readers familiar with these concepts may omit section 7.2 without loss of continuity.

Section 7.2.2 also identifies some of the principal contributors to post-war research programmes in optimisation and mathematical economics. These initiatives begun in the context of the Cold War led to a small research programme on the 'optimal allocation of resources'. Quite unexpectedly, this research resulted in the formulation and analysis of an optimisation problem suitable for forecasting urban travel and route flows over congested road networks.

Proceeding chronologically, these developments are described with other studies occurring in parallel, in some cases stimulated by transportation studies in Detroit and Chicago (Chapter 2). Once the significance of these early findings began to be recognised, additional research was undertaken, often by Ph.D. students in operations research. These studies are described chronologically for each version of the following problems:

1. deterministic network equilibrium problem with fixed demand;
2. stochastic network equilibrium problem with fixed demand;
3. deterministic multi-modal network equilibrium problem with variable demand;
4. implementation, estimation and validation studies of the optimisation formulations.

Then, generalisations of the original optimisation formulation are considered:

1. non-linear complementarity and variational inequality;
2. solution algorithms and extensions;
3. prototype solutions of the asymmetric assignment problem;
4. public transport assignment on congested road networks.

Finally, the roles of international symposia and academic journals in the development of the field are described, followed by a brief conclusion.

7.2 ASSUMPTIONS AND MATHEMATICAL APPROACH

7.2.1 Assumptions about Travel on Transportation Networks

Underlying travel forecasting models defined on multi-modal urban transportation networks are several assumptions that determine the conceptual and analytical approach.

First, travel patterns tend to repeat themselves regularly, day after day. In the absence of such repetition, individuals would have little basis for deciding when to travel, by which route, to a given destination, or even for choosing their destinations. Regular travel patterns are distorted by unexpected events, such as accidents, or by somewhat predictable events such as weather conditions. Even so, these regularities are sufficiently strong to make an assumption of 'perfect information' about network conditions worth exploring. Historically, such information was based on one's experience. Recently, technological advances have provided current travel information, which may be regarded as 'very good information'.

Second, travellers independently and non-cooperatively tend to minimise the time and cost of their journeys over road and public transport networks. The extent of this tendency depends on the type of choice (e.g., route, mode or destination) and the definition of time, cost and importance among other considerations. An implication of this assumption is the existence of an 'equilibrium' in which the objectives of all travellers are simultaneously satisfied. In this chapter, we refer to this construct as a 'network equilibrium'. An equivalent term is 'user equilibrium'.

The objective of some travellers may be to travel as quickly as possible to their destinations. Travel time includes actual driving or riding time, as well as access time to the network, and waiting time for public transport services, which depends on the frequency of service. Other travellers may also consider the monetary cost of travel, such as the vehicle operating cost, including tolls and parking fees, or the fares paid for public transport or taxis. Reliability of travel is another consideration, perhaps represented by the variation in travel time from trip to trip. Still other factors relate to less tangible considerations such as comfort and convenience. A weighted sum of these various costs is called the generalised travel cost, formerly known as 'impedance'; see section 2.3.4 for the early use of this term. An example of generalised travel cost is the travel time plus the monetary travel cost divided by the traveller's value of time. Travellers may be grouped into user classes according to their values of time and other attributes of their generalised cost functions. In the following, 'travel cost' means generalised cost, including travel time.

The origins of the assumption concerning an individual's minimisation of travel cost are noteworthy. Johann Georg Kohl [1808–1878] was a German travel writer, historian and geographer.[3] His main scientific work concerned 'road traffic and human settlement and their dependence on surface terrain'. Kohl described different types of transportation over land routes. He proposed that the least expensive, most prompt, direct and cautious, and least dangerous type of transport is the best, considering: (a) the kind of goods to be shipped (quick or slow transport, weight and volume of goods, etc.); and (b) the available routes for the specified types, and particularly their friction: the less the friction of a road surface and the greater its smoothness, the more perfect it is (Kohl, 1841, 77–78).[4] Peter Steenbrink (1974b, 26) remarked that the statement 'everybody traveling from *a* to *b* chooses a path [route] that has the lowest value for the user costs' was made in 1841 by J.G. Kohl. Michael Patriksson (1994, 29) stated that Kohl (1841, 76) 'recognized that the routes chosen by travelers were those that were individually perceived as being the shortest under prevailing traffic conditions'.

The subject of route choice over a two-route road network was considered by Arthur Cecil Pigou [1877–1959] in his 'most enduring contribution', *The Economics of Welfare* (Pigou, 1918).[5] Pigou made an error in an example (omitted in subsequent editions), which attracted the attention of Frank Knight [1885–1972].[6] Knight (1924) was the first to describe the conditions governing route choice on a two-route road network:

> Suppose that between two points there are two highways, one of which is broad enough to accommodate without crowding all the traffic which may care to use it, but is poorly graded and surfaced; while the other is a much better road, but narrow and quite limited in capacity. If a large number of trucks operate between the two termini and are free to choose either of the two routes, they will tend to distribute themselves between the roads in such proportions that the cost per unit of transportation, or effective result per unit of investment, will be the same for every truck on both routes. As more trucks use the narrower and better road, congestion develops, until at a certain point it becomes equally profitable to use the broader but poorer highway (Knight, 1924, 584–585).

In a survey paper presented in 1952, John Wardrop [1920–1989][7] subsequently stated:

> Consider two alternative criteria based on these journey times which can be used to determine the distribution on the routes, as follows:
> (1) The journey times on all the routes actually used are equal, and less than those which would be experienced by a single vehicle on any unused route.
> (2) The average journey time is a minimum (Wardrop, 1952, 344–345).

His first criterion became known as Wardrop's first principle. Wardrop was a staff member of the Road Research Board of the UK Department of Scientific and Industrial Research. In the five pages devoted to the subject of route choice in his 38-page paper, Wardrop explored a simple analysis of several alternative routes, ending with the realisation that 'In the case of a network of roads the theoretical problem becomes very complicated' (Wardrop, 1952, 348).

Third, the travel time over a link, a short segment of the road network or a segment of a bus line depends on the number of vehicles or travellers on the segment. For a road link, travel time is typically assumed to increase indefinitely in relation to the link's own flow, as shown in Figure 7.1 for the traditional BPR volume-delay (travel time-flow) function for a link with a nominal capacity of 1000 vehicles per hour (vph) (see section 2.5.5) (US DoC, 1964).[8] A related function, also shown in Figure 7.1, is the total time incurred by vehicles on the link, which equals the time incurred by each vehicle at a given flow multiplied by the link flow. If the travel time on a link approaching an intersection depends on the flows of all links

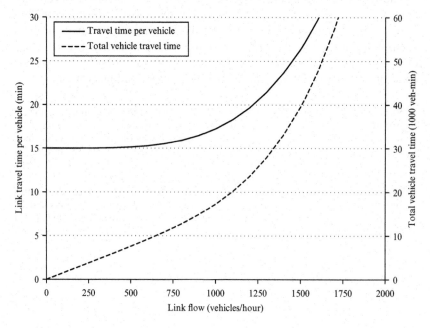

Source: Computed from the traditional Bureau of Public Roads volume-delay function.

Figure 7.1   Link travel time and total vehicle travel time in relation to link flow

entering the intersection, as well as the traffic signal or other intersection controls, a more challenging problem is defined. In the case of a bus line, the travel time may also increase with passenger occupancy, assuming that the vehicle capacity, service frequency and route are fixed.

Fourth, representation of generalised travel costs on the network, and travellers' perceptions of these costs, is a matter of extensive study. At one extreme, these costs are regarded as deterministic functions of flow and other network variables. At the other, travel costs are defined as random variables, reflecting several sources of variability and uncertainty of the individual traveller and in the network, as well as the lack of knowledge of the modeller (Chapter 4). Variations in the way travellers weight the various characteristics of individual links (e.g., times, distance, safety, scenic value) reflect part of that lack of knowledge. The modeller might invoke random variables to express both the 'taste variation' among travellers and unmeasured factors.

If perception errors are assumed not to be present, and travellers have perfect information and perceive network conditions in the same way without taste variation, the model is 'deterministic', and a single generalised cost is associated with each link. If travellers differ in the way they perceive and value conditions on the network, and this is represented by a probability distribution, but the network conditions are assumed to be described by the same time-flow functions, then the model is generally termed 'stochastic'; 'semi-stochastic' might be a better name, since the travel times are deterministic.

If the link travel times are considered to be random variables, reflecting variations in reality, then an additional assumption about the travellers' attitudes towards risk in the choice of route is required. Travellers may be risk-prone, risk-averse or risk-neutral. For example, risk-prone travellers favour routes with lower mean times, even though they have higher variances; risk-averse travellers favour routes with longer mean times, but with lower variances; risk-neutral travellers ignore the variance and follow minimum mean time routes. If perception errors and taste variations are assumed, and network conditions are random variables, then 'fully stochastic' may better describe such formulations.

Generally, the travel cost over a route is assumed to be the sum of the costs over the links constituting that route. A non-additivity assumption, in which the disutility of the route travel time is a non-linear function of the total route time, was studied by Gabriel and Bernstein (1997) and Larsson et al (2002). Additivity of link costs, however, is nearly always assumed.

Fifth, from the outset of urban travel forecasting in the US in the 1950s, travel forecasts were made for a 24-hour weekday, and sometimes for shorter periods of the day, such as the morning peak commuting period. Trips were considered to flow continuously from origins to destinations at constant rates per hour or per day. The interactions of these flows occur over links of the network, but not over clock time intervals during the period of interest. These models are now called 'static'.

Since the 1980s, models have been proposed in which the flows also interact through clock time as well as over links of the network.[9] In these models, the forecast period is divided into short intervals, such as 15 minutes. Link flows, and therefore link costs, are assumed to change from interval to interval. For these models to represent network flows over these short intervals, departure rates from origins must be defined by interval. These departure rates may be fixed by interval, or vary by interval in response to network conditions. An example of the former model is CONTRAM (section 9.3.1). The latter case has been the subject of recent research on dynamic traffic assignment and of biannual scientific workshops since 2006. Algorithms for solving the dynamic traffic assignment problem are now beginning to be applied in urban travel forecasting (Chiu et al, 2011).

Sixth, demand is either 'fixed' or 'variable' from the viewpoint of transportation network models. Fixed demand is constant with respect to travel costs, regardless of any changes in the network. Variable demand is sensitive to network conditions, and is generally assumed to decrease with travel costs. If flow on a link is zero, the travel cost corresponds to 'free-flow conditions'.

To illustrate the potential complexity of the network equilibrium problem, consider two simple cases: (a) a two-link, fixed demand problem; and (b) a one-link, variable demand problem. For the case of a single origin–destination pair with a fixed total flow over two routes, the problem of finding the user-equilibrium flows may be solved graphically, as shown in Figure 7.2 for links with nominal capacities of 1000 and 2000 vehicles per hour and a fixed demand of 4000 vehicles per hour. In this case the network equilibrium occurs when the travel times over the two routes are equal to 27.1 minutes, with flows of 1522 and 2487 vehicles per hour on links 1 and 2.

The second case is illustrated in Figure 7.3, for a negative exponential demand function with a cost sensitivity parameter equal to 0.01, and one link with a free-flow travel time of 30 minutes and a nominal capacity of 500 vehicles per hour, as depicted by the BPR volume-delay function. The graphical solution to this fixed point problem representing demand and cost is found by determining the point where demand equals flow, as shown by the 45-degree line in Figure 7.3.

The solution of both problems for large numbers of origins, destina-

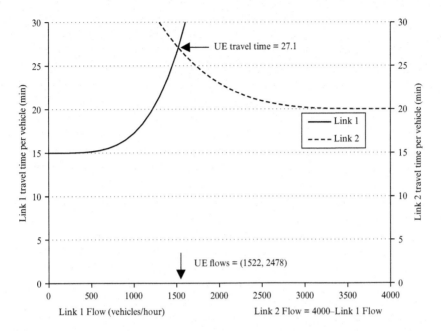

UE travel time = 27.1

Link 1
Link 2

UE flows = (1522, 2478)

Link 1 Flow (vehicles/hour)   Link 2 Flow = 4000–Link 1 Flow

Source: Computed from BPR functions; based on Beckmann et al (1956, 83).

Figure 7.2   User-equilibrium (UE) link flows and travel times over a two-link network

tions, links and routes, and for several modes and classes of travellers, is now well understood and computationally tractable for models with deterministic travel times.

7.2.2   Mathematics of Optimisation and Equilibria

An overview of the mathematics that forms the basis for network equilibrium models is offered in this section. This intuitive orientation to the subject is primarily for the benefit of readers who have not had an opportunity or desire to study this subject in more depth. For those desiring more advanced knowledge, this section may provide guidance on how to proceed.

To express the equilibrium of choices of routes, modes and destinations over a transportation network, two kinds of information are required:

1. a representation of the network in terms of its basic elements: nodes, or intersections; links, or segments of roads or public transport services,

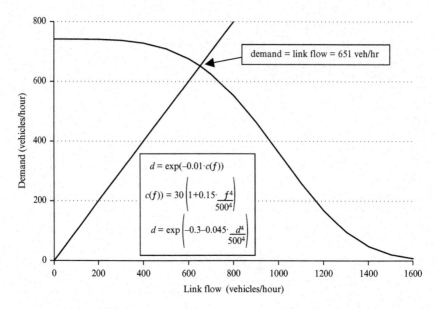

The equations shown in the figure:

$$d = \exp(-0.01 \cdot c(f))$$

$$c(f)) = 30\left(1 + 0.15 \cdot \frac{f^4}{500^4}\right)$$

$$d = \exp\left(-0.3 - 0.045 \cdot \frac{d^4}{500^4}\right)$$

demand = link flow = 651 veh/hr

Source: Computed by the authors from the equations shown in the figure.

Figure 7.3   *Fixed point function relating demand (d), user-equilibrium link cost (c(f)) and flow (f)*

including their operating characteristics; and zones, or spatial division of the area of interest;

2. mathematical relationships expressing the assumptions in the previous section in terms of flows of persons and vehicles with respect to generalised costs.

With the experience of 60 years of transportation research, and two centuries of mathematical advances, we can state these equilibrium relationships directly. It may be beneficial, however, to proceed in the way that the transportation network equilibrium field developed, which was not always intuitive or straightforward. The field actually developed in five steps:

1. Formulate an optimisation problem representing the elements of the network equilibrium.
2. Derive the mathematical conditions characterising the optimal solution, realising that these conditions describe the desired equilibrium stated in the assumptions.

3. Reformulate these conditions into a system of equations and inequalities.
4. Realise this system corresponds to other representations of equilibria investigated in other fields, including physics and economics.
5. Exploit this related knowledge to create methods (algorithms) for solving the system.

Why formulate an optimisation problem to characterise equilibrium travel conditions? Actually, the answer is very interesting. But, first, let us define an 'optimisation problem'. To state an optimisation problem, we require a mathematical expression defined in terms of the variables of interest, called an 'objective function'. For an increasing function, for which a straight line joining any two points lies above the function, the function is called 'strictly convex'; a strictly convex function has a unique minimum. We assume the variables are continuous (real valued).

Now, suppose we place one or more 'linear constraints' on the values of the variables; for example, the sum of the flows on two links equals some fixed amount. Such a constraint was represented in Figure 7.2 by the horizontal axis equal to 4000 vehicles per hour. A strictly convex objective function subject to linear constraints is called a 'convex programming problem' or more generally a 'non-linear optimisation problem'.

Minimisation of a convex function subject to linear equations was introduced by Joseph Louis Lagrange [1736–1813].[10] The method of Lagrange multipliers is a strategy for finding the local minima of a convex objective function subject to equality constraints. A 'Lagrangian equation' is formed by adding the products of each constraint times a new unknown, called a 'Lagrange multiplier', to the objective function. Minimising the Lagrangian equation with respect to each unknown variable defines a set of equations called 'optimality conditions'. The solution of these conditions for the unknown variables and Lagrange multipliers yields new relationships among the variables, as well as the numerical values of the unknown variables, if desired (Lagrange, 1813, 1888).

Lagrange considered only the case in which the constraints are equations, also called 'equalities'. The other possibility is that the constraint is an 'inequality'; for example, the variable must be greater than or equal to zero, or 'non-negative'. Solution of a constrained optimisation problem subject to inequalities as well as equalities waited a much longer time to be considered. Our historical account of how this problem was solved now briefly diverges to consider the special case of minimisation of a linear function subject to linear constraints.

Experiences during the Second World War with the application of mathematics to military problems stimulated interest in optimisation methods by the US Department of the Air Force, where George Dantzig [1914–2005],[11] Saul Gass [1926–2013] and others worked on project planning methods in the late 1940s.[12] Dantzig devised his 'simplex method' for solving linear optimisation problems with linear constraints, which he called the 'linear programming problem' (Dantzig, 1949, 1982, 2002).

In 1948 Dantzig met Tjalling Koopmans [1910–1985], a Dutch mathematical economist, who migrated to the US in 1940, and was then director of research at the Cowles Commission for Research in Economics and professor of economics at the University of Chicago.[13] Koopmans (1949) had earlier devised a solution method for a special case of a linear programming problem, the minimisation of the total cost of commodity shipments subject to linear constraints on the supply of the commodity at each production location and the requirements for each commodity at each consumption location. The 'transportation problem of linear programming', as it became known, was studied earlier by Frank Hitchcock (1941), and independently by Leonid Kantorovich [1912–1986].[14]

The interest of economists in linear programming, and more generally mathematical programming, stemmed from papers presented at a symposium organised by Koopmans in 1949, sometimes referred to as Symposium 0 (Balinski, 1991). Koopmans (1951) published selected papers in an edited volume, *Activity Analysis of Production and Allocation*. He chose the title carefully to represent a field of inquiry broader than linear programming, as well as an emerging view of optimisation of activities of private firms as well as public agencies. Its contents, however, pertained almost exclusively to linear programming. A few papers examined the theory of resources allocation, and methods for allocating resources. In 1951, the (first) Symposium on Linear Inequalities and Programming included several of the same speakers as in 1949 (Orden and Goldstein, 1952). This symposium also was almost exclusively devoted to linear programming. The Second Symposium on Linear Programming held in 1955 also nearly exclusively concerned linear programming (Antosiewicz, 1955). Hence, linear programming dominated research on constrained optimisation during this time.

During a chance meeting with George Dantzig, Albert Tucker [1905–1995], a professor of mathematics at Princeton University, noted that Dantzig's description of linear programming 'sounded like Kirchhoff's Laws' (Kuhn, 1976, 1991, 2002). Tucker suggested to David Gale [1921–2008] and Harold Kuhn [1925–2014] that they write a sequel to an earlier paper (Gale et al, 1951), generalising the 'duality' properties of linear programs to quadratic programs.[15] Kuhn wrote the paper with an emphasis 'on the general non-linear case and the properties of convexity that imply the necessary conditions for an optimum are also sufficient', given a constraint qualification added later. A revised version of 'Nonlinear Programming' was presented by Kuhn and Tucker at the Second Berkeley Symposium on Mathematical Statistics and Probability in 1950, the first conference presentation of the classic Kuhn–Tucker theorem. Their paper became a starting point for subsequent theoretical and algorithmic research, as well as applications to economic and engineering problems.

Hence, the generalisation of the Lagrangian problem of minimising a convex function subject to linear constraints to include inequality constraints was proposed by Harold Kuhn and Albert Tucker (1951) and is known as the Kuhn–Tucker theorem. However, William Karush [1917–1997] was later recognised as having proved the same result in 1939 in his M.Sc. thesis.[16] Therefore, these conditions are now known as the Karush–Kuhn–Tucker (KKT) optimality conditions.[17] The role of the KKT conditions in the formulation of the network equilibrium problem is described in section 7.3.2.

Concerning the significance of Kuhn and Tucker's paper, Akira Takayama [1932–1996] stated in his classic textbook *Mathematical Economics*: 'nonlinear programming theory . . . is probably the most important mathematical technique in modern economic theory' (Takayama, 1985, xix).[18] Although the origins of non-linear programming are complex, the paper by Kuhn and Tucker decisively introduced this technique to economics, as well as to operations research and related fields of engineering.[19]

The interpretation of the KKT optimality conditions is quite intuitive. Basically, one examines alternative or 'complementary' cases, such as for a non-negativity constraint on a variable. First, suppose the variable is positive; then, what is the solution determined by the other conditions? Second, suppose the variable is zero; then, what is the solution? In general, one considers the complementary cases, and solves the resulting conditions. The KKT conditions include the constraints on the variables, as well as inequalities related to the derivatives of the objective function.

Typically, one examines the KKT conditions to determine if an interpretation can be found. Often the conditions provide additional understanding of the stated optimisation problem, for example the minimisation of total travel costs. This type of problem is termed a direct optimisation problem, since the function being minimised is directly interesting to a decision maker. However, an indirect, or artificial, optimisation problem is also possible: the optimality conditions correspond to a set of behavioural assumptions, and the objective function is constructed so as to obtain those conditions. This situation describes how an optimisation problem could characterise a network equilibrium (section 7.3.2).

The KKT conditions are a complete statement of the optimisation or

equilibrium problem, even though they do not include the objective function. Therefore, it seems natural to ask whether they can be expressed in
other forms. One form is to define an array consisting of the unknown
variables plus the Lagrange multipliers in such a manner that they are all
non-negative. Corresponding to each of these unknowns is an inequality
or equality condition, including the derivatives of the Lagrangian equation
and the constraints. These conditions may also be arranged so that they are
also non-negative. Then, the pairwise products of the conditions times their
unknown variables must equal zero, which is called a 'complementarity
condition'. The entire structure is a 'non-linear complementarity problem',
which has been extensively studied since 1968, initially in its linear form.[20]

A second form of the KKT conditions is the 'finite-dimensional variational inequality problem', which may provide a more general statement
of the network equilibrium problem.[21] Its structure is similar to the non-
linear complementarity problem in so far as the function and variables are
concerned. The mathematical theory of variational inequalities was initially developed to analyse various equilibrium problems, and was studied
in mathematics, physics, economics, finance and game theory, thereby
providing many results applicable to transportation network equilibrium.

Next we consider some further questions that pose difficulties for such
methods. Does a solution to the network equilibrium problem exist? Is the
solution unique? The quick answer is 'yes', for simple cases, and 'maybe',
for more realistic cases. One simple case refers to link cost functions that
depend only on the link's own flow, called 'separable', the type almost
always used in travel forecasting practice. For this case, the matrix of
partial derivatives of link cost functions with respect to the link flows,
called the Jacobian matrix, is symmetric with positive values on its main
diagonal and zeros elsewhere. In this case, the optimisation formulation,
the non-linear complementarity problem and the variational inequality problem are equivalent, and their solutions generally exist and are
uniquely determined by the optimality conditions, if the link costs are
strictly increasing with link flows.

In the 'non-separable' case, the link cost function is more realistically
defined upon each link's own flow plus the flows on conflicting and opposing links at a downstream intersection. For this case, the Jacobian matrix
is unlikely to be symmetric (section 7.4.1.2). Such link cost functions
are called 'asymmetric'; in such cases the value of the objective function
may not be 'well defined' (Patriksson, 1994, 51–54). For such cases the
variational inequality problem may offer a more useful representation
of certain network equilibrium problems. However, the solution of these
problems, if they exist, may be characterised by local optima; that is, the
optimality conditions do not determine a unique optimal solution.

Solution methods for variational inequality formulations of transportation network equilibrium problems often involve solving a sequence of optimisation problems with separable link cost functions; these methods are sometimes called diagonalisation or relaxation methods (Patriksson, 1994, 165). The basic idea is that the problem is solved for each link's own flows, holding constant the effect of other link flows on that link's cost; then the effects of the other flows on the link costs are updated, and the process repeated. Moreover, for these more realistic functions, the link cost may not be strictly increasing with flows. Until now, large-scale implementations of problem formulations with these attributes were not studied extensively from a computational viewpoint.

7.3   A NOVEL TRANSPORTATION NETWORK EQUILIBRIUM MODEL

Completely unrelated to the emerging field of urban transportation planning in the 1950s, a research project on the 'theory of resources allocation' provided the conditions for a study of congested road networks with important and lasting consequences for urban travel forecasting methods. The study was undertaken at a research centre on mathematical economics at the University of Chicago during 1951–55 by three researchers in mathematical economics.

In brief, their study of road transportation contributed the following innovations:

1. a mathematical representation of a road network in which travel costs on road segments increase in relation to traffic flows;
2. a mathematical statement of the 'equilibrium' among origin–destination flows (demand, assumed to decrease in relation to travel cost), equal costs over the routes actually travelled from origin to destination (assumed to be the 'shortest' ones under prevailing traffic conditions), and flows over road segments (link volumes), thereby providing a mathematical formulation of Wardrop's first criterion (section 7.2.1);
3. a mathematical statement of the related 'efficiency' problem of finding the origin–destination, route and link flows that minimise the total system costs for a road network, interpreting the additional required costs (or subsidies) as efficiency tolls, thereby providing a mathematical statement of Wardrop's second criterion.

The numerical solution of the system of equations and inequalities for the equilibrium and efficiency cases did not concern the authors, as time and resources for the study were limited. Despite the publication of their findings in a book, *A Study of Highway Transportation*, Part I of *Studies in the Economics of Transportation*, by Martin Beckmann, Bartlett McGuire and Christopher Winsten (1956),[22] for over a decade no one pinpointed the connection between their contribution and concurrent urban transportation studies. Then, academic researchers gradually began to probe the properties of these formulations, and by the early 1970s had identified solution methods, and tested them on small problems.

Throughout the next decade these findings slowly made their way into travel forecasting practice, but only in so far as the solution of the practitioners' traffic assignment problem with fixed demand was concerned. Efforts to solve the more general problem of the equilibrium of origin–destination, mode and route flows were also undertaken, as an alternative to the sequential travel forecasting procedure, but with little impact on practice. Had early practitioners and researchers recognised the correspondence between their model formulation and the procedures being applied in practice, the development of the field in the late 1950s and early 1960s could have been markedly different. In fact, these early formulations represent a missed opportunity that was only later realised.

7.3.1 Research on the Theory of Resources Allocation

Transportation research at the Cowles Commission, located at the University of Chicago, stemmed from the appointment of Tjalling Koopmans as a staff member in 1944 and director of research in 1948. According to Carl Christ (1952, section 7), a research project on the 'theory of resources allocation' was initiated in 1949 with the support of the RAND Corporation 'on the application of activity analysis to problems of transportation and location'. One of RAND's interests, it seems, was how to relocate the civilian population in the event of a military attack.

According to the Cowles Foundation website,[23] Martin J. Beckmann joined the Commission in July 1951, C. Bartlett McGuire [1925–2006] in January 1952, and Christopher B. Winsten [1923–2005] in October 1952. At the time of their appointments, their ages ranged from 26 to 29. Beckmann was born in Germany and received his Doctor rerum politicarum (Doctor of Economics) degree in 1950 from the University of Freiburg, after studying mathematics from 1945 to 1948 at the University of Göttingen. Prior to 1945, he had served in the German army as a radio operator. Beckmann came to the University of Chicago in 1950 as a post-doctoral fellow. McGuire pursued undergraduate studies in economics and political science at the University of Minnesota, in 1946–49, and graduate studies in economic theory, statistics and mathematics at the University of Chicago, receiving his MA degree in economics in 1952. Following graduation from high school in 1943, he had served in the US Navy as an electronics technician. Winsten was educated at the University of Cambridge, and served in the British armed forces during the war. His interests included probability and queuing theory and Prais–Winsten regression analysis (Prais and Winsten, 1954).[24]

A Cowles Commission report for the period ending January 1952 stated that Beckmann was constructing a model of 'flows of transport to a given network of roads or railroads connecting a finite number of locations at which supply and demand is concentrated. . . . [T]his introduces the new problem of congestion.' In a letter to Oskar Morgenstern [1902–1977][25] at Princeton University in April 1954, McGuire related:

> Our original hope was that this work would give us some insight into the economics of city layout so that if a long-run policy of city dispersal were initiated, primarily for defense purposes, we could say something about where things should be dispersed to, and the costs or benefits thereof. . . . While from this point of view I don't feel we have been very successful, I do think the work has led us to a better understanding of highway economics in general.[26]

Shortly after joining the Cowles Commission, Beckmann (1951) wrote a discussion paper, 'Optimum Transportation on Networks'. By late 1952 he had produced two more discussion papers, 'Efficient Transportation in Networks' (Beckmann, 1952) and 'Road Utilization under Conditions of Individual Choice', according to a reference of McGuire. The first was later revised into Discussion Papers 2049A and 2049B (Beckmann, 1952, 1953). The second paper on conditions of individual choice was evidently never issued, but became the basis for Chapter 3 of *Studies* (Beckmann et al, 1956).[27] During the same period, McGuire (1952) completed 'Highway Capacity and Traffic Congestion'.

By October 1953, their work had progressed to the point that a book outline was prepared. Beckmann's proposal for Part I largely conformed to the published version, but was somewhat more ambitious. In addition to Part II on rail transportation, he proposed Part III on location, one of his keen interests. A month later, he wrote a ten-page note describing his ideas for Part I. Evidently, the idea of publishing a book was problematic. On 14 October, he wrote: 'Even if the plan of a book is shelved, I should argue for an integrated, though perhaps not so broadly written, article or a series of articles, on highway transportation, following the outline.'

About the same time, Beckmann and McGuire (1953) completed a nontechnical discussion paper issued as RAND P-437, 'The Determination of Traffic in a Road Network – An Economic Approach'. The paper described problems of road transportation in relation to the present state of traffic engineering knowledge. Three levels of the problem of traffic forecasting were described: (a) the structure of individual choices affecting traffic; (b) repercussions of traffic conditions on these choices; and (c) traffic equilibrium in a network. The basic principles of route choice and demand on a network were described verbally. The paper was submitted to *Traffic Quarterly* and rejected.[28] At the time, *Traffic Quarterly* was arguably the leading journal in English serving multi-disciplinary interests in traffic and transportation.

By June 1954, the book manuscript was hurriedly finished, as funding from the RAND Corporation for the project was exhausted. Beckmann departed for Germany, his first trip home since 1950. Correspondence between Beckmann and McGuire on technical and editorial points of the book continued throughout the summer and autumn, stimulated by many questions, comments and suggestions by Koopmans. A letter dated May 1954 to William Vickrey [1914–1996] offered $150 as 'partial compensation' for a review of the manuscript. Vickrey, an economics professor at Columbia University, had a keen interest in transportation economics.[29] Detailed written comments reveal that Vickrey made extensive suggestions. Editing and revisions continued throughout the remainder of 1954. The completed manuscript was issued as RAND Memorandum 1488 in May 1955. Yale University Press considered the book for publication in 1955, in conjunction with Koopmans moving to Yale University as professor of economics; in May 1955, it agreed to publish the book. McGuire attended to editorial details, and the book appeared in late 1955.

Following the publication of *Studies*, Beckmann was sometimes asked who devised the mathematical formulation of the network equilibrium model. He steadfastly maintained that the formulation was a joint effort of the three authors. In 1999, David Boyce posed that question to McGuire. 'Why, of course, it was Martin's idea', he replied. He recalled many discussions in which he sought Beckmann's explanation of the mathematics of the formulation. In this account, therefore, we refer to the formulation as Beckmann's and to the book as Beckmann et al (1956).

7.3.2 Beckmann's Model Formulation

Part I of *Studies in the Economics of Transportation* contains numerous innovations regarding how to conceptualise the modelling of vehicle flows on a congested road network. As the authors were breaking entirely new ground, they clearly struggled to organise concepts in a way that provided for a tractable mathematical formulation. Among these were whether to treat delays at intersections of roads separately from delays on road segments, and how to separate directional flows from total flows on two-lane roads. For this exposition, these details are suppressed to focus on their fundamental contribution of the formulation of two closely related transportation network problems with variable origin–destination flows, one related to equilibrium and the other to efficiency. The terms 'equilibrium' and 'efficiency' were the titles of Chapters 3 and 4, respectively. The two formulations are described next.[30]

Consider a road network represented by sets of nodes and links. Unknown origin–destination flows, or demands, occur between certain pairs of nodes, i and k. Directional link flows corresponding to the flow terminating at each destination node are also unknown. The sums of these destination-specific link flows equal the unknown total flow on each link. Conservation of vehicle flows through each node of the network is described by an identity defined for each pair of nodes (Beckmann et al, 1956, 61–62).

Link flows terminating at node k may arrive at and depart from every other node on the network. The flows in and out of each node i may be described as follows:

1. If no flow originates or terminates at node i, then its arriving flow equals its departing flow.
2. If flow originates at node i and terminates at node k, then that originating flow plus any arriving flow that terminates at node k must equal the departing flow from node i that terminates at node k.
3. If flow terminates at node k, then the arriving flow terminating at node k must equal the terminating flow.

In the subsequent literature, each pair of originating and terminating flows was defined as a 'commodity', and the conservation of flow relationships defined for each commodity.[31] In order to represent these flows completely, Beckmann wrote a set of 'conservation of flow' equations for the above three cases for each pair of nodes i on the network and nodes k with terminating flow, as follows:

Total flow departing from any node i and terminating at node k equals total flow arriving at node i and terminating at node k plus the flow originating at node i and terminating at node k.

If no flow originates at node i and terminates at node k, then the third term is zero, and the arriving flow equals the departing flow at node i for each terminating node k.[32]

Next, 'complementarity conditions' on the choice of shortest routes were defined in terms of link costs: the cost of the shortest route from any node to the terminating node must be less than or equal to the cost from that node to a node connected by one link plus the cost from the connected node to the terminating node. According to the assumption that travellers use the shortest route, if there is flow from the first node through the connected node to the terminating node then the difference in costs from the two nodes to the terminating node must equal the cost of the connecting link. If the difference in costs is less than the cost of the connecting link, then there can be no flow over that link to the destination (Beckmann et al, 1956, 62).

To formulate the model, Beckmann defined separable functions of demand and link flows:

1. Origin–destination (O-D) flow (demand) is a positive and strictly decreasing function of the O-D travel cost; therefore, the travel cost can also be expressed as an inverse function of the O-D flow (demand). This travel cost is the minimum cost from the origin to destination (Beckmann et al, 1956, 57).
2. Link travel cost is a non-decreasing function of the link's own flow, which is called a capacity function, whose costs increase indefinitely as a certain flow level, the absolute capacity limit, is approached (Beckmann et al, 1956, 58).

To define a separable function for O-D flow (demand), the flow depends only on the cost of that O-D pair, and not on the cost of other O-D pairs; likewise, to define a separable link cost function, the link cost depends only on the link's own flow, and not on the flow of other links (Patriksson, 1994, 34, 51). Given this description of origin–destination flows, and link flows, Beckmann proposed to maximise the difference between two artificial functions of O-D demand and link flow (Beckmann et al, 1956, 63) subject to the conservation of flow equations stated above and non-negativity of flows:[33]

1. integral from zero to the unknown O-D flow of the inverse demand function for node pair (i, k), summed over all O-D pairs;
2. integral from zero to the unknown total link flow of the link travel cost function, summed over all links.

By applying the Kuhn–Tucker theorem, Beckmann demonstrated that maximising the difference of these functions with respect to O-D flows and the link flows terminating at a node, subject to the above conservation of flow constraints and non-negativity conditions, yields the following complementarity conditions for each O-D pair (Beckmann et al, 1956, 64):

1. If a link flow terminating at node k is positive, then the difference in costs from the two nodes connected by the link to the termination node must equal the cost of the connecting link, as determined by its total flow for all links and termination nodes.
2. If a link flow terminating at node k is zero, then the difference in costs from the two nodes connected by the link to the termination node must be less than or equal to the cost of the connecting link, as determined by its total flow for all links and termination nodes.
3. If the difference in costs from the two nodes connected by the link to the termination node is less than the cost of the connecting link, as determined by its total flow, then the flow on the connecting link terminating at node k must be zero for all links and termination nodes.
4. If the O-D flow is positive, then the inverse demand function evaluated at that flow must equal the O-D cost for all node pairs; if the O-D flow is zero, then the inverse demand function evaluated at zero flow must be less than or equal to the O-D cost between that pair of nodes for all node pairs.

Or, as they stated:

> Demand refers to trips and capacity refers to flows on roads. The connecting link is found in the distribution of trips over the network according to the principle that traffic follows shortest routes in terms of average cost. The idea of equilibrium in a network can then be described as follows. The prevailing demand for transportation, that is, the existing pattern of originations and terminations, gives rise to traffic conditions that will maintain that same demand. Or, starting at the other end, the existing traffic conditions are such as to call forth the demand that will sustain the flows that create these conditions (Beckmann et al, 1956, 59).

Three principles corresponding to the above two points were stated as follows:

1. If between a given origin and a given destination more than one route is actually travelled, the cost of transportation to the average road user, as indicated by the average-cost capacity curves, must be equal on all these routes.
2. Since the routes used are the 'shortest' ones under prevailing traffic conditions, average cost on all other possible routes cannot be less than that on the route or routes travelled.
3. The amount of traffic originated per unit of time must equal the demand for transportation at the trip cost which prevails (Beckmann et al, 1956, 60).

By the end of 1954 Beckmann had mathematically formulated the transportation network equilibrium problem with variable demand as a constrained optimisation problem, integrating in a single formulation the trip distribution problem with fixed origin–destination costs and the traffic assignment problem with fixed origin–destination flows, problems which were only then beginning to be tackled in practice. His formulation was the first to use the new method of non-linear programming to investigate the behavioural properties of the complex phenomena of traffic congestion experienced daily by urban travellers. Moreover, he analysed the mathematical properties of this formulation, which could provide the basis for forecasting the use of new roads and other facilities, if the resulting system of equations and inequalities was solved for large networks.

This formulation is one of the few cases of the indirect representation of behaviour by maximising an artificial function, with the hypothesised behaviour corresponding to the optimality, or equilibrium, conditions. In contrast, most applications of mathematical programming involve the direct optimisation of a function whose behavioural meaning is clear. Presumably, by working backwards from the desired optimality conditions, Beckmann defined an artificial functional form whose optimality conditions corresponded to the desired equilibrium.[34]

In Chapter 4, the authors considered the question of transportation network efficiency. By replacing the sum of the integrals of link cost functions with the total cost of travel on the network, Beckmann devised a second maximisation problem whose solution corresponds to the minimum of the total travel cost with variable demand (Beckmann et al, 1956, 91–94).[35] In this case, travellers follow routes of equal marginal travel cost. The authors interpreted the difference between these marginal costs, and the average costs normally experienced by the travellers as 'efficiency tolls'. As with their 'equilibrium' analysis, these 'efficiency' results were completely novel, although they had been understood by Knight (1924) for a two-link network.[36]

The exposition of these results required about 40 pages, plus introductory chapters on supply and demand, and a concluding chapter on unsolved problems. The presentation is neither straightforward nor simple to understand. Even today when the results are understood, thanks to the efforts of several generations of researchers, the exposition is difficult to follow. As Beckmann stated in 1998, 'The book was hard to read.'[37]

Did the authors fully grasp the significance of their result? Clearly, they understood they had derived a new theory of traffic equilibrium and efficiency containing both behavioural and societal aspects. Did they understand it was potentially useful for travel forecasting? Based on responses to questions posed to Beckmann and McGuire, the answer was frankly no. As both discussed in interviews, they did not appreciate its practical significance for two reasons:

1. In 1954 as they completed their manuscript, there were no computers available to them to solve even an eight-link example (Beckmann et al, 1956, 73–79). Therefore, they regarded the model as being theoretical.
2. Despite their efforts to understand current research on traffic and to interact with traffic engineers, they were unaware that urban transportation studies were under way to predict future road traffic and to devise plans for its accommodation (section 2.4).[38]

What is the relation of Chapters 3 and 4 to the route choice 'criteria' of Wardrop (1952)? Wardrop's paper was listed in the bibliography of Beckmann et al (1956), but was not cited in the text. McGuire stated that he became aware of Wardrop's paper in late 1952. Beckmann agreed that he learned of Wardrop's criteria from McGuire after completing the first draft of the book. Hence, Beckmann's formulation of the network equilibrium model occurred independently of, and effectively concurrently with, Wardrop's statement of his two criteria.

7.3.3 Response to the Book

The RAND Corporation report was released in May 1955; the Yale University Press edition appeared in December 1955. By 1959, three printings of the book had been issued in the US, and in the UK through Oxford University Press.[39] A Spanish edition, *Economía del transporte*, was issued in 1959. In 2010, the WorldCat List of Records showed 421 copies of the Yale edition held by libraries worldwide, 16 copies of the RAND report and six copies of the Spanish edition.[40]

Studies in the Economics of Transportation was reviewed in nine economics and operations research journals. All of the reviews praised the book. None of the reviewers, it appears, understood the significance of Part I. Perhaps the reviewer best able to appreciate the work was William Prager [1903–1980], a German-born applied mathematician, who left Germany in 1933, and later was a professor at Brown University.[41] He had also investigated the network equilibrium problem. Even so, Prager (1956–57) doubted that the model would 'yield valid numerical results'. Perhaps the most noted reviewer in the transportation field was R.J. Smeed [1909–1976] of the UK Road Research Laboratory.[42] Smeed (1957) stated: 'it is refreshing to read a book that attempts to tackle the subject of road transport in a comprehensive and fundamental way'. The reviewer perhaps best able to understand the economic analysis was Edwin

Mansfield [1930–1997]. Although noting the use of the Kuhn–Tucker theorem to study equilibrium and efficiency, Mansfield (1959) did not seem to appreciate the significance of the findings.[43] In a note to McGuire in February 1960 concerning the book reviews, Beckmann wrote: 'It is fascinating and depressing at the same time. How little we are understood!'

What is clear from today's perspective is that *Studies* was a difficult book. It was one of the first uses of the Kuhn–Tucker theorem to study a societal problem, notably urban traffic congestion. The authors struggled conceptually with their model. Their explanation did not do justice to their results. Even in a later paper written to 'popularise' the ideas in the book, Beckmann (1967b) did not connect the results with travel forecasting activities of urban transportation planning agencies.

As noted in section 7.2.2, non-linear programming was a new field in 1950 when Kuhn and Tucker presented their paper (Kuhn, 1976). It developed in the shadow of linear programming, which had a slight head-start and seemed more useful in applications, despite its restriction to linear problems. The inability of the authors, or anyone else, to foresee that large-scale versions of such problems might be solved computationally may have limited interest further. Whatever discussions took place at the time were of a theoretical nature.

Some 50 years later, sessions at two academic conferences examined the impact of the book. A panel discussion at the North American Regional Science Meetings in November 2003 discussed its significance (Boyce et al, 2005). At the Meeting of the Institute for Operations Research and the Management Sciences in November 2005, a panel of leading researchers reviewed the history of the book and its impact on the field. On this occasion, a citation was presented to Professors Beckmann and McGuire by the Cowles Foundation for Research in Economics at Yale University, the successor to the Cowles Commission.

7.3.4   Concurrent Research on Network Equilibrium and Efficiency

Equilibrium and efficiency in road networks was not an entirely new subject when Beckmann and his co-authors began their research in 1952. Papers preceding the completion of *Studies* in 1955 are reviewed here, as well as research undertaken subsequently without knowledge of its publication. These papers pertain to partial formulations of the equilibrium or efficiency models and share some of their attributes. These models consider only fixed origin–destination flows (demand); no other model with variable flows was proposed.

What was new in Beckmann et al (1956) was the mathematical treatment of equilibrium flows in a network; however, even this idea was not entirely novel. Richard Duffin [1909–1996], later recognised for his seminal contributions to geometric programming, wrote several papers on the behaviour of electrical networks (Duffin, 1947).[44] Although the context is unfamiliar, it seems clear that Duffin did understand that the integral of a 'conductivity function' defined on arcs connecting pairs of nodes of an electrical network was the key to proving that 'a network of quasi-linear conductors has a stable state of currents, and this state is unique'. Duffin used 'quasi-linear' to contrast with the linear case, known as Ohm's law. He also described the functions as 'nondecreasing'. Duffin's paper was motivated by a desire to generalise the Kirchhoff–Maxwell laws.

William Prager (1954) informally posed the network equilibrium problem, including the integral of travel time as a linear function of opposing flows on a two-way road. Motivated by the criteria of Wardrop (1952), Prager described the equal journey times of routes in terms of the differences in potentials between nodes of the network. Hence, he was also thinking along the same lines as Duffin, but without the benefit of the Kuhn–Tucker theorem. Prager was aware of the earlier results of Koopmans (1949), and proposed a formulation for the efficient transportation of goods in which the total shipment cost is a quadratic function of the flows on the network, a special case of the formulation of Beckmann (Prager, 1955). Prager was unclear about the source of origin–destination flows. In his 1955 paper, they are unspecified, and in his 1954 paper they appear to be specified in terms of net outflows and inflows of a single commodity.

Abraham Charnes [1917–1992] and William Cooper [1914–2012] described a traffic network equilibrium formulation for the case of fixed origin–destination flows (Charnes and Cooper, 1958; Cooper, 2002, 38). They also knew of the formulation of Prager (1954) and 'the principles' of Wardrop. They were evidently the first to recognise the relation of their model to the non-cooperative game theory of John Forbes Nash, Jr. (Nash, 1951).[45] The paper is written in the terminology of electrical networks with references to Kirchhoff's laws. Like their colleague Duffin, they proposed minimising the sum of 'integrated resistance functions' of total arc flow, which they refer to as 'branch resistances'. While they never specified an actual resistance function, it is clearly non-decreasing.

At the first symposium on the theory of traffic flow in 1959 (Herman, 1961), Charnes and Cooper (1961) proposed to use multicopy linear programming techniques to solve an example pertaining to a small Indiana town (11 origin–destination pairs, 22 nodes, 27 links). The example was provided by staff of the Chicago Area Transportation Study, indicating that Charnes, then a professor at Northwestern University, was in contact with the first generation of travel forecasting professionals (section 2.4.5).

Also at the first symposium, Wardrop (1961) presented a paper on the theory of travel demand on a simple road system without congestion. Included is a reference to Beckmann et al concerning demand.

The next event in this chronology concerns the MS thesis research of a Danish graduate student, Niels Jorgensen, at the University of California, Berkeley. Jorgensen was a graduate student in transportation engineering, and a research assistant of Robert Oliver, professor of industrial engineering and operations research.[46] Jorgensen had studied network flow and traffic flow models with Oliver, who suggested the problem of network equilibrium to him as an MS thesis topic. Oliver also brought the papers of Charnes and Cooper to Jorgensen's attention, but not Beckmann et al.

In his 39-page unpublished thesis, Jorgensen (1963) formulated the network equilibrium and network efficiency problems with fixed origin–destination flows. Using the Kuhn–Tucker theorem together with Wardrop's first criterion, he derived the sum of the integrals objective function. In contrast to all earlier works on the subject, Jorgensen's treatment is a picture of clarity. He investigated several cases, and in particular explored a specific travel time-flow function based on the assumption that link speed is a linear, decreasing function of total link flow; equivalently, travel time is a non-linear increasing function of flow. Jorgensen did not attempt to devise a solution algorithm, but he did solve several simple examples. In response to a question about the origins of his work, he stated: 'I believe the user-equilibrium formulation was my own. I recall that it gave me a kind of "aha-feeling", but in reality it was just a reinvention of Beckmann's formulation, which I should have known.' Jorgensen also worked with an electrical analogy.

When Jorgensen returned to Denmark, he continued his research, writing a paper for the third symposium on the theory of traffic flow held in New York in 1965. However, lacking travel funds, he did not attend the symposium. His interest in the work waned, because Danish practitioners did not like the model's property that route flows are not unique, later recognised as a basic property of network equilibrium models (Rossi et al, 1989; Patriksson, 1994, 44).[47] Jorgensen's thesis report was cited by early researchers on network equilibrium, including Stella Dafermos (section 7.4.1.2).

A recent English translation of the paper in which Dietrich Braess (1968) introduced his 'paradox of traffic planning' revealed another independent formulation of the network equilibrium problem (Braess et al, 2005).[48] According to Nagurney and Boyce (2005), Braess, a young applied mathematician, was introduced to traffic models in a seminar in 1967 given by W. Knödel at the University of Münster, Germany. Intrigued by what he had heard, Braess studied the problem of traffic network equilibrium, identifying the counter-intuitive 'paradox' that the addition of a link to a traffic network with flow-dependent, user-equilibrium travel times may lead to an increase in the total time of travel. Further, he formulated the network equilibrium problem with fixed origin–destination flows, and identified the conditions for which the solution exists and is unique. Although his result was published 12 years after Beckmann et al (1956), Braess was unaware of earlier research on the problem.

The first known academic paper that examined Beckmann's model is a 1959 discussion paper on road pricing (Walters, 1961) by the British economist Alan Walters [1926–2009].[49] Walters drew extensively on the material in Chapter 4 of *Studies*, as well as the earlier works of Pigou and Knight, to perform a two-road graphical analysis. Following the graphical analysis of the effect of a bottleneck on one road, he presented a mathematical analysis of a network of roads. In a footnote to this analysis, Walters stated:

> The Beckmann model distinguishes between the 'trip' and the 'route'. The 'trip' is from the origin to the destination, and this may be achieved by running over various roads, i.e. by various 'routes'. The demand function has the number of trips as the quantity variable, whereas the cost function relates to the quantity of traffic on particular roads. I think this is an excellent way of organizing the material. But I have not followed their lead in this paper, partly because I can add nothing to their treatment in this respect, and partly because it would introduce much complication into the notation (Walters, 1961, 682).

In his treatment, Walters implicitly proposed a model of several independent roads connecting two points. Unlike Beckmann, he examined the cross-elasticities of road costs on demand, but did not consider that two routes might use some parts of the same link.

William Garrison [1924–2015] and Duane Marble (1958) offered a paper with a linear programming formulation of highway network design, which cited Beckmann et al (1956), but did not describe their model.[50] Later Garrison agreed that he did not appreciate their contribution until Beckmann explained the model to him in 1961.[51] Richard Quandt (1960, 107–108) also cited Beckmann et al (1956), and referred to their discussion of long-run problems of network extent and layout.[52]

7.4 EXTENSIONS TO BECKMANN'S FORMULATION

Although Beckmann's formulation assumed that travel demand decreases with travel cost, early research based on his formulation assumed demand was fixed. Later, if demand was assumed to decrease with travel cost, it was sometimes called 'elastic', but no specific restrictions on the demand function were implied by this term. Elsewhere, demand was described as the distribution of traffic between zones, called trip distribution. Here, 'variable demand' refers to all cases in which travel demand is not fixed.

Several streams of network equilibrium research resulted directly or indirectly from Beckmann's formulation. These are reviewed below in sections organised by topic, rather than chronologically. The first section provides an overview of early research inspired by Beckmann's formulation.

These research streams may be classified as follows:

1. extensions of the deterministic optimisation formulation with fixed demand;
2. relaxation of the perfect information assumption of the optimisation formulation;
3. extensions of Beckmann's variable demand formulation to specific choice functions;
4. implementation, estimation and validation studies of optimisation formulations.

7.4.1   Early Contributions to Network Equilibrium Research

7.4.1.1   European research during the 1960s
Research on the traffic assignment problem, as defined by urban transportation practitioners, continued during the 1960s, when its relation to Beckmann's formulation was first recognised. Joyce Almond (1967) was the first to relate the traffic assignment problem to Beckmann's formulation in her presentation at the third symposium on theory of traffic flow. In solving the problem of traffic assignment on congested roads, she recognised that a method should involve shortest routes; she explored cases of two and three links with graphical methods. Although aware of Beckmann et al, she did not use a diagram like Figure 7.3, based on Beckmann et al (1956, 83). Instead, she appeared to be influenced by the graphical approach of her colleague John Wardrop.

In the section of her paper dealing with the method of solution for a network, Almond (1967) described a procedure for averaging a sequence of all-or-nothing assignments, in which each assignment is based on updated link travel times. She used a weighted averaging scheme in which the sum of the weights assigned to the current solution and the all-or-nothing assignment based on that current solution are equal to one. Although her method is equivalent to the method of successive averages (MSA), it was justified by its performance in solving small problems. Patriksson (1994,

22–23) discussed this point in detail; see also section 7.4.3.1 for details about MSA.

At the same symposium, Knud Overgaard (1967, 217) described the results of a test of a traffic assignment algorithm with averaging of both route and link flows by a procedure akin to the method of successive averages. The link travel time function is a generalisation of the one proposed by Robert Smock (1963, 15) (section 2.5.6). Niels Jorgensen's formulation of the network equilibrium problem was stated, but not explored further (section 7.3.4). Although Overgaard was concerned about the convergence of his heuristic, he did not use Jorgensen's objective function to monitor its convergence. Overgaard (1967, 221) ended his paper with the statement: 'We may conclude that the traffic assignment problem still offers great opportunities for mathematical thinking as well as for engineering experimentation.'

Martin Beckmann (1967a) also presented a paper at the third symposium, his first in this series. His paper was related to the 'Efficiency' chapter of *Studies*, but did not present the network formulations found there. Instead, he discussed problems of optimal tolls on two competing roads with variable demand. Hence, ten years after the publication of *Studies*, Beckmann's interest related to theoretical models from which policy insights might be gained, and not to travel forecasting methods.

M. Bruynooghe, a civil engineer at the Institut de Recherche des Transports, at Arcueil near Paris, wrote several papers during 1967–72 on the network equilibrium traffic assignment problem with fixed demand, and on the traffic assignment problem integrated with the distribution of traffic (Bruynooghe, 1967, 1969).[53] In a paper presented at the fourth symposium on the theory of road traffic flow at Karlsruhe, Germany, Bruynooghe, with Alain Gibert and Michel Sakarovitch,[54] proposed two algorithms for solving the network equilibrium problem with fixed demand (Bruynooghe et al, 1969), one of the first proposals to solve a variant of the problem stated by Beckmann et al (1956).

Bruynooghe et al (1969) formulated the problem in terms of the link flows specified by origin. Necessary and sufficient conditions for the existence of the solution were derived. The proposed solution algorithms were proven to converge to the unique solution. The first is a linearisation algorithm of the type proposed by Marguerite Frank and Philip Wolfe (1956). The second algorithm requires finding both the minimum and maximum cost routes for each origin–destination pair; then the origin–destination flow on the maximum cost route is shifted to the minimum cost routes. Their paper had little impact on practice in the US or UK.

Maurice Netter, also at the Institut de Recherche des Transports, authored two theoretical papers on network equilibrium and marginal cost pricing with multiple user classes (Netter, 1972a, 1972b), and a working paper with J.G. Sender (Netter and Sender, 1970). These papers examined the conditions for the existence and uniqueness of solutions to formulations of the network equilibrium problem for the case of multiple user classes and for marginal cost pricing. The papers explored mathematical properties of Beckmann's formulation extended to multiple user classes, and offered warnings about the non-convexity of certain formulations.[55]

7.4.1.2   Theoretical analyses and algorithms of Dafermos

Stella Dafermos [1940–1990] was born in Greece and graduated from the National Technical University of Athens in 1964, majoring in civil engineering. She enrolled at Johns Hopkins University in operations research, graduating with a Ph.D. in 1968. Dafermos and Sparrow (1969, 1971) reported the findings of her thesis. In the first, she explored the mathematical properties of the network equilibrium problem with fixed demand. One motivation for her research was the practitioners' 'traffic assignment problem', as the research was supported by the US National Bureau of Standards (Nemhauser, 1991, 115). The second concerned the problem of efficient planning for improvements to an existing network.

Despite the practice-oriented source of her support, Dafermos attacked the problem in a highly abstract manner, building on earlier results by Wardrop (1952), Beckmann et al (1956), Jorgensen (1963), Charnes and Cooper (1958, 1961), Tomlin (1966) and Almond (1967). She proposed the terms 'user-optimized' and 'system-optimizing' to describe the two 'criteria' of Wardrop, and extensively explored the properties of the two problem formulations (Dafermos and Sparrow, 1969, 94). At the same time as Bruynooghe et al (1969), she proposed solution algorithms with proofs of convergence. She introduced the link-route form of the conservation of flow conditions (Patriksson, 1994, 34–39). Although her algorithms used shortest routes, they required knowing the shortest and longest used routes between each O-D pair in the current solution, sets of routes that might be computationally difficult to identify. Therefore, her proposed algorithms were not practical for the problems of several thousand links being considered at that time.[56]

Following completion of her degree, Dafermos moved to Cornell University with her husband, Constantine Dafermos.[57] Supported partly by George Nemhauser's contract with the Federal Highway Administration, she addressed fundamental properties of network equilibrium models with fixed demand (Dafermos, 1971, 1972, 1973). All three papers considered generalisations of Beckmann's network equilibrium formulation, in which the travel cost of each two-way link was assumed to be a non-decreasing function of the sum of the two-way flows on the link (Beckmann et al, 1956, 61–62).

Dafermos (1971) considered a generalisation of Beckmann's model in which the cost of each link depends, in principle, on the flow on every link in the network. She showed that Beckmann's optimisation formulation of the network equilibrium problem would apply only if the following symmetry condition was met: for each pair of links, the derivatives of the link cost functions with respect to the other link's flow must be equal. Her detailed analysis of the system-optimising and user-optimising cases substantially extended Beckmann's findings.

Dafermos (1972) considered the question of the effect of multiple user classes, such as passenger cars and trucks, on the link cost function. She showed (1972, 79) that the matrix of pairwise partial derivatives of the class link cost functions with respect to the class link flows must be symmetric in order to satisfy the mathematical requirements of the network equilibrium problem. While she argued that this assumption could be met, she admitted that the user-optimised case was not as general as the system-optimised one, where no such requirement is needed. Dafermos also introduced the concept of hypernetworks, which she called 'modified networks', in which a multi-class model is formulated as a more complex single class model.

Dafermos (1973) examined the effects of tolls in multi-class networks, finding that similar symmetry conditions must be satisfied for the user-optimised formulation to hold. In these three papers, Dafermos not only analysed the properties of the network equilibrium model in depth, but also laid the foundation for developments ten years later (section 7.5.1).

7.4.1.3 Centre for Research on Transportation at Montreal

The Centre for Research on Transportation (CRT) at the University of Montreal was established in 1970 with a grant from Transport Canada. In 1972 a basic research programme in transportation was initiated with an unrestricted grant from the Ford Motor Company of Canada to the University of Montreal (Florian, 2008). The first faculty members in the Centre were Michael Florian, Marc Gaudry and Pierre Robillard.

Michael Florian was born in 1939 in Bucharest, Romania.[58] He moved to Montreal in 1957, earned an engineering degree from McGill University in 1962, and worked for the Canadian National Railway until 1964. After two years with the Canadian International Paper Company, and graduating from Columbia University with a doctoral degree in operations research, he joined the Department of Computer Science and Operations Research at the University of Montreal in 1969. In 1973, he was appointed director of CRT.

Florian initiated research with his early graduate students Sang Nguyen and Renée Dionne on urban travel forecasting methods. The extensive results of this research are described in sections 7.4.2.1, 7.4.2.4 and 7.5.1. He also organised conferences on traffic network equilibria and supply in 1974, 1977 and 1981, which established CRT internationally as a leading academic research centre in the field (Florian, 1976; Florian and Gaudry, 1980). In 1976, he founded the transportation planning software company INRO (section 10.5.1.7).

7.4.2   Deterministic Network Equilibrium Models with Fixed Demand

7.4.2.1   Link-based algorithms

Although Bruynooghe et al (1969) and Dafermos and Sparrow (1969) proposed solution algorithms to the network equilibrium problem, the first algorithms applied to realistic, albeit small, test networks were those of Larry LeBlanc (1973) and Sang Nguyen (1974a, 1974b). For his Ph.D. thesis, LeBlanc realised that the quadratic programming algorithm of Frank and Wolfe (1956) might provide a convergent and relatively efficient solution method for the network equilibrium problem, especially since the linearised subproblem could be solved efficiently as a shortest route problem, rather than as a linear programming problem as in the general case.[59] From the standpoint of travel forecasting practice in the US at that time, traffic assignment methods that converged to a stable solution were effectively unknown.[60] LeBlanc tested his implementation of the Frank–Wolfe linearisation method on a small test network he devised for the city of Sioux Falls, South Dakota (24 centroids, 24 nodes, 76 links).[61] In his papers (LeBlanc et al, 1974, 1975), LeBlanc referred to his proposed method as the 'Frank–Wolfe algorithm', the name now often used (Patriksson, 1994, 96). LeBlanc's linearisation method provided the basis for the algorithm introduced into US DoT's Urban Transportation Planning System (UTPS) (section 10.3.3).[62]

For his Ph.D. thesis, Sang Nguyen (1974a) stated and tested algorithms based on the convex-simplex method for solving the network equilibrium problem with fixed and variable demand in the space of link flows, origin-based flows and origin–destination route flows (Nguyen, 1974b). Later he compared his algorithm with LeBlanc's but found that neither was dominating for his test networks on the computers of that day (Nguyen, 1976). Validation studies performed by Nguyen are described in section 7.4.2.4.

John Murchland (1969) and Suzanne Evans (1973b) each proposed link-based assignment algorithms, with features in common with LeBlanc's algorithm, as portions of model formulations that combined trip distribution and assignment (sections 7.4.4.1, 7.4.4.2). Van Vliet and Dow (1979) also described link-based algorithms with features in common with the Frank–Wolfe method.

Experts in constrained optimisation methods found the challenge of speeding up the 'linearisation method', as applied to the network equilibrium problem, to be almost irresistible. The literature pertaining to these efforts is reviewed by Florian and Hearn (1995, 502–513, 535–537; 1999). While somewhat useful in speeding convergence on the computers with limited memory, the findings were not as helpful as hoped. Although the method was adopted by several software developers, further advances were not found to improve substantially the speed of convergence of this method. The method served practitioners well, however, when computers were slow and expensive, and memory was limited.

7.4.2.2 Route-based algorithms

The first known proposal of a route-based algorithm was a computer science working paper by Bothner and Lutter (1982) of the University of Bremen, Germany. The motivation for the paper is unknown. Its existence might not be known if it had not been the basis for the method incorporated into PTV's VISUM system by Thomas Schwerdtfeger (section 10.5.1.6).

Michael Patriksson (1994, Chapter 4) stated a formal mathematical classification of algorithms for solving the network equilibrium problem. His interest was undoubtedly sparked in part by his own contribution to this problem (Larsson and Patriksson, 1992). In view of the slow convergence of the link-based method, solving the problem in the space of route flows might be advantageous.

Larsson and Patriksson (1992) proposed a new algorithm called disaggregated simplicial decomposition (DSD). With the Frank–Wolfe algorithm, the solution proceeds in terms of finding and averaging together the link flows from a sequence of all-or-nothing assignments to shortest route trees. In the DSD algorithm, in contrast, the all-or-nothing assignments are averaged together at the route level. The number of routes with user-equilibrium flow is larger than the number of origin–destination pairs with flow; how much larger depends upon the size of the networks and the level of congestion. Therefore, the number of routes may be much larger than the number of links.

Jayakrishnan et al (1994) proposed another route-based method, where shifts are based on a gradient projection. They reported achieving higher precision than the link-based methods prevailing in research and practice at that time. Subsequently, Florian et al (2009, 10) proposed 'a new adaptation of Rosen's projected gradient algorithm . . . in which the origin–destination pairs are considered sequentially'. This route-based method is related to earlier adaptations of the gradient projection method and restricted simplicial decomposition, but the details of the algorithm are quite different. According to Florian et al (2009), their projected gradient method has the advantage that all route 'flows are adjusted simultaneously by shifting flow from routes that have a cost higher than the average route cost to routes that have a cost lower than the average route cost', which is 'somewhat similar to the algorithm of Jayakrishnan et al'. One difference is that the 'gradient projection method uses a constant that must be chosen in some way to obtain the best results', whereas Florian's projected gradient algorithm 'uses a line search to determine the step size for flow changes' (Florian et al, 2009, 11).

7.4.2.3 Origin-based, bush-based and segment-based algorithms

Despite the sophistication of Patriksson's DSD algorithm, studies by Donald Hearn and colleagues into the simplicial decomposition approach (Hearn et al, 1985, 1987), and the gradient projection algorithm of Jayakrishnan et al (1994), few advances were reported during the 1990s. Then, 30 years after the first convergent algorithms were identified, three new algorithms with a similar approach were proposed in a relatively short period: (a) origin-based assignment (OBA) by Hillel Bar-Gera (2002); (b) algorithm B by Robert Dial (2006); and (c) local user cost equilibrium (LUCE) by Guido Gentile (2014). Yu Nie (2010, 2012) reviewed and compared these algorithms.

All bush-based algorithms proposed so far share a few important features. They 'construct and maintain a bush for each origin (or destination) and restrict the traffic assignment only to these bushes' (Nie, 2010, 74). The term 'bush' was originally introduced by Dial (1971) in a slightly different context. A bush is an acyclic subnetwork that includes all of the user-equilibrium shortest routes from the origin node to all destination nodes. Acyclicity exploits the property that user-equilibrium flows from an origin do not contain cycles, that is, routes that pass through the same node more than once. Moreover, when the user-equilibrium flows on all bushes are found, the entire network is equilibrated. Therefore, the use of bushes not only offers efficiency, but also assures optimality, in the sense that user-equilibrium flows can be represented by equilibrated bushes. Bush-based algorithms construct user-equilibrium bushes by iterating between two subproblems, bush construction and bush equilibration (Bar-Gera, 2010; Nie, 2010; Gentile, 2014).

Bush-based algorithms differ from each other with regard to their equilibration methods, and can be classified as route-based or origin-based according to the flow aggregation level in the bush equilibration subproblem. Dial's algorithm B is in the former category, and equilibrates bushes

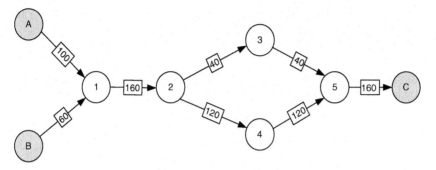

Source: Based on Boyce et al (2010, 7).

Figure 7.4 Pair of alternative segments serving flows from zones A and B to zone C

by swapping flows between the longest and shortest routes, as proposed by Dafermos and Sparrow (1969). Bar-Gera's origin-based algorithm is in the latter category; flows are represented by proportions of traffic arriving at each node from its predecessor links. Gentile's LUCE has a similar structure to OBA, differing mainly in the way the bushes are equilibrated. Jun Xie et al (2013) studied differences in performance of LUCE and OBA.

Until recently, an unresolved issue concerning the formulation and solution of the network equilibrium problem was that only link flows are uniquely determined. Many different route flow solutions may correspond to the same link flows as a result of possible swaps of flows between origin–destination pairs across a 'pair of alternative segments' with a common diverge and merge node, as shown in Figure 7.4 for two origins and one destination. In order to determine route flows uniquely, an additional condition is required. Hillel Bar-Gera (2010) proposed the term 'proportionality condition', and a new algorithm to solve for user-equilibrium route and link flows satisfying proportionality, traffic assignment by paired alternative segments (TAPAS). The proportionality condition states 'that the proportion of travelers on each of the two alternative segments should be the same regardless of their origin or their destination' (Bar-Gera, 2010, 1026); an example with two alternative segments connecting two O-D pairs is shown in Figure 7.4.

The same concept applies to the assignment of multiple classes of traffic with the same generalised cost function, such as travel time. In this case, the class link flows (e.g., cars and trucks) are also not uniquely determined. Imposing the condition of proportionality determines class link flows and class route flows uniquely. Imposing the condition of proportionality in a single class problem is effectively equivalent to maximising the entropy of route flows (Bar-Gera, 2010, 1027).

The underlying mathematical basis for TAPAS, the maximisation of route entropy, is studied in Bar-Gera (2006). Bar-Gera et al (2012) compared TAPAS with other algorithms. Inoue and Maruyama (2012) evaluated the performance of several of these algorithms on large-scale networks.

7.4.2.4   Convergence and validation of solutions

Formulation of the network equilibrium problem as a convex optimisation problem led not only to the development of convergent algorithms, but also to the specification of measures of convergence to the network equilibrium. As the mathematical theory for constructing these measures progressed, it was adopted in transportation research, but more slowly in practice. The specification and application of these measures are considered here and in section 2.5.6.

The convex optimisation formulation of the network equilibrium problem with fixed and variable demand provided the basis for a well-defined convergence criterion based on the objective function (Patriksson, 1994, 96–98). Moreover, the criterion for the fixed demand problem has a direct interpretation in terms familiar to practitioners. Consider a current feasible solution to the fixed demand traffic assignment problem, such as an initial solution generated by the assignment of a trip matrix to shortest routes defined on free-flow link travel times. Using that solution's link flows to evaluate the link cost functions, find the shortest routes from origins to destinations, and perform an all-or-nothing assignment of the trip matrix to these routes. The resulting assignment is a 'minimum cost assignment', given the link flows and corresponding link costs from the current solution. The total travel cost of the current solution (TC) less the total travel cost of the minimum cost assignment is called the Gap, also known as the total excess cost.[63] As the current solution converges towards the network equilibrium solution, the Gap tends to zero. One definition of the Relative Gap is the ratio of the Gap to TC, denoted RG(TC).[64] The value of the Relative Gap is independent of a specific network and trip matrix.[65]

Alternatively, a lower bound (LB) on the objective function of the network equilibrium problem may be defined as the objective function value minus the Gap. The lower bound must be less than or equal to the objective function value.[66] As the solution converges, however, the LB does not necessarily increase (monotonically) with each iteration towards the objective function value. Accordingly, a best lower bound (BLB), the maximum value of the LB achieved so far, is required to monitor convergence. Therefore, another version of the Relative Gap, denoted RG(OF), is defined as the ratio of the objective function value less the BLB to the BLB. Since the current total travel cost is greater than the current value of the BLB for a congested network, RG(TC) is somewhat less than RG(OF). Generally, the orders of magnitudes of the two values are the same, so the stopping criterion is not greatly affected by the choice.

Practitioners sometimes speak of an assignment process 'reaching closure'. The term 'closure' may stem from its use by Brokke and Mertz (1958, 82). In the context of a discussion of the application of the Fratar (1954) growth factor method, they stated: 'A measure of the efficiency of the various forecasting methods is the rapidity with which the individual zone growth factors converge toward the limiting F factor of 1.0 in successive iterations. . . . It can be seen . . . that the Fratar method is extremely efficient in its rate of closure.' Hence 'rate of closure' meant the rate of convergence of the solution procedure.

The term 'closure' is generally used, however, in the sense that a well-defined solution has been reached, as in 'reaches closure', rather than as the rate of convergence. For traffic assignment problems found in professional practice, no exact solution is possible. Rather, the assignment process converges towards the network equilibrium solution, but never reaches it exactly. Therefore, the issue faced by practitioners is when to stop the solution process. The Relative Gap provides useful guidance for such decisions.

The first statement of a stopping criterion based on the objective function, or Gap, appears to be Bruynooghe et al (1969, 201–202), who proposed two variants of the solution algorithm now known as the Frank–Wolfe method (Gibert, 1968b). LeBlanc (1973) and Nguyen (1974a) each proposed algorithms for solving the network equilibrium problem (section 7.4.2.1). LeBlanc stated a lower bound on the objective function value and described its use as a stopping criterion. However, he did not report its value in computational experiments with his Sioux Falls network (LeBlanc et al, 1974, 1975).

Nguyen (1974b, 1976) investigated three algorithms for solving the fixed demand network equilibrium problem; one was the method initially proposed by Bruynooghe et al (1969) and independently proposed by LeBlanc (1973). The second was a modified reduced gradient method suggested by Dafermos and Sparrow (1969). The third was based on the convex-simplex method. All three algorithms included well-defined stopping criteria. Nguyen investigated the performance of these algorithms on a network for Hull, Ontario, Canada (27 zone centroids, 155 nodes, 376 links) and Winnipeg, Manitoba, Canada (146 zone centroids, 1035 nodes, 2788 links). Criteria for the termination of each solution process were not described, although 18 solutions were compared. His principal interest was the execution times of the alternative algorithms, and not their convergence characteristics.

Michael Florian and Sang Nguyen (1976) performed the first comparison of the solution of the network equilibrium traffic assignment problem with a convergent algorithm to road traffic counts, using network and O-D data for the Winnipeg, Canada network for 1971 (140 zone centroids, 1035 nodes, 2789 links).[67] Two algorithms were applied: (a) the Frank–Wolfe method; and (b) Nguyen's convex-simplex method. The authors referred to other papers for detailed descriptions of the algorithms, so stopping criteria were not discussed. For the Frank–Wolfe algorithm, the authors stated: 'convergence was achieved in 15 to 18 cycles' (iterations). No reason was given for terminating the solution process at that point. Detailed plots compared link flows, link times and route times from the solution with observed link flows, and with link times and route times computed from the observed flows.

In spite of these advances during the mid-1970s, and the incorporation of network equilibrium traffic assignment into US DoT's Urban Transportation Planning System, few professional practitioners in the US adopted the new method. One reason was that the initial implementation in UTPS was flawed, temporarily delaying its adoption. Another was that some transportation planning agencies continued to use the capacity restraint assignment program in PLANPAC (US DoT, 1977a, 189–193) (section 10.3.3).

Ronald Eash et al (1979) introduced the Frank–Wolfe method into PLANPAC by performing the line search and averaging of link flows, demonstrating its superiority in terms of convergence and stability of link flows. Their paper explained and illustrated the method to practitioners, which was not provided in UTPS training manuals (US DoT, 1977b). A common solution procedure for capacity restraint assignment at that time was to perform four iterations, each based on the link costs from the last iteration, and average together the link flows from the third and fourth iterations. For comparison with this procedure, four iterations of the Frank–Wolfe method were performed on the DuPage County network (904 zone centroids, 9400 nodes, 25000 links). Values of the objective function showed their proposed method achieved better convergence; the Gap was not reported. Comparison of link volumes from the two methods with observed counts showed similar goodness-of-fit.

During the next 20 years, practitioners slowly adopted the Frank–Wolfe method, first in UTPS and later using commercial software systems. As computer speed and memory increased, the number of iterations performed also increased. Still, practitioners complained about the instability of their assignment results, especially in scenario analyses, often incorrectly blaming the problem on the algorithm, rather than on insufficient convergence. David Boyce, Biljana Ralevic-Dekic and Hillel Bar-Gera (2004) performed analyses with the network of the Delaware Valley Regional Planning Commission (2510 zone centroids, 13 389 nodes, 40 003 links). They compared two assignments with and without a proposed freeway connection, showing that a Relative Gap < 0.0001 (0.01 per cent) was necessary to assure stability of link flows throughout the network.

7.4.3 Stochastic Network Equilibrium Models with Fixed Demand

The network equilibrium problem formulated by Beckmann is deterministic. Drivers are assumed to choose their minimum cost routes on the basis of precise generalised travel costs of each route from their origins to their destinations, although these costs are determined by the simultaneous route choices of all travellers. As Beckmann's deterministic formulation became better known, several efforts sought to relax this assumption. Research reviewed here mainly attacked this problem by extending Beckmann's optimisation framework.

7.4.3.1 Stochastic formulations for uncongested networks
Early attempts to include user perceptions in a model of route choice with fixed travel costs were proposed by Abraham (1961), Von Falkenhausen (1966), Burrell (1969) and Dial (1971). All were motivated by travel forecasting practice, and the need to forecast link flows more realistically than was possible with either the all-or-nothing or the capacity restraint procedures. Dial's STOCH method in the US (section 2.5.6) and Burrell's method in the UK (section 3.6.3) were designed to introduce dispersion of route flows into assignments.[68] The proportion of trips selecting each route was (a) specified over an enumerated set of routes, or generated by path splitting at different nodes in the network (Dial), or (b) through random sampling from link cost distributions (Burrell).

Dial proposed two algorithms, which he called 'single pass' and 'double pass'. Dial's double-pass algorithm corresponds to a multinomial logit route choice model in which route flows occur over 'efficient routes', routes in which, for each link, the node at the head of the link is closer to the destination and farther from the origin than the node at the tail of the link. Since Dial considered only the case of fixed link costs, efficient routes were determined independently of route flows.

Michael Florian and Bennett Fox (1976) and Huw Williams (1977a), among others, noted that the logit function implied by Dial's double-pass method violated the independence from irrelevant alternatives (IIA) property owing to overlapping routes. In this case two routes may share a sequence of links between a given origin–destination pair, which may lead to implausible route proportions, possibly yielding unrealistic route and link flows. In a highway or public transport network, the existence of common links on alternative routes was a clear source of similarity and correlation between the costs of a set of overlapping routes. Morton Schneider (1974) summarised the 'virtues and faults' of Dial's method, noting that it 'is a frankly mechanical procedure without explanatory pretensions, designed to spread trips around in a more or less reasonable way'. Pierre Robillard (1974, 119), in deriving a maximum likelihood method for estimating the parameter in Dial's method, noted that the method 'does not lend itself to flow-dependent assignment'.

The 'overlapping route problem' was critically examined by Carlos Daganzo and Yossi Sheffi (1977). In proposing an alternative approach, reminiscent of Burrell's method, they assumed that drivers choose their routes in terms of perceived travel time, which equals the deterministic route travel time plus a random error term, thereby generalising Wardrop's first criterion as 'no user believes he can improve his travel time by unilaterally changing routes'.[69] Their stated motivation was to offer a model applicable to uncongested networks. If drivers' perceived route times are multivariate Gumbel distributed, then logit stochastic routes are obtained; if the perceived times are normally distributed, then probit stochastic routes result (Daganzo et al, 1977; Daganzo, 1979). Although their early formulations were developed for fixed link costs, their papers pointed the way to the stochastic network equilibrium problem.

A further contribution of Sheffi and Daganzo (1978) was the representation of the multiple choices available to a traveller (e.g., location, mode and route) through the concept of route choice within an abstract network called a hypernetwork (section 7.4.1.2).[70] They discussed the selection of hyperpaths through this network whose links had normally distributed costs. The probit model was used to elaborate on the problems of correlation between the utilities in the various choice dimensions, including those arising from common links on street networks, and also to formulate a consistent approach to determining equilibrium between demand and level-of-service throughout a complex choice model.

7.4.3.2   Stochastic network equilibrium

Caroline Fisk (1980) formulated the stochastic network equilibrium problem as a generalisation of Beckmann's deterministic network equilibrium problem with fixed origin–destination flows. By adding an entropy function defined on route flows to Beckmann's link cost function, she showed that the solution of this problem yields a logit function defined on the equilibrium travel costs of each route between each origin and destination.[71] Moreover, if the routes are restricted to efficient routes and the link costs are fixed, 'it is clear that the solution . . . will be identical to that obtained by using Dial's model' (Fisk, 1980, 245). Fisk investigated the properties of the solution, but did not propose a solution algorithm.

Assuming fixed travel demand and separable link cost functions, two unconstrained optimisation problems for the stochastic network equilibrium problem were formulated by Carlos Daganzo (1982) and by Yossi Sheffi and Warren Powell (1982, 195), who showed the stochastic user-equilibrium problem could be formulated without the direct use of probabilistic assumptions.[72] Sheffi and Powell (1981) compared solutions computed from the logit and probit models. They noted that a fixed set of routes must be predetermined for solving the problem (Powell and Sheffi, 1982, 52). Such a set could be defined on zero-flow link travel times using Dial's concept of 'efficient routes'. The use of non-equilibrium link times to determine the set of efficient routes, however, is a drawback of the method.

The solution of the logit route choice formulation was facilitated by the rediscovery by Powell and Sheffi (Powell and Sheffi, 1982; Sheffi and Powell, 1982) of the method of successive averages in the context of statistical approximation methods (Robbins and Monroe, 1951; Blum, 1954). MSA may be used to average a sequence of solutions with predetermined step sizes. A commonly used step size is $1/n$, where n is the iteration, and the quantity being averaged with the current solution is the difference between the new solution and the current solution. Hence, the new solution, which is based on the current solution, is given a weight of $1/n$, and the current solution a weight of $(n-1)/n$. Assuming the objective function of the problem has a unique minimum, this method is known to converge, albeit slowly. Sheffi (1985, section 12.5) described in detail the evolution of these ideas.

Takashi Akamatsu (1996, 1997) investigated the relation of Dial's double-pass method for fixed link costs to stochastic user-equilibrium models of the logit type. He showed that the logit route choice user-equilibrium model could be formulated in terms of link flow variables as well as route flow variables. He discussed solution algorithms, thoroughly integrating the literature up to that time. More recent developments include Bekhor and Prashker (2001) and a review by Meng and Liu (2012), followed by their formulation and solution algorithm for the probit-based asymmetric stochastic network equilibrium problem with elastic demand.

The first known application of the stochastic network equilibrium formulation of Sheffi was by Howard Slavin et al (1988) to an analysis of commuter rail ridership in the New York region. The model was applied to forecast choices among hundreds of combinations of mode, access mode, commuter rail station and car parks for travel from 50 zones to a single destination. The model was solved by the method of successive averages for fixed car park capacities.

Although Sheffi's stochastic network equilibrium formulation sparked considerable interest, there was little discussion of the model's limited stochastic attributes. Only the perception error is a random variable. The remainder of the model is deterministic, as in Beckmann's original formulation. In a truly stochastic network equilibrium problem, link travel times are random variables. Such a model was proposed by Pitu Mirchandani and Hossein Soroush (1987). Examination of their detailed exposition enables one to envisage the difficulty of such a formulation and the requirements for its solution.

One requirement of the formulation is an assumption concerning the attitude of the traveller towards risk: risk-prone, risk-averse or risk-neutral. For example, risk-prone travellers are inclined to favour routes with lower mean travel times and higher variances than risk-averse travellers, who might choose routes with higher mean travel times and lower variances. This assumption raises the question of whether travellers could be identified with regard to this attribute.

7.4.4 Deterministic Network Equilibrium Models with Variable Demand

Beckmann's formulation related travel demand between each pair of nodes of the network to a decreasing function of the travel costs over the shortest route for each node pair. A decade following its publication, researchers began to explore his formulation in more depth, and relate it to travel forecasting practices of that period. These papers are reviewed in this section; research aimed at implementing these models is examined in section 7.4.5.

7.4.4.1   Early combined trip distribution and assignment formulations
John Murchland, a British applied mathematician, established the Transport Network Theory (TNT) Unit in 1964, first in the London School of Economics and Political Science, and subsequently in the London Graduate School of Business Studies. The initial focus of his research was methods for computing shortest routes through networks. Murchland wrote three of his widely distributed notes, the first and third on traffic assignment, and the second on the gravity model of trip distribution and an equivalent optimisation formulation (Murchland, 1966a, 1966b, 1967). The first hints at an algorithm for solving the congested traffic assignment problem. The second suggests an equivalent optimisation formulation of the gravity model. In his second paper, Murchland stated:

I think the main role of this equivalent maximization problem will be in formulating more general models, in which distribution is just one aspect. . . .
In reality most road networks are subject to some degree of congestion. . . .
A possible way of carrying out this congested calculation would be to repeat
the gravity distribution model calculation, and the assignment of the resulting
traffic to the given network, alternately till no further changes occurred. . . . I
only want to draw attention here to an attractive feature of the maximization
formulation of the distribution model. In the iteration mentioned above, the
assignment calculations must necessarily be a so-called 'multi-commodity'
one. . . . [I]f the assignment and distribution calculations could be combined
(by using the maximization formulation of the latter) the resulting calculation
would be a simpler 'single-commodity' calculation (Murchland, 1966b, 15–16).

These fragments of his text show Murchland was trying to imagine how
the distribution and assignment problem could be 'combined' into a
single problem. Perhaps the difficulty Murchland encountered was that
he appeared to think in terms of algorithms, or computational procedures, rather than model formulations. In his note on the gravity model,
Murchland cites Beckmann et al (1956) in connection with a discussion of
consumer surplus, revealing that he was aware of that work. However, at
that time he had evidently not yet considered Beckmann's network equilibrium formulation with variable demand.

Alain Gibert evidently visited Murchland's TNT Unit in July 1968,
when he wrote a note on 'the traffic assignment problem when demand
is elastic' (Gibert, 1968a). His note is closely related to his co-authored
paper, Bruynooghe et al (1969). The note is primarily concerned with
the equivalence of Beckmann's objective function and the network equilibrium conditions, the existence of solutions to this problem, and the
convergence of his proposed algorithm for solving the traffic assignment
problem with elastic demand.

By 1970 John Murchland had moved to Karlsruhe, Germany;[73] he proposed a formulation of the network equilibrium problem with variable
demand (Murchland, 1969), based on the convex programming theory of
R.T. Rockafellar (1967). He acknowledged Beckmann for his 'complete
exposition' of 'the problem of the steady-state distribution of traffic on
a road network'.[74] Although the presentation of his formulation seems
rather obscure from today's perspective, Murchland did succeed in defining and analysing the model, as shown by the detailed exposition and
analysis of his model by Evans (1973b, section 4.4). In the section of his
paper on a solution algorithm, Murchland acknowledges the contribution
of Gibert (1968a, 1968b) and Bruynooghe et al (1969) to his proposal.
Although Murchland did not publish any computational results, by 1970
he had a working computer program.[75] Murchland later advised on the
implementation of the Frank–Wolfe method for solving the fixed demand

traffic assignment problem in UTPS, and continued writing his notes and occasional papers (e.g., Murchland, 1977).

Concurrently, and in conjunction with his co-authored paper on fixed demand assignment presented in 1968, M. Bruynooghe (1969) wrote a 67-page working paper on the distribution and assignment of traffic on a network. This paper proposed a unified formulation of the distribution and assignment problems. The properties of the formulation were studied, two algorithms for its solution were described and their convergence properties were examined. The references listed in this paper show Bruynooghe was well informed about developments in trip distribution and traffic assignment in the US and the UK. The conclusions to the paper suggest Bruynooghe was planning to extend his formulation to a model for simultaneously distributing trips to destinations, modes and routes (1969, 53).

John Tomlin (1971) proposed another formulation of a combined model of trip distribution and assignment. In this case, assignment was formulated as the minimisation of total travel costs; however, link costs and therefore O-D costs were fixed. A solution algorithm was proposed.

The findings of Gibert, Murchland, Bruynooghe and Tomlin set the stage for several contributions that effectively solved the problem of formulating the origin–destination, mode choice and road traffic assignment problems as an integrated model, in contrast to the sequential procedure of early practitioners (sections 2.3.4, 2.4.4, 2.5.7 and 3.7). By proposing convergent algorithms, these authors also addressed the question of how to solve their models computationally, thereby offering insights into the question of how to iterate the sequential procedure to an equilibrium solution.

7.4.4.2 Formulation and algorithms of Evans

For her 1973 Ph.D. thesis, Suzanne Evans (1973b) independently assembled the network equilibrium formulations proposed by Beckmann, Gibert, Murchland, Tomlin and others, analysed the properties of these models with the convex analysis theory of Rockafellar (1967), proposed a 'combined model of trip distribution and traffic assignment', devised a new algorithm for its solution, and offered proofs of convergence and lower bounds. The problem of combining distribution and assignment was suggested by her advisor, Richard Allsop, who recognised the need for an integrated model from policy questions arising in the UK, and from his participation in the fourth symposium on the theory of traffic flow (Allsop, 1968).[76]

In Chapter 3 of her thesis, Evans thoroughly reviewed the pertinent formulations of the trip distribution problem, analysed its properties and discussed procedures for its solution. In Chapters 4 and 5, she reviewed formulations of the traffic assignment problem with fixed and elastic demand, and algorithms for their solution, including the algorithm of Murchland. In Chapter 6, she presented her novel synthesis of the combined trip distribution and traffic assignment (CDA) model. Then she proposed a new partial linearisation, link-based algorithm, which may be seen to be a generalisation of the linearisation method (Patriksson, 1993; 1994, 105–110, 145–146). Evans defined two test quantities for monitoring the convergence of her proposed solution algorithm (Evans, 1976b, 47–49).

In contrast to the theses of LeBlanc and Nguyen on traffic assignment with fixed demand, Evans's thesis and two subsequent papers were theoretical. That said, her 311-page thesis was the most extensive synthesis of formulations and their mathematical properties for the period 1950–70, as well as the most rigorous analysis of a model and solution algorithm performed up to that time. Her papers remain the most detailed analysis of convergence measures for a combined model. Evans presented her findings in 1974 (Evans, 1976b) and published a detailed paper on her principal results (Evans, 1976a). Although she maintained contact with the traffic equilibrium field, she made no further contributions and devoted her academic research career to applied statistics and communication networks.

7.4.4.3   Subsequent model formulations and algorithms
Following the model and solution algorithm proposed by Murchland, and the definitive formulation and partial linearisation solution algorithm of Evans, further progress in combined models was achieved by extending the basic formulation to include the nested logit structures being proposed by demand modellers (Chapter 5). As assignment algorithms began to be extended to route-based and origin-based network representations, those solution methods were integrated into the combined model framework. The refinement of the model formulations, and their integration with more advanced assignment algorithms are reviewed in this section for optimisation formulations of the traffic assignment model with separable link cost functions. Research aimed at the implementation, estimation and validation of these models is described in section 7.4.5. Formulations for non-separable link cost functions and related asymmetric models are considered in section 7.5.

Michael Florian and Sang Nguyen (1974) were the first to publish computational results on the traffic assignment problem with elastic demand, as originally formulated by Beckmann. Building on the suggestion of Gibert (1968a), they proposed an algorithm based on generalised Benders decomposition, and reported solutions for the network of Hull, Canada (27 zones, 155 nodes, 376 links). Florian et al (1975) proposed two solution algorithms for a formulation of the combined trip distribution and traffic assignment problem, previously studied by Tomlin (1971) and Evans (1973b). Florian and Nguyen (1978) expanded their formulation to include mode choice, again proposing a full linearisation algorithm.

At the symposium on traffic equilibrium methods organised by Michael Florian in 1974, Stella Dafermos (1976) described a formulation intended to represent the sequential procedure found in practice as a single model. She used the term 'integrated model' to describe her formulation. In this manner she proposed a concept similar to Suzanne Evans's 'combined model', presented at the same symposium (section 7.4.4.2).

Sven Erlander (1977) proposed an interesting reformulation of Evans's model. In the same manner as Beckmann, Evans viewed the two non-linear terms in her objective function as an artificial optimisation problem, whose solution gave the desired trip distribution function and network equilibrium conditions. The demand-related term is an entropy function defined on the O-D flows, which equals to the integral of the inverse demand function when demand is described by a negative exponential function.

Erlander moved the entropy term into the constraint set. In this manner he suggested its interpretation as a measure of 'interactivity', which might also be termed 'dispersion of O-D flows' (Erlander and Stewart, 1978, 1990; Erlander et al, 1979). His reformulation suggested the notion of a set of entropy constraints pertaining to mode, origin–destination and trip frequency to subsequent researchers.

Erlander (1990) proposed a reformulation of Fisk (1980) to include origin–destination flows (section 7.4.3.2). He called this model the continuous dispersed equilibrium (CDE) model, which is related to but different from the combined distribution and assignment (CDA) model of Evans. Erlander compared the properties of these two models as follows:

> The CDA model is constructed in a very ingenious way so as to get an equilibrium solution, which assumes that travellers choose shortest routes. This assumption seems to be very natural provided that the travellers have full information. In the CDE model, on the other hand, there is still a tendency to choose short routes, but the trips are spread out, in principle over all routes. However, many routes will have large origin–destination costs and will thus carry very small flows, since the routes are determined by the exponential function. This result might be reasonable in cases where the travellers do not have full information about which routes are the shortest ones. Another advantage with the CDA model is that it produces gravity model solutions for the trip distribution. However, the intriguing question remains: Can the CDA model be motivated in a more direct way and not only by the fact that it is a good optimization problem giving the wanted result? Can the optimization problem itself be said to have some meaning? Why does this optimization problem produce such good results? (Erlander, 1990, 367).

Since 1968 David Boyce had lectured on urban travel forecasting methods, focusing often on the contributions of Alan Wilson (1970). In 1976 he proposed a synthesis of the urban location model of Wilson (1970, Chapter 4) with the network equilibrium problem of Evans (Boyce, 1978).[77] Interest in this paper led to his review and synthesis of urban location models with endogenous travel costs (Boyce, 1980) in which he posed questions related to the incorporation of mode choice into the location–travel choice function, the representation of congestion during peak time periods of the day, and parameter estimation of the cost function.

In her Ph.D. thesis, Carolyn Frank (1978) compared the algorithms proposed by Florian et al (1975) and Evans (1976a) for solving the combined model of trip distribution and assignment. Florian et al (1975) proposed a full linearisation of the objective function, whereas Evans proposed linearising only the term related to link costs. The former algorithm required the solution of an $n \times n$ linear programming (LP) problem, where n is the number of zones. Evans's algorithm required the solution of an $n \times n$ doubly-constrained trip matrix. The conjecture addressed by Frank was whether the LP problem could be solved more efficiently than balancing the trip matrix. For the network of Hull, Canada (27 zones, 155 nodes, 376 links), the LP problem was indeed solved somewhat faster than balancing the trip matrix; however, each LP-generated trip matrix contained only $(2n-1)$ positive O-D flows, as compared with the full flow matrix obtained by balancing the trip matrix. Therefore, the full linearisation algorithm of Florian et al (1975) converged very slowly compared to the partial linearisation algorithm of Evans.

Convergence of the two algorithms may be compared with their Relative Gaps.[78] Scenarios were solved for two cost sensitivity parameter values. The objective function value achieved by the full linearisation method after 20 iterations was surpassed after eight iterations of the partial linearisation method for the smaller parameter value and after four iterations for the larger value. For comparable levels of convergence, therefore, Evans's algorithm was substantially faster. LeBlanc and Farhangian (1981) made a similar comparison for a combined mode choice and assignment model with LeBlanc's Sioux Falls test problem (24 centroids, 24 nodes, 76 links). In agreement with Frank, they demonstrated that Evans's partial linearisation approach converged much faster than the linearisation method.[79]

David Boyce and Larry LeBlanc began to collaborate in 1979 in order to improve their mutual understanding of the combined model framework of Evans. They formulated a family of travel choice models that synthesised the composite cost formulations of Williams (1977a)[80] with the combined network equilibrium model formulation of Evans. The key idea was how to formulate a set of nested entropy constraints corresponding to the nested logit structure of Williams. Their goal was to derive this model structure, estimate its parameters and compute solutions for a network of manageable size, given the limitations of the mainframes of the early 1980s; model formulations were reported in Boyce et al (1983, 1985) and Boyce (1984, 1990) (sections 7.4.5.2, 7.4.5.3).

Yossi Sheffi (1985, Chapters 6, 7) proposed a formulation of the network equilibrium problem with variable demand, and described a linearisation algorithm for its solution, which he called the convex combination method. He reviewed several variants of the doubly-constrained trip distribution problem with user-equilibrium costs, and presented alternative algorithms, arguing that the linearisation method was preferable. His conclusion was reached without the benefit of computational experiments, which could have demonstrated the superiority of the partial linearisation approach of Evans.

Safwat and Magnanti (1988) described an extension of the combined model concept to include trip generation. Their paper reviewed various approaches and recommended a full linearisation algorithm. Applications to intercity passenger travel and to urban travel were briefly described. Helmut Schittenhelm (1990) described a combined model formulation based on the route-based assignment algorithm of Bothner and Lutter (1982) (section 7.4.2.2). He performed computational tests on a network for Lilienthal, Germany (21 nodes, 293 links), citing the superiority of his method over those of Florian and Evans. Boyce and Lundqvist (1987) and Abrahamsson and Lundqvist (1999) estimated and evaluated alternative nested logit formulations of combined models of origin–destination, mode and route flows for the Stockholm region (section 7.4.5.3).

7.4.4.4 Cost-efficiency principle of Smith and Erlander

Tony Smith, first independently, and later in collaboration with Sven Erlander, proposed a new theoretical foundation for the derivation of log-linear models, which included the logit function, models derived with maximum entropy methods, and models of origin–destination–mode–route interaction (Smith, 1978a, 1978b, 1983, 1988; Erlander, 1985, 1990, 2010; Sen and Smith, 1995). Erlander and Smith (1990, 173) noted that it was 'long recognized that many types of population behaviour exhibit cost-minimization tendencies at the macro level. With respect to human populations in particular, the explicit recognition of this tendency dates from the work of' George Zipf [1902–1950], an American linguist who studied the rank–size rule in languages and 'proposed a principle of "least effort" governing human activity' (Zipf, 1949).[81]

The cost-efficiency principle, formally stated in Smith (1978a), postulated an explicit principle of human spatial interaction behaviour, asserting at each level of activity that spatial interaction patterns with lower total costs are always at least as probable as those with higher total costs. Smith showed that this macro-statistical principle characterised the classical family of exponential gravity models, and hence accounted in part for the robustness of these models. Subsequently, the cost-efficiency principle was recognised to have much broader implications for the full class of log-linear probability models. Erlander (1985) offered a more general interpretation leading to characterisations of a wide range of models in statistical mechanics and other branches of applied probability.

Initially, Smith developed his cost-efficiency principle for fixed travel costs. Later, he extended the theory to congested networks in which travel costs depend upon the cost-minimising route choices of travellers (Smith, 1983, 1988; Erlander and Smith, 1990). Erlander (2005) explored these and related constructs, including related points of view such as the additive random utility maximising model and models derived with Lagrangian analysis. In his book Erlander (2010) also synthesised several related constructs, including welfare, freedom of choice and composite utility in the logit model.

The extension of Smith's cost-efficiency principle to congested transportation networks is based on the definition of a 'cumulative user-cost function' for discrete (individual) trips. He described his cost-efficiency principle of travel behaviour for congested networks as follows:

> consider travel behavior on the network over a sequence of comparable daily time periods. If we are now able to observe only *macro* trip activity levels (in terms of the trip origin and destination totals at each location), . . . which micro trip-pattern sequences are most likely to have generated this activity. Under the conditions of the micro cost-minimization hypothesis, one would expect on average to observe daily trip patterns with lower rather than higher levels of cumulative user-costs. Hence, if we now consider the mean daily level of cumulative user-costs associated with each possible pattern sequence, then, as a macro extension of this cost-minimization hypothesis, one may expect that pattern sequences with lower mean cost levels will be more likely (Smith, 1983, 439).

Later in the paper, Smith related this theory to network equilibrium models, as follows:

> In these continuous flow models [Beckmann et al, 1956] it is postulated that a *user-equilibrium* is characterized by equal flow costs on all routes used between any pair of locations (and by higher flow costs on all routes not used). The behavioral meaning here is simply that (under conditions of full information) traffic flows will always shift to cheaper (quicker) routes until all [costs] are equated on the routes used.[82]

The present class of exponential trip-pattern models reflect this same type of equilibrium behavior in a probabilistic way. In particular, if trip makers are not perfect cost-minimizers (because of imperfect information, or other preference considerations, for example), but still exhibit definite cost-minimizing tendencies in their route choices (that is, satisfy the micro cost-minimizing hypothesis), then one might expect user-equilibrium trip patterns to emerge as the *most probable states* within a distribution of possible states. This is precisely the behavior exhibited by exponential trip-pattern models (Smith, 1983, 443).

Erlander (2010, Chapter 8) showed how Smith's cost-efficiency formulation with discrete variables could be approximated with continuous variables to yield a Beckmann-type model.

7.4.4.5 Oppenheim's synthesis with random utility theory

Norbert Oppenheim (1993a) explored a formulation of destination choice in the context of a combined model of travel choice by introducing a congestion function at the destination, as well as adding an entropy term to the objective function. The resulting trip distribution model took the form of a logit model with cost terms related to travel time and endogenous destination costs. He also showed how his result related to random utility theory, and proposed a variant of Evans's partial linearisation algorithm for its solution. Oppenheim (1993b) used a similar approach to formulate a combined model of personal travel and goods movement. Both models embraced the framework of Evans to propose an algorithm for finding the equilibrium flows; neither offered computational results.

Two years later, Oppenheim (1995) published *Urban Travel Demand Modeling*. He first offered a synthesis of route choice models for uncongested and congested networks. Then, he explained how to expand this modelling framework to include mode, destination and travel frequency in a random utility theory framework. He showed how the network equilibrium model could be reformulated as an economic model of a representative traveller, providing a new interpretation of the Beckmann–Evans objective function, proposing the first substantive interpretation for Beckmann's sum of the integrals of the link cost function. In the process he embraced the entropy-constrained formulation of Erlander. Then, he proposed how to estimate the parameters of the models using maximum likelihood methods. Finally, he considered the bi-level formulation of the network design problem, including network pricing.

For such an innovative and far-reaching synthesis, Oppenheim would seem to have garnered much praise. In fact, he did not, and experienced stinging disappointment. Why did this result occur, one might ask? His synthesis of random utility theory and user-equilibrium models meant that few colleagues were ready to understand the joint product. While some would agree that Oppenheim's text provided 'an opportunity to move our field substantially forward', as Boyce stated in his foreword to the book, the field was clearly not ready to embrace this approach in 1995, and certainly did not move substantially in this direction in the succeeding two decades. The field's traditional sequential procedure was too deeply ingrained in practice to be displaced by Oppenheim's more scientific and rigorous paradigm. Moreover, other challengers were already appearing in the form of tour-based and activity-based models. From the perspective of 20 years later, the latter gained the higher ground.

Oppenheim's solution algorithms were based on Evans's link-based algorithm, the state of the art at the time. By the time of the book's publication, new assignment techniques were beginning to appear, suggesting revisions to algorithms for solving combined travel choice models. The first of these was Patriksson's route-based algorithm (Larsson and Patriksson, 1992). Jan Lundgren and Michael Patriksson (1998) proposed a combined distribution and assignment model building on this advance.

Bar-Gera and Boyce (2003) synthesised Bar-Gera's origin-based assignment algorithm with the doubly-constrained trip distribution and mode choice model. Solutions for the Chicago regional network and zone system (1790 zones, 12 982 nodes, 39 018 road links) compared their proposed algorithm with an implementation of Evans's algorithm and the sequential procedure, which clearly demonstrated the superiority of their approach. These findings were summarised by Boyce (2002), who asked whether the four-step, sequential procedure is counter-productive in the sense that it focuses attention on the individual steps and away from the consistent formulation of the overall forecasting model.

In summary, the findings of Evans, LeBlanc, Florian, Nguyen, Boyce and Oppenheim, together with the earlier proposals of Bruynooghe, Gibert, Murchland and Tomlin, completed the circle from the sequential procedure of Douglas Carroll and other practitioners in the mid-1950s to Martin Beckmann's network equilibrium formulation in 1956. Given the concerns of practitioners in the US after 1991 with solving the sequential procedure with feedback, these combined models might have provided the insights needed to formulate a procedure in which travel demand models and transportation network models were truly integrated, and to provide the basis for solving them efficiently in practice. In fact, these proposals were largely ignored. The research performed to implement and test the algorithms proposed to solve combined models is considered next.

7.4.5 Implementation, Estimation and Validation Studies

Following the formulation of the trip distribution, mode choice and traffic assignment problems as combined models, and proposals for algorithms to solve these models, several implementation studies were performed.

7.4.5.1 Origins of EMME/2
Michael Florian and his group at the Centre for Research on Transportation, University of Montreal, implemented and validated the first generation of a user-equilibrium, two-mode travel forecasting model called EMME (Florian et al, 1979).[83] To implement the model proposed by Florian (1977) (section 7.5.1), a survey-based single class trip matrix for Winnipeg, Canada was allocated to car and bus modes by a multinomial logit function, and integrated with user-equilibrium assignment of the two trip matrices to the road and public transport networks. The data analysis and parameter estimation were described in detail for three mode choice functions.

Tests were performed jointly for the Winnipeg road and bus networks (147 zones, 1040 road nodes, 2836 road links, 56 bus lines, 800 bus nodes, 1755 line segments). Iterative results or convergence measures were not reported. Solution of the model required about 80 minutes on the CDC Cyber 176, a mainframe widely used in university research. The authors concluded: 'the use of such sophisticated models . . . is feasible and the simulation of scenarios results in refined and fully detailed evaluations, which would not be possible otherwise' (Florian et al, 1979, 22). Subsequent publications referred to this model as EMME/2; see section 10.5.1.7.

7.4.5.2 Three models of the Chicago region
David Boyce and his students, in collaboration with Ronald Eash and Dean Englund of the Chicago Area Transportation Study, studied several combined models for the Chicago region. The first project implemented models that combined a single class, singly-constrained origin–destination–mode function with a user-equilibrium (UE) assignment of cars and trucks to an aggregated network (317 zones, 820 nodes, 2422 links) (Boyce et al, 1983, 1985, 1992; Boyce, 1984). The second project performed sensitivity analyses on a similar model with a doubly-constrained origin–destination–mode choice function (Boyce et al, 1992; Tatineni et al, 1994). The third project implemented, estimated and validated a two-class, doubly-constrained origin–destination–mode choice function with a UE assignment of cars and trucks to a detailed zone system and road network (1790 zones, 12 982 nodes, 39 018 road links) (Boyce and Bar-Gera, 2003). The solution method for each project was the Evans algorithm.

Computational facilities available to the first project consisted of the IBM System/370, on which the Urban Transportation Planning System (US DoT, 1977b) was available (see sections 2.6 and 10.3.3). The model was implemented with user-coded subroutines inserted through entry points in the UROAD module of UTPS. Data available for the first model were synthesised from a 1975 household survey, the 1970 census of population, and a survey-based truck trip matrix, factored to the two-hour morning peak period. Generalised cost functions for travel by car were defined as a weighted sum of in-vehicle travel time, operating cost and access–egress walking time. For public transport, the cost function included in-vehicle time, fare, access–egress time, transfer time and waiting time. Parameters were borrowed from earlier studies. Convergence was severely restricted by the integer-valued origin–destination–mode flows and link flows in UTPS.

Four combined models were solved, listed with their Relative Gaps (RG) (section 7.4.2.4):

1. UE assignment of a fixed vehicle matrix (cars and trucks) to the road network: nine iterations, RG < 0.02;
2. mode choice function applied to a fixed trip matrix, and UE assignment of the car trip matrix with the fixed truck matrix: five iterations, RG < 0.02;
3. destination location and mode choice function, given residential locations, and UE assignment of the resulting car matrix with truck trip matrix: nine iterations, RG < 0.01;
4. residential location and mode choice function, given destination locations, and UE assignment of the resulting car matrix with truck trip matrix: nine iterations, RG < 0.02.[84]

Values of the two cost sensitivity parameters related to mode choice, and to destination or origin choice, were identified in relation to the dispersion (entropy) of the observed trip matrices, as suggested by an entropy-constrained formulation of the combined model. The model calibrations explored the parameter space in detail, in order to understand the properties and performance of the models.[85]

An enhanced version of the model was implemented during the second project as a doubly-constrained origin–destination–mode choice model with UE assignment of cars and trucks as real-valued flows. Parameters were estimated with maximum likelihood methods (Boyce et al, 1992; Boyce and Zhang, 1998). The model was solved in 20 iterations with RG < 0.01. Sensitivity analyses were performed on the model inputs including public transport fares, fuel price and employment location (Tatineni et al, 1994). Paul Metaxatos and David Boyce, with Michael Florian and Isabelle Constantin, implemented the Evans algorithm in EMME/2 (Metaxatos et al, 1995); this procedure is now a standard option of Emme (section 10.5.1.7).

During 1997–2000, a third project was undertaken to: (a) implement a combined model of origin–destination–mode choice and UE assignment for two user classes (home–work, other travel), plus background flows of trucks for the two-hour morning peak period; and (b) estimate and validate this model for the detailed zone system and road network used for transportation planning in the Chicago region. The solutions converged in seven iterations to a RG < 0.001. This model was estimated with data from the 1990 CATS household travel survey. The estimation of model parameters was performed using the experimental statistical method of Sacks et al (1989) to identify the best parameter values on the maximum likelihood response surface. Model validation was performed for home–work travel with the 1990 census journey-to-work data (US DoT, 1995).

Two choice functions were estimated for origin–destination–mode choice: the multinomial logit function and the nested logit function (D/M/A). Although the nested logit function performed slightly better, conditions on the relative size of the cost sensitivity coefficients for the nested logit function were satisfied only for home–work travel and were not satisfied for other travel. This finding suggested the 'reverse' model formulation of Mattsson (1987, 258–260) for other travel; see also Anderstig and Mattsson (1991, 171–173).

The validation of predicted home–work travel for 1990 was performed by comparing the predicted interzonal home–work person trips with the corresponding interzonal census data for one-mile straight-line distance intervals from 0 to 30 miles. Public transport share and modal travel times were similarly compared. The proportions of predicted and observed travel were aggregated to 12 districts constituting the Chicago region to compare the predicted and observed proportions in terms of their ratios and differences (Boyce and Bar-Gera, 2003).

7.4.5.3 Two models of the Stockholm region

David Boyce and Lars Lundqvist, with their students, implemented two combined models for the Stockholm region (Boyce and Lundqvist, 1987; Abrahamsson and Lundqvist, 1999), which led to the maximum likelihood estimation of a doubly-constrained, origin–destination–mode choice model with UE assignment. Parameter estimation was performed with the 1975 Swedish census home–work travel by mode. The model was solved for the road network (175 zones, 3000 links) with travel times and monthly fares of the public transport network serving the Stockholm region. Four nested logit functions were hypothesised corresponding to alternative assumptions about the form of the dispersion constraints. Each set of models was estimated for zero public transport fares and for monthly transit fares pro-rated per day.[86]

Subsequently, Torgil Abrahamsson performed parameter estimation for alternative combined model formulations, the most detailed exploration of the traditional and reverse nested logit functions to that time. The model was estimated on aggregated single class data for the Stockholm region (45 zones, 417 nodes, 964 road links). From 12 to 41 iterations of the Evans algorithm were required to achieve an RG < 0.0005, depending upon values of the cost sensitivity parameters. Two cases were estimated: (a) the traditional nested logit function in which mode choice is conditional on origin–destination choice; and (b) the reverse nested logit function in which origin–destination choice is conditional on mode choice at the origin. The estimation results suggested rejection of the traditional function.

7.4.5.4 Travel forecasting in the German Democratic Republic

During 1950–90, academic researchers and practitioners in the German Democratic Republic (DDR or East Germany) developed travel forecasting models largely independently of research in Western Europe and North America. These models, based on mathematical foundations similar to others reviewed in this chapter, were extensively applied and documented in East German publications. After German reunification in 1990, the models became better known through their incorporation into PTV's VISUM (section 10.5.1.6).

The Department of Transportation Sciences was founded at the Technical University Dresden, DDR, in 1950. Two years later the department was transferred to the newly formed University of Transportation Friedrich List.[87] After 1992, the Faculty of Transportation Sciences was re-established at Technical University Dresden, consolidating programmes in mechanical engineering and civil engineering with the University of Transportation.

The DDR Central Transportation Research Institute began to implement and apply urban travel forecasting models, such as the trip matrix factoring method of Fratar (1954) and shortest route search routines, by the early 1960s. Travel surveys were begun in 1972 by the Technical University Dresden, recording household travel as well as freight vehicle traffic every five years. The ninth survey was conducted in 2008 in 76 cities throughout Germany. These travel surveys may well be the most extensive long-term record of urban travel in the world (Christfreund et al, 1969; Ahrens et al, 2009).[88]

During the 1970s, Dieter Lohse[89] began developing personal travel models (Lohse, 1977), including solution methods for non-linear systems of equations called 'MULTI-models'. These models were initially used to extrapolate a survey-based trip matrix to a forecast year, and to solve trip distribution and modal split models based on marginal constraints. In the 1980s, Lohse extended his approach into an integrated system of trip generation, trip distribution and modal split models, called Erzeugung–Verteilung–Aufteilung (EVA), the German terms for these models. Simultaneous distribution and modal split models were stated as a system of non-linear equations with inelastic or elastic constraints and marginal constraints including consideration of location attractiveness and constraints at destinations (e.g., parking restrictions). Trip generation, trip distribution and modal split were functionally specified and connected in EVA. In addition to public transport and cars, pedestrian and bicycle traffic were included in the model. In the 1980s, EVA and MULTI-model were utilised for transportation master planning in several cities including Berlin, Dresden, Magdeburg, Frankfurt (Oder) and Rostock.

After 1984 the model VERBER (VERkehrsplanerische BERechnungen, or transportation planning calculations) was developed at the DDR Central Transportation Research Institute in collaboration with Lohse's research group. It included demand matrix calculation (trip generation, trip distribution, modal split) and traffic assignment. A method for assigning traffic with capacity limitations, called 'the learning procedure' (Lernverfahren), was proposed and tested (Lätzsch and Lohse, 1980). Lohse's learning procedure appears to be an intuitive method for averaging a sequence of all-or-nothing assignments to shortest route trees, and is probably equivalent to the linearisation method solved with the method of successive averages. The learning procedure is implemented in two versions: (a) a shortest route search; or (b) an n-best route algorithm. The n-best-route version is also referred to as 'stochastic user equilibrium' (Lohse, 2011, 431–441).

Network and demand modelling for public and private passenger travel and freight transportation was performed with VERBER in many cities including Berlin, Cottbus, Eisenhüttenstadt, Erfurt, Frankfurt (Oder), Chemnitz and Schwerin. EVA was further improved during the 1990s, leading to the development of VISEVA for modelling urban travel and goods movements. Since 2005 parts of VISEVA have been implemented by PTV in VISUM (section 10.5.1.6). This research and model implementation was documented in a two-volume German text and reference, Lohse (1997, 2011),[90] and in Lohse et al (1997, 2005).

7.5 GENERALISATIONS OF STATIC NETWORK EQUILIBRIUM PROBLEMS

Beckmann's optimisation formulation assumed separable demand and link cost functions for a single class of vehicles (section 7.3.2). In fact, the optimisation formulation is somewhat more general than the separable case (section 7.4.1.2). Suppose the link cost functions representing flows into a four-way intersection depend on all four link flows entering the intersection. If the $n \times n$ (Jacobian) matrix of the pairwise derivatives of the n link travel cost functions with respect to the n link flows is symmetric everywhere, the optimisation formulation involving the sum of the integrals of the link cost functions is mathematically 'well defined' (Patriksson, 1994, 51–54) (section 7.2.2). Otherwise, the functions are termed 'asymmetric'. Analogous results pertain to demand or mode choice functions.

If flows of two or more classes of vehicles occur on the same link, then another type of symmetry problem arises: how do the link flows of each class of vehicles affect the link costs of the other classes? As above, if the derivatives of the link cost function with respect to each of the class flows are equal, then symmetry holds and the formulation is well defined.

The effects of the symmetry assumption were studied by Dafermos, Netter and others during the early 1970s. Two new formulations of the network equilibrium problem were proposed in 1979 that circumvented some of the limitations of Beckmann's integral-based objective function: the non-linear complementarity problem, and the variational inequality problem. These closely related formulations led to intensive research activities to understand their implications for network equilibrium models (section 7.5.1). Solution algorithms were proposed and applied to test problems (section 7.5.2). A few large-scale applications were performed (section 7.5.3).

Thomas Magnanti (1984) reviewed recent developments concerning these formulations. Patrick Harker and Jon-Shi Pang (1990) surveyed the theory, algorithms and applications of finite-dimensional variational inequality and non-linear complementarity problems. Patriksson (1994, Chapter 3) synthesised the theory related to network equilibrium, which Patrice Marcotte and Michael Patriksson (2007) extensively updated. Anna Nagurney (1993) synthesised the basic theory and described its application to several network problems, including transportation.

The introduction of the public transport mode into network equilibrium models poses additional challenges, which extend beyond the question of asymmetric link cost functions. Moreover, different behavioural assumptions may pertain to models of public transport (section 7.5.4).

7.5.1   Variational Inequality and Non-linear Complementary Problems

Dafermos (1971, 1972, 1973) and Netter (1972a, 1972b) explored the restrictions imposed by the symmetry condition on optimisation formulations (section 7.4.1). Michael Hall and Richard Asmuth addressed basic properties of network equilibrium formulations with variable demand (Hall, 1978; Asmuth et al, 1979).

Michael Florian (1977, 1978) described an integrated model of two classes of vehicles (cars and buses) interacting on links of the network. In his model of network equilibrium car flows with variable demand by car and bus, the link times were determined by the variable flow of cars and fixed flow of buses on each link of the network. A solution algorithm was described with computational results for the Hull, Canada network. His findings stimulated further research on non-linear Jacobi methods (Florian and Spiess, 1982, 1983).

Mustafa Abdulaal and Larry LeBlanc (1979) investigated problems arising from the representation of cars and buses on a road network, where the demand for each mode is given by a multinomial logit function. Their paper was closely related to the problem of Florian. They concluded that an equivalent optimisation problem for this model does not exist unless the symmetry conditions related to modal costs and modal flows are met. They described a solution algorithm for a sequence of optimisation problems in which the modal link flows are fixed in each iteration, later called the diagonalisation method. Subsequently, LeBlanc and Abdulaal (1982) extended this model to include origin–destination flows, as well as mode and link flows, for two groups of travellers. A solution algorithm was tested on the Sioux Falls network (24 centroids, 24 nodes, 76 road links, 5 bus routes).

Michael Smith (1979) investigated the properties of an equilibrium in which the costs of each link depend upon the vector of link flows in the network. He stated a set of conditions governing these equilibria in terms of inequalities defined on link costs for the equilibrium flows, the vector of equilibrium flows and any feasible flow vector satisfying the origin–destination demands. He proved the existence of the equilibrium described by his inequalities, and uniqueness under certain assumptions. Furthermore, Smith identified the properties of a network equilibrium for determining signal-setting policies, which corresponded to a variational inequalities problem (VIP).

H. Z. Aashtiani and Thomas Magnanti (1981) explored the non-linear complementarity problem (NCP), a related formulation that avoids the problematic integral of the link cost function in Beckmann's objective function. They showed that the optimality conditions of the network equilibrium problem with variable demand correspond to a system of non-linear equations and inequalities defined on the link cost functions, demand equations and non-negative link flows. Under certain conditions on the cost functions, the solution to this problem exists and is unique. The authors proposed a linearisation algorithm for solving the equation system. Braess and Kohl (1979) proposed a related proof of the existence of equilibria in asymmetrical multi-class-user transportation networks.

Stella Dafermos (1980) forged the connection between her own earlier research, Beckmann et al (1956) and Smith (1979) by exploring the relation between Smith's formulation and the variational inequality problem for the general traffic assignment problem with fixed demand. She established the existence and uniqueness of the solution under the assumption of strong monotonicity, proposed a solution algorithm and studied its convergence properties.[91] Subsequently, Dafermos (1982a) extended her model to include variable multi-modal demand. In this model, link costs depend upon the vector of link flows in the entire network, and origin–destination flows depend on the equilibrium costs for all O-D flows and modes. A solution algorithm was described. In Dafermos (1982b), she described relaxation algorithms for a single mode network equilibrium problem with variable demands, and the general problem with multiple modes. Linear convergence of the relaxation algorithms was established under the assumption that the link cost functions were not 'too asymmetric', or that the cost interaction of the modes was relatively weak.

Caroline Fisk and Sang Nguyen (1981) expressed the conditions in the model of Florian (1977) as a system of non-linear equations. Drawing on empirical conditions from an application of the model (Florian et al, 1979), they concluded that the network equilibrium symmetry conditions were not satisfied by the equations, and explored the conditions required for a unique solution of the equations. They also noted that the conditions described by Aashtiani's NCP and Dafermos's VIP were not satisfied by these equations. Fisk and Nguyen (1982) investigated the solution characteristics of several algorithms proposed to solve the general traffic assignment problem with fixed demand. Following a synthesis of the theoretical results, they tested five algorithms, including two proposed by Dafermos and the diagonalisation method (section 7.2.2). The cost functions of the test networks were highly asymmetric. All five algorithms achieved effectively the same results, but with rather different computational times. The diagonalisation method had the lowest computational requirements.

Michael Florian and Heinz Spiess (1982) studied further the convergence properties of the diagonalisation method, showing that local convergence is assured if a certain condition is satisfied. Dmitri Bertsekas and Eli Gafni (1982) proposed another solution algorithm for the VIP with fixed demand based on a projection method. Pang and Chan (1982, 284) studied 'both the local and global convergence of various iterative methods for solving the variational inequality and non-linear complementarity problems with applications to traffic equilibria'. Friesz (1981) identified an equivalent optimisation problem for combined multi-class distribution, assignment and modal split that circumvents symmetry restrictions.

Three subsequent papers synthesised and extended the basic models proposed by Aashtiani, Smith and Dafermos. Florian and Spiess (1983) described a variational inequality reformulation of a two-mode and link flow equilibrium, and studied the convergence of the diagonalisation method to solve the proposed model. Then, Fisk and Boyce (1983) synthesised, generalised and extended several earlier results of Dafermos, of Florian and Spiess and of Smith. Fisk placed these results in a non-linear equation framework to address questions of asymmetry from the viewpoint of fixed point theory, concluding that the non-linear equation framework:

> is an attractive alternative to other frameworks proposed so far. Additional computational experience is necessary before definitive statements as to the effectiveness of each approach can be made. One factor impeding such a study
> . is that link-cost functions which realistically represent interactions between conflicting flows have yet to be developed' (Fisk, 1984, 77) (section 7.5.3).

7.5.2 Extensions and Solution Algorithms

Sang Nguyen and Clermont Dupuis (1984) proposed a small test network for the asymmetric network equilibrium problem, which was widely used subsequently. Using this network (4 zones, 13 nodes, 19 links), they compared the performance of their new algorithm with the diagonalisation method. They applied the same algorithm to the Hull, Canada network (23 zones, 501 nodes, 798 links) and the Winnipeg, Canada network (147 zones, 1052 nodes, 2836 links), reporting solutions within 0.4 per cent of the lower bound on the objective function.

Siriphong Lawphongpanich and Donald Hearn (1984) proposed a simplicial decomposition algorithm for solving the asymmetric problem, reporting computational results in the form of the Relative Gap, perhaps for the first time. Hearn et al (1984) synthesised the VIP formulations of Smith and Dafermos, identified cases in which equivalent convex optimisation formulations exist and examined the implications for solution algorithms (Hearn, 1982). Patrice Marcotte proposed a new algorithm and reported results for the network of Nguyen and Dupuis and for Hull, Canada (Marcotte, 1985; Marcotte and Guélat, 1988). Marcotte and Wynter (2004) examined the multi-class network equilibrium problem with asymmetric costs, identified a natural decomposition approach, and proposed a convergent solution algorithm.

Stella Dafermos (1982a, 1982b, 1983a, 1983b, 1988), Dafermos and Nagurney (1984a, 1984b) and Nagurney (1986) continued to explore the mathematical properties of the variational inequality formulation. Dafermos was particularly interested in the cost-flow symmetry conditions that characterise formulations of her 'extended model'. The extent of the asymmetry determines whether the solution exists and is unique. Like Smith (1984), she investigated the theoretical convergence of solution algorithms to these problems, and made contributions to the general theory of variational inequalities, well beyond traffic equilibria.

Anna Nagurney was the first Ph.D. student of Stella Dafermos, and her frequent co-author from 1984 until the untimely death of Dafermos in 1990 at age 49 (Nagurney, 1991). Nagurney (1993) published *Network Economics*, a synthesis of the theory, solution algorithms and applications of the variational inequalities problem to several equilibrium problems defined on networks, and arising in perfect and imperfect competition and general equilibrium. Nagurney and Zhang (1996) extended the analysis of the transportation network equilibrium problem from the point of view of projected dynamical systems, thereby providing insights into the dynamic behaviour of travellers in making their decisions concerning travel demand and route choices.

Torbjörn Larsson and Michael Patriksson (1994, 1995, 1999) explored a different approach to representing the traffic equilibria more realistically, 'traffic equilibria with side constraints'. One of their objectives was to impose capacity constraints on these models.

7.5.3 Prototype Solutions of Asymmetric Assignment Problems

Unlike the separable link cost functions used in travel forecasting practice, in reality link costs are basically asymmetric. Travel times experienced by vehicles approaching a signal-controlled intersection are determined not only by the link's own flow, but also by opposing and conflicting flows. The effects of these flows on link travel times are generally asymmetric. The same situation occurs in two-way stop sign-controlled intersections, in which one street has higher flows, and higher priority, than the other. Anna Nagurney (1986) tested the relative efficiencies of two computational techniques that solved for traffic equilibria in multi-modal networks, the relaxation and projection methods.

Claudio Meneguzzer (1995, 1997) explored the application of realistic link cost functions in an asymmetric traffic assignment problem. His cost functions were drawn from the *Highway Capacity Manual* (Transportation

Research Board, 1985), which was based in part on the seminal research of Rahim Akçelik (1981, 1988). Meneguzzer devised link cost functions, analysed their properties with respect to asymmetry assumptions of the traffic assignment problem, and conducted experiments on a realistic street network (72 zone centroids, 413 nodes, 934 links). He concluded that 'the algorithm converged in all test cases, even though the sufficient conditions for convergence were not satisfied' (Meneguzzer, 1995).

Building on this experience, Stan Berka implemented a much larger network model based on the 1985 *Highway Capacity Manual* for a 300 square mile subregion of the Chicago region (447 zones, 2552 nodes, 7850 links). Signalised intersections were assumed to be timed optimally and independently. During the most congested periods of the weekday, the algorithm converged satisfactorily in about 20 diagonalisation iterations (Berka and Boyce, 1996). The Frank–Wolfe method was applied to solve the diagonalised subproblems.

Alan Horowitz (1989, 1997) tested the performance of various traffic assignment techniques, including with cost functions based on the 1994 update of the *Highway Capacity Manual*. S.C. Wong, Chao Yang and Hong Lo (2001) implemented a similar approach based on the traffic engineering software system TRANSYT. Properties of the Jacobian matrix were studied for the travel cost function for a small network (4 zones, 9 nodes, 62 links). Three solution methods were tested and thoroughly compared.

7.5.4 Public Transport Assignment on Congested Road Networks

Early methods for assigning passengers to public transport networks relied on simplified network representations, with assignment of public transport trip matrices to minimum cost routes defined by scheduled travel times and fares. Although the development of travel forecasting software for public transport began in the US in the mid-1960s (section 2.6), little progress was made in extending these early methods to more realistic models, in terms of incorporating timetables directly into assignment procedures and in modelling user behaviour in complex public transport networks with multiple route choices. Guy Desaulniers and Mark Hickman (2007) comprehensively reviewed public transport models.

During the 1980s, the Montreal group again led the way in formulating and solving more complex models, incorporating generalised optimisation methods. Heinz Spiess and Michael Florian (1989) proposed a public transport assignment model for both uncongested and congested public transport networks based on the concept of 'strategies', travel on the shortest hyperpaths connecting an origin to a destination. A hyperpath is

a combination of public transport routes connecting an origin and destination; a shortest hyperpath takes into account the frequency of service on
those routes. Their formulation of the congested public transport assignment problem was a non-linear mixed integer programming problem,
which was transformed into 'a compact linear program. The proposed
assignment procedure has the flavor of a shortest route algorithm.' Sang
Nguyen and Stefano Pallottino (1988, 177) extended this formulation into
a variational inequality defined on a graph-theoretic framework for public
transport equilibrium assignment, and proposed several formulations of
the model and algorithms for computing equilibrium flows.

A series of papers by Joaquín de Cea and Enrique Fernández, and
Michael Florian, Jia Hao Wu, Shuguang He and Patrice Marcotte, collaboratively or separately, thoroughly explored formulations and solution algorithms to the public transport assignment problem defined on
congested roads and separate rail lines, sometimes integrated with mode
choice and trip distribution models (de Cea and Fernández, 1993; Wu
and Florian, 1993; Fernández et al, 1994; Wu et al, 1994). These efforts
led to the development of a new software system, ESTRAUS (de Cea et
al, 2001, 2005) (section 10.5.2.5), and STGO, an application in EMME/2
(Florian et al, 2002) (section 10.5.1.7). Both software systems were
employed in a major public transport planning study in Santiago, Chile
(12 modes or network types, 11 modal combinations, 264 zones, 13 classes
of travellers – combinations of household incomes and car ownership,
1091 nodes, 5606 links, 1273 public transport lines, 45 753 line segments,
3 trip purposes; Florian et al, 2002). By far the largest implementation
of a combined model of congested road and public transport systems to
date, the model was used to plan a major reform of the Santiago public
transport system.[92]

Cominetti and Correa (2001) extended the models of Wu et al (1994) to
incorporate an 'effective frequency' model of transit assignment that considered possible congestion on the boarding links. Transportation modellers in the public transport-rich environment of Hong Kong extended
some of the above model formulations to the stochastic network equilibrium case, as well as providing additional details concerning transfers,
non-linear fare structures and other attributes found in reality (Lam et al,
1999, 2002; Lo et al, 2003, 2004). A further extension of Cominetti and
Correa was undertaken by Cepeda et al. (2006); computational results for
networks from practice demonstrated the applicability of the method.

Nielsen (2000) implemented a stochastic user-equilibrium model with
a probit model based on congested waiting times and in-vehicle discomfort, and solved a stochastic user-equilibrium assignment model on the
Copenhagen regional public transport network (297 zones, 2200 nodes,

3497 links, 435 lines, 4190 route segments, 1301 terminals). Nielsen (2004) gave further developments based on a nested logit model.

7.6 CONTRIBUTIONS OF INTERNATIONAL SYMPOSIA AND JOURNALS

At the time of the publication of Beckmann et al (1956), no international conferences, symposia or speciality journals served academic transportation research in the US or UK. Although the nascent fields of operations research and regional science provided forums for papers on urban transportation from the mid-1950s, no speciality conferences served this new field. Robert Herman [1914–1997] organised the first international symposium on the theory of traffic flow in 1959, which included a few papers on network equilibrium models (Herman, 1961) (see also section 12.2.2).[93] Subsequent symposia were held in 1963 (London), 1965 (New York), 1968 (Karlsruhe), 1971 (Berkeley), 1974 (Sydney), 1977 (Kyoto), 1981 (Toronto) and every three years to 2004, when a biennial format was adopted. Although highly specialised, these symposia played an important role in the development of this interdisciplinary field.

In 1967, Robert Herman founded *Transportation Science* under the aegis of the Transportation Science Section of the Operations Research Society of America, now the Institute for Operations Research and the Management Sciences (INFORMS), serving as editor from 1967 to 1973. In the same year, Frank Haight [1919–2006] founded *Transportation Research*. Haight served as editor-in-chief of Parts A and B of the expanded journal from 1967 to 2003.[94] Two journals were founded more recently: *Networks and Spatial Economics* by Terry Friesz in 2001, and *Transportmetrica* by William Lam and his colleagues in 2005.

Michael Florian organised international symposia at the University of Montreal in 1974, 1977 and 1981 on traffic network equilibrium methods and related topics (Florian, 1976; Florian and Gaudry, 1980). Florian also organised a short course on transportation networks at Amalfi, Italy in 1982 (Florian, 1984a). Since 1991, faculty at the University of Montreal and others have organised the Triennial Symposium on Transportation Analysis (TRISTAN). Related conferences organised by the Working Group on Transportation of the Association of European Operational Research Societies (EURO) (Bell, 1998; Patriksson and Labbé, 2002) also contributed to ongoing research on transportation network equilibrium.

7.7 CONCLUSION

When viewed with hindsight, academic research sometimes seems to proceed along a twisted path, but then reaches rather unexpected results. If one wanted to explore this conjecture empirically, transportation network equilibrium could provide a highly suitable case study. The seminal formulation of the network equilibrium model with variable demand by Beckmann occurred during a research project with general and relatively vague objectives. Although the authors found their formulation interesting, they had little idea about its significance for urban travel forecasting. In fact, their model had a profound influence on the future development of this subject.

Dafermos took up the problem in the mid-1960s as a doctoral student, and made fundamental contributions to the theory of network equilibrium. Several other graduate students in the UK, the US and Canada during the early 1970s, motivated by practical problems of travel forecasting, devised and tested efficient solution algorithms. These findings gradually began to impact travel forecasting practice. Progress was slow, however; opportunities to stress the convergent properties of the new algorithms and to assess the precision of solutions were sometimes overlooked.

In the following decade academic researchers generalised and deepened their understanding of these formulations, and began to experiment with their implementations on large-scale networks. By and large, these developments were ignored by transportation planning practitioners, who retained their non-analytic, heuristic approaches. This situation began to change when start-up software developers began to offer travel forecasting systems for mini- and microcomputers, gradually replacing the mainframe programs of US DoT. Chapter 10 offers further details about these software developments.

For these reasons, we characterise the original formulation of the network equilibrium problem as 'a missed opportunity'. While one could speculate about how the history of this field might well have evolved very differently, the fact is that it did not. The lessons of this experience are two-fold: (a) be vigilant with regard to the potential application of new research findings, whatever their origin or motivation; and (b) do not expect that research specifically targeted to solve a problem arising in practice will necessarily be successful in producing the most useful innovations.

NOTES

1. An earlier version of parts of sections 7.3 and 7.4 was published in Boyce (2007b).
2. The US Department of the Air Force established the RAND Corporation in 1948 as 'an independent nonprofit organization' in Santa Monica, California, to continue research on mathematical programming, game theory and related topics (www.rand.org/about/history.html, accessed 21 January 2014). During the 1950s many significant contributors to mathematical programming and mathematical economics worked at RAND or were supported by its contracts.
3. en.wikipedia.org/wiki/Johann_Georg_Kohl (accessed 2 August 2013).
4. Walter Buhr found and translated this statement in Kohl (1841) in response to a request from David Boyce.
5. In his treatise on welfare economics, Pigou introduced the concept of an externality and the idea that externality problems could be corrected by the imposition of what later became known as a Pigovian tax (en.wikipedia.org/wiki/Arthur_Cecil_Pigou, accessed 12 February 2014).
6. en.wikipedia.org/wiki/Frank_Knight (accessed 3 August 2013).
7. en.wikipedia.org/wiki/John_Glen_Wardrop (accessed 2 August 2013).
8. Nominal capacity may mean the volume at level-of-service C or D, as assumed by the modeller.
9. Merchant and Nemhauser (1978) were the first to propose such a model.
10. en.wikipedia.org/wiki/Joseph_Louis_Lagrange (accessed 13 March 2013).
11. en.wikipedia.org/wiki/George_Dantzig (accessed 3 August 2013).
12. Saul Gass (2002) described the working environment and the role of computers in the project.
13. en.wikipedia.org/wiki/Tjalling_Koopmans (accessed 3 August 2013).
14. en.wikipedia.org/wiki/Leonid_Kantorovich (accessed 3 August 2013). Kantorovich and Koopmans shared the Sveriges Riksbank Prize in Economic Sciences in Memory of Alfred Nobel (Nobel Prize in Economic Sciences) in 1975 for 'their contributions to the theory of optimum allocation of resources' (nobelprize.org/nobel_prizes/economics/laureates/1975/, accessed 21 March 2013).
15. en.wikipedia.org/wiki/Albert_W._Tucker; en.wikipedia.org/wiki/Harold_W._Kuhn; en.wikipedia.org/wiki/David_Gale (all accessed 3 August 2013).
16. en.wikipedia.org/wiki/William_Karush (accessed 3 August 2013).
17. en.wikipedia.org/wiki/Karush-Kuhn-Tucker_conditions (accessed 13 March 2013). The history of these developments was described by Kjeldsen (2000). Prekopa (1980) provided a fascinating review of the history of non-linear programming.
18. Henry Thompson (1996) compiled a memoir on the life and accomplishments of Akira Takayama.
19. Robert Dorfman [1916–2002] was evidently the first economist to apply the Kuhn–Tucker theorem. In a short monograph consisting of his doctoral dissertation on an application of linear programming to the theory of the firm, plus the addition of a new section on quadratic programming to Chapter 3 on production scheduling for monopolized products, Dorfman (1951) showed that the well-known profit maximising properties of a linear model of production and a linear demand function, which correspond to a quadratic profit function, could be derived by applying the Kuhn–Tucker theorem. In a review article for economists on the new field of mathematical programming, Dorfman was the first to cite Kuhn and Tucker (1951) in an economics journal. In discussing models in which prices are variable, Dorfman (1953, 823) stated: 'The general mathematical theory of dealing with variable prices has been investigated and practical methods of solution have been developed for problems where the demand and supply curves are linear.'
20. en.wikipedia.org/wiki/Nonlinear_complementarity_problem; en.wikipedia.org/wiki/Complementarity_theory (both accessed 15 March 2013).
21. en.wikipedia.org/wiki/Variational_inequality (accessed 15 March 2013).

22. Part II of *Studies* concerned rail transportation, which is not considered here.
23. cowles.econ.yale.edu/ (accessed 19 February 2013).
24. Boyce and Nagurney (2006) provided further details on the careers of McGuire and Winsten.
25. en.wikipedia.org/wiki/Oskar_Morgenstern (accessed 3 August 2013).
26. This account is based upon the original project files of Bartlett McGuire, which he gave to David Boyce in 1999, and an interview of McGuire by David Boyce.
27. Letter from Martin Beckmann to David Boyce, 2004.
28. No correspondence about the rejected paper survived, except a memo by Koopmans puzzling over the result.
29. en.wikipedia.org/wiki/William_Vickrey. William Vickrey shared the Nobel Prize in Economic Sciences in 1996 (www.nobelprize.org/nobel_prizes/economic-sciences/laureates/1996/, accessed 1 February 2014).
30. A detailed mathematical analysis of Beckmann's equilibrium model was offered in Boyce (2013). To facilitate comparisons with the book, the models are presented using the authors' original notation, including their link-node representation, rather than the link-route representation more commonly used now.
31. Michael Patriksson (1994, 36–39) further explained these representations.
32. In mathematical terms, consider a road network consisting of nodes i and links ij. Flow from origin node i to termination node k is represented by $x_{i,k}$. A link flow from node i to node j is designated x_{ij}, and a link flow terminating at node k is designated $x_{ij,k}$. Accordingly, $x_{ij} = x_{ji} = \sum (x_{ij,k} + x_{ji,k})$. Hence, the total flow on a link is non-directional. Link flows must be non-negative: $x_{ij} \geq 0$. Conservation of flows of vehicles through nodes of the network is specified by the equations $\sum_j x_{ij,k} = \sum_j x_{ji,k} + x_{i,k}$, for all pairs of originating nodes i and terminating nodes k. The relationship between link flows and link costs is given by the 'capacity function', $y_{ij} = h_{ij}(x_{ij})$. The demand function is defined as $x_{i,k} = f_{i,k}(y_{i,k})$. The inverse of the demand function is $y_{i,k} = g_{i,k}(x_{i,k})$, which exists because the function is assumed to be strictly decreasing (monotonic). The authors pointed out that demand may be perfectly elastic ('a small rise in the prevailing transportation costs would induce a substantial decrease in demand') or fixed ('perfect inelasticity') (Beckmann et al, 1956, 57–58).
33. Given the above description, maximise the following objective function for the equilibrium model:

$$\max_{(x)} \left[\sum_{i,k} \int_0^{x_{i,k}} g_{i,k}(s)\,ds - \frac{1}{2}\sum_{ij} \int_0^{x_{ij}} h_{ij}(s)\,ds \right]$$

The insertion of (1/2) before the second term reconciles the double-counting of the links.
34. Boyce (2013, 50) offered an interpretation of how Beckmann may have arrived at his formulation.
35. The objective function for the efficiency model is:

$$\max_{(x)} \left[\sum_{i,k} \int_0^{x_{i,k}} g_{i,k}(s)\,ds - \frac{1}{2}\sum_{ij} h_{ij}(x_{ij})x_{ij} \right]$$

36. Robin Lindsey (2006) reviewed all known literature on efficiency and road pricing.
37. Interview of Martin Beckmann by David Boyce, August 1998.
38. The Chicago Area Transportation Study was begun in 1955, a year after Beckmann and McGuire left the city.
39. The prices were $4 (US) and 32 shillings (UK) respectively.
40. The RAND monograph was recognised as a RAND Classic in 2003; to download the 359-page file without charge, go to www.rand.org/pubs/research_memoranda/RM1488/ (accessed 19 February 2013). The Yale University Press version of the monograph is available online through the courtesy of the Cowles Foundation at cowles.econ.yale.edu/archive/reprints/specpub-BMW.pdf (accessed 19 February 2013).

41. en.wikipedia.org/wiki/William_Prager (accessed 2 August 2013).
42. en.wikipedia.org/wiki/Reuben_Smeed (accessed 2 August 2013).
43. en.wikipedia.org/wiki/Edwin_Mansfield (accessed 2 August 2013).
44. en.wikipedia.org/wiki/Richard_Duffin (accessed 2 August 2013).
45. en.wikipedia.org/wiki/John_Forbes_Nash,_Jr. John Nash shared the Nobel Prize in Economic Sciences in 1994 (www.nobelprize.org/nobel_prizes/economic-sciences/lau reates/1994/, accessed 1 February 2014).
46. Oliver co-authored an early text on urban transportation models with Renfrey Potts (Potts and Oliver, 1972).
47. Jorgensen shifted his interests to traffic safety research, completed a Ph.D. and served on the faculty of the Technical University of Denmark.
48. Readers of *Transportation Research* were informed of Braess's paradox by John Murchland (1970b).
49. en.wikipedia.org/wiki/Alan_Walters (accessed 25 January 2014).
50. en.wikipedia.org/wiki/William_Garrison_(geographer) (accessed 29 January 2014).
51. Interview of William Garrison by David Boyce in 1999.
52. en.wikipedia.org/wiki/Richard_E._Quandt (accessed 29 January 2014).
53. William Jewell [1932–2003] completed his D.Sc. thesis on optimal flows through networks at MIT, and joined the operations research faculty of the University of California Berkeley in 1960. During 1965–66, Jewell was a Fulbright Scholar at the Société d'Économie et de Mathématiques Appliquées in Paris. Reporting on discussions in France about traffic assignment, Jewell (1967) described the traffic assignment problem with fixed demand from the viewpoint of electrical circuits, the multi-commodity network flow literature and the Kuhn–Tucker theorem. His paper is useful in understanding the status of traffic assignment in France at the time.
54. Michel Sakarovitch studied civil engineering in Paris, and wrote his Ph.D. thesis on the multi-commodity maximum flow problem at the University of California, Berkeley. In his thesis Sakarovitch cited Tomlin (1966) concerning multi-commodity network flow, Charnes and Cooper (1961) and Jorgensen (1963), as examples of the application of multi-commodity network flow models to traffic problems, but not Beckmann et al (1956).
55. After 1972, the research record of the French group ends. Fabien Leurent, a senior French researcher, speculated to David Boyce in 2013 that changes in research priorities may have been the reason.
56. Leventhal et al (1973) subsequently showed how shortest routes can be generated as needed, which they called 'column generation'. Column generation can be used in conjunction with the route-based algorithms of Dafermos to greatly reduce computer memory requirements.
57. According to her curriculum vitae dated December 1989, Stella Dafermos was an instructor and assistant professor at Cornell University during 1968–71; after moving to Brown University, she was: assistant professor (research), 1972–78; associate professor (research), 1978–82; and professor, 1982–90.
58. fr.wikipedia.org/wiki/Michael_Florian (accessed 2 December 2013).
59. Interview of Larry LeBlanc by David Boyce in 2003.
60. The incremental assignment algorithm contained in CDC's TRANPLAN may be an exception to this statement, but its convergence properties were not recognised at that time (section 2.5.6).
61. Larry LeBlanc included the data for his 24-node, 76-link test network in his 1975 paper; it has since been used as a test network for many papers related to road traffic networks. The network data and solutions may be found at www.bgu.ac.il/~bargera/tntp/. The network is atypical of networks used in practice in that each node also represents an origin and destination.
62. Personal communication with Robert Dial by David Boyce in 2008.
63. This property was described by Donald Hearn (1982, 71).

64. Dirck Van Vliet (1976, 139) proposed a slightly different definition, the ratio of the Gap to the total cost of the minimum cost assignment given the current link flows.

65. The definitions of the two versions of the Relative Gap are:

$Gap^k = \sum_{(ij) \in A} f_{ij}^k \cdot t_{ij}(f_{ij}^k) - \sum_{(ij) \in A} y_{ij}^k \cdot t_{ij}(f_{ij}^k)$, where y_{ij}^k is the link flow given by an all-or-nothing assignment to $(t_{ij}(f_{ij}^k))$.

$RG^k(TC) = \dfrac{Gap^k}{TC^k}$, where $TC^k = \sum_{(ij) \in A} f_{ij}^k \cdot t_{ij}(f_{ij}^k)$

66. The definition of the lower bound (LB) at iteration k is:

$$LB^k = \sum_{(ij) \in A} \int_0^{f_{ij}^k} t_{ij}(s)\,ds - \sum_{(ij) \in A} t_{ij}(f_{ij}^k) \cdot (f_{ij}^k - y_{ij}^k)$$

If the best lower bound (BLB) is set initially to $-\infty$, then the BLB at iteration k is:
$BLB^k = \max(BLB^{k-1}, LB^k)$

$$RG^k(OF) = \dfrac{(OF^k - BLB^k)}{BLB^k}$$

67. One of several versions of the Winnipeg network may be found at www.bgu. ac.il/~bargera/tntp/.

68. Dirck Van Vliet (1976, 154) evaluated alternative stochastic assignment methods for a large-scale network.

69. Subsequently, other authors substituted 'perceives' for 'believes'.

70. They noted that 'the idea of hypernetworks has been latent in the literature for some time', citing A.G. Wilson's reference to the concept as early as 1972 (Sheffi and Daganzo, 1978, 115). See also Dafermos (1972).

71. Caroline Fisk extended Beckmann's formulation for the case of fixed origin–destination flows as follows:

$$\min_{(\mathbf{h},\mathbf{v})} Z(\mathbf{h},\mathbf{v}) = \frac{1}{\theta} \sum_{pq} \sum_r h_{pqr} \ln h_{pqr} + \sum_a \int_0^{v_a} t_a(v)\,dv$$

subject to : $\sum_r h_{pqr} = d_{pq}$, all pq

where $v_a = \sum_{pq} \sum_r h_{pqr} \delta_{pqr}^a$, all a

where h_{pqr} is the flow from origin p to destination q by route r;
d_{pq} is the fixed flow from origin p to destination q;
v_a is the flow on link a;
δ_{pqr}^a is a (0,1) indicator whose value is 1 if link a belongs to route r from origin p to destination q, and 0 otherwise;
$t_a(v_a)$ is a travel time function for link a defined on its own flow, v_a.
Solution of this constrained minimisation problem yields the condition that:

$h_{pqr} = d_{pq} \cdot \dfrac{\exp(-\theta c_{pqr})}{\sum_s \exp(-\theta c_{pqs})}$, all routes r connecting origin p to destination q.

where $c_{pqr} = \sum_a \delta_{pqr}^a \cdot t_a(v_a)$.

72. Using the above definitions, Sheffi and Powell's formulation may be stated as follows:

$$\min_{(\mathbf{v})} Z(\mathbf{v}) = \frac{1}{\theta} \sum_{pq} d_{pq} \ln\left(\sum_r \exp(-\theta c_{pqr}) \right) + \sum_a v_a \cdot t_a(v_a) - \sum_a \int_0^{v_a} t_a(v)\,dv$$

Solution of this problem in terms of link flows yields link costs, which can be used to determine the route flows using the logit function.

73. John Murchland (1970c) completed the requirements for the Doctor of Economic Science at Universität Fridericiana at Karlsruhe, Germany on 31 July 1970.

74. His paper was subsequently published in German (Murchland, 1970a).

75. John Murchland offered David Boyce a printout of a computer program for solving his model, as well as a copy of his 1969 paper, when they first met in August 1970 in Karlsruhe, Germany.

76. Remarks of Richard Allsop to David Boyce, July 2004.

77. Questions of Stephen Putman, his colleague at the University of Pennsylvania, stimulated Boyce's interest in the problem.

78. The Relative Gap for the combined distribution and assignment problem is similar to that of the fixed demand problem plus a term related to the logarithm of the zone-to-zone vehicle flows.

79. Michael Florian (1984b, 145) agreed that computational results of Frank (1978) and LeBlanc and Farhangian (1981) supported the intuitively better search direction of the partial linearisation algorithm.

80. A chance visit by David Boyce to the University of Leeds in November 1980 enabled Huw Williams to suggest a clarification of Boyce's recently formulated network equilibrium model of origin–destination and mode choice.

81. en.wikipedia.org/wiki/George_Kingsley_Zipf; en.wikipedia.org/wiki/Zipf's_law (both accessed 17 October 2013).

82. Smith wrote: 'until all flows are equated on the routes used'; clearly, he intended to write 'costs', not 'flows'.

83. EMME was an acronym for 'équilibre multimodal–multimodal equilibrium'.

84. For the assignment problem with variable mode choice, the Gap was defined as follows:

$$\sum_a c_a^h(f_a^h) \cdot (g_a^h - f_a^h) + \sum_{ij} c_{ij}^t(q_{ij}^t - p_{ij}^t) \cdot T + \frac{T}{\mu}\sum_{ijm} \ln q_{ij}^m(q_{ij}^m - p_{ij}^m)$$

where $c_a^h(f_a^h)$ is the generalised travel cost of a vehicle on the road network with flow f_a^h per hour; g_a^h is the corresponding flow in the subproblem solution; c_{ij}^t is the fixed generalised travel cost per person by public transport from zone i to zone j; p_{ij}^t is the proportion of the total origin–destination flow T among all zone pairs from zone i to zone j on the public transport network; q_{ij}^t is the corresponding subproblem flow; m is the cost sensitivity parameter value for mode choice. The partially linearised lower bound on the objective function is:

$$LB^k = \sum_a c_a^h(f_a^{kh}) + \sum_a c_a^h(f_a^{kh}) \cdot (g_a^{kh} - f_a^{kh}) + \sum_{ij} c_{ij}^t(q_{ij}^{kt}) \cdot T + \frac{T}{\mu}\sum_{ijm} \ln q_{ij}^{km}(q_{ij}^{km})$$

where the superscript k on link flows and origin–destination–mode flows denotes the kth iteration.

85. Yong Jae Lee calibrated these models based on values of the entropy constraints. Chi-Kang Lee estimated the cost function parameters with the maximum likelihood method for the 1980 census journey-to-work data. His research was the first to use the Cray X-MP, and was performed with his own codes, in contrast to the earlier studies using UTPS. The expanded memory of the Cray X-MP substantially simplified the solution process with real-valued representation of flows. References to their theses are found in Boyce (1990).

86. Solution and estimation of the Stockholm model were performed by Chi-Kang Lee on the Cray X-MP.

87. Friedrich List, a German economist, promoted railway development in Germany in the nineteenth century (en.wikipedia.org/wiki/Friedrich_List, accessed 6 August 2013).

88. tu-dresden.de/die_tu_dresden/fakultaeten/vkw/ivs/srv/dateien/staedtepegel_srv2008. pdf (accessed 8 August 2013).

89. Dieter Lohse was professor of theory of transport planning, Technical University Dresden, from 1970 to 2010.

90. www.beuth.de/de/artikel/strassenverkehrstechnik (accessed 28 October 2013).

91. Under rather general conditions suited to traffic equilibria, the NCP can also be stated as a VIP, and more generally as a fixed point problem, as noted by Magnanti (1984).

92. The reform, Transantiago, is described at en.wikipedia.org/wiki/Transantiago (accessed 15 August 2013).

93. Robert Herman, an academic physicist with broad interests and major accomplishments, became interested in 'traffic science' and joined General Motors Research Laboratories at age 42 in 1956; later he retired from General Motors, and joined the faculty of the University of Texas at Austin in 1979. His biography may be found at www.ph.utexas. edu/utphysicshistory/UTexas_Physics_History/Robert_Herman.html (accessed 23 October 2013); his complete publication list is at scholar.google.com/citations?user=7 Yiedy4AAAAJ&hl=en.

94. The *Journal of Transport Economics and Policy* also began publication in 1967, edited by Denys Munby and Michael Thomson, and published by the London School of Economics and Political Science.

8.   Tradition and innovation in US practice

8.1   INTRODUCTION

Following initiation of 'urban transportation studies' in the US in the 1950s, the 1962 Federal-Aid Highway Act mandated the preparation of urban transportation plans as a condition for urbanized areas to receive construction funds (Weiner, 1997, 23). The focus of this requirement was the preparation of long-range plans for roads and public transport. Shortly afterwards, the Bureau of Public Roads issued memoranda requiring metropolitan areas to undertake 'a continuing, comprehensive, and cooperative (3C) planning process' consisting of:

> establishing an organization to carry out the planning process; development of local goals and objectives; surveys and inventories of existing conditions and facilities; analyses of current conditions and calibration of forecasting techniques; forecasting of future activity and travel; evaluation of alternative transportation networks resulting in a recommended transportation plan; staging of the transportation plan; and identification of resources to implement it (Weiner, 1997, 25).

These transportation plans pertained to a 'target year' some 20 to 25 years in the future, updated at least every ten years.[1]

By 1970 comprehensive transportation plans for major roads and rail public transport were in place in most large metropolitan areas for target years between 1980 and 2000 (Boyce et al, 1970, 24). In agreement with the 3C requirement, these plans were regularly updated by the designated metropolitan planning organisations (MPOs) in response to regional population and employment trends. As the MPOs became more adept at their tasks, the plans were also prepared in more detail. For example, plans for freeway systems were extended to include major arterial roads, a plan element little emphasised in the earlier efforts.

During 1970–90, state and local road and public transport agencies also initiated planning and engineering studies related to short-term travel demand management (TDM). In some cases these activities were undertaken by MPOs; in others, they were performed by planning and engineering agencies at the state or local level. Generally, these TDM studies did not directly utilise the sequential travel forecasting procedure maintained by MPOs or their consultants. In some cases individual models, especially mode choice, were applied, but the use of the full sequential or four-step procedure was quite limited.

For example, Thomas Lisco (1975) performed evaluations of demand for proposed public transport projects using mode choice models based on market surveys, household surveys, census data and transit operations data;[2] Thomas Higgins (1990) described empirical TDM case studies of employer-based demand management strategies; and Erik Ferguson (1990) reviewed experimental studies undertaken by various governmental agencies to determine the effectiveness of TDM strategies. In these studies and in TDM case studies reviewed by Comsis Corporation (1990), no reference was made to the sequential procedure.

Even in the late 1980s, travel forecasting was largely based on the sequential procedure solved on mainframe computers with UTPS or PLANPAC. Agencies with the expertise to apply these mainframe programs were the travel forecasting units of MPOs, sometimes housed within state DOTs. Traffic engineering departments at the state and local level were separate agencies, working with their own methods. Few public transport agencies had access to mainframe computers for applying UTPS. MPO staffs were heavily loaded with responsibilities for regional and subregional travel forecasts in the preparation of long-range transportation plans. These practices began to change in the late 1980s, however, with the introduction of personal computers.

Given this background, this chapter examines the abrupt changes in travel forecasting for urban transportation planning that began in 1990. New legislation at the federal level mandated changes in the travel forecasting practices of the MPOs, aptly described as a 'wake-up call' for a new era (section 8.2). In response, the Federal Highway Administration (FWHA) initiated its Travel Model Improvement Program (TMIP), which sought to move the field forward. The Federal Transit Administration (FTA), formerly the Urban Mass Transportation Administration, implemented its New Starts Program (section 8.3.1).

Events conspired, however, to divert the modest funding for TMIP to a novel systems approach, dubbed TRANSIMS, intended to displace the venerable sequential procedure. In the end, however, this revolution did not occur (section 8.4.1). Instead, a few MPOs and their consultants forged cautiously ahead with their activity-based models (Chapter 6; section 8.4.2). Completing the chapter are reviews of land use models (section 8.5) and urban goods movement models (section 8.6).

8.2   EVOLVING REQUIREMENTS FOR URBAN TRAVEL FORECASTING

8.2.1   Origins of the Wake-Up Call

A major call to improve urban travel forecasting practice came from a somewhat unexpected source, federal legislation to improve air quality.[3] Problems with air quality stemming from emissions from stationary and mobile sources led to the enactment of the Clean Air Act of 1955, amendments in 1959, 1963 and 1965, the Air Quality Act of 1967 and the Clean Air Act of 1970. Among these problems were the severe smog conditions experienced in southern California from atmospheric chemical reactions of oxides of nitrogen, carbon monoxide and hydrocarbons emitted by cars and trucks. Major reductions in emissions from cars were achieved through the introduction of catalytic converters, which required eliminating tetraethyl lead as a petrol additive in 1975.[4]

The Clean Air Act Amendments of 1977 required transportation planners to incorporate air quality goals into their planning procedures to qualify for federal aid for road projects (Garrett and Wachs, 1996, 3). The US Environmental Protection Agency (US EPA) and the US DoT issued joint guidelines in 1980 to establish the 'conformity of transportation plans, improvement programs and projects with state implementation plans',[5] as mandated by the amendments of 1977.[6]

The alleged failure of the Metropolitan Transportation Commission (MTC) serving the San Francisco Bay Area to comply with the Act led to a lawsuit in a federal court in which the commission agreed to modify its procedures to better address air quality concerns. The concerns raised in the lawsuit pertained partly to travel forecasting models, as represented by the sequential travel forecasting procedure, and partly to the relationship between transportation system investment and the distribution of economic development and residential population in a region undergoing growth.[7] More specifically, the lawsuit resulted in discussions about how to improve MTC's travel forecasting procedure (Kollo and Purvis, 1989; HCG, 1997, 46; and, in particular, Garrett and Wachs, 1996, Chapter 3). Part of the lawsuit concerned interrelationships among the 'models' (steps) of the sequential procedure, how to achieve a 'reasonable equilibrium' among the models, such as between mode choice and traffic assignment, and how to structure a feedback procedure that would properly 'account for how changes in the transportation network would affect trip patterns and even redistribute population and development in the region' (1996, 89). In their concluding chapter, the authors addressed questions of the interrelationships among the models (steps):

An understanding of the important limitations of existing travel forecasting modeling technology emerges from this history of travel demand models. The question of feedback among the models . . . is one good example. If each model in the sequence is really independent of all the others, the models lack realism in part because of the absence of feedback, which in practical terms means that the earlier models in the sequence are not influenced or affected by the later models in the sequence. . . . The modeling process, however, does not provide for such adjustments unless feedback exists from later models in the sequence to earlier ones (Garrett and Wachs, 1996, 199).

Another question pertained to the feasibility of forecasting travel and air quality at points five, ten or 20 years into the future for the purpose of reaching decisions about regulations (Transportation Research Board, TRB, 1995, 5–6; Garrett and Wachs, 1996, 202–203). Before the Bay Area lawsuit was settled, however, the US Congress passed the Clean Air Act Amendments of 1990 and the Intermodal Surface Transportation Efficiency Act in 1991, which further impacted the status of travel forecasting methods.

8.2.2 Clean Air Act Amendments of 1990

One impetus for the revitalisation of travel forecasting procedures in US transportation planning practice was the Clean Air Act Amendments of 1990 (CAAA). The history of these requirements was examined by Weiner (1997, 201–207; 2013) and US DoT (2010).[8] Our objective is to explore the meaning of modelling terms in relation to this Act, and to understand how detailed requirements for travel forecasting were incorporated into the regulations implementing this legislation.

To begin, we note that 'transformation conformity' is defined as a 'process to assess the compliance of any metropolitan transportation plan, program, or project with air quality implementation plans. The conformity process is defined by the Clean Air Act (CAA) and regulated by the conformity rule' (US DoT, 2010, 22). In areas experiencing air quality problems, 'the CAA requires metropolitan transportation plans, TIPs [transportation improvement programs], and Federal projects conform to the purpose of the State Implementation Plan', 'the air quality plan for meeting the National Ambient Air Quality Standards' (US DoT, 2010, 6, 22). Conformity to the purpose of that plan means that the transportation activities will not cause new violations of the National Ambient Air Quality Standards, worsen existing violations or delay timely attainment of the standards. These regulations are described in sections quoted below to illustrate their specific relation to travel forecasting methods. (Italics are added to emphasise points discussed following the Regulations.)

The requirements imposed on the states, and their constituent agencies, for conformity analysis in the Clean Air Act Amendments of 1990 are stated in the following Federal Regulations:

§ 93.122 Procedures for determining regional transportation-related emissions.[9]
(a) General requirements. [Items 1–5 concerned with emissions analyses are omitted.]
(b) Regional emissions analysis in (certain) nonattainment areas must meet the requirements of paragraphs (b) (1) through (3) if their metropolitan planning area contains an urbanized area population over 200,000.
1) By January 1, 1997, estimates of regional transportation-related emissions used to support conformity determinations must be made . . . using *network-based travel models* according to procedures and methods that are available and in practice. Network-based travel models must at a minimum satisfy the following requirements:
    i.   Network-based travel *models must be validated against observed counts* (peak and off-peak, if possible) for a base year that is not more than 10 years prior to the date of the conformity determination. Model forecasts must be analyzed for reasonableness and compared to historical trends and other factors, and the results must be documented;
    ii. Land use, population, employment, and other network-based travel model assumptions must be documented and based on the best available information;
    iii. Scenarios of land development and use must be consistent with the future transportation system alternatives for which emissions are being estimated. The distribution of employment and residences for different transportation options must be reasonable;
    iv. A *capacity-sensitive assignment methodology must be used*, and emissions estimates must be based on a methodology which differentiates between peak and off-peak link volumes and speeds and uses speeds based on final assigned volumes;
    v.   *Zone-to-zone travel impedances used to distribute trips between origin and destination pairs must be in reasonable agreement with the travel times that are estimated from final assigned traffic volumes.* Where use of transit currently is anticipated to be a significant factor in satisfying transportation demand, these times should also be used for modeling mode splits; and
    vi. Network-based travel models must be reasonably sensitive to changes in the time(s), cost(s), and other factors affecting travel choices.
2) Reasonable methods in accordance with good practice must be used to estimate traffic speeds and delays in a manner that is sensitive to the estimated volume of travel on each roadway segment represented in the network-based travel model.

The requirements are interesting for what they did and did not include. First, the regulations stated that network-based models that differentiate between peak and non-peak travel must be applied with capacities, and validated 'if possible'. For the first time in the history of US travel forecasting, MPOs were required to perform assignments for periods shorter than the 24-hour weekday. Previously, some MPOs performed capacity restraint assignments in which the capacities in the volume-delay function were factored to represent an effective 24-hour capacity based on peak periods of the weekday. The factor was the ratio of 24-hour link flows to peak hour link flows. The use of such factors circumvented the partitioning of the 24-hour trip matrix into peak and off-peak period matrices, which would require multiple assignments. Implicitly, the regulations pertained to the conventional 'static' definition of traffic assignment. In static models, flows and generalised costs do not change during the time period of the assignment.

Second, 'zone-to-zone travel impedances' must be in agreement with travel times estimated from final road and transit assignments. This requirement, commonly known as solving the travel forecasting procedure with 'feedback', was seldom observed by MPOs prior to these regulations. The use of the term 'impedance' in this regulation clearly means zone-to-zone travel time. See section 2.3.4 for a discussion of the origins of 'impedance'.

Third, transit as well as road times must be used in forecasting mode choice. Apparently, no requirement is stated with regard to trip distribution, implying that road times and costs could be used for trip distribution. Moreover, no general requirement for combining road and transit times and costs into a single impedance measure at the origin–destination (O-D) level was stated.

Even so, these regulations represented a major departure from earlier travel forecasting practice. No longer could travel forecasts represent only the 24-hour weekday. No longer could the discrepancy among impedances assumed in trip distribution and the impedances implied by the road traffic assignments be ignored. No requirement was imposed, however, on how peak and off-peak travel was to be determined. Typically, this allocation was made by factoring 24-hour trip matrices on the basis of proportions observed in base-year household travel surveys, thereby ignoring the effect of different levels of congestion by time of day on peak and off-peak travel choices. Finally, no mention was made of the ordering of the trip distribution and mode split steps in the sequential procedure or of how these two steps should be linked (sections 3.5.3, 9.5.3).

We were told that the regulations were a compromise between US EPA and FHWA, the agencies charged with their preparation.[10] Generally US EPA, a regulatory agency, wanted more prescriptive regulations, whereas FHWA saw its role as advisory to the MPOs. In any event the resulting regulations did not inform practitioners of the methods needed for their implementation. In fact, few knew how to implement the feedback requirement satisfactorily (section 8.3.2.3). Finally, these regulations were changing partially the purposes for which forecasts were produced from infrastructure planning to the regulation of air quality.

Although the regulations were imposed in principle by the CAAA, it would be years before the regulations were written and finalised. Shrouds (1995) traced this history in detail. The first publication of these requirements occurred in late 1993.[11] Following challenges and court decisions, 'final' rules were published in 1999, 2004 and 2006.

8.2.3   Intermodal Surface Transportation Efficiency Act of 1991

The Intermodal Surface Transportation Efficiency Act (ISTEA) of 1991 represented a new direction in legislation pertaining to surface transportation, which had not changed substantially since 1962. Subsequently, legislation with similar titles was enacted every five to six years. Therefore, ISTEA served as a further wake-up call to MPOs. More flexible funding was provided to states for roads, transit, safety and research, and specific requirements were imposed, a change of great significance (Weiner, 1997, 217):

1. preparation of a long-range (typically at least 20-year) plan, generally updated every five years, that identifies a transportation facilities system plan, including a five-year financial plan and a transportation improvement programme;
2. an assessment of capital investment and other measures to make the most efficient use of existing facilities to relieve congestion;
3. (in regions that had not met the federally mandated air quality objectives) the coordination of the long-range plan with transportation control measures required under the CAAA;
4. consideration of 15 interrelated factors in the development of the long-range plan, including the effect of transportation decisions on land use and development;
5. preparation of a congestion management system for the effective management of new and existing facilities through the use of travel demand reduction and operations strategies.

The Act also initiated new capital investment programmes for construction of new fixed guideway systems and extensions, which evolved from 1997 into the New Starts Program of the Federal Transit Administration (section 8.3.1). The implications of ISTEA and its successors were substantial; however, specific requirements were not prescribed in the legislation or by US DoT in subsequent regulations. A heavy burden was placed on MPOs to implement travel forecasting methods for performing alternatives analyses more adequately. As a result, most large MPOs performed 'model updates' on their forecasting procedures, including 'peer reviews' by knowledgeable modellers from other MPOs, consultants and universities (section 8.3.2).

8.3 RESPONSES TO THE EVOLVING REQUIREMENTS

8.3.1 Initiatives of US DoT

In response to ISTEA, FHWA established the Travel Model Improvement Program.[12] TMIP sought to identify shortcomings in travel forecasting methods and to initiate consulting and research activities to address them. TMIP consisted of four tracks: outreach; near-term improvements; longer-term improvements; and data collection in support of the first three tracks (Garrett and Wachs, 1996, 221; Weiner and Ducca, 1996).

In 1992, FHWA called for proposals for new approaches to the modelling of travel demand, as part of its longer-term improvement programme. Small contracts were issued to four organisations to expand their short proposals into research projects. Each of the selected proposals advocated what is now known as an activity-based model[13] (sections 6.5.1, 8.4.2). FHWA's objective was to develop one or more demand models that might be later integrated with a dynamic network model. Ensuing developments, however, were not what was envisaged. Section 8.4 traces some of the activities that actually transpired.

In 2003 a peer review programme was implemented (Culp et al, 2006), providing travel funds and staff support for experienced practitioners, consultants and academics to meet on a volunteer basis with the travel forecasting team of an MPO, including its consultant, to review the status of its models and offer advice on how to proceed with improvements.[14]

By 2013 TMIP included an extensive clearing house of technical reports, operated a listserve, was actively used by professionals to send queries to its members and offered seminars by webcast. The programme was making a positive contribution to practitioners, graduate students and university faculty and academic researchers. TMIP generally refrained from recommending specific methods or travel forecasting software.

In contrast to FWHA's advisory-oriented approach, FTA established strict guidelines and procedures for preparing proposals for federal capital grants in an effort to reduce past tendencies to overestimate future transit ridership and underestimate investment costs (Pickrell, 1989, 1992; Flyvbjerg et al, 2003).[15] The procedures specified are the following:[16]

1. The horizon year used for the travel forecasts is 2030.
2. Ridership forecasts are based on a single set of projections and policies consistent with the regional transportation plan and held constant for the preparation of travel forecasts for the New Starts Baseline and New Starts Build alternatives, including:
   a) the highway network, except as modified for changes inherent to the Build alternative (such as the conversion of traffic lanes to transit-only rights-of-way);
   b) transit service policies regarding geographic coverage, span of service, and headways, modified;
   c) where necessary to integrate transit guideways into the bus system;
   d) pricing policies (fares, highway tolls, and parking costs);
   e) transit capacity provided given projected transit volumes, productivity standards, and loading standards.
3. Travel models used to prepare the forecasts were developed and tested with the best available data on current conditions in the urban area, collected in year ___, including:
   a) highway speed data;
   b) transit travel-time data;
   c) home interview/travel-diary data;
   d) transit on-board survey data.
4. Except for the impacts of physical changes introduced by the alternatives themselves, the performance of the highway and transit systems is held constant between the New Starts Baseline and New Starts Build alternatives, including:
   a) highway congestion levels;
   b) transit operating speeds in mixed traffic;
   c) maximum access and egress distances to/from transit services, as well as representations of walking, waiting, and transfer times.
5. Transit-mode-specific constants describing unmeasurable attributes of individual modes are either the same across all transit line-haul modes or are derived from ridership experience on existing transit modes in the metropolitan area, and have magnitudes that are within acceptable ranges as reviewed and approved by FTA.
6. Service levels in both the New Starts Baseline and New Starts Build alternatives were adjusted to meet projected ridership levels using consistent vehicle-loading standards.
7. Forecasts of ridership and transportation benefits were subjected to quality-assurance reviews designed to identify and correct large errors that would threaten the usefulness of the information in project evaluation.
8. The forecast of ridership using park/ride access to an individual transit stop/station does not exceed the capacity of the associated park/ride lot, as reported in the current planning and/or environmental documents for the alternatives (US DoT, 2009, 14).

Hence, the alternatives analysis procedures for new transit proposals required the use of a single O-D trip matrix for all alternatives (items 2, 4). Any effects of the proposed alternative plan on land use, household location and interzonal travel must be ignored (item 2). FTA procedures also relied heavily on a standardised method for summarising travellers' use of each alternative to aggregate forecasts and benefits measures to districts, allowing analysts and decision makers to understand the large amount of detail generated by travel forecasting methods.[17]

8.3.2 Responses of the MPOs

8.3.2.1 Model updates

At the time of the legislative mandates in 1990 and 1991, many MPOs had not updated their travel forecasting models since the 1970s; household surveys for recalibrating the models were outdated. Development of US DoT's Urban Transportation Planning System had ended, and software systems for personal computers were entering the market (section 10.3.3).

Model updates built on and refined the traditional sequential procedure. Models for specific steps were reformed, including trip generation based on household characteristics, use of 'logsums' (composite costs) to connect the trip distribution and mode split models, factoring of 24-hour trip matrices into periods, and introduction of a feedback procedure. Model validation studies were performed to check whether the base-year forecasts were improved by the updated procedure. Relatively few MPOs embarked on new approaches (section 8.4.2).

Model updates were often performed by travel forecasting consultants. Through their own model development activities and contracts with other MPOs, consultants were able to bring recent model developments to an agency. The detailed manual by Greig Harvey [1950–1997] and Elizabeth Deakin provided early and useful guidance (Harvey and Deakin, 1993). Later, NCHRP Report 716 provided detailed descriptions of current practice, including typical parameter values (Cambridge Systematics et al, 2012). Table 8.1 summarises changes that occurred in the applications of models of a typical large MPO.

8.3.2.2 Model calibration and forecast accuracy

The model update process raised numerous model calibration issues. In general, past models were calibrated with regard to a recent household survey and related data. Model validation studies were performed on base-year road vehicle counts and public transport system boardings.

One important issue concerned the representation of generalised cost in the trip distribution and mode split models. Formerly, these costs often reflected only road network travel times. Now, with improved understanding of the representation of these costs in the mode split model, practitioners were advised to adopt a 'composite cost' measure, which practitioners

Table 8.1   Models applied in the sequential procedure before and after model updates

Model or step	Prior version	Updated version
Trip generation	Zone-based rates	Household-based rates
Trip distribution	Gravity model with friction factors	Doubly-constrained gravity model based on 'logsums'; or destination choice model
Mode split	Diversion curves	Logit function
Traffic assignment	24-hour, all-or-nothing; 24-hour all trips matrix, capacity restraint	24-hour user-equilibrium assignment; peak hour and off-peak matrices by class factored from 24-hour matrices with user-equilibrium assignment
Transit assignment	All-or-nothing to generalised cost	All-or-nothing to generalised cost
Feedback	Generally not performed	Three iterations, often without averaging

Note: More detailed models pertaining to car ownership, car occupancy and time of day of travel are omitted from this overview.

Source: Based in part on Institute of Transportation Engineers (ITE) (1994); feedback was not included in the ITE report.

generally call a 'logsum', corresponding to the natural logarithm of the denominator term of a logit mode split model. The use of 'logsums' to represent the composite cost of travel by car and public transport modes became widely accepted in practice.

Practitioners have seldom recognised that their model parameter values calibrated on recent surveys imply assumptions about these values in the design or target year of the plan. Underlying this issue is the question of how mean travel times change between a base year and target year. Lee et al (2009) reported a 'marked increase' in mean metropolitan commuting times from the four national travel surveys undertaken between 1983 and 2001: mean private car travel times increased 28 per cent from 1983 to 2001; mean public transport travel times increased 40 per cent over the same period.[18] Their research examines 'reasons for this dramatic change' from past results, which had exhibited little change from survey to survey (Lee et al, 2009, 78; Gordon et al, 1991). The observed changes appear to relate to the spatial redistribution of residences and workplaces, which may actually have the effect of moderating trip lengths, and not only the effect of increasing congestion. Their research raised important questions for travel forecasting: what assumption should be made about commuting travel times in the future?

In conjunction with the post-ISTEA model updates and related concerns about model calibration, one could expect that MPOs might have undertaken comparisons of the forecasts of their first transportation plans and the measured outcomes, as represented by the 1980–2010 decennial censuses and other recent surveys. Only two published papers on this subject from US research were found. A committee of the Institute of Transportation Engineers (1980) compared early regional population forecasts and outcomes for the Southeastern Wisconsin region, the Chicago region and the Puget Sound region during the 1970s. Given the few studies examined, no overall conclusions were drawn.

John McDonald (1988) compared 1980 Census of Population counts with the 1980 population forecast in the first plan for the Chicago region (Chicago Area Transportation Study, 1959, 1960, 1962). He found that the regional population forecast was too high (+27 per cent), whereas the forecast of car ownership rate per person forecast was too low (−28 per cent). As a result these errors cancelled: the forecast number of cars was within 6 per cent of the outcome. McDonald's paper remains an excellent example of the difficulties of performing an assessment of forecast accuracy. Mackinder and Evans (1981) performed a detailed study of forecast accuracy of 12 aggregate variables for 44 transportation studies in the UK (section 3.7). Their report also depicted the difficulty of performing such studies, in that the values of many of the desired forecast variables were largely unobservable, and had to be estimated from other data sources.

8.3.2.3 Solving the sequential procedure with feedback

Technically, solving the sequential procedure with feedback is substantially more difficult than it may appear. The underlying mathematical problem of bringing the solution variables of a system of non-linear variables, equations and constraints into consistent agreement is not easy to solve. This difficulty may be further exacerbated by the system not having a unique solution or not converging smoothly to an acceptably precise solution.

Although 'feeding back' the solution of one problem as an input to an earlier problem in the sequence of forecasting models appears simple enough, several necessary choices make the problem more complex. The first concerns what information to feed back. The second is whether to average the values that are fed back and, if so, how the averaging should be performed. The third concerns how to assess whether a stable result is achieved, technically called convergence. Examining how practitioners have responded to these choices suggests an inadequate understanding of the underlying problem.

Following the issuance of the initial regulations from the Clean Air Act Amendments of 1990 (section 8.2.2), a session at the TRB Transportation Planning Applications Conference in 1993 considered solutions to the feedback problem. The presentations offered a very wide variety of solutions. For example, the variables suggested for feedback included not only zone-to-zone travel times or impedances, sometimes referred to as 'skims', but also link travel times and link speeds. Most practitioners had not yet considered whether to compute weighted averages of the values of variables from successive solutions of the models, or how to assess the stability of the solution.

In an effort to provide advice on this matter, FHWA awarded a task order to Comsis Corporation (1996). The study encountered difficulties. Comsis applied its own software system MINUTP (section 10.5.1.3) to perform tests of alternative ways of performing feedback, which imposed serious limitations on what experiments could be conducted. Hence, the project did not provide the desired guidance. During the same period, a method for solving the sequential procedure with feedback based on the combined model formulation of Evans (1976b) was implemented by Metaxatos et al (1995) in EMME/2. A discussion on TMIP Online, 'Technical Synthesis – Feedback Loops', based on email exchanges between 2005 and 2009, however, suggested this issue remained unresolved (TMIP Online, 2009). Boyce et al (2008) described another way to perform feedback calculations on a trip distribution–assignment procedure with VISUM.

8.4   INITIATIVES TO DEVELOP NEW TRAVEL
FORECASTING METHODS

Perhaps stimulated by the CAAA and ISTEA legislation, as well as expanding computing technology in the early 1990s, academic researchers and planners were eager to explore new approaches to travel forecasting. The traditional sequential procedure, with its emphasis on aggregate cross-sectional forecasts, appeared less appropriate for new technologies being proposed in the early 1990s. Calls for consideration of travel dynamics of all modes, including non-motorised travel, were regularly expressed.

In this environment, offers of totally new approaches seemed especially appealing. One proposal surprisingly emerged from an energy laboratory known historically for its role in the creation of nuclear weapons. Others came from academic research, as new behavioural concepts and new mathematical methods began to be understood (Chapters 6, 7). In this section, two of these developments are examined: TRANSIMS, and activity-based models. A third new approach is dynamic traffic assignment (DTA). Departure choice models were recently added to earlier DTA models, thereby making these models more behaviourally plausible. Sufficient experience for their review here is not yet available (Chiu et al, 2011).

8.4.1 The TRANSIMS Project

Following the disintegration of the Soviet Union in August 1991, American defence laboratories were encouraged to address civilian or societal technology problems with small grants from the US Department of Energy (US DoE). At Los Alamos National Laboratory (LANL), a US DoE facility, a team of systems scientists led by Christopher Barrett proposed a transportation analysis simulation system (TRANSIMS). Barrett had received his Ph.D. in bio-information systems from the California Institute of Technology in 1985, followed by six years of experience at LANL. Altogether, Barrett worked at LANL for 17 years, was leader of the Basic and Applied Simulation Science Group, and 'built up a research group active in theoretical and applied research in intelligent systems, distributed systems and advanced computer simulation'.[19]

David Albright, director of research at New Mexico DoT, was a proponent of the LANL proposal, which sought to design from first principles a systems dynamics approach to modelling urban transportation systems in response to the requirements of the CAAA and ISTEA (Donnelly et al, 2010).[20] Soon after the long-term research programme of TMIP was initiated, Federal Highway administrator Thomas Larson [1928–2006] directed that the initial development of TRANSIMS be funded at the level of $1 million.[21] Larson was co-founder and first director of the Pennsylvania Transportation and Safety Center (now the Larson Transportation Institute) at Pennsylvania State University; subsequently, he was Pennsylvania secretary of transportation.[22] Larson had little technical experience regarding urban travel forecasting; being aware of the need for major innovations in the field, however, he evidently viewed the LANL proposal as an opportunity to move the field forward.

The Committee for Determination of the State of the Practice in Metropolitan Area Travel Forecasting of TRB summarised the funding of the project:

TRANSIMS was funded primarily by congressional appropriation and administered through the Federal Highway Administration's Travel Model

Improvement Program. From 1992 to 2003, $38 million was spent on TRANSIMS, about three-quarters of which went to Los Alamos for basic research and development. After 2003, a 3-year hiatus occurred during which no funding was available for TRANSIMS development or implementation. The Safe, Accountable, Flexible, Efficient Transportation Equity Act (2009) allocates $2 million annually to TRANSIMS, some of which is to support implementation by MPOs and other operating agencies and some of which is to support TRANSIMS related development activities (TRB, 2007, 98).

Subsequently, the TRANSIMS Open Source Community was established in 2006 to support the further development and application of TRANSIMS. Additional studies were undertaken by AECOM and by the Transportation Research and Analysis Computing Center of Argonne National Laboratory.

8.4.1.1 Objectives of the project

An informal description of the intended capabilities of TRANSIMS was presented in 1994:

> In the model every individual has a set of activities that he or she wants to engage in. . . . Those activities and their destinations together with data on the behavior of individual people in the household, their income, and various demographic variables, feed into the trip planner. The planner determines what particular roadway segments, bus segments and rail segments that each individual will use. Implicit in the trip planner are intermodal decisions. . . . For the entire population for the entire twenty-four hours, we account for each trip decision implicitly. Drivers and households resolve conflicts among themselves as they do in the real world. They decide to leave earlier in order to avoid congestion. They decide which route to take and/or which mode and so forth. The information that feeds the trip planner is obtained from demographic and land use planning models. The demand is estimated for people and individuals, and for commodities and freight. . . . TRANSIMS tracks every car, every driver, every stoplight, acceleration, deceleration, braking and turning. We also use information on roadway grade. All of that is done for one second intervals, and that feeds the environmental model (Morgeson, 1994, 40).[23]

The computational requirements of TRANSIMS were considered daunting by many; the following comment responded to that concern:

> The work reported here is requirement and policy driven, starting with the questions of what is the computational framework which will satisfy those issues. This work was not restricted to use the computing power on your desktop today, personal computers and the current generation of computational technology. The work is aimed at machines that will be affordable and effective by the end of the [twentieth] century (Morgeson, 1994, 39).[24]

A more detailed description of the design of TRANSIMS follows:

The TRANSIMS Project objective is to develop a set of mutually supporting realistic simulations, models, and data bases that employ advanced computational and analytical techniques to create an integrated regional transportation systems analysis environment. By applying forefront technologies and methods, it will simulate the dynamic details that contribute to the complexity inherent in today's and tomorrow's transportation issues. The integrated results from the detailed simulations will support transportation planners, engineers, and others who must address environmental pollution, energy consumption, traffic congestion, land use planning, traffic safety, intelligent vehicle efficacies, and the transportation infrastructure effect on the quality of life, productivity, and economy.

TRANSIMS predicts trips for individual households, residents, freight loads, and vehicles rather than for zonal aggregations of households. The Household and Commercial Activity Disaggregation Module creates regional synthetic populations from census and other data. Using activity-based methods and other techniques, it produces a travel representation of each household and traveler.

The Synthetic Populations submodule creates a regional population imitation whose demographics closely match that of the real population. The imitation's households also are distributed spatially to approximate the regional population distribution. The synthetic population's demographics are provided to the Activity Demand submodule to derive individual and household activities requiring travel.

The purpose of the Household and Commercial Activity Disaggregation's Activity Demand submodule is to generate household activities, activity priorities, activity locations, activity times, and mode and travel preferences. The activities and preferences are functions of the household demographics created by the Synthetic Population submodule.

The Intermodal Route Planner involves using a demographically defined travel cost decision model particular to each traveler. Vehicle and mode availability are represented and mode choice decisions are made during route plan generation. The method estimates desired trips not made, induced travel, and peak load spreading. This allows evaluation of different transportation control measures and travel demand measures on trip planning behaviors.

The Travel Microsimulation executes the generated trips on the transportation network to predict the performance of individual vehicles and the transportation system. It attempts to execute every individual's travel itinerary in the region. For example, every passenger vehicle has a driver whose driving logic attempts to execute the plan, accelerates or decelerates the car, or passes as appropriate in traffic on the roadway network.

The Travel Microsimulation produces traffic information for the Environmental Models and Simulations to estimate motor vehicle fuel use, emissions, dispersion, transport, air chemistry, meteorology, visibility, and resultant air quality. The emissions model accounts for both moving and stationary vehicles (Smith et al, 1995, 1–4).

The above description should be interpreted as a 'requirements specification' for the desired capability of the proposed method, and not a description of a working capability. That interpretation agrees with the following perspective on its development:

> To provide greater, more timely interaction and feedback from the TRANSIMS user community, we have formulated an approach for TRANSIMS development in which we will develop an interim operational capability (IOC) for each major TRANSIMS module. When the IOC is ready, we will complete a specific case study to confirm the IOC features, applicability, and readiness. We will complete the specific case study with the collaboration of the staff of a selected MPO. This approach should give us quicker feedback from the user community and provide interim products, capabilities, and applications. This approach maintains our goal of an integrated framework for predicting individual travel behavior and for supporting transportation planners from travel demand forecasting to assessments of transportation system modifications (Smith et al, 1995, 10).

TRANSIMS was intentionally designed to be modular so that improvements or substitutions could be made to individual modules. This feature can be observed in the activity estimator, which was originally designed as a statistical sampling technique. In later applications, the activity estimator was replaced by other activity-based models. The following description of the TRANSIMS modules should be interpreted in relation to concurrent and subsequent modelling efforts (sections 6.5, 8.4.2).

8.4.1.2 Description of the resulting method

As implemented, TRANSIMS consisted of five modules: Population Synthesizer, Activity Generator, Route Planner, Traffic Microsimulator and Emissions Estimator (LANL, 2003). These modules are described below based on explanations in LANL (2003) and Hobeika (2005). Original documents concerning TRANSIMS are used wherever possible. Short explanatory comments follow the description of each module.

> Using census data and population demographic projections, the Population Synthesizer generates a synthetic population of households and individuals distributed geographically and demographically as within the real metropolitan region. Also from census or other data, TRANSIMS assigns vehicles to each household. Households, work places, schools, stores and shops, etc., are placed at 'activity locations' along the transportation network (LANL, 2003, Volume 3, Chapter 1, 3).

The Population Synthesizer applied the classic method of iterative proportional fitting (Deming and Stephan, 1940; Fratar, 1954; McFadden et al, 1977a) to the Public Use Microdata Sample (PUMS) to generate the desired synthetic population. As applied in the Portland Case Study, the Population Synthesizer determined a base-year synthetic population from the 1990 Census PUMS. To prepare a synthetic population for a future year, the marginal proportions for that year would need to be forecast by other methods (Beckman et al, 1996).

Matching each household's demographics against those from household travel and activity surveys, the Activity Generator builds an activity list for each household individual. Each list includes activity type (in-home, work, school, shopping, etc.), start time, stop time, travel time to the activity, and travel mode(s). TRANSIMS selects a likely activity location for each activity from network travel times and the activity locations' attractiveness as determined from, for example, the number of retail employees or retail-store floor space (LANL, 2003, Volume 3, Chapter 1, 4).

The activity list prepared by the Activity Generator is determined by a household travel survey in so far as home-based daily travel patterns are concerned. A discrete choice model based on land use data and travel times determines the locations of the destination activities, given the base activity pattern. Work locations were chosen first. Other activities are added using a multinomial logit model. Initial travel times between activity locations are estimated with average times for activity types and modal preferences (LANL, 2003, Volume 3, Chapter 3, 5).

'The Route Planner finds each traveler's fastest (or minimal cost) route to each activity during the day. The activity information and the trip plans (including route timetables) constitute each traveler's (initial) expectation of the transportation system's performance' (LANL, 2002, Volume 3, Chapter 1, 4). The Route Planner computes the shortest route, subject to modal constraints, for each traveller in the system based on the congested cost of each link in the transportation network. Constraints are provided by modal preferences for different legs of the trip (LANL, 2003, Volume 3, Chapter 4, 4). The algorithm underlying the TRANSIMS Route Planner is the classical Dijkstra algorithm, which finds the shortest routes in a weighted, directed graph.

When combined, the Population Synthesizer, Activity Generator, and Route Planner create individual travel plans. However, to simulate realistic traffic, individuals must interact with the environment and with each other. The Traffic Microsimulator, the module that follows, is designed to meet this need. The Traffic Microsimulator executes each traveler's trip plans, second-by-second, simulating the movement of individuals throughout the transportation network, including their use of vehicles such as cars or buses. A Cellular Automata (particle-hopping) model of individual vehicle interactions produces traffic dynamics calibrated and validated against real-world data (LANL, 2003, Volume 3, Chapter 1, 4).

The Traffic Microsimulator simulates the movements and interactions of travelers in a metropolitan region's transportation system. . . . Using a cellular automata (CA) approach, the Traffic Microsimulator provides the computational speed necessary to simulate an entire region at the individual traveler level. . . . Each link in the transportation network is divided into a finite number of cells. . . . We evaluate the fidelity and performance limits of the Traffic Microsimulator to establish the computational detail that supports the fidelity necessary to meet analysis requirements (LANL, 2003, Volume 3, Chapter 5, 1).

Kai Nagel's model of freeway traffic simulation was one starting point for the development of the Traffic Microsimulator (Nagel and Schreckenberg, 1992).[25] The TRANSIMS Microsimulator was one of several efforts to develop microsimulators for large networks.

Using iteration and feedback directed by the Selector/Iteration Database, this virtual world of travelers and vehicles eventually mimics the traveling and driving behavior of real people in the region. Furthermore, this realistic simulation captures the predicted performance of the proposed transportation system as a whole and as observed by each traveler. At this point, the modules can execute extremely realistic traffic simulations. Adding to the reality of such simulations is the Emissions Estimator, which is designed to take data acquired during a traffic simulation and calculate vehicle emissions (LANL, 2003, Volume 3, Chapter 1, 4).

These quotations describe the intended performance of TRANSIMS, since the full system was not yet implemented on a case of the intended size and complexity. The proposed use of feedback to solve the system and produce a realistic result is described hypothetically in LANL (2002, Volume 3, Chapter 6).

8.4.1.3 Case studies

The Traffic Microsimulation module of TRANSIMS was initially tested for a 25 square mile suburban area of Dallas, Texas (LANL, 1998). Trips passing through or within the area were extracted from an O-D trip matrix. The case study examined how roadways would respond to improvements, such as adding a freeway lane or modifying arterial street intersections. Based on performance measures computed with and without the improvements, the developers were satisfied that the simulations reproduced the observed traffic patterns and effects of the improvements.

Following the initial Dallas test, additional case studies and software development proceeded as parallel efforts. In 1999, FHWA initiated an application of TRANSIMS with Portland Metro, the MPO of Portland, Oregon (Donnelly et al, 2010, 58). This effort was undertaken by LANL, PBConsult, AECOM and IBM. Metro procured the computing resources, developed data resources and began model development. To use the Portland region as a proof of concept test case for a large-scale implementation of activity-based microsimulation techniques, LANL developed a regional network that contained all of the local streets and transit routes within the greater Portland metropolitan area. This 'all-streets' network was intended for use in the initial model development and software evaluation efforts using trip-based demand from Metro's travel model (LANL, 2002; AECOM, 2006, 1).

In 2002, FHWA initiated a full implementation of TRANSIMS for the Portland metropolitan area designed to evaluate the feasibility of using the networks and trip matrices from existing regional planning models as input to a TRANSIMS microsimulation. By comparing the results of this effort to the more detailed 'all-streets' implementation of LANL, FHWA sought to evaluate the relative costs and benefits of pursuing a microsimulation-only approach. The Router–Microsimulator implementation was based on the following travel and road-transit networks: 24-hour travel period with 4.9 million trips connecting 28 814 activity locations in 1260 zones; road network consisting of 8375 links, 1370 signals and over 250 transit routes. Sensitivity tests of this system were completed with reasonable responses for changes in traffic signal timing, a bridge closing and a 15 per cent increase in traffic.[26]

A full implementation of an activity-based, full second-by-second network microsimulation of the location, duration and type of activities and movements of individuals, vehicles and households over a 24-hour period was also initiated. The tour and destination choice models were calibrated and validated, the mode choice model was specified and partially calibrated, and the model feedback mechanisms were specified. According to the lessons learned:

> The project demonstrated that standard regional networks and trips tables can be used effectively to simulate travel demand on a time-dependent network. A user equilibrium convergence process was developed to incrementally identify a travel path for each vehicle that minimized the travel impedance of each traveler while stabilizing the network performance.
>
> It also demonstrated that loading transit trip tables to schedule-based transit routes can effectively reproduce transit ridership data by route. The impedance parameters used for selecting the transit paths, however, tend to be significantly different from the conventional wisdom of traditional travel demand forecasting. In this case, the weighting of out-of-vehicle travel time is nearly equal to in-vehicle travel time and transfer penalties relate to the attributes of the stop location and the reliability of the transit service (AECOM, 2009, 37).

Following the completion of this work, further activities were halted for lack of funds (TMIP, 2005, 13). Portland Metro shifted its staff priorities to New Starts analyses in support of transit proposals (Donnelly et al, 2010, 58).

Additional applications of TRANSIMS were subsequently funded by FHWA. One was the White House Area Transportation Study, a study to reroute traffic away from the residence and offices of the president in Washington, DC. This study was the first application of a portion of the TRANSIMS software, requiring detailed simulations of the time-of-day dynamics of traffic operations in Washington, DC. AECOM expanded and enhanced the tools developed for Portland to include a new micro-simulator, replacing the cellular automata concepts with actual vehicle locations and speeds (Roden, 2009).

AECOM and the Mid-Ohio Regional Planning Commission (MORPC) undertook a study to route and simulate the daily activity patterns generated by MORPC's tour-based model on a fine-grained TRANSIMS network (AECOM, 2011). Tours from MORPC's activity-based model were converted to trip matrices by time of day, routed over the road network by the TRANSIMS Router, and assigned with a static assignment algorithm as a first solution. Then, this solution was refined by applying the TRANSIMS Microsimulator.

8.4.1.4   Software development and dissemination

TMIP Online (1999) issued 'Early Deployment of TRANSIMS', concerning the release of TRANSIMS to MPOs.[27] The Early Deployment Program consisted of several elements: complete the model development, which was ongoing at the time; hire a software contractor team; complete the Portland Case Study; select local transportation planning agencies; train agency staff and consultants; collect data for TRANSIMS; and apply TRANSIMS.

A workshop on commercialisation and deployment opportunities for TRANSIMS was held at Santa Fe, New Mexico in June 1999. '[F]irms with an interest in the commercialization process received a technical overview of TRANSIMS, learned the requirements for the commercial software, met with the LANL development team, potential end users, and other organizations with which they could team' (Fisher, 2000).[28] Subsequently, a contract was let to PricewaterhouseCoopers, a public accounting firm, for the development of a commercial software system based on LANL's research software. This aspect of TRANSIMS deployment was not mentioned again in TRANSIMS or TMIP reports.

In 2006, LANL and FHWA released a version of TRANSIMS from a LANL-developed version, further developed by AECOM. These versions were released under a software open source agreement to make them available as a public resource on a Google website.[29] TRANSIMS Open Source

Community members, funded by FHWA and other sources, continued to refine TRANSIMS code, methods and documentation based on this version.

Argonne National Laboratory, a US DoE facility, initiated a multi-year programme with the support of US DoT in 2006, to establish the Transportation Research and Analysis Computing Center (TRACC).[30] The early objectives of TRACC were to establish a high performance computing centre for use by US DoT research teams, including those from Argonne and its university partners, and to use advanced computing and visualisation facilities for the performance of focused computer research and development programs in areas of interest for US DoT. Tasks to enhance the performance and utility of TRANSIMS included improved interfaces and parallelisation.

By late 2013, the activities of TRACC related to TRANSIMS were completed.[31] Further development of TRANSIMS may be continuing at AECOM as in the past. TRANSIMS open source, however, has shown no activity since early 2011.[32]

8.4.1.5　Conclusions

Although TRANSIMS, as proposed by LANL and its proponents, was a 'novel' approach to modelling urban travel, it contained, and indeed it had to contain, if developed at a micro-level, many aspects of demand and network modelling that were already the subject of substantial research efforts. For example, by the 1990s the microsimulation approach was well established for solving models specified at the micro-level (section 5.4.3); population synthesis had been applied in transportation for two decades (Ireland and Kullback, 1968; McFadden et al, 1977a); activity-based models were a decade old (Recker et al, 1986; Kitamura, 1988; Chapter 6); discrete choice models applied to modal and destination choice were commonplace (Ben-Akiva and Lerman, 1985; Chapter 5); estimation and solution of detailed network equilibrium models were being implemented at realistic scales (Florian et al, 1979). A new network microsimulation method was being proposed (Daganzo, 1994). What was new about TRANSIMS was the unprecedented spatial and temporal resolution of the proposed solutions, particularly in network representation and analy-sis, and the scale proposed for its solution and application, microsimulat-ing entire cities rather than subarea networks.

TRANSIMS was undertaken at great expense, relative to contemporary and subsequent research support, and outside the main travel forecast-ing research and software development community. Documentation and publication of its findings and experience were highly limited, especially in view of its professed scientific, basic research orientation. Hence, 20 years later TRANSIMS remains a controversial subject, and still evokes a wide range of opinions for a project that had limited success in achieving its original terms of reference. Model design principles suggest that TRANSIMS's proposed level of space-time detail may be neither necessary nor desirable for the strategic analysis of policies with intermediate and longer-term impacts.

In some respects, however, TRANSIMS remains a work in progress. Just as TRANSIMS built upon past research, its proposed approach will be more widely adopted in the future, but predominantly for particular purposes, such as exploring the consequences of short-term responses to intelligent transportation systems and other traffic management issues. For example, one contribution of TRANSIMS is the ongoing development of a system for multi-agent transportation simulation (MATSim) by Kai Nagel, a participant in the TRANSIMS project, and Kay Axhausen. Although working papers are available on their websites, few contributions to the archival literature were found.[33]

The one area in which the original TRANSIMS team was prescient concerns the rapid progress in computing power and speed over the past 20 years. Few transportation researchers in the early 1990s anticipated the enormous advances in computing capability that ensued (section 10.2.3). Even with these advances in processor speed, memory and networking, however, the implementation originally proposed remains beyond reach.

One fascinating attribute of urban travel modelling over the past 60 years is that the desired level of detail continues to expand faster than advances in computing capability. There is no apparent end to this dilemma. Therefore, a challenge continuing to face modellers is to fit the spatial, temporal, behavioural and physical system representation to the questions for which answers are desired, given the computing resources available. In our view, while the TRANSIMS experience broadened the discussion, it has yet to contribute insights concerning what answers it is feasible to obtain. In this respect it joins past attempts to revolutionise the questions being asked, but without contributing new solutions or guidelines for answering them. Other examples are the Penn Jersey Transportation Study (section 2.7.2), land use – transportation studies (section 8.5) and perhaps even dynamic traffic assignment.

8.4.2 Applications of Tour-Based and Activity-Based Models

Throughout the TRANSIMS project, parallel innovations occurred with regard to activity-based travel models. These studies were supported by FHWA as well as the US National Science Foundation and metropolitan planning agencies (Resource Decision Consultants, RDC, 1995; Kitamura et al, 1996; Bowman et al, 1999) (section 6.5). Recent progress with the application of these models is reviewed here, beginning with a discussion of their historical basis.

Origin–destination surveys conducted by early urban transportation studies interviewed household members concerning their daily travel tours. For the purpose of trip generation analysis, however, these tours were segmented into trips and related to land uses at each trip's origin and destination. Little debate occurred at that time concerning the adoption of this trip-based approach (section 2.5.2). The reasons were highly pragmatic: individual trips could be associated with land uses. Since the objective was to predict 24-hour travel, moreover, the time of day of travel was not an issue.

The classification of trips as home-based and non-home-based in US practice in the 1960s may be viewed as a simplified way of dealing with the representation of tours within a trip-based paradigm. A 'home-based trip production' depicts the beginning of a tour from home and the termination of a tour at home. All other one-way trips were defined as 'non-home-based' trips. The origins of this representation are obscure. The terminology is first found in US DoT (1967); the conversion of production–attraction matrices to origin–destination matrices was explained in US DoC (1963a, III-2, VI-1 – VI-5). Otherwise, forecasting of travel on the basis of tours did not occur in early US practice (section 6.3).

Practising transportation planners and academic researchers became interested during the 1980s in more detailed and realistic representations of urban travel. In particular, they sought representations that recognised that:

1. individuals make a sequence of linked trips over the weekday, and not separate trips;
2. choice of a mode for the first trip in the sequence may constrain that choice in subsequent trips;
3. family members sometimes travel together, both by car and by public transport.

The trip-based representation did not capture these and other travel attributes. These ideas encouraged tour-based concepts, later called activity-based models, when the activities generating travel were added.

By 2010 activity-based models had been designed and at least partially implemented in a few metropolitan areas in the US: New York, Portland, San Francisco County, Sacramento, Columbus and Phoenix (VHB, 2007; Donnelly et al, 2010, 32–35, 58–63; Association of Metropolitan Planning Organizations, 2011). Model implementation efforts were reported by

MPOs in Atlanta, Denver, Houston, Minneapolis–Saint Paul, San Diego and Seattle.[34] Forecasts of activity-based tours were converted to zone-to-zone trip matrices by mode and time of day, and assigned to the road and public transport networks with static assignment methods. So far as can be understood, the travel times, on which the activity-based tours were based, were not necessarily consistent with respect to demand and network generalised costs. Solving activity-based models with 'feedback' remained a challenge for the future. Bowman (2009) reviewed the status of these models (section 6.6.1). More recently, an integrated microsimulation model of activity-travel demand and dynamic traffic assignment was solved along a continuous time-of-day axis for a suburban region of Phoenix (Pendyala et al, 2012; Konduri et al, 2014).

The Committee for Determination of the State of the Practice in Metropolitan Area Travel Forecasting addressed the status of activity-based models (TRB, 2008) in its summary: 'Although a number of agencies have begun to use tour- and activity-based models, many believe that these models are not fully ready for implementation. There are valid concerns about the costs associated with the new models and the amount of data needed to specify, calibrate, and validate them' (TRB, 2008, 6).

The committee recommended that US DoT: 'a) support and provide funding for the continued development, demonstration, and implementation of advanced modeling approaches, including activity-based models; b) continue support for the implementation of activity-based modeling and other advanced practices, and considerably expand this support through deployment efforts in multiple urban areas' (TRB, 2008, 11).

At a more detailed level, the committee stated:

> Travel models can be improved by being based on a more comprehensive understanding of the activities of households. Also needed is a more complete representation of the supply-side network to account for the details of congested operations throughout the day. No one new modeling approach can address these and other needs. Rather, a suite of related approaches, taken together, shows promise for greatly improving modeling practice. These approaches include improved land use modeling, tour-based models, activity-based models, discrete-choice modeling, traffic micro-simulation, and dynamic traffic assignment (TRB, 2008, 115).

In 2009, the Strategic Highway Research Program (SHRP 2) of the Transportation Research Board initiated two large projects with the objective of integrating an activity based model with a dynamic traffic assignment model. RSG et al (2014) integrated the DaySim population synthesiser and activity-based model of the Sacramento, California region with the TRANSIMS Router and Microsimulator.[35] Cambridge

Systematics et al (2014) implemented SACSIM, the regional travel model of the Sacramento Area Council of Governments with DynusT, a mesoscopic traffic simulation model, and FAST-TrIPS, a transit simulation model.[36]

8.5   LAND USE – TRANSPORTATION MODELS

The initial development and application of land use models in urban transportation planning from 1959 to 1973 in the US was relatively unsuccessful (section 2.7.5), ending on a distinctly negative note with the 'Requiem for Large-Scale Models' (Lee, 1973). This section traces developments from that period to the present.

Several reviews were published after 1973. Stephen Putman (1975) described the state of the art at the time of Lee's Requiem, and offered a first 'integrated land use and transportation network model'. Britton Harris (1985) reviewed the field from the perspective of an early effort to forecast land use; later Harris updated his analysis (Oryani and Harris, 1997). Eric Miller (2003) summarised the recent status of land use and transportation models from a transportation planning point of view, Michael Wegener (2004) provided an overview from an urban planning viewpoint, and Hunt et al (2005) described operational modelling frameworks for land use and transportation.

The literature pertaining to land use – transportation models is actually not strictly about either land use or transportation. Land use forecasting models primarily forecast the locations where urban activities occur, and not always the use of the land on which they occur. The models concern the locations of households in residences and employees in workplaces, as well as the locations where individuals engage in retail and service activities; hence, urban activity location models might be a better name. The choice of household location also determines the amount of land in residential use. Moreover, the choice of a location at which to perform shopping activities, or obtain services, also determines the amount of land use at that location engaged in retail and service trade. When these models of urban activity location were linked to, or integrated with, a transportation network model, the resulting model was a travel forecasting model, based on a representation of the transportation system.

The implementation and application of urban activity/land use models is reviewed in section 8.5.1. Research on operationally oriented models is then considered in section 8.5.2, emphasising research that benefited from the participation of MPOs.

8.5.1 Applied Land Use Models

Following the disappointing experiences during the 1960s with the consideration of alternative land use – transportation plans, and the use of models for their elaboration, many agencies focused on refinement of transportation systems plans as new data became available from the 1970 Census and other sources. After some time, however, the need for land use forecasts again became apparent. Efforts to implement operational models inspired by the prototype model of Lowry (1964) were a favoured approach. Stephen Putman installed his 'disaggregate residential allocation and employment allocation' (DRAM/EMPAL) model for numerous MPOs.[37] By 2000, these models were available at over 40 planning agencies, more than any other land use model (US EPA, 2000, A-15).[38] He reported his research concerning the development of these models in Putman (1983, 1991, 1998, 2001).

DRAM/EMPAL forecasts employment and household location by five-year increments from the base year to the target year:

> The employment allocation submodel, EMPAL, forecasts the location of future employment by economic sector to spatially contiguous zones overlaying the metropolitan area . . . by taking into account the following variables:
> 1. zone-specific employment levels (total and by economic sector) for a specified time;
> 2. number of households (population) in each zone, by income level, for a specified time;
> 3. regional level of target year employment (growth trends);
> 4. regional level of target year employment (growth trends);
> 5. travel time between zones, or other zone-specific measures of accessibility to the work force;
> 6. total land area of each zone.
> EMPAL uses this information to estimate the likelihood of a site for future employment primarily based on how often it was selected in the past, given the distribution of households and ease of reaching that zone from other zones.
> DRAM forecasts the future location of households given this distribution of employment and the attractiveness (including accessibility) of the zones . . . considering the following variables:
> 1. employment, by type, in each zone from EMPAL;
> 2. impedance (travel time and cost) between zones;
> 3. percent of households, by type, per zone;
> 4. various land uses (vacant developable land (acres), developed land (%), residential acres (%).
> DRAM also contains trip distribution models and can project home-to-work, home-to-shop and work-to-shop trips (US EPA, 2000, B-10).

DRAM/EMPAL were the two major components of an integrated set of models known as an integrated transportation and land use package

(ITLUP). Forecasts from DRAM/EMPAL were used to perform standard travel forecasts including trip generation and distribution, modal choice, and traffic assignment. The question of how to link DRAM/EMPAL to a travel forecasting model engaged Stephen Putman for many years; he summarised the findings from tests for five metropolitan areas in Putman (1998, 2001).[39]

Aside from the insights and conclusions drawn from the tests performed, Putman's analysis brought sharply into focus some of the practical difficulties of aggregate land use forecasting experienced in practice from 1960 to 2000. Zone sizes used for land use forecasting were generally larger than zone sizes used for travel forecasting by a factor of two to ten (Putman, 2001, 25–26). In order to link a land use model to a travel model, employment and household forecasts by class for land use zones must be disaggregated to traffic zones. Similarly, travel times between pairs of traffic zones must be aggregated to pairs of land use zones. Such a disaggregation and aggregation process introduced substantial elements of arbitrariness into the models. These practical considerations, and related issues pertaining to travel within zones, led to the application of more detailed models: more zones; more classes of households, employment and travel; more detailed network representations; and more time-of-day periods. Fortunately, the huge expansion of computing memory and storage, as well as increased processor speed, facilitated the application of these larger models.

At the time of the US EPA (2000) review, UrbanSim was being implemented by Paul Waddell for the Eugene–Springfield area in Oregon. Further development and application of UrbanSim proceeded rapidly (Waddell, 2000, 2002, 2011; Waddell et al, 2003, 2007; Waddell and Ulfarsson, 2004).[40] 'UrbanSim is a software-based simulation system for supporting planning and analysis of urban development, incorporating the interactions between land use, transportation, the economy, and the environment.'[41] UrbanSim consists of a set of interacting models representing major actors and choices in the urban system, including households moving to residential locations, business choices of employment locations and developer choices of locations and types of real estate development. It is based on a highly disaggregated representation of individual households, jobs, land use developments and location choices using grid cells of 150 × 150 metres (about 0.1 × 0.1 mile) in size, and simulates the evolution over years in locations of individual households and jobs from choices by families and employers, and the evolution within each grid cell resulting from actions of real estate developers.

Theoretical urban models are often based on unrealistic assumptions about behaviour, such as agents having perfect information of all the alternative locations in the metropolitan area, transactions being costless, and markets being perfectly competitive. Observed market imperfections motivated the use of less restrictive assumptions in UrbanSim. Rather than calibrating the model to cross-sectional or base-year conditions, statistical methods were devised to calibrate UrbanSim with data over a multiple-year period (Ševčíková et al, 2007).

UrbanSim is an agent-level model system, but unlike some agent-based models it does not focus exclusively on the interactions of adjacent agents. Households, businesses or jobs, buildings, and land areas, represented either by parcels or by grid cells, are used to represent the agents and locations within a region. Parcel-level modelling applications allow the representation of accessibility at a walking scale, which cannot be effectively achieved at higher levels of spatial aggregation.

UrbanSim was refined in collaboration with a core development team and a community of researchers. Waddell collaboratively linked UrbanSim with an activity-based travel model and a dynamic traffic assignment model (Pendyala et al, 2012; Konduri et al, 2014). Following its release in 1998, UrbanSim was adopted for use in the US, Europe, Asia and Africa, and in university research settings.

8.5.2 Prototype Land Use Models

Michael Wegener (1994, 1998, 2004) wrote three detailed reviews of prototype land use models. Among the models he described, two that were applied in US practice are reviewed: the Chicago region combined model, and METROSIM, a land use model for the New York region. Then, Wegener's own model of the Dortmund region in Germany is described. T. John Kim's three-dimensional, urban activity model is reviewed in section 8.6.

Putman's implementation of DRAM/EMPAL linked a land use model to a travel forecasting model in order to determine the zone-to-zone travel times on which to base the land use forecast. His effort to link models computationally was one approach to solving the problem of basing location choices on the congested travel times that correspond to those choices.

Another approach to linking of models is to formulate a mathematical problem of the relationships among location and travel such that the congested travel times are endogenous to the solution. This approach, which initially grew out of discussions with Putman, was explored by David Boyce based on the trip distribution and assignment formulation of Evans (1976a) (section 7.4.4.2). Boyce (1980) reformulated the quasi-dynamic model of Wilson (1970, Chapter 4) to make travel costs endogenous. A key to the reformulation was restating the entropy function in Wilson's formulation as a constraint (Erlander, 1977).[42]

The implementation of an urban location model with endogenous travel costs was undertaken by Boyce and his students in collaboration with Ronald Eash at the Chicago Area Transportation Study (Boyce et al, 1985). The model was implemented on a sketch planning network of 317 zones, about as large as could be solved at that time with the computers available; additional details are found in section 7.4.5.2.[43]

US EPA (2000) inventoried several land use models that were implemented a limited number of times. Among the most noteworthy was METROSIM, described as 'an operational large-scale computer simulation model that uses an economic approach to forecast the interdependent effects of transportation and land use systems and of land use and transportation policies at the metropolitan level' (US EPA, 2000, 91). METROSIM was one of a series of models formulated and applied by Alex Anas (Anas and Duann, 1985; Anas, 1995).

METROSIM was the basis for the New York Land Use Model, a component of the Best Practice Model of the New York Metropolitan Transportation Council (NYMTC) (Alex Anas & Associates, 2002, 2005). The purpose of the NYMTC Land Use Model was:

> to allocate employed residents and jobs among the 3586 zones comprising the NYMTC modeling region, consisting of parts of New York, New Jersey and Connecticut and also to model how floor spaces and vacant land stocks in each of these zones is altered in each five-year period over the time horizon from 1996 to 2020 by the construction and demolition decisions of developers (Alex Anas & Associates, 2005, 5–141).

The land use model was linked to a travel model to obtain zone-to-zone travel times by mode. The travel model began with congested travel times calculated for the base-year land use and socio-economic/demographic pattern. New congested travel times were calculated for the five-year target year. Composite congested travel times were fed back into the land use model. Based on these new travel times, the land use model then produced a new land use pattern for the target year, which was input to the travel model. The cycle continued until convergence was achieved (Alex Anas & Associates, 2005, 5–136).

Three methods of seeking convergence were described, but not the actual convergence criteria (Parsons Brinckerhoff Quade & Douglas, 2005).[44] Subsequently, Anas and Liu (2007) implemented a dynamic general equilibrium model, RELU-TRAN, with aggregated data for the Chicago region. A spatial computable general equilibrium model, RELU-TRAN2, was also solved (Anas and Hiramatsu, 2012).

The development of a model of intraregional location and mobility decisions in a metropolitan area by Michael Wegener (1985, 2011a) has been ongoing since the 1980s at the Institute of Spatial Planning, University of Dortmund (IRPUD).[45] A brief summary of the IRPUD model is found in US EPA (2000, B-17 – B-20). Activities in the model are represented by zones connected by important links of the public transport and road networks. The temporal dimension of the model is represented by periods of one or more years. For each period the model predicts the intraregional location decisions of industry, residential developers and households, the resulting migration and travel patterns, construction activity and land use development and the impacts of public policies on industrial development, housing, public facilities and transportation. Wegener described his model as a 'simulation' model; however, it is not a microsimulation model in that it does not represent the behaviour of individual agents (travellers, households or employers).

IRPUD consists of six integrated submodels:

1. transportation – facilities and services, including car ownership;
2. ageing of stock variables – population, employment, residential and non-residential buildings;
3. public programmes – land use, housing, non-residential buildings, public facilities, transportation;
4. private construction – investment and locational behaviour of private developers;
5. regional labour market – new hires, redundancies and changes of jobs;
6. regional housing market – intraregional migration decisions of households.

Together, the six submodels form a comprehensive stand-alone model system. The major stock variables of the model are: population, employment, residential buildings and non-residential buildings (industrial and commercial workplaces and public facilities). Actors representing these stocks are individuals or households, workers, housing investors and firms.

These actors interact in five urban submarkets. The submarkets and the market transactions occurring in them are:

1. labour market (new hires and lay-offs);
2. non-residential building market (new firms and firm relocations);
3. housing market (in-migration, out-migration, new households and moves);
4. land and construction market (changes of land use through new construction, modernisation or demolition);
5. travel market (trips) (US EPA, 2000, B-17).

Choice in the submarkets is constrained by supply (jobs, vacant housing, vacant land, vacant industrial or commercial floor space) and guided by attractiveness, which in general terms is an aggregation of neighbourhood quality, accessibility and price.

IRPUD has a modular structure and is solved in a recursive manner on a common spatio-temporal database. The transportation submodel is a network equilibrium model solved for a point in time. All other submodels refer to a calendar time interval. The models are solved sequentially for each period. By making the periods short, such as one year, the interactions among the submarkets occur over time, and are not solved to an equilibrium. IRPUD has been applied in numerous projects funded by the German Research Council, the European Commission and national authorities.

8.6 URBAN GOODS MOVEMENT

Forecasting the movement of urban goods, also known as urban commodity or urban freight transportation, is the neglected step-child of urban personal travel forecasting in the US. An examination of the urban goods movement literature, nevertheless, revealed a small, but committed, group of scholars and practitioners from the mid-1960s onwards. The literature on this subject extended well beyond forecasting to policy, data, regulation and so on. Kenneth Ogden (1992) offered a comprehensive summary. Proceedings of conferences on urban goods transportation between 1973 and 1988 indicated the breadth and depth of this subject (e.g., Chatterjee et al, 1989).

This section overviews the principal contributors and the general approaches to modelling urban goods movement since 1970. Studies before 1970 were described in section 2.5.8. Recent reviews of forecasting methods for urban goods movement were offered by Holguín-Veras et al (2001) and Southworth (2003, 2011). Holguín-Veras et al (2001, 15) noted: 'Standard practices of freight transportation modeling roughly resemble the traditional passenger transportation modeling framework: trip generation, trip distribution, mode split and traffic assignment. . . . For the most part, trip generation, mode split and traffic assignment are conducted using the same techniques as in passenger transportation.'[46]

A principal difference among approaches is whether the model is trip-based or commodity-based. Trip-based models rely on surveys of truck movements, whereas commodity-based models rely on surveys of commodity shipments. Trip-based models assume that the vehicle movement is the unit of demand, rather than the commodity being transported.

Commodity-based models focus on the flows among economic sectors, usually represented by an inter-industry model, and then disaggregate these flows to an appropriate geography. Some reviews state that 'the commodity-based approach should lead to more realistic and robust models' (Giuliano et al, 2010, 75–77). A third modelling approach models the behaviour of individual actors in the logistical supply chain by representing commercial vehicle movements as a multi-stop tour.

A clear analogy with personal travel is apparent. In the traditional approach to modelling personal travel, elements of trip tours, or trips, are aggregated by trip purpose and other attributes of the traveller. The modeller then focuses on the prediction of these trips, without concern for the effect of the larger tour on specific travel choices. In traditional urban goods movement models, aggregate commodity flows among industrial sectors may be represented, but actual shipments are not. Decisions about size and frequency of shipments in relation to inventory, for example, and their effects on choice or type of carrier (private truck, common carrier truck, delivery service, use of multi-modal services, etc.) are suppressed, in the same way as personal and multi-person tours are suppressed.

In response to early interest in urban goods movement, the Highway Research Board organised a conference on urban commodity flow in 1970. The scope of the conference included problem definition, public policy, data requirements, planning process and research and demonstration programmes. The ensuing report embraced the commodity-based approach described above, recommending the development of five separate models for analysing commodity flows (French and Watson, 1971, 135; Hoel, 1971, 7–8):

1. industry network location, in relation to labour, rent, transportation facilities and other factors;
2. inter-industry transactions, to determine outputs of industries and demand for commodities required from other industries;
3. freight flow, to determine the magnitude of commodity flows over the transportation system in relation to industries or traffic zones;
4. choice of means for transporting commodities between industries or traffic zones (analogous to mode choice);
5. network assignment of transported commodities to the transportation system (French and Watson, 1971, 137–138).

These recommendations were ambitious, taking into account short- and long-term perspectives, sequential or simultaneous solution of the models, and micro versus macro concepts of demand for commodities. Recommendations on data noted that urban commodity flow data are severely lacking (Goeller, 1971). No programmes to develop urban commodity flow models were implemented in response to the recommendations.

At the same conference, Charles Hedges characterised similarities and differences between personal urban travel and urban goods movement. The similarities were:

> Both are sensitive to the level of economic activity; both have pronounced peaks during weekdays; except in the most densely-populated cities, both are carried predominately by motor vehicles and frequently over the same rights-of-way; and for both the bulk of the travel occurs during the daylight hours on weekdays.

The differences included:

> Passenger movements usually are two-way (round-trip) movements, while goods movements usually are a series of one-way flows; trip ends for commodities are not as dispersed as those for passengers; trucks, particularly delivery trucks and those with two or more axles, make more trips per day than automobiles; goods movements require more modal interchanges and transfers; documentation is essential in goods movements; and freight data are more difficult to obtain than passenger data (Hedges, 1971, 145).

As with personal travel forecasting, our review emphasises who performed the early studies of urban goods movement and when the work was undertaken. Section 8.6.1 examines early attempts to forecast the movement of urban goods with the vehicle-based approach, which led to the preparation of guidebooks. Section 8.6.2 then examines the commodity-based approach, which is found largely in the academic literature, while section 8.6.3 examines a microsimulation approach.

8.6.1 Evolution of the Vehicle-Based Approach

Urban transportation studies conducted in Detroit and Chicago during the 1950s inventoried truck movements in relation to land uses. So far as can be determined from the study reports, truck movements were not included in the traffic forecasts prepared for the alternative plans. More comprehensive studies of truck movements were performed in the Toronto and New York regions (section 2.7).

Fresko et al (1972) described an urban goods movement forecasting procedure similar to the sequential forecasting procedure for personal travel. They explored 'the distinguishing characteristics between people and goods movement' and sought to identify 'where one could adapt person travel techniques to goods movement'. The difficulties of

identifying requirements for goods from household and industrial activities at the zonal level were addressed. An inter-industry model, as well as
gravity model concepts, was recommended with a frank realisation of the
difficulties and a call for research.

Peter Watson (1972, 1975) initiated research on urban goods movement, performing statistical analyses of trucking activities in relation to
industrial activities. Research plans for the commodity-based approach
were abandoned when Watson accepted a position at the World Bank.
David Zavattero (1974), who had studied with Watson, moved to the
Chicago Area Transportation Study. He characterised an early urban
goods movement forecasting model intended for implementation as
follows: 'In so far as the standard transportation models consider goods
movements at all, they typically assume freight-oriented trips to be some
(constant) proportion of person trips and obtain estimates of commercial
vehicle traffic by applying these trip rates to the previously calculated
person trips' (Zavattero, 1974, 1).

His model followed the conventional generation–distribution–vehicle
loading–assignment concept. Originating and attracted freight flows by
zone were assumed to be related to land use by type and commodity. An
inter-industry structure was envisaged in the manner proposed by the 1970
conference. A gravity model was proposed to distribute shipments from
origins to destinations, resulting in flows from origin zone to destination
zone by land use at the origin and destination, and by commodity type.
Data from a 1970 commercial vehicle survey were available to calibrate
and test the model. Michael Demetsky (1974) also proposed a data collection scheme for urban goods movements in support of similar modelling
proposals.

Arnim Meyburg and Peter Stopher (1974) advanced the case for modelling of urban goods movements by defining the requirements for forecasting and exploring approaches to model development. An important
contribution of their paper was the identification of the consignment, that
is, 'a good or group of goods with a single origin and destination', as the
appropriate unit for data collection, analysis and prediction. They identified the consignment, analogous to the individual traveller, as the basic
unit of analysis. Their proposal differed from surveys of truck movements
at that time, since an individual truck may transport one or many consign-
ments. In two detailed figures, the authors presented their proposal for
'urban freight demand estimation' analogous to the sequential procedure
for modelling personal travel.

The authors noted the substantially additional complexity of the urban
goods movement model: 'intraurban truck movements comprise multiple
collection and delivery operations' so that 'a large part of the vehicle route

may be determined by the location of the collection and delivery points, which leaves little, if any, assignment problem'. What they noted is that the nature of the problem of routeing trucks over the network is radically different from the traditional assignment of person trips by car, and resembles the travelling salesperson problem of finding the shortest route connecting a list of stopping points, perhaps constrained by time window requirements. The authors also stated that the choice of mode and vehicle loading for shipments depends in part upon the delivery travel times and costs, and may require an iterative solution.

Howard Slavin (1976) reported on a detailed demand analysis of urban goods movement. Two aggregate models were estimated on a truck survey for the Boston area. The first model related the density of trip ends (origins plus destinations) to five types of employment densities, population density, the proportion of heavy trucks and a location variable. The second model was a direct demand model of light goods vehicle trips made by food manufacturers within a 16-zone suburban area of Boston. Several functional forms were evaluated. The final form related interzonal aggregate trip density to retail and population zonal densities and a power function of travel time. His findings are interesting because they explored new functional forms.

These research efforts and applications primarily addressed questions related to the production and attraction of truck trips and the estimation of interzonal flows. Related studies by planning agencies, such as in Chicago and New York, emphasised the generation of truck trips in relation to land use. However, these studies did not yet constitute an urban goods movement model. Perhaps the first model to include freight generation, distribution and assignment was proposed and implemented by Frank Southworth and David Zavattero at the Chicago Area Transportation Study. They proposed and tested several innovations. One was an attempt to depict conceptually the circuits that delivery trucks follow in the network from terminal to terminal, in contrast to assigning O-D truck-equivalent commodity flows to shortest routes (Southworth, 1982). A second was a method for restricting truck flows to designated truck routes in a network equilibrium traffic assignment of all road traffic, as one element of a complete motor freight planning model (Southworth et al, 1983a, 1983b). This model sought to provide a tool for locating motor freight terminals of for-hire carriers. In this manner, a contribution to the planning of terminals was undertaken, a significant step beyond the usual estimation of truck traffic on the road network. Southworth subsequently devoted a substantial portion of his career to urban and interregional freight modelling.

Professional practice stemming from these pioneering studies continued during the 1980s and 1990s, leading to the preparation of guidebooks and manuals in the forecasting of urban goods movement. The report of Earl Ruiter [1939–2008] (1992) is a fine example. A guidebook prepared by Cambridge Systematics (1997) was followed a decade later by the quick response manual by Beagan et al (2007).[47]

8.6.2 Development of the Commodity-Based Approach

Building on the proposal of Hedges (1971), several research efforts explored models for forecasting urban goods movements as flows among industry groups, based on inter-industry or input–output analysis. Edwin Mills (1972) proposed an abstract general equilibrium model of urban production, consumption, trade and housing formulated as a relatively abstract linear programming model representing inter-industry flows across a grid of locations. One novel aspect of the model was the inclusion of building densities and land rents. Movements of commodities and persons followed a grid network. Imports into the grid, and exports from it, occurred from the centre, where a harbour or railhead was assumed to be located. Local transportation costs over the grid increased with flow to represent congestion.

T. John Kim (1978) introduced a second mode into Mills's model, a continuous subway system for use by workers. The solution of the linear program yielded an efficient assignment of activities to locations and the efficient use of the transportation system. As a result, it is possible to model the interactions between urban activities (land uses) and transportation systems. The principal objective of the models proposed by Mills and Kim was to gain insights into urban structure and function under the assumption of an efficient allocation of activities to land and the efficient pricing of the transportation systems.

Subsequently, Kim (1989, Chapter 5) and Rho and Kim (1989) sought to make the model more behaviourally realistic, while retaining its novel features regarding the intensity of development. They synthesised the contributions of Leontief and Strout (1963) and Wilson (1970, Chapter 3) by introducing a combined inter-industry and spatial interaction model at the metropolitan level, and incorporating the user-equilibrium route choice principle for both commodities and persons. The resulting nonlinear programming model remained abstract, but had the possibility to be solved on a quasi-realistic network representation and land zoning system. The model was implemented with a 74-zone representation of the Chicago region with four industrial sectors (manufacturing, trades, services and households) and three modes (cars, transit and trucks). The results were described in detail with respect to land use intensity and values, as well as travel.[48]

Genevieve Giuliano and Peter Gordon, and their students, implemented a model for estimating intra-metropolitan freight flows on a road network. The steps of the model were:

1. Estimate commodity-specific interregional and international productions and attractions for those locations where airports, seaports, rail yards or regional highway entry–exit points are located.
2. Utilize a regional input–output transactions table to estimate intraregional commodity-specific trip attractions and trip productions at the level of small-area units.
3. Create regional commodity-specific origin–destination matrices using estimates from steps 1 and 2.
4. Load the O-D matrices on to a regional road network with known passenger (car) flows (Giuliano et al, 2010, 77).

They summarised the implementation of this procedure as follows. Interregional commodity flows in dollars within the Los Angeles five-county metropolitan area (LA), between LA and the remainder of the US, and the remainder of the world, were estimated for 2001 for nine commodities. Using a regional inter-industry matrix and small-area employment data, productions and attractions for the nine commodities corresponding to the interregional flows were estimated for 3203 zones in the LA area. These quantities, converted from annual dollars to daily tons, were used to estimate a single O-D truck matrix with a conventional gravity model. Finally, that truck matrix in car equivalent units was assigned with exogenously provided person flows to the Southern California road network using deterministic network equilibrium assignment. Validation studies were performed using truck counts at screen-lines.

The model, based on widely available data sources, could be applied in scenario analyses of international trade through the large port serving the region, road improvements, road pricing and changes in the location of employment. This model is representative of the approach described in 1971 by Hedges and by French and Watson. As with the vehicle-based approach, it does not attempt to represent the actual delivery routes of trucks over the road network, but rather the zone-to-zone commodity flows implicit in those deliveries.[49]

A final issue concerns the estimation of empty trucks on the road network, known as empty backhauls. Holguín-Veras and Patil (2008, 312) noted empty trucks represent 30 to 40 per cent of all truck trips, and proposed a simple method of estimating these truck flows. Just as the vehicle-based and commodity-based models do not seek to represent the actual truck flows over the network, the movements of empty trucks to and from loading points were not represented in many models; however,

Giuliano et al (2010) included a factor representing these flows. The issue of empty trucks reminds us that modelling urban goods movements is highly complex, and that the current state of practice presents many challenges (section 9.7).

8.6.3   Agent-Based Microsimulation Approach

As in related fields of travel forecasting, agent-based approaches solved with microsimulation were considered relatively recently. Hunt and Stefan (2007) explored a tour-based microsimulation of urban commercial truck movements, based on an unusually detailed data set collected for Calgary, Canada. Although a partial model, as compared with the more comprehensive models described above, modelling of truck tours contributes a dimension that was largely missing in those earlier efforts. Another formulation in the same class models was proposed by Wang and Holguín-Veras (2008).

Donnelly (2009) formulated a more comprehensive model and implemented it with data for the Portland, Oregon region. The resulting model was described as 'a proof of concept of a radically different way of approaching urban freight modeling'. The microsimulation was defined in terms of the firms and households forming a regional economy. The activities of those 'agents' generated commodity flows, made destination and transshipment choices, and generated daily shipments, carriers and vehicles, which are allocated to trucks and itineraries for delivery. Those itineraries in turn determined the truck flows assigned to the road network.

8.7   CONCLUSION

The traditional travel forecasting approach to the preparation of long-range metropolitan transportation plans continues much in the way it began in the 1950s. Specific models comprising the sequential procedure have improved, but the basic approach is unchanged:

1. reliance on a cross-sectional, weekday forecast of travel over one or more hypothesised networks for a single target year;
2. representation of the demand for travel as actions of individuals, largely unconstrained by their daily schedules, household requirements and timing during the day;
3. static representation of the time and cost of travel, in which individual trips compete for scarce capacity on road and public transport

networks, but do not actually experience the timing consequences of those choices in terms of the congestion resulting from them;

4. disregard for the long-term evolution of the metropolitan land use and activity system with respect to its adjustment to congestion, the monetary cost of travel and externalities produced (e.g., emissions, accidents, noise).

A major review of this process (TRB, 2007) suggested relatively marginal refinements. The main tradition of practice was unchallenged, and may be expected to continue in a 'business as usual' manner. In Chapter 11, we present our thinking for changes in this direction.

An effort to invent a new approach to travel forecasting, unprecedented in scale and resources provided, TRANSIMS, has not impacted long-term travel forecasting practice as was hoped. The history of this effort was described in detail, with the hope that lessons may still be learned from this experience. Few reports from the project are available online or in print to document what occurred.

Other efforts to creating new kinds of forecasting models occurred on the basis of grass-roots efforts. Among these are efforts of a few innovative staff members and their consultants to create tour-based and activity-based models. While this is still a work in progress, we are impressed with their commitment and findings. The same positive appreciation may be offered to those few individuals devoted to modelling land use and urban goods movements.

We call attention to what has not been attempted since 1980, by which time a fairly mature understanding of demand and network models had been achieved. Despite the surveys performed, the measurements and data collection on the transportation system operation, as well as efforts of the US Census, little is known empirically about short- or long-term trends in urban travel by mode or trends in utilisation of road and public transport systems. Suppose one wanted to examine long-term trends in travel for a sample of major metropolitan areas: number of weekday trips by mode, person-hours and vehicle-miles of travel by car, vehicle-miles of travel for trucks, passenger-hours of travel by public transport, car availability and occupancy, public transport load factors, and so on. Few MPOs have data available on such trends. Moreover, trends for subregions and periods of the day do not exist. Yet we claim to evaluate proposals for the improvement and operation of these systems in future decades. We return to these issues in section 11.5.2.

NOTES

1. The Detroit and Chicago transportation studies used the term 'target year' to designate a future year in which the population, employment and related forecasts would probably occur. The precise year was not considered to be as important as the level of activities represented by the forecasts (Detroit Metropolitan Area Traffic Study, 1956, 15; Chicago Area Transportation Study, 1960, 3).
2. Thomas Lisco (1967) served earlier as transportation economist at the Chicago Area Transportation Study, following completion of his Ph.D. in economics on the value of travel time.
3. This section draws on a detailed analysis by Garrett and Wachs (1996).
4. en.wikipedia.org/wiki/Catalytic_converter (accessed 17 December 2013).
5. A State Implementation Plan is a specific plan to attain the standards for each area designated to be in violation (nonattainment) of National Ambient Air Quality Standards. www.epa.gov/oar/urbanair/sipstatus/index.html (accessed 9 February 2014).
6. www.fhwa.dot.gov/environment/air_quality/ (accessed 4 June 2014).
7. The lawsuit also led to the report *Expanding Metropolitan Highways* (Transportation Research Board, TRB, 1995).
8. www.fhwa.dot.gov/environment/air_quality/conformity/guide/basicguide2010.pdf (accessed 8 October 2013); the 2005 version of the guide is found at www.ampo.org/assets/25_bguide05.pdf (accessed 9 October 2013).
9. Title 40: Protection of Environment, Part 93 – Determining Conformity of Federal Actions to State or Federal Implementation Plans, Subpart A – Conformity to State or Federal Implementation Plans of Transportation Plans, Programs, and Projects Developed, Funded or Approved under Title 23 U.S.C. or the Federal Transit Laws, Electronic Code of Federal Regulations, ecfr.gpoaccess.gov/ (accessed 7 October 2013).
10. Frederick Ducca, discussions with David Boyce.
11. Rule Criteria for Determining Conformity to State or Federal Implementation Plans of Transportation Plans, Programs, and Projects Funded or Approved under Title 23 U.S.C. or the Federal Transit Act, Final Rule, Federal Register, 24 November 1993.
12. TMIP now has two websites: www.fhwa.dot.gov/planning/tmip/ and tmiponline.org/ (accessed 30 August 2013).
13. Their responses were summarised by Bruce Spear (1996).
14. Peer review reports were posted at www.fhwa.dot.gov/planning/tmip/publications/peer_review_reports/ (accessed 3 October 2013).
15. www.fta.dot.gov/documents/Release_FY11_Reporting_Instructions.pdf (accessed 7 October 2013).
16. The procedures are quoted verbatim from US DoT (2009, 14–15) except for minor editorial changes.
17. www.fta.dot.gov/documents/Discussion_11_Summit_Example_Calcs.xls (accessed 7 October 2013).
18. The data sources for their analyses were the 1995 Nationwide Personal Transportation Survey, the 2001 National Household Travel Survey and the 1990 and 2000 decennial censuses.
19. Christopher Barrett was director, Network Dynamics and Simulation Science Laboratory, and professor, Virginia Bioinformatics Institute and Department of Computer Science, Virginia Tech, Blacksburg, Virginia (www.vbi.vt.edu/faculty/personal/Christopher_Barrett, accessed 8 February 2014).
20. NCHRP Synthesis 406 (Donnelly et al, 2010, 15–16) describes how TRANSIMS began.
21. Frederick Ducca, personal interview with David Boyce, January 2011.
22. www.pti.psu.edu/larsonBio, www.pti.psu.edu/news-detail.php?ID=50 (accessed 31 August 2013).

23. Morrison and Loose (1995), TRANSIMS Model Design Criteria as Derived from Federal Legislation, ntl.bts.gov/DOCS/462.html (accessed 7 October 2013).
24. Intel Corporation's fifth generation microarchitecture, first released under the Pentium brand in March 1993, and its predecessors were in widespread use in travel forecasting practice at the time of this statement. Faster processors were offered by Sun Microsystems or its competitors, such as the Sun SPARC series, 1989–95, followed by the Sun Ultra series, 1995–2001 (en.wikipedia.org/wiki/Comparison_of_CPU_architectures, accessed 7 October 2013). See Figure 10.1 for a comparison of processing speeds. In related documents, LANL described high-speed networks of engineering workstations, which are now common for PCs.
25. en.wikipedia.org/wiki/Nagel-Schreckenberg_model (accessed 9 February 2014). Carlos Daganzo (1994) on the cell transmission model included references to Nagel's model among others.
26. Frederick Ducca described the status of the Portland Case Study in a presentation dated 8 September 2005, at the time work was suspended.
27. media.tmiponline.org/clearinghouse/issue_paper/issue_paper.pdf (accessed 8 October 2013).
28. www.fhwa.dot.gov/publications/publicroads/00marapr/transims.cfm (accessed 10 February 2014).
29. TRANSIMS Open Source, code.google.com/p/transims/ (accessed 28 March 2014).
30. www.tracc.anl.gov/index.php/transportation-research/transportation-systems-modeling (accessed 28 March 2014). The description of TRANSIMS activities in the text is no longer available on the TRACC website.
31. Hubert Ley, discussion with David Boyce, 4 October 2013.
32. Use of TRANSIMS open source may continue; however, a Google web search did not verify this conjecture.
33. For websites related to MATSim, see: www.matsim.org/; www.vsp.tu-berlin.de/publications/; and www.ivt.ethz.ch/vpl/publications (all accessed 29 September 2013).
34. www.trb.org/Main/Blurbs/169685.aspx (accessed 5 November 2014).
35. www.trb.org/Main/Blurbs/170759.aspx, www.trb.org/main/blurbs/170877.aspx (accessed 5 November 2014).
36. 14th TRB National Transportation Planning Applications Conference, Columbus, OH, 2013, www.trbappcon.org/program.aspx (accessed 30 September 2013).
37. Stephen Putman's research leading to DRAM/EMPAL was supported by contracts from US DoT to the University of Pennsylvania. His report *Integrated Transportation and Land Use Forecasting: Sensitivity Tests of Alternative Model Systems Configuration*, Travel Model Improvement Program, US DoT, is available at ntl.bts.gov/lib/18000/18300/18370/PB2001108460.pdf (accessed 7 January 2013).
38. www.epa.gov/reva/docs/ProjectingLandUseChange.pdf (accessed 13 October 2013).
39. ntl.bts.gov/lib/18000/18300/18370/PB2001108460.pdf (accessed 7 January 2013).
40. en.wikipedia.org/wiki/UrbanSim (accessed 8 October 2013). Development of UrbanSim was supported in the US by grants from the National Science Foundation, the Environmental Protection Agency and the Federal Highway Administration, as well as states, MPOs and research councils in Europe and South Africa.
41. www.urbansim.org (accessed 8 October 2013).
42. Boyce and Mattsson (1999) applied a similar approach to reformulate Lars-Göran Mattsson's integrated model of residential and employment location (IMREL); see Anderstig and Mattsson (1991).
43. The maximum memory available to the user on the IBM System/370 was 512 KB. The memory required to hold the integer-valued trip matrix in memory was at least 400 KB. Therefore, all trip matrix computations were performed row by row or column by column. For comparison, an off-the-shelf desktop computer purchased in 2012, and used to write this book, has a memory of 8 GB, or about 16000 times 512 KB.
44. www.nymtc.org/project/BPM/model/bpm_finalrpt.pdf (accessed 8 October 2013).

45. www.spiekermann-wegener.com/mod/pdf/AP_1101_IRPUD_Model.pdf (accessed 2 April 2014).
46. www.utrc2.org/research/assets/6/regionalfreight1.html (accessed 9 April 2012).
47. ops.fhwa.dot.gov/freight/publications/qrfm2/qrfm.pdf (accessed 10 October 2013).
48. Jeong H. Rho implemented a similar model for Seoul, Korea.
49. Oppenheim (1993b) proposed a related model incorporating network equilibrium concepts (section 7.4.4.5).

9. Tradition and innovation in UK practice

9.1 INTRODUCTION

In this chapter we describe some of the major developments in urban travel forecasting practice in the UK over the past 30 years, with particular emphasis on recent times. This review examines the refinement of traditional methods as well as significant innovations. The coverage is wide-ranging, but as in Chapter 8 it is necessarily selective. We intend to give a flavour of developments in a country with, according to Shepherd et al (2006b, 313), 'a strong culture of transport modelling', albeit one exhibiting wide variations in practice. We do not intend to offer a detailed history, description or critique of modelling practice – tasks undertaken by others (as we discuss below in this section) – but to introduce significant developments and the motivation for them.

We adopt terminology in widespread use in UK practice. In agreement with British usage, we describe travel forecasts as the product of a 'transport model' or 'multi-stage model', in contrast to the 'multi-step procedure' or 'sequential procedure' terminology commonly found in US practice. In US practice, a 'model' generally refers to an individual step of the procedure, such as the 'trip distribution model'. In section 9.4, 'scheme' refers to a specific project proposed for consideration.

Reports and reviews on transportation planning practice are usually subject to a range of caveats; we mention three at this stage. Firstly, circumstances can change fairly rapidly, and descriptions of particular travel forecasting models can soon become dated as refinements and upgrades are made. Secondly, this comment also applies to the status of advice and guidance emanating from the UK Department for Transport (UK DfT) as its documentation passes from consultative through to definitive status, and is subject to updating. Thirdly, because of the need to respect client confidentiality, some innovative material simply does not reach wider circulation among professional or academic audiences. Our discussion, therefore, mentions few specific studies, but emphasises distinct points of theory and method, and comparative issues, where these exist, and their significance in our story so far.

As noted in Chapter 3, in the early days of the discipline, the UK followed where the US led. That period, which included the 1960s and early
1970s, was one of considerable build-up of expertise in urban travel forecasting. It was also a time of innovation in technical and theoretical development in some UK universities, the larger consultancies and government
agencies. We emphasised the key role that the Mathematical Advisory Unit
(MAU) played in an extraordinary period of innovation in the mid-1960s,
and we claimed that the SELNEC 'mathematical model', which implemented numerous important advances, was one of the most sophisticated
in the world at that time. That early momentum foundered, and a relative
decline of modelling capability set in for a variety of reasons: (a) closure of
the MAU; (b) change of governments in 1970 and 1979; (c) abolition of the
Greater London Council and metropolitan county councils; (d) the privatisation and deregulation agenda of the early 1980s; (e) increasing scarcity
of funding; (f) a further wave of antipathy towards large-scale models; and
even (g) some scepticism towards the deployment of economics and the
scientific method to guide policy and decision making. The role, extent and
continued relevance of such factors are still matters of opinion and debate.

In the late 1970s and 1980s, 'comprehensive' urban transportation
modelling initiatives in the UK were infrequently requested. The financial
stringencies of this period resulted in the dissipation of expertise from
local authorities, which were under pressure to 'out-source' specialist services.[1] Privatisation of local public transport services and local authority
out-sourcing changed the need for multi-modal urban models into more
project-specific models for a more dispersed set of problems and clients.
While many authorities retained the level of technical skills required for
minor transportation design and some planning functions, most of the
larger tasks were increasingly undertaken by the private sector. Here
national and international consultancies, sometimes acting as consortia,
were more than able to apply traditional forecasting methods for personal
travel and goods movement, and undertake their refinement and further
development. The UK would not, however, witness the level of ambition
that occurred at the cutting edge of practice in the US, or in some European
countries, notably the Netherlands, particularly in regard to developments
at the micro-level of tour-based and activity-based analyses of personal
travel. Although there were many disaggregate studies of modal choice in
various contexts, and a number of UK studies which adopted tour-based
representations (e.g., the Greater Manchester Strategy Planning Model
and the Leeds Transport Model), we note only one major conurbation-
wide application of a tour-based travel demand model estimated with
disaggregate data and methods (PRISM, section 9.5.2) and one using
activity-based modelling techniques (section 9.5.2).

It is worth emphasising again, as in Chapter 1, that the contexts of urban travel forecasting are very wide-ranging. We stress the generic nature of modelling within the cross-sectional approach. We refer to a number of reviews and reports into the nature and form of UK transportation models conducted during this period: Webster et al (1988); Standing Advisory Committee on Trunk Road Assessment (SACTRA) (1994, 1999); Bly et al (2001, 2002); WSP et al (2002); Bates et al (2003); MVA (2005); Shepherd et al (2006a, 2006b); Coombe (2009a); and other reports prepared for or by UK DfT. Some reviews were specifically related to the theoretical underpinnings and analytic content of models; others were closely related to the world of practice, exploring particular features of forecasting models across several studies; and yet others examined the extent to which the methods of demand analysis and forecasting embodied the guidelines or advice laid down or proposed by UK DfT.

In section 9.2 we describe in more detail some of the contexts within which travel forecasting has been conducted in the UK. Without attempting to evaluate its impact, we also discuss the nature and role of official advice and guidance emanating from UK DfT and its predecessors, particularly in the last 15 years or so.[2] To avoid confusion for the reader not familiar with changes in the organisation and governance of the UK transportation sector, we simply refer to the UK Department for Transport, or simply 'the Department', as the central government body responsible for that sector, although references will cite the name of the specific department existing at any particular time.

In section 9.3 we review some of the innovations that occurred in transportation network modelling. In particular, we consider specialised assignment models developed to incorporate traveller and traffic behaviour at a higher level of spatial and temporal resolution. We describe some aspects of the commercial software systems SATURN and CONTRAM, and note their origin and development. We then note the increasing popularity of microsimulation approaches for more intricate applications in both road and public transport systems analysis.

Although the deliberations of the Standing Advisory Committee on Trunk Road Assessment relate to road developments predominantly outside or on the periphery of urban areas, there are four reasons why we must consider SACTRA's influential 1994 report:

1. In the late 1980s, concerns were expressed about whether new and improved roads led to significantly more 'generated' traffic and travel than anticipated; the consequences for forecasting and evaluating its effects under congested conditions were being questioned.

2. Related to the above, the adequacy of simplified methods of appraisal and, in particular, those based on the 'fixed demand' or 'fixed matrix' approximation (section 7.4.2) came under particular scrutiny at that time.
3. The report and its findings had important implications for future research on travel demand and particularly for model structures and elasticities for both highway assessment and policy appraisal more generally.
4. The methods discussed in the report are directly related to the central issues of Chapter 7, namely the specification and solution of equilibrium models and the 'laws of traffic' embodied within them.

In section 9.4 we summarise the background, objectives, main findings and legacy of the 1994 SACTRA report *Trunk Roads and the Generation of Traffic*.

In section 9.5 we focus in more detail on those variously described multi-step, multi-stage, multi-level or hierarchical travel forecasting procedures based on the nested logit model, which by the 1990s had become the international 'work-horse' of travel demand studies (Ortúzar, 2001). We consider the widely applied UK practice of implementing the nested logit model in 'incremental' or 'pivot-point' form and the structures and parameters that accompanied its use, and note the state of the art of disaggregate modelling in the UK. From the extensive documentation of official UK DfT guidance and advice, we also sample some aspects relating to the specification, calibration, equilibration, validation and use of multi-stage models.

As in the US, two areas in which significant compromises are usually made between technical sophistication and practical considerations concern the development of integrated land use – transportation models and the forecasting of urban and regional goods movement. In sections 9.6 and 9.7, we examine the circumstances that encouraged their development and refinement. We consider the particularly successful land use models that originated at the Martin Centre, University of Cambridge, and the work of small consultancies and researchers associated with it.

The chapter concludes with a brief assessment of the developments and states of practice in the UK.

9.2 EVOLVING REQUIREMENTS FOR URBAN TRAVEL FORECASTING AND APPRAISAL

9.2.1 The Context

We shall refer to many model developments and specific reviews of model applications that accompanied the planning of urban and regional transportation projects and policies dating back to the early 1980s. Our main focus, however, is on applications during the past two decades, especially those resulting from the initiatives of the New Labour Government elected in 1997. In particular, we draw on three reports of modelling and appraisal studies in order to derive information and insights on the range of methods adopted for particular purposes, as well as specific technical issues, and the practical compromises involved in travel forecasting. The contexts of studies by Bates et al (2003), Shepherd et al (2006b) and Coombe (2009a) are important and are noted briefly. All contain interesting reviews of models and methods and comments on their application.

Bates et al (2003) was an assessment of the conduct of the so-called 'multi-modal studies' (MMS) initiated in 1999. These studies were meant to analyse and propose solutions for addressing problems on particular parts of the trunk road network suffering from 'severe transportation stress'. A key requirement was that they should develop packages of projects and interventions adopting a wide range of policy instruments. The studies were diverse in nature; six of the 17 were specifically associated with conurbations or the periphery of major urban areas, including Tyneside, South-East Manchester, West Midlands and areas around London. Other studies were mainly concerned with inter-urban corridors, but contained parts of conurbations or large towns.

To achieve a broadly common approach, the methods that supported this initiative were subject to central government advice, *Guidance on the Methodology for Multi-Modal Studies* (UK Department of the Environment, Transport and the Regions, DETR, 2000), better known by the (most unattractive) acronym GOMMMS. The advice was quite detailed in its appraisal procedures (see below), but 'generally extremely non-prescriptive on the modelling detail' (Bates et al, 2003, 9), which allowed considerable discretion on the part of the professionals involved. Each MMS involved teams of prominent UK-based consultants and was conducted over about two years. In terms of the requirements to acquire suitable information, develop appropriate models, and test and evaluate a wide variety of policies and plans, the consultants were under 'massive pressure . . . to handle this volume of demanding work' (Bates et al, 2003, 6). As we note below (section 9.5.1), these conditions had an important influence on the approaches adopted for travel forecasting.

In order to address transportation issues at the local level, in 2000 the New Labour Government instituted a ten-year programme built around five-year integrated transportation strategies. Local authorities in England (outside London) were encouraged to put integrated transportation planning into practice with greater emphasis on public transport, cycling and walking. Local transport plans (LTPs) were the instruments by which authorities would put forward bids for capital spending, and were submitted by authorities of widely differing size and urban geography. As with the multi-modal studies, the initial guidance in relation to modelling was not detailed, although it was considered that the advice pertaining to large schemes, greater than £5 million, was sufficient.

Anthony May and his colleagues at the Institute for Transport Studies (ITS), University of Leeds, have conducted a large amount of research on the generation and evaluation of urban transportation plans and policies, and associated methods for improved decision making, along with barriers to their implementation, over the past two decades (Shepherd et al, 2006b; May and Matthews, 2007; May et al, 2008; May, 2013). The study by Shepherd et al (2006b) is particularly revealing about the range of analytic procedures adopted and attitudes towards modelling in UK local authorities; we draw on this publication in the following discussion.

The authors reviewed and conducted accompanying interviews on the modelling approaches used in the first round of LTPs.[3] Unsurprisingly, given the variation in the size and composition of the authorities, travel forecasting was found to be considerably more sophisticated in those areas where consortia of authorities could utilise existing or recently applied models, such as Greater Manchester and West Yorkshire. To assess the various forecasting methods adopted and their particular context of application, Shepherd et al (2006b, 310) developed a hierarchy, listed in Table 9.1, which includes no quantitative model (1) and linked land use – transportation models (9). We note aspects from this table in later discussion (section 9.3.1). This paper contained many interesting comments on the complexity of models and the world of practice, and included what must be regarded as a core belief of the travel forecasting community:

In most circumstances, methodologies further up the hierarchy are more expensive to develop, mainly because of greater data collection costs. However, with respect to the estimation of travel demand, they typically generate more accurate forecasts than models lower down in the hierarchy. . . . There is thus a trade-off between accuracy and cost. As a general principle to help resolve this trade-off, high cost models can be justified for situations where the potential

Table 9.1 *Hierarchy of modelling methodologies used to support local transport planning in the UK*

1.	No quantitative model – purely qualitative estimates (perhaps relying on expert judgement or previous results)
2.	Simple cost-based – add financial costs to (1)
3.	Spreadsheet model
4.	Sketch planning model
5.	Network assignment model in isolation without elastic assignment
6.	Network assignment model in isolation with elastic assignment
7.	Network assignment model in conjunction with external demand/mode choice model
8.	Four-stage model
9.	Land use – transportation interaction (LUTI) model
10.	Strategic transport/environment model

Source: Derived from Shepherd et al (2006b, 310).

costs and benefits of the schemes or plans are large, but not for smaller schemes or plans (Shepherd et al, 2006b, 310).

In preparation for the second round of LTPs, UK DfT (2004) published a report by the team at the University of Leeds that discussed the applicability of various forecasting models and methods to authorities of different types.

In contrast to the reports by Bates et al (2003) and Shepherd et al (2006b), which addressed the methods actually applied in specific planning or policy initiatives, that by Coombe (2009a) assessed the readiness and modelling capability to support the Department's approach to long-term regional transportation planning (its Delivering a Sustainable Transport System or DaSTS initiative) based on policies, packages and major schemes. Coombe's review focused on the characteristics and applicability of 30 transportation models, many of these having been put forward by consortia of authorities, centred on subregions, conurbation(s) and key urban areas. Coombe's study gave particular attention to the degree of compliance with official advice, the identification of what was considered to be best practice, and suggestions about how modelling capabilities could be improved.

These three studies, Bates et al (2003), Shepherd et al (2006b) and Coombe (2009a), touched on many of the essential aspects of model development: (a) model complexity; (b) the large diversity of methods applied for travel forecasting; and (c) attitudes towards maintaining databases and forecasting capabilities. Between them, the studies considered travel forecasting for a wide range of policy instruments, including: (a) land use policies; (b) highway projects; (c) heavy rail, modern bus, tram and light rail transport (LRT) systems; (d) highway capacity reallocation; (e) central area parking and park-and-ride proposals; (f) road pricing schemes of varying description; (g) priority for 'slow modes' (bicycle and walk); and increasingly (h) a range of policies to promote 'smart travel choices'. We shall draw comments on these at different points in the chapter.

A few remarks about London are relevant here. By virtue of its sheer size, the extent and intensity of its transportation problems, the nature of travel demand in the city, the range of public transport options, the distinct organisation and control of public transport, and its urban governance,[4] London is a special case among UK cities. Unlike most other conurbations and urban areas, almost continuous transportation model development has occurred in London since the early 1960s. As in many great cities of the world, a large number of proposals relating to urban development, large investment projects across several modes, traffic restraint schemes and so on are under constant test, revision and possible abandonment. We mention a number of forecasting models for the whole or parts of London, including: (a) conventional four-stage multi-modal models, London Transportation Studies 1981 (LTS81) and London Transportation Studies 1991 (LTS91); (b) a strategic model developed to test road pricing policies; and (c) an innovative goods movement model.

The delegation of powers to the Mayor of London following 2000 gave significant authority to this office, which was considered crucial in establishing in 2003 the largest congestion charging scheme in the world; see Richards (2006) for a discussion of the policy and its impact. Transport for London (TfL), the authority responsible for ground transportation modes relevant to travel within the city, has performed a wide variety of modelling exercises with a range of transportation modelling software systems in support of the Mayor's strategy for the city.

9.2.2   Travel Forecasting and Appraisal at the UK Department for Transport

Since the 1960s, UK DfT and its predecessors have played a significant role in the provision of advice for the analysis, and particularly the evaluation, of transportation proposals to be applied in different contexts. Much of the detailed development work on appraisal of the economic and environmental effects was originally undertaken in relation to the evaluation of highway schemes. Over the years, and particularly since the early 1980s, there has been a concerted attempt to develop a unified evaluation framework to be applied without bias to projects and policies involving all modes, and incorporating a wide range of impacts.

Accompanying the multi-modal studies, UK DfT introduced the 'new approach to appraisal' (NATA), which has been continuously updated, and remains 'the corner stone of transport appraisal practice' (UK DfT, 2009a, 2009b).[5] NATA drew together and extended prior work on appraisal and is a form of a multi-criteria analysis with impacts relating to five government objectives (environment, safety, economy, accessibility and integration). These impacts are expressed through qualitative and/or quantitative indicators. Where it was considered theoretically convincing and practically feasible, several of these were expressed in monetary form. The framework, and its presentation and summary on a single sheet of paper were designed to counter a widely perceived potential bias in favour of those factors that could be quantified and, in particular, monetary components of the economic appraisal.

The quantification of time savings and its variation over different segments of the travel market remains at the heart of the appraisal process and is subject to periodic updating (Mackie et al, 2001, 2003). As noted in Chapter 5, since the 1990s the influence of travel time reliability on individual decisions and the contribution of changes in this attribute to project appraisal became important issues of research and practice in the UK (see, for example, Bates et al, 2001; Noland and Polak, 2002; UK DfT, 2009b).

The wider work on appraisal and forecasting by the Department (UK DfT, 2012) has included: (a) forecasting growth in transportation use; (b) assessing the impact of transportation using strategic models developed in-house; (c) developing and supporting methods for impact assessment of transportation improvements; and (d) setting the framework, and producing and supporting software for assessing whether transportation projects are good value for money. To these ends, a number of tools have been provided to assist those undertaking modelling and appraisal, including:

1. data sources, such as the trip-end model presentation program TEMPro, which provided forecasts of travel demand at a detailed geographical level;[6]
2. advice and guidance on modelling and appraisal known as webTAG;
3. a national transport model;
4. a programme of research work on modelling, appraisal and evaluation.

In seeking to promote 'robust decision making' founded on a sound evidence base, UK DfT and its predecessors for some years have provided guidance and advice to local authorities and consultants on travel forecasting and appraisal of projects and policies. Much of this support has occurred over the last 15 years or so, and is under continual development and updating. Since 2003 different sources have been brought together in the web-based 'Transportation Analysis and Guidance' (webTAG) documentation, which built on earlier publications, particularly GOMMMS (UK DETR, 2000) and the *Design Manual for Roads and Bridges* (UK DoT, 1997). webTAG grew into an extensive interconnected set of documents at various stages of refinement that range in content between the rather non-committal or partial to the highly prescriptive. With regard to the status of the information in webTAG, 'The guidance should be seen as a requirement for all projects/studies that require government approval. For projects/studies that do not require government approval TAG should serve as a best practice guide' (UK DfT, 2011a).

In the evolution of webTAG, UK DfT sought a balance between standardisation in content and promoting consistency of methods among different areas of the UK, while seeking to accommodate local variation (in context, data capabilities, etc.). The general approach to modelling and appraisal has been reinforced many times, and is probably best captured in the following:

> the quality of an appraisal should not be judged by the size of its traffic model, nor by its apparent sophistication, but by the efficiency with which it can provide the information needed to make and justify decisions. The use of more sophisticated methods can only be justified if they provide a significant reduction in the risk of wrong decisions being made and the appraisal itself provides good value for money (UK DoT, 1997, 2/1, para 2.5).

Although expressed over 15 years ago in the context of highway appraisal, this basic philosophy describes the current approach and underpins the official advice offered. Perhaps the reliance on incremental improvements in methodology can best be described in terms of a 'cost–benefit' analysis of the modelling process itself. It was this emphasis on the design of models – if changes are to be made, they only should be sufficient to match the sophistication of the modelling to the complexity of the policy and the significance of its impact, and the resources required – that permeated the advice given to practitioners by UK DfT.

Much of the advice provided by the Department relates to basic modelling methodology founded on generic concepts. From a strictly theoretical viewpoint, the advice on urban travel demand forecasting, for example, draws heavily on discrete choice random utility modelling and is specifically related to the appropriate application of the multinomial and nested logit models.

9.3 DEVELOPMENTS IN NETWORK MODELLING

9.3.1 The Quest for Greater Detail

At the international level, several travel forecasting software systems link road and public transport network analyses (assignment) with travel demand models. Most have been under development for many years. The report by UK DfT (2006b) observed that the most widely used travel forecasting systems were TRIPS, now part of the Citilabs' CUBE software system, INRO's Emme, and PTV's VISEM and VISUM. The history and characteristics of these software systems are described in Chapter 10.

In the case of public transport networks, differences in specifications gave rise to a range of specialist assignment models that address particular features of the services along fixed lines. Such differences, sometimes subtle, exist in relation to: (a) definition of generalised costs; (b) treatment of multi-modal options, incorporation of taste variation and limited knowledge; (c) path building and selection; and (d) allocation to services at the assignment stage. A detailed comparison of the characteristics and functionality of eight commercial public transport systems was conducted by UK DfT (2006b, section 14) on the basis of their treatment of: (a) walk access, egress, transfer and waiting times; (b) fare structures; (c) crowding effects; (d) treatment of common lines and identification of acceptable paths; (e) assignment methods (frequency-based/schedule-based; stochastic/deterministic); (f) definition of composite costs over several paths; and (g) data input, output and graphical capabilities. Data sources to calibrate, validate and, where crowding effects are relevant, equilibrate such models are discussed in this report.

Two specialised highway network analysis models gained considerable appeal. Development of SATURN (simulation and assignment of traffic in urban road networks) and CONTRAM (continuous traffic model) began in the late 1970s, and evolved in contrasting ways. SATURN developed from link-based traffic equilibrium assignment to cater to more complex and realistic simulation of traffic behaviour at selected junctions (see also section 10.5.2.1). CONTRAM broadened from a detailed junction analysis to a general network analysis tool that included route choice and traffic simulation with dynamic queuing at intersections. One of the defining features of both systems is their functionality to model flow metering and 'blocking back'.

SATURN was introduced by Dirck Van Vliet, Luis Willumsen, Michael Hall and John Bolland as 'a modern assignment model' (Hall et al, 1980; Van Vliet, 1982). Van Vliet, a former physicist trained at McGill and Cambridge universities, had been responsible for highway assignment at the Greater London Transportation Study (GLTS) before moving to the Institute for Transport Studies at the University of Leeds in 1974. From his experience with GLTS networks, Van Vliet was well aware of the need for the large area-wide link-based equilibrium assignments. In certain applications, the need for greater precision and detail was clear, particularly for the analysis of relatively small-scale traffic management schemes requiring detailed modelling of vehicle behaviour at junctions (intersections).

SATURN provided these twin functions within a combined representation. It enabled area-wide network modelling within state-of-the-art equilibrium assignments based on optimisation techniques. Through a 'windowing function', it could represent and model a subset of junctions in more detail. Here, the build-up and dispersal of queues were treated by simulation using a platoon dispersal model similar to that in TRANSYT (Robertson, 1969), the signal coordination software developed at the UK Road Research Laboratory. With his colleagues Luis Willumsen, Michael Hall and John Bolland, who had academic backgrounds in transportation engineering, mathematics and operational research, respectively, Van Vliet developed SATURN into a traffic assignment model used extensively for network planning, exploring the local traffic implications of urban development projects, and traffic management purposes (e.g., one-way streets, changes in junction control, bus-only streets). A long-standing partnership of the Institute for Transport Studies and WS Atkins, which distributed the software, as well as contributing to its development, was important to the successful deployment of SATURN.

An attractive feature of SATURN was its very early use of methods for matrix estimation derived from traffic counts on links (including turning movements) for deriving least biased (or maximum likelihood) estimates of those matrices. This innovation included the possibility of using prior trip information as a means of breathing fresh life into ageing O-D matrices. Luis Willumsen, who also made a major contribution to the early conceptual development of SATURN, created the program ME2 (matrix estimation by maximum entropy) for estimating the most probable trip matrix consistent with: (a) any prior trip matrix, (b) independent information provided by traffic counts, and (c) assumptions underpinning the user-equilibrium assignments (Willumsen, 1978, 1981; Van Zuylen and Willumsen, 1980). Over the years this approach has been widely applied in the UK. A full discussion of the method is given by Ortúzar and Willumsen (2011, section 12.4).

Progressively, SATURN was refined and extended to include: (a) improved representations of vehicle behaviour; (b) stratifications on the demand side to include multiple user classes and time periods (Van Vliet et al, 1986); (c) demand-responsive assignment (Hall et al, 1992; Bates et al, 1999); and (d) multi-modal capabilities (Willumsen et al, 1993). Following the official response to the SACTRA report of 1994, applications of SATURN with elastic demand models for highway project appraisal became widespread (see Table 9.1).

Apart from its role in many transportation studies internationally, SATURN also became a framework for theoretical analysis, computational investigations, and network design experimentation. Several successful research studies at ITS were based on SATURN, including: (a) algorithms for efficient solution of equilibrium assignments (Arezki and Van Vliet, 1990); (b) combined optimal signal setting and reassignment (Van Vliet et al, 1987); (c) detailed junction representations for forecasting energy consumption and emissions generation in networks (Ferreira, 1981; Matzoros and Van Vliet, 1992); and (d) economic and environmental effects of induced traffic in networks with and without road pricing (Williams et al, 2001a, 2001b). SATURN was also applied to investigations of the design and impact of novel road charging instruments (May and Milne, 2004). Furthermore, SATURN was linked to the microsimulation model DRACULA (dynamic route assignment combining user learning and microsimulation), under development at ITS since 1993 (Liu et al, 1995, 2006). Development, maintenance and support of SATURN by Dirck Van Vliet are ongoing.[7]

While the development of SATURN was largely an academic effort, CONTRAM (Leonard and Tough, 1979; Taylor, 2003) began its life at the UK Transport Research Laboratory (formerly the UK Road Research Laboratory and UK Transport and Road Research Laboratory). This former government agency, which was privatised in 1996, established over many years a formidable international reputation for the development of software for junction design, signal optimisation and coordination, and urban traffic control (including PICADY, ARCADY, OSCADY, TRANSYT and SCOOT). As a specialised dynamic assignment model, CONTRAM modelled time-varying demand and congestion by combining multiple time slices of the trip matrix and route choice behavioural rules with the dynamic build-up and decay of queues at junctions, which were modelled in detail. The time-dependent queuing relationships were consistent with those in ARCADY (roundabouts), PICADY (priority intersections) and OSCADY (signals). In this way dynamic assignment of trips based on time-varying demand could readily accommodate the treatment of journeys extending over several time slices, which allowed over-capacity periods to be rigorously treated. Suitably specified and furnished with required data for time-dependent trip matrices, CONTRAM spanned the requirements for testing policies and projects within transportation planning, demand management and traffic control, including the effects of driver information systems and real-time traffic control.[8]

9.3.2 The Growing Popularity of Microsimulation

Microsimulation has long been used for solution of stochastic queuing problems at uncontrolled and signal-controlled junctions for detailed design. Beginning in the 1980s computational power became sufficient to handle larger configurations involving a network of junctions. Thereafter, in the UK and elsewhere, great interest developed in this approach by local authorities and consultants as a means of addressing a wide range of problems relating to infrastructure design, traffic management and control measures.

The approach involved increasingly sophisticated behavioural models of individual agents (some or all of car and truck drivers, public transport vehicles, cyclists and pedestrians) as they interact with each other and their physical environment and respond to detailed regulation and traffic information. Such methods represent travel in typically, but not necessarily, complex junctions and small transportation networks. While several of these applications are outside our scope, they are mentioned here for two reasons. Firstly, some problems in network design and traffic management are now being treated by models specified at different scales, involving macro-, meso- or micro-specifications, which raises the issue of the relative merit of the different approaches. Secondly, as in the case of demand, the specification of network models at the macro- and meso-level often involves assumptions at the micro-level that may be investigated with microsimulation. Over the past 15 years, several reports have examined the conditions favouring the use of the microsimulation technique over other, often more simplified, approaches, and the extent to which they are dependent on: (a) the details necessary for a valid representation of the problem; (b) the resources involved; and (c) the output information required (see, for example, Transport for London, TfL, 2003).

The network simulation systems applied most widely over the last decade by local authorities and consultants in the UK have been PTV's VISSIM and SIA's PARAMICS, with Transport Simulation Systems' AIMSUN a more recent popular addition. The guidance note prepared by Transport for London contained a detailed comparison of VISSIM and PARAMICS across the following range of items: 'data input, network changes, calibration, validation, option testing, animation, pollution modelling, pedestrian modelling, output, literature availability' (TfL, 2003). Recent technical comparisons of microsimulation systems for various types of urban traffic operations can be found in Hydas (2005) and Ratrout and Rahman (2009).[9]

9.4 SACTRA'S INFLUENTIAL REPORT *TRUNK ROADS AND THE GENERATION OF TRAFFIC*

9.4.1 Background

As has long been accepted, major transportation projects and policies can give rise to a wide range of behavioural responses, including land use changes, relocation of activities, modal substitution, and time-of-day period and route switching, as well as more subtle changes involving trip consolidation and reallocation of tasks within the family (see also Chapter 6). What was, and remains, the subject of debate and research is: (a) whether these various responses contribute significantly to changes in network, economic and environmental conditions; (b) how these responses vary with different policies, projects and geographical environments within which they are applied; and (c) the adequacy of different assumptions, approximations and simplifications for forecasting and appraisal.

Traditionally, in the UK the four-stage 'transport model' was the mainstay for urban travel forecasting in major investigations, although the specification of such models varied considerably in structure and detailed form. Typically, behavioural responses underpinning forecasts with the four-stage model include the possibility of route, mode and destination changes accompanying any modification to network generalised costs; in contrast, changes in trip generation and frequency were rarely considered. In the UK such models were sometimes referred to as 'variable demand models' (VDM). They were linked to assignment models for the 'feedback' of travel costs in attempts to achieve mutually consistent travel demand and cost matrices, both for a 'do-nothing' state and for a test policy or project coded into the network; see also sections 2.3.4, 7.4.4, 8.2 and 8.3.

For practical expediency, particularly for small road projects outside or on the periphery of urban areas, model simplifications were often made. Notably the effects of 'variable demand' (e.g., destination and modal substitution effects) were considered to be sufficiently small that they could be neglected. In its so-called 'fixed demand' traffic assignments, travel demand on the road network was assumed to change over time under the influence of exogenous factors (such as GDP, car ownership, the real price of fuel, and anticipated land use changes), but, apart from route-switching effects, was considered insensitive to changes in the level-of-service either in the 'do-nothing/minimum' state or as a result of the road project itself;

see section 7.4.2 for a description of other uses of the term 'fixed demand'. For major road projects, estuary crossings and so on, a more sophisticated form of travel demand analysis incorporating other behavioural responses would usually be applied.

Two issues in the late 1980s raised concerns about methods for assessing road projects both by the conventional four-stage approach and by fixed demand assignments which limited the responses to route switching. Firstly, routine road traffic forecasts at the end of the 1980s during an economic boom suggested traffic on the UK trunk road network would increase substantially, by between 85 and 142 per cent by 2025 (UK DoT, 1989). These forecasts implied that many road improvements being planned could become congested for significant periods of their lifetime. Secondly, empirical evidence of significant additional traffic and travel being 'generated' by road improvements was accumulating (see Beardwood and Elliott, 1989; SACTRA, 1994, Chapters 2–5; Goodwin, 1996). In particular, significantly more flow than had been forecast was being observed on sections of the recently completed London orbital motorway (M25). Although the M25 and its constituent links were not typical schemes of the road programme, this high profile case cast doubt on traffic forecasts generally and particularly those in or near large urban areas.

The concern was that increasing congestion over time would, through a variety of behavioural mechanisms, suppress some of the growth of demand (below the level it would otherwise be on the road network) and that this would in whole or part be released under capacity expansion. Further, any calculations which excluded contributions from induced traffic in such congested conditions might significantly *overstate* rather than *understate* the benefits derived from the scheme computed under a fixed demand approximation (Thomson, 1970; Bonsall et al, 1990; Williams and Moore, 1990; Williams et al, 1991; Williams and Yamashita, 1992; Mackie, 1996). The UK Department of Transport asked SACTRA to examine these issues, which were starting to become controversial in respect of both the technicalities of forecasting and the substantive case for new and expanded roads themselves.

9.4.2 Objectives, Findings, Recommendations and Legacy of SACTRA (1994)

SACTRA's report itself contained no new theory of travel behaviour or of transportation systems in equilibrium, but a detailed assessment of the evidence and synthesis of theoretical and empirical findings on 'suppressed' and 'induced' demand[10] from various choice mechanisms in 'un-priced' road networks and the contexts in which they were likely to be important. The committee addressed four questions:

1. Did new roads and expanded capacity give rise to a significant amount of induced traffic?
2. What were its consequences for the planning, design and evaluation of road schemes?
3. In what contexts was it likely to be important?
4. What modifications to existing methods were required in these cases?

Evidence was sought from a range of sources (SACTRA, 1994, Chapters 4, 5): (a) opinions of professionals achieved through a Delphi survey; (b) differential traffic growth rates in corridors or on major roads that were attributed to different levels of congestion; (c) evidence derived from econometric and other studies of travel demand relating to short-term and long-term responses to travel cost changes; (d) comparison of forecast and observed traffic on improved roads from routine monitoring and specific case studies; and (e) evidence derived from a range of modelling studies. The last included both numerical investigations and results from major transportation studies in which network flows and highway project benefits were assessed with a variety of methods ranging across: (a) simplified elasticity methods in which several responses (except rerouteing) were subsumed into a model with a single elasticity parameter (the so-called 'own-elasticity' or 'simple elasticity' demand model); (b) the traditional four-stage approach, incorporating both singly-constrained and doubly-constrained distribution models; and (c) land use – transportation interaction models. This evidence from modelling studies was reviewed in Chapter 10 of the report, and subsequently summarised and critically discussed by Coombe (1996).

Among the conclusions reached by the committee were the following:

> induced traffic can and does exist, probably quite extensively, though its size and significance are likely to vary widely with different circumstances. . . . Based on the evidence we are convinced that there are circumstances where induced traffic can seriously affect the design, environmental appraisal and economic value of schemes. . . . The evidence suggests that induced traffic will be of greatest importance in the following circumstances:
> 1. where the network is operating or is expected to operate close to capacity;
> 2. where the elasticity of demand with respect to travel costs is high;
> 3. where the implication of a scheme causes large changes in travel costs (SACTRA, 1994, 205).

In advocating that variable demand models become the normal basis for forecasting traffic on the trunk road system the committee made a

series of additional recommendations for interim and longer-term implementation, for road schemes of different types, including the issuing by
UK DfT of 'general advice on good practice in developing conventional
four-stage transportation models. . . . [W]here necessary, existing models
should be enhanced, so that they are able to estimate all the important
demand responses to road provision, including trip frequency and choice
of time of travel' (SACTRA, 1994, 207).

Following the 1994 SACTRA report, a wide range of reflections and
reviews and much specific technical and policy-related commentary and
research were published; see Noland and Lam (2002) and Litman (2010)
for reviews of UK and US publications on this subject. Research on
demand mechanisms and elasticities was initiated by UK DfT in response
to the report, which we describe in sections 9.5.3 and 9.5.4.[11] The report
also stimulated research on the converse mechanism to the 'generated
traffic' phenomenon, sometimes referred to as the 'degeneration of
traffic' under capacity reductions and reallocation (e.g., pedestrianised
streets and bus and bicycle lanes), which were increasingly included in
urban transportation proposals in the late 1990s (Cairns et al, 1998;
MVA, 1998).

The most direct opportunities to examine travel responses arising from
new highway infrastructure come from 'before and after' studies, examined in conjunction with mathematical models. While there is routine
monitoring of the impact of highway schemes, this is usually confined
to the effect on traffic flows. A number of post-SACTRA investigations
initiated by the UK Department for Transport have however sought to
identify travel responses to new roads and expanded capacity. The most
detailed of these is a study of the recently completed motorway scheme
around Manchester (the M60) (Rohr et al, 2012). In this case disaggregate
hierarchical demand models that incorporated frequency, mode, destination and time-of-day choices were deployed in order to identify the impact
of the M60 project. The authors concluded:

> The models indicated that the M60 scheme is likely to have induced traffic at
> the level of a 15–17% increase across the most relevant screenline counts of
> which the majority were due to destination switching and less to mode shift.
> Time-of-day effects were found to be negligible, although in the M60 situation,
> journey time changes across time periods were broadly similar. . . . [T]he model
> results reinforce the need for transport planners to take account of induced
> traffic effects when considering the benefits of a new transport infrastructure
> (Rohr et al, 2012, 2, 28).

9.4.3 The Wider Context: Relationship to the 'Laws of Traffic'

To put the SACTRA report in its wider context, and relate it to the network equilibrium framework in Chapter 7, we next examine related issues on transportation systems equilibria. Propositions espoused by Anthony Downs were not specifically examined in the SACTRA report; however, the report did pose the notion of 'latent' demand somewhat more generally, and its possible consequences. Downs (1962, 2004) addressed the difficulty of removing peak hour congestion through road building and capacity expansion with his 'triple convergence' theory: in a multi-modal, multi-temporal spatial context, route switching ('spatial convergence'), time period of travel switching ('time convergence') and mode switching ('modal convergence') jointly conspire to offset initial peak period benefits of added capacity.[12]

SACTRA's report did however briefly consider the Downs–Thomson (or Pigou–Knight) paradox[13] regarding the possible counter-productive effects of road capacity expansion in a multi-modal system which might arise as a result of the responses from public transport operators to the loss of demand (Thomson, 1977; Mackie and Bonsall, 1989; Arnott and Small, 1994; Williams, 1998). The possibility of flat demand curves (infinite elasticity) would seem to suggest that the worst case scenario would be that the expansion of road capacity would result in zero additional benefits to users (SACTRA, 1994, Chapter 9; Mackie, 1996). However, if the Downs–Thomson paradox applied, expansion of a highway system as a remedy to congestion would not only be ineffective but might also be counter-productive. Referring to 'Mogridge's conjecture', SACTRA stated the paradox in the following way: 'if journey costs on public transport are increased as a result of loss of demand, then the new equilibrium cost will be at a higher level than before. Increasing road capacity thus increases journey costs for cars' (SACTRA, 1994, 128).

The implications of the paradox have been widely examined and publicised by Martin Mogridge [1940–2000], notably for London in his book *Travel in Towns: Jam Yesterday, Jam Today and Jam Tomorrow?* Mogridge dedicated a considerable part of his professional life to arguing the folly of road capacity expansion in major urban areas and the desirability, indeed the imperative, of expanding the capacity of public transport (Mogridge, 1990, 1997). The SACTRA committee gave support to additional study on the effect, concluding that 'this argument does merit consideration in the context of capacity improvements to radial routes in metropolitan areas, where public transport has a significant share of the travel market and some mode switching may occur' (SACTRA, 1994, paras 9.21–9.23).

Several theoretical studies have explored the characteristics of equilibria resulting from capacity increases in bi-modal systems in which a travel market is shared according to the relative modal costs, and (a) the car travel cost increases in relation to the vehicle flow to capacity ratio, while (b) the public transport travel cost falls (rises) under increased (reduced) load. Under general demand conditions, this relatively simple system is capable of quite complex behaviour: the nature of the equilibrium states, along with their uniqueness and stability, depends on the elasticity of demand and the slopes of the travel cost functions. The Downs–Thomson paradox provides us with a cautionary tale that remains the object of curiosity and the subject of ongoing research on its relevance to policies and infrastructure investment for multi-modal systems, particularly in rapidly growing and highly congested cities.

Although the issue of pricing was not considered, the findings of SACTRA were consistent with the broad conclusions of transport economists over the last 40 years. Kenneth Small stated the generally held view succinctly:

> If demand is highly elastic, policies that attempt to significantly reduce congestion by limiting demand or increasing capacity are likely to fail. . . . In contrast, congestion pricing would make a large difference, because it moves the equilibrium level of average cost below the demand curve instead of shifting along the demand curve (Small, 1992, 112).

9.5 MULTI-STAGE DEMAND MODELS: STRUCTURES, PARAMETERS AND POLICY ANALYSIS

9.5.1 Development and Application of the Incremental Nested Logit Model

By the 1990s the four-stage approach was being more widely applied in the UK in a nested logit (NL) form, with the 'logsum' linking the destination and modal choice stages, and interpreted behaviourally within a discrete choice framework. Applications were made at various spatial scales, ranging from detailed to very coarse zone systems according to the context of study, and sometimes within hierarchical spatial representations. Examples are the LTS81 and LTS91 models applied in London; see MVA (2005), as well as section 9.5.3.

We also saw a growing tendency to apply models in incremental form (also known as pivot-point analysis) in which the base matrix derived from observed data sources served as a reference from which growth and network changes were assessed. This approach arose from the recognition that establishing close fits of a travel demand model to the base pattern may be difficult without inserting a substantial number of additional parameters. This situation arises especially at the distribution stage, where travel patterns reflect historic processes that may be difficult to model using relatively simple choice representations for a given cross-section (Van Vuren, 2010). Pivot-point/incremental analyses thus focus on directly modelling behavioural *changes* arising from network modifications.

The expression and application of the NL model in incremental form had major implications for travel demand forecasting in the UK. To the authors' knowledge, this formulation was devised independently by Bates et al (1987) and by Martinez (1987). A full discussion of the pivoting process and application to multi-stage models was given by Daly et al (2005). Just as the MNL model was formulated and applied in incremental/pivot-point form, so too could the NL model be expressed in terms of changes in demand from a base or reference state arising from the change in the generalised and composite costs ('logsums') of any or all of its component choices. As with the incremental MNL model, the spread of trips in the base trip pattern, or 'dispersion characteristics', could effectively be 'decoupled' from the demand response or elasticity characteristics. In the same way that elasticity parameters for the incremental MNL model could be transferred from other studies, so too could response parameters for the incremental nested logit (INL) model be derived locally, or transferred from elsewhere, or recommended in official advice. This property was particularly appealing where locally calibrated models were unavailable, either because particular data or the resources required for full model development were unavailable.

Importantly, the INL model could be adapted to explore the implications of different demand structures with compatible response parameters accompanying individual decisions in a hierarchy, such as frequency, destination, mode, time-of-day period and route. This mutually consistent ordering of choices in the NL demand model and the response parameters satisfying required inequality constraints (section 5.2) could now be achieved, if necessary, by construction. What those structures should be, and the numerical values of the response parameters included, would depend on available evidence and/or official advice.

In the 1990s we began to see the wider use of INL models in strategic analyses, where some sacrifice in spatial detail is offset by greater market segmentation, particularly in relation to person type, purpose and time periods. Early examples were the START (Bates et al, 1991; Roberts and Simmonds, 1997) and APRIL models (Williams and Bates, 1993; Bates et al, 1996). We note the application of START in section 9.6.

Building on the travel model component of MEPLAN (Hunt and

Simmonds, 1993), described in section 9.6, APRIL was developed for UK DoT for the analysis of alternative road pricing proposals for London.[14] These proposals included point, cordon, distance or time-based policies, with the ability to vary prices according to location, time period of day and vehicle type. The model contained 'a number of less widely available features', including: (a) simple tours for mode and time period of day choice; (b) incremental models for most choice procedures to provide an exact match to the base-year travel pattern; (c) uncertainty in travel times on user behaviour; (d) public transport overcrowding; (e) capacity restraint on car parking; and (f) consistent representation of mode switching to and from slow modes (Williams and Bates, 1993, 1). In the purpose-dependent, multi-level choice model used to represent decisions on mode and time period, the linear-in-parameters disutility function included monetary cost, travel time, reliability and degree of modal overcrowding.

For the London application, eight time-of-day periods were defined. Four home-based purposes and two non-home-based purposes were distinguished, the former representing primary destination tours, with residual movements treated as non-home-based trips. Within each home-based purpose, typically seven person types accounted for differences in: (a) trade-offs between money and time; (b) accessibility to a car; and (c) parking availability. Four travel modes were distinguished: (a) car driver and passenger; (b) bus; (c) rail; and (d) slow modes (walk and bicycle). The choices incorporated in the INL model included route, travel time, mode, destination and frequency. Time-dependent charging policies were applied by modifying the generalised cost on the separate legs of return trips occurring in the various time periods. APRIL was applied in conjunction with more detailed transportation network models; and LASER (section 9.6) was used to assess the land use impacts of pricing policies (Bates et al, 1996).

The INL model was also widely applied in the multi-modal studies where:

> very little demand model calibration has been carried out. . . . There has been a general reliance on incremental models, which is in line with good practice. However, in most cases the actual demand functions have either made use of existing models, or existing parameters/elasticities. . . . In some cases the model is limited to managing the mode choice between car and public transport, with a small number of demand segments being distinguished. In other cases most demand responses are in fact addressed, including time of day choice and impacts on land use. Partly, of course, this variation reflects the availability of existing models as well as the amount of effort required for data collection (Bates et al, 2003, 13).

Discussions of demand models in the late 1990s and subsequent years were dominated by observations, debates and recommendations about:

(a) what behavioural responses would be significant and justified in different travel forecasting contexts; (b) what ordering of choices should appear in model structures; and, crucially, (c) what were illustrative values and ranges for response parameters for different journey purposes and market segments. These questions were considered in reviews of previous models and formed the basis for later official recommendations in policy testing situations.

9.5.2 Application of PRISM, an Advanced Tour-Based Micro-Model

The application of the disaggregate approach to urban travel forecasting in the MTC study (Ruiter and Ben-Akiva, 1978) was quickly followed by similar applications in the Netherlands, Sweden and France (see section 5.5.3). By comparison, the UK adoption of such models was slow to develop, and it would be many years before Britain would see a conurbation-wide study of the type that had been applied in San Francisco in the mid-1970s, Amsterdam in the early 1980s and Stockholm, Copenhagen and Sydney in the 1990s. Certainly by the 1990s disaggregate modal choice models were being increasingly applied with both stated preference and revealed preference data sets, and particularly for evaluating projects such as new or extended urban light rail systems. The case for the applicability of more general disaggregate methods in the UK was presented as late as the mid-1990s (Van Vuren et al, 1995).

The development of PRISM (policy-responsive integrated strategy model) for the West Midlands region (Van Vuren et al, 2004; Van Vuren, 2010) has been the most significant application of the disaggregate approach to urban travel forecasting in the UK. A tour-based model solved with the VISUM software system incorporated in a detailed manner the following choices or responses: car ownership, tour frequency, destination, mode, time-of-day period of travel, and route. PRISM is highly segmented in its representation of travel demand and modal networks; four time periods in the highway model and two in the public transport model are defined.

Initially implemented between 2002 and 2004 and subsequently refined, PRISM is the product of the consultants Mott MacDonald and RAND Europe, on behalf of the seven West Midland metropolitan authorities, the Highways Agency and CENTRO, the West Midland Public Transport Executive. The objectives of the model relate to a range of policy initiatives, including capacity increases in road and rail, light rail extensions, road user charging, park-and-ride initiatives, and policies promoting walking and cycling.

The PRISM travel forecasting system consists of four separate components: (a) population model; (b) travel demand models; (c) a processing model; and (d) assignment of travel to the road and public transport networks (Van Vuren et al, 2004; Van Vuren, 2010). The first, employing a prototypical sampling procedure, is solved to provide a description of the West Midland population representative of the future socio-economic and spatial distribution of the population. The demand model then applies the frequency, mode, destination, public transport access mode and station choice, and time-of-day period models. The structure of the travel forecasting model is shown in Figure 9.1. Its most detailed form is used for home-based models for commuting, shopping and other travel. The processing step converts the tours to trips for each mode, purpose and time period, applies the pivoting procedure,[15] and then adds freight, external trips and trips to and from Birmingham International Airport. An updated version of the model has been developed with 2011 as the base year. Further details of the model, its calibration and its application are available in Van Vuren et al (2004) and Van Vuren (2010) and on the PRISM website.[16]

Applications of activity-based models of the type described in sections 6.5 and 6.6 are rare in the UK. One example was undertaken by Davidson et al (2006) and Clarke et al (2008) in Truro by migrating from an existing multi-modal model. A synthetic population with associated activities was applied in an NL model structure representing the choice combination of mode, time period, destination, journey timing (for peak spreading) and car park selection, and solved by agent-based microsimulation. The model was used to investigate alternative approaches to constraining parking demand, pricing of workplace parking charges, and effects on peak spreading.

9.5.3   Alternative Demand Model Structures: Sources of Evidence

Greater interest shown in the 1990s towards market segmentation, the range of travel responses arising from policies and projects, and the associated elasticity values did not begin with SACTRA's investigations. Deliberations and recommendations of the committee and subsequent research programmes of UK DfT certainly added to their study and emphasis. The intention of UK DfT's variable demand modelling (VDM) research programme was to clarify the specifications and ranges for the associated parameters of multi-stage demand models in various situations relating to the nature, scale and location of an investment. Such models were to include some or all of the behavioural responses incorporated in the traditional four-stage approach as well as the choice of journey timing, which was by now starting to be recognised as of particular significance

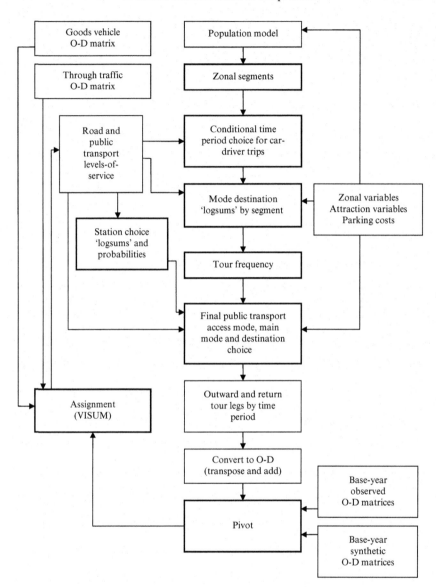

Source:　Tom Van Vuren, personal communication, 2014.

Figure 9.1　Structure of the PRISM model

and importance (SACTRA, 1994; Bates, 1996; Bates et al, 1996). The VDM programme of research was initially concerned with the appraisal of highway schemes but would later form the basis for much wider thinking and advice on policy and project analysis.

Three significant studies contributed to the assessment and recommendation of model structures and their accompanying elasticity parameters. A systematic review of travel demand models was initiated by UK DfT in 2001 and conducted in several phases as a basis for issuing what was called 'user-friendly multi-stage modelling advice' (UFMMA). The second and third phases by Bly et al (2001, 2002) had considerable value in their own right for their recording, comparison, critical review of modelling practice, and examination of options for modelling. A further influential study by MVA (2005) critically reviewed the response parameters for different market segments and the relative positions of the destination and modal choices in hierarchical structures in a number of their studies. In a further study, RAND Europe (Rohr, 2005) specifically investigated the structure and parameters for destination, mode and time-of-day period choices, and adopted the disaggregate demand model incorporated in PRISM. Because of their significance, we comment briefly on each.

Bly et al (2001) reviewed 24 multi-stage models that included 'the large majority of travel demand models extant in this country'; it was an important survey of UK practice of the prior 15 years. The models ranged greatly in complexity from simple MNL models applied to split modal demand, linking assignments to public and private networks, through traditional four-stage approaches, to six-level hierarchical logit formulations involving time-of-day period decisions and submodal split between several public transport modes. Where time-of-day period was explicitly considered, evidence was sought on the representation of 'macro' and 'micro' time period of day choices, a distinction introduced by Bates (1996). The former involved time-of-day choice with possible substitution behaviour over periods several hours apart, while the latter, 'micro-time period choice', referred to journey timing responses involving a matter of minutes (as, for example, in responses to increasing congestion).

The review recorded the spread of values for the sensitivity parameters associated with the various demand responses incorporated in the different studies. The sensitivity of trip generation to travel costs was found to be very small, and dependent on whether 'slow modes' were incorporated at a later modal split stage. The sensitivities of distribution and mode split were found to be larger and fairly similar in size; the sensitivity for peak spreading was greater still. In the light of our comments in section 5.2.1.6 on the formation of consistent model structures, a significant finding of this review related to the sizes of the response parameters for models combining distribution and modal split. Bly et al noted: 'In most of the models mode choice occurs *after* distribution, yet overall the mode split sensitivity is smaller than that for distribution' (Bly et al, 2001, 63, our emphasis).

A review by MVA (2005) had considerable further influence on official views (UK DfT, 2006a, section 1.11). Seven studies conducted by MVA were reviewed: two in London (LTS81, LTS91), two in Scotland, and three from medium-sized cities in England. The consultants noted that all seven models, which involved aggregate (zonal) specifications:

> have mode and destination choice structures based on the hierarchical logit model. The relative positioning of mode and destination choice in the hierarchy has in all cases been justified by the relative magnitudes of the calibration parameters. In all cases destination choice has been determined to be more sensitive than mode choice. The resultant model structure therefore has mode choice applied at the trip end level and destination choice at the matrix level by mode/car availability segment. In some cases alternative structures have been investigated and rejected due to the relative magnitudes of the resultant parameters (MVA, 2005, 2).[17]

A further study by RAND Europe investigated the ordering of destination and mode choices for a variety of journey purposes for the NL travel demand model in PRISM (Rohr, 2005). Several different tree structures were examined and the structural parameter θ, the coefficient of the 'logsum' in the higher level of the nest, was recorded (see section 5.2). For the commuting purpose, the parameter θ was not significantly different from unity, indicating that an MNL model over destination–mode combinations was appropriate. For primary, secondary and tertiary education, shopping, and other travel, a value of θ significantly less than unity was achieved for the structure in which destination choice follows modal choice, indicating that such an ordering was appropriate.

Official advice from UK DfT, based on the accumulated evidence, supported the view that main mode choice should precede destination choice as 'main mode choice was less sensitive than destination choice. . . . [T]he main mode choice scaling parameters are all less than or equal to one' (UK DfT, 2006a, paras 1.9.16, 1.11.15).

Table 9.2 provides evidence on the ranges of the scaling parameters, which are defined as the ratio of the sensitivity of the main mode choice to destination choice. These investigations by Bly et al (2001, 2002), MVA (2005) and RAND Europe (Rohr, 2005) led to broadly consistent conclusions with regard to the joint decisions over mode and destination, with no investigation supporting the traditional structure with destination preceding modal choice.

The ordering of choices involving journey timing alternatives has given

Table 9.2   Evidence on the scaling parameters (ratio of sensitivity of main mode choice relative to destination choice) in MID model structures

Trip purpose	Minimum	Median	Maximum	Sample
Home-based work	0.50	0.68	0.83	6
Home-based employer's business	0.26	0.45	0.65	2
Home-based other	0.27	0.53	1.00	4
Non-home-based employer's business	0.73	0.73	0.73	1
Non-home-based other	0.62	0.81	1.00	2

Note: The shaded boxes correspond to an **M-D** structure.

Source: UK Department for Transport (2006a, para 1.11.15).

rise to further complexity and uncertainty, and took on a new importance in the 1990s for the purpose of incorporating both peak spreading and time-dependent pricing policies. Such decisions and their combination with other choices involved the way in which preferred arrival and/or departure times would be traded off against journey travel times and costs. Clearly these decisions were always going to prove theoretically and empirically challenging tasks. The identification of the choice alternatives, the representation of scheduled utility, the incorporation and measuring of other explanatory variables, the distribution of population tastes, and the pattern of substitutability among the different choices have resulted in a range of deterministic and stochastic choice models over the years. As we described in section 5.7.2, these issues constitute a vigorous research area (e.g., Small, 1982; Bates, 1996; Bly et al, 2001, 2002; de Jong et al, 2003; UK DfT, 2006a; Hess et al, 2007).

In their summary of the available evidence on those structures, which include choice of time-of-day period, UK DfT came to the following view:

> Less evidence is available about the sensitivity of the macro-time period choice than either main mode or destination choice. Recent research conducted for the Department suggests that the sensitivity of the choice between relatively long periods, such as three hours or so, should be about the same as that of main mode choice. The research also suggests that, as the time periods are reduced the sensitivity increases. Thus, when long time periods, of the order of three hours, are being modelled macro-time period choice should be positioned either just before or just after main mode choice, with parameter values similar in magnitude to the main mode choice parameter values. Peak spreading, or micro-time period choice that will include a schedule disutility term, if included in the model, should be positioned after destination choice (UK DfT, 2006a, para 1.11.17).

There remains considerable debate about how micro-time changes should be incorporated into travel forecasting models for routine urban applications, the appropriate manner depending on the categorisation of time intervals (choice sets) (e.g., within the peak and between the peak and off-peak) and whether deterministic or stochastic models should be applied to account for the dispersion of preferences and information available to travellers. While many studies purported to incorporate a peak spreading mechanism, details are often hard to discern (Bly et al, 2001). Stochastic models are typically based around the MNL or NL models in absolute or incremental form.

While emphasising the preference for deriving parameters and compatible demand model structures on the basis of locally calibrated models, default structures and associated parameters were proposed by the Department in the way described. Unsurprisingly, highway project appraisal received the most detailed discussion and advice; the selection of a demand model depended on the categorisation of the highway project. For complex schemes, the recommended approach calls for each response to be considered separately within an incremental approach: 'The Department's preference for road-scheme appraisal is to use an incremental form of model whether pivot-point or based on incremental application of absolute estimates, unless there are strong reasons for not doing so' (UK DfT, 2006a, para 1.5.24).

An example of the choice hierarchy **F/M/T/D/t/R**, involving frequency (F), main mode (M), destination (D), macro- and micro-time period choices, (T) and (t), and route choice (R), was discussed. 'In the absence of any information to the contrary, this is . . . the hierarchy which should be adopted' (UK DfT, 2006a, para 1.9.16).

UK DfT sought to give advice not only on the structure of travel forecasting models and their associated response parameters, but also on a framework within which such hierarchical models can be easily implemented and equilibrated to arrive at internally consistent cost and volume information. This facility was considered particularly relevant to authorities that would not have the resources to develop demand models 'from scratch'. To this end the Department initiated a research programme resulting in the development of the DIADEM (dynamic integrated assignment and demand modelling) software by Mott MacDonald, 'designed to enable practitioners to easily set up variable demand models that are consistent with other webTAG advice on model structures' (UK DfT, 2011d, 2011f).

9.5.4   Realism Testing and the Validation of Models

Over the past 15 years, travel forecasting models have been increasingly required to be subjected to 'realism testing'. Traditionally, model validation was often solely confined to assignment and trip matrix validation, whereas the treatment of demand responses was restricted and sometimes non-existent (Coombe, 2009a, 2009b). By the late 1990s, however, goodness-of-fit at the cross-section was officially recognised as an insufficient basis for validating travel forecasting models, even when model validation involved 'reserved' data not used in the calibration of the model.

Testing the 'realism' of modelled responses was now considered necessary for policy analysis. This testing compared the (arc-)elasticities inherent in a calibrated model with independent information on elasticities accumulated from research studies and wider reviews (e.g., MVA and John Bates Services, 2000; Balcombe et al, 2004; Goodwin et al, 2004; Graham and Glaister, 2004; UK DfT, 2011d). The model elasticities were derived numerically from incremental changes in demand resulting from incremental changes in various cost and time components.[18] The comparison with external values of the elasticity of public transport demand for categories of travel by time period to changes in fare or service frequency, and/or of car travel demand to fuel cost or journey time or parking cost, often formed the basis for such realism tests 'to ensure that the model responds rationally and with acceptable elasticities . . . and accords with experience' (UK DfT, 2006a, paras 1.9.17, 1.11.4).

Such tests are now considered necessary, whether the parameters of the model are derived from calibration to local data or based on illustrative values. Relevant ranges of the elasticity parameters are given in UK DfT (2011d). Values outside the ranges would trigger model parameter adjustment.

On the basis of reviews and interviews Coombe (2009a, 2009b) has documented the characteristics of some 30 urban and regional models, either in existence or under development, in order to 'understand better the modelling capacity of the regions and their ability to undertake strategic appraisal, including an identification of best practice and how their capability can be improved'. In addition to identifying the uses made of the models and questions they could address, Coombe identified areas and examples of good practice, along with some common model deficiencies, including: (a) interpretation and misuse of vehicle count data; (b) expression of trip matrices in O-D (origin–destination) rather than P-A (production–attraction) format (see UK DfT, 2011e); (c) adoption of model hierarchical structures with inconsistent sensitivity parameters; and (d) use of calibrated or transferred models with elasticity parameters outside officially recommended ranges. These points were augmented by more policy-specific weaknesses, including: (a) network interventions with inadequate assignment models; (b) road pricing models with inadequate assignments and no income segmentation; and (c) parking policies with inadequate treatment of the supply constraints.

9.5.5 A Note on Some Policy- or Project-Specific Issues

We do not intend to review the documents offering guidance and advice on modelling the impact of specific policies. Given the generic nature of the modelling framework and the 'universal' behavioural specification based largely on random utility theory and standard linear disutility (generalised cost) functions, doing so would involve much repetition. A few comments, however, are relevant to the wider scope of this book.

Much of the official advice available in webTAG draws directly on the variable demand modelling framework, the core document being UK DfT (2006a) and its updated version in 2009, with different policies represented as changes in measurable components of standard generalised cost functions and modification to any relevant capacities (affecting parking, highway and public transport networks). Typically, advice documents concern the familiar process of model building with reference to data sources, network building, assignment and demand model specification, calibration, validation, equilibration, sensitivity analysis and forecasting. Each policy instrument is considered to evoke specific responses over the time period considered, with implications for travel choice hierarchies, while individuals may be subject to distinct patterns of behaviour, differing choice sets, and variation of tastes (with implications for market segmentation). Some of the relevant documentation for a selection of policy instruments are found as follows: highways (UK DoT, 1997; UK DfT, 2006a, 2006b); public transport (UK DfT, 2005a, 2006a, 2006b, 2006c, 2006d, 2007a); road pricing (UK DfT, 2007b);[19] and parking, including city centre, park-and-ride and workplace policies (UK DfT, 2011b).

There are few instances where the challenge of travel forecasting is more acute, and the call for further research more frequently heard, than in the appraisal of policies representing 'smarter travel choices'. Such policies take many different forms, either separately or as part of 'packages': 'workplace travel plans, school travel plans, personalised travel planning, public transport information and marketing, real-time transport information, travel awareness campaigns, car clubs, car sharing schemes, bicycle hire schemes, walking and cycling schemes, as well as teleworking, teleconferencing, and home shopping' (UK DfT, 2011c). These policies have been widely proposed and are now at the heart of many urban transportation initiatives in the UK, Europe and elsewhere. Such policies often consist of 'hard measures' (represented as changes in measurable attributes of generalised costs) or 'soft measures' (designed to evoke changes in perception, attitudes and tastes) or combinations thereof.

It is generally recognised that the modelling of such choices is notoriously difficult. Although expanding rapidly, the evidence base for such policies remains relatively low (see, for example, Cairns et al, 2008; Moser and Bamberg, 2008; Sloman et al, 2010; UK DfT, 2011c). With regard to the modelling of 'soft measures', Coombe expresses a common sentiment:

> No model deals adequately with the soft measures often found in smarter choice packages, not least because there is a paucity of reliable evidence about the effects of soft measures. Smarter choice packages, such as workplace and school travel plans often involve a mixture of hard measures, such as parking (not often modelled well) and public transport improvements, and soft measures, about which little is known for sure (Coombe, 2009a, para 19).

A wide range of assumptions underpins modelling practice in this area, sometimes relying on little more than guess work. When time is short, recourse to transfer of results from selected demonstration projects and international experience moderated by a few local assumptions, and local attitudinal or stated preference studies, is often likely to trump extensive model development. In an attempt to provide a systematic and logical approach to such policies, the Department has issued advice on forecasting practice (UK DfT, 2011c, section 1.3). Modelling difficulties and uncertainties accompanying 'smart choices' are not confined to UK practice; this area remains a major challenge to the profession.

9.6 APPLICATION OF LAND USE – TRANSPORTATION MODELS

No formal land use models were applied in urban transportation studies in the UK during the 1960s (see section 3.2.3.2). Exogenous forecasts of land use of an *ad hoc* nature were supplied to the trip generation and other stages of the travel forecasting model. This situation, with few exceptions, still broadly prevailed at the urban level in the mid-1990s even though a number of operational integrated land use – transportation models had become available. For urban transportation studies the potential improvement in concept and accuracy which formal land use or integrated models might bring was not considered to exceed the additional resources required for their implementation.

For the purpose of this overview of UK practice, we characterise land use – transportation (LUT) models as one of two forms: (a) those fully integrated models in which parts of the transportation model, usually the generation and distribution models, are replaced by spatial interaction/ allocation models within a combined whole; and (b) those linked models in which land use and transportation models are developed in tandem with information exchanged between them (David Simmonds Consultancy, 1998; UK DfT, 2005b). We refer to these two forms as integrated (ILUT) and linked (LLUT) models, respectively. Both have been applied within a comparative static and quasi-dynamic framework (see section 8.5.1).

By the late 1980s about eight operational integrated land use – transportation models were at various stages of development and refinement internationally. Detailed comparisons of these early operational models and full documentation and assessment of their mechanisms, theoretical basis and empirical development are found in Webster et al (1988), Webster and Paulley (1990), Paulley and Webster (1991), Wegener (1994, 1998, 2004) and David Simmonds Consultancy (1998). A number of these models were developed in the UK.

Roger Mackett's 'Leeds integrated land use transport model' (LILT), which stemmed from his doctoral studies at the University of Leeds, was applied in several research studies (Mackett, 1983, 1990a). To the authors' knowledge, LILT is no longer operational. During this period Mackett wrote extensively on the development of travel, location and integrated models at the macro- and micro-levels. His subsequent research on a 'micro-analytic simulation of transport, employment and residence' (MASTER) model is also noteworthy (Mackett, 1990b, 1990c).

In terms of their significance for applied forecasting and policy analysis, a set of spatial economic models were successfully developed at the Martin Centre, University of Cambridge and related small consultancies of academics and graduates from that centre. A special issue of *Environment and Planning B*, edited by Owers and Echenique (1994), recorded early developments at the Cambridge Centre and the wide applications at urban and regional levels in the UK, Europe and the developing world (see, in particular, Hunt and Simmonds, 1993; de la Barra, 1994; Echenique, 1994; Hunt, 1994; Jin, 1994; Simmonds, 1994; and Williams, 1994). Many of those who studied at the Martin Centre went on to distinguished careers in consultancy and/or academia.

Two of these models, MEPLAN and TRANUS, derived from common research programmes extending over several years since the late 1960s, had several similarities. The broad framework employed in MEPLAN and TRANUS, in which transportation flows are derived from interacting economic agents and the associated factor markets, is shown in Figure 9.2.

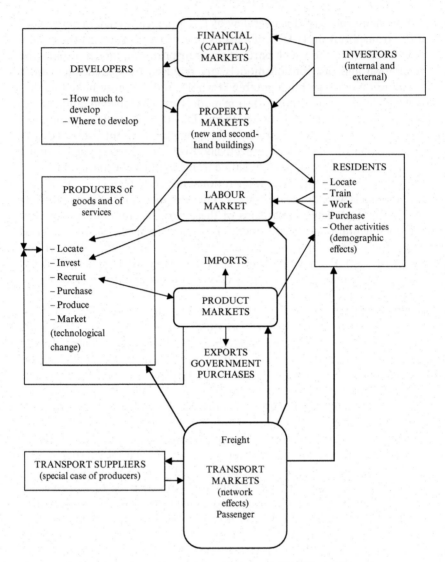

Source: Redrawn from David Simmonds Consultancy (1998, Figure 2.1).

*Figure 9.2   Actors and markets in land use – transportation interaction
           models*

Both models depict the demand for and supply of land (floor space) and the location decisions of households, firms and developers; spatial input–output models are used to derive the associated demand for movement of goods and people. The location and modal choice behaviour of individuals and households in these models are based on discrete choice theory and represented by hierarchical logit models implemented at the zone level. The assumption of market clearance in each time period allowed the incomes and rents in the labour and property markets to be determined (de la Barra, 1989; Echenique et al, 1990; David Simmonds Consultancy, 1998; Echenique, 2004). These are fully integrated (ILUT) models in the sense that the transportation model and its interactions were embedded in the land use model; the generation and distribution stages of the multi-stage approach were replaced by the input–output and spatial allocation models.

MEPLAN and TRANUS reached operational status by the mid-1980s, and were being applied both in the UK and in the developing world, notably in rapidly growing South American cities and regions where a strong mutual dependency between land development, transportation flows and infrastructure projects was found (Echenique, 1986; de la Barra, 1989, 1994). Over the next 25 years, these models were applied in many countries in urban, regional, national and international settings, the context determining the design and detailed specification of each model (Owers and Echenique, 1994; Echenique, 2004).

In urban applications, an early example was the model for the London and south-east region (LASER) (Williams, 1994), where particular emphasis was placed on travel-related decisions accompanying residential location, car ownership and the journey to work and to school. In regional applications (e.g., the EUNET Trans-Pennine model), more emphasis was placed on modelling goods movement arising from industrial location decisions and development of the regional economy (UK DfT, 2005b; WSP, 2005). MEPLAN continues in use by UK DfT and Transport for London.[20] Further details and discussion of the theoretical basis of MEPLAN and TRANUS, the assumptions involved in their specification, and their place in the typology of integrated land use – transportation models are found in Wegener (1994, 2004), David Simmonds Consultancy (1998), Echenique (2004), UK DfT (2005b) and Simmonds and Feldman (2011).

An alternative to the fully integrated model is a land use model linked with an existing or purpose-built travel forecasting model. These models typically focus on the various processes of change affecting the demand for and supply of land use and are also more highly segmented in terms of their socio-economic variables. In the current most widely applied LLUT forms, discrete choice models specified at the zonal level are adopted for locating activities.

One example is MENTOR, designed specifically for local authority use, which builds on the theoretical structures of MEPLAN. MENTOR has been applied by a number of local and national agencies in the UK. Another notable example of an operational land use model is DELTA, which has been under development by the David Simmonds Consultancy since 1994 (Simmonds and Still, 1998; Simmonds, 2001; Feldman et al, 2006). Both MENTOR and DELTA have been applied in conjunction with externally developed travel forecasting models, and are linked through the exchange of land use and accessibility variables between the travel forecasting and land use models, respectively. DELTA was first applied to Edinburgh (Simmonds and Still, 1998) and Greater Manchester (Copley et al, 2000) in conjunction with the transportation model START (Bates et al, 1991; Roberts and Simmonds, 1997). Simmonds and Feldman (2011) compared the treatment of the decisions of households, firms and developers in selected models, including MEPLAN and DELTA.

Several substantive and theoretical factors contributed to the greater interest in and use of formal land use – transportation models since the early 1990s. Substantive factors included: (a) investigations of the land use and induced traffic effects arising from significant infrastructure projects (SACTRA, 1994; Coombe, 1996) and in particular those associated with the multi-modal studies; (b) increased interest in congestion charging initiatives and their implications for land use (Williams and Bates, 1993; Bates et al, 1996); (c) the impact and improved evaluation of major regeneration schemes; (d) a long-standing search for more sustainable urban environments and their associated land use and transportation arrangements (Breheny, 1992; Echenique, 2005; May et al, 2005; Shepherd et al, 2006c; Lautso and Wegener, 2007; Marshall and Banister, 2007; May and Matthews, 2007);[21] and (e) recent attempts to improve integrated models of the space economy and goods movement at national, regional and conurbation levels (WSP et al, 2002; UK DfT, 2003; WSP, 2010) (see also section 9.7).

A reason for renewed theoretical interest in land use – transportation interaction was the limitations of traditional approaches for estimating the amount and distribution of benefits arising from infrastructure investments when the factor markets (for land, housing and labour) are subject to imperfect competition and agglomeration effects. These impacts were the specific focus of *Transport and the Economy*, a report by SACTRA (1999), which analysed in depth the assumptions underpinning existing operational integrated land use – transportation models and other more general but (currently) spatially more limited computable general equilibrium models. This report, drawing on the review by David Simmonds Consultancy (1998), examined the consequences of imperfect competition and scale economies in production and distribution for estimating the responses to transportation improvements and implications for scheme benefits. The report provided a summary of the ways that integrated models are able to capture such effects. The linkage and choice mechanisms embodied in the DELTA/START model, the MEPLAN model (in its LASER and EUNET forms), and the computable general equilibrium model (CGEM) of Venables and Gasiorek (1998) are illustrated and contrasted within the framework shown in Figure 9.2 (see SACTRA, 1999, Figures 10.1–10.4). The substantial data and estimation problems of introducing imperfect competition and agglomeration effects in operational models were emphasised in this analysis. More detail on the nature, data requirements and assessment of alternative approaches (particularly those embodied in MEPLAN, MENTOR, TRANUS and DELTA) may be found in David Simmonds Consultancy (1998), Hunt et al (2005), UK DfT (2005b) and Simmonds and Feldman (2011).

9.7 FORECASTING URBAN GOODS MOVEMENT

9.7.1 Goods Vehicle Forecasting: The Poor Relation to Personal Travel Forecasting

As in the US, the time and resources allocated to urban goods movement forecasting models in the UK have been very modest compared with those devoted to corresponding personal travel demand modelling. Traditional methods, and in particular those based on simple growth factor methods, survived for similar reasons: (a) the complexity of and resources needed to develop, calibrate and validate alternatives; and (b) what might be seen among practitioners to be the adequacy of available techniques for the purposes required, where more detailed models might be considered both extravagant and unnecessary. That said, since the 1970s perennial calls have been made for more sophisticated forecasting in this sector, where current practice was seen to be subject to poor behavioural foundations and policy insensitivity (SACTRA, 1999; Neffendorf et al, 2001). This observation is especially true in the context of responses to transportation improvements, where 'the current practice of modelling freight operator responses in general and the responses of goods vehicle movement in particular is relatively primitive and unsatisfactory' (SACTRA, 1999, 223).

Although over a decade has passed, this remark still holds with considerable force. As SACTRA emphasised, while goods vehicle trips may account for a relatively small proportion of overall traffic in a given situation, they contribute much more significantly to the overall benefits of transportation improvements because of the relatively high value of time associated with these journeys. Flows of goods vehicles, particularly heavy goods vehicles, are also an important component of atmospheric emissions and noise.

Again, as in the US, many differences between personal travel and goods movement bearing on the forecasting problem were widely recognised (UK DfT, 2003), and the challenge of improving the forecasting of commercial vehicles was acknowledged as being even more formidable than for personal travel. Factors cited in recent studies include: (a) heterogeneity of the shippers, receivers and commodities transported, and differences in the importance of generalised costs for each; (b) complexities of the supply chain and the decisions made along it; (c) the scope for and economics of 'backhauling'; (d) the 'tour-based' nature of many urban deliveries; (e) the paucity and commercial confidentiality of much relevant data; (f) the dynamic nature of the sector in relation to social, economic and technological trends; and, some have argued, (g) lack of a satisfactory conceptual framework for analysis (Neffendorf et al, 2001; WSP et al, 2002; Ortúzar and Willumsen, 2011, Chapter 13).

Over the last two decades several factors contributed to increasing interest in goods movement, and addressing the conceptual weaknesses of traditional forecasting models (Williams et al, 2007). These factors related to: (a) relatively rapid economic and technological changes affecting production and logistical practices in the business sector; (b) social changes and urban policies affecting the spatial and temporal organisation of activities in cities; (c) a need for greater understanding of the link between goods vehicle growth and the development of the economy as a whole; (d) changes in the growth of goods vehicles of varying sizes on roads of different type; (e) a need to evaluate the responses of goods vehicles to congestion charging and other policy instruments; and (f) an increasing emphasis on reducing or containing the environmental consequences of goods distribution (SACTRA, 1999; Neffendorf et al, 2001; Williams et al, 2007).

If the SACTRA report of 1994 contributed to the scrutiny of personal travel demand models, the SACTRA report of 1999, *Transport and the Economy*, performed a rather similar role for goods movement. It advocated a thorough review of forecasting methods both for the growth of demand for goods movement and for the responses to changes to the transportation system. Responding to this recommendation, UK DfT initiated a major review of the sector in 2000 (WSP et al, 2002) as a prelude to issuing interim advice and guidance to those appraising schemes or forecasting goods movement (Williams et al, 2007).

For routine urban modelling, the standard multi-step model described in section 8.6 served widely as a broad conceptual framework, although 'freight transportation logistics professionals would not recognise the four-step paradigm as applied to their industry' (Neffendorf et al, 2001, 3). Given the traditional transportation study emphasis on flow, congestion and capacity problems, a 'vehicle-based' rather than 'commodity-based' approach has almost invariably been adopted, although its conceptual deficiencies have been noted:

> models have usually involved gathering data only on vehicle movements, creating observed traffic flow matrices and then using growth factors for future projections. The results have been unsatisfactory because the vehicle trip volumes show little correlation with land use data. In addition the matrices are usually poor, having little or no behavioural basis, and with no sensitivity for tests of policy issues or forecasting variables (Shahkarami and Raha, 2002).

In fact, given the almost complete reliance of goods movement on the road sector in and around many urban areas, forecasting methods are often applied in simple terms by expanding O-D matrices of vehicle movements with growth factors based on national road traffic forecasts, distinguishing heavy goods vehicles (HGVs) and light goods vehicles (LGVs). This approach has two significant practical problems: (a) the difficulty of creating a good quality matrix for the base year from count data and roadside interview surveys; and (b) the changes in growth trends since the late 1990s among vehicles of different size and commodity carried 'illustrates the risks inherent in extrapolating past trends of freight transportation demand patterns through future years without having sound economic models to explain these trends' (Williams et al, 2007).

In the review of the sector, various methods for forecasting the origin–destination pattern of goods movement were considered, each involving 'different assumptions about the role of costs and interdependency between the commodity groups and their relation to the spatial economy' (UK DfT, 2003). These included: (a) simple or differential factoring methods; (b) spatial interaction models; and (c) spatial input–output models. With regard to recommendations, the Department noted:

> For individual urban areas or small corridors the factoring methods are probably the only ones directly applicable, since too large a proportion of freight movements will have one or both ends well outside the area. . . . The interaction and input–output models are likely to be applicable if the modelled area represents at least most of a region, and best applicable for studies which need to model more than one region (UK DfT, 2003, para 1.1.10).

In the UK, to a greater extent than in the US, the development of urban/ conurbation commodity-based goods movement forecasting, derived through input–output modelling, has been closely allied to the development of integrated land use – transportation modelling initiatives, particularly with the development of MEPLAN and TRANUS. However, it is generally recognised that, in the input–output modelling approach, which almost invariably was implemented in units of value, 'the conversion of trade by value into physical units of freight . . . is a critical but relatively under-researched topic' (UK DfT, 2003, para 1.1.9). In this conversion of commodity forecasts into vehicle-kilometres of freight traffic, several key assumptions are involved, relating to value density, modal split, handling factors, average length of haul, load factors and empty running (Netherlands Economic Institute, 1997; SACTRA, 1999, para 6.51). We describe below an approach to freight forecasting based on the functionalities available in MEPLAN.

As in the personal travel sector, firms have at their disposal a potentially large number of short- and longer-term shipment choice alternatives that may be invoked to respond to urban infrastructure investments and pricing policies. Available evidence of firm location and operational behaviour at the urban level is scarce; the evidence on HGVs and LGVs and vehicle-kilometres travelled in relation to the London congestion charge was summarised by Williams et al (2007, 12–13).

9.7.2 Beyond Traditional Approaches: Incorporating Logistical Features in a Strategic Model

A model representing the derived demand for goods movement at a strategic level and incorporating choice theoretic principles for the underpinning decisions is the multi-modal freight model FiLM (Freight in London Model) developed for Transport for London (Deane et al, 2010; WSP, 2010). This study built on and proposed a similar modelling approach to previous studies by the consultants WSP and, in particular, the earlier EUNET model of goods movement in the Trans-Pennine corridor (WSP, 2005), as well as research undertaken for the national freight model (WSP, 2010).

Although London is rather atypical of urban areas, and the model is more applicable to regional contexts, FiLM is highlighted here because it is innovative in a number of important ways: (a) freight flows are derived from a spatial input–output model in which distinct logistical channels are distinguished for a wide range of commodity groups, allowing a more satisfactory treatment of customer sourcing, mode and vehicle-type choices strongly dependent on distribution stages within the overall logistical system; (b) detailed consideration is given to the movement of light commercial vehicles (LCVs) travelling for freight, commuting and service delivery purposes; and (c) a wide set of economic and land use data sources are included, such as detailed consideration of freight hubs, to generate modal trip matrices and to provide estimates of the beginning and termination of goods vehicle movements. We elaborate on the first two of these features.

The model draws directly on the functionality of MEPLAN, deriving the interzonal movement of goods and services from the final and intermediate demand of the spatial input–output model. For each of a wide range of product groups, the pattern of logistics is categorised by the number of stages in the distribution channels linking the zonal production (P) and consumption (C) of goods. Combinations of distribution legs generate a variety of distribution channels, each sequence of distribution legs connected from the producer (P) through to the consumer (C) being a separate channel (WSP, 2010, 25). As they have distinct transportation characteristics, the model explicitly distinguishes primary, secondary and tertiary distribution stages for a wide range of individual commodities. Primary distribution legs are those from producers to distribution centres or to major individual consumers; secondary distribution legs refer, for example, to the linkage from distribution centres to major retail outlets or to local distributors; and tertiary distribution legs involve distribution to dispersed small-scale consumers, representing the multi-drop pattern of collection and delivery that is carried out mainly in LGVs and smaller HGVs (Deane et al, 2010, 5).

The model outputs are freight flows and tonnages by origin and destination, commodity type, logistical stage and transportation mode, representing all domestic freight moved to, from and within London by heavy goods vehicles, light commercial vehicles, rail and water-borne freight movement on the River Thames. FiLM was developed with a spatial disaggregation of 700 zones (400 within the M25 motorway), and six road freight vehicle types in addition to rail and shipping, and considers 16 commodities split into three distribution stages. Further details of the calibration and application of the model are given by Deane et al (2010) and WSP (2010).

9.8 CONCLUSION

The conceptual development of urban travel demand modelling over time reflects a progression from trip-based, through tour-based, towards activity scheduling-based approaches developed at the micro-level. In this perspective, the experience of UK travel demand modelling over the last 30 years must be regarded as traditionally trip-based, with only limited forays into tour-based and activity-based approaches. As the large majority of travel forecasting models applied internationally are the traditional aggregate trip-based multi-stage form, important comments and interesting developments may be noted about the specification, calibration and validation of such models.

Furthermore, as is made clear in official advice, to judge models solely by their technical sophistication would be to miss the important point of developing forecasting procedures at an appropriate level of detail for the problem at hand with the available resources. Bates et al (2003) and Shepherd et al (2006b) clearly stated that the challenges faced by UK travel forecasters in the last 10–15 years were sometimes almost of a different order from those of perhaps only a decade earlier, in terms of: (a) the combination of instruments in plan generation and testing; (b) the range of information required by appraisal frameworks; and (c) often limited resources available to conduct studies – time, money and, occasionally, required skills. The need for parsimony in the technical aspects of travel forecasting was ever present, and the adoption of simplified techniques and the practice of transferring models, methods or (elasticity) parameter values, where these were available, seemed eminently sensible strategies.

At its most sophisticated level, the core of travel demand modelling practice is now predominantly cast around the multinomial and nested logit models, often expressed in incremental form at both the aggregate (zonal) and the disaggregate (micro-) levels, and founded on discrete choice random utility theory. It is now generally accepted that an appropriate model structure relates to the relative sensitivity of the different response mechanisms involved, which may vary with different travel purposes and possibly different segments of the travel market. Any adopted multi-stage travel demand model with response parameters inconsistent with that structure (as determined by the required inequalities), which was widely observed in modelling practice as late as 2000, would no longer be considered 'fit for purpose' (Coombe, 2009a, 2009b). In this regard, review and research over the last 15 years corroborated some of the findings of UK research from the mid-1970s (Williams and Senior, 1977; Daly and Zachary, 1978). While it would be too strong a conclusion to say that the traditional 'post-distribution modal split' demand model form **G/D/M/A** has been decisively rejected, there now appears little general support for adopting this model form as a default. The reverse treatment of the destination and modal choices **G/M/D/A** (with its special case **G/M-D/A**) appears to be increasingly acknowledged and supported. In this regard, validation of models, in respect to (a) their goodness-of-fit at the cross-section; (b) the 'realism' of their elasticity properties; and (c) their equilibration for secure evaluation/benefit calculations and sensitivity analysis, are now much more prominent features of model development and testing than perhaps only a decade ago.

As more refined temporal information was required from models and time-of-day-dependent pricing policies became more common, temporal substitution mechanisms both of macro-shifting among different daily time periods and of micro-shifting within the peak period are now widely recognised as potentially important and in some cases prominent behavioural responses. However, quantitative evidence remains rather scarce, and time-of-day period decisions continue to pose modelling challenges both in respect of ordering within nested model structures and in their detailed specification. Recognition and research into the importance of the travel time reliability, both in its influence in individual decision making and in the accompanying evaluation of schemes, have increased considerably.

In both land use – transportation interaction and goods movement modelling, significant practical advances have been made in the UK. However, these topics still pertain to specialist areas with relatively few expert practitioners. Calls for more behaviourally realistic and policy-sensitive models of goods movement will continue to be heard. Incorporating concepts of firm logistics, particularly multi-stop journeys, to analyse and forecast the transportation of goods and services under a wide range of policies remains an outstanding practical task. Difficulties in acquiring appropriate data and the scale of resources required for implementation make models such as FiLM an exception rather than the rule. For the large majority of urban transportation planning requirements, it seems likely that the vehicle-based growth factor expansion of base trip matrices will continue to play the dominant role in routine goods vehicle forecasting. As in the personal travel sector, the derivation of quality base matrices will continue to pose practical challenges.

There are significant variations in the complexity of models applied in practice. The approach taken for common forecasting tasks may vary greatly, as occurred in both the multi-modal studies and particularly in local transportation planning, owing to the limited time and resources available for the tasks at hand. Among some practitioners and those responsible for commissioning technical studies a view persists that 'modelling is too complex, too expensive, incomplete in its coverage of policy instruments, and difficult to undertake due to a lack of necessary skills' (Shepherd et al, 2006b, 316). It also remains the case that many transportation planning authorities do not have the resources to maintain databases or the tools and expertise to develop models to address the considerable demands placed on them (Coombe, 2009a).

It is inevitable, even among professional modellers, that a wide range of opinions will continue to be held on: (a) the state of practice; (b) the priority areas for model development; (c) the areas requiring local discretion in the application of particular models; and (d) a longer-term agenda for research. In the UK as elsewhere, these are matters for debate at conferences, and comment in professional and academic journals. We offer some further comments on these issues in Chapters 11 and 12.

NOTES

1. During the late 1980s and early 1990s some major studies were carried out by consortia of authorities, despite the fragmentation of local government. These included integrated transport studies mostly at metropolitan/city-region level, e.g., BITS (Birmingham), JATES (Edinburgh) and MerITS (Merseyside).
2. More information on the political and institutional structures and transportation planning process can be found on the UK DfT website and, in particular, in webTAG documentation found at www.gov.uk/transport-analysis-guidance-webtag. For details of local transportation planning and changing responsibilities over time, see Shepherd et al (2006b) and May (2013).
3. A more detailed discussion and assessment of the development of local transport planning, and the three rounds of local transport plans, can be found in May (2013).
4. Under the Greater London Authority Act 1998 the Greater London Authority and Transport for London (TfL) came into being in 2000. Ken Livingstone became Mayor of London in 2000.
5. Although the use of the term NATA has been discontinued, its framework continues to provide the basis for evaluation.
6. TEMPro provided access to the national Trip End Model Presentation Program of growth in travel demand (www.gov.uk/government/collections/tempro). The program allows forecasts of trip ends for small areas (sub-divisions of local authorities) to be output from the National Car Ownership Model (NATCOP) and the National Trip End Model (NTEM). Forecasts to 2041, cross-stratified by a number of variables (such as mode, time of day and trip purpose), can be output for multi-modal trip ends based on changes in demographic and socio-economic variables, but excluding the effects of travel costs (www.transport-assessment.com/tempro.htm, accessed 27 August 2014).
7. The status of SATURN can be found at www.saturnsoftware.co.uk (accessed 14 March 2014).
8. Our understanding is that development work on CONTRAM has now ceased.
9. Further description of the current capabilities of VISSIM, PARAMICS and AIMSUN can be found on the respective websites: www.vissim.de, www.sias.co.uk and www.aimsun.com (all accessed 14 March 2014).
10. In their investigations and reporting, a distinction was made between those responses to road schemes from *existing* journeys which could result in changes in vehicle mileage on a network ('induced traffic') and responses which could result in extra journeys ('induced trips'). Changes in route, the retiming of journeys and travel to new locations belong to the former while, for example, modal switching, frequency responses and land use changes could contribute *locally* to additional journeys by car.
11. One particular conclusion resulting from UK DfT research related to the use of alternative simplifications to the fixed demand assumption; because the use of 'own cost' or

simple elasticity models fails to reflect the subtleties of demand responses to network changes it may give rise to significant bias in the evaluation of road schemes (UK DfT, 2006a, paras 1.2.1–1.2.5).

12. In his 'Law of Peak Hour Expressway Congestion', Anthony Downs (1962) stated: 'on urban commuter expressways, peak hour traffic congestion rises to meet maximum capacity'. en.wikipedia.org/wiki/Anthony_Downs (accessed 13 March 2014).

13. en.wikipedia.org/wiki/Downs-Thomson_paradox (accessed 16 March 2014).

14. The context and content of this application are extensively discussed in the six related papers (various authors) under the title The London Congestion Charging Research Programme, *Traffic Engineering and Control* (1996), 37 (2), 66–71; 37 (3), 178–183; 37 (4), 277–282; 37 (5), 334–339; 37 (6), 403–409; 37 (8), 436–441.

15. The pivoting procedure, described in Van Vuren (2010), is performed in the following way:

$$V_f = V_b\left(\frac{S_f}{S_b}\right) \text{ or } V_f = \left(\frac{V_b}{S_b}\right)S_f$$

where:
V_f = forecast travel demand
V_b = observed base-year travel demand
S_f = (synthetically) modelled forecast demand
S_b = modelled base-year demand.
Special procedures are applied for cases in which elements in the base matrix, synthetic base matrix or synthetic future matrix are zero.

16. Detailed reports on the model, its calibration and its application are found at www.prism-wm.com (accessed 13 March 2014).

17. In their report (MVA, 2005) the consultants add the following interesting comment: 'Although the relative positioning of mode and destination choice in the model hierarchy has been found to be the same in the models reported there are circumstances where a different structure might be expected. Two examples where this might be the case are:
(1) Study areas with large, highly aggregated zone systems. Here the proportion of intra-zonal trips might be relatively high and the coarseness of the zone system could hide changes in origin destination trip patterns; and
(2) Models of freestanding monocentric areas where a single urban centre provides almost all of the employment and shopping opportunities' (MVA, 2005, 2).

18. An elasticity is the ratio of the percentage change in the model output variable (e.g., demand) to the percentage change in the input variable (e.g., costs or time).

19. The challenge of representing and modelling different road user charging policies has benefited from a very wide range of theoretical and empirical studies over the last 50 years; many modelling studies have been conducted on UK cities, including London, where examinations of supplementary licensing and area pricing were the subject of extensive model-based studies by the Greater London Council in the 1970s. More recently, a substantial programme of investigations of proposed road pricing schemes in the capital was undertaken prior to the introduction of the London congestion charge (see note 14; ROCOL Working Group, 2000; Richards, 2006). Paulley (2002) and UK DfT (2007b) discussed key issues in road pricing and modelling of various schemes. Road pricing policies continue to be of practical interest in the UK, Europe and elsewhere. Koh and Shepherd (2006) examined some European experience and models of urban road pricing. The continual monitoring of the London congestion charge scheme is an important source of information on travel behaviour along with congestion and environmental effects (www.tfl.gov.uk).

20. Marcial Echenique sold the company, ME&P, in 2001; the model became the property of WSP.

21. Several collaborative studies, conducted under European funding initiatives, related to the development of methods for analysing and optimising integrated strategies to promote sustainable land use – transportation arrangements in European cities. See,

for example, Marshall and Banister (2007), particularly the chapters by Lautso and Wegener (2007) and May and Matthews (2007), as well as www.konsult.leeds.ac.uk (accessed 14 March 2014). In this regard, a number of models, simplified in their spatial and network representations, or omitting detailed assignment components, were developed for land use and transportation analysis and to inform policy at the strategic level. See, for example, STM and TPM, developed at the UK Transport Research Laboratory (2002) and MARS (metropolitan activity relocation simulator) (Pfaffenbichler et al, 2007).

10. Computing environment and travel forecasting software

10.1 INTRODUCTION[1]

This chapter addresses the evolution of computer programs used for travel forecasting from the packages, batteries or suites developed for mainframe computers from the late 1950s to the 1980s to the modern software systems designed for personal computers. The review emphasises the software systems developed for solving the traditional four-step, or sequential, travel forecasting procedure. These systems came into use during the 1980s and are now the primary 'toolkits' used in practice to solve a range of models; to some extent they are also used in research. Software for supporting analysis and parameter estimation was sometimes incorporated into these systems. By and large, this supporting software is not considered here, but is reviewed in the chapters where those methods are described.

As personal computers became more powerful during the 1990s, and operating systems evolved to facilitate their use (e.g., Microsoft Windows, Linux), other computer applications related to traditional travel forecasting also emerged. One was the microsimulation of road traffic based on car-following concepts or theories of traffic flow (section 8.4.1). Traffic microsimulation software applied in the UK is reviewed in section 9.3.2. The solution of variants of the dynamic traffic assignment problem that relaxes the static traffic assignment problem's implicit assumption that route and link flows occur uniformly over a period of one or more hours of the 24-hour day is an active area of research and software development. Software for dynamic traffic assignment is not included in this review (Chiu et al, 2011).

The chapter begins with a brief overview of the computing environment from 1951 onwards, including an analysis of the characteristics of computers in terms of speed and memory. The evolution of government-provided computer programs to a private software development niche, which now characterises the field, is then traced. The status of these systems is described into the early 2000s.

10.2   OVERVIEW OF THE COMPUTING
ENVIRONMENT

Digital computers, and programs for their use, had a profound effect on the development of travel forecasting methods from the very beginning of the field. Urban transportation planning, and specifically travel forecasting, is arguably one of the first civilian applications of computing. During the period examined in this review, 1950–2000, computing hardware and travel forecasting software progressed to such an extent that novices to this field may not be able to imagine the conditions that prevailed at its outset. A brief overview of the development of computing hardware and software is provided to address this gap in knowledge and experience.[2]

10.2.1   Mainframe Computing

From the introduction of computers into urban transportation studies and the Bureau of Public Roads (BPR) in the late 1950s until well into the 1980s, travel forecasting models in the US were solved on mainframe computers, predominantly produced by IBM.[3] They included the first generation (vacuum-tube) computers, such as the IBM 704 and 709 during the 1950s, the second generation (transistor) computers, such as the IBM 7090 and 7094 from the late 1950s well into the 1960s, and the third generation (integrated circuit) computers, the IBM System/360 and System/370 from the 1960s onwards. Smaller computers such as the IBM 650, 1401 and 1620 were used for secondary computations, or to prepare magnetic tapes from punched cards for input to mainframes. Operating systems for first and second generation IBM computers, such as IBSYS and OS/360, evolved with the hardware. Prior to and during the first years of mainframe usage, processing of survey data files was performed with IBM electromechanical accounting machines (Figure 2.2(a)) (sections 2.3.3, 2.4.5).

The IBM 704 computer (Figure 2.2(b)) was the first mass-produced computer with core memory and floating point arithmetic. The IBM 700 series were binary computers with 32 000 words of 36-bit length. The IBM 709 added overlapped input and output, indirect addressing, and decimal instructions. 'The IBM 7090 was a 709 with transistor logic. The 36-bit 700- and 7000-series were IBM's scientific computers from 1952 until the introduction of the 32-bit System 360 in 1964.'[4]

The IBM System/360 (S/360) was a third generation mainframe introduced in 1964.[5] It was the first computer with several compatible designs at different prices. Computers used for travel forecasting were often the largest models available, such as the S/360 65. The S/360 introduced the 8-bit byte, byte-addressable memory, as contrasted with word-addressable memory with 32-bit words. For the IBM System/370 (S/370) announced in 1970, IBM maintained backward compatibility with the S/360. New architectural features included: (a) standard dual-processor capability; (b) full support for virtual memory; and (c) 128-bit floating point arithmetic. S/370 computers were replaced by subsequent IBM mainframes. The transition to minicomputers and microcomputers effectively ended the dominance of the mainframe for travel forecasting.

In addition to IBM, seven smaller competitors produced mainframe computers in the US. Most noteworthy among these for travel forecasting was Control Data Corporation (CDC), whose chief designer was Seymour Cray [1925–1996],[6] later the designer of the Cray supercomputer during the 1970s.[7] The CDC 6600 mainframe was delivered in 1964.[8]The CDC 3000 and 6600 series gained some market share during the late 1960s, especially in universities, succeeded by the CDC Cyber series after 1970.

IBM and CDC mainframes suitable for travel forecasting were initially too expensive to be owned by planning agencies, or state and local governments. Computer time was purchased from service bureaus (facilities established to provide computer services), a large corporate computing facility, leading research universities or a federal agency, such as the US National Bureau of Standards. Execution of programs was performed by programmers physically visiting the service bureau, as remote terminals were initially not available.

10.2.2   Transition to Minicomputers and Microcomputers

During the 1970s and 1980s, computing hardware choices available to engineering consulting firms, universities and public agencies began to broaden. Minicomputers were introduced, most successfully by Digital Equipment Corporation (DEC) with its PDP and VAX computers with VBS or UNIX operating systems. These minicomputers were physically smaller and much less expensive, so that a consulting firm or a university department could aspire to own one. Software applications were either custom made or highly specialised. As described below, travel forecasting software for use by practitioners began to be developed for these systems, as well as for university research.

As computer processor technology evolved, the next development stage was the Apple II microcomputer, offered by Apple in 1977.[9] Then IBM introduced its Personal Computer (IBM PC) in 1981.[10] The CP/M-86 (Control Program for Microcomputers) operating system first used by these computers was soon eclipsed by MS-DOS (disk operating system) of Microsoft.[11] The IBM design team built its PC with 'off-the-shelf' parts from a variety of original equipment manufacturers, which established an open architecture. In this manner IBM determined the standards for personal computers, which other manufacturers soon followed. The IBM PC-compatible computer was soon established as the standard for office computing. This seemingly unintended standardisation allowed software producers to develop and market software which would operate on hardware systems produced by many firms. In addition to general purpose software for spreadsheet analysis, statistics and word processing, specialised travel forecasting software began to be produced.

Paralleling the development of personal computers was the engineering workstation, a higher performance desktop microcomputer designed to be used by one person at a time, but also accessed remotely by other users as necessary. At first, workstations offered better performance than the IBM PC, especially with respect to graphics, processing power and multitasking ability. The workstation operating systems were some 'flavour' of the UNIX operating system, an innovation of Bell Laboratories in the 1960s.[12] In the early 1990s, when these UNIX-based workstations were considerably more powerful than PCs, it was unclear which computing platform should be used for travel forecasting. Further technical development and price competition from PC producers gradually tipped the balance in favour of the evolving PC, relegating engineering workstations to more specialised engineering and research tasks, as well as servers for larger-scale computing systems.

10.2.3 Comparisons of Computing Speed, Memory and Cost

How can the performance of computers used in the early period of travel forecasting be compared with those in use today? Computer scientists interested in this question have performed tests during the past 40 years. Perhaps the most noteworthy comparisons were made by Jack Dongarra.[13] One metric for comparisons is the number of floating point operations per second (flops) for solving a system of linear equations. Figure 10.1 shows two data series for this measure for computers introduced between 1951 and 2010. The data series from Strohmaier et al (2005) shows floating point operations per second for several computers introduced between 1951 and 2005. The second and more detailed series is based on measurements performed by Dongarra. The points shown are a small selection of the measurements he performed. The trend established by the early mainframe computers and extended by Cray supercomputers and more exotic machines continues to this day.

Early IBM mainframes had 32 kilowords of memory, each word consisting of 36 bits; therefore, their memory was roughly equivalent to 256 kilobytes (KB). The IBM S/360 and S/370 had up to 512 KB of memory,

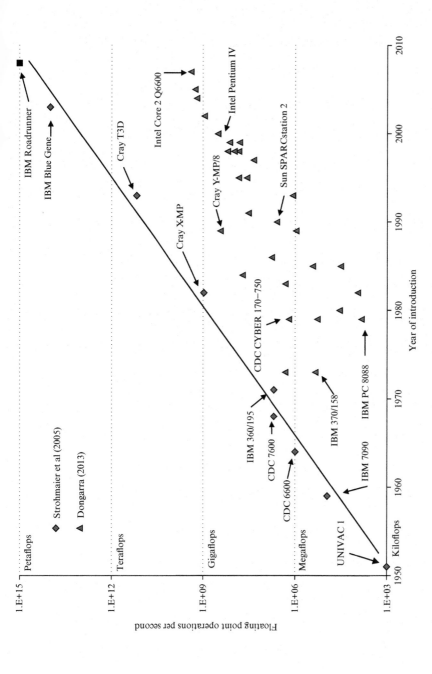

Sources: Drawn from data in Strohmaier et al (2005); and Dongarra (2013), www.netlib.org/utk/people/JackDongarra/papers.htm (accessed 2 March 2014).

Figure 10.1   Performance of mainframe, super-, mini- and microcomputers, 1951–2008

where a byte consists of 8 bits. The maximum memory available in early minicomputers and engineering workstations was also typically 512 kilobytes. Subsequently, the memory of PCs expanded to 1024 KB or 1 megabyte (MB) per 32-bit processor. As 64-bit PCs became available, memory limits expanded to 4096 MB or 4 gigabytes (GB) up to 16 GB. PCs with multiple CPUs or cores began to be offered after 2000, greatly expanding the processing speed and memory available to software applications.

Related to the increasing speed and memory of computers is the phenomenon known as Gordon Moore's law: 'over the history of computing hardware, the number of transistors on an integrated circuit has doubled approximately every two years'.[14] A shorter period often quoted was stated by Intel executive David House, 'who predicted that chip performance would double every 18 months',[15] a combination of the effect of more transistors and their faster speed. Figure 10.2 shows the log-linear relationship between the number of transistors on an integrated circuit and the date of its introduction.

Before the advent of minicomputers and especially microcomputers, commercial mainframe computing time could cost as much as $2000 per CPU hour. Estimation of a logit model on a mainframe, for example, could cost several hundred dollars. The use of travel forecasting models was prohibitively costly unless one was affiliated with a university or a public agency. The use of microcomputers to perform analyses in a form useful to clients, therefore, offered a compelling business opportunity. To reap the benefits of PC technology, practitioners would clearly require extensive software. With the introduction and ongoing development of the IBM PC, some software developers believed that the cost of computing would become nominal, once the acquisition cost of computer hardware was amortised.[16]

10.3 TRAVEL FORECASTING WITH MAINFRAME COMPUTERS

10.3.1 Programs for the IBM 700/7000 Series

The first mainframes used by urban transportation studies, BPR and their consultants were the IBM 700/7000 series, in particular the IBM 704 and 709, and the IBM 7090/7094.[17] These computers were used by the Detroit and Chicago transportation studies from 1956 onwards for trip distribution and traffic assignment (sections 2.3.3, 2.4.5). In some cases the IBM 650 was used for small problems. Douglas Carroll (1956) summarised the state of traffic assignment practice in 1956, noting that computers were

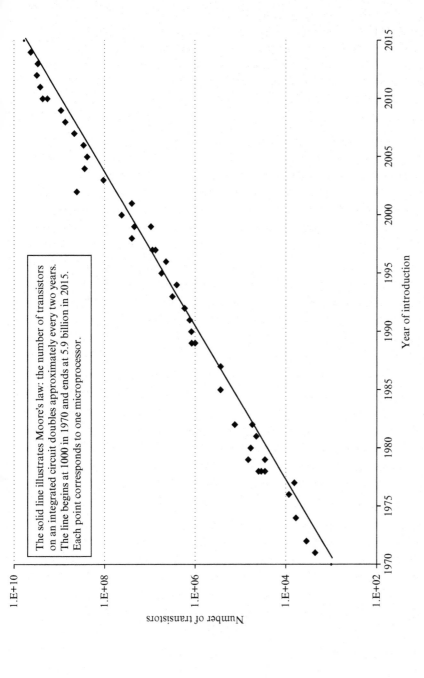

The solid line illustrates Moore's law: the number of transistors on an integrated circuit doubles approximately every two years. The line begins at 1000 in 1970 and ends at 5.9 billion in 2015. Each point corresponds to one microprocessor.

Source: Drawn from data in Wikipedia: Moore's law (en.wikipedia.org/wiki/Moore's_law); and Microprocessor chronology (en.wikipedia.org/wiki/Microprocessor_chronology) (both accessed 24 August 2014).

Figure 10.2 Number of microprocessor transistors on an integrated circuit, 1971–2014

just beginning to automate the preparation of diversion curves for allocating traffic to proposed facilities (section 2.3.3).

In parallel with the Detroit and Chicago studies, Glenn Brokke and Lee Mertz at BPR began development of computer programs to solve trip distribution models of the gravity type, and apply traffic assignment methods based on Edward Moore's algorithm for finding the shortest routes through a network (Brokke and Mertz, 1958; Brokke, 1959, 1969; Mertz, 1960a, 1960b) (section 2.5.1). Programs for calibrating and testing a gravity model were initially written for the IBM 704 and later modified for use on the IBM 7090/94 (US DoC, 1963a, ii). Programming for assignment programs was initiated for the IBM 704 in 1958 under contract to the General Electric Computer Department, Phoenix, Arizona. 'This project produced a battery of high-speed computer programs that would assign nondirectional interzonal traffic movements', including an option of using a diversion or all-or-nothing assignment. These programs were extended in 1960 to permit directional assignments as well as turn penalties and prohibitions (US DoC, 1964, I-3). Following the transition from first to second generation computers during 1961–62, BPR combined its programs into a library.

Mertz (1961) surveyed transportation studies in California, Chicago, Detroit, Minnesota, Toronto and Washington, DC with regard to solving traffic assignments with the IBM 650 and IBM 704 computers, including the size of problems that could be solved, the cost of program preparation and use, and efforts to share programs. Computer use charges for traffic assignments were $1000 to $2000 per assignment for a large mainframe computer.[18]

The Transportation Planning Computer Exchange Group (T-PEG), consisting of early computer programmers, met from 1963 until 1973 under the leadership of BPR. Seventeen meetings had been held by 1973, when the group evidently disbanded. Newsletters issued by BPR documented the discussions and news from members of the group.[19]

Transportation engineering consultants began to offer the capabilities required by many metropolitan area studies. One example was Wilbur Smith and Associates, founded in 1952 by Wilbur Smith [1911–1978], associate director of Yale University's Bureau of Highway Traffic. In Canada, Neal Irwin and H.G. von Cube, Traffic Research Corporation under contract to the Metropolitan Toronto Planning Board, implemented an innovative traffic assignment method together with trip generation and trip distribution models (Irwin et al, 1961). Subsequently, Irwin and von Cube (1962) described how to solve a relatively detailed travel forecasting model with feedback (Mertz, 1961, 100).

Alan Voorhees [1922–2005],[20] an early advocate of urban travel forecasting models, formed Alan M. Voorhees and Associates (AMV) in 1961 in response to the requirements of urban transportation planning studies for travel forecasting capabilities (Voorhees, 1955, 1958; Voorhees and Morris, 1959). Walter Hansen [1931–2008] joined the firm soon after. AMV soon established itself as a leading provider of travel forecasts and computer programs.

The Urban Mass Transportation Act of 1964, as amended in 1966, assigned responsibility for 'urban mass transportation' systems planning to the US Department of Housing and Urban Development (US HUD) (Weiner, 1997, Chapters 4, 5; 2013). Charles Graves, a land use planner formerly with the Puget Sound Regional Transportation Study, Seattle, proposed that US HUD develop a mass transit planning computer program battery comparable to BPR's highway program battery. The effort was called the 'Urban Mass Transit Planning Project'. A contract was awarded to AMV for development of programs for modal split, transit assignment and related peripheral functions for the IBM 7090/94 (section 2.6). Walter Hansen headed the project; initially, the programmers were Richard Bunyan and Robert Dial.

Robert Dial joined AMV in 1965 at age 27, after working at the Puget Sound Regional Transportation Study. His undergraduate major in mathematics was the basis for his first position as a statistician. There he became 'enthralled' by the modelling and computational challenges of this emerging field, and gained experience with the use of early computers. To advance his knowledge and standing, Dial studied transportation engineering with Edgar Horwood [1919–1985], a geographical information system pioneer at the University of Washington.[21] For his MSE thesis, Dial created an early geographic information system, which he implemented on the IBM 709.

For the US HUD contract, Bunyan prepared a process diagram, similar to BPR's highway package, which consisted of seven modules: (a) network description; (b) transit path builder; (c) O-D travel times; (d) mode split model calibration; (e) mode split model application; (f) load trip table; and (g) report generator (Dial and Bunyan, 1968).[22] Robert Dial's early contributions to the representation of transit networks and pathfinding in transit networks stem from this project. The programs were written in FORTRAN except for the pathfinding routines, a 2000-line code written in assembly language to achieve practical running times (Dial, 1967). Dial also wrote a 500-line pathfinder code in FORTRAN to test his algorithm's design. AMV's US HUD package offered the essential components of a mass transit planning system for the first time.[23]

Interestingly, while working at Freeman, Fox, Wilbur Smith and Associates in the UK, John Wootton (1967) presented a paper on 'The

Analysis of Public Transport Systems' to the British Computer Society Symposium in Edinburgh. He later described his paper as 'the first description of a minimum path assignment algorithm for allocating passengers to public transport services. The algorithm was subsequently used in the Greater London Transportation Studies (TRANSITNET) and other transportation studies (MINITRAMP).' Elements of the program were used in his subsequent programs providing support for public transport operations.[24] It seems that Robert Dial and John Wootton made original contributions to finding shortest routes over public transport networks at the same time (see also section 3.7.2).

10.3.2 Programs for the CDC 3600

With the introduction of the CDC 3600 in 1963, Control Data Corporation became a principal competitor of IBM for its mainframe business.[25] In that year, CDC began to develop its own travel forecasting program package TRANPLAN, a transportation planning system for the Control Data 3600 (CDC, 1965). CDC's motivation was to sell computer time at its Data Centers (i.e., service bureaus) by offering an alternative to the travel forecasting programs developed for the IBM 7090/94 by BPR and later US HUD.

CDC's *Urban Affairs* newsletter stated:

> 3600 TRANPLAN is an integrated system of computer programs which not only performs the data processing functions traditionally employed by transportation planners, but also contains several advantages over previously implemented systems. The system developed for the 3600 computer by CDC, in association with a number of leading transportation planning consultants, is a powerful tool for the transportation planning process. 6600 HUDTRAN is a series of computer programs ... used for planning public transportation systems. The programs were designed and written by Alan M. Voorhees and Associates, Inc. under contract to the Department of Housing and Urban Development. Conversion of the programs to the CDC 6600 was done by Data Services personnel to complement 3600 TRANPLAN.[26]

The 'previously implemented systems' to which the newsletter refers were BPR's battery of trip distribution and assignment programs, as well as programs developed by AMV for its consulting practice. Brokke (1969, 36) noted that CDC 'has developed at their own expense a battery of CDC 3600 programs that are capable of handling larger networks than can be accommodated on the 7090/94'. AMV was the principal consultant in the development of TRANPLAN beginning in 1964.[27] After 1966, AMV became a primary user. The CDC newsletters issued during 1969 also reported applications of TRANPLAN in urban transportation studies in the mid-western and western US.

Upon completion of the US HUD transit planning system, AMV received a terse letter from CDC demanding all of the US HUD source code under the US Freedom of Information Act.[28] AMV promptly complied; at that time results accomplished at the taxpayer's expense were considered to be in the public domain. Once CDC received the source code, it noticed that the transit path builder was written in assembler language, contrary to portability requirements for computer program development supported by the US government. In response to a complaint, Robert Dial offered CDC his FORTRAN path builder test code. Without this program to guide it, CDC might not have achieved substantial use of the program.[29]

In its *Urban Affairs* newsletter of December 1969, CDC announced the planned release of TRANPLAN II in July 1970 for the CDC 6600 and 3300 computers, recently introduced at seven CDC Data Centers in a nationwide network called CYBERNET Service, accessible by voice-grade or wideband telecommunication lines. TRANPLAN II was described as offering: (a) a comprehensive, integrated set of transportation planning functions; (b) application of key advances within the computer industry; (c) problem-oriented command and control language; and (d) capability to insert or change individual modules. The basic functions of TRANPLAN II were to include: (a) data capture; (b) highway and transit network builder; (c) highway and transit path builder; (d) highway and transit network loader; (e) gravity and Fratar trip distribution; (f) modal choice; (g) file utilities; (h) report generator; and (i) graphic displays. The capability to execute the programs from remote terminals was emphasised. The September 1970 newsletter then stated that TRANPLAN II was scheduled for release in January 1971. As the archived newsletters ended with the January 1971 issue, the effort was evidently abandoned after 1970.

The project leader of CDC's TRANPLAN effort from 1963 to 1966, Franklin Goodyear, related in correspondence in 2010:

> We assembled a team of about four to seven computer programmers to create the package, as designed by AMV. We at CDC did not have subject matter expertise in the field of transportation planning. Our role was to create a functioning system which would run efficiently on the CDC 3600 in use at CDC Data Centers. We relied completely on our consultants to design the functions to be programmed. Our primary contact with AMV was Richard Bunyan, who provided the specifications of each component of TRANPLAN.[30]

Goodyear stated that in his opinion CDC abandoned the development of TRANPLAN because it was unsuccessful in selling it to users. CDC management determined that $300 should be charged for user manuals.

Evidently, prospective customers were unable to obtain funds for this purpose, which was small compared to charges for the 3600 itself.[31]

10.3.3   Programs for the IBM System/360 and System/370

In 1964 after IBM announced its System/360, BPR realised that its program library would need to be adapted to third generation computers (US DoT, 1972a, I-8 – I-9). According to Brokke (1969, 37), BPR's S/360 computer installation replaced three second generation machines, and handled a problem twice as large at the same speed and one-third the cost. The computer programs implemented for the IBM S/360 for the Federal Highway Administration (FHWA) were designated as the Urban Planning System 360 for Trip Distribution and Traffic Assignment (US DoT, 1969a, 1969b). The trip distribution model formulations described and implemented in this report and associated computer programs were the same empirical gravity models found in US DoC (1963a) plus Schneider's intervening opportunities model (sections 2.4.3, 2.5.3).

In 1967 the Ontario Department of Transportation contracted with AMV to write a new highway modelling package. The code development was undertaken by three programmers under the direction of Robert Dial and implemented on the S/360; it included: (a) a highway network builder; (b) a highway network path builder; (c) a path skimmer; (d) a gravity trip distribution model; and (e) matrix manipulation tools. Programs developed or modified during this project had the prefix OV for 'Ontario Voorhees'. AMV also transferred its US HUD modal split and transit assignment programs to the IBM S/360, thereby completing a travel forecasting capability for IBM's third generation computer system (US HUD, 1966, 1967, 1968).[32] The resulting program package was named TRIPS (TRansportation Improvements Programming System). TRIPS became the basis for much work performed by AMV, but was not sold commercially.

In 1966, the US Department of Transportation (US DoT) was created. Following a transition period, the Bureau of Public Roads became the Federal Highway Administration. Responsibility for mass transit in US HUD was also reconsidered; the Urban Mass Transportation Administration (UMTA) was created in US DoT in 1968.[33] Computer program development activities at US HUD were transferred to UMTA. FHWA continued the development and dissemination of its travel forecasting programs for the IBM S/360 and S/370. Later, the FHWA battery was renamed PLANPAC/BACKPAC, a core set of programs used in travel forecasting and other related utilities (US DoT, 1973a, 1974, 1977a).

Robert Dial returned to Seattle in 1968 and pursued a Ph.D. at the University of Washington with Edgar Horwood, while continuing to work part time for AMV. His thesis research led to his probabilistic multi-path assignment model (Dial, 1971) (section 2.5.6). Following completion of his Ph.D. in 1970, Dial joined the UMTA's Office of Research, Development and Demonstrations, where he led the development of the UMTA Transportation Planning System (UTPS) (US DoT, 1972b). AMV donated TRIPS to UMTA, thereby sparing itself the cost of maintaining TRIPS.[34] The initial version of UTPS was accomplished by changing the *AV* and *OV* prefixes of TRIPS programs to *U*. The first release was just TRIPS in a different wrapper, but then development of TRIPS and UTPS diverged. Since UTPS documentation was provided in the form of line printer output, little documentation has survived.

FHWA later joined with UMTA in the further development and enhancement of an integrated system of programs for road and transit planning, renamed the Urban Transportation Planning System (also UTPS) for the IBM S/370. UTPS consisted of eight principal modules, including those in TRIPS, plus INET and UROAD, a capacity restraint assignment module with network equilibrium assignment (sections 2.5.5, 7.4.2) (Dial, 1976; Dial and Quillian, 1980; Dial et al, 1980). In addition to government staff, consultants to UMTA and FHWA participated in the development of UTPS programs, documentation and training manuals (US DoT, 1976, 1977b).

Robert Dial led the development of UTPS at UMTA through the 1970s. By 1981, computer technology was rapidly evolving. Minicomputers (e.g., Digital Equipment Corporation's PDP series) were approaching the speed and memory of mainframes at substantially lower costs, and microcomputers began entering the market in 1977 (section 10.2.2). Although Dial did not write much code at UMTA, the opportunity to experiment with these new computers proved irresistible to him. In 1981 he joined the faculty of the University of Texas at Austin; no further development of UTPS was undertaken after that time, although substantial improvements in its functionality and performance continued. UTPS training courses were also offered by UMTA to 1987.

10.4   TRAVEL FORECASTING WITH MINICOMPUTERS AND MICROCOMPUTERS

As computing hardware evolved from mainframes to minicomputers to microcomputers in the late 1970s, universities and consultants began to develop and offer programs for travel forecasting, learning from their research (section 7.4) and FHWA's PLANPAC and UMTA/FHWA's UTPS experience. About 1980, certain private firms complained to US DoT that its agencies were developing software in competition with the private sector. Such complaints may have received a sympathetic hearing by the Reagan administration, which began in January 1981. In any event, UMTA and FHWA ceased further development of UTPS and PLANPAC. FHWA also terminated development of its Quick Response System (QRS), and gave the rights to its developer, Alan Horowitz (section 10.5.2.2).

Evolving computer technology together with this change in policy had a huge impact on the travel forecasting software sector. In the eyes of some, it also hampered the ability of US DoT to advance the state of practice in travel forecasting methods. With the emergence of software development by the private sector, FHWA also no longer offered advice to planning agencies and consultants concerning what software they should use. Software systems being developed and offered to state DoTs and metropolitan planning organisations (MPOs) differed in their capabilities. Users of these systems had modest abilities to evaluate the qualities of the systems, which sometimes produced different results. Moreover, standards and protocols for travel forecasting software did not emerge, as sometimes occurs in other software sectors.

To facilitate the exchange of information about this emerging software, UMTA and FHWA compiled 'Microcomputers in Transportation' (US DoT, 1982).[35] A new series called 'PCs in Transportation Software Directory' appeared in July 1988 and continued for several years. Although the reports issued during the 1980s cannot be regarded as definitive, they do offer insights into the activities of that period. The 1984 and 1987 editions of 'Microcomputers in Transportation' showed that several software systems were under development, as listed in Table 10.1 in the order in the publication. Early editions of these reports also reported software under development by Marvin Manheim[36] at MIT and Robert Dial at the University of Texas at Austin.

Ferguson et al (1992) provided another benchmark in the development of travel forecasting software. At that time, software was primarily oriented to the IBM PC-compatible with the 80286/80386/80486 series CPU operating under MS-DOS, 640 KB of RAM, at least 60 MB of disk storage and a graphics monitor (VGA/SVGA). Some developers used engineering workstations as their development platform, and therefore also offered systems for one or more UNIX-based computers. In their review, the authors identified eight vendors offering software suited to both road and public transport models used in the four-step travel forecasting procedure. In alphabetical order, the systems were: EMME/2;

Table 10.1   *Microcomputer travel forecasting software developed in the mid-1980s*

Name	Developer	Computing environment
MicroTrans	TRANSWARE Systems	IBM PC-MS-DOS
TMODEL	Robert Shull, Professional Solutions	Apple, IBM PC-MS-DOS
MINUTP	Larry Seiders, Comsis Corporation	IBM PC-MS-DOS
MTPS	San Diego Systems	Apple, IBM PC
TGDA	Wayne Kittleson, CH2M Hill	Apple
UMOT	Mobility Systems	Apple
TP-System	Kenneth Roberts & Associates	Altos 68000-UNIX
TRANPLAN	James Fennessy, DKS Associates	IBM PC-MS-DOS
MicroTRIPS	PRC Voorhees/MVA Systematica	IBM PC-MS-DOS
EMME/2	Michael Florian, INRO	Pixel 100/AP-UNIX
MOTORS	Bob Lewis, M.M. Dillon	IBM PC-MS-DOS
QRS II	Alan Horowitz, AJH Associates	IBM PC-MS-DOS
VISUM/VISEM	T. Schwerdtfeger, PTV	HP 1000-UNIX
SATURN	Dirck Van Vliet, University of Leeds	IBM PC-MS-DOS

MINUTP; QRS II; System II;[37] TMODEL2; TRANPLAN; TransCAD; and TRIPS. Other contemporary systems were VISUM/VISEM of PTV in Germany and SATURN of the University of Leeds, UK.

These software systems varied substantially in size of model (numbers of zones, nodes and links), graphics and network editing capabilities (limited graphics to a full GIS), interactive capabilities (batch, menu-driven, mouse) and price (nominal to quite expensive). Most developers offered training programmes and technical support. Thus, only ten years after the advent of the IBM PC, a specialised software niche had emerged, based on the rapidly expanding capabilities of microcomputers. While large planning organisations continued to rely to a considerable extent on mainframes, and UTPS and PLANPAC software, the conversion to commercial software systems for the PC and UNIX-based computers was clearly the trend for the future.

10.5 TRAVEL FORECASTING SOFTWARE DEVELOPERS AND PRODUCTS

Software evolved for minicomputers and microcomputers in three ways. First, mainframe programs were rewritten for minis and micros. The authors of these early mainframe-based systems were often the same programmers, practitioners and consultants who wrote the code for the mainframes. Second, as academic research on travel forecasting methods began to catch up with practice in the late 1960s, academic research-based developers initiated software systems that were distinctly different from their practice-based counterparts (section 7.4.2). Third, several software systems were created by practitioners and consultants based on their experience and their interest in applying the emerging technology.

In the first group, there were three development streams, which later merged to form Citilabs:

1. TRIPS, based on the pioneering efforts of AMV, and the basis for CDC's TRANPLAN (sections 2.5.6, 10.5.1.2);
2. MicroTRIPS, which also evolved from the original TRIPS of AMV;
3. MINUTP, based in part on its developer's earlier experience with BPR.

In the following sections, these are presented in this order, with a summary of their merged status in Citilabs. The fourth member of this group is TRACKS, an early product of a New Zealand consultant, Gabites Porter; initially TRACKS was also a mainframe application.

The second group consists of seven academic/research-related firms that began in the 1980s:

1. VISUM, developed by PTV, based on research at the University of Karlsruhe, and located in Karlsruhe, Germany;
2. Emme, developed by INRO, based on research at the Centre for Research on Transportation, University of Montreal, and located in Montreal, Canada;
3. TransCAD, developed by Caliper Corporation, Newton, Massachusetts, US, initially based on academic research of the 1990s;
4. SATURN, based on research of Dirck Van Vliet and others at the Institute for Transport Studies, University of Leeds, UK, and distributed by Atkins Global;
5. QRS II, based on research at the University of Wisconsin-Milwaukee, and located in Milwaukee, Wisconsin, US;

6. EVA, based on research at the University of Transportation Friedrich List, in Dresden, DDR, and from the 1990s onward on research at the Technical University Dresden, Germany;
7. ESTRAUS, developed by MCT, based on research at the Department of Transportation Engineering, Pontificia Universidad Católica de Chile, Santiago, and located in Santiago, Chile.

The first three systems, VISUM, Emme and TransCAD, developed into generalised travel forecasting software systems, comparable in scope to the evolving products of Citilabs. Descriptions of these software products are presented in section 10.5.1 roughly in the order that they entered the market in the 1980s.

The latter four systems, SATURN, QRS II, EVA and ESTRAUS, which are more specialised, are described in section 10.5.2, together with a third group of smaller software developers, sometimes one person working alone: TMODEL, UFOSNET, STRADA and OmniTRANS. Two of these, EVA and TMODEL, were later merged into PTV's VISUM. Software systems serving regional markets, such as in Germany, are not included in this review.

The following descriptions are based on responses to a questionnaire by knowledgeable principals and software developers. Claims and other statements concerning the capabilities of the software, and which was first to achieve them, are not included, since the authors have no way to verify them. Likewise, information on market penetration and share at various points in time is not included for lack of verification. Further development of many of these systems is ongoing. Since any historical account is out of date by the time that it is published, any detailed descriptions are for historical purposes, and generally end about 2000. Current information may be obtained from the referenced websites.

10.5.1   Generalised Travel Forecasting Software Systems

10.5.1.1   TRANPLAN[38]
James Fennessy first used TRANPLAN in 1965 at Wilbur Smith and Associates. He joined Control Data Corporation's Palo Alto Data Center in 1967 to support and enhance TRANPLAN, based on his experience with urban transportation studies. Following the demise of TRANPLAN II, Fennessy joined DeLeuw, Cather & Company (DCCO) in San Francisco. About that time, FHWA released PLANPAC for the IBM S/360; according to Fennessy, this software was initially error-prone and unreliable. Given its need to apply travel forecasting models, and with no reliable software and hardware available, DCCO developed a new software system

for the CDC 6600 based on TRANPLAN. This development effort was led by Fennessy, and supported by Raif Kulunk, who had earlier worked on the initial development of TRANPLAN.

TRANPLAN, as redeveloped by DCCO, was licensed to CDC to run on its 6000 series computers. During the same period, UMTA and FHWA were jointly developing UTPS for the IBM S/370. With UTPS being offered free by US DoT, TRANPLAN usage declined. When minicomputers were introduced by DEC and PR1ME in the late 1970s, TRANPLAN was converted to these platforms. Given the high computing costs of applying UTPS and TRANPLAN at service bureaus, some agencies began to purchase TRANPLAN licences in the early 1980s for use on these less expensive minicomputers. TRANPLAN was next rewritten for the IBM PC. In 1984, Fennessy founded Urban Analysis Group (UAG) to continue the distribution and development of TRANPLAN, which was acquired by UAG and Raif Kulunk from DCCO.

10.5.1.2 TRIPS and MicroTRIPS[39]

AMV's TRIPS was brought to the UK for the Tyne Wear Plan Study, and AMV Ltd was formed. Brian Martin, who had returned to the UK to serve as chief transport planner of the Greater London Council, following an extended period of study and research in the US, was named managing director of the UK subsidiary. In 1976, the company was renamed Martin and Voorhees Associates (MVA) in recognition of Brian Martin's contributions.[40] Later the software business of MVA, led by Hugh Neffendorf, was called MVA Systematica.

AMV lost interest in the further development of TRIPS because UTPS was being enhanced and was available free if one had access to an IBM S/360. However, UTPS was not well suited to British transportation planning, because some US modelling concepts were quite different from UK practice. Accordingly, Hugh Neffendorf, who had joined AMV Ltd as a member of the Tyne Wear Plan team in 1969, began to extend TRIPS, by writing a gravity model program with car ownership segmentation and a partial matrix technique for matrix estimation developed with John Wootton. These new programs had the prefix MV. In the following years, Edwin Ecob wrote a highway assignment package for UK practice, and Chris Querée began the gradual conversion of TRIPS to portable FORTRAN for use on other computers. By the early 1980s a FORTRAN suite of programs could operate on a range of mainframes (IBM, Honeywell, ICL, CDC) and minicomputers (PR1ME, DEC VAX, DEC PDP11) in either batch or interactive mode. The suite included modules for trip distribution and assignment as well as survey processing and data analysis.

A parallel product called MicroTRIPS was developed in the early 1980s for CP/M-based micros, and later for the IBM PC. Bruce Ramsey wrote the first version of MicroTRIPS, which ran under the CP/M with 56 KB of memory. Martin Bach developed MVGRAF, an interactive network graphics program. Miles Logie developed MVESTM, a matrix estimation program. Gier Kiste wrote TRIPSWIN, a TRIPS supervisor program, which added usability and model quality assurance. MicroTRIPS, later named TRIPS again, was actively developed as MS-DOS expanded the capability of personal computers. In 1992, MVA was acquired by Systra, a transportation consultant based in Paris. Systra sponsored the design of TRIPS 2000, but it was never completed.

A significant change in the approach to TRIPS/MicroTRIPS occurred when it began to be sold to government agencies, consulting firms and universities. This change was important, because its use became extensive internationally and became the main driver for its ongoing development.

10.5.1.3   MINUTP[41]

Development of a third software system based on emerging minicomputer–microcomputer hardware was undertaken by Larry Seiders, working in the California office of Comsis Corporation, a consulting firm involved in the development of PLANPAC and UTPS. Seiders had worked for BPR in the early 1960s. Seiders first developed MINUTP for certain minicomputers in the late 1970s; it was rewritten for the IBM PC with MS-DOS. Most restrictions on the PC version were due to its limited memory and compiler capabilities. Many standard modelling procedures were included: (a) generation; (b) shortest route search; (c) distribution; and (d) assignment with capacity restraint. Stochastic assignment and transit-related procedures were added, and the initial procedures were improved and enhanced. Seiders described MINUTP as similar in nature and function to larger, more complicated systems such as UTPS, PLANPAC and CDC's TRANPLAN, but simpler to use (US DoT, 1982).

There was no graphical user interface for MINUTP or other software in the early 1980s. Network viewing and editing were extremely difficult and time consuming. In the late 1980s Seiders developed NetVue, based on the Hercules monochrome graphic standard. The MS-Windows-based successor to MINUTP was TP+, originally proposed as a joint development effort of Comsis, the Hague Consulting Group and Steer Davies Gleave.

Seiders initiated development of TP+ in the mid-1990s. He acquired the rights to MINUTP and TP+ when he retired from Comsis in 1997, and continued its development in collaboration with Victor Siu. Seiders and Siu joined UAG in 1997, where they concentrated on further software development, Seiders on TP+, and Siu on his user interface, VIPER, which began as a network editor and as a multi-data (text, database, network, matrix, model scripts) viewer/editor. VIPER also managed the application and presented results in a single, integrated environment.

10.5.1.4 CUBE[42]

Citilabs was created in 2001 by the merger of MVA's Software Products Division (TRIPS) and Urban Analysis Group (TRANPLAN, MINUTP, TP+). Their origins can be traced to TRIPS developed by AMV and TRANPLAN developed by CDC in the 1960s. TRIPS, TP+ and VIPER were consolidated by Citilabs into two parts: CUBE BASE, the user interface; and travel forecasting procedures. CUBE BASE consisted of three parts: (a) VIPER, a graphical user interface; (b) Application Manager from TRIPS, based on the TRIPSWIN flowchart interface for laying out, developing and managing the modelling process; and (c) Scenario Manager, a new element for creating, managing and batching scenarios developed at Citilabs. The travel forecasting procedures in the legacy software systems acquired by Citilabs, except MINUTP, could be applied with CUBE BASE. In 2003, Citilabs began to distribute CUBE VOYAGER, initially the merger of TP+ and a transit planning module for networks, path building, skimming and assignment. Development of CUBE is ongoing in response to user needs and algorithmic and computational advances.

10.5.1.5 TRACKS[43]

TRACKS is a suite of over 50 modules developed since 1975 by Grant Smith of Gabites Porter Consultants, Christchurch and Hamilton, New Zealand, for land use and transportation planning. The only travel forecasting programs in use in New Zealand prior to its development were ICES-Transet and UTPS.[44] The functional areas of TRACKS are: 'land use and data preparation; trip generation; trip distribution and modal split; parking; network assignment; public transport; evaluation; and matrix and file manipulation'. TRACKS solves the four-step procedure with various options, and links to SIDRA[45] and MapInfo.[46]

TRACKS began as a suite of FORTRAN programs for solving a three-step model: (a) category analysis trip generation; (b) gravity-type trip distribution; and (c) all-or-nothing assignment. The first applications were in 1976 on an IBM S/370, later converted to a Burroughs mainframe. Core programs were retained, but assignment was extended to include capacity restraint. Several calibration and evaluation modules were added. By 1980 the software was ported to a DEC PDP 11/03 with 32 KB of memory and two 128 KB floppy disk drives, requiring that matrix operations be performed row by row, and assignments be performed tree by tree.

Even so, models adequate for New Zealand cities were solved. Input was through screens and keyboard. The system was converted to the IBM PC with MS-DOS in 1983. The PC's graphics capability enabled a GIS-based graphical network editor to be developed by the late 1980s. In 1993, the system was converted to MS-Windows.

TRACKS incorporated intersection delays in 1981 as a statistical function of opposing flow. Later, calculation of approach delay was implemented as a function of conflicting flows, based on formulae in Australian Road Research 123 for signals (Akçelik, 1981) and Tanner's queuing theory for priority intersections and roundabouts. By the mid-1990s, the assignment procedures allowed delays to be calculated by turning movement. Cycle times and phase splits were determined endogenously depending on the flows on each movement at each iteration of the assignment.

10.5.1.6   VISUM[47]

PTV (originally, Planungsbüro Transport und Verkehr GmbH) was founded as a consulting company in Karlsruhe, Germany, in 1979. After Thomas Schwerdtfeger joined the company in 1985, he participated in a project on the evaluation of traffic calming concepts. To meet the project objectives, he undertook the development of a traffic assignment program based on a route-based traffic assignment algorithm of Bothner and Lutter (1982). This program was the beginning of the VISUM software system.

During the same period, Schwerdtfeger implemented a second system, VISEM, an activity-based demand model based on the research of Uwe Sparmann at the University of Karlsruhe (Fellendorf et al, 1997) (see also section 6.3.2). Subsequently, a public transport model was added to VISUM as a separate component, owing to memory constraints of that era. As more memory became available in PCs, and MS-Windows 3.0 was released, PTV offered three modules as separate systems: (a) VISUM – Private Transport; (b) VISUM – Public Transport; and (c) VISEM. As a result of the emphasis in the US on the four-step procedure, these were later integrated into a single system.[48] VISUM combines all aspects of strategic planning with operational planning, allowing the user to integrate real-time data directly into the strategic planning process.

In 2004, TMODEL Corporation, the software company of Robert Shull, the developer of TMODEL2, was acquired by PTV and merged with Innovative Transportation Concepts, PTV's partially owned subsidiary specialising in microscopic simulation, transit signal priority and traffic engineering, to form a new PTV subsidiary, PTV America (section 10.5.2.4).

PTV staff, often in collaboration with academic researchers, extended the capabilities of VISUM in several ways. One is the provision of capabilities for detailed modelling of public transport systems based on timetables, including the use of search methods in preparing timetables and crew scheduling for operations planning (Friedrich et al, 2000, 2001). Another is the modelling of boarding and alighting in frequency-based transit assignment (Nökel and Wekeck, 2009). A bi-criterion approach to road traffic assignment, Tribut, was implemented, which allows time and money costs of routes to be considered separately with the value of time chosen as a random variable. EVA, a model that combines trip generation, distribution and mode choice, was implemented in VISUM, based on research and applications in East Germany (sections 7.4.5.4, 10.5.2.3). Recently, LUCE, the bush-based road traffic assignment algorithm of Gentile (2014), was added to the traffic assignment options.

Development of VISUM continues in response to user needs, algorithmic and computational advances, and the contributions of PTV's computer scientists.

10.5.1.7   Emme[49]

During the 1970s, Michael Florian was director of the Centre for Research on Transportation (CRT) at the University of Montreal (section 7.4.1.3). With Sang Nguyen, Heinz Spiess and others, Florian initiated research on urban travel forecasting models (section 7.4.5.1). Transport Canada supported development of an experimental code for the model of Florian (1977) for the City of Winnipeg, which resulted in a model called équilibre multimodal–multimodal equilibrium (EMME). It was implemented computationally as a FORTRAN code for validation and model calibration on a CDC Cyber 176 (Florian et al, 1979).

At that time, there was considerable scepticism regarding the use of rigorous algorithms for congested traffic assignments, since heuristic methods, such as incremental assignment and variants of the capacity restraint method, were generally used in practice. This perspective motivated Florian to develop experimental software for combining the components of the conventional travel forecasting procedure into a single integrated model, which could be solved iteratively, in contrast to solving the four-step procedure with feedback.

INRO, founded by Michael Florian in 1976, obtained the rights for EMME from the University of Montreal in 1984. During 1980–83, the EMME experimental code was rewritten and implemented with interactive graphics on a CDC Cyber with Tektronix graphic terminals. One of the main contributors to its development was Heinz Spiess. All of the code was written for 32-bit minicomputers and microcomputers that were not yet available. A strategy-based public transport assignment model developed at this time was added (Spiess and Florian, 1989). Florian (2008, 44–45) described the development of EMME/2.

EMME/2 was ported to 32-bit UNIX and VMS microcomputers. The first commercial implementation in 1981was on a VAX 11/750 for the Stockholm County Council, followed in 1983 by a Pixel UNIX system at Metro, the MPO of Portland, Oregon. Afterwards EMME/2 rapidly evolved into a toolkit for modelling multi-modal networks and providing for full integration of transit and car modes, which featured: (a) matrix manipulation tools allowing implementation of a wide variety of travel demand models; (b) assignment methods based on convergent network equilibrium algorithms; (c) interactive calculators for evaluation and impact analysis methods; (d) a macro language for automating repetitive procedures; and (e) graphic display capabilities. Examples of additional features were: (a) a capability to implement virtually any spatial interaction model; (b) multi-class assignment based on generalised costs; (c) comprehensive route analysis capabilities; (d) triple index matrix operations; (e) O-D matrix adjustment for road and transit; (f) congested and capacitated transit assignments; and (g) stochastic road and transit assignment. The modular nature of the system enabled the development of model variants by defining macro procedures that used the building blocks of the software. An example is the solution of the sequential procedure with feedback with a convergent method devised by Metaxatos et al (1995).

About 2007 the software system was renamed Emme. Its development is ongoing in response to scientific advances and greatly enhanced computer capabilities.

10.5.1.8   TransCAD[50]

Caliper Corporation was founded in 1983 by Howard Slavin and Eric Ziering, who had conducted market research for Charles River Associates and contributed to its travel forecasting projects. Caliper's original goals were to serve business and government by focusing on market research, travel forecasting and logistics, as well as development of custom software for clients to implement the recommended solutions.

Caliper undertook a variety of software projects during its first few years, discovering that developing custom software for each project was difficult and expensive. From this experience emerged the concept for TransCAD, a platform for implementing such applications. Initially, TransCAD was intended to be a platform for new methods found in the expanding research literature. Ironically, only when the legacy methods found in PLANPAC or UTPS were added to TransCAD did it take off in the market.

From the beginning TransCAD was both a geographical information system (GIS) and a transportation modelling system with a common inter-face and common data structures. Hence, Caliper was an early innovator in the use of GIS in support of transportation modelling (Slavin, 2004). Routines were provided for: (a) network building and editing; (b) comput-ing shortest routes and trees; (c) traffic assignment (incremental, capac-ity restraint, deterministic and stochastic network equilibrium); (d) the travelling salesperson problem; (e) spatial interaction models (entropy model solution and calibration); (f) minimum cost network flows; and (g) arc-node partitioning.

TransCAD was written in C language for IBM PC-compatible comput-ers, had a user interface, and could accommodate large databases and networks. Its functions were accessible through menus integrating GIS graphics and database functionality with travel forecasting methods. An MS-DOS version of TransCAD was first offered in 1988; early adopters were the Metropolitan Transportation Authority of New York and Volpe National Transportation Systems Center.

A version released in 1996 for MS-Windows 3.0 introduced a script-ing language for both modelling and GIS functionality, including: (a) pre-packaged procedures for trip generation; (b) support for estimation and application of multinomial logit models; (c) new traffic assignment options; (d) trip table estimation from counts; (e) tools for accessing US census transportation planning products;[51] and (f) methods for represent-ing transit systems more precisely.

In 2000 Caliper added more features and supported more complex modelling procedures for large MPOs: (a) an enhanced user interface for solving models and managing scenarios; (b) additional options for transit pathfinding and assignment; (c) multi-modal multi-class assignments; and (d) nested logit applications. Solution of the four-step procedure with feedback was added by applying the method of successive averages to link flows. Subsequently, Caliper has pioneered in high performance comput-ing applications by introducing parallel processing, multi-threading and 64-bit computing. Rapidly converging link-based, origin-based and route-based network equilibrium assignment algorithms were added.

Development of TransCAD continues in response to user needs and computational advances.

10.5.2 Specialised Travel Forecasting Software Systems

10.5.2.1 SATURN[52]
SATURN is a flexible network analysis software system developed since 1976 by Dirck Van Vliet, initially in collaboration with Luis Willumsen, Michael Hall and others at the Institute for Transport Studies, University

of Leeds, UK (Hall et al, 1980, 1992). Since 1981, SATURN has been distributed by Atkins Global, an international consultancy. SATURN's initial innovation was that delays in various turning movements could be identified on the basis of detailed traffic simulations of junctions. This feature enabled SATURN to model the flow metering of traffic down-stream of bottlenecks and to avoid double-counting of queuing delays (section 9.3.1).

'SATURN is primarily a multi-function traffic assignment suite with additional facilities for matrix manipulation and demand estimation from counts. Its strengths lie in its flexibility and the analysis features offered, including its comprehensive display capabilities' (see also Van Vliet, 1982).[53] SATURN includes some of the basic features of four-step proce-dures, but with additional options not found in other systems. SATURN has six basic functions, paraphrased as follows: (a) combined traffic simulation and assignment for the analysis of road investment schemes for networks ranging from local road systems to major infrastructure improvements; (b) conventional traffic assignment for the analysis of larger networks; (c) simulation of individual intersections; (d) network editor; (e) matrix manipulation capabilities; and (f) travel demand model with basic elements of trip distribution and modal split.[54] Origin-based assignment was incorporated for both single and multiple user classes, which can achieve precise network equilibrium solutions. SATURN links to MapInfo for GIS capabilities.[55]

10.5.2.2 QRS II[56]

Quick Response System II (QRS II) was developed by Alan Horowitz, University of Wisconsin-Milwaukee, and is maintained and distributed by AJH Associates, Whitefish Bay, Wisconsin. Initially, QRS referred to manual techniques described in NCHRP Report 187 (Sosslau et al, 1978). FHWA released a microcomputer version of QRS in 1981. QRS II was an entirely new implementation of the philosophy stated in the NCHRP report that methods should be fast and tailored to the problem size.

QRS II, first released in 1987, included an MS-DOS-based graphics editor, a shortest route search routine, traffic assignment, multi-path transit assignment, and a logit-based mode split model. A feedback proce-dure based on the method of successive averages was added. An integrated land use model, a constrained Lowry–Garin activity allocations method with full feedback from equilibrium traffic assignment, was added next (Horowitz, 1989, 1991). Since 1992, link delays in the traffic assignment step have been calculated using traffic operations analysis methods for signalised intersections, two-way stops, all-way stops and two-lane roads from the 1985 *Highway Capacity Manual* (Transportation Research

Board, TRB, 1985). More types of traffic control were implemented later (Horowitz, 1992, 1997).

The initial system was developed for early IBM PCs with MS-DOS. As traffic engineering and travel forecasting evolved, the 1985 HCM was replaced by the 2000 HCM (TRB, 2000), path building was replaced by vine building, and methods were added from NCHRP Report 365 (Martin and McGuckin, 1998). As PC memory and disk storage expanded, limitations on the number of zones were relaxed. QRS II has continued to expand by offering a wider range of capabilities consistent with the traditional sequential procedure.

10.5.2.3   EVA[57]

EVA was a computer system and a related class of models based on a consistent traffic demand theory related to solution procedures for non-linear equation systems with side constraints developed by Dieter Lohse, University of Transportation Friedrich List, Dresden, DDR, and Technical University Dresden, Dresden, Germany during the period 1970–2010. The name EVA corresponds to the first letters of generation, distribution and modal split of traffic in German (section 7.4.5.4).

EVA is a disaggregated system related to personal travel: (a) traffic zones; (b) classes of travellers by age, life cycle status, gender and vehicle availability; (c) origin or destination locations defined by residence, workplace, school, shopping and leisure; (d) origin and destination groups defined by location (home to work, work to shopping, etc.); (e) competing modes of travel (pedestrian, bicycle, public transport, car, etc.); and (f) time of day. Trip generation, trip distribution and modal split were functionally specified and interconnected in EVA. No stepwise solution of the model was performed; rather, origin and destination flows by mode were determined by each complete solution. A traffic assignment procedure known as 'Lohse's learning procedure' was also implemented and is now available in VISUM.[58]

In urban applications, the use of four modes of travel (pedestrian, bicycle, public transport, car) was common. A non-linear equation system of travel demand (trip distribution and modal split on competing modes of transportation) was solved, resulting in three-dimensional traffic flow matrices (origin, destination and mode). EVA included options for the interpretation and illustration of results: (a) simple matrix operations; (b) travel distance and travel time distributions; (c) comparison of matrices with a linear regression analysis; and (d) matrix aggregation according to macro zones. Complex traffic demand calculations with simultaneous traffic distribution and modal split were implemented. For metropolitan Dresden with a population of 1.2 million, models with 900 traffic zones, four modes of transportation and 17 classes were solved. EVA was used in many applications for road, public transport and rail planning in Germany.

10.5.2.4   TMODEL[59]

Robert Shull initiated TMODEL in 1982 as a planning agency tool for analysis of urban development in Washington County, Oregon. It had a modular design based on the four-step procedure, but also included: (a) pre-distribution and post-distribution mode split options; (b) digitiser and plotter support; (c) matrix editor; (d) screen-line and scattergram assignment analysis; (e) import/export utilities; (f) path saving/editing; (g) link level-of-service analysis; (h) emissions analysis; (i) select link/ zone capabilities; (j) multi-point assignment; and (k) intersection (node) delays. Intersection capacity analysis tools, including TRC 212 and HCM methods for signalised and unsignalised intersections, were accessible from TMODEL's menus. In 1982, Shull founded Professional Solutions to develop and support TMODEL full time. David Larrabee made important contributions, including digitiser, plotter, and analysis utilities, and improved assignment and graphics editor features.

TMODEL was released for the Apple II in 1983. A modular system design with open, documented data formats allowed users to add their own functionality for data processing. The first version was capable of modelling 80 zones on an Apple II, later expanded to over 1000 zones on the IBM PC. The first application of screen graphics was implemented in 1984 on the Apple II and HP Touchscreen computer. TModel Corporation merged with Innovative Transportation Concepts in 2004 to form PTV America (section 10.5.1.6).

10.5.2.5   ESTRAUS[60]

Joaquín de Cea and Enrique Fernández, Pontificia Universidad Católica de Chile, Santiago, Chile, and Modelos Computacionales de Transporte (MCT), developed ESTRAUS with support from the Secretaria Interministerial de Planificatión de Transporte, Chile (SECTRA). ESTRAUS was developed in response to the government's goal of reforming Santiago's public transport system, especially the bus system.[61] ESTRAUS solves an integrated travel forecasting problem, satisfying network equilibrium route choice principles for both car and transit modes as well as the internal consistency requirements of the travel models, in contrast to solving the sequential procedure with feedback (de Cea et al, 2005).

ESTRAUS is suitable for the analysis and evaluation of strategic transportation plans, such as subway lines, highways, roadway concessions, segregated bus corridors, road pricing, public transit fare integration, and so on. The software provides for: (a) multiple user classes (e.g., income level, car availability, trip purpose); (b) multi-modal networks (pure and combined); (c) congestion in all networks and capacity constraints in public transport; (d) flexible and hierarchical structure for travel choice models; (e) doubly-constrained entropy-based trip distribution; (f) hierarchical logit modal split; (g) deterministic equilibrium assignment in public and private transportation networks; and (h) interactive network and database editing through a graphical user interface or external GIS. ESTRAUS is solved on a standard PC with the Linux operating system.

10.5.2.6   UFOSNET[62]

UFOSNET is a PC-MS-Windows-based travel forecasting software system with integrated GIS and GPS technologies developed by Robert Tung, RST International, Bellevue, Washington, US. It was originally written as a network design tool for solving network equilibrium assignment problems. Tung continued its development as an MS-DOS system and gradually expanded it to a general purpose planning tool. It was migrated to MS-Windows in 1991. The software was first offered commercially in 1993.

UFOSNET, built on the four-step sequential procedure, provides all essential tools for users to make travel forecasts for small to large urban areas. The core tools are: (a) network equilibrium traffic assignment; (b) capacity-constrained transit assignment; (c) network calculator; (d) matrix calculator; (e) network editor; and (f) scripting language. Trip distribution and mode choice models are provided with the scripting language. These modules are accessed through a menu-driven user interface. UFOSNET's GIS capabilities enable geographical analysis and mapping, including built-in GPS tools for conducting travel time and speed analyses. UFOSNET's assignment model is able to simulate node delays using HCM methodology.

10.5.2.7   STRADA[63]

The Japan International Cooperation Agency (JICA) initiated the development of STRADA (System for Travel Demand Analysis) for use in its transportation study projects in developing countries. JICA's objective was to provide a common tool of transportation planning and to build a common database for its technical assistance programmes. The software development effort began in 1993, led by Hideo Nakamura, University of Tokyo, Japan; subsequently, Yoshio Yoshida developed and applied STRADA, which was first released in 1997 for MS-Windows. STRADA consists of the traditional four-step procedure plus a disaggregate modal split model, O-D matrix calibrator, stochastic network equilibrium assignment, time-of-day network equilibrium assignment, a combined modal split and assignment model, an intersection analysis model and a GIS data converter.

10.5.2.8   OmniTRANS[64]

OmniTRANS was initially developed by Goudappel Coffeng, a transportation and traffic engineering consulting firm in the Netherlands. Henk Goudappel, a pioneering transportation planner in the Netherlands, established Goudappel Coffeng in 1963. Goudappel Coffeng became the Dutch distributor of TRANPLAN in 1972 (section 10.5.1.1). During the following 25 years, although many extensions and improvements were added to TRANPLAN, the firm realised that the core software was not satisfying its needs. In 1998, Goudappel Coffeng began development of OmniTRANS to meet its needs.

OmniTRANS was introduced in 1999, at which time all Dutch users of TRANPLAN adopted the new system. OmniTRANS International was established in 2003 to separate the ongoing development of OmniTRANS from Goudappel Coffeng. OmniTRANS has an object-oriented design, a relational database management system and a graphical user interface, with project management, land use – transportation interaction, trip distribution, discrete modal choice, path building and assignment, matrix estimation, environmental reporting, mapping and alternative analysis capabilities.

10.6   CONCLUSION

Urban travel forecasting with data processing equipment dates from 1953 (section 2.3.3). Computers with the potential to forecast urban travel (Univac 1 and IBM 704) soon became available. Hence, one may say that travel forecasting and computers for civilian use have common origins. Although difficult to demonstrate, urban travel forecasting was probably the first application of digital computing in the civilian public sector.

Anyone who witnessed all or much of the transition from that early period to the present day stands in awe of the accomplishments achieved. And yet, at nearly every point during this 60-year period, the challenges facing the users of computing hardware and software were formidable. This statement seems just as true today as it was at each point in the past. No doubt, novices entering the field today feel just as intimidated and fascinated as their predecessors.

Perhaps what has advanced even more than computer hardware is the software now available for travel forecasting applications. An active and flourishing software niche serving travel forecasting emerged during the past 30 years. Four software companies compete worldwide, and several more compete in regional markets. Each has a different approach to implementation of methods, to distribution and training, and even to the pricing of its products. That all four continue successfully is itself a remarkable and positive attribute of this field.

During the past decade new approaches to forecasting travel have come to the forefront at the level of general and specific problems to exploit the enormous and seemingly never-ending increases in computing speed, memory and data storage. Microsimulation-based models of activity-travel-network systems, such as TRANSIMS, MATSim and DynusT,[65] are examples that have benefited from ongoing increases in computing power and advanced computing languages. Solution of larger and more detailed traffic assignment problems is another. For both of these examples, more remains to be accomplished, so much more that future increases in computer power will undoubtedly be productively applied for many years to come.

Where do experienced or novice practitioners and students entering the field stand relative to this history? Clearly, all are challenged as never before to learn, perform their roles and contribute. But, in the same spirit as those who came before them, they are undoubtedly fascinated and inspired by the opportunities to utilise these technologies to solve problems facing our field at all levels. Equally challenged are those who strive to be their teachers and to address the widening array of research opportunities and problems offered by these computing technologies.

NOTES

1. An earlier version of sections 10.1 to 10.4 was published by Boyce and Bar-Gera (2012).
2. Much of the description was gleaned from Wikipedia (www.wikipedia.org/, accessed 26 January 2013).
3. en.wikipedia.org/wiki/IBM_mainframe (accessed 28 February 2014).
4. www.columbia.edu/cu/computinghistory/ (accessed 26 January 2013).
5. en.wikipedia.org/wiki/IBM_System/360   (en.wikipedia.org/wiki/IBM_System/370, accessed 26 January 2013).
6. en.wikipedia.org/wiki/Seymour_Cray (accessed 23 August 2013).
7. A supercomputer is a computer at the forefront of processing capacity, particularly speed of calculation, at the time of its introduction. Supercomputers introduced in the 1960s were designed primarily by Seymour Cray at CDC, and led the market into the 1970s, when Cray left to form Cray Research. Cray dominated the supercomputer market with his new designs, leading the supercomputing field in the late 1980s. Today, supercomputers are typically one-of-a-kind custom designs produced by companies such as Cray, Inc. and IBM (en.wikipedia.org/wiki/supercomputer, accessed 26 January 2013).

8.   en.wikipedia.org/wiki/CDC_6600 (accessed 26 January 2013).
9.   en.wikipedia.org/wiki/Apple_II (accessed 28 February 2014).
10. en.wikipedia.org/wiki/IBM_Personal_Computer (accessed 26 January 2013).
11. en.wikipedia.org/wiki/Ms-dos (accessed 28 February 2014).
12. en.wikipedia.org/wiki/Unix (accessed 28 February 2014).
13. en.wikipedia.org/wiki/Jack_Dongarra (accessed 24 August 2013).
14. en.wikipedia.org/wiki/Moore's_law (accessed 11 February 2013).
15. en.wikipedia.org/wiki/Moore's_law (accessed 11 February 2013).
16. Comments by Howard Slavin to David Boyce.
17. en.wikipedia.org/wiki/IBM_700/7000_series (accessed 20 January 2013).
18. At the time of the survey, the salary of an entry-level civil engineer was about $500 per month.
19. books.northwestern.edu/viewer.html?id=inu:inu-mntb-0005779868-bk (accessed 22 August 2013); Daniel Brand drew the attention of David Boyce to this newsletter.
20. en.wikipedia.org/wiki/Alan_Voorhees (accessed 23 August 2013).
21. en.wikipedia.org/wiki/Geographic_information_system (accessed 28 February 2014).
22. These modules, whose names began with AV for Alan Voorhees, are described in US HUD (1966, 1967, 1968).
23. Based on comments of Robert Dial received by David Boyce on 11 April 2012.
24. Curriculum vitae of John Wootton, received in July 2008.
25. en.wikipedia.org/wiki/CDC_3000. The history of Control Data Corporation is found at en.wikipedia.org/wiki/Control_Data_Corporation (both accessed 31 January 2013) and described by Worthy (1995).
26. Control Data Corporation, *Urban Affairs: A Data Services Newsletter Covering the Application of Computer Sciences to Urban Affairs*, issued monthly by Data Centers Division Marketing Staff, Minneapolis, MN, 3 September 1969, p. 3, Archives of Control Data Corporation, Charles Babbage Institute, University of Minnesota, Minneapolis, MN.
27. Richard Bunyan reported in the *T-PEG Newsletter*, August 1964: 'AMV has entered into a joint venture . . . to give technical assistance to CDC in reprogramming the traffic assignment battery of programs on the CDC 3600. The 3600 will have a 48 bit word length, 65 K memory. . . . [A]n extremely efficient package will accommodate 8100 nodes and 2000 zones.'
28. Contained in a 16-page letter from Robert Dial dated 15 August 2007.
29. Comments of Robert Dial received by David Boyce, 11 April 2012.
30. Richard Bunyan was the project leader of the CDC project. Raif Kulunk wrote CDC's tree builder based on Bunyan's explanation of the algorithm written earlier by General Electric. Based on an interview with Robert Dial in November 2003, and extensive notes provided in August 2007.
31. In 1966, Goodyear left CDC to become assistant director of data processing of the Metropolitan Washington Council of Governments, where he spent the remainder of his career. A brief description of TRANPLAN is given in Schofer and Goodyear (1967, 247).
32. By that time, AMV had acquired its first in-house computer, a leased IBM S/360 Model 40 with 128 kilobytes of memory, four tape drives and one disk.
33. Later, UMTA was renamed the Federal Transit Administration.
34. Personal communication from Frank Spielberg to David Boyce.
35. The first issue was dated August 1982, and the last evidently appeared in June 1987.
36. Early research-based computer models included an ambitious effort to develop an experimental teaching and research system, DODOTRANS, by Marvin Manheim and Earl Ruiter (1970).
37. System II was offered by JHK and Associates in the early 1990s.
38. Based on an interview with James Fennessy.
39. Based on interviews with Hugh Neffendorf and Dudley Morrell.
40. www.mvaconsultancy.com/history.html (accessed 5 February 2013).

41. Based on interviews with Larry Seiders and Victor Siu.
42. Based on interviews with Michael Clarke. www.citilabs.com (accessed 5 February 2013).
43. Based on an interview with Grant Smith. www.gabites.co.nz (accessed 5 February 2013).
44. The Integrated Civil Engineering System (ICES) was developed by Daniel Roos (1966) at MIT; the Transet subsystem was written by Earl Ruiter.
45. www.sidrasolutions.com (accessed 5 February 2013).
46. www.pbinsight.com/welcome/mapinfo/ (accessed 5 February 2013).
47. Based on interviews with Thomas Schwerdtfeger, Robert Shull and Klaus Nökel. www.ptvgroup.com/en/ (accessed 5 February 2013).
48. For an example of the use of VISUM for solving the sequential procedure, see Boyce et al (2008).
49. Based on interviews with Michael Florian and Heinz Spiess. www.inro.ca (accessed 5 February 2013).
50. Based on interviews with Howard Slavin with David Boyce. www.caliper.com (accessed 5 February 2013).
51. www.fhwa.dot.gov/planning/census_issues/ctpp/ (accessed 28 February 2014).
52. Based on comments by Dirck Van Vliet. www.saturnsoftware.co.uk (accessed 5 February 2013).
53. www.saturnsoftware.co.uk/downloads/pdfs/Saturn_Brochure_300.pdf, p. 2.
54. www.saturnsoftware.co.uk/7.html, p. 1 (accessed 28 March 2014).
55. www.pbinsight.com/welcome/mapinfo/ (accessed 5 February 2013).
56. Based on an interview with Alan Horowitz. my.execpc.com/~ajh/ (accessed 5 February 2013).
57. Based on notes provided by Birgit Dugge in consultation with Dieter Lohse.
58. Lohse's learning method appears to be equivalent to the linearisation method (Frank–Wolfe) solved with the method of successive averages.
59. Based on an interview with Robert Shull.
60. Based on discussions with Justin Siegel and Alexandra Soto. www.MCTsoft.com (accessed 5 February 2013).
61. Additional details are found at en.wikipedia.org/wiki/Transantiago (accessed 5 February 2013).
62. Based on information provided by Robert Tung. www.ufosnet.net (accessed 5 February 2013).
63. Based on information provided by Yoshio Yoshida. www.intel-tech.co.jp/strada/stradae (accessed 5 February 2013).
64. Based on information provided by John Morris. www.omnitrans-international.com/en (accessed 5 February 2013).
65. www.matsim.org/; dynust.net/ (both accessed 11 March 2014).

11. Achievements, current challenges and future prospects

11.1 INTRODUCTION

Our survey of historical developments in urban travel forecasting is almost complete. The journey, which began in the US in the 1950s, has covered much ground. The theory, methods and practice of travel forecasting evolved into a worldwide phenomenon, and were adapted and developed to meet local needs to varying degrees. In this chapter we offer our personal and inevitably selective views on the nature of progress in the field over the last six decades, outline what we see as current challenges, and identify some unanswered questions and possible areas of investigation. We hope to stimulate or rekindle debate about research priorities in this field.

How has urban travel forecasting changed over the past 60 years? To this simple question there are many answers. Some are based on factual developments, as previous chapters testify. Some strongly depend on personal expectations. Others are conditioned by the huge variation in the real world of practice and the contexts in which models are built and applied. To assess this change and the status of the subject, we consulted the international literature and corresponded with pioneers and current theoreticians and practitioners. A huge range and many shades of opinions emerged, spanning high praise in addressing some of the major problems of society[1] to downright disbelief that the methods and models that generated self-fulfilling prophecies and consistently fed our addiction for car travel and the problems associated with it remain dominant. Given the variations in practice, we would contend there is some truth in all of these assessments. Considerably greater agreement, however, was found with the view that the gap between the world of 'theory and research models' and the world of 'practice' has for many years been large and is growing in some areas.

We explore these issues against some of the themes we specified in Chapter 1, now by charting developments over time and drawing examples from the past. Further themes thread through our discussion, in particular: (a) the role of simplification in the development of theories and models; (b) what alternative methods were or are available for generating required information at any particular time; and (c) the question of why the field failed to respond adequately and in a timely manner to the range of criticisms directed at models and methods.

Although we have already noted many areas of current research and unanswered technical questions in individual chapters, notably in Chapters 5, 6 and 7, here we seek to broaden the discussion by adopting a wider perspective. In section 11.2 we summarise our view of the major developments in different eras that significantly influenced travel forecasting in either research or planning practice. We emphasise that this progression does not necessarily refer to the temporal development of methodology applied in any particular country. Internationally, elements from all these different eras may currently be found across the many different project and policy applications.

In section 11.3 we examine the challenge over the years to develop a 'behavioural' approach to travel forecasting – the problems of model validation, particularly with the cross-sectional approach – and consider the ongoing tensions between the description, explanation and forecasting of the behaviour of land use – transportation systems. In section 11.4 we summarise the contribution of equilibrium analysis developed within the formulation introduced by Beckmann et al (1956) with respect to: (a) the validity and realism of link cost functions; (b) the consistency between the demand for and cost of travel for a wide variety of models; (c) the scope for further investigations with combined equilibrium models; and (d) the prospect of going beyond the comparative static equilibrium framework to achieve more dynamic representations.

In section 11.5 we turn to several aspects relating to the predictive performance and validity of models, ranging from the purely technical to the darker side of forecasting where, owing to the uncertainties in specification, variable projections, parameter values and key assumptions, forecasts may become vulnerable to those who would manipulate them for commercial or political ends. We make some specific recommendations for greater transparency in the assumptions underpinning forecasts and evaluation measures, and offer some views on improving the performance of forecasts over time. In section 11.6 we address the world of practice, the alternative methods and models available, and the common dilemmas faced in their selection. Again, we discuss the tension between complexity and sophistication in the representation of behaviour and the pressure to develop simplified models and methods.

In a concluding section we offer some views on the changing context of travel forecasting and on what we see as the field's approach to critical assessment.

Throughout this chapter, we give our personal views and make specific suggestions for further investigations. Because the prime purpose of this book is to provide an introduction to the field to as wide a range of participants as possible, we present our discussion in general terms, setting out current issues and future prospects within their historical context.

11.2 EVOLUTION AND DEVELOPMENT OF URBAN TRAVEL FORECASTING MODELS

11.2.1 Establishment of the Multi-Step Approach: Early 1950s to Mid-1960s

The multi-step procedure was developed and applied to examine the implications of growth of population, employment and car ownership, and its outward suburbanisation, for alternative highway network plans. Later these were extended to alternative land uses as well as public transport networks. Its main features were:

1. establishment of a 'systems approach' based on cross-sectional analyses of large-scale household and commercial vehicle surveys initially in US and Canadian cities;
2. analysis of the influence of land use on personal travel and movement of goods, and the reciprocal role of accessibility in determining the location of urban activities;
3. extrapolation of car ownership rates based on time series data;
4. development of trip-based models for home-based and non-home-based trip purposes;
5. partitioning of travel markets spatially by origin and destination zones, and with minimal socio-economic segmentation;
6. creation of a three-step procedure for forecasting road traffic based on a **G/D/A** structure:
    a) trip generation (**G**) models based on regression methods at the zonal level;
    b) trip distribution (**D**) based on gravity and related models expressed in terms of empirically derived trip deterrence functions, or growth factor techniques such as for commercial vehicle trips;
    c) 24-hour assignment (**A**) based on route diversion curves, with later adoption of assignment of origin–destination flows to computed minimum travel cost routes;

    d)   modal split developed for two composite motorised modes (public and private), initially applied at the 'trip ends' in 'four-step' **G/M/D/A** structures, and later **G/D/M/A** structure developed based on empirically derived diversion curves for modal split;

7.   development of link-based travel time–volume relationships and rudimentary capacity restraint assignment;

8.   application of electromechanical accounting machines and mainframe computers for data reduction, analysis and forecasting.

11.2.2   Consolidation towards Hybrid Multi-Stage Models: Late 1960s to Present

This evolving methodology was applied to the preparation of land use – transportation infrastructure plans, and later to restraint schemes. In addition to the developments set out in section 11.2.1, we note:

1.   greater emphasis on market segmentation; household classes as units of analysis for trip generation; category analysis adopted to forecast trip generation and car ownership;

2.   much greater concern for public transport, with line- or service-based network representations and assignments;

3.   assignment of flows to 24-hour and later peak periods, as user-equilibrium solution methods were identified and applied;

4.   generalised costs, defined by linear combinations of in-vehicle time, out-of-vehicle time and out-of-pocket costs, are estimated from micro-studies of modal choice; these are applied with interzonal times and costs; policies interpreted in terms of changes in link capacities and components of generalised costs;

5.   multinomial logit models (MNL) applied at the aggregate level in distribution and modal split analyses and interpreted through entropy maximising or information theory;

6.   maximum likelihood and related methods used to estimate model parameters;

7.   analytic models in hierarchical structures of **G/M/D/A**, **G/D/M/A** and later **G/D-M/A** form, in which MNL share models are linked through composite costs;

8.   'feedback' of generalised costs recognised and applied in an *ad hoc* limited way.

11.2.3 Discrete Choice Approach to Travel Demand: Early 1970s to Present

Discrete choice formulations were applied in a wide range of travel forecasting situations, emphasising the short-term, but increasingly the longer-term, requirements of urban transportation planning organisations:

1. interpretation of travel patterns as the result of choices by individuals or households among discrete sets of alternatives;
2. discrete choice, random utility maximising (RUM) approach used as an organising framework for the development of a wide range of travel-related models;
3. '*post-hoc* rationalisation' of the binary modal choice models of the 1960s based on compensatory decision models within the RUM framework;
4. MNL models widely applied at the micro-level to modal choice and increasingly to various travel-related contexts; its strengths and weaknesses are recognised;
5. model parameters estimated from small samples of revealed preference data using maximum likelihood methods;
6. hypothesis of model transferability examined and applied in practice;
7. aggregation problem addressed in depth, and various practical procedures developed;
8. alternative hypotheses of the trip decision process based on 'simultaneous' and 'sequential' decision making proposed and resultant model structures explored;
9. nested logit structures derived within the RUM framework, in which the hierarchy is determined by the pattern of similarity among alternative choices, and the ordering of choices by the relative sizes of behavioural responses; empirical testing of appropriate ordering through response parameter inequalities;
10. links between discrete choice RUM models and economic welfare measures established;
11. increasing use of models of individual and household behaviour, including limited intra-household interactions;
12. practical applications of 'disaggregate models' for short-term and long-range forecasting for large urban areas, initially in the US and the Netherlands;
13. four-stage aggregate models **G/M/D/A**, **G/D/M/A** and **G/D-M/A** recast in nested logit form, and given behavioural interpretations; previously applied **G/D/M/A** models found to violate parameter inequalities;

14. stated preferences methods introduced and, in conjunction with revealed preference approach, enter the mainstream of travel forecasting;
15. range of 'closed' and 'open' forms of RUM models developed, the former within a generalised extreme value (GEV) framework, the latter solved by simulation techniques;
16. discrete choice RUM approach used to model choices in competitive urban markets, forging integration of urban economics, spatial behaviour and transportation planning.

11.2.4 Activity-Travel Frameworks and the Quest for Greater Behavioural Realism: 1980s to Present

A grand synthesis of 'constraint-based' and 'choice-based' approaches emerged within an activity-travel framework, with limited applications, although it was increasingly applied to a range of policies, particularly those influencing the timing of activities and journeys:

1. explicit rationale for travel and its purpose within the context of activities undertaken by individuals and households;
2. focus on the totality of daily activities, with the travel of individuals and households, and travel variation, related to the structure of the household, and its stage in the life cycle;
3. range of constraints on individual action recognised; constraints on daily activities in space and time expressed through 'prisms';
4. wider variety of activity-travel choices and more complex patterns of substitution in response to policies considered within a space-time and household context; timing of activities and travel emerges as a key dimension of choice;
5. tour-based approaches introduced to preserve continuity in mode choice and timing of journeys, and applied in practice;
6. behavioural choice process considered in greater depth and alternative decision models proposed;
7. various practical urban travel forecasting models developed in terms of daily schedules; distinctions between econometric and rule-based computational process models;
8. microsimulation widely applied to solve and aggregate increasingly sophisticated activity-travel models;
9. corresponding micro-level developments to consider logistical aspects within the activities of firms.[2]

11.2.5 Network Equilibrium for Expanded Richness and Realism: Late 1960s to Present

Elaborating on the formulation of Beckmann et al (1956), an expanding and increasingly sophisticated representation of network-based models of travel choices emerged:

1. solution and application of the fixed demand case as an alternative to 'capacity restraint' assignment heuristics;
2. extension of the deterministic model to several stochastic formulations of route choice;
3. exploration of network equilibrium with variable demand as an alternative to the four-step procedure;
4. identification of alternative mathematical formulations of network equilibrium, with the potential for more realistic representation of link and network travel times;
5. extensions to public transport systems with complex travel choice alternatives;
6. experimentation with (agent-based) microsimulation of travel over detailed modal networks;
7. evolution of a software development niche offering increasingly sophisticated modelling alternatives in combination with network and geographical information systems.

11.2.6 Summary

We can now reflect on this complex development of urban travel forecasting models as having progressively greater concern for:

1. nature of the way that travel demand is expressed: from 'trip' to 'tour' to 'daily schedule';
2. variation of individual and household behaviour and segmentation of the travel market, determined by current patterns of behaviour, responses to policies and developments over time;
3. range of variables and their combination through which policies are expressed;
4. range of individual choices sensitive to level-of-service (LOS) variables and patterns of substitution in response to policies; from original concern for frequency, destination, modal and route choice to a range of further choices, notably including journey timing;
5. different methods for exploring preferences and estimating the parameters of models;

6. analytic models based on information theory, entropy maximisation and choice theories;
7. synthesis between constraint-based and choice-based approaches;
8. detail in which networks are represented and movement through them expressed;
9. consistency between demand, flows and LOS variables throughout the model;
10. corresponding developments for goods vehicle movements, in terms of organisation and logistics, to bring models of the firm more in line with those of the household.

11.3 CHALLENGE OF BEHAVIOURAL TRAVEL MODELLING

11.3.1 Limitations of the Cross-Sectional Approach

We first consider a set of issues, relating to forecasting validity of cross-sectional models, which are long-standing in our field. Because of their importance, several points are worthy of emphasis. Travel forecasting with cross-sectional models evolved with little concern that the correlations between travel demand and socio-economic and transportation variables, observed in cross-sectional surveys, do not necessarily imply causation related to changes in the relevant variables. Over the last 60 years, cross-sectional 'goodness-of-fit' has dominated the criteria by which a model is deemed acceptable in practice, a situation that continues to have potentially severe consequences. The leap of faith that correlation implies causation has been problematic ever since the impressive goodness-of-fits found for trip generation regression models based on zonal data in the 1950s and 1960s. As seen in numerous studies over the years, many models can pass standard statistical 'goodness-of-fit' tests, but give rise to quite inappropriate travel forecasts (see, for example, section 5.2).

Because there is little tradition of confronting and confirming predictions of cross-sectional models with outcomes in either back-casting or detailed before-and-after studies, refutation by evidence in the classic scientific style (Popper, 1959) is absent.[3] The inadequacy of calibration and goodness-of-fit as a basis for model validation has been explicit or implicit in many critiques since the 1960s, as exemplified by comments of Yacov Zahavi [1926–1983]:[4]

> Most travel demand models are calibrated to – namely, adjusted to – the observed travel measures which they are asked to reproduce as a final output.

Thus, the verification of such a model is self-fulfilling, in the sense that the model's validity is tested by the ability to reproduce the same observed travel characteristics upon which it is calibrated (Zahavi, 1978, 1).

The use of 'hold-back' samples – which are often endowed with similar data structure and extent of statistical variation to those used in model calibration – does little to alter this proposition.

Efforts to improve goodness-of-fit have led to the widespread incorporation of additional model variables or parameters without an adequate explanatory basis. Comments of such problems created in a forecasting context are not new (e.g., Wilson et al, 1969). As Chandra Bhat recently remarked:

> while a model with several adjustment factors may be a super-fit for the base conditions, it can be a disaster for forecasting. The obsession with the use of ground counts as the ultimate or dominating validation measure of model performance constitutes an Achilles heel in our pursuit of developing good forecasting models (Bhat, 2014).

The problems of inference of causation from patterns of activity-travel behaviour have been considered in some detail (e.g., Handy et al, 2005). In the context of exploring the extent to which the physical environment is a determinant of travel, Susan Handy reminded us that 'finding a strong relationship between urban form and travel patterns is not the same as showing that a change in urban form will lead to a change in travel behaviour, and finding a strong relationship is not the same as understanding that relationship' (Handy, 1996, 162).

At any point in time, human behaviour is the result of many demographic, social, economic and cultural determinants arising at various times in the past. It is not surprising that the credibility of inferring the response to policies and projects from the variability of behaviour between individuals at the cross-section has so often been called into question, or that incremental models that distinguish the dispersion in travel patterns from the response properties of models have gained a following among some practitioners (see, for example, section 9.5).

There is often a significant gap between the theoretical basis for models applied in practice and the behaviour they purport to represent. This is particularly true of simple location models involving longer-term decisions (e.g., housing choice and location, and workplace choice and location). Here, information on available options and their attributes is far from perfect, and decisions involve complex and interdependent social, economic and demographic processes (Fotheringham and Wegener, 2000). Even that most venerable class of model, spatial interaction models of MNL form, based on generalised costs and applied at both the individual and the zone level, requires further research to assess whether the parameters estimated from the dispersion in cross sectional travel data are suitable for forecasting the response to policies. Furthermore, because parameter values can be very sensitive to the specification of models, indirect supporting evidence from meta-studies (review and synthesis of parameters such as value of time and elasticities from a wide variety of approaches and studies including panel and time series studies) has proved to be essential to maintain credibility in the forecasting approach from cross-sectional models.

It is now generally seen as desirable that forecasts from cross-sectional urban travel models should rely on checks against a range of criteria, in addition to goodness-of-statistical-fit, including:

1. parameter value inequalities in nested logit applications;
2. comparison of model parameters (e.g., value of time) with ranges from meta-studies;
3. 'realism tests' in which marginal changes predicted by the model are compared with ranges of elasticities derived from meta-studies;
4. indirect evidence, such as geographical transferability of relationships and parameters over space and time;
5. any evidence obtained from back-casting or before-and-after studies of the model (or similar model specification) where such confirming evidence is available.

In many practical applications, few of this wider range of checks are applied. In both the US and the UK, recent guidelines on the validation of models (Cambridge Systematics, 2010; UK DfT, 2011d) are available for 'realism testing' (section 9.5.4). Before-and-after studies at the level of detail of McFadden's BART project in the mid-1970s (section 4.3.4) or the recent study conducted in Manchester by Rohr et al (2012) (section 9.5.3) are difficult and expensive, but invaluable. The importance of monitoring the response to and collating evidence from a wide range of policies and projects cannot be overstated (e.g., Pratt et al, 2000).

The limitations of the cross-sectional approach should be more widely recognised, and the culture of model validation strengthened whenever opportunities arise. Ongoing international collaboration is needed to collate the results from major before-and-after studies for general conclusions to be drawn.

11.3.2 Debate over 'Macro'- versus 'Micro'-Models

We have already discussed in some detail the problems and possibilities of developing forecasting models at different levels at which data are collected and grouped, models specified, parameters determined and forecasts made. In particular we have contrasted the 'aggregate' and 'disaggregate' approaches (sections 4.1, 4.3, 4.7, 5.5) and noted McFadden's (1976b, 8) observation on disaggregation and market segmentation (section 4.7). The issues and problems of developing models with different measures of trip or activity (the trip, tour and schedule), at different levels of aggregation and detail of their underpinning behavioural models, are sometimes cast in terms of a 'macro–micro' debate.

Over the years the travel forecasting field has been characterised by an approach in which increasingly intricate expressions of system behaviour have been proposed as the basis for modelling and predicting aggregate demand. The 'disaggregate behavioural' approach introduced in the late 1960s and the 1970s was based on a powerful proposition: observed behaviour is best represented, explained and forecast at the micro-level where individuals' decisions are made. Much of the current thinking about this macro–micro question is predicated on a view that suitable models can be achieved at the micro-level. Indeed, the 'disaggregate behavioural' approach has often been taken as self-evident. But, as Daniel Brand protested in the early 1970s, 'The often-used term "disaggregate behavioural" models gives the impression that individual-choice models have a monopoly on incorporating travel behaviour. That is clearly unfair, for travel demand models can be derived from behavioural assumptions independently of whether they will use aggregate or disaggregate data' (Brand, 1973, 240).

The quest for sophisticated micro-behavioural explanations and the finer and finer representation of behaviour within activity-travel frameworks have resulted in ever greater theoretical and empirical modelling challenges for temporal and policy-related forecasting.

Hani Mahmassani, reflecting on the appropriate level at which to develop behavioural models, came to the following view 25 years ago when the activity-travel field was still young:

> As one surveys the vast landscape of contributions in this area, one might wonder if researchers have been somewhat overwhelmed looking for the complexity of activity participation, scheduling, intra-household interaction and travel behaviour, rather than seeking whatever underlying simplicity or 'repeatability' might be present and could be taken advantage of for the purpose of meaningful predictive work. Admittedly, the microscopic details of the phenomena under consideration are extremely complex. Miring in this complexity

may have precluded some coarser though no less useful relations and processes (Mahmassani, 1988, 36).

We suggest his views remain relevant today. More recently, in an assessment of the state of the art in activity-travel analysis, Ortúzar et al (2012), referring to Kenneth Train's view 'There is a limit to what we can learn from that we cannot see' (Train, 2009, 141), offered their own thinking: 'To what extent is it really possible to identify real underlying behaviour? Even with the most gloriously sophisticated models at our disposal it is practically impossible to disentangle all the various effects that could be underpinning a given observed or declared set of choices by individuals' (Ortúzar et al, 2012, 357).

The appropriate means of specifying, estimating, aggregating, testing and validating models for complex urban systems remains a vigorous area of ongoing research (section 6.6). Its resolution will depend on the demands on data, what policies are to be tested, and what information is required (e.g., whether detailed network flows are required).

The lack of a consensus on the specification of models of activity-travel behaviour requires the ongoing comparison and evaluation of models of different levels of complexity and aggregation.

We return to this issue in section 11.6.3.

11.3.3 The 'Standard Model' of Choice and Beyond

We would argue that the standard econometric models of choice based on rational decision making and random utility maximisation (RUM)[5] have been remarkably successful in addressing many fundamental problems first encountered in the 1960s and the 1970s (Chapters 4, 5; section 11.2). The choice theoretic RUM approach was also a framework capable of much development (section 5.7). Recently, debate has continued over where to place more emphasis in research, on the systematic component of utility in contrast to 'blindly trying to "extract more juice" from stochastic error components' (Ortúzar et al, 2012, 357).

Even in the standard approach based on MNL and NL models of choice and compensatory decision rules, however, many questions of the most fundamental kind remain to be addressed. Among these is the appropriate functional form of the representative utility component in terms of explanatory variables, where the linear difference model, widely found in practice, has been questioned for many years (e.g., Gaudry and Wills, 1978; Gaudry et al, 1989; Daly, 2010; Gaudry and Quinet, 2011; Daly et al, 2014). The latter noted:

In the last decade, modelling methodology has switched to the estimation of models, with error defined on the log time and log cost difference scale, and with VOT [value of time] distributed randomly in the population. These models appear to give a better explanation of observed SC [stated choice] responses (Daly et al, 2014, 215).

With regard to value-of-time (VOT) research in general, those authors add: 'while major improvements have been made in the development of estimation methods for VOT since the 1960s, the problems have not yet all been solved and further research is required to maintain the credibility of this important parameter' (Daly et al, 2014, 217). This view is supported by Kenneth Small (2012, 2), who starts his review: 'After decades of study, the value of travel time remains incompletely understood and ripe for further theoretical and empirical investigation.' We consider a related issue in section 11.5.3.

Some areas of the economics profession have been under considerable pressure following the 2008 financial crash.[6] Students have even revolted in some university economics departments for the slavish adherence to, and teaching of, mathematical models which have failed to take on board the insights and 'realities' gleaned in other disciplines, notably psychology. This tension between standard utility formulations and more 'realistic' models of behaviour was to some extent anticipated in our field in the 1980s (section 6.2.2). Since that time, travel forecasting model research, and micro-economic approaches in particular, have drawn freely from other disciplines, notably geography and, increasingly since the 1990s, psychology. Their study is currently enjoying a fresh lease of life.

We have discussed proposed embellishments of, or alternatives to, the standard decision rules and assumptions underpinning RUM models that were introduced in the 1980s and 1990s (sections 6.3, 6.5). Alternative hypotheses relating to limited information, memory, habit, thresholds,[7] alternative decision rules,[8] learning mechanisms and the contexts and processes of choice have been explored within static and dynamic frameworks (sections 6.2, 6.6; Ben-Akiva et al, 1997, 1999, 2002a, 2012; de Palma et al, 2008). While important in a research context, to date these efforts have made little impression on travel forecasting models applied in routine practice.

At the time of writing, *Horizon*, the highly respected science programme on BBC television, has, sandwiched between 'The Hunt for the Higgs'[9] and 'Man on Mars: Mission to the Red Planet', an exploration of 'How You Really Make Decisions' (24 February 2014), affirming the scientific basis for this activity. The programme highlighted the findings of Nobel laureate Daniel Kahneman and charted the rise of what is now referred to as behavioural economics.[10] This research has explored and confirmed multiple sources of cognitive bias and 'non-rationality' in human decision making in choice contexts, especially where uncertainty and risk are key elements in economic, social and political processes (Kahneman, 2011). In the past these investigations drew the often-quoted quip from Daniel McFadden (1999, 79): 'This work has both fascinated and dismayed economists; it has been like watching master carpenters construct the scaffold for your hanging.' Suggestions for relaxing the standard views on optimality and delving into the 'black box' of decision making are now major themes in the literature on discrete choice modelling (see Ben-Akiva et al, 1999, 2012; McFadden, 1999; de Palma et al, 2008; Cherchi, 2012). We note only one prominent area of concern.

Nearly 35 years since its initial proposal by Kahneman and Tversky (1979), later followed by a 'cumulative' version (Tversky and Kahneman, 1992), the application of prospect theory of decision making to travel-related behaviour has over the last decade been increasingly widely and critically studied for its applicability, and differences with standard approaches emphasized.[11] Important differences between prospect theory and standard utility theories are:

1. preferences are not fixed and well defined, but may vary with context;
2. alternatives are 'framed' as changes relative to a reference state;
3. loss aversion exists in which a higher value is associated with a loss compared with an increase of the same size.

See van de Kaa (2010, 772-774) and Li and Hensher (2011) for a detailed discussion of the theory and its implications for travel forecasting.

Where comparisons were feasible among the 106 studies examined, van de Kaa (2010, 771) concluded: 'the joint application of the assumptions of an extended prospect theory might provide a better understanding of human choice behaviour over the whole range of travel-related contexts'.

Andre de Palma et al (2008) have more formally discussed the 'cross-fertilizations of random utility models with the study of decision making under risk and uncertainty'. Here the differences between standard expected utility models and non-expected utility models, including those derived from prospect theory, were examined within a discrete choice framework.

Of all the many potential embellishments of the standard econometric approach to travel modelling, forecasting and evaluation, some consensus around the priorities would be helpful to direct further theoretical and empirical research. Although its formal study is over three decades old, in our view the role of uncertainty and reliability in many travel decisions warrants a higher priority.

While most current applications involving uncertainty and, in particular, randomness about travel times have occurred in the journey timing and modal choice situations, their extension to most choice and joint choice processes is warranted. Including uncertainty and reliability without making the models too complex is a topic requiring further theoretical research and practical testing.

Within the context of travel choice and demand modelling generally, major changes are occurring in the way that data are being collected (Richardson et al 1995; Stopher and Greaves 2007). Large differences between reported attributes and measured attributes, familiar since the 1960s, are still a matter for concern in understanding and predicting travel-related behaviour. Advances in data collection technology, notably through GPS data capture, are informing research on this issue. For a full discussion of the impact of modern technology on travel choice and activity-travel surveys, see Stopher et al (2005) and Bonnel et al (2009). The emergence of an era of 'big data' may transform travel analysis and forecasting in quite unexpected ways.

11.3.4 Empirical Regularities and Alternative Forecasting Assumptions

Examination of travel in terms of the trip, the tour and the daily schedule has prompted the following question: at what level of detail and grouping of trips should empirical regularities be sought, hypotheses developed, explanations proffered and forecasts of travel applied? Since John Wootton and Gerry Pick's use of residential density as a proxy for locational effects in trip rate category analysis (section 3.3.1), various empirical and methodological frameworks have emerged for exploring the influence of socio-economic, demographic, location (density and neighbourhood characteristics) and level-of-service or accessibility effects on activities and travel.[12] Such studies are increasingly informing policy on such issues as 'smart growth' and the 'densification of cities'.

We wish to comment on the development of alternative hypotheses to the common modelling assumption of constancy of trip rates for different socio-economic groups in various density bands. The possibility that the amount of time and money that people spend in travelling per day might be approximately the same, or stable, under different conditions for people of given characteristics has been an issue in transportation research ever since the seminal paper by John Tanner (1961). This 'promoted the possibility that forecasts might be improved by incorporating estimates of travel expenditure' (Kirby, 1981, 1). Howard Kirby added: 'The two key

questions for practice might be put as follows: (a) how does the forecasting ability of methods based on travel expenditure rates compare with that
for methods based on trip rates? (b) how could one use travel expenditure
rates in forecasting?' (Kirby, 1981, 1).

The approximate stability of travel budgets, applied at the levels of
groups rather than individuals, and the implications for forecasting,
evaluation and policy development, have been issues of sustained interest
for the last five decades.[13] The topic continues to provoke much interest,
controversy and research.

Yacov Zahavi (1974) was an early contributor to the development of
models focused on regularities in household daily travel time and money
expenditures which 'are observed to be transferable both spatially and
temporally'. In proposing his unified mechanism of travel (UMOT)
model, Zahavi sought to avoid what he saw as the circularity implied
by the calibration of standard models. 'The UMOT approach generates
simultaneous estimates of travel components, such as daily travel distance,
modal shares, car ownership levels and household locational patterns,
which are compared with observed data – not calibrated to them – for
model validation' (Zahavi et al, 1981, Abstract).

Patricia Mokhtarian and Cynthia Chen summarised their meta-analysis
of aggregate and disaggregate studies of travel time (and sometimes
money) expenditure as follows:

> We conclude with prior research that travel time expenditures are not constant
> except, perhaps, at the most aggregate level. Nevertheless individuals' travel
> time expenditures do show patterns that can partly be explained by measurable
> characteristics (e.g., income level, gender, employment status and car owner-
> ship) attributes of activities at destination and characteristics of residential
> areas (e.g., density, spatial structure and level-of-service). To the extent that
> travel time expenditures *are* constant at the aggregate level, the underlying
> mechanisms explaining that regularity are not well understood (Mokhtarian
> and Chen, 2004, 643).

Many still see the possibility of developing travel forecasting models and
exploiting empirical regularities, not at the individual but at a group level.
Goodwin (2005, 17) expressed the view: 'we would probably make more
accurate forecasts if we start from the assumption that the average total
travel time is constant and then seek special reasons why it might not be
in particular cases'.

To David Metz (2008), the empirical regularities and near constancy of
time budgets had an extra significance for evaluation and policy. In his
provocative paper 'The Myth of Travel Time Saving', he pondered the
destiny of travel time savings following transportation investments, and

challenged the conventional approach to their evaluation and the policy of speeding up travel, if it simply leads to longer journeys. For a spirited response, see Mackie (2008).

Over 40 years ago Alan Wilson (1973b, 1974) considered the hierarchical construction of demand relations within a Strotz-type framework (section 3.5.4), an issue yet to be fully resolved.

The reconciliation of demand relations based on trips or tours and daily schedules and corresponding travel expenditure on time and money within a hierarchical framework warrants further study.

11.4 SEARCH FOR INTERNAL CONSISTENCY: EQUILIBRIUM MODELS AND BEYOND

11.4.1 Toward Valid and More Realistic Road Network Link Costs

Over 50 years ago, engineers at the Bureau of Public Roads plotted an empirical relationship between travel time and volume on a link as a basis for testing their initial ideas concerning 'capacity restraint' assignment (US DoC, 1964). They assumed a link's travel time increased as a (separable) function of the total volume on the link, ignoring the effects of vehicle classes and of opposing and conflicting traffic at the link's downstream intersection. In the succeeding decades, methods for solving for user-equilibrium flows with these simple functions was improved in several elegant ways. However, the venerable BPR function remained the common representation of the relation of time and total flow on a link.

The mathematical understanding of the requirements for realistic and meaningful travel time-flow functions has steadily advanced since the 1980s, as understanding and solution of the variational inequality problem flourished (Florian and Hearn, 1995; Marcotte and Patriksson, 2007). The means to acquire, record and manipulate traffic flow and intersection attribute data are now available with GIS software. Likewise, computational speeds have advanced to the point that user-equilibrium flows based on realistic functions defined on all interacting flows can be solved with reasonable effort.

Still, practitioners and researchers alike continue to ignore the interaction of class flows at intersections, as well as the interaction of class link flows within links. From a network equilibrium and network cost perspective, this issue is perhaps one of the most blatant shortcomings of the state of practice and the state of the art.

The implementation and solution of a hierarchy of link cost functions of increasing detail and complexity representing the interactions of class link flows through signalised and priority intersections on a par with advanced highway capacity models are a high priority for both practice and research. Algorithms suitable for solving a hierarchy of problems at the regional, subregional and local scale require specification, testing and dissemination. Travel forecasting software developers seem likely to respond to the challenge of implementing these enhanced modelling tools if and when they are requested by the practitioner community.

11.4.2   Internal Consistency and the Multi-Stage Approach

The problem of generating travel forecasts in which interzonal demand, link flows and network level-of-service variables have mutually consistent values throughout the model was recognised early in the development of the multi-stage approach. Although the theoretical and computational aspects of this problem are now fairly well understood, much lip service continues to be paid in practice to the procedure of 'feeding back' travel times and costs with few iterations (sections 8.2.2, 8.3.2.3). Two different aspects involved in this process are: (a) model specification issues, requiring mechanisms (e.g., the form of composite costs in nested logit models) by which times and costs are represented in different parts of the procedure, and through which the effects of policies are transmitted; and (b) algorithmic issues concerning equilibration of the resulting values.

The aggregate demand network cost equilibrium formulation of Beckmann et al (1956) was elaborated over time to incorporate various demand specifications, such as nested logit structures and integrated land use – transportation models. As discussed in some detail in Chapter 7, the framework provided:

1. an optimising formulation within which equilibrium solutions were sought;
2. the existence and uniqueness properties of equilibrium solutions;
3. the means for investigating the properties and performance of solution algorithms;
4. implied prices that could be associated with network links to convert the user equilibrium into a system-optimal state.

The internal consistency between travel demand and network cost was central to the formulation of this approach. Now a wealth of (academic) experience exists for solving such models to a high level of precision for particular demand functions specified at the aggregate (zonal) level. However, many currently applied models, whether formulated in terms of the trip, tour or daily activity, are specified and estimated at the micro-level; if equilibration is attempted, it relies on a 'feedback' sequence after trip matrices are compiled and assigned to the network.

Over 25 years ago the failure to achieve internal consistency of level-of-service variables, demand and link flows was cited as a key criticism of practical travel modelling, and one aspect of a planning process subject to litigation (Garrett and Wachs, 1996). Yet there is still no accepted or agreed-upon procedure to address the topic of 'feedback' in practice and little testing of convergence. One software system, TransCAD, incorporated the method of successive averages (section 10.5.1.8) on the grounds that it can be proven mathematically to converge. This property has little bearing, however, on the implications for achieving a precise solution computationally. The effectiveness of the method was unsatisfactory in one test with a network of realistic size (Boyce et al, 2008).

A comprehensive analysis of equilibrium-seeking procedures for a range of multi-stage demand models of increasing complexity with realistic cost functions is a compelling research priority for large-scale, multi-modal, multi-class networks. As part of this investigation, convergence criteria should be established for use in policy testing for network flows, suppressed and induced demand, and evaluation measures including user benefits and environmental impacts. The criteria should be useful for policies such as transportation infrastructure investments and for restraint schemes.

11.4.3 Scope for Further Application

The numerical solution of user-equilibrium models of all forms (trip-, tour- and schedule-based), and the significance of inconsistencies between travel demand and network cost (LOS) variables on forecasts and evaluation measures warrant extensive study and testing. In view of their practical relevance, we also advocate the in-depth study of consistency and convergence, involving:

1. discrete choice micro-models of nested logit structure in trip-, tour- and schedule-based representations, including a range of demand responses, such as trip timing, and additional level-of-service variables, including reliability;
2. multi-modal, multi-class, multi-temporal systems, including the case in which public transport service levels are dependent on market share, allowing the practical investigation of the Downs–Thomson effect (section 9.4.3);
3. dynamic traffic assignment models in deterministic and stochastic representations.

Further investigations within the network modelling framework of the user-equilibrium and system-optimal models should explore the nature and extent of inefficiencies and bias in the 'without' (reference) state and 'with project' states for evaluating transportation policies and, in particular, transportation investments.

11.4.4　The End of Equilibrium?

It is widely accepted that land use – transportation systems are never actually in a state of equilibrium, but subject to dynamic adjustments over different time scales under the influence of external factors and transportation policies.[14] The comparative static economic equilibrium assumption has been applied as an approximation to more sophisticated dynamical models under the assumption that 'equilibrium is, for practical purposes, a reasonably unbiased approximation to the dynamic reality' (Goodwin, 1998). Although dynamic behaviour and disequilibrium models have been widely considered in our field since at least the 1970s (e.g., Wilson, 1974; Echenique and de la Barra, 1977), the failure to adopt dynamic representations continues to be debated in different contexts, from modal split to the land use – transportation interaction (Goodwin, 1998; Simmonds et al, 2013).

For Phil Goodwin (1998), from whose chapter the title of this section is taken (with the addition of a question mark), and his former University College London contemporary, Martin Mogridge (Mogridge, 1997; section 9.4.3), inappropriate forecasts and policy prescriptions are directly influenced by our failure to understand the processes of change, and the (in-)adequacy of the assumptions underlying current mathematical models. Goodwin's unease was not confined to differences between long-run and short-run elasticities, but more generally to the very foundations of the model and its focus on 'end states' at the expense of behavioural processes and dynamical adjustments.

Interpreting data and specifying relationships, and estimating their parameters under assumptions of equilibrium, may lead to systematic biases or may, as Goodwin has suggested, simply be wrong. These considerations suggest that:

> ignoring dynamic factors could give misleading results not only for behavioural forecasts, but also for interpretation of the values and utilities underpinning them. It is not, of course, self evident that errors of this type are necessarily larger than those arising from the many other known (and unknown) imperfections in forecasting practice, but their particular importance derives from the likelihood of systematic bias, which has the danger of making some policies seem worse than they are, and others better (Goodwin, 1998, 132).

Goodwin, among others, has consistently argued since the 1980s for process-oriented approaches in which the role of memory, habit, and discontinuous and non-reversible change are accommodated, for which the cross-sectional approach is not well suited. Whether these can be suitably included in models without invoking major increases in complexity continues to be debated in the profession.

Detailed consideration of the potential additional accuracy and practical implications of dynamic models over comparative static equilibrium forms is needed to identify: (a) conditions where the former may offer significant advantages in practice; and (b) under what circumstances particular simplifications are justified. These investigations should include the current generation of dynamic microsimulation models.

11.5 PERFORMANCE OF MODELS AND THE ASSUMPTIONS UNDERLYING FORECASTS

11.5.1 Predictive Accuracy of Urban Travel Forecasts

In the early days of travel forecasting, the professional effort and computational requirements involved in assembling data, calibrating models and preparing forecasts were so large that little consideration was given to sources of error and uncertainty, let alone computing confidence intervals for point estimates of key outputs. Using sensitivity analysis, some early studies did explore how errors in planning variables and model parameters propagate through multi-step land use – transportation forecasting models (e.g., CONSAD Research, 1968; Bonsall et al, 1977). More recently these analyses have been considerably extended by Kara Kockelman and her students (Pradhan and Kockelman, 2002; Zhao and Kockelman, 2002; Krishnamurthy and Kockelman, 2003).

Studies of the performance of models necessarily awaited the target year outcomes from major studies conducted in the 1950s, 1960s and 1970s, as discussed in Chapters 2 and 3 (Institute of Transportation Engineers, 1980; Mackinder and Evans, 1981; McDonald, 1988). There is now a growing literature on the uncertainty and errors in forecasts arising from the multiple sources: (a) the projections of exogenous factors (land use, income, population, employment, car ownership, etc.); (b) the specification of models; (c) the parameters and their estimation; (d) model assumptions; (e) data errors; and (f) human error. Incorporating uncertainty and confidence intervals in forecasts arising only from the first of the above sources is now a fairly standard requirement, but only for some modelling purposes (e.g., de Jong et al, 2007a; UK DfT, 2009c; Rasouli and Timmermans, 2012).

Individual in-depth and meta-studies of predictive accuracy of forecasts in common contexts (e.g., long-range forecasts of vehicle traffic or public transport demand over time; impact of heavy rail, light rail and express bus schemes; impact of toll roads, etc.) have been required to draw general conclusions.[15] These reviews, surveys and analyses attest to the very large errors that often accompany travel forecasts, and arise from the sources listed above and the institutional factors that influence them.

Paul Timms (2008) questioned whether it is reasonable to expect any travel forecasting model to produce accurate results over a medium- or long-term time horizon, even if the effects of inaccurate exogenous inputs are 'screened out'. In response to this question, he appealed to several philosophy of science issues associated with travel forecasting models and the production of forecasts.

Other viewpoints are more immediate and practical. The notion of objective, value-free forecasts has long been challenged in the critical literature on the use of models for informing public policy. Optimism on the part of forecasters is not a new phenomenon; see Mackinder and Evans (1981) and section 3.7.4. However, the terms 'optimism bias', 'boosterism' and 'naïve and wishful thinking' have only relatively recently entered the critical vocabulary on the extent to which the scope for uncertainty can be exploited for political, planning or commercial ends. Martin Wachs (1982, 1989, 1990) described the conflicts that some professionals face:

> Forecasting is one of the most important activities performed by professionals in support of public policymaking. . . . Many of the most interesting and complex ethical dilemmas facing these professionals arise from the complexity of the forecasting task and from the enormous political consequences of their forecasts. Forecasts are presented to the public as the results of unbiased scientific procedures, yet they are in reality often highly subjective exercises in advocacy. Professionals who must prepare forecasts are frequently confused by mixed signals which they get. According to law, and in the eyes of the public, their forecasts are expected to provide analyses aimed at clarifying choices among courses of action. But their direct superiors and clients expect them to produce forecasts which will become part of the supporting documentation justifying a course of action which has already been chosen for political reasons (Wachs, 1990, 141).

The extent to which this concern is widespread in various contexts in which travel forecasters perform their tasks is not known, although it is likely to vary with the size of the project and its regional and national importance. Recent articles on the accuracy of traffic forecasts have cited the results of Bent Flyvbjerg, Mette Skamris Holm and Søren Buhl (2006), derived from their extensive study of 210 infrastructure projects; see also Flyvbjerg et al (2003). Although these are not confined to urban situations, the general message is clear:

> forecasters generally do a poor job of estimating the demand for transportation infrastructure projects. The result is substantial downside financial and economic risk. Forecasts have not become more accurate over the 30 year period studied. If techniques and skills for arriving at accurate demand forecasts have improved over time, as often claimed by forecasters, this does not show in the data. For nine out of ten rail projects, passenger forecasts are overestimated; average overestimation is 106%. For 72% of rail projects, forecasts are overestimated by more than two thirds. For 50% of road projects, the difference between actual and forecasted traffic is more than ±20%; for 25% of road projects, the difference is larger than ±40%. Forecasts for roads are more accurate and more balanced than for rail, with no significant difference between the frequency of inflated versus deflated forecasts. But for both rail and road projects, the risk is substantial that demand forecasts are incorrect by a large margin. The causes of inaccuracy in forecasts are different for rail and road projects, with political causes playing a larger role for rail than for road (Flyvbjerg et al, 2006, 1).

These risks are 'typically ignored or downplayed by planners and decision makers, to the detriment of social and economic welfare'. Flyvbjerg and his colleagues call for more accountability and reference class forecasting.[16] Robert Bain (2009) reached similar conclusions on forecasting error and bias from his extensive studies of road projects.

To David Hartgen, the greatest knowledge gap in US travel forecasting practice is the 'unknown accuracy of road traffic forecasts' arising from multiple sources:

> Modeling weaknesses leading to these problems (non-behavioral content, inaccuracy of inputs and key assumptions, policy insensitivity, and excessive complexity) are identified. In addition, the institutional and political environments that encourage optimism bias and low risk assessment in forecasts are also reviewed. Major institutional factors, particularly low local funding matches and competitive grants, confound scenario modeling efforts and dampen the hope that technical modeling improvements alone can improve forecasting accuracy. The fundamental problems are not technical but institutional (Hartgen, 2013, 1133).

To address these problems, Hartgen advocated

> a multi-decade effort to substantially improve model forecasting accuracy over time by monitoring performance and improving data, methods and understanding of travel, but also by deliberately modifying the institutional arrangements

that lead to optimism bias . . . [and], to openly quantify and recognize the inherent uncertainty in travel demand forecasts and deliberately reduce their influence on project decision-making. . . . However to be successful either approach would require monitoring and reporting accuracy, standards for modeling and forecasting, greater model transparency, educational initiatives, coordinated research, strengthened ethics and reduction of non-local funding ratios so that localities have more at stake (Hartgen, 2013, 1133–1134).

We strongly support these views and the need to provide further in-depth study of different sources of error and uncertainty in a wide variety of forecasting contexts relating to projects and policies.

11.5.2 Improving the Performance of Models with Multiple Cross-Sectional Data

Our emphasis in this book has almost without exception concerned the use of single cross-sectional forecasting models and data for their estimation. However, we wish to comment further on the use of longitudinal data[17] in the form of multiple cross-sectional data sets based on independent samples, to test the transferability of model parameters over time and to examine their changes, and thereby improve the quality of forecasts.[18]

Two recent examples illustrate the benefits of models based on multiple cross-sectional data. Nobuhiro Sanko (2014) has studied the choice of rail, bus or car mode in the Nagoya region of Japan using cross-sectional data on journey times and several dummy variables for 1971, 1981, 1991 and 2001. His results confirmed that: (a) a model framework with time-dependent parameters can provide better forecasts than a model using only the most recent data; (b) alternative-specific constants change significantly over time, a result consistent with previous studies; and (c) using older data enables analysis of historical changes in travel behaviour, thereby providing more insights into actual travel behaviour.

Sabreena Anowar, Naveen Eluru and Luis Miranda-Moreno (2014) analysed household car ownership in the Montreal region with a generalised order logit formulation using cross-sectional data for 1998, 2003 and 2008. Although the three surveys were not based on the same set of households, the authors concluded that the surveys 'still provide us an opportunity to examine the impact of technology, altering perceptions of road and transit infrastructure, changing social and cultural trends across the population on vehicle ownership. Further, pooled datasets allow us to identify how the impact of exogenous variables has altered with time' (Anowar et al, 2014, 13).

Many countries have conducted national travel surveys, often dating back to the 1970s, to assess the evolution of key indicators and to support the development of local transportation planning and policy. Furthermore, ongoing model development has occurred in many major cities of the world over the last 50 years based on periodically collected major household and smaller project-based surveys. After five decades our field is approaching the point when several O-D surveys have been conducted in many metropolitan regions. For most US metropolitan areas, however, trends in the key indicators, such as trip rates, mean trip lengths and departure times disaggregated by trip purpose and mode, are seldom available.

Despite these data resources, a single cross-sectional approach to urban travel forecasting has generally continued up to the present. When a new O-D survey is undertaken, then a new model, often improved over the previous one, is estimated on the new survey, and applied in forecasting travel for the next target year, typically ten years beyond the previous one. In US studies, detailed comparisons of a new survey with earlier surveys are rarely performed. Differences in survey questions and methods, as well as changes in zoning systems, can make comparisons difficult. Even so, such comparisons are generally not regarded as a priority.

We suggest studies with both aggregate and disaggregate models to address the following questions:

1. What uses have been made of multiple cross-sectional data for model development and forecasts at the urban and regional level?
2. How should travel forecasting models with temporally defined parameters be specified with multiple cross-sectional data to improve the confidence intervals of forecasts?
3. What improvement of accuracy can be achieved by using multiple cross-sectional data rather than basing model forecasts on the last available survey?
4. How should periodically collected small samples be used efficiently to test the temporal changes in parameters and the resulting forecasts?

Knowledge of trends in key travel-related variables and analysis of multiple cross-sectional data have more value than satisfying historical curiosity. These trends should be further exploited for monitoring changes in behaviour and assessing the plausibility of forecasts for the target year and for intermediate years.

11.5.3 Exposing Methods and Assumptions to Wider Scrutiny

Calls for greater transparency in both the transportation planning process and the technical procedures that lie at its heart are long-standing and now persistent. In the UK, the approach adopted by land use – transportation studies was subject to detailed scrutiny in 1972 by a House of Commons Expenditure Committee, which recommended that: 'The assumptions made and the methods used in transportation studies should be made more comprehensible to the layman' (UK HoC, 1972, para 165). The travel forecasting community has been unsuccessful in effectively conveying to both the planning profession and interested citizens the range and implications of key assumptions underpinning forecasts and scheme evaluation.

In reporting the results of travel forecasts, evaluation measures and decisions, a statement of the significance of uncertainty in influential key variables, parameters and assumptions would be useful. For some exogenous factors, such as GDP or population forecasts, such statements might be routinely supplied. In many cases, however, the effort is partial, very limited or absent. Neither the public, professional planners nor many travel forecasters are aware of the numerical significance of errors or uncertainty of many key parameters and assumptions.

Take, for example, that most venerable parameter at the heart of our profession, the value of time, central to forecasts and the evaluation of policies and projects. This parameter is sometimes recorded to a quite spurious accuracy, in some cases to two decimal places. There are few instances where the assumptions in the value of model parameters are more important or the implications of proposed alternative assumptions so dramatic as in the arguments surrounding the money value of small travel time savings within the social cost benefit analysis of projects and plans.

A limited amount of documented evidence suggests that for many urban projects, and particularly those in mature and dense urban networks, a significant proportion of the total economic benefit of schemes, even major projects, results from very modest changes in travel times, on average perhaps a couple of minutes or less. Impressive figures for aggregate benefits often result from a very large number of trips enjoying small time savings (e.g., Welch and Williams, 1997). This situation is not widely appreciated by planning professionals or the public because standard forecasting and evaluation software typically reports only aggregate information (e.g., aggregate net present value, benefit to cost ratio, internal rate of return) rather than the frequency distribution of time savings and benefit measures disaggregated by the amount of time saved. We know of only a few cases internationally where time savings by time band are presented;[19] these bands are often not appropriate to a wide range of projects and policies.

The general debate over the measurement, valuation and significance of small time savings within the whole forecasting and evaluation framework is one of very long standing – at least since the first applications of cost–benefit analysis in the transportation sector. The arguments concern the assumption of a constant unit value of time, independent of the length and direction of time saved,[20] against the alternative proposition that very small time savings should be discounted, although not necessarily to zero. The arguments and counter-arguments relating to these key assumptions are variously philosophical, theoretical, empirical and practical and have been well rehearsed over the years in the academic literature.[21] Although international practices vary, many countries assume a constant unit value of time saved in benefit calculations; a few make special provision for small time savings. The theoretical and empirical arguments for either approach cannot however be described as strong, and 'many countries have taken the decision to use a uniform value for pragmatic reasons' (Daly et al, 2014, 214).[22]

The controversy over the variation in the value of time (in relation to the length of journey, the extent of time change gains and losses, and whether differences should accompany the forecasting and evaluation processes) often gets disinterred when major value-of-time studies are considered or their results published, and then reburied when the fuss dies down. For example, following a major UK value-of-time study in 2001, which offered support for the use of a unit value independent of the sign and size of time saving, an editorial appeared in the professional publication *Local Transport Today* under the banner 'Timelords Need Challenging'. It could not have been clearer in its comments and recommendations regarding the controversy over the accumulation of vast numbers of trips enjoying small time savings, which leads to many citizens 'scratching their heads'. In the light of a lack of consensus among professionals, and its significance in practice, the editorial concluded with the recommendation: 'The issues need to be exposed to wider debate than between just a handful of specialist timelords' (*Local Transport Today*, 2003, 13).

Following several previous calls over the years we recommend that information should be routinely produced on the distribution of time savings by length and direction of time saved (+/−) for both person and commercial vehicle trip purposes, with time intervals appropriate to the project and policy at hand. Within the context of practical multi-criteria and cost–benefit evaluation frameworks, in which time savings are monetised, the distribution of scheme benefits should be documented by length and direction of time saved. The sensitivity of a range of standard evaluation indicators to the valuation of small time savings should be identified. These analyses could be conducted at the aggregate and disaggregated levels, the latter involving the experience of a sample of journeys before and after a network change.

11.6 COMPROMISES OF PRACTICE AND RESEARCH: WHAT ARE THE ALTERNATIVES?

11.6.1 Why Has Progress Been So Slow in Adopting 'Advanced Techniques'?

Over the years a wide range of increasingly powerful software products, often with visually attractive display features, have been developed at the macro-, meso- and micro-levels for the analysis, evaluation and design of highway, public transport and pedestrian networks (see Chapter 10). These products serve the diverse needs of land use and transportation planning, demand management, and traffic operations and control.

Forecasts are now often and rightly subject to an *ex post* assessment against outcomes at some time in the future. Only in this way will the assumptions underpinning model specifications and forecasts of exogenous variables be subject to scrutiny and improvements made. The practical challenge at any particular time, however, is the *ex ante* position of selecting a method of analysis, typically involving readily available software, that generates the information to the required precision and minimises the risk of coming to different and inappropriate decisions, within the practical constraints encountered. Here, context is everything: the limitations of data, the knowledge base, the software available, and the time and other resources to do the job at hand. In this regard we argue below that insufficient information is currently available on the merits of alternative approaches, particularly in relation to 'advanced techniques'.

Two of the most often posed questions in our field are: (a) Why has the four-step approach, often in an archaic form, survived for over 50 years? (b) Why, with the exception of modal choice investigations, has the adoption of 'advanced techniques', including disaggregate methods based on the trip, tour or schedule, been so limited?

Concepts ultimately survive for a variety of reasons: because they continue to serve a purpose; the costs 'sunk' in present practices and software and human expertise are high; and the transfer costs to alternatives are prohibitive. We can assume that the propensity to change practices is inversely related to the difference between the new and current methodologies (Resource Decision Consultants, 1995). Furthermore, there is abundant evidence in the literature that knowledge of the merits of alternative approaches is limited, and we shall address this point further in section 11.6.3.

A further reason why the traditional forecasting procedure has survived is that metropolitan planning organisations (MPOs) in the US are still required to conduct rather similar forecasting exercises every decade, exercises that have long been served by the four-step procedure. In striving for consistency among a series of such forecasts, the penalty for changing methods becomes high. For example, the Sacramento Area Council of Governments decided to maintain two independent travel forecasting procedures, at least for some period of time, in order to ensure consistency with past analyses.[23]

Anecdotal reports also offer an additional reason: senior and mid-level staff of planning agencies and their consultants may be resistant to changing methods or procedures. Software developers routinely offer new or improved procedures, providing more precise solutions with less computing effort. Adoption of these methods, however, is often slow or simply does not occur. The apparent reason is the reluctance of supervisors to try a new method, whose properties may not be apparent or may be beyond their knowledge or comfort zone. Even experimental evaluation of new methods by curious staff seems to be discouraged.

Recently, however, there is some evidence of change, at least in the US, where:

> At the beginning of the 21st century, clear indications of a paradigm shift in transportation modeling are apparent. A growing number of agencies ... are abandoning established traditional modeling techniques and exploring advanced practices in travel forecasting ... defined as those practices that go beyond the traditional four-step travel demand modeling approach (Donnelly et al, 2010, 1).

Among the main findings of that report are:

> There is widespread agreement that human assets are the key factor limiting the adoption of advanced models. In almost all instances – and certainly in the most successful ones – a visionary champion was clearly identified as the sustaining force behind the adoption of advanced models. It was widely believed that this champion, with the support of upper management in the agency, was the single most important ingredient for success. Although a consultant can play this role the results to date have been less satisfactory. Absent strong federal leadership in this area it is likely that the importance of the champion – from both management and technical standpoints – will remain high in the move towards advanced models. ... An equally significant human constraint is the lack of agency staff capable of creatively and competently building and using advanced models (Donnelly et al, 2010, 65).

Change in forecasting practice can be rewarding, invigorating and exciting to agency staff. Opportunities to encourage change in practice should be welcomed and embraced, following prudent evaluation. At the same time, change brings risk and expense. Ways of mitigating such risk should be sought, and are worthy of study and exploration.

Ultimately, the reasons for the adoption of new methods relate to policy impacts and information requirements, as discussed in detail and summarised (Donnelly et al, 2010, Table 4), and this is likely to be the case in future as more profound changes occur in lifestyles, activity patterns and targeted transportation policies.

11.6.2   Gap between 'Research' and 'Practice'

The characterisation of a tension between 'research', particularly academic research, and 'practice' is somewhat problematic. Over the years some of the most distinguished theoreticians and academic researchers, moving between universities, government agencies and research-intensive consultancies, have been at the forefront of bringing new ideas and methods into practice. Nevertheless, by wide consensus there is a large gap between the research frontier and the activities of the practising planner, with no difference in esteem implied here. Furthermore, the methods and language of both are often remote or incomprehensible to the large majority of citizens whose lives are profoundly affected by the tools of the trade and the ideas that underpin them. We shall have more to say about this latter aspect in section 12.3. Here we comment on the former aspect – the gap between research, and particularly academic research, and practice.

The explanation is as straightforward as it is difficult to resist. Our discipline began in the era of the large transportation studies, with much 'learning on the job', where significant innovations occurred over two or three years. Although travel forecasting became an interdisciplinary subject *par excellence*, and thrived in transportation centres throughout the world, over time it also became prominent in individual academic disciplines, particularly econometrics and optimisation, with their own language, research methods and traditions. While this situation led to regular advances in technique, it has also resulted in increasing specialisation and compartmentalisation, both between and within the multiple disciplines which bear on travel behaviour and its forecasting. For interesting comments on the disciplinary and professional perspectives on travel forecasting, particularly accompanying activity-travel research, see Kitamura (1988), Mahmassani (1988), Bhat and Koppelman (1999a) and Pinjari and Bhat (2011).

Although the distinction between the academic travel behaviour or network equilibrium researcher and the practitioner planner is often not a sharp one, the motivations of the two seldom coincide. Both would consider themselves as 'practical problem solvers', but the former are often drawn through intellectual curiosity to that endless quest to forge ahead, to push the boundaries, in return for the rewards of the modern academic:

publications in prestigious international journals, contributions to major national and international conferences, research grants and a following of research students, and possibly a role in consultancy. Such activities are encouraged by institutional competition and publication of modern international metrics of academic esteem. These incentives are different from the requirements of the practitioner working in the public or private sector, often under severe commercial pressures and/or resource constraints of time pressures and limited budgets. No less laudable in intent, practitioners often search for the simplest tools in the toolbox to do the job and value a sense of consensus and stability. Many research-based consultants have their feet in both camps, and some have been highly successful in bringing innovative techniques to the market.

11.6.3 Complexity, Simplification and Model Design: What Really Matters?

A large number of excellent studies conducted over many years resulted in a progression from 'trip-based' through 'tour-based' to practical 'activity-travel' models, most although not all within the micro-behavioural tradition. Many problems still exist, as we discussed in section 6.6. John Bowman, a leading authority on activity-based models, concluded a review of practical applications in upbeat terms:

> Practical model systems now microsimulate full day itineraries for synthetic populations of entire metropolitan regions, representing the influence of real-world constraints and influences with increased realism. We expect that the realism of activity-based travel decision microsimulation models will continue to improve, that activity-based demand models will be integrated with highway and public transport microsimulation models, and that the usage of these models for practical planning and policy analysis will become more widespread in the years ahead (Bowman, 2009, 318).

Some of John Bowman's predictions on the refinement, uptake and enhancement of this approach are already occurring (Donnelly et al, 2010), although our own view is that further complex integrated activity-travel models linking demand and network models within a microsimulation framework may have limited applicability. One of the useful by-products of the current generation of such models will be to identify and test suitable model simplifications.

A cautionary view has also been expressed by Michael Wegener (2011b), a senior contributor to and commentator on land use – transportation models, who has questioned the trend towards microsimulation modelling of activity-travel systems in planning practice. His reservations are on technical, theoretical and philosophical grounds in the light of the range of problems facing planning practice in the twenty-first century:

> While recognising these advances the paper calls attention to the problems of disaggregate models in terms of data requirements, computing time and stochastic variation[24] and shows that in the light of new challenges cities are facing, such as energy scarcity and climate change, not further refinement but more focus on basic needs and constraints is needed to make the models more useful to planning practice (Wegener, 2011b, 161).

One of his technical concerns is the computational costs and implications of Monte Carlo variability, which he referred to as 'stochastic variation', for examining the differences between equilibrium states in policy analysis. Although this problem has been increasingly studied over the last decade, the general implications for the adoption of the approach are still unclear.

Wegener also saw these issues as part of the model design process of identifying the policy and information requirements within which microsimulation, or models for which microsimulation is a solution method, is an appropriate approach. As a possible approach to the macro–micro debate, he called for 'a theory of multi-level models according to which for each planning task there is an appropriate level of conceptual, spatial and temporal resolution' (Wegener, 2011b, 161).

Although we share Wegener's views we also acknowledge an alternative argument, for which Chandra Bhat is a leading proponent (Bhat et al, 2013; Bhat, 2014). In all of the discussion above, we may have given the impression that more behavioural realism necessarily implies less practical applicability. Bhat and his colleagues suggest that the movement toward more conceptually accurate modelling approaches need not necessarily imply more time-consuming and 'cumbersome' models:

> There are ways that more theoretically sound and new methodologies can lead to models that are computationally efficient and even simpler to understand/ implement. For example, rather than have a series of single discrete choices of participation in different activity purposes, one can model this with a more theoretically sound multiple discrete choice model of participation that recognizes satiation effects in activity participation while also predicting activity participation choices in one stroke (Bhat, 2014).

As noted in Chapter 9, to judge a model solely on its mathematical or technical sophistication is to miss the point. We only require a model sufficiently detailed to reduce to an acceptable level the risk of making poor decisions. To misquote a famous scientist, the practitioner's task is to 'Make your model as simple as possible, but no simpler.'[25] Of course, ahead of this decision we may not know the relative merits of alternatives, and it is here that we believe relatively large gains can be made quickly. Many crucial issues relate to model design – the development of models appropriate to the problem at hand, which will deliver the information required. Practitioners need to know to what extent and in what contexts the claims for model improvements are justified.

In our view one of the most pressing research priorities at the heart of travel forecasting modelling is to bring to fruition the task set out long ago by Ian Heggie and Peter Jones (1978) to identify the 'domains of validity' of different models (section 6.1.1):

1. *Of the wide range of trip-, tour- and schedule-based models specified and estimated at different levels of aggregation, what models are available to address particular questions and are appropriate in different contexts, for generating the required information?*
2. *How should simplifications in models be systematically identified and tested (e.g., in relation to the presence and absence of various behavioural responses of individuals and households) and their practical implications made clearer?*
3. *To what extent are more complex models more accurate, and for what information and what decisions? How can the trade-off between accuracy and cost of technique be clarified (Chapter 9)?*

Progress is being made on all these issues, but few general results based on numerical testing on large networks are as yet available (e.g., Walker, 2005; Ferdous et al, 2012).

The testing of complex models against progressively simpler models to detect the likely size of errors and bias in key indicators needs to be an ongoing task, as relevant to current as to future innovations, in passenger, commercial vehicle and integrated land use – transportation models. In the absence of the above knowledge, the merits of different practical approaches remain rather imprecise and may be subject to a fog of claim and counter-claim.

In the past often only one model or method was available for undertaking a particular task. In the future, several may be available; models should be judged against the 'next best' alternative, and the traditional four-step model should no longer be considered the sole basis for comparison.

11.7   CONCLUSION

We have described a field that evolved rather irregularly over time, with great variation in the models developed in research studies and those applied in practice. The astonishing amount of material that is now being produced in ever more specialised journals and conferences suggests the field is in rude health. Should we therefore be sanguine about the state of travel forecasting? While there is room for optimism in the recognition of certain problems and the exploration of different theoretical approaches, there is also rather little evidence that the technical sophistication of some currently promoted models and methods is matched by improved accuracy. Clearly, there is still much to do and, in the various technical chapters and the preceding sections, we have given our personal views on some of the priorities facing researchers.

In this chapter, and perhaps in the book more generally, we might be accused of failing to convey the 'bigger picture' of forecasting – the dependence of travel forecasts on future trends in population, migration, employment changes, development, the car market, technological innovation and so on. These are all immensely important issues, and any detailed consideration of uncertainty in future estimates of travel would necessarily involve several of these aspects. To do them full justice and to discuss inevitable country-specific issues would have lengthened the book considerably, and partly taken us into the realms of deep speculation. Our focus in this chapter has been firmly on the development of theory, techniques and assumptions underpinning forecasts. In closing this chapter we touch briefly on two further issues: one is speculative – the changing contexts within which travel forecasting may occur; and one is always topical – the contribution of the critic.

We presented the innovations and developments in urban travel forecasting as associated with, sometimes conditioned by, a broadening range of objectives and information requirements, the latter usually involving greater spatial and temporal detail over time. We have made the assumption that this information and its accuracy matter. We have also perhaps implied in our discussion that the systems approach, the scientific method and decisions based on evidence can now be taken for granted and that travel forecasters will be given time to do their job. While the nature of the transport planning process, and role of forecasting models within it, has and will evolve differently in different parts of the world, there is no guarantee whatsoever that in the future any of the above assumptions will survive changes in technology, the political environment, and more pressing problems of the twenty-first century being thrust upon us. It is likely that travel forecasting in some form will still be an important part of the planning process, but the relevance of the questions we have raised throughout this chapter will almost certainly change as what is regarded as important, and how it is touched by technology, also changes.

Finally, we comment on the contribution of the critic. We accept that the field of travel forecasting and policy assessment is not characterised by a cosy consensus of views, but is subject to many uncertainties and criticisms. This has always been true. We must always be aware of the extent to which the problems of the present and past have been addressed and dealt with to the satisfaction of most. The policy insensitivity of models, failure to generate information of the required precision, theoretical limitations, the over-complexity of models and now the inaccuracy of forecasts tend to be the most widely cited. Criticism comes both from professionals within the field and from those who observe from the sidelines, be they politicians, journalists or interested and concerned citizens, as they become acquainted with the decisions of planners and perhaps also the methods they adopt. There is a danger that our field, particularly academic contributions to forecasting, will become an inward-looking profession, dispersed into research enclaves where proponents can and do preach to the converted, and where minority views are isolated. Some have suggested that this has long been the case.

Our view is that critics serve a vital role in stimulating research questions. How should the travel forecasting community deal with issues outside the 'mainstream', which may have unpalatable consequences for method, planning and policy? Is it possible to forge a consensus on what is agreed within the current approaches and, more importantly, on what there is disagreement, in order to identify those problems that are or can be subject to theoretical and empirical investigation? Let us also recognise that over the last six decades there are many who have seen travel forecasting as part of the problem rather than the solution to the dilemmas of urban transportation. If not directly through 'predict and provide' planning approaches, it has been suggested that, through simply embedding past and current preferences of individuals in forecasting models and evaluation procedures, we cannot hope to address the very culture of car use, place limits on mobility by car, and redesign our transportation systems and cities as part of addressing the major problems of the twenty-first century. The objective, it is argued, is not to 'forecast' but to fundamentally 'change' behaviour not just through standard policy instruments but by addressing attitudes and tastes more directly. Travel forecasters need to understand what these issues mean and relate their own methods and theories to statements in a range of other planning philosophies and approaches.

In presenting some of these viewpoints in this chapter, we have not had the intention of running amok in the proverbial travel forecasting china shop, for there is much to be preserved. However, we urge our colleagues to revisit past and present critiques and debates where these are still unresolved. If the field is confident in its foundations, then it can be confident to face its critics more openly and actively than in the past in order to promote research and advance its methods. If the house is built on sand, it is best the occupants be told. In the spirit of debate we challenge the field to be open, address its critics more directly, and be more eclectic in its outlook.

NOTES

1. It was put to us this way by Alan Horowitz: 'The modern travel forecasting model is one of the greatest achievements of mankind. It took hundreds, maybe thousands, of extremely smart and dedicated people, all working toward a single goal, to get where we are today' (personal communication with David Boyce, 2013).
2. For examples of the discussion of recent advances in the behaviour, microanalysis and simulation of urban goods movements, see Hensher and Figliozzi (2007), Hunt and Stefan (2007), Liedtke (2009) and Chow et al (2010).
3. Lipsey (1989) discussed the 'refutation by evidence' and 'confirmation by evidence' approaches to theory testing. In his view the latter approach is hazardous, since 'the world is sufficiently complex for *some* confirming evidence to be found for almost any theory, no matter how unlikely the theory may be' (Lipsey, 1989, 24).
4. www.surveyarchive.org/zahavi.html (accessed 22 April 2014).
5. The model was once described to Huw Williams as 'an intellectual game puffed up by mathematics'.
6. See, for example, 'After the Crash, We Need a Revolution in the Way We Teach Economics' by Ha-Joon Chang and Jonathan Aldred, Viewpoint, *Guardian*, 11 May 2014, 36.
7. For a discussion of the incorporation of inertia and thresholds within the discrete choice framework, see Cantillo et al (2006) and Ortúzar and Willumsen (2011).
8. Good recent discussions of embedding alternative decision rules in discrete choice models can be found in the papers by Timmermans (2010), Hess et al (2012) and Leong and Hensher (2012).
9. Higgs boson, an exotic elementary particle postulated in 1964, whose existence was confirmed in 2012 at CERN, the European Organization for Nuclear Research (home. web.cern.ch/).
10. www.dailymotion.com/video/x1mp2je_bbc-horizon-2014-how-you-really-make-decisions-720p-hdtv-x264-aac-mvgroup-org_news (accessed 23 May 2014).
11. Several papers on the application of behavioural economics, and the applicability of prospect theory specifically, to travel choice situations have appeared since 2000, including the contributions by Avineri and Prashker (2003), Avineri and Chorus (2010), Timmermans (2010), van de Kaa (2010), Li and Hensher (2011) and Metcalfe and Dolan (2012).
12. See, for example, Handy (1996), Cervero and Kockelman (1997), Kitamura et al (1997b), Handy et al (2005), Maat et al (2005) and Ewing and Cervero (2010).
13. The papers by Tanner (1961, 1981), Gunn (1981), Kirby (1981), Schafer and Victor (2000), Mokhtarian and Chen (2004), Van Wee et al (2006) and Metz (2008) survey the issues and implications of the topic.
14. See Goodwin (1998, Table 5.2, 119) and Simmonds et al (2013, Table 1) for suggested adjustment times accompanying projects and policies.
15. See, for example, Pickrell (1989, 1992), Kain (1990), Mackett and Edwards (1998), Flyvbjerg et al (2006), de Jong et al (2007a), Bain (2009), Li and Hensher (2010), Parthasarathi and Levinson (2010), Hartgen (2013) and Rose and Hensher (2014).
16. Reference class forecasting is 'the method of predicting the future, through looking

at similar past situations and their outcomes . . . developed by Daniel Kahneman and Amos Tversky' (en.wikipedia.org/wiki/Reference_class_forecasting, accessed 17 May 2014).

17. Various forms of longitudinal data designs have been used in practice. The use of panel data, in which observations on the travel choices of the same sample of individuals are taken at different points in time, has long been advocated and widely applied in research studies. For a full discussion of the various forms of longitudinal data designs, their relative advantages and disadvantages, along with significant applications, see, for example, Kitamura (2000), Ortúzar and Willumsen (2011) and Ortúzar et al (2011).

18. A large literature dating from the 1970s exists on the stability of certain key indicators and, in particular, trip rates (e.g., Downes and Gyenes, 1976; Kostyniuk and Kitamura, 1984). Similarly, multiple cross-sectional data has been used to test the constancy and transferability of the parameters in spatial interaction models (e.g., Elmi et al, 1999). For a fine discussion of the spatial and temporal transferability of value-of-time parameters, see Gunn (2001).

19. In the revised version of NATA (UK DfT, 2009a), for example, time savings in the following six bands were required: less than -5 minutes, -5 to -2 minutes, -2 to 0 minutes, 0 to 2 minutes, 2 to 5 minutes, greater than 5 minutes.

20. For a project saving ten minutes the value of the first minute saved is the same as that of the tenth.

21. For a full discussion of the relevant issues, see Waters (1995), Welch and Williams (1997), Mackie et al (2001), Small (2012) and Daly et al (2014).

22. The pragmatic reasons are to avoid: (a) the 'creeping congestion' problem (at what stage do changes in levels-of-service become significant?); (b) the so-called 'adding-up' problem in which a large project warranting a constant unit value assumption could be sub-divided to an extent where the individual parts might merit a different (discounted) unit value of time; and (c) potential bias in favour of large projects under certain evaluation indicators.

23. John Bowman, discussion with David Boyce, 2013.

24. Wegener is here referring to the Monte Carlo variation, the variation in output measures arising from drawing random numbers in the process of solving the models; see Wegener (2011b).

25. 'Make your theory as simple as possible, but no simpler' (A. Einstein).

12. Conclusion

12.1 INTRODUCTION

In Chapter 11 we discussed several technical advances made over the years, as well as current challenges, as possible pointers to future research requirements. In this concluding chapter we wish to address some further rather more general questions. The first is to ask how progress was achieved, as a means of identifying the preconditions for the creation, diffusion and adoption of new ideas. Then, we want to consider how the accumulated experience of the field can be passed on, particularly to new generations of urban transportation planners and travel forecasters, as well as interested citizens. At several points we shall express personal views, hoping that they will stimulate or rekindle debate.

12.2 HOW WAS PROGRESS ACHIEVED?

12.2.1 History of Innovation and Ideas

Although we do not intend to draw deep comparisons between the evolution of our field and the great scientific and technological achievements of the past, some parallels about the evolution of ideas are worth noting. The history of innovation and ideas in science and technology is a well-established field of study (Kuhn, 1962; Koestler, 1964; Johnson, 2010), where questions such as the following are addressed:

1. Did a particular field move in a smooth progression or was it interspersed with 'quantum jumps'?
2. Were old ideas overthrown, or did they survive in particular circumstances?
3. Where did breakthrough ideas come from?
4. Did innovations come 'out of the blue', or did they arise through building incrementally on prior efforts?

5. Was an innovation in response to new requirements, availability of new data, enhanced computing technology, unusually clear thinking over a sustained period, or simply a single bright idea?
6. Was it the result of serendipity, or closely related to other developments, possibly in a related field?
7. Was it the product of the lone researcher, or of several individuals working in a well-resourced research consultancy or institute, multidisciplinary academic centre or government agency?
8. How were the new ideas received?
9. Over what time period did the impact occur?
10. Are good ideas inevitable?

These questions are of interest in their own right, and we have already made remarks on several of them in the previous chapters. As Steven Johnson (2010) notes, one of their main values is to identify the environments in which new ideas occurred as a basis for having more of them. We wish to make a few additional remarks on some of these issues and their relevance to our field.

12.2.2 Progress through a Series of Paradigm Changes?

Over the last 60 years, travel forecasting models, and their conceptual frameworks, have been applied to an extensive range of policies and projects for generating information relating to an ever expanding range of objectives. Not infrequently, the progression of planning priorities and travel forecasting methods has been discussed in terms of the transfer between different paradigms that 'strongly affects the kinds of problems that are identified, how they are framed and diagnosed, the methods that are used for analysis and the policy solutions that are subsequently generated' (Jones, 2012, 3).

Although differences exist in the number and description of these paradigms, and the dates and countries to which they apply, this perspective is fairly common: transitions between different epochs subject to different planning philosophies, requiring appropriate methods and models for analysis, forecasting and evaluation. Further examples include a transition from an era of 'predict and provide' in planning, specifically relating to highway capacity, to one of 'predict and prevent' through demand restraint (Owens, 1995), or to an era in which a 'new realism' in transportation planning emerges in which 'we cannot build ourselves out of the congestion problem'.

Few examples of major urban highway construction programmes are currently found in mature cities in advanced industrialised countries.

However, in many countries and certainly internationally, we still see in the urban sector the whole range of planning and policy instruments requiring analysis: (a) from major land use changes to detailed neighbourhood planning; (b) from heavy investment in prestigious public transport and highway projects to capacity reallocation and local transportation systems management; (c) demand restraint through a variety of instruments; and (d) planning for non-motorised modes. In addition, in the US and some other countries, long-range forecasts of 20 and 30 years remain a requirement for urban transportation and air quality planning, and have been so for five decades, while demand management has a lesser role (Chapters 2, 8). In other countries, congestion charging is the cornerstone of the attack on urban transportation problems. In earlier chapters we have noted the development of objectives that have guided planners over the years, from operational requirements to a whole range involving efficiency, equity, environment, development, regeneration, and resource scarcity, with information requirements that have generally increased in spatial and temporal detail. Which planning approach and priorities prevail in any particular place and time depends on a wide variety of local contexts.

In a useful summary of the international transportation research and policy agenda over the last 50 years, Peter Jones (2012) has described five different perspectives of planning practice and its accompanying methodology, from an initial vehicle-based approach to trip-based, activity-based, attitude-based and finally dynamics-based perspectives. Jones discussed these different approaches not in terms of an evolution of distinct paradigms, in which one set of issues supplanted another, but as a 'successive paradigm enlargement' to apply to different planning contexts.[1]

In the internationally complex evolution of travel forecasting models over the years, revolutionary changes have occurred in the conceptualisation of travel behaviour, transportation networks and the travel forecasting problem and implementation of models. As described in section 11.2, the original four-step approach slowly evolved, as it fed off various innovations. However, for reasons described in section 11.6, the 'old regime' has survived and co-exists with relatively minor modifications among a variety of approaches that differ greatly in their theoretical and practical sophistication. Our view of the development of methods, therefore, is similar to the view of Jones: conceptual jumps with a substantial enlargement of the methods applied in practice. No 'knock-out' blows were delivered, but the fight is not over (sections 11.2, 11.6).

12.2.3   Where Do 'Good' Ideas Come From?

Before proceeding, it is important to note that what constitutes a 'good idea' may be a very contentious issue indeed. To one person a 'breakthrough idea' supporting or strengthening the status quo may be acknowledged as a real step forward. On the other hand, it might be anathema to another who is unswerving ideologically to either an alternative approach or alternative policies (e.g., those who see nothing other than an individual behavioural approach as a basis for forecasting, or those who support greater provision for 'non-motorised' modes over the historical priority given to motorised modes in urban transportation policy).

Some might argue, often with the benefit of hindsight, that certain ideas simply delayed the introduction or development of an alternative, more fruitful approach. We have witnessed this situation, both in the literature and at conferences, in relation to the entropy maximising approach, utility maximising approaches, and models or methods that treat travel separately from the activities of households.

What distinguishes 'breakthrough ideas' is their power for explanation and synthesis and their enduring contribution, even if their implications for forecasts are relatively small. In Richard Lipsey's terms, these have allowed us to see the world in a different way (section 1.3). Insights provided by the activity-travel framework (Chapter 6) offer the clearest example of a breakthrough idea.

Computational opportunities created by early mainframe computers in the 1950s, perhaps, were the first breakthrough in our field. The ability to solve the shortest route problem on road networks initially led to crude heuristics for the traffic assignment problem, and later to convergent solution algorithms. Trip distribution models, later supplemented by mode split models, built on this advance, resulting in a capability to solve the four-step procedure on mainframes. Iterative solutions (solving the four-step procedure with feedback) turned out to be too costly in terms of computing resources and staff time.

With the advent of microcomputers in the 1980s, computers became more widely available. Private software developers, sometimes with strong connections to academic research, followed. Initially, their response was to support and extend the ingrained four-step paradigm; primarily, they continue today in this manner, supplying the tools sought by most planning agencies. More recent huge advances in computing speed, memory and fast disk storage enabled microsimulation of travel demand and network performance for entire regions. So far, however, only a few consultants and academics, as well as adventurous practitioners, have responded to this opportunity.

Paralleling the technological innovations in computing in the early 1950s, academic leaders in applied mathematics, mathematical economics and the analytically oriented social sciences founded new academic and professional societies that provided the environment and stimulation for innovative thinking. One of the first was the Operations Research Society of America (ORSA) in 1952, followed in 1954 by the slightly more management-oriented association, the Institute of Management Sciences (TIMS).[2] Simultaneously in the UK, the Operational Research Society was established in 1953. Each of these organisations had their roots in the applications of mathematics for military purposes during the Second World War, in both the UK and the US. The origins of mathematical programming can be traced to these organisations and their founders (see section 7.2.2).

Operations research provided a fertile environment for a former academic physicist, Robert Herman [1914–1997], to propose the Transportation Science Section of ORSA. Herman was the founding editor of the section's journal, *Transportation Science*, which began publication in 1967. In 1956 Herman had:

> joined the General Motors Research Laboratory, as head of the basic science group, later renamed the theoretical physics department. He introduced science into the affairs of his employer by inventing . . . traffic science. Drawing upon his background in physics, he first directed his attention to the description of the microscopic behaviour of traffic: the detailed manner in which individual drivers avoid coinciding with each other in space and time, at least most of the time.[3]

In 1959, Herman organised the first international symposium on the theory of traffic flow, which continues biennially today. The Robert Herman Lifetime Achievement Award was initiated in his honour in 1991.[4]

The Cowles Commission for Research in Economics was founded in 1932 by a Colorado businessman, Alfred Cowles, at Colorado Springs. The Commission moved to Chicago in 1939, and was affiliated with the Department of Economics of the University of Chicago until 1955, when it then moved to Yale University as the Cowles Foundation (see section 7.3).[5] Many prominent staff members of the Cowles Commission were leaders of the Econometric Society, 'an international society founded in 1930 for the advancement of economic theory in relation to statistics and mathematics'.[6]

In 1954 the Regional Science Association (RSA) was founded in the US by a group of economists, quantitative geographers and urban planners with interests in industrial location theory, input–output models (industrial inter-industry analysis), mathematical programming and methods of urban and regional analysis. The leader of this group was Walter Isard [1919–2010], a maverick economist at Harvard University. Today, Isard is remembered as the founder of the field of regional science, as well as the field's first periodicals: *Papers of the RSA* and the *Journal of Regional Science*. Several members of this group had interests in urban travel forecasting. During the 1960s, Isard stimulated the interest of European economists and geographers in regional science by organising congresses and urging the formation of language-based sections of the RSA.

From the early 1950s these academic and professional societies provided an environment and context for the new field of urban travel forecasting, just as mainframe computers offered the means for implementing the new methods. The main developments in urban travel forecasting during this period stemmed from a few papers and research monographs responsible for both consolidating the existing approach and opening up new vistas. The initial statement of the sequential procedure with feedback by Douglas Carroll, the network equilibrium theory proposed by Martin Beckmann and his co-authors, the entropy maximising approach advocated by Alan Wilson, the discrete choice approach based on random utility theory developed by Daniel McFadden, and the activity-travel framework proposed by Torsten Hägerstrand and Stuart Chapin, and later adopted and extended by Peter Jones and his colleagues, were distinguished by power of explanation and the sheer number of good ideas. Sooner or later, each of these innovations changed the way that the urban travel forecasting problem was viewed and solved in practice.

One might argue that the ideas of Carroll and Beckmann came 'out of the blue'. The proposal of Carroll and his team (Roger Creighton, John Hamburg, Irving Hoch and Morton Schneider) was to: (a) decompose a complex problem into more manageable steps; (b) realise that the input and output variables of the steps were interrelated; and (c) recognise that an iterative solution was therefore required. Schneider devised an ingenious method, for that time, to solve the trip distribution and traffic assignment problem in a way that incorporated the interaction between these two models. Beckmann envisaged that non-linear programming, a novel optimisation formulation, could combine point-to-point travel demand functions with network flows based on shortest routes. He derived optimality (equilibrium) conditions corresponding to aggregate behavioural postulates about flows over shortest routes determined by endogenously determined route costs. Both Carroll and Beckmann participated in Regional Science meetings in 1954 and thereafter. They probably also presented their thinking at early operations research meetings.[7] Carroll was also active in the Highway Research Board, the principal academic-professional organisation related to the new field of urban transportation.

Although entropy maximising methods and discrete choice theory were drawn from prior thinking in other fields, the challenges of making urban travel forecasts stimulated Alan Wilson and Daniel McFadden to examine basic problems in new ways. Entropy maximising methods drew on established methods in statistical mechanics as well as the new field of information theory. The disaggregate behavioural discrete choice approach drew on developments in the analysis of discrete data and on psychological and economic theories of behaviour. In asking the question 'What about people in regional science?', Torsten Hägerstrand was responding to the early annals of regional science research by proposing a new approach based on conditions imposed on the everyday lives of urban dwellers (Hägerstrand, 1970, 11). His activity-travel framework can be seen as a natural outgrowth of the Swedish school of geography.

Some innovations took many years to be fully understood, refined and assimilated into the mainstream of practice or to be accepted as alternatives. The time interval varied according to the difference in concept, method and software from the current practice of that time. Some innovations provided a *post-hoc* rationalisation for and strengthened an existing approach – both entropy maximising and discrete choice theory served this role. It is partly for that reason that they were very successful. As we noted in Chapter 3, the entropy maximising method made a rapid and relatively seamless transition into practice in the UK, whereas in the US it was ignored by practitioners and many academics. Later, however, models based on the new approach were incorporated into many modern software systems.

One of the most significant innovations in our field was the introduction of analytical models rather than empirical functions into the analysis and forecasting of behaviour. For example, the MNL model based on linear generalised costs (or disutility) gave new insights into behaviour and allowed policies to be more easily represented. In our field the practice of '*post-hoc* rationalisation' provided a powerful means of strengthening the prevailing set of ideas. Over the years the demand model implicit in the four-step approach simply 'morphed' into a more satisfactory nested logit-type demand structure, allowing the framework to take on behavioural clothes. These are examples of what Steven Johnson referred to as 'the adjacent possible' form of innovation:

> In human culture, we like to think of breakthrough ideas as sudden accelerations on the timeline, where a genius jumps ahead fifty years and invents something that normal minds, trapped in the present moment, couldn't possibly

have come up with. But the truth is that technological (and scientific) advances rarely break out of the adjacent possible; the history of cultural progress is, almost without exception, a story of one door leading to another door, exploring the palace one room at a time (Johnson, 2010, 36).

In our view, even the loudly trumpeted TRANSIMS can be seen as an incremental development of existing micro-behavioural practice. Within the broader scheme of things, its innovation lay in its treating demand and network use at an unprecedented level of detail and as solved through microsimulation, both of which already enjoyed a substantial tradition. The innovations were technical and computational, rather than theoretical.

Was something 'in the air' at a particular time, which required a conceptual development, improved computational capabilities or new data, to resolve a particular issue? There are examples of this notion – the development of the nested logit model in the early 1970s was a clear response to the problem of finding a workable model, and in particular a generalisation of the MNL model, that was not subject to the independence from irrelevant alternatives property, but still consistent with utility maximisation.

The development of the field has been the product of some remarkable people whose influence has been exerted in many ways: consulting to solve immediate problems; writing software; organising and leading research programmes; editing journals; authoring textbooks that synthesised earlier innovations; advising theses of students who subsequently emerged as leaders of the field; organising conferences; and inspirational teaching. We have already mentioned many in this book. Some have contributed centrally to the development of the subject and moved to other related fields. Others have stayed to make multiple contributions over several decades. If one considers the forecasting of travel behaviour, few would dissent from the view that Daniel McFadden has been a towering influence. Likewise, Martin Beckmann's and Alan Wilson's early contributions were inspiring and lasting examples to many. Others made significant contributions over three or four decades.

To support this view, one may consult the Lifetime Achievement Awards of the International Association of Travel Behaviour Research: Frank Koppelman (2003), Moshe Ben-Akiva (2006), Ryuichi Kitamura (2006), David Hensher (2009), Andrew Daly (2012) and Juan de Dios Ortúzar (2012). And one may also consult the Robert Herman Lifetime Achievement Awards of the Transportation Science and Logistics Society of the Institute for Operations Research and the Management Sciences (INFORMS): Martin Beckmann (1994), Michael Florian (1998), David Boyce (2003), Michael Smith (2007), Nathan Gartner (2011) and Carlos Daganzo (2013).

12.2.4 Environments within Which Innovations Occur

In his assessment of innovations in science and technology, Steven Johnson mused on what he referred to as 'patterns of creativity'. In particular, he asks why it is that 'some environments squelch new ideas; [while] other environments seem to breed them effortlessly' (Johnson, 2010, 16). It is not our intention to say what is the best environment for the creation and nurturing of innovation, or whether, as Johnson (2010) would put it, 'the connected hive mind is smarter than the lone thinker'.

Whatever is the answer, unsurprisingly the existence of highly imaginative individuals is a common requisite. In our field good ideas arose in many different environments, some from highly competitive university environments, or academics working in concert with research-oriented consultancies, while others emerged from collaborative ventures within government bodies. Many of the more important ideas in our field have been the product of lone thinkers; others are from what approximates to Johnson's 'hive mind'. The allocation of research funding to selected centres of excellence in elite institutions, in which a strong research culture thrives, rather than spread throughout research networks, is an old dilemma and one which may differ from country to country.[8]

The role of government in identifying, supporting, and promoting 'best practice', while laudable in standardising an approach and lessening bias and even distortion in decision making, inevitably also has the potential to inhibit innovation. Moreover, in a commercial environment governmental agencies may well be reluctant to undertake software development, or encourage the adoption of new methods for which there are only a few suppliers. These concerns may act as a serious brake on innovation. Variations in the local situation need to be acknowledged, and flexibility allowed on advice, as is generally well understood. Without suitable financial support for monitoring innovations in forecasting methods and active two-way links of government agencies with the international research and practitioner communities, the danger of ossification of official advice is ever present. In section 11.7 we argued that the critic often provides stimulus for research questions that may subsequently be the creative force for innovation and development.

12.2.5 Are 'Good' Ideas Inevitable?

In response to a question from a newspaper reporter, Daniel McFadden reflected modestly on his award of the 2000 Nobel prize in economic sciences. He was asked whether someone else would have eventually developed what he had done. McFadden said that his innovations were in response to the increasing availability of data on the discrete choices made by individuals; if he had not developed the theory and methods for handling such data, it was inevitable that someone else would. The same response would seem to apply to the early contributions of Douglas Carroll and Martin Beckmann. Indeed, partial derivations related to Beckmann's formulation did occur before his results became widely known.

We cannot image any situation in our field where this statement would not be true. Of course, when, where and by whom such innovations would emerge, and the alternative path of history of a field, are entirely speculative. The implications of these comments, however, are clear and practical, and relate to the need for the field to identify relevant research questions and pose them in a form amenable to research. Once solutions emerge, it is another matter how they will impact mainstream practice. We would recommend that specialist bodies, such as government agencies, professional societies and academic interest groups, such as the conferences of the International Association of Travel Behaviour Research, the International Symposia on Transportation and Traffic Theory and the Symposia of the European Association for Research on Transportation, with inputs from theoreticians and practitioners, regularly seek to identify and pose key questions to challenge the field, as is sometimes done at international conferences and symposia. Alongside this thrust forward, we must always ask whether the challenges posed in earlier times were all addressed satisfactorily.

When key questions or identified problems are posed clearly, then one or more solutions will eventually emerge. If there was 'something in the air', it will not be surprising if similar solutions emerge at the same time and several people or groups working independently claim the solution. As is usually the case with research, when questions are suitably posed, then similar solutions will be generated. In this interdisciplinary subject *par excellence*, it is also not surprising that many innovations are the result of contacts with related fields: the natural sciences, mathematics and statistical theory, and the social sciences.

12.3 HANDING ON THE EXPERIENCE AND LEARNING IN THE PROCESS

Because the questions addressed, the research methodology and the language of discourse are often conducted within well-defined academic traditions, it may be expected, and perhaps is inevitable, that the product may sometimes appear jargon bound and poorly packaged. Even within the social sciences, tensions between quantitative and qualitative research methods serve to compartmentalise the field. With due humility for any part we have played to the contrary, we would advocate an urgent need to convey research results in a user-friendly way and, with due respect to cultural differences, in plain English.

The culture of research and the means of conveying research material have changed dramatically over the last 20 years, especially since the advent of the World Wide Web. While the demise of the traditional lecture has been predicted at least since the 1970s, and a similar fate is often predicted for the book, these still serve centrally as the means of transmitting knowledge. Today, in contrast to the situation five decades ago, vastly improved methods and materials are available for teaching and conveying complex ideas through distance-learning and self-study programmes. Access to and dissemination of these programmes, delivered through attractive multimedia, serve to demystify the techniques and dispel the veneer of certainty and accuracy in travel forecasting, widely seen as a consequence of its tradition and language.

Suitable learning materials related to travel forecasting could be specifically tailored to politicians, civil servants, academics, practising planners and interested citizens. At the present time there exist substantial materials for pedagogic purposes, such as webTAG in the UK and TMIP in the US, but there is considerably more scope for user-friendly developments.

Through these means we may also reach out to the interested citizen where there is a dearth of relevant material; see Beimborn et al (n.d.).[9] It is beyond the scope of this book to debate whether citizens should be allowed to challenge travel forecasts in public inquiries or through the legislative process; clearly in some societies they are at liberty to do so, while in many others they are not. The formation of well-constructed national advisory panels may be a means for resolving contentious technical issues that would otherwise bring a planning process to a juddering halt, and for avoiding the acrimony and delay of litigation.

The search for more transparency and accountability in planning extends to its methodology, a view promulgated in section 11.5. As in so many areas of public policy and planning, the interested citizen has a view. To assume that many citizens, either acting alone or in special interest groups, cannot acquire the necessary skills and expertise to understand the basis for forecasting would be both naïve and arrogant. Citizens are entitled to know the technical basis on which planning decisions are made, whether from the traffic implications of housing developments, the impact of highways or congestion-charging systems, or the introduction of bus and bicycle lanes. Appropriate documentation in an accessible language, linked to further technical information, is required for this purpose.

The major developments in this field may well be associated with innovations in policy and projects in the rapidly emerging economies of Asia and Latin America, where cities and transportation systems are developing with different emphases on innovative technology, behavioural modification and city organisation in culturally diverse contexts. Access to transportation networks may be very different from the present in terms of time, space, price and regulation. The transfer of experiences to and from different cultures may prove to be centrally important to the further development of transportation planning and the methods that support it.

12.4 SOME FINAL REMARKS

12.4.1 How Will Future Progress Be Judged?

There is no reason to suppose that we are at a particularly privileged time in the development of travel forecasting models and methods. Much as in the past, what now appears relatively sophisticated may be found wanting or simply misdirected when viewed from one, two or three decades hence.

Progress will be judged in many ways and, we would suggest, according to: (a) how the problems of the past and present are identified, prioritised and addressed; (b) timely responses to existing and new requirements, whether these are technical or policy related; (c) whether existing critiques were answered; (d) whether the evidence base was suitably expanded; (e) whether the methods were suitably clarified to stake-holders; and (f) whether currently existing scholarly and professional networks are suitable for the transfer of knowledge.

As a further stimulation to innovate, our field should clarify what is known and not known, and what technical, theoretical and practical issues are subject to dissent. With regard to allocation of resources for research and development, we offer no prescription. With a lot of hindsight and a modest amount of foresight, we suggest that the allocation of very large sums of money to specific projects which appear to offer a panacea may well be sub-optimal in terms of the opportunities forgone.

12.4.2 For Those New to the Field

We welcome newcomers to a challenging and rewarding profession of immense practical significance to the future quality of life in cities. We ask you to expect a contested field, with many expressions of the state of the art in terms of both practice and theory. We ask the newcomer to expect to find a wide range of opinions on the adequacy of models and methods, and points of contention relating to the philosophy of forecasting, the policy issues addressed, theories of behaviour underpinning models, methods of analysis, and practical implementation issues.

Travel forecasting is an amalgam of a large number of practical problems. Some are amenable to precise mathematical specification and detailed technical analysis, and are largely uncontested. Others are much more diffuse issues relating to the behaviour of individuals, households and firms, particularly in relation to its evolution over time and responses to policies within highly uncertain political, economic and technological contexts. For those not attracted to the field especially for its mathematical content, we ask you not to be intimidated by its complexity and the sheer weight of past research. Behind the technical language and apparent sophistication lie relatively simple ideas.

The history of our field has shown that key innovations and important new ideas sometimes came from people relatively new to the field, unencumbered by past conceptions of travel behaviour and forecasting. These individuals transferred ideas, on occasion, from the natural and social sciences, bringing with them useful insights from these traditions. They either built on established ideas or bucked the trend and questioned widely held assumptions and the basis for them.

While they delve into the technicalities and practicalities of the field in standard texts, we urge newcomers also to be aware of the writing of those who offered critiques of the nature and use of models, the technical and political challenges, and the philosophy of forecasting itself. The writings of Douglass Lee (1973, 1994), Andrew Sayer (1976), Martin Wachs (1982, 1990), Michael Wegener (1994, 2011b), Bent Flyvbjerg, Mette Holm and Søren Buhl (2006), Paul Timms (2008) and David Hartgen (2013) are good starting points.

The political and planning contexts within which travel forecasting exists in the future will no doubt change greatly, but will always influence the methods applied. As suggested in section 11.7, in the future some governments may not remain persuaded that evidence-based planning and detached assessment of alternatives, with its unwieldiness and expense, will be preferred to a limited and more overtly political process. Whether the future turns out to be much like the present, or is based on currently unimaginable technological changes and radical policies on the organisation of cities, the process of forecasting travel to anticipate the effects of alternative courses of action will probably remain with us and continue to be complex, fascinating and always controversial.

Innovations in method may result from the need to respond to new questions, the aspiration to develop more sophisticated models, or the discovery of new approaches. We will need to examine any available alternatives, and to seek to characterise and be aware of the differences in methods and models at any particular time. The need will remain to question conventional accounts, the credibility of models and their forecasting assumptions, and the inherent uncertainties in forecasting, always asking where, why and when proposed modifications in theory or method matter. In the world of practice, context will be important, always.

Ultimately it will be the analyst's job to be the last defence against wishful thinking, boosterism, and the platitudes of some politicians. Where at all possible we must seek out the evidence base for policy and always bear in mind Andreas Schleicher's wise words that pertain to us all: 'without data, you are just another person with an opinion'.[10]

NOTES

1. Communication of Huw Williams with Peter Jones, May 2014.
2. These two societies merged in 1995 to form the Institute for Operations Research and the Management Sciences (INFORMS), now 'the largest society in the world for professionals in the field of operations research, management science, and analytics' (www. informs.org/, accessed 23 March 2014).
3. en.wikipedia.org/wiki/Robert_Herman (accessed 23 March 2014).
4. www.informs.org/Community/TSL/Prizes-and-Awards (accessed 23 March 2014).
5. cowles.econ.yale.edu/ (accessed 23 March 2014).
6. en.wikipedia.org/wiki/Econometric_Society (accessed 25 March 2014).
7. Records of these meetings are no longer available.
8. For a history of the evolution of academic transport studies in the UK, see Dudley and Preston (2013).
9. www4.uwm.edu/cuts/blackbox/blackbox.pdf (accessed 24 March 2014).
10. The catchphrase attributed to Andreas Schleicher, special adviser on educational policy at the Organisation for Economic Co-operation and Development, by Peter Wilby, education correspondent, *Guardian*, 26 November 2013, www.theguardian.com/educa tion/2013/nov/26/pisa-international-student-tests-oecd (accessed 25 March 2014).

References

Aashtiani, H.Z. and T.L. Magnanti (1981) Equilibria on a congested transportation network, *SIAM Journal of Algebraic and Discrete Methods* 2 (3), 213–226.

Abdulaal, M. and L.J. LeBlanc (1979) Methods for combining modal split and equilibrium assignment models, *Transportation Science* 13 (4), 292–314.

Abraham, C. (1961) La répartition du trafic entre itinéraires concurrents: réflexions sur le comportement des usagers, application au calcul des péages, *Revue générale des routes et aérodromes* 357, 57–60, 65–72, 75–76.

Abrahamsson, T. and L. Lundqvist (1999) Formulation and estimation of combined network equilibrium models with applications to Stockholm, *Transportation Science* 33 (1), 80–100.

Adler, T. and M.E. Ben-Akiva (1975) A joint frequency, destination and mode choice model for shopping trips, *Transportation Research Record* 569, 136–150.

Adler, T. and M.E. Ben-Akiva (1979) A theoretical and empirical model of trip chaining behaviour, *Transportation Research Part B* 13, 243–257.

AECOM (2006) Using Traditional Model Data as Input to TRANSIMS Microsimulation, Federal Highway Administration, US Department of Transportation, Washington, DC.

AECOM (2009) Revisiting the Portland GEN2 Modeling Process with TRANSIMS Version 4.0 Software Methods, Research Summary, Federal Highway Administration, US Department of Transportation, Washington, DC.

AECOM (2011) Interfacing Activity Model Outputs with TRANSIMS Microsimulation, Federal Highway Administration, US Department of Transportation, Washington, DC.

Ahrens, G.-A., F. Liesske, R. Wittwer and S. Hubrich (2009) Endbericht zur Verkehrserhebung, Mobilität in Städten – SrV 2008, und Auswertungen zum SrV-Städtepegel, Im Auftrag von Städten, Verkehrsunternehmen, Verkehrsverbünden und Bundesländern bearbeitet durch die Lehrstuhl Verkehrs- und Infrastrukturplanung, Technische Universität Dresden, Dresden, Germany.

Akamatsu, T. (1996) Cyclic flows, Markov process and stochastic traffic assignment, *Transportation Research Part B* 30 (5), 369–386.

Akamatsu, T. (1997) Decomposition of path choice entropy in general transport networks, *Transportation Science* 31 (4), 349–362.

Akçelik, R. (1981) Traffic Signals: Capacity and Timing Analysis, Research Report ARR No. 123, Australian Road Research Board, Melbourne.

Akçelik, R. (1988) The Highway Capacity Manual delay formula for signalized intersections, *ITE Journal* 58 (1), 23–27.

Albright, R.L., S.R. Lerman and C.F. Manski (1977) Report on the Development of an Estimation Program for the Multinomial Probit Model, Federal Highway Administration, Cambridge Systematics, Cambridge, MA.

Alex Anas & Associates (2002) The NYMTC-Land Use Model, Final Report for the New York Metropolitan Transportation Council, New York, www.nymtc.org/data_services/LUM/files/FR_LUM_020807.pdf (accessed 8 January 2013).

Alex Anas & Associates (2005) Land Use Model, Section 5.8, Transportation Models and Data Initiative, General Final Report, New York Best Practice Model, Parsons Brinckerhoff Quade & Douglas, for the New York Metropolitan Transportation Council, New York, 5–135 – 5–152, www.nymtc.org/project/bpm/model/bpm_finalrpt.pdf (accessed 8 January 2013).

Algers, S., A.J. Daly, P. Kjellman and S. Widlert (1996) Stockholm model system (SIMS): application, in *World Transport Research*, Volume 2, D. Hensher, J. King and T.H. Oum (eds), Pergamon, Amsterdam, 345–361.

Algers, S. and J. Eliasson (2006) Microsimulating the SIMS Model – Model Simplifications, Department of Transport and Economics, Royal Institute of Technology, Stockholm.

Algers, S., J. Eliasson and L.-G. Mattsson (2005) Is it time to use activity-based urban transport models? A discussion of planning needs and modelling possibilities, *Annals of Regional Science* 39, 767–789.

Allaman, P.M., T.J. Tardiff and F.C. Dunbar (1982) *New Approaches to Understanding Travel Behavior*, Report 250, National Cooperative Highway Research Program, Transportation Research Board, Washington, DC.

Allsop, R.E. (1968) Fourth International Symposium on Theory of Traffic Flow, *Traffic Engineering and Control* 10, 263–264.

Almendinger, V.V. (1961) Topics in the Regional Growth Model: I, PJ Paper No. 4, Penn Jersey Transportation Study, Philadelphia.

Almond, J. (1965) Traffic assignment to a road network, *Traffic Engineering and Control* 6, 616–617, 622.

Almond, J. (1967) Traffic assignment with flow-dependent journey times, in *Vehicular Traffic Science*, L.C. Edie, R. Herman and R. Rothery (eds), American Elsevier, New York, 222–234.

Amemiya, T. (1975) Qualitative response models, *Annals of Economic and Social Measurement* 4, 363–372.

Ampt, E., J. Swanson and D. Pearmain (1995) Stated preference: too much deference?, Transportation Planning Methods, Summer Annual Meeting, Planning and Transport Research and Computation Co., Warwick.

Anas, A. (1973) A dynamic disequilibrium model of residential location, *Environment and Planning* 5, 633–647.

Anas, A. (1982) *Residential Location Markets and Urban Transportation*, Academic Press, New York.

Anas, A. (1983) Discrete choice theory, information theory and the multi-nomial logit and gravity models, *Transportation Research Part B* 17, 13–23.

Anas, A. (1984) Discrete choice theory and the general equilibrium of employment, housing, and travel networks in a Lowry-type model of the urban economy, *Environment and Planning A* 16, 1489–1502.

Anas, A. (1995) Capitalization of urban travel improvements into residential and commercial real estate: simulations with a unified model of housing, travel mode and shopping choices, *Journal of Regional Science* 35 (3), 351–375.

Anas, A. and L.S. Duann (1985) Dynamic forecasting of travel demand, residential location and land development: policy simulations with the Chicago Area Transportation/Land Use System, *Papers, Regional Science Association* 56, 38–58.

Anas, A. and C.M. Feng (1988) Invariance of expected utilities in logit models, *Economic Letters* 27, 41–45.

Anas, A. and T. Hiramatsu (2012) The effect of the price of gasoline on the urban economy: from route choice to general equilibrium, *Transportation Research Part A* 46 (6), 855–873.

Anas, A. and Y. Liu (2007) A regional economy, land use, and transportation model: formulation, algorithm design, and testing, *Journal of Regional Science* 47 (3), 415–455.

Anderson, S.P., A. de Palma and J.-F. Thisse (1992) *Discrete Choice Theory of Product Differentiation*, MIT Press, Cambridge, MA.

Anderstig, C. and L.-G. Mattsson (1991) An integrated model of residential and employment location in a metropolitan region, *Papers in Regional Science* 70 (2), 167–184.

Anowar, S., N. Eluru and L.F. Miranda-Moreno (2014) Analysis of vehicle ownership evolution in Montreal, Canada, using pseudo panel analysis,

Paper 14–3023 online, Transportation Research Board, Washington, DC.

Antosiewicz, H.A. (ed) (1955) *Proceedings of the Second Symposium in Linear Programming*, Volumes 1 and 2, National Bureau of Standards, US Department of Commerce, and Directorate of Management Analysis, DCS Comptroller, US Air Force, Washington, DC.

Arentze, T.A. and H.J.P. Timmermans (2004) A learning-based transportation oriented simulation system, *Transportation Research Part B* 38, 613–633.

Arentze, T.A. and H.J.P. Timmermans (2007) Modelling Dynamics of Activity-Travel Behaviour, Urban Planning Group, Eindhoven University of Technology, Eindhoven.

Arezki, Y. and D. Van Vliet (1990) A full analytic implementation of the PARTAN/Frank–Wolfe algorithm for equilibrium assignment, *Transportation Science* 24, 58–62.

Arnott, R. and K. Small (1994) The economics of traffic congestion, *American Scientist* 82, 446–455.

Asmuth, R., B.C. Eaves and E.L. Peterson (1979) Computing economic equilibria on affine networks with Lemke's algorithm, *Mathematics of Operations Research* 4 (3), 209–214.

Association of Metropolitan Planning Organizations (2011) Advanced Travel Modeling Study, Phase 1 Final Report, Washington, DC.

Atherton, T. and M.E. Ben-Akiva (1976) Transferability and updating of disaggregate travel demand models, *Transportation Research Record* 610, 12–18.

Avineri, E. and C. Chorus (2010) Recent developments in prospect theory-based travel behaviour research, *European Journal of Transport and Infrastructure Research* 10, 293–298.

Avineri, E. and J.N. Prashker (2003) Sensitivity to uncertainty: need for a paradigm shift, *Transportation Research Record* 1854, 90–98.

Axhausen, K.W. (ed) (2007) *Moving through Nets*, Elsevier, Oxford.

Axhausen, K.W. and T. Gärling (1992) Activity-based approaches to travel analysis: conceptual frameworks, models and research problems, *Transport Reviews* 12, 323–341.

Axhausen, K.W. and R. Herz (1989) Simulating activity chains: German approach, *ASCE Journal of Transportation Engineering* 115, 316–325.

Bain, R. (2009) Error and optimism bias in toll road traffic forecasts, *Transportation* 36, 469–482.

Balcombe, R., R. Mackett, N. Paulley, J. Preston, J. Shires, H. Titheridge, M. Wardman and P. White (2004) The Demand for Public Transport: A Practical Guide, TRL Report, Transportation Research Laboratory, London.

Balinski, M.L. (1991) Mathematical programming: journal, society and recollections, in *History of Mathematical Programming*, J.K. Lenstra, A.H.G. Rinnooy Kan and A. Schrijver (eds), Elsevier, Amsterdam, 5–18.

Balmer, M., K. Meister, M. Rieser, K. Nagel and K.W. Axhausen (2008) Agent-based simulation of travel demand: structure and computational performance of MATSim-T, *Innovations in Travel Modeling*, Portland, Transportation Research Board, Washington, DC.

Banister, D. (1978) The influence of habit formation on modal choice - a heuristic model, *Transportation* 7, 5–18.

Bar-Gera, H. (2002) Origin-based algorithm for the traffic assignment problem, *Transportation Science* 36 (4), 398–417.

Bar-Gera, H. (2006) Primal method for determining the most likely route flows in large road networks, *Transportation Science* 40 (3), 269–286.

Bar-Gera, H. (2010) Traffic assignment by paired alternative segments, *Transportation Research Part B* 44 (8–9), 1022–1046.

Bar-Gera, H. and D. Boyce (2003) Origin-based algorithms for combined travel forecasting models, *Transportation Research Part B* 37 (5), 403–422.

Bar-Gera, H., D. Boyce and Y. Nie (2012) User-equilibrium route flows and the condition of proportionality, *Transportation Research Part B* 46 (3), 440–462.

Bates, J.J. (1988) Econometric issues in stated preference analysis, *Journal of Transport Economics and Policy* 22, 46–59.

Bates, J.J. (1996) Time Period Choice Modelling: A Preliminary Review, Report for the UK Department for Transport, London.

Bates, J.J., D.A. Ashley and G. Hyman (1987) The nested incremental logit model: theory and application to modal choice, Transportation Planning Methods, Annual Summer Meeting, Planning and Transport Research and Computation Co., Bath.

Bates, J.J., M. Brewer, P. Hanson, D. McDonald and D.C. Simmonds (1991) Building a strategic model for Edinburgh, Summer Annual Meeting, Planning and Transport Research and Computation Co., Brighton.

Bates, J.J., D. Coombe, S. Porter and D. Van Vliet (1999) Allowing for variable demand in highway scheme assessment, Transportation Planning Methods, European Transport Conference, Cambridge.

Bates, J.J., P. Mackie, J. Nellthorp and D. Forster (2003) Evaluation of the Multi-Modal Study Process: Modelling and Appraisal, Report for the UK Department for Transport, London.

Bates, J.J., J. Polak, P. Jones and A. Cook (2001) The valuation of reliability for personal travel, *Transportation Research Part E* 37, 191–229.

Bates, J.J. and M. Roberts (1986) Value of time research: summary of methodology and findings, Summer Annual Meeting, Planning and Transport Research and Computation Co., Brighton.

Bates, J.J., I. Williams, D. Coombe and J. Leather (1996) The London congestion charging research programme: 4. the transport models, *Traffic Engineering and Control* 37, 334–339.

Batley, R. (2007) Marginal valuations of travel time and scheduling, and the reliability premium, *Transportation Research Part E* 43, 387–408.

Batley, R. and A. Daly (2006) On the equivalence between elimination-by-aspects and generalised extreme value models of choice behaviour, *Journal of Mathematical Psychology* 50, 456–467.

Batty, M.J. (1972) Recent developments in land use modelling: a review of British research, *Urban Studies* 9, 151–177.

Batty, M. (1994) A chronicle of scientific planning, *Journal of the American Planning Association* 60, 7–16.

Batty, M.J. and S. Mackie (1972) The calibration of gravity, entropy and related models of spatial interaction, *Environment and Planning* 4, 205–233.

Beagan, D., M. Fischer and A. Kuppam (2007) Quick Response Freight Manual II, Federal Highway Administration, Cambridge Systematics, Cambridge, MA.

Beardwood, J.E. and J. Elliott (1989) Roads generate traffic, Highway Appraisal and Design, Planning and Transport Research and Computation Co., Brighton.

Beckman, R.J., K.A. Baggerly and M.D. McKay (1996) Creating synthetic baseline populations, *Transportation Research Part A* 30, 415–429.

Beckmann, M. (1951) Optimum Transportation on Networks, Cowles Commission Discussion Paper: Economics No. 2023, Cowles Commission for Research in Economics, Chicago.

Beckmann, M. (1952) Efficient Transportation in Networks, Cowles Commission Discussion Paper: Economics No. 2049, with the assistance of C.B. McGuire; revised as Efficient Transportation in Networks, Cowles Commission Discussion Paper: Economics No. 2049A, Cowles Commission for Research in Economics, Chicago.

Beckmann, M. (1953) Efficient Transportation in Networks Continued, Cowles Commission Discussion Paper: Economics No. 2049B, Cowles Commission for Research in Economics, Chicago.

Beckmann, M.J. (1967a) On optimal tolls for highways, tunnels and bridges, in *Vehicular Traffic Science*, L.C. Edie, R. Herman and R. Rothery (eds), American Elsevier, New York, 331–341.

Beckmann, M.J. (1967b) On the theory of traffic flow in networks, *Traffic Quarterly* 21 (1), 109–117.

Beckmann, M.J. and T.F. Golob (1972) On the metaphysical foundations of traffic theory: entropy revisited, *Traffic Flow and Transportation*, G.F. Newell (ed), American Elsevier, New York.

Beckmann, M. and C.B. McGuire (1953) The Determination of Traffic in a Road Network – An Economic Approach, P-437, RAND Corporation, Santa Monica, CA.

Beckmann, M., C.B. McGuire and C.B. Winsten (1956) *Studies in the Economics of Transportation*, Yale University Press, New Haven, CT; Rand-RM-1488-PR, RAND Corporation, Santa Monica, CA, 1955.

Beesley, M.E. (1965) The value of time spent in travelling: some new evidence, *Economica* 32, 174–185.

Beggs, S., S. Cardell and J. Hausman (1981) Assessing the potential demand for electric cars, *Journal of Econometrics* 17, 1–19.

Beimborn, E., R. Kennedy and W. Schaefer (n.d.) Inside the Blackbox: Making Transportation Models Work for Livable Communities, A Guide to Modeling, University of Wisconsin-Milwaukee, Citizens for a Better Environment and the Environmental Defense Fund, Washington, DC.

Bekhor, S. and J.N. Prashker (2001) Stochastic user equilibrium formulation for generalized nested logit model, *Transportation Research Record* 1752, 84–90.

Bell, M.G.H. (ed) (1998) *Transportation Networks*, Elsevier, Amsterdam.

Bell, M.G.H. and Y. Iida (1997) *Transportation Network Analysis*, Wiley, Chichester, West Sussex.

Ben-Akiva, M.E. (1973) Structure of Passenger Travel Demand Models, Ph.D. thesis, Civil Engineering, Massachusetts Institute of Technology, Cambridge, MA.

Ben-Akiva, M.E. (1974) Structure of passenger travel demand models, *Transportation Research Record* 526, 26–42.

Ben-Akiva, M.E. (1981) Issues in transferring and updating travel-behavior models, Chapter 38 in *New Horizons in Travel Behavior Research*, P.R. Stopher, A.H. Meyburg and W. Brög (eds), Lexington Books, Lexington, MA, 665–686.

Ben-Akiva, M.E. and T. Atherton (1977) Methodology for short-range travel demand predictions, *Journal of Transport Economics and Policy* 11, 224–261.

Ben-Akiva, M.E. and M. Bierlaire (1999) Discrete choice methods and their applications to short term travel decisions, in *Handbook of Transportation Science*, R.W. Hall (ed), Kluwer, Boston, 5–33.

Ben-Akiva, M.E. and D. Bolduc (1996) Multinomial Probit with a Logit Kernel and a General Parametric Specification of the Covariance Structure, working paper, Department d'Économique, Université de Laval, Québec, and Department of Civil and Environmental Engineering, Massachusetts Institute of Technology, Cambridge, MA.

Ben-Akiva, M.E., D. Bolduc and M. Bradley (1993) Estimation of travel choice models with randomly distributed values of time, *Transportation Research Record* 1413, 88–97.

Ben-Akiva, M.E., D. Bolduc and J. Walker (2001) Specification, Identification and Estimation of the Logit Kernel (or Continuous Mixed Logit) Model, working paper, Department of Civil Engineering, Massachusetts Institute of Technology, Cambridge, MA.

Ben-Akiva, M.E. and J.L. Bowman (1998) Activity based travel demand model systems, Chapter 2 in *Equilibrium and Advanced Transportation Modelling*, P. Marcotte and S. Nguyen (eds), Kluwer, Boston, 27–46.

Ben-Akiva, M.E., J.L. Bowman and D. Gopinath (1996) Travel demand model system for the information era, *Transportation* 25, 241–55.

Ben-Akiva, M., M. Bradley, T. Morikawa, J. Benjamin, T. Novak, H. Oppewal and V. Rao (1994) Combining revealed and stated preferences data, *Marketing Letters* 5, 335–349.

Ben-Akiva, M.E., A. de Palma, D. McFadden, M. Abou-Zeid, P.-A. Chiappori, M. de Lapparent, S.N. Durlauf, M. Fosgerau, D. Fukuda, S. Hess, C. Manski, A. Pakes, N. Picard and J. Walker (2012) Process and context in choice models, *Marketing Letters* 23, 439–456.

Ben-Akiva, M.E. and F.S. Koppelman (1974) Multidimensional choice models: alternative structures of travel demand models, *Behavioral Demand Modeling and Valuation of Travel Time*, Special Report 149, Transportation Research Board, Washington, DC, 129–142.

Ben-Akiva, M.E., B.C. Kullman, L. Sherman and A.J. Daly (1978) Aggregate forecasting with a system of disaggregate travel demand models, Transport Models, Summer Annual Meeting, Planning and Transport Research and Computation Co., Warwick.

Ben-Akiva, M.E. and S.R. Lerman (1979) Disaggregate travel and mobility choice models and measures of accessibility, in *Behavioural Travel Modelling*, D.A. Hensher and P.R. Stopher (eds), Croom Helm, London, 654–679.

Ben-Akiva, M.E. and S.R. Lerman (1985) *Discrete Choice Analysis*, MIT Press, Cambridge, MA.

Ben-Akiva, M., D. McFadden, M. Abe, U. Böckenholt, D. Bolduc, D. Gopinath, T. Morikawa, V. Ramaswamy, V. Rao, D. Revelt and D. Steinberg (1997) Modeling methods for discrete choice analysis, *Marketing Letters* 8 (3), 273–286.

Ben-Akiva, M., D. McFadden, T. Gärling, D. Gopinath, J. Walker, D. Bolduc, A. Börsch-Supan, P. Delquié, O. Larichev, T. Morikawa, A.

Polydoropoulou and V. Rao (1999) Extended framework for modeling choice behaviour, *Marketing Letters* 10 (3), 187–203.

Ben-Akiva, M., D. McFadden, K. Train, J. Walker, C. Bhat, M. Bierlaire, D. Bolduc, A. Börsch-Supan, D. Brownstone, D. Bunch, A. Daly, A. de Palma, D. Gopinath, A. Karlstrom and M.A. Munizaga (2002a) Hybrid choice models: progress and challenges, *Marketing Letters* 13 (3), 163–175.

Ben-Akiva, M.E. and T. Morikawa (1990) Estimation of travel demand models from multiple data sources, *Transportation and Traffic Theory*, M. Koshi (ed), Elsevier, New York, 461–476.

Ben-Akiva, M.E., J. Walker, A.T. Bernardino, D.A. Gopinath, T. Morikawa and A. Polydoropoulou (2002b) Integration of choice and latent variable models, Chapter 21 in *In Perpetual Motion*, H.S. Mahmassani (ed), Elsevier, Oxford, 431–470.

Bennett, J. and R.K. Blamey (eds) (2001) *The Choice Modelling Approach to Environmental Evaluation*, Edward Elgar Publishing, Cheltenham, UK, and Northampton, MA, USA.

Berka, S. and D.E. Boyce (1996) Generating highway travel times with a large-scale, asymmetric user equilibrium assignment model, in *Advanced Methods in Transportation Analysis*, L. Bianco and P. Toth (eds), Springer, Berlin, 29–61.

Bertsekas, D.P. and E.M. Gafni (1982) Projection methods for variational inequalities with application to the traffic assignment problem, *Mathematical Programming Study* 17, 139–159.

Bhat, C.R. (1995) A heteroscedastic extreme value model of intercity mode choice, *Transportation Research Part B* 29, 471–483.

Bhat, C.R. (1998) Accommodating variations in responsiveness to level-of-service variables in travel mode choice modeling, *Transportation Research Part A* 32, 495–507.

Bhat, C.R. (2000) Flexible model structures for discrete choice analysis, Chapter 5 in *Handbook of Transport Modelling*, D.A. Hensher and K.J. Button (eds), Pergamon, Amsterdam, 71–90.

Bhat, C.R. (2001) Quasi-random maximum simulated likelihood estimation of the mixed multinomial logit model, *Transportation Research Part B* 35, 677–693.

Bhat, C.R. (2003) Simulation estimation of mixed discrete choice models using randomized and scrambled Halton sequences, *Transportation Research Part B* 37, 837–855.

Bhat, C.R. (2005) A multiple discrete-continuous extreme value model: formulation and application to discretionary time-use decisions, *Transportation Research Part B* 39, 679–707.

Bhat, C.R. (2007) Econometric choice formulations: alternative model structures, estimation techniques and emerging directions, Chapter 3 in *Moving through Nets*, K. Axhausen (ed), Elsevier, Oxford, 45–80.

Bhat, C.R. (2011) The maximum approximate composite marginal likelihood estimation of the normally-mixed multinomial logit model, *Transportation Research Part B* 45, 923–939.

Bhat, C.R. (2014) Remarks at a workshop on 50 years of travel demand forecasting, Annual Meeting, Transportation Research Board, Washington, DC.

Bhat, C.R. and S. Castelar (2002) A unified mixed logit framework for modeling revealed and stated preferences: formulation and application to congestion pricing analysis in the San Francisco Bay Area, *Transportation Research Part B* 36, 593–616.

Bhat, C.R. and S.K. Dubey (2013) A New Estimation Approach to Integrate Latent Psychological Constructs in Choice Modeling, Department of Civil, Architectural and Environmental Engineering, University of Texas at Austin, Austin.

Bhat, C.R. and N. Eluru (2010) The multiple discrete-continuous extreme value (MDCEV) model: formulation and applications, Chapter 4 in *Choice Modelling*, S. Hess and A. Daly (eds), Emerald, Bingley, West Yorkshire, 71–100.

Bhat, C.R., K.G. Goulias, R.M. Pendyala, R. Paleti, R. Sidharthan, L. Schmitt and H.-H. Hu (2013) A household-level activity pattern generation model with an application for Southern California, *Transportation* 40, 1063–1086.

Bhat, C.R., J.Y. Guo, S. Srinivasa and A. Sivakumar (2004) A comprehensive econometric microsimulator for daily activity-travel patterns, *Transportation Research Record* 1894, 57–66.

Bhat, C.R. and F.S. Koppelman (1993) A conceptual framework of individual activity program generation, *Transportation Research Part A* 27, 433–446.

Bhat, C.R. and F.S. Koppelman (1999a) Activity-based modeling of travel demand, Chapter 3 in *Handbook of Transportation Science*, R.W. Hall (ed), Kluwer, Boston, 39–65.

Bhat, C.R. and F.S. Koppelman (1999b) A retrospective survey of time-use research, *Transportation* 26, 119–139.

Bhat, C.R. and R.M. Pendyala (2005) Modeling intra-household interactions and group decision making, *Transportation* 32, 443–448.

Bierlaire, M. (2002) The network GEV model, Second Swiss Transportation Research Conference, Ascona, Switzerland.

Bierlaire, M. (2006) A theoretical analysis of the cross-nested logit model, *Annals of Operational Research* 144, 287–300.

Birkin, M. and M. Clarke (1988) SYNTHESIS – a synthetic spatial information system for urban and regional analysis: methods and examples, *Environment and Planning A* 20, 1645–1671.

Black, A. (1990) The Chicago Area Transportation Study: a case study in rational planning, *Journal of Planning Education and Research* 10 (1), 27–37.

Blum, J.R. (1954) Multidimensional stochastic approximation methods, *Annals of Mathematical Statistics* 25 (4), 737–744.

Bly, P., P. Emmerson, N. Paulley and T. Van Vuren (2002) User-Friendly Multi-Stage Modelling Advice, Phase 3: Multi-Stage Modelling Options, project report, Transport Research Laboratory, Crowthorne, Berkshire.

Bly, P., P. Emmerson, T. Van Vuren, A. Ash and N. Paulley (2001) User-Friendly Multi-Stage Modelling Advice, Phase 2: Modelling Parameters, Calibration and Validation, project report, Transport Research Laboratory, Crowthorne, Berkshire.

Bock, R.D. and L.V. Jones (1968) *The Measurement and Prediction of Judgement and Choice*, Holden-Day, San Francisco.

Bolduc, D. and R. Alvarez-Daziano (2010) On estimation of hybrid choice models, Chapter 11 in *Choice Modelling*, S. Hess and A. Daly (eds), Emerald, Bingley, West Yorkshire, 259–289.

Bonnel, P., M. Lee-Gosselin, J. Zmud and J.-L. Madre (eds) (2009) *Transport Survey Methods*, Emerald, Bingley, West Yorkshire.

Bonsall, P.W. (1980) The simulation of organised car sharing: description of the models and their calibration, *Transportation Research Record* 767, 12–21.

Bonsall, P.W. (1982) Microsimulation: its application to car sharing, *Transportation Research Part A* 15, 421–429.

Bonsall, P.W. (1983) Transfer price data – its use and abuse, Summer Annual Meeting, Planning and Transport Research and Computation Co., Brighton.

Bonsall, P.W., A.F. Champernowne, A.C. Mason and A.G. Wilson (1977) Transport modelling: sensitivity analysis and policy testing, *Progress in Planning* 7, 153–237.

Bonsall, P.W., P.J. Mackie and S. Pells (1990) Traffic generation, *Surveyor* 174, 18–19.

Börsch-Supan, A. (1987) *Econometric Analysis of Discrete Choice*, Lecture Notes in Economics and Mathematical Systems, Volume 296, Springer, Berlin.

Bothner, P. and W. Lutter (1982) Ein direktes Verfahren zur Verkehrsumlegung nach demersten Prinzip von Wardrop, Arbeitsbericht Nr. 1, Forschungsbereich Verkehrssysteme, Universität Bremen, Bremen, Germany.

Bowman, J.L. (1995) Activity Based Travel Demand Model System with Daily Activity Schedules, M.S. thesis, Civil Engineering, Massachusetts Institute of Technology, Cambridge, MA.

Bowman, J.L. (2009) Historical development of activity-based models: theory and practice, *Traffic Engineering and Control* 50, 59–62, 314–318.

Bowman, J.L. and M.E. Ben-Akiva (2001) Activity-based disaggregate travel demand model system with activity schedules, *Transportation Research Part A* 35 (1), 1–28.

Bowman, J.L., M. Bradley, Y. Shiftan, T.K. Lawton and M.E. Ben-Akiva (1999) Demonstration of an activity based model system for Portland, *World Transport Research*, Volume 3, H. Meersman, E. van de Voorde and W. Winkleman (eds), Pergamon, Amsterdam, 171–184.

Boyce, D.E. (1978) Equilibrium solutions to combined urban residential location, mode choice and trip assignment models, in *Competition among Small Regions*, W. Buhr and P. Friedrich (eds), Nomos, Baden-Baden, Germany, 246–264.

Boyce, D.E. (1980) A framework for constructing network equilibrium models of urban location, *Transportation Science* 14 (1), 77–96.

Boyce, D.E. (1984) Network models in transportation/land use planning, in *Transportation Planning Models*, M. Florian (ed), North-Holland, Amsterdam, 475–498.

Boyce, D.E. (1990) Network equilibrium models of urban location and travel choices: a new research agenda, in *New Frontiers in Regional Science*, M. Chatterji and R.E. Kuenne (eds), New York University Press, New York, 238–256.

Boyce, D. (2002) Is the sequential travel forecasting procedure counter-productive?, *ASCE Journal of Urban Planning and Development* 128 (4), 169–183.

Boyce, D. (2007a) An account of a road network design method: expressway spacing, system configuration and economic evaluation, in *Infrastrukturprobleme bei Bevölkerungsrückgang* [Infrastructure problems under population decline], X. Feng and A.M. Popescu (eds), Berliner Wissenschafts, Berlin, 131–159.

Boyce, D. (2007b) Forecasting travel on congested urban transportation networks: review and prospects for network equilibrium models, *Networks and Spatial Economics* 7 (2), 99–128.

Boyce, D. (2013) Beckmann's transportation network equilibrium model: its history and relationship to the Kuhn–Tucker conditions, *Economics of Transportation* 2 (1), 47–52.

Boyce, D. and H. Bar-Gera (2003) Validation of multiclass urban travel forecasting models combining origin–destination, mode, and route choices, *Journal of Regional Science* 43 (3), 517–540.

Boyce, D. and H. Bar-Gera (2012) The role of computing in urban travel forecasting: how transportation planning practice shaped software, and software impacted transportation planning practice, Chapter 12 in *Societies in Motion*, A. Frenkel, P. Nijkamp and P. McCann (eds), Edward Elgar Publishing, Cheltenham, UK, and Northampton, MA, USA, 271–295.

Boyce, D.E., K.S. Chon, M.E. Ferris, Y.J. Lee, K.T. Lin and R.W. Eash (1985) Implementation and Evaluation of Combined Models of Urban Travel and Location on a Sketch Planning Network, University of Illinois at Urbana-Champaign, Urbana, and Chicago Area Transportation Study, Chicago.

Boyce, D.E., N.D. Day and C. McDonald (1970) *Metropolitan Plan Making*, Regional Science Research Institute, Philadelphia.

Boyce, D.E., L.J. LeBlanc, K.S. Chon, Y.J. Lee and K.T. Lin (1983) Implementation and computational issues for combined models of location, destination, mode and route choice, *Environment and Planning A* 15 (9), 1219–1230.

Boyce, D.E. and L. Lundqvist (1987) Network equilibrium models of urban location and travel choices: alternative formulations for the Stockholm region, *Papers, Regional Science Association* 61, 91–104.

Boyce, D.E., H.S. Mahmassani and A. Nagurney (2005) A retrospective on Beckmann, McGuire and Winsten's *Studies in the Economics of Transportation, Papers in Regional Science* 84 (1), 85–103.

Boyce, D. and L.-G. Mattsson (1999) Modeling residential location choice in relation to housing location and road tolls on congested urban highway networks, *Transportation Research Part B* 33 (8), 581–591.

Boyce, D. and A. Nagurney (2006) In memoriam: C. Bartlett McGuire (1925–2006) and Christopher B. Winsten (1923–2005), *Transportation Science* 40 (1), 1–2.

Boyce, D., Y. Nie, H. Bar-Gera, Y. Liu and Y. Hu (2010) Field Test of a Method for Finding Consistent Route Flows and Multiple-Class Link Flows in Road Traffic Assignments, Federal Highway Administration, Washington, DC, www.transportation.northwestern.edu/docs/research/Boyce_FieldTestConsistentRouteFlows.pdf (accessed 5 October 2013).

Boyce, D., C. O'Neill and W. Scherr (2008) Solving the sequential travel forecasting procedure with feedback, *Transportation Research Record* 2077, 129–135.

Boyce, D., B. Ralevic-Dekic and H. Bar-Gera (2004) Convergence of traffic assignments: how much is enough?, *ASCE Journal of Transportation Engineering* 130 (1), 49–55.

Boyce, D., M. Tatineni and Y. Zhang (1992) Scenario Analyses for the Chicago Region with a Sketch Planning Model of Origin–Destination,

Mode and Route Choice, Report to the Illinois Department of Transportation, University of Illinois at Chicago, Chicago.

Boyce, D.E. and H.C.W.L. Williams (2005) Urban travel forecasting in the USA and UK, Chapter 3 in *Methods and Models in Transport and Telecommunications*, A. Reggiani and L. Schintler (eds), Springer, Berlin, 25–44.

Boyce, D. and Y. Zhang (1998) Parameter estimation for combined travel choice models, Chapter 10 in *Network Infrastructure and the Urban Environment*, L. Lundqvist, L.-G. Mattsson and T.J. Kim (eds), Springer, Berlin, 177–193.

Boyd, J. and J. Mellman (1980) The effect of fuel economy standards on the U.S. automotive market: a hedonic demand analysis, *Transportation Research Part A* 14, 367–378.

Bradley, M.A., J.L. Bowman and B. Griesenbeck (2009) Activity-based model for a medium sized city: Sacramento, *Traffic Engineering and Control* 50, 73–79.

Bradley, M. and A.J. Daly (1991) Estimation of logit choice models using mixed stated preference and revealed preference information, in Les Méthodes d'Analyse des Comportements de Déplacements pour les années 1990 – 6e Conférence Internationale sur les Comportements de Deplacements, Château Bon Entente, Québec.

Bradley, M. and A.J. Daly (1993) New analysis issues in stated preference research, Summer Annual Meeting, Planning and Transport Research and Computation Co., Manchester.

Bradley, M., P.M. Jones and E. Ampt (1987) An interactive household interview method to study bus provision policies, Transport Planning Methods, Planning and Transport Research and Computation Co., Bath.

Bradley, M., P. Marks and M. Wardman (1986) A summary of four studies into the value of travel time savings, Transportation Planning Methods, Planning and Transport Research and Computation Co., Brighton.

Braess, D. (1968) Über ein Paradoxon aus der Verkehrsplanung, *Unternehmensforschung* 12, 258–268.

Braess, D. and G. Kohl (1979) On the existence of equilibria in asymmetrical multiclass-user transportation networks, *Transportation Science* 13 (1), 56–63.

Braess, D., A. Nagurney and T. Wakolbinger (2005) On a paradox of traffic planning, translated from the original German, *Transportation Science* 39 (4), 446–450.

Brand, D. (1973) Travel demand forecasting: some foundations and a review, *Urban Travel Demand Forecasting*, Special Report 143, Highway Research Board, Washington, DC, 239–282.

Brand, D. and M.L. Manheim (eds) (1973) *Urban Travel Demand Forecasting*, Special Report 143, Highway Research Board, Washington, DC.

Breheny, M.J. (ed) (1992) *Sustainable Development and Urban Form*, European Research in Regional Science 2, Pion, London.

Brög, W. and E. Erl (1983) Application of a model of individual behaviour (situational approach) to explain household activity patterns in an urban area and to forecast behavioural changes, in *Recent Advances in Travel Demand Analysis*, S. Carpenter and P. Jones (eds), Gower, Aldershot, Hampshire, 250–270.

Brokke, G.E. (1959) Program for assigning traffic to a highway network, *Highway Research Bulletin* 224, 89–97.

Brokke, G.E. (1969) Urban transportation planning computer system, paper to the American Association of State Highway Officials Conference, May 1967, in Urban Planning System 360, Traffic Assignment and Peripheral Programs, Federal Highway Administration, US Department of Transportation, Washington, DC, 32–68.

Brokke, G.E. and W.L. Mertz (1958) Evaluating trip forecasting methods with an electronic computer, *Highway Research Bulletin* 203, 52–75; also in *Public Roads* 30 (4), 77–87.

Brownstone, D. and K.A. Small (2005) Valuing time and reliability: assessing the evidence from road pricing demonstrations, *Transportation Research Part A* 39, 279–293.

Brownstone, D. and K.E. Train (1998) Forecasting new product penetration with flexible substitution patterns, *Journal of Econometrics* 89, 109–129.

Bruton, M.J. (1975) *Introduction to Transportation Planning*, 2nd edn, Hutchinson, London.

Bruynooghe, M. (1967) Affectation du trafic sur un multi-réseau, Institut de Recherche des Transports, Arcueil, France.

Bruynooghe, M. (1969) Un modèle intégré de distribution et d'affectation du trafic sur un réseau, Institut de Recherche des Transports, Arcueil, France.

Bruynooghe, M., A. Gibert and M. Sakarovitch (1969) Une methode d'affectation du trafic, in *Beiträge zur Theorie des Verkehrsflusses*, W. Leutzbach and P. Baron (eds), Straßenbau und Straßenverkehrstechnik, Heft 86, Herausgegeben von Bundesminister für Verkehr, Abteilung Straßenbau, Bonn, 198–204.

Buchanan, C. (1963) *Traffic in Towns*, Her Majesty's Stationery Office, London; a shortened edition was published by Penguin Books, Harmondsworth, Middlesex, 1964.

Buchanan, C. and G.P. Crow (1963) Towards an amalgam of town and traffic planning, *Traffic Engineering and Control* 5, 36–37.

Buliung, R.N. and P.S. Kanaroglou (2007) Activity-travel behaviour research: conceptual issues, state of the art, and emerging perspectives on behavioural analysis and simulation modelling, *Transport Reviews* 27, 151–187.

Burnett, K.P. and S. Hanson (1979) Rationale for an alternative mathematical approach to movement as complex human behaviour, in *Behavioural Travel Modelling*, D.A. Hensher and P.R. Stopher (eds), Croom Helm, London, 116–134.

Burnett, K.P. and S. Hanson (1982) The analysis of travel as an example of complex human behaviour in spatially-constrained situations: definition and measurement issues, *Transportation Research Part A* 16, 87–102.

Burnett, K.P. and N.J. Thrift (1979) New approaches to understanding traveller behaviour, Chapter 4 in *Behavioural Travel Modelling*, D.A. Hensher and P.R.Stopher (eds), Croom Helm, London, 116–134.

Burrell, J.E. (1969) Multiple route assignment and its application to capacity restraint, *Beiträge zur Theorie des Verkehrsflusses*, W. Leutzbach and P. Baron (eds), Straßenbau und Straßenverkehrstechnik, Heft 86, Herausgegeben von Bundesminister für Verkehr, Abteilung Straßenbau, Bonn, 210–219.

Button, K.J., A.D. Pearman and A.S. Fowkes (1982) *Car Ownership Modelling and Forecasting*, Gower, Aldershot, Hampshire.

Cairns, S., C. Hass-Klau and P. Goodwin (1998) *Traffic Impact of Highway Capacity Reductions*, Landor, London.

Cairns, S., L. Sloman, C. Newson, J. Anable, A. Kirkbride and P. Goodwin (2008) Smarter choices: assessing the potential to achieve traffic reductions using 'soft measures', *Transport Reviews* 28, 593–618.

Cambridge Systematics (1997) *A Guidebook for Forecasting Freight Transportation Demand*, Report 388, National Cooperative Highway Research Program, Transportation Research Board, Washington, DC.

Cambridge Systematics (2010) Travel Model Validation and Reasonableness Checking Manual, 2nd edn, Federal Highway Administration, Cambridge, MA.

Cambridge Systematics, Sacramento Regional Council of Governments, University of Arizona, University of Illinois, Chicago, Sonoma Technology, Fehr and Peers (2014) Dynamic, Integrated Model System: Sacramento-Area Application, Volume 1, Summary Report, SHRP 2 Report S2-C10B-RW-1, Volume 2, Network Report, SHRP 2 Report S2-C10B-RW-2, Transportation Research Board, Washington, DC.

Cambridge Systematics, Vanasse Hangen Brustlin, Gallop Corporation, C.R. Bhat, Shapiro Transportation Consulting and Martin/Alexiou/ Bryson (2012) *Travel Demand Forecasting: Parameters and Techniques*,

Report 716, National Cooperative Highway Research Program, Transportation Research Board, Washington, DC.

Campbell, M.E. (1952) Foreword, traffic assignment, *Highway Research Bulletin* 61, iii.

Cantillo, V., B. Heydecker and J. de D. Ortúzar (2006) A discrete choice model incorporating thresholds for perception in attribute values, *Transportation Research Part B* 40, 807–825.

Cardell, N.S. and F.C. Dunbar (1980) Measuring the societal impact of automobile downsizing, *Transportation Research Part A* 14, 423–434.

Cardell, N.S. and B. Reddy (1977) A Multinomial Logit Model Which Permits Variations in Tastes across Individuals, working paper, Charles River Associates, Boston.

Carlstein, T., D. Parkes and N. Thrift (eds) (1978) *Timing Space and Spacing Time*, Edward Arnold, London.

Carpenter, S. and P. Jones (eds) (1983) *Recent Advances in Travel Demand Analysis*, Gower, Aldershot, Hampshire.

Carrasco, J.A. and J. de D. Ortúzar (2002) Review and assessment of the nested logit model, *Transport Reviews* 22, 197–218.

Carrion, C. and D.M. Levinson (2012) Value of travel time reliability: a review of current evidence, *Transportation Research Part A* 46, 720–741.

Carroll, J.D., Jr. (1949) Some aspects of home work relationships of industrial workers, *Land Economics* 25 (4), 414–422.

Carroll, J.D., Jr. (1952) The relation of homes to work places and the spatial pattern of cities, *Social Forces* 30 (3), 271–282.

Carroll, J.D., Jr. (1955) Spatial interaction and the urban-metropolitan regional description, *Papers, Regional Science Association* 1, 59–73.

Carroll, J.D., Jr. (1956) General discussion of traffic assignment by mechanical methods, *Highway Research Bulletin* 130, 76–77.

Carroll, J.D., Jr. (1959) A method of traffic assignment to an urban network, *Highway Research Bulletin* 224, 64–71.

Carroll, J.D., Jr. and H.W. Bevis (1957) Predicting local travel in urban regions, *Papers, Regional Science Association* 3, 183–197.

Carroll, J.D., Jr. and R.L. Creighton (1957) Planning and urban area transportation studies, *Proceedings*, Highway Research Board, Washington, DC, 1–7.

Carroll, J.D., Jr. and G.P. Jones (1960) Interpretation of desire line charts made on a Cartographatron, *Highway Research Bulletin* 253, 86–108.

Cascetta, E. (2009) *Transportation Systems Analysis*, 2nd edn, Springer, Berlin.

Cascetta, E., A. Nuzzolo and V. Velardi (1993) A System of Mathematical Models for the Evaluation of Integrated Traffic Planning and Control

Policies, unpublished report, Laboratorio Richerche Gestione e Controllo Traffico, Salerno, Italy.

Cepeda, M., R. Cominetti and M. Florian (2006) A frequency-based assignment model for congested transit networks with strict capacity constraints: characterization and computation of equilibria, *Transportation Research Part B* 40 (6), 437–459.

Cervero, R. and K. Kockelman (1997) Travel demand and the 3Ds: density, diversity and design, *Transportation Research Part D* 2, 199–219.

Chapin, F.S., Jr. (1974) *Human Activity Patterns in the City*, Wiley, New York.

Chapman, R.G. and R. Staelin (1982) Exploiting rank ordered choice set data within the stochastic utility model, *Journal of Marketing Research* 19, 288–301.

Charles River Associates (1972) A Disaggregate Behavioral Model of Urban Travel Demand, Federal Highway Administration, Boston.

Charles River Associates (1976) The independence of irrelevant alternatives property of the multinomial logit model, in Disaggregate Travel Demand Models, Project 8–13: Phase I Report, National Cooperative Highway Research Program, Transportation Research Board, Washington, DC.

Charnes, A. and W.W. Cooper (1958) Extremal principles for simulating traffic flow in a network, *Proceedings of the National Academy of Sciences* 44 (2), 201–204.

Charnes, A. and W.W. Cooper (1961) Multicopy traffic networks, in *Theory of Traffic Flow*, R. Herman (ed), Elsevier, Amsterdam, 85–96.

Chatterjee, A., G.P. Fisher and R.A. Stanley (eds) (1989) *Goods Transportation in Urban Areas*, Fifth Conference, American Society of Civil Engineers, New York.

Cherchi, E. (2012) Modelling individual preferences, state of the art, recent advances, and future directions, in *Travel Behaviour Research in an Evolving World*, R.M. Pendyala and C.R. Bhat (eds), www.Lulu.com, 207–248.

Cherchi, E. and J. de D. Ortúzar (2008) Empirical identification in the mixed logit model: analysing the effect of data richness, *Networks and Spatial Economics* 8, 109–124.

Cherchi, E. and J. de D. Ortúzar (2010) Can mixed logit infer the actual data generating process? Some implications for environmental assessment, *Transportation Research Part D* 15, 428–442.

Cherchi, E., J. Polak and G. Hyman (2004) The impact of income, tastes and substitution effects on the assessment of user benefits using discrete choice models, European Transport Conference, Strasbourg.

Chicago Area Transportation Study (1959) *Survey Findings*, Volume I, Chicago.

Chicago Area Transportation Study (1960) *Data Projections*, Volume II, Chicago.

Chicago Area Transportation Study (1962) *Transportation Plan*, Volume III, Chicago.

Chiou, L. and J.L. Walker (2007) Masking identification of discrete choice models under simulation methods, *Journal of Econometrics* 141, 683–703.

Chiu, Y.-C., J. Bottom, M. Mahut, A. Paz, R. Balakrishna, T. Waller and J. Hicks (2011) *Dynamic Traffic Assignment, A Primer*, Transportation Research Circular E-C153, Transportation Research Board, Washington, DC.

Chow, J.Y., C.H. Yang and A.C. Regan (2010) State-of-the-art of freight forecast modeling: lessons learned and the road ahead, *Transportation* 37, 1011–1030.

Christ, C.F. (1952) History of the Cowles Commission, 1932–1952, in Economic Theory and Measurement, Cowles Commission for Research in Economics, Chicago, cowles.econ.yale.edu/P/reports/1932-52.htm#7 (accessed 3 June 2014).

Christfreund, W., G. Förschner and U. Böhme (1969) Schriftliche Verkehrsbefragungen als Grundlage der Generalverkehrsplanung, *Wissenschaft und Technik im Straßenwesen*, Heft 11, Transpress, Berlin.

Clark, C.E. (1961) The greatest of a finite set of random variables, *Operations Research* 9, 145–162.

Clarke, M. and E. Holm (1987) Microsimulation methods in spatial analysis and planning, *Geografiska Annaler* 69, 145–164.

Clarke, M., P. Keys and H.C.W.L. Williams (1981) Microanalysis and simulation of socio-economic systems: progress and prospects, in *Quantitative Geography in Britain*, N. Wrigley and R.J. Bennett (eds), Routledge, Oxford, 248–256.

Clarke, M.I. (1980) The Formation and Initial Development of an Activity Based Model of Household Travel Behaviour, Working Paper 116, Transport Studies Unit, University of Oxford, Oxford.

Clarke, P., P. Davidson and R. Culley (2008) Using Truro's activity-based parking model to investigate optimum pricing for workplace parking charging, European Transport Conference, Noordwijkerhout, Netherlands.

Cochrane, R.A. (1975) A possible economic basis for the gravity model, *Journal of Transport Economics and Policy* 9, 34–49.

Coelho, J.D. and H.C.W.L. Williams (1978) On the design of land use plans through locational surplus maximisation, *Papers, Regional Science Association* 40, 71–85.

Cominetti, R. and J. Correa (2001) Common-lines and passenger assignment in congested transit networks, *Transportation Science* 35 (3), 250–267.

Comsis Corporation (1990) Evaluation of Travel Demand Management Measures to Relieve Congestion, US Department of Transportation, Washington, DC.

Comsis Corporation (1996) Incorporating Feedback in Travel Forecasting, Travel Model Improvement Program, US Department of Transportation, Washington, DC.

CONSAD Research Corporation (1968) Systematic Sensitivity Analysis of the Urban Travel Forecasting Process, Bureau of Public Roads, US Department of Transportation, Washington, DC.

Control Data Corporation (1965) *Transportation Planning System for the Control Data 3600 Computer*, Users' Manual, Data Centers Division Applications Program No. 7, Minneapolis, MN.

Coombe, D. (1996) Induced traffic: what do transportation models tell us?, *Transportation* 23, 83–101.

Coombe, D. (2009a) Regional and Local Strategic Modelling and Appraisal Capability, Final Report to the UK Department for Transport, Denvil Coombe Practice, London.

Coombe, D. (2009b) DaSTS: are our models and modellers up to it?, Transport Modelling, Fourth Annual Forum, Local Transport Today, London.

Cooper, W.W. (2002) Abraham Charnes and W. W. Cooper (et al.): a brief history of a long collaboration in developing industrial uses of linear programming, *Operations Research* 50 (1), 35–41.

Coopers and Lybrand Associates (1973) *Channel Tunnel: Economic Report*, Part 2, Section 2, Freight Studies, Main Report, Chapter 4: Statistical models of mode and route choice, British Channel Tunnel Company and Société Française du Tunnel sous La Manche.

Copley, G., A. Skinner, D. Simmonds and J. Laidler (2000) Development and application of the Greater Manchester strategic planning model, Transport Modelling, European Transport Conference, London.

Cosslett, S.R. (1981) Efficient estimation of discrete choice models, Chapter 2 in *Structural Analysis of Discrete Data with Econometric Applications*, C.F. Manski and D. McFadden (eds), MIT Press, Cambridge, MA, 51–111.

Coventry City Council (1973) *Coventry Transportation Study*, Coventry.

Creighton, R.L. (1970) *Urban Transportation Planning*, University of Illinois Press, Urbana.

Creighton, R.L., I. Hoch and M. Schneider (1959) The optimum spacing of arterials and of expressways, *Traffic Quarterly* 13 (3), 477–494.

Creighton, R.L., I. Hoch, M. Schneider and H. Joseph (1960) Estimating efficient spacing for arterials and expressways, *Highway Research Bulletin* 253, 1–43.

Cullen, I. and V. Godson (1975) Urban networks: the structure of activity patterns, *Progress in Planning*, Volume 4, Part 1, Pergamon, Oxford.

Culp, M., E. Lee and A.M. Steffes (2006) Summary of recommendations from Travel Model Improvement Program's peer review program, *Transportation Research Record* 1981, 50–55.

Dafermos, S.C. (1971) An extended traffic assignment model with applications to two-way traffic, *Transportation Science* 5 (4), 366–389.

Dafermos, S.C. (1972) The traffic assignment problem for multiclass-user transportation networks, *Transportation Science* 6 (1), 73–87.

Dafermos, S.C. (1973) Toll patterns for multi-class user transportation networks, *Transportation Science* 7 (3), 211–223.

Dafermos, S.C. (1976) Integrated equilibrium flow models for transportation planning, in *Traffic Equilibrium Methods*, M. Florian (ed), Springer, Berlin, 106–118.

Dafermos, S. (1980) Traffic equilibrium and variational inequalities, *Transportation Science* 14 (1), 42–54.

Dafermos, S. (1982a) The general multimodal network equilibrium problem with elastic demand, *Networks* 12 (1), 57–72.

Dafermos, S. (1982b) Relaxation algorithms for the general asymmetric traffic equilibrium problem, *Transportation Science* 16 (2), 231–240.

Dafermos, S. (1983a) An iterative scheme for variational inequalities, *Mathematical Programming* 26 (1), 40–47.

Dafermos, S. (1983b) Convergence of a network decomposition algorithm for the traffic equilibrium model, in *Transportation and Traffic Theory*, V.F. Hurdle, E. Hauer and G.N. Steuart (eds), University of Toronto Press, Toronto, 143–145.

Dafermos, S. (1988) Sensitivity analysis in variational inequalities, *Mathematics of Operations Research* 13 (3), 421–434.

Dafermos, S.C. and A. Nagurney (1984a) Sensitivity analysis for the asymmetric network equilibrium problem, *Mathematical Programming* 28 (2), 174–184.

Dafermos, S.C. and A. Nagurney (1984b) Stability and sensitivity analysis for the general network equilibrium-travel choice model, in *Transportation and Traffic Theory*, J. Volmuller and R. Hamerslag (eds), VNU Science, Utrecht, 217–231.

Dafermos, S.C. and F.T. Sparrow (1969) The traffic assignment problem for a general network, *Journal of Research of the National Bureau of Standards* 73B, 91–118.

Dafermos, S.C. and F.T. Sparrow (1971) Optimal resource allocation and toll patterns in user-optimized transportation networks, *Journal of Transport Economics and Policy* 5 (2), 184–200.

Daganzo, C.F. (1979) *Multinomial Probit*, Academic Press, New York.

Daganzo, C.F. (1982) Unconstrained extremal formulation of some transportation equilibrium problems, *Transportation Science* 16 (3), 332–360.

Daganzo, C. (1994) The cell transmission model: a dynamic representation of highway traffic consistent with the hydrodynamic theory, *Transportation Research Part B* 28, 269–287.

Daganzo, C.F., F. Bouthelier and Y. Sheffi (1977) Multinomial probit and qualitative choice: a computationally efficient algorithm, *Transportation Science* 11, 338–358.

Daganzo, C.F. and Y. Sheffi (1977) On stochastic models of traffic assignment, *Transportation Science* 11 (3), 253–274.

Dale, H.M. (1973) Trip generation and analysis of variance, Urban Traffic Models, Planning and Transport Research and Computation Co., Brighton.

Dale, H.M. (1977) Trip generation: what should we be modelling?, Chapter 3 in *Urban Transportation Planning*, P. Bonsall, M.Q. Dalvi and P.J. Hills (eds), Abacus, Tunbridge Wells, Kent, 23–29.

Dalvi, M.Q. and A.J. Daly (1976) The Valuation of Travelling Time: Theory and Estimation, Report T72, Local Government Operational Research Unit, Reading, Berkshire.

Dalvi, M.Q. and K. Martin (1973) Urban Transport Evaluation Procedures: A Review, Working Paper 23, SRC Transportation Planning Project, Institute for Transport Studies, University of Leeds, Leeds.

Daly, A.J. (1987) Estimating 'tree' logit models, *Transportation Research Part B* 21, 251–267.

Daly, A.J. (2001) Recursive Nested Extreme Value Model, Working Paper 559, Institute for Transport Studies, University of Leeds, Leeds.

Daly, A.J. (2010) Cost Damping in Travel Demand Models, for the UK Department for Transport, RAND Europe, Cambridge.

Daly, A. (2013) Forecasting behaviour: with applications to transport, Chapter 2 in *Choice Modelling*, S. Hess and A. Daly (eds), Edward Elgar Publishing, Cheltenham, UK, and Northampton, MA, USA, 48–72.

Daly, A.J. and M. Bierlaire (2006) A general and operational representation of GEV models, *Transportation Research Part B* 40, 285–305.

Daly, A.J., J. Fox and J.G. Tuinenga (2005) Pivot-point procedures in practical travel demand forecasting, 45th Congress, European Regional Science Association, Amsterdam.

Daly, A.J. and H.F. Gunn (1986) Cost-effective methods for national-level demand forecasting, in *Behavioural Research for Transport Policy*, VNU Science, Utrecht, 193–215.

Daly, A.J. and C. Rohr (1998) Forecasting demand for new travel alternatives, Chapter 19 in *Theoretical Foundations of Travel Choice Modeling*, T. Gärling, T. Laitila and K. Westlin (eds), Elsevier, Amsterdam, 451–471.

Daly, A.J., F. Tsang and C. Rohr (2014) The value of small time savings for non-business travel, *Journal of Transport Economics and Policy* 48, 205–218.

Daly, A.J. and H.H.P. van Zwam (1981) Development of travel demand models for the Zuidvleugel Study, Summer Annual Meeting, Planning and Transport Research and Computation Co., Warwick.

Daly, A.J., H.H.P. van Zwam and J. van der Valk (1983) Application of disaggregate models for a regional transport study in the Netherlands, World Conference on Transport Research, Hamburg.

Daly, A.J. and S. Zachary (1975) Commuters' Values of Time, Report T55, Local Government Operational Research Unit, Reading, Berkshire.

Daly, A.J. and S. Zachary (1978) Improved multiple choice models, Chapter 10 in *Identifying and Measuring the Determinants of Modal Choice*, D.A. Hensher and M.Q. Dalvi (eds), Saxon House, London, 335–357.

Damm, D. (1983) Theory and empirical results: a comparison of recent activity-based research, in *Recent Advances in Travel Demand Analysis*, S. Carpenter and P. Jones (eds), Gower, Aldershot, Hampshire, 3–33.

Damm, D. and S.R. Lerman (1981) A theory of activity scheduling behaviour, *Environment and Planning A* 13, 703–718.

Dantzig, G.B. (1949) Programming of inter-dependent activities II, mathematical model, Project SCOOP Report No. 6, Headquarters, US Air Force, Washington, DC; in T.C. Koopmans (ed) (1951) *Activity Analysis of Production and Allocation*, Wiley, New York, 19–32.

Dantzig, G.B. (1982) Reminiscences about the origins of linear programming, *Operations Research Letters* 1 (2), 43–48.

Dantzig, G.B. (2002) Linear programming, *Operations Research* 50 (1), 42–47.

David Simmonds Consultancy (1998) Review of Land Use/Transport Interaction Models, Report for the Standing Advisory Committee on Trunk Road Assessment (SACTRA), with Marcial Echenique & Partners, Cambridge.

Davidson, J.D. (1973) Forecasting traffic on STOL, *Operational Research Quarterly* 4, 461–469.

Davidson, P., P. Clarke and I. Sverdlov (2006) Modelling congestion from travel derived from activities, Applied Methods, European Transport Conference, Strasbourg.

Davidson, W., R. Donnelly, P. Vovsha, J. Freedman, S. Ruegg, J. Hicks, J. Castiglione and R. Picado (2007) Synthesis of first practices and operational research approaches in activity-based travel demand modeling, *Transportation Research Part A* 41, 464–488.

Davies, A.L. and K.G. Rogers (1973) Modal Choice and the Value of Time, Report C143, Local Government Operational Research Unit, Reading, Berkshire.

Davinroy, T.R., T.M. Ridley and H.J. Wootton (1963) Predicting future travel, *Traffic Engineering and Control* 5, 366–371.

de Cea, J. and J.E. Fernández (1993) Transit assignment for congested public transport systems, *Transportation Science* 27 (2), 133–147.

de Cea, J., J.E. Fernández, V. Dekock and A. Soto (2005) Solving network equilibrium on multimodal urban transportation networks with multiple user classes, *Transport Reviews* 25 (3), 293–317.

de Cea, J., J.E. Fernández and A. Soto (2001) ESTRAUS: a simultaneous equilibrium model to analyze and evaluate multimodal urban transportation systems with multiple user classes, World Conference on Transport Research, Seoul.

de Jong, G., A. Daly, M. Pieters, S. Miller, R. Plasmeijer and F. Hofman (2007a) Uncertainty in traffic forecasts: literature review and new results for the Netherlands, *Transportation* 34, 375–395.

de Jong, G., A. Daly, M. Pieters and T. van der Hoorn (2007b) The logsum as an evaluation measure: review of the literature and new results, *Transportation Research Part A* 41, 874–889.

de Jong, G., A. Daly, M. Pieters, C. Vellay, M. Bradley and F. Hofman (2003) A model for time of day and mode choice using error components logit, *Transportation Research Part E* 39, 245–268.

de Jong, G., E. Kroes, R. Plasmeijer, P. Sanders and P. Warffemius (2004) The value of reliability, European Transport Conference, Strasbourg.

de la Barra, T. (1989) *Integrated Land Use and Transport Modelling*, Cambridge University Press, Cambridge.

de la Barra, T. (1994) From theory to practice: the experience in Venezuela, *Environment and Planning B* 21, 611–617.

de Neufville, R. and J.H. Stafford (1971) *Systems Analysis for Engineers and Managers*, McGraw-Hill, New York.

de Palma, A., M. Ben-Akiva, D. Brownstone, C. Holt, T. Magnac, D. McFadden, P. Moffatt, N. Picard, K. Train, P. Wakker and J. Walker (2008) Risk, uncertainty and discrete choice models, *Marketing Letters* 19 (3–4), 269–285.

Deane, G., I. Williams, Y. Zhu, J. Pharoah, D. Kabeizi and B. Khan (2010)

FiLM – a model of freight and LGV movements in London, Regional and National Freight Models, European Transport Conference, Glasgow.

Debreu, G. (1960) Review of R.D. Luce, *Individual Choice Behavior*, *American Economic Review* 40, 186–188.

Delaware Valley Regional Planning Commission (1967) *1985 Regional Projections for the Delaware Valley*, Plan Report No. 1, Philadelphia.

Delaware Valley Regional Planning Commission (1969) *1985 Regional Transportation Plan*, Plan Report No. 5, Technical Supplement, Philadelphia.

Demetsky, M.J. (1974) Measurement of urban commodity movements, *Transportation Research Record* 496, 57–67.

Deming, W.E. and F.F. Stephan (1940) On a least squares adjustment of a sampled frequency table when the expected marginal tables are known, *Annals of Mathematical Statistics* 11, 427–444.

Desaulniers, G. and M.D. Hickman (2007) Public transit, Chapter 2 in *Transportation*, C. Barnhart and G. Laporte (eds), Handbooks in Operations Research and Management Science, Volume 14, Elsevier, Oxford, 69–127.

Detroit Metropolitan Area Traffic Study (1955) *Data Summary and Interpretation*, Part I, Detroit.

Detroit Metropolitan Area Traffic Study (1956) *Future Traffic and a Long Range Expressway Plan*, Part II, Detroit.

Dial, R.B. (1967) Transit pathfinder algorithm, *Highway Research Record* 205, 67–85.

Dial, R.B. (1971) A probabilistic multipath traffic assignment model which obviates path enumeration, *Transportation Research* 5, 83–111.

Dial, R.B. (1976) The Urban Transportation Planning System: UTPS philosophy and function, *Transportation Research Record* 619, 43–48.

Dial, R.B. (2006) A path-based user-equilibrium traffic assignment algorithm that obviates path storage and enumeration, *Transportation Research Part B* 40 (10), 917–936.

Dial, R.B. and R.E. Bunyan (1968) Public transit planning system, *Socio-Economic Planning Sciences* 1, 345–362.

Dial, R.B., D. Levinsohn and G.S. Rutherford (1980) Integrated transit-network model (INET): a new urban transportation planning system program, *Transportation Research Record*, 761, 33–40.

Dial, R.B. and L.F. Quillian (1980) Introduction to aggregate data analysis by using UTPS: UMATRIX, *Transportation Research Record* 771, 17–22.

Domencich, T.A., G. Kraft and J.P. Valette (1968) Estimation of urban passenger travel behaviour: an economic demand model, *Highway Research Record* 238, 65–78.

Domencich, T.A. and D. McFadden (1975) *Urban Travel Demand*, North-Holland, Amsterdam.

Dongarra, J.J. (2013) Performance of Various Computers Using Standard Linear Equations Software, Linpack Benchmark Report, Computer Science Technical Report, CS-89-85, University of Tennessee, Knoxville.

Donnelly, R. (2009) A Hybrid Microsimulation Model of Urban Freight Transport Demand, Ph.D. thesis, Civil Engineering, University of Melbourne, Australia.

Donnelly, R., G.D. Erhardt, R. Moeckel and W.A. Davidson (2010) *Advanced Practices in Travel Forecasting*, Synthesis 406, National Cooperative Highway Research Program, Transportation Research Board, Washington, DC.

Dorfman, R. (1951) *Application of Linear Programming to the Theory of the Firm, Including an Analysis of Monopolistic Firms by Nonlinear Programming*, University of California Press, Berkeley.

Dorfman, R. (1953) Mathematical, or 'linear', programming: a nonmathematical exposition, *American Economic Review* 43 (5), 797–825.

Douglas, A.A. (1973) Home based trip end models – a comparison between category analysis and regression analysis procedures, *Transportation* 2, 53–70.

Douglas, A.A. and R.J. Lewis (1970) Trip generation techniques: (1) introduction; (2) zonal least squares regression analysis, *Traffic Engineering and Control* 12, 362–365, 428–431.

Douglas, A.A. and R.J. Lewis (1971) Trip generation techniques: (3) household least squares regression analysis; (4) category analysis and summary of trip generation techniques, *Traffic Engineering and Control* 12, 477–479, 532–535.

Downes, J.D. and L. Gyenes (1976) Temporal Stability and Forecasting Ability of Trip Generation Models in Reading, TRRL Report LR726, Transport and Road Research Laboratory, Crowthorne, Berkshire.

Downs, A. (1962) The law of peak hour expressway congestion, *Traffic Quarterly* 16, 393–409.

Downs, A. (2004) *Still Stuck in Traffic*, Brookings Institution, Washington, DC.

Drake, G.L. (1963) London Traffic Survey – Phase II, *Traffic Engineering and Control* 5, 80–85.

Dudley, G. and J. Preston (2013) Historical narrative and the evolution of academic transport studies in the UK, *Transport Reviews* 33, 131–147.

Duffin, R.J. (1947) Nonlinear networks, IIa, *Bulletin of the American Mathematical Society* 53 (10), 963–971.

Eash, R.W., B.N. Janson and D.E. Boyce (1979) Equilibrium trip assignment: advantages and implications for practice, *Transportation Research Record* 728, 1–8.

Echenique, M.H. (1986) The practice of modelling in developing countries, in *Advances in Urban Systems Modelling*, B. Hutchinson and M. Batty (eds), North-Holland, Amsterdam, 275–297.

Echenique, M.H. (1994) Urban and regional studies at the Martin Centre: its origins, its present, its future, *Environment and Planning B* 21, 517–534.

Echenique, M.H. (2004) Econometric models of land use and transportation, Chapter 12 in *Handbook of Transport Geography and Spatial Systems*, D.A. Hensher, K.J. Button, K.E. Haynes and P.R. Stopher (eds), Elsevier, Oxford, 185–202.

Echenique, M.H. (2005) Forecasting the sustainability of alternative plans, the Cambridge Futures experience, Chapter 6 in *Future Forms and Design for Sustainable Cities*, M. Jenks and H. Dempsey (eds), Elsevier, Boston, 113–133.

Echenique, M. and T. de la Barra (1977) Compact land-use/transportation models, Chapter 8 in *Urban Transportation Planning*, P. Bonsall, Q.M. Dalvi and P.J. Hills (eds), Abacus, Tunbridge Wells, Kent, 111–125.

Echenique, M.H., A.D. Flowerdew, J.D. Hunt, T.R. Mayo, I.J. Skidmore and D.C. Simmonds (1990) The MEPLAN models of Bilbao, Leeds and Dortmund, *Transport Reviews* 10, 309–322.

Elmi, A.M., E.A. Badoe and E.J. Miller (1999) Transferability analysis of work-trip-distribution models, *Transportation Research Record* 1676, 169–176.

Erlander, S. (1977) Accessibility, entropy and the distribution and assignment of traffic, *Transportation Research* 11, 149–153.

Erlander, S. (1985) On the principle of monotone likelihood and log-linear models, *Mathematical Programming Study* 21, 108–123.

Erlander, S. (1990) Efficient population behavior and the simultaneous choices of origins, destinations and routes, *Transportation Research Part B* 24 (5), 363–373.

Erlander, S. (2005) Welfare, freedom of choice and composite utility in the logit model, *Social Choice and Welfare* 24 (3), 509–525.

Erlander, S. (2010) *Cost-Minimizing Choice Behavior in Transportation Planning*, Springer, Berlin.

Erlander, S., S. Nguyen and N.F. Stewart (1979) On the calibration of the combined distribution–assignment model, *Transportation Research Part B* 13 (3), 259–267.

Erlander, S. and T.E. Smith (1990) General representation theorems for efficient population behavior, *Applied Mathematics and Computation* 36 (3), 173–217.

Erlander, S. and N.F. Stewart (1978) Interactivity, accessibility and cost in trip distribution, *Transportation Research* 12 (4), 291–293.

Erlander, S. and N.F. Stewart (1990) *The Gravity Model in Transportation Analysis*, VSP, Utrecht.

Ettema, D., A.W.J. Borgers and H.J.P. Timmermans (1993) Simulation model of activity-scheduling behaviour, *Transportation Research Record* 1413, 1–11.

Ettema, D. and H.J.P. Timmermans (1997) Theories and models of activity patterns, in *Activity-Based Approaches to Travel Analysis*, D. Ettema and H.J.P. Timmermans (eds), Pergamon, Oxford, 1–36.

Evans, A.W. (1971) The calibration of trip distribution models with exponential and similar functions, *Transportation Research* 5, 15–38.

Evans, S.P. (1973a) A relationship between the gravity model of trip distribution and the transportation problem in linear programming, *Transportation Research* 7, 39–61.

Evans, S.P. (1973b) Some Applications of Optimisation Theory in Transport Planning, Ph.D. thesis, Civil Engineering, University College London, London.

Evans, S.P. (1976a) Derivation and analysis of some models for combining trip distribution and assignment, *Transportation Research* 10 (1), 37–57.

Evans, S.P. (1976b) Some models for combining the trip distribution and assignment stages in the transport planning process, in *Traffic Equilibrium Methods*, M. Florian (ed), Springer, Berlin, 201–228.

Ewing, R. and R. Cervero (2010) Travel and the built environment, *Journal of the American Planning Association* 76, 265–294.

Feldman, O., D. Simmonds and A. Dobson (2006) The use of land-use/economic modelling in transport planning: experience with DELTA, David Simmonds Consultancy, Cambridge.

Fellendorf, M., T. Haupt, U. Heidl and W. Scherr (1997) PTV Vision: activity based demand forecasting in daily practice, Chapter 3 in *Activity-Based Approaches to Travel Analysis*, D. Ettema and H.J.P. Timmermans (eds), Pergamon, Oxford, 55–72.

Ferdous, N., L. Vana, J.L. Bowman, R.M. Pendyala, G. Giaimo, C.R. Bhat, D. Schmitt, M. Bradley and R. Anderson (2012) Comparison of four-step versus tour-based models for prediction of travel behavior before and after transportation system changes, *Transportation Research Record* 2303, 46–60.

Ferguson, E. (1990) Transportation demand management planning, development and implementation, *Journal of the American Planning Association* 56 (4), 442–456.

Ferguson, E., C. Ross and M. Meyer (1992) PC software for urban transportation planning, *Journal of the American Planning Association* 58 (2), 238–243.

Fernández, E., J. de Cea, M. Florian and E. Cabrera (1994) Network equilibrium models with combined modes, *Transportation Science* 28 (3), 182–192.

Ferreira, L.J.A. (1981) The role of comprehensive traffic management in energy conservation, Summer Annual Meeting, Planning and Transport Research and Computation Co., Warwick.

Fisher, K.M. (2000) TRANSIMS is coming!, *Public Roads* 63 (5).

Fisk, C. (1980) Some developments in equilibrium traffic assignment, *Transportation Research Part B* 14 (4), 243–255.

Fisk, C. (1984) A nonlinear equation framework for solving network equilibrium problems, *Environment and Planning A* 16 (1), 67–80.

Fisk, C.S. and D.E. Boyce (1983) Alternative variational inequality formulations of the network equilibrium-travel choice problem, *Transportation Science* 17 (4), 454–463.

Fisk, C. and S. Nguyen (1981) Existence and uniqueness properties of an asymmetric two-mode equilibrium model, *Transportation Science* 15 (4), 318–328.

Fisk, C. and S. Nguyen (1982) Solution algorithms for network equilibrium models with asymmetric user costs, *Transportation Science* 16 (3), 361–381.

Fleet, C.R. and S.R. Robertson (1968) Trip generation in the transportation planning process, *Highway Research Record* 240, 257–289.

Florian, M. (ed) (1976) *Traffic Equilibrium Methods*, Springer, Berlin.

Florian, M. (1977) A traffic equilibrium model of travel by car and public transit modes, *Transportation Science* 11 (2), 169–179.

Florian, M. (1978) Rejoinder: a traffic equilibrium model of travel by car and public transit modes, *Transportation Science* 12 (2), 176.

Florian, M. (ed) (1984a) *Transportation Planning Models*, Elsevier, Amsterdam.

Florian, M. (1984b) An introduction to network models used in transportation planning, in *Transportation Planning Models*, M. Florian (ed), Elsevier, Amsterdam, 137–152.

Florian, M. (2008) Models and software for urban and regional transportation planning: contributions of the CRT, *INFOR* 46, 29–50.

Florian, M., R. Chapleau, S. Nguyen, C. Achim, L. James-Lefebvre, S. Galarneau, J. Lefebvre and C. Fisk (1979) Validation and application of an equilibrium based two-mode urban transportation planning method (EMME), *Transportation Research Record* 728, 14–23.

Florian, M., I. Constantin and D. Florian (2009) A new look at projected gradient method for equilibrium assignment, *Transportation Research Record* 2090, 10–16.

Florian, M. and B. Fox (1976) On the probabilistic origin of Dial's multipath traffic assignment model, *Transportation Research* 10 (5), 339–341.

Florian, M. and M. Gaudry (eds) (1980) *Transportation Supply Models, Transportation Research Part B* 14 (1/2).

Florian, M. and D. Hearn (1995) Network equilibrium models and algorithms, Chapter 6 in *Network Routing*, M.O. Ball, T.L. Magnanti, C.L. Monma and G.L. Nemhauser (eds), Handbooks in Operations Research and Management Science, Volume 8, Elsevier Science, Amsterdam, 485–550.

Florian, M. and D. Hearn (1999) Network equilibrium and pricing, Chapter 11 in *Handbook of Transportation Science*, R.W. Hall (ed), Kluwer, Boston, 361–393.

Florian, M. and S. Nguyen (1974) A method for computing network equilibrium with elastic demands, *Transportation Science* 8 (4), 321–332.

Florian, M. and S. Nguyen (1976) An application and validation of equilibrium trip assignment methods, *Transportation Science* 10 (4), 374–389.

Florian, M. and S. Nguyen (1978) A combined trip distribution modal split and assignment model, *Transportation Research* 12 (4), 241–246.

Florian, M., S. Nguyen and J. Ferland (1975) On the combined distribution–assignment of traffic, *Transportation Science* 9 (1), 43–53.

Florian, M. and H. Spiess (1982) The convergence of diagonalization algorithms for asymmetric network equilibrium problems, *Transportation Research Part B* 16 (6), 477–483.

Florian, M. and H. Spiess (1983) On binary mode choice/assignment models, *Transportation Science* 17 (1), 32–47.

Florian, M., J.H. Wu and S. He (2002) A multi-class multi-mode variable demand network equilibrium model with hierarchical logit structures, Chapter 8 in *Transportation and Network Analysis*, M. Gendreau and P. Marcotte (eds), Kluwer, Dordrecht, 119–133.

Flyvbjerg, B., N. Bruzelius and W. Rothengatter (2003) *Megaprojects and Risk*, Cambridge University Press, Cambridge.

Flyvbjerg, B., M.K.S. Holm and S.L. Buhl (2006) Inaccuracy in traffic forecasts, *Transport Reviews* 26, 1–24.

Fosgerau, M. (2006) Investigating the distribution of the value of travel time savings, *Transportation Research Part B* 40, 688–707.

Fosgerau, M. and M. Bierlaire (2007) A practical test for the choice of mixing distribution in discrete choice models, *Transportation Research Part B* 41, 784–794.

Fosgerau, M. and M. Bierlaire (2009) Discrete choice models with multiplicative error terms, *Transportation Research Part B* 43, 494–505.

Fosgerau, M. and A. Karlstrom (2010) The value of reliability, *Transportation Research Part B* 44, 38–49.

Fosgerau, M., D. McFadden and M. Bierlaire (2013) Choice probability generating functions, *Journal of Choice Modelling* 8, 1–18.

Foster, C.D. and M.E. Beesley (1963) Estimating the social benefit of constructing an underground railway in London, *Journal of the Royal Statistical Society*, Series A (General) 126, Part 1, 46–92.

Fotheringham, A.S. and M. Wegener (2000) *Spatial Models and GIS*, Taylor & Francis, London.

Fowkes, A.S. (1986) The UK Department of Transport Value of Time project, *International Journal of Transport Economics* 13, 197–207.

Fowkes, A.S. (1998) The Development of Stated Preference Techniques in Transport Planning, Working Paper 479, Institute for Transport Studies, University of Leeds, Leeds.

Fowkes, A.S., C.A. Nash and G. Tweddle (1991) Investigating the market for inter-modal freight technologies, *Transportation Research Part A* 25, 161–172.

Fowkes, A.S. and G. Tweddle (1988) A computer guided stated preference experiment for freight mode choice, Transport Planning Methods, Summer Annual Meeting, Planning and Transport Research and Computation Co., Bath.

Fox, M. (1995) Transport planning and the human activity approach, *Journal of Transport Geography* 3, 105–116.

Frank, C. (1978) A Study of Alternative Approaches to Combined Trip Distribution–Assignment Modeling, Ph.D. thesis, Regional Science, University of Pennsylvania, Philadelphia.

Frank, M. and P. Wolfe (1956) An algorithm for quadratic programming, *Naval Research Logistics Quarterly* 3 (1–2), 95–110.

Fratar, T.J. (1954) Vehicular trip distribution by successive approximations, *Traffic Quarterly* 8 (1), 53–65.

Freeman, Fox, Wilbur Smith and Associates (1966) London Traffic Survey, Volume II: Future Traffic and Travel Characteristics in Greater London, Greater London Council, London.

Freeman, Fox, Wilbur Smith and Associates (1967) *Transportation Analysis Programs*, London.

French, A. and P.L. Watson (1971) Demand forecasting and development of a framework for analysis of urban commodity flow, conference panel report, *Urban Commodity Flow*, Special Report 120, Highway Research Board, Washington, DC, 135–141.

Fresko, D., G. Shunk and F. Spielberg (1972) Analysis of need for goods movement forecasts, *ASCE Journal of the Urban Planning and Development Division* 98 (UP1), 1–16.

Friedrich, M., I. Hofsaess and S. Wekeck (2001) Timetable-based transit assignment using branch and bound techniques, *Transportation Research Record* 1752, 100–107.

Friedrich, M., P. Mott and K. Nökel (2000) Keeping passenger surveys up to date, *Transportation Research Record* 1735, 35–42.

Friesz, T.L. (1981) An equivalent optimization problem for combined multi-class distribution, assignment and modal split which obviates symmetry restrictions, *Transportation Research Part B* 15 (5), 361–369.

Gabriel, S.A. and D. Bernstein (1997) The traffic equilibrium problem with nonadditive path costs, *Transportation Science* 31 (4), 337–348.

Gale, D., H.W. Kuhn and A.W. Tucker (1951) Linear programming and the theory of games, in *Activity Analysis of Production and Allocation*, T.C. Koopmans (ed), Wiley, New York, 317–329.

Gallo, G. and S. Pallottino (1984) Shortest path methods in transportation models, in *Transportation Planning Models*, M. Florian (ed), Elsevier, Amsterdam, 227–287.

Gapper, J. and C. Rolfe (1968) Modal Split: Factors Determining the Choice of Transport for the Journey to Work, Report C32, Local Government Operational Research Unit, Reading, Berkshire.

Gärling, T., T. Kalen, J. Romanus, M. Selart and B. Vilhelmson (1998a) Computer simulation of household activity scheduling, *Environment and Planning A* 30, 665–679.

Gärling, T., M. Kwan and R. Golledge (1994) Computational process modelling of household activity scheduling, *Transportation Research Part B* 28, 355–364.

Gärling, T., T. Laitila and K. Westin (eds) (1998b) *Theoretical Foundations of Travel Choice Modeling*, Elsevier, Amsterdam.

Garrett, M. and M. Wachs (1996) *Transportation Planning on Trial*, Sage, Thousand Oaks, CA.

Garrison, W.L. and D.M. Levinson (2006) *The Transportation Experience*, Oxford University Press, New York.

Garrison, W.L. and D.F. Marble (1958) Analysis of highway networks: a linear programming formulation, *Proceedings*, Highway Research Board, Washington, DC, 1–17.

Gass, S.I. (2002) The first linear-programming shoppe, *Operations Research* 50 (1), 61–68.

Gaudry, M.J., S.R. Jara-Diaz and J. de D. Ortúzar (1989) Value of time sensitivity to model specification, *Transportation Research Part B* 23, 151–158.

Gaudry, M. and E. Quinet (2011) Shannon's Measure of Information and the Utility of Multiple Network Path Use in Transport Demand Estimation and Project Appraisal, Working Paper AJD-142, Agora Jules Dupuit, Economics Department, University of Montreal, Canada, and Paris-Jourdan Sciences Économiques (PSE), École des Ponts ParisTech (ENPC), Paris.

Gaudry, M.J.I. and M.I. Wills (1978) Estimating the functional form of travel demand models, *Transportation Research* 12, 257–289.

Gendreau, M. and P. Marcotte (2002) *Transportation and Network Analysis*, Kluwer, Dordrecht.

Gentile, G. (2014) Local user cost equilibrium: a bush-based algorithm for traffic assignment, *Transportmetrica*, 10 (1), 15–54.

Gibert, A. (1968a) A Method for the Traffic Assignment Problem When Demand Is Elastic, LBS-TNT-85, Transport Network Theory Unit, London Graduate School of Business Studies, London, July.

Gibert, A. (1968b) A Method for the Traffic Assignment Problem, LBS-TNT-95, Transport Network Theory Unit, London Graduate School of Business Studies, London, August.

Giuliano, G., P. Gordon, Q. Pan, J. Park and L. Wang (2010) Estimating freight flows for metropolitan area highway networks using secondary data sources, *Networks and Spatial Economics* 10 (1), 73–91.

Goeller, B.F. (1971) Freight transport in urban areas: issues for research and action, *Urban Commodity Flow*, Special Report 120, Highway Research Board, Washington, DC, 149–162.

Goldner, W. (1971) The Lowry model heritage, *Journal of the American Institute of Planners*, 37 (2), 100–110.

Goldner, W., S.R. Rosenthal, J.R. Meredith and M.M. Reynolds (1972) Projective Land Use Model – PLUM, three volumes, Institute of Transportation and Traffic Engineering, University of California Berkeley, Berkeley.

Golob, J.M. and T.F. Golob (1983) Classification of approaches to travel behavior analysis, *Travel Analysis Methods for the 1980s*, Special Report 201, Transportation Research Board, Washington, DC, 83–107.

Golob, T.F. (2001) Travelbehavior.com: activity approaches to modeling the effects of information technology on personal travel behaviour, chapter 6 in *Travel Behaviour Research*, D.A. Hensher (ed), Pergamon, Oxford, 145–183.

Golob, T.F. and M.J. Beckmann (1971) A utility model for travel forecasting, *Transportation Science* 5, 79–90.

Golob, T.F. and A.C. Regan (2001) Impact of information technology on personal travel and commercial vehicle operations: research challenges and opportunities, *Transportation Research Part C* 9, 87–121.

Goodwin, P.B. (1983) Some problems in activity approaches to travel demand, Chapter 16 in *Recent Advances in Travel Demand Analysis*, S. Carpenter and P. Jones (eds), Gower, Aldershot, Hampshire, 470–474.

Goodwin, P.B. (1996) Empirical evidence on induced traffic, *Transportation* 23, 35–54.

Goodwin, P.B. (1998) The end of equilibrium, Chapter 5 in *Theoretical Foundations of Travel Choice Modeling*, T. Gärling, T. Laitila and K. Westlin (eds), Elsevier, Amsterdam, 103–132.

Goodwin, P. (2005) The remarkable consistency of travel time: comment, *Local Transport Today* 432, 17.

Goodwin, P.B., J. Dargay and M. Hanly (2004) Elasticities of road traffic and fuel consumption with respect to price and income: a review, *Transport Reviews* 24, 275–292.

Goodwin, P.B., M.C. Dix and A.D. Layzell (1987) The case for heterodoxy in longitudinal analysis, *Transportation Research Part A* 21, 363–376.

Gordon, P., H.W. Richardson and M.-J. Jun (1991) The commuting paradox: evidence from the top twenty, *Journal of the American Planning Association* 57 (4), 416–420.

Graham, D.J. and S. Glaister (2004) Road traffic demand elasticity estimates: a review, *Transport Reviews* 24, 261–274.

Green, P.E. and V.R. Rao (1971) Conjoint measurement for quantifying judgmental data, *Journal of Marketing Research* 8, 355–363.

Greene, W.H. and D.A. Hensher (2003) A latent class model for discrete choice analysis: contrasts with mixed logit, *Transportation Research Part B* 37, 681–698.

Gumbel, E.J. (1958) *Statistics of Extremes*, Columbia University Press, New York.

Gunn, H.F. (1981) Travel budgets: a review of evidence and modelling implications, *Transportation Research Part A* 15, 7–23.

Gunn, H.F. (1984) An analysis of transfer price data, Annual Summer Meeting, Planning and Transport Research and Computation Co., Brighton.

Gunn, H. (2001) Spatial and temporal transferability of relationships between travel demand, trip cost and travel time, *Transportation Research Part E* 37, 163–189.

Gunn, H.F., A.I.J.M. van der Hoorn and A.J. Daly (1989) Long range country-wide travel demand forecasts from models of individual choice, *Travel Behaviour Research*, Avebury, Aldershot, Hampshire.

Hägerstrand, T. (1970) What about people in regional science?, *Papers, Regional Science Association* 24, 7–21.

Hague Consulting Group (1985) Developments in Modelling Urban and Regional Travel Demand in the Netherlands since 1977, The Hague.

Hague Consulting Group (1997) A Review of Current World Practice, Report 6090–4, prepared for New South Wales Department of Transport, Australia, The Hague.

Haikalis, G. and H. Joseph (1961) Economic evaluations of traffic networks, *Highway Research Bulletin* 306, 39–63.

Hall, M.A. (1978) Properties of the equilibrium state in transportation networks, *Transportation Science* 12 (3), 208–216.

Hall, M.D., T. Fashole-Luke, D. Van Vliet and D.P. Watling (1992) Demand responsive assignment in SATURN, Summer Annual Meeting, Planning and Transport Research and Computation Co., Manchester.

Hall, M.D., D. Van Vliet and L.G. Willumsen (1980) SATURN – a simulation-assignment model for the evaluation of traffic management schemes, *Traffic Engineering and Control* 21, 168–176.

Hall, R.W. (ed) (1999) *Handbook of Transportation Science*, Kluwer, Boston.

Handy, S.L. (1996) Methodologies for exploring the link between urban form and travel behaviour, *Transportation Research Part D* 1, 151–165.

Handy, S.L., X. Cao and P. Mokhtarian (2005) Correlation or causality between the built environment and travel behavior? Evidence from Northern California, *Transportation Research Part D* 10, 427–444.

Hansen, W.G. (1959) How accessibility shapes land use, *Journal of the American Institute of Planners* 25 (2), 73–76.

Hansen, W.G. (1962) Evaluation of gravity model trip distribution procedures, *Highway Research Bulletin* 347, 67–76.

Hanson, S. (1979) Urban travel linkages: a review, in *Behavioural Travel Modelling*, D. Hensher and P. Stopher (eds), Croom Helm, London, 81–100.

Harker, P.T. and J.-S. Pang (1990) Finite-dimensional variational inequality and nonlinear complementarity problems: a survey of theory, algorithms and applications, *Mathematical Programming* 48 (1–3), 161–220.

Harris, A.J. and J.C. Tanner (1974) Transport Demand Models Based on Personal Characteristics, Supplementary Report 64 UC, UK Transport and Road Research Laboratory, Crowthorne, Berkshire; in *Transportation and Traffic Theory*, D.J. Buckley (ed), Elsevier, New York.

Harris, B. (1961) Some problems in the theory of intra-urban location, *Operations Research* 9, 695–721.

Harris, B. (1963) Linear Programming and the Projection of Land Uses, PJ Paper No. 20, Penn Jersey Transportation Study, Philadelphia.

Harris, B. (1985) Urban simulation models in regional science, *Journal of Regional Science* 25 (4), 545–567.

Harris, B. (1994) The real issues concerning Lee's 'requiem', *Journal of the American Planning Association* 60 (1), 31–34.

Harrison, A.J. and D.A. Quarmby (1969) The value of time in transport planning: a review, *6th Round Table*, European Conference of Ministers of Transport, Paris; Mathematical Advisory Unit Note 154, UK Department of the Environment, London, 1970.

Hartgen, D.T. (1974) Attitudinal and situational variables influencing urban mode choice: some empirical findings, *Transportation* 3, 377–392.

Hartgen, D.T. (1983) Executive summary, *Travel Analysis Methods for the 1980s*, Special Report 201, Transportation Research Board, Washington, DC, 3–4.

Hartgen, D.T. (2013) Hubris or humility? Accuracy issues for the next 50 years of travel demand modeling, *Transportation* 40, 1133–1157.

Hartgen, D.T. and G.H. Tanner (1971) Investigations of the effects of traveler attitudes in a model of mode choice behavior, *Highway Research Record* 369, 1–14.

Harvey, G. and E. Deakin (1993) *A Manual of Regional Transportation Modeling Practice for Air Quality Analysis*, Deakin Harvey Skabardonis, Berkeley, CA.

Hausman, J.A. and D.A. Wise (1978) A conditional probit model for qualitative choice: discrete decisions recognising interdependence and heterogeneous preferences, *Econometrica* 46, 403–426.

Havers, G. and D. Van Vliet (1974) Greater London Transport Study Models: The State-of-the-Art, GLTS Note 71, Greater London Council, London.

Heanue, K.E. and C.E. Pyers (1966) A comparative evaluation of trip distribution procedures, *Highway Research Record* 114, 20–50.

Hearn, D.W. (1982) The gap function of a convex program, *Operations Research Letters* 1 (2), 67–71.

Hearn, D.W., S. Lawphongpanich and S. Nguyen (1984) Convex programming formulations of the asymmetric traffic assignment problem, *Transportation Research Part B* 18 (4/5), 357–365.

Hearn, D.W., S. Lawphongpanich and J.A. Ventura (1985) Finiteness in restricted simplicial decomposition, *Operations Research Letters* 4, 125–130.

Hearn, D.W., S. Lawphongpanich and J.A. Ventura (1987) Restricted simplicial decomposition: computation and extensions, *Mathematical Programming Study* 31, 99–118.

Hedges, C.A. (1971) Demand forecasting and development of a framework for analysis of urban commodity flow: statement of the problem, *Urban Commodity Flow*, Special Report 120, Highway Research Board, Washington, DC, 145–148.

Heggie, I.G. (1978a) Behavioural dimensions of travel choice, Chapter 3 in *Determinants of Travel Choice*, D.A. Hensher and Q.M. Dalvi (eds), Saxon House, Farnborough, Hampshire, 100–125.

Heggie, I.G. (1978b) Putting behaviour into behavioural models of travel choice, *Journal of the Operational Research Society* 29, 541–550.

Heggie, I.G. and P.M. Jones (1978) Defining domains for models of travel demand, *Transportation* 7, 119–135.

Heightchew, R.E., Jr. (1979) TSM: revolution or repetition?, *ITE Journal* 48 (9), 22–30.

Helvig, M. (1964) Chicago's External Truck Movements: Spatial Interactions between the Chicago Area and the Hinterland, Research Paper No. 90, Department of Geography, University of Chicago, Chicago.

Hensher, D.A. (1976) The structure of journeys and nature of travel patterns, *Environment and Planning A* 8, 655–672.

Hensher, D.A. (1994) Stated preference analysis of travel choices: the state of practice, *Transportation* 21, 107–133.

Hensher, D.A., P.O. Barnard and T.P. Truong (1988) The role of stated preference methods in studies of travel choice, *Journal of Transport Economics and Policy* 22, 45–58.

Hensher, D.A. and M.A. Figliozzi (2007) Guest editorial: behavioural insights into the modeling of freight transportation and distribution, *Transportation Research* B 41, 921–923.

Hensher, D.A. and W.H. Greene (2003) The mixed logit model: the state of practice, *Transportation* 30, 133–176.

Hensher, D.A. and L.W. Johnson (1981) *Applied Discrete Choice Modelling*, Croom Helm, London.

Hensher, D.A. and J.J. Louviere (1979) Behavioural intentions as predictors of very specific behaviour, *Transportation* 8, 167–182.

Hensher, D.A., P.B. McLeod and J.K. Stanley (1975) Usefulness of attitudinal measures in investigating the choice of travel mode, *International Journal of Transport Economics* 2, 51–75.

Hensher, D.A., J.M. Rose and W.H. Greene (2005) *Applied Choice Analysis*, Cambridge University Press, Cambridge.

Hensher, D.A., J.M. Rose and W.H. Greene (2008) Combining RP and SP data: biases in using the nested logit 'trick' – contrasts with flexible mixed logit incorporating panel and scale effects, *Journal of Transport Geography* 16 (2), 126–133.

Hensher, D.A. and P.R. Stopher (eds) (1979) *Behavioural Travel Modelling*, Croom Helm, London.

Herbert, J.D. and B.H. Stevens (1960) A model of the distribution of residential activity in urban areas, *Journal of Regional Science* 2 (1), 21–36.

Herman, R. (ed) (1961) *Theory of Traffic Flow*, Elsevier, Amsterdam.

Herriges, J.A. and C.L. Kling (1999) Nonlinear income effects in random utility models, *Review of Economics and Statistics* 81, 62–72.

Hess, S., M. Bierlaire and J.W. Polak (2005) Estimation of value of travel-time savings using mixed logit models, *Transportation Research Part A* 39, 221–236.

Hess, S. and A. Daly (eds) (2013) *Choice Modelling*, Edward Elgar Publishing, Cheltenham, UK, and Northampton, MA, USA.

Hess, S., J.W. Polak, A. Daly and G. Hyman (2007) Flexible substitution patterns in models of mode and time of day choice: new evidence from the UK and the Netherlands, *Transportation* 34, 213–238.

Hess, S., A. Stathopoulos and A. Daly (2012) Allowing for heterogeneous decision rules in discrete choice models: an approach and four case studies, *Transportation* 39, 565–591.

Higgins, T.J. (1990) Demand management in suburban settings – effectiveness and policy considerations, *Transportation* 17, 93–116.

Hill, D.M. (1965a) A growth allocation model for the Boston region, *Journal of the American Institute of Planners* 31, 111–120.

Hill, D.M. (1965b) A model for prediction of truck traffic in large metropolitan areas, *Papers, Transportation Research Forum* 6, 167–182.

Hill, D.M., D. Brand and W.B. Hansen (1965) Prototype development of a statistical land use prediction model for the greater Boston region, *Highway Research Record* 114, 51–70.

Hill, D.M. and H.G. von Cube (1963) Development of a model for forecasting travel mode choice in urban areas, *Highway Research Record* 38, 78–96.

Hillman, M., I. Henderson and A. Whalley (1973) Personal Mobility and Transport Policy, Publication 342, Political and Economic Planning, London.

Hillman, M., I. Henderson and A. Whalley (1976) Transport Realities and Planning Policy: Studies of Friction and Freedom in Daily Travel, Publication 42, Political and Economic Planning, London.

Hitchcock, F.L. (1941) The distribution of a product from several sources to numerous localities, *Journal of Mathematics and Physics* 20, 224–230.

Hobeika, A. (2005) TRANSIMS Fundamentals, Chapters 1–7, Virginia Polytechnic, Blacksburg, VA.

Hoch, I. (1959) A comparison of alternative inter-industry forecasts for the Chicago region, *Papers, Regional Science Association* 5, 217–235.

Hoel, L.A. (1971) Summary of conference proceedings, *Urban Commodity Flow*, Special Report 120, Highway Research Board, Washington, DC, 4–10.

Hoinville, G. and E. Johnson (1971) *The Importance and Values Commuters Attach to Time Savings*, Social and Community Planning Research, London.

Holguín-Veras, J., G.F. List, A.H. Meyburg, K. Ozbay, R.E. Paaswell, H. Teng and S. Yahalom (2001) An Assessment of Methodological Alternatives for a Regional Freight Model in the NYMTC Region, New York Metropolitan Transportation Council, New York.

Holguín-Veras, J. and G.R. Patil (2008) A multicommodity integrated freight origin–destination synthesis model, *Networks and Spatial Economics* 8 (2–3), 309–326.

Horowitz, A.J. (1989) Convergence properties of some iterative traffic assignment algorithms, *Transportation Research Record* 1220, 21–27.

Horowitz, A.J. (1991) Convergence of certain traffic/land-use equilibrium assignment models, *Environment and Planning A* 23 (3), 371–383.

Horowitz, A.J. (1992) Implementing travel forecasting with traffic operational strategies, *Transportation Research Record* 1365, 54–61.

Horowitz, A.J. (1997) Intersection delay in regionwide traffic assignment: implications of the 1994 update of the Highway Capacity Manual, *Transportation Research Record* 1572, 1–8.

Horowitz, J. (1985) Travel and location behaviour: state of the art and research opportunities, *Transportation Research Part A* 19, 441–453.

Hotelling, H. (1938) The general welfare in relation to problems of taxation and of railway and utility rates, *Econometrica* 6, 242–269.

Hunt, J.D. (1994) Calibrating the Naples land use and transport model, *Environment and Planning B* 21, 569–590.

Hunt, J.D., D.S. Kriger and E.J. Miller (2005) Current operational urban land-use-transport modeling frameworks: a review, *Transport Reviews* 25 (3), 329–376.

Hunt, J.D. and D.C. Simmonds (1993) Theory and application of an integrated land-use and transport modelling framework, *Environment and Planning B* 20, 221–244.

Hunt, J.D. and K.J. Stefan (2007) Tour-based microsimulation of urban commercial movements, *Transportation Research Part B* 41, 981–1013.

Hutchinson, B.G. (1974) *Principles of Urban Transport Systems Planning*, McGraw-Hill, New York.

Hydas, P. (2005) A functional evaluation of the AIMSUN, PARAMICS and VISSIM microsimulation models, *Road and Transport Research* 14, 45–59.

Hyman, G.M. (1969) The calibration of trip distribution models, *Environment and Planning* 1, 105–112.

Hyman, G.M. and A.G. Wilson (1969) The effects of changes in travel costs on trip distribution and modal split, *High Speed Ground Transportation Journal* 3, 79–85.

Ingram, G.K., J.F. Kain, J.R. Ginn, H.J. Brown and S.P. Dresch (1972) The Detroit Prototype of the NBER Urban Simulation Model, National Bureau of Economic Research, New York.

Inoue, S. and T. Maruyama (2012) Computational experience on advanced algorithms for user equilibrium traffic assignment problem and its convergence error, *Procedia – Social and Behavioral Sciences* 43, 445–456.

Institute of Transportation Engineers (1980) Evaluation of the accuracy of past urban transportation forecasts, Technical Council Committee 6F-13, *ITE Journal* 50 (2), 24–34.

Institute of Transportation Engineers (1994) Travel Demand Forecasting Processes Used by Ten Large Metropolitan Planning Organizations, Technical Council Committee 6Y-53, An Informational Report, Washington, DC.

Ireland, C.T. and S. Kullback (1968) Contingency tables with given marginals, *Biometrika* 55, 179–188.

Irwin, N.A. (1965) Review of existing land-use forecasting techniques, *Highway Research Record* 88, 182–216.

Irwin, N.A., N. Dodd and H.G. von Cube (1961) Capacity restraint in assignment programs, *Highway Research Bulletin* 297, 109–127.

Irwin, N.A. and H.G. von Cube (1962) Capacity restraint in multi-travel mode assignment programs, *Highway Research Bulletin* 347, 258–289.

Isard, W. (1960) *Methods of Regional Analysis*, Wiley, New York.

Jara-Diaz, S. (2007) *Transport Economic Theory*, Elsevier, Amsterdam.

Jayakrishnan, R., W.K. Tsai, J.N. Prashker and S. Rajadhyaksha (1994) A faster path-based algorithm for traffic assignment, *Transportation Research Record* 1443, 75–83.

Jewell, W.S. (1967) Models for traffic assignment, *Transportation Research* 1 (2), 31–46.

Jin, Y. (1994) The YEZTS transport model: a discussion of the empirical findings on modal split, *Environment and Planning B* 21, 591–602.

Johnson, R.M. (1974) Tradeoff analysis of consumer values, *Journal of Marketing Research* 11, 121–127.

Johnson, S. (2010) *Where Good Ideas Come From*, Penguin, London.

Johnston, R.H. (1988) Some mechanisms of speed similarity in urban areas, *Traffic Engineering and Control* 29, 6–9.

Jones, P.M. (1977) Travel as a manifestation of activity choice: trip generation revisited, Chapter 4 in *Urban Transportation Planning*, P.W.

570 *Forecasting urban travel*

Bonsall, Q.M.Dalvi and P.J. Hills (eds), Abacus, Tunbridge Wells, Kent, 31–49.
Jones, P.M. (1979a) 'HATS': a technique for investigating household decisions, *Environment and Planning A* 11, 59–70.
Jones, P.M. (1979b) New approaches to understanding travel behaviour: the human activity approach, Chapter 2 in *Behavioural Travel Modelling*, D.A. Hensher and P.R. Stopher (eds), Croom Helm, London, 55–80.
Jones, P.M. (1985) Interactive travel survey methods: the-state-of-the-art, in *New Survey Methods in Transport*, E.S. Ampt, A.J. Richardson and W. Brög (eds), VNU Science, Utrecht, 99–127.
Jones, P.M. (2012) The role of an evolving paradigm in shaping international transport research and policy agendas over the past 50 years, Chapter 2 in *Travel Behaviour Research in an Evolving World*, R.M. Pendyala and C.R. Bhat (eds), www.lula.com, 3–34.
Jones, P.M., M. Bradley and E.S. Ampt (1989) Forecasting household response to policy measures using computerised, activity-based stated preference techniques, in *Travel Behaviour Research*, Avebury, Aldershot, 41–63.
Jones, P.M., M.C. Dix, M.I. Clarke and I.G. Heggie (1983) *Understanding Travel Behaviour*, Gower, Aldershot.
Jones, P.M., F.S. Koppelman and J.-P. Orfeuil (1990) Activity analysis: the state of the art and future directions, in *Developments in Dynamic and Activity-Based Approaches to Travel Analysis*, P.M. Jones (ed), Avebury, Aldershot, 34–55.
Jorgensen, N.O. (1963) Some Aspects of the Urban Traffic Assignment Problem, ITTE Graduate Report No. 1963:9, M.S. thesis, Civil Engineering, University of California Berkeley, Berkeley.
Kahneman, D. (2011) *Thinking, Fast and Slow*, Farrar, Straus and Giroux, New York.
Kahneman, D. and A. Tversky (1979) Prospect theory: an analysis of decision under risk, *Econometrica* 47, 263–291.
Kain, J.F. (1990) Deception in Dallas: strategic misrepresentation in rail transit promotion and evaluation, *Journal of the American Planning Association* 56, 184–196.
Kain, J.F. and W.C. Apgar (1985) *Housing and Neighborhood Dynamics*, Harvard University Press, Cambridge, MA.
Kim, T.J. (1978) Effects of subways on urban form and structure, *Transportation Research* 12 (1), 231–239.
Kim, T.J. (1989) *Integrated Urban Systems Modeling*, Kluwer, Dordrecht.
Kirby, H.R. (ed) (1981) Personal Travel Budgets, *Transportation Research Part A* 15, 1–106.

Kitamura, R. (1988) An evaluation of activity-based travel analysis, *Transportation* 15, 9–34.

Kitamura, R. (2000) Longitudinal methods, Chapter 7 in *Handbook of Transport Modelling*, D.A. Hensher and K. Button (eds), Pergamon, Amsterdam, 113–129.

Kitamura, R., C. Chen, R.M. Pendyala and R. Narayanan (2000) Microsimulation of daily activity-travel patterns for travel demand forecasting, *Transportation* 27, 25–51.

Kitamura, R. and S. Fujii (1998) Two computational process models of activity-travel choice, in *Theoretical Foundations of Travel Choice Modeling*, T. Gärling, T. Laitila and K. Westin (eds), Elsevier, Amsterdam, 251–279.

Kitamura, R., S. Fujii and E.I. Pas (1997a) Time-use data, analysis and modeling: towards the next generation of transportation planning methodologies, *Transport Policy* 4, 225–235.

Kitamura, R., P.L. Mokhtarian and L. Laidet (1997b) A microanalysis of land use and travel in five neighborhoods in the San Francisco Bay Area, *Transportation* 24, 125–158.

Kitamura, R., E.I. Pas, C.V. Lula, T.K. Lawton and P.E. Benson (1996) The sequenced activity mobility simulator (SAMS): an integrated approach to modeling transportation, land use and air quality, *Transportation* 23, 267–291.

Kitamura, R., T. van der Hoorn and F. van Wijk (1997c) A comparative analysis of daily time use and the development of an activity-based travel-benefit measure, in *Activity-Based Approaches to Travel Analysis*, D.F. Ettema and H. Timmermans (eds), Pergamon, Oxford, 171–187.

Kjeldsen, T.H. (2000) A contextualized analysis of the Kuhn–Tucker theorem in nonlinear programming: the impact of World War II, *Historia Mathematica* 27 (4), 331–361.

Klosterman, R.E. (1994) An introduction to the literature on large-scale models, *Journal of the American Planning Association* 60, 41–44.

Knight, F.H. (1924) Some fallacies in the interpretation of social cost, *Quarterly Journal of Economics* 38 (4), 582–606.

Kocur, G., T. Adler, W. Hyman and B. Aunet (1982) Guide to Forecasting Travel Demand and Direct Utility Assessment, Urban Mass Transportation Administration, US Department of Transportation, Washington, DC.

Koenig, J.-G. (1975) A theory of urban accessibility: a new working tool for the urban planner, Urban Traffic Models, Annual Summer Meeting, Planning and Transport Research and Computation Co., Warwick.

Koestler, A. (1964) *The Act of Creation*, Macmillan, New York.

Koh, A. and S. Shepherd (2006) Issues in the Modelling of Road User

572   *Forecasting urban travel*

Charging, Appendix A, Issues in the Modelling of Road User Charging, Distillate Project F, Institute for Transport Studies, University of Leeds, Leeds, www.its.leeds.ac.uk/projects/distillate/outputs/reports.php.

Kohl, J.E. (1841) Der Verkehr und die Ansiedelungen der Menschen in ihrer Abhängigkeit von der Gestaltung der Erdoberfläche [Road traffic and human settlement and their dependence on surface terrain], Dresden Arnoldische Buchhandlung, Dresden, Germany.

Kollo, H.P.H. and C.L. Purvis (1989) Regional Travel Forecasting System for the San Francisco Bay Area, *Transportation Research Record* 1220, 58–65.

Konduri, K.C., R.M. Pendyala, D. You, Y.-C. Chiu, M. Hickman, H. Noh, P. Waddell, L. Wang and B. Gardner (2014) The application of an integrated behavioral activity-travel simulation model for pricing policy analysis, in *Data Science and Simulation in Transportation Research*, D. Janssens, A.-U.-H. Yasar and L. Knapen (eds), IGI Global, Hershey, PA, 86–102.

Koopmans, T.C. (1949) Optimum utilization of the transportation system, *Econometrica* 17 (supplement), 136–146.

Koopmans, T.C. (ed) (1951) *Activity Analysis of Production and Allocation*, Wiley, New York.

Koppelman, F.S. (1975) Travel Prediction with Models of Individual Choice Behavior, Ph.D. thesis, Civil Engineering, Massachusetts Institute of Technology, Cambridge, MA.

Koppelman, F.S. (1976) Guidelines for aggregate travel predictions using disaggregate choice models, *Transportation Research Record* 610, 19–24.

Koppelman, F.S. and M.E. Ben-Akiva (1977) Aggregate forecasting with disaggregate travel demand models using normally available data, World Conference on Transport Research, Rotterdam.

Koppelman, F.S. and C. Bhat (2006) A Self Instructing Course in Mode Choice Modeling: Multinomial and Nested Logit Models, Federal Transit Administration, US Department of Transportation, Washington, DC, www.transportation.northwestern.edu/people/koppelman.

Koppelman, F. and J. Hauser (1979) Destination choice for non-grocery shopping trips, *Transportation Research Record* 673, 157–165.

Koppelman, F. and V. Sethi (2000) Closed-form discrete choice models, Chapter 13 in *Handbook of Transport Modelling*, D.A. Hensher and K.J. Button (eds), Pergamon, Amsterdam, 211–227.

Koppelman, F.S. and C.H. Wen (2000) The paired combinatorial logit model: properties, estimation and application, *Transportation Research Part B* 34 (2), 75–89.

Koppelman F.S. and C.G. Wilmot (1982) Transferability analysis of disaggregate travel choice models, *Transportation Research Record* 895, 18–24.

Kostyniuk, L.P. and R. Kitamura (1984) Temporal stability of urban travel patterns, *Transport Policy and Decision Making* 4, 481–500.

Kraft, G. (1963) Demand for Intercity Passenger Travel in the Washington–Boston Corridor, Systems Analysis and Research Corporation, Boston.

Kraft, G. and M. Wohl (1967) New directions for passenger demand analysis and forecasting, *Transportation Research* 1, 205–230.

Kreibich, V. (1979) Modelling car availability, modal split and trip distribution by Monte-Carlo simulation: a short way to integrated models, *Transportation* 8, 153–166.

Krishnamurthy, S. and K.M. Kockelman (2003) Propagation of uncertainty in transportation land use models: investigation of DRAM– EMPAL and UTPP predictions in Austin, Texas, *Transportation Research Record* 1831, 219–229.

Kroes, E.P. and R.J. Sheldon (1988) Stated preference methods: an introduction, *Journal of Transport Economics and Policy* 22, 11–24.

Kuhn, H.W. (1976) Nonlinear programming: a historical view, *Nonlinear Programming*, R. Cottle and C.E. Lemke (eds), *SIAM–AMS Proceedings* 9, 1–26.

Kuhn, H.W. (1991) Nonlinear programming: a historical note, in *History of Mathematical Programming*, J.K. Lenstra, A.H.G. Rinnooy Kan and A. Schrijver (eds), North-Holland, Amsterdam, 82–96.

Kuhn, H.W. (2002) Being in the right place at the right time, *Operations Research* 50 (1), 132–134.

Kuhn, H.W. and A.W. Tucker (1951) Nonlinear programming, in *Proceedings of the Second Berkeley Symposium on Mathematical Statistics and Probability*, J. Neyman (ed), University of California Press, Berkeley, 481–492.

Kuhn, T.S. (1962) *The Structure of Scientific Revolutions*, University of Chicago Press, Chicago.

Kutter, E. (1973) A model of individual travel behaviour, *Urban Studies* 10, 233–255.

Lagrange, J.L. (1813) *Théorie des Fonctions Analytiques*, M.V. Courcier, Paris.

Lagrange, J.L. (1888) *Mécanique Analytique*, 4th edn, Gauthier-Villars et fils, Paris.

Lakshmanan, T.R. and W.G. Hansen (1965) Market potential model and its application to a regional planning problem, *Highway Research Record* 102, 19–41.

Lam, W.H.K., Z.Y. Gao, K.S. Chan and H. Yang (1999) A stochastic user equilibrium assignment model for congested transit networks, *Transportation Research Part B* 33 (5), 351–368.

Lam, W.H.K., J. Zhou and Z.-H. Sheng (2002) A capacity restraint transit assignment with elastic line frequency, *Transportation Research Part B* 36 (10), 919–938.

Lancaster, K.J. (1966) A new approach to consumer theory, *Journal of Political Economy* 84, 132–157.

Lane, R., T.E. Powell and P. Prestwood-Smith (1971) *Analytic Transport Planning*, Gerald Duckworth, London.

Langdon, M. (1976) Modal split models for more than two modes, Urban Traffic Models, Annual Summer Meeting, Planning and Transport Research and Computation Co., Warwick.

Langdon, M.G. and C.G.B. Mitchell (1978) Personal Travel in Towns: The Development of Models That Reflect the Real World, TRRL Supplementary Report 369, Transport and Road Research Laboratory, Crowthorne, Berkshire.

Larsson, T., P.O. Lindberg, M. Patriksson and C. Rydergren (2002) On traffic equilibrium models with a nonlinear time/money relation, Chapter 2 in *Transportation Planning*, M. Patriksson and M. Labbé (eds), Kluwer, Dordrecht, 19–31.

Larsson, T. and M. Patriksson (1992) Simplicial decomposition with disaggregated representation for the traffic assignment problem, *Transportation Science* 26 (1), 4–17.

Larsson, T. and M. Patriksson (1994) Equilibrium characterizations of solutions to side constrained asymmetric traffic assignment models, *Le Matematiche* 49, 249–280.

Larsson, T. and M. Patriksson (1995) An augmented Lagrangean dual algorithm for link capacity side constrained traffic assignment problems, *Transportation Research Part B* 29 (6), 433–455.

Larsson, T. and M. Patriksson (1999) Side constrained traffic equilibrium models: analysis, computation and applications, *Transportation Research Part B* 33 (4), 233–264.

Lätzsch, L. and D. Lohse (1980) Straßennetzberechnung mit Kapazitätsbeschränkungen, *Die Straße* 20 (5), 148–154.

Lautso, K. and M. Wegener (2007) Integrated strategies for sustainable urban development, Chapter 8 in *Land Use and Transport*, S. Marshall and D. Banister (eds), Elsevier, Amsterdam, 153–175.

Lave, C.A. (1969) A behavioural approach to modal split forecasting, *Transportation Research* 3, 463–480.

Lawphongpanich, S. and D.W. Hearn (1984) Simplicial decomposition of the asymmetric traffic assignment problem, *Transportation Research Part B* 18 (2), 123–133.

LeBlanc, L.J. (1973) Mathematical Programming Algorithms for Large Scale Network Equilibrium and Network Design Problems, Ph.D. thesis, Industrial Engineering and Management Sciences, Northwestern University, Evanston, IL.

LeBlanc, L.J. and M. Abdulaal (1982) Combined mode split–assignment and distribution-model split-assignment models with multiple groups of travelers, *Transportation Science* 16 (4), 430–442.

LeBlanc, L.J. and K. Farhangian (1981) Efficient algorithms for solving elastic demand traffic assignment problems and mode-split assignment problems, *Transportation Science* 15 (4), 306–317.

LeBlanc, L.J., E.K. Morlok and W.P. Pierskalla (1974) An accurate and efficient approach to equilibrium traffic assignment on congested networks, *Transportation Research Record* 491, 12–23.

LeBlanc, L.J., E.K. Morlok and W.P. Pierskalla (1975) An efficient approach to solving the road network equilibrium traffic assignment problem, *Transportation Research* 9 (5), 309–318.

Lee, B., P. Gordon, H.W. Richardson and J.E. Moore, II (2009) Commuting trends in U.S. cities in the 1990s, *Journal of Planning Education and Research* 29 (1), 78–89.

Lee, D.B., Jr. (1973) Requiem for large-scale models, *Journal of the American Institute of Planners* 39, 163–178.

Lee, D.B. (1994) Retrospective on large-scale models, *Journal of the American Planning Association* 60, 35–40.

Lee, N. and M.Q. Dalvi (1969) Variations in the value of travel time, *Manchester School of Economic and Social Studies* 37, 213–236.

Lenntorp, B. (1976) Paths in space-time environments: a time geographic study of movement possibilities of individuals, *Lund Studies in Geography, Series B* 44, Lund University, Lund.

Lenntorp, B. (1978) A time-geographic simulation model of individual activity programmes, Chapter 9 in *Human Activity and Time Geography*, Volume 2, T. Carlstein, D. Parkes and N. Thrift (eds), Edward Arnold, London, 162–180.

Leonard, D.R. and J. Tough (1979) Validation work on CONTRAM – a model for use in the design of traffic management schemes, Summer Annual Meeting, Planning and Transport Research and Computation Co., Warwick.

Leonardi, G. and R. Tadei (1984) Random utility demand models and service location, *Regional Science and Urban Economics* 14, 399–431.

Leong, W. and D.A. Hensher (2012) Embedding decision heuristics in discrete choice models: a review, *Transport Reviews* 32, 313–331.

Leontief, W.W. and A. Strout (1963) Multi-regional input–output analysis, in *Structural Independence and Economic Development*, T. Barna (ed), Macmillan, London.

Lerman, S.R. (1976) Location, housing, automobile ownership, and mode to work: a joint choice model, *Transportation Research Record* 610, 6–11.

Lerman, S. and M.E. Ben-Akiva (1975) Disaggregate behavioural model of automobile ownership, *Transportation Research Record* 569, 43–51.

Lerman, S.R. and J.J. Louviere (1978) On the use of functional measurement to identify the functional form of the utility expression in travel demand models, *Transportation Research Record* 673, 78–86.

Lerman, S.R. and C.F. Manski (1979) Sample design for discrete choice analysis of travel behaviour: the state of the art, *Transportation Research Part A* 13, 29–44.

Lerman, S.R. and C.F. Manski (1981) On the use of simulated frequencies to approximate choice probabilities, in *Structural Analysis of Discrete Data with Econometric Applications*, C.F. Manski and D. McFadden (eds), MIT Press, Cambridge, MA, 305–319.

Leventhal, T., G.L. Nemhauser and L. Trotter, Jr. (1973) A column generation algorithm for optimal traffic assignment, *Transportation Science* 7 (2), 168–176.

Levinson, H.S. and K.R. Roberts (1965) System configuration in urban transportation planning, *Highway Research Record* 64, 71–83.

Li, Z. and D.A. Hensher (2010) Toll roads in Australia: an overview of characteristics and accuracy of demand forecasts, *Transport Reviews* 30, 541–569.

Li, Z. and D.A. Hensher (2011) Prospect theoretic contributions in understanding traveller behaviour: a review and some comments, *Transport Reviews* 31, 97–115.

Li, Z., D.A. Hensher and J.M. Rose (2010) Willingness to pay for travel time reliability in passenger transport: a review and some new empirical evidence, *Transportation Research Part E* 46, 384–403.

Liedtke, G. (2009) Principles of micro-behavior commodity transport modeling, *Transportation Research Part E* 45 (5), 795–809.

Lindberg, P.O., E.A. Eriksson and L.-G. Mattsson (1995) Invariance of achieved utility in random utility models, *Environment and Planning A* 27 (1), 121–142.

Lindsey, R. (2006) Do economists reach a conclusion on road pricing? The intellectual history of an idea, *Econ Journal Watch* 3 (2), 292–379.

Liou, P.S. and A.P. Talvitie (1974) Disaggregate access mode and station choice models for rail trips, *Transportation Research Record* 526, 42–65.

Lipsey, R.G. (1989) *An Introduction to Positive Economics*, 6th edn, Oxford University Press, Oxford.

Lisco, T.E. (1967) The Value of Commuters' Travel Time: A Study in Urban Transportation, Ph.D. thesis, Economics, University of Chicago, Chicago.

Lisco, T.E. (1975) Contemporary use of demand models in transportation project evaluation, Workshop on Recent Research Developments in Practical Transportation Planning, Committee on Traveler Behavior and Values, Annual Meeting, Transportation Research Board, Washington, DC.

Litman, T. (2010) Generated Traffic and Induced Travel: Implications for Transport Planning, Victoria Transport Policy Institute, Victoria, British Columbia.

Liu, R., D. Van Vliet and D. Watling (1995) DRACULA: dynamic route assignment combining user learning and microsimulation, Planning and Transport Research and Computation Co., Warwick.

Liu, R., D. Van Vliet and D. Watling (2006) Microsimulation models incorporating both demand and supply dynamics, *Transportation Research Part A* 40, 125–150.

Lo, H., C.W. Yip and K.H. Wan (2003) Modeling transfers and nonlinear fare structure in multi-modal network, *Transportation Research Part B* 37 (2), 149–170.

Lo, H., C.W. Yip and Q.H. Wan (2004) Modeling competitive multi-modal transit services: a nested logit approach, *Transportation Research Part C* 12 (3–4), 251–272.

Local Transport Today (2003) Editorial Comment: Timelords Need Challenging, LTT 366, 13.

Lohse, D. (1977) Berechnung von Personenverkehrsströmen [Calculation of passenger flows], *Wissenschaft und Technik im Straßenwesen*, Heft 17, Transpress, Berlin.

Lohse, D. (1997) *Verkehrsplanung*, Band 2, *Grundlagen der Strassenverkehrstechnik und Strassenverkehrsplanung* (with W. Schnabel), Verlag für Bauwesen, Berlin.

Lohse, D. (2011) *Verkehrsplanung*, Band 2, *Grundlagen der Strassenverkehrstechnik und der Verkehrsplanung* (with W. Schnabel) [Transport planning, Volume 2, Fundamentals of traffic engineering and transportation planning], Beuth, Berlin, www.beuth.de/de/artikel/strassenverkehrstechnik (accessed 11 November 2013).

Lohse, D., H. Teichert, B. Dugge and G. Bachner (1997) *Ermittlung von Verkehrsströmen mit n-linearen Gleichungssystemen unter Beachtung von Nebenbedingungen einschließlich Parameterschätzung (Verkehrsnachfragemodellierung: Erzeugung, Verteilung, Aufteilung)*, Schriftenreihe des Instituts für Verkehrsplanung und Straßenverkehr, Technische Universität Dresden, Dresden, Germany.

Lohse, D., H. Teichert, B. Dugge and G. Bachner (2005) *VISEVA – Simultanes Verkehrsnachfragemodell für den Personen- und Wirtschaftsverkehr Programmsystem*, Institut für Verkehrsplanung und Straßenverkehr, Technical University Dresden, Dresden, Germany.

Los Alamos National Laboratory (1998) The Dallas Case Study, TRANSIMS, DOT-T-99–04, US Department of Transportation, Washington, DC, media.tmiponline.org/clearinghouse/DOT-T-99–04/DOT-T-99–04.pdf (accessed 8 October 2013).

Los Alamos National Laboratory (2002) TRANSIMS Portland Study Reports, Volumes 0–5, 7, ndssl.vbi.vt.edu/transims-docs.php (accessed 7 October 2013).

Los Alamos National Laboratory (2003) TRANSIMS, Version 3.1, Volumes 2–7, ndssl.vbi.vt.edu/transims-docs.php (accessed 7 October 2013).

Louviere, J.J. (1979a) Modelling individual residential preferences: a totally disaggregated approach, *Transportation Research Part A* 13, 374–384.

Louviere, J.J. (1979b) Attitudes, attitudinal measurement and the relationship between attitudes and behaviour, Chapter 36 in *Behavioural Travel Modelling*, D.A. Hensher and P.R. Stopher (eds), Croom Helm, London, 782–794.

Louviere, J.J. (1988) Conjoint analysis modelling of stated preferences: a review of theory, methods, recent developments and external validity, *Journal of Transport Economics and Policy* 22, 93–119.

Louviere, J.J., D.H. Henley, G. Woodworth, R.J. Meyer, I.P. Levin, J.W. Stoner, D. Curry and D.A. Anderson (1980) Laboratory simulation versus revealed preference methods for estimating travel demand models, *Transportation Research Record* 794, 42–51.

Louviere, J.J. and D.A. Hensher (1982) On the design and analysis of simulated choice or allocation experiments in travel choice modelling, *Transportation Research Record* 890, 11–17.

Louviere, J.J. and D.A. Hensher (1983) Using discrete choice models with experimental design data to forecast consumer demand for a unique cultural event, *Journal of Consumer Research* 10, 348–361.

Louviere, J.J., D.A. Hensher and J. Swait (2000) *Stated Choice Methods*, Cambridge University Press, Cambridge.

Louviere, J.J., R. Meyer, F. Stetzer and L.L. Beavers (1973) Theory, Methodology and Findings in Mode Choice Behaviour, Working Paper No. 11, Institute of Urban and Regional Research, University of Iowa, Iowa City.

Louviere, J.J. and G.G. Woodworth (1983) Design and analysis of simulated choice or allocation experiments: an approach based on aggregate data, *Journal of Marketing Research* 20, 350–367.

Lowry, I.S. (1964) A Model of Metropolis, RAND Corporation, Santa Monica, CA.

Lowry, I.S. (1965) A short course in model design, *Journal of the American Institute of Planners* 31, 158–166.

Lowry, I.S. (1968) Seven models of urban development: a structural comparison, *Urban Development Models*, Special Report 97, Highway Research Board, 121–146.

Luce, R.D. (1959) *Individual Choice Behavior*, Wiley, New York.

Luce, R.D. and P. Suppes (1965) Preference, utility and subjective probability, in *Handbook of Mathematical Psychology*, Volume III, R.D. Luce, R. Bush and E. Galanter (eds), Wiley, New York.

Luce, R.D. and J.W. Tukey (1964) Simultaneous conjoint measurement: a new type of fundamental measurement, *Journal of Mathematical Psychology* 1, 1–27.

Lundgren, J.T. and M. Patriksson (1998) An algorithm for the combined distribution and assignment model, Chapter 16 in *Transportation Networks*, M.G.H. Bell (ed), Elsevier, Oxford, 239–253.

Maat, K., B. van Wee and D. Stead (2005) Land use and travel behaviour: expected effects from the perspective of utility theory and activity-based theories, *Environment and Planning B* 32, 33–46.

Mackett, R.L. (1983) Leeds Integrated Land-Use Transport Model (LILT), Supplementary Report SR791, Transport and Road Research Laboratory, Crowthorne, Berkshire.

Mackett, R.L. (1985) Micro-analytical simulation of locational and travel behaviour, Transportation Planning Methods, Summer Annual Meeting, Planning and Transport Research and Computation Co., Brighton.

Mackett, R.L. (1990a) The systematic application of the LILT model to Dortmund, Leeds and Tokyo, *Transport Reviews* 10, 323–338.

Mackett, R.L. (1990b) Comparative analysis of modelling land-use transport interaction at the micro and macro levels, *Environment and Planning A* 22, 459–475.

Mackett, R.L. (1990c) MASTER Model (Micro-Analytic Simulation of Transport, Employment and Residence), Report CR 237, Transport and Road Research Laboratory, Crowthorne, Berkshire.

Mackett, R.L. and M. Edwards (1998) The impact of new urban public transport systems: will the expectations be met?, *Transportation Research Part A* 32, 231–245.

Mackie, P.J. (1996) Induced traffic and economic appraisal, *Transportation* 23, 103–119.

Mackie, P.J. (2008) Who knows where the time goes?, A response to David Metz, *Transport Reviews* 28, 692–694.

Mackie, P.J. and P.W. Bonsall (1989) Traveller response to road improvements: implications for user benefits, *Traffic Engineering and Control* 30 (9), 411–416.

Mackie, P.J., S. Jara-Diaz and A.S. Fowkes (2001) The value of travel time savings in evaluation, *Transportation Research Part E* 37, 91–106.

Mackie, P.J., M. Wardman, A.S. Fowkes, G. Whelan, J. Nellthorp and J. Bates (2003) Values of Travel Time Savings in the UK, Final Report to UK Department for Transport, Institute for Transport Studies, University of Leeds, Leeds.

Mackinder, I.H. and S.E. Evans (1981) The Predictive Accuracy of British Transport Studies in Urban Areas, TRRL Supplementary Report 699, Transport and Road Research Laboratory, Crowthorne, Berkshire.

MacNicholas, M.J. and F.M. Collins (1971) A Transport Policy Model for Work Trips to a High Density City Centre, Universities Transport Study Group, University of Sheffield, Sheffield.

Magnanti, T.L. (1984) Models and algorithms for predicting urban traffic equilibria, in *Transportation Planning Models*, M. Florian (ed), Elsevier, Amsterdam, 153–185.

Mahmassani, H.S. (1988) Some comments on activity-based approaches to the analysis and prediction of travel behaviour, *Transportation* 15, 35–40.

Manheim, M.L. (1973) Practical implications of some fundamental properties of travel demand models, *Highway Research Record* 422, 21–38.

Manheim, M.L. (1979) *Fundamentals of Transportation Systems Analysis*, MIT Press, Cambridge, MA.

Manheim, M.L. and E.R. Ruiter (1970) DODOTRANS I: a decision-oriented computer language for analysis of multimode transportation systems, *Highway Research Record* 314, 135–163.

Mansfield, E. (1959) Book review of *Studies in the Economics of Transportation, Journal of Political Economy* 67 (5), 540.

Manski, C.F. (1977) The structure of random utility models, *Theory and Decision* 8, 229–254.

Manski, C.F. and S.R. Lerman (1977) The estimation of choice probabilities from choice based samples, *Econometrica* 45, 1977–1988.

Manski, C.F. and D. McFadden (1981) Alternative estimators and sample designs for discrete choice analysis, in *Structural Analysis of Discrete Data*, C.F. Manski and D. McFadden (eds), MIT Press, Cambridge, MA, 2–50.

Marcotte, P. (1985) A new algorithm for solving variational inequalities with application to the traffic assignment problem, *Mathematical Programming* 33 (3), 339–351.

Marcotte, P. and J. Guélat (1988) Adaptation of a modified Newton method for solving the asymmetric traffic equilibrium problem, *Transportation Science* 22 (2), 112–124.

Marcotte, P. and M. Patriksson (2007) Traffic equilibrium, Chapter 10 in *Transportation*, Handbooks in Operations Research and Management Science, Volume 14, C. Barnhart and G. Laporte (eds), Elsevier, Oxford, 623–713.

Marcotte, P. and L. Wynter (2004) A new look at the multiclass network equilibrium problem, *Transportation Science* 38 (3), 282–292.

Marschak, J. (1960) Binary choice constraints and random utility indicators, in *Mathematical Methods in the Social Sciences*, K. Arrow, S. Karlin and P. Suppes (eds), Stanford University Press, Stanford, CA, 312–329.

Marshall, S. and D. Banister (eds) (2007) *Land Use and Transport*, Elsevier, Amsterdam.

Martin, B.V. and M. Manheim (1965) A research program for comparison of traffic assignment techniques, *Highway Research Record* 88, 69–84.

Martin, B.V., F.W. Memmott, 3rd and A.J. Bone (1961) Principles and Techniques of Predicting Future Demand for Urban Area Transportation, Research Report No. 38, Massachusetts Institute of Technology, Cambridge, MA.

Martin, W.A. and N.A. McGuckin (1998) *Travel Estimation Techniques for Urban Planning*, Report 365, National Cooperative Highway Research Program, Transportation Research Board, Washington, DC.

Martinez, F.J. (1987) La forma incremental del modelo logit: aplicaciones, Actas del III Congreso Chileno de Ingenieria de Transporte, Universidad de Concepcion, Chile, 223–239.

Martinez, F.J. (1992) The bid-choice land use model: an integrated economic framework, *Environment and Planning A* 24, 871–885.

Mattsson, L.-G. (1987) Urban welfare maximisation and housing market equilibrium in a random utility setting, *Environment and Planning A* 19 (2), 247–261.

Mattsson, L.-G., J. Weibull and P.O. Lindberg (2014) Extreme values, invariance and choice probabilities, *Transportation Research Part B* 59, 81–95.

Matzoros, A. and D. Van Vliet (1992) A model of air pollution from road traffic, based on the characteristics of interrupted flow and junction control: Part 1 – model description; Part 2 – model results, *Transportation Research Part A* 26, 315–330, 331–355.

May, A.D. (2013) Balancing prescription and guidance for local transport plans, *Proceedings of the Institution of Civil Engineers – Transport* 166 (TR1), 36–48.

May, A.D. and B. Matthews (2007) Improved decision-making for sustainable transport, Chapter 15 in *Land Use and Transport*, S. Marshall and D. Banister (eds), Elsevier, Amsterdam, 335–361.

May, A.D. and D.S. Milne (2004) Effects of alternative road pricing schemes on network performance, *Transportation Research Part A* 34, 407–436.

May, A.D., M. Page and A. Hull (2008) Developing a set of policy support tools for sustainable urban transport in the UK, *Transport Policy* 15, 328–340.

May, A.D., S.P. Shepherd, G. Emberger, A. Ash, X. Zhang and N. Paulley (2005) Optimal land use – transport strategies: methodology and application to European cities, *Transportation Research Record* 1924, 129–138.

Mayberry, J.P. (1970) Structural requirements for abstract-mode models of passenger transportation, Chapter 5 in *The Demand for Travel*, R.E. Quandt (ed), Heath Lexington Books, Lexington, MA, 103–125.

McDonald, J.F. (1988) The first Chicago Area Transportation Study projections and plans for metropolitan Chicago in retrospect, *Planning Perspectives* 3, 245–268.

McFadden, D. (1968) The Revealed Preferences of a Government Bureaucracy, Technical Report W-17, Institute of International Studies, University of California Berkeley, Berkeley.

McFadden, D. (1973) Conditional logit analysis of qualitative choice behaviour, in *Frontiers in Econometrics*, P. Zarembka (ed), Academic Press, New York, 105–142.

McFadden, D. (1974) The measurement of urban travel demand, *Journal of Public Economics* 3, 303–328.

McFadden, D. (1976a) Quantal choice analysis: a survey, *Annals of Economic and Social Measurement* 5, 363–390.

McFadden, D. (1976b) The Theory and Practice of Disaggregate Demand Forecasting for Various Modes of Urban Transportation, Working Paper 7623, Urban Travel Demand Forecasting Project, University of California Berkeley, Berkeley; reprinted in T.H. Oum et al (eds) (1997) *Transport Economics*, Harwood, Amsterdam, 51–80.

McFadden, D. (1978) Modeling the choice of residential location, Chapter 3 in *Spatial Interaction Theory and Residential Location*, A. Karlqvist, L. Lundqvist, F. Snickars and J. Weibull (eds), North-Holland, Amsterdam, 75–96.

McFadden, D. (1981) Econometric models of probabilistic choice, in *Structural Analysis of Discrete Data*, C. Manski and D. McFadden (eds), MIT Press, Cambridge, MA, 198–272.

McFadden, D. (1986) The choice theory approach to market research, *Marketing Science* 5, 275–297.

McFadden, D. (1989) A method of simulated moments for estimation of discrete response models without numerical integration, *Econometrica* 57, 995–1026.

McFadden, D. (1997) Measuring willingness-to-pay for transportation improvements, Chapter 15 in *Theoretical Foundations of Travel Choice Modeling*, T. Gärling, T. Laitila and K. Westlin (eds), Pergamon, Oxford, 339–364.

McFadden, D. (1999) Rationality for economists?, *Journal of Risk and Uncertainty* 19 (1–3), 73–105.

McFadden, D. (2000a) Daniel L. McFadden – Autobiography, Nobel Prize, Stockholm, nobelprize.org/nobel_prizes/economics/ laureates/ 2000/mcfadden.html.

McFadden, D. (2000b) Disaggregate Behavioural Travel Demand's RUM Side: A 30-Year Retrospective, Department of Economics, University of California Berkeley, Berkeley; also in *Travel Behaviour Research*, D. Hensher (ed) (2001), Pergamon, Oxford, 17–63.

McFadden, D. (2001) Economic choices, *American Economic Review* 91, 351–378.

McFadden, D. (2002) The path to discrete choice models, *Access*, University of California Transportation Center, Berkeley, 2–7.

McFadden, D., S. Cosslett, G. Duguay and W. Jung (1977a) Demographic Data for Policy Analysis, Urban Travel Demand Forecasting Project, Phase I Final Report Series, Volume 8, Institute of Transportation Studies, University of California Berkeley, Berkeley.

McFadden, D. and F. Reid (1975) Aggregate travel demand forecasting from disaggregate demand models, *Transportation Research Record* 534, 24–37.

McFadden, D. and P.A. Ruud (1994) Estimation by simulation, *Review of Economics and Statistics* 76 (4), 591–608.

McFadden, D. and K. Train (1978) The goods/leisure trade-off and dis-aggregate work trip mode choice models, *Transportation Research* 12, 349–353.

McFadden, D. and K. Train (2000) Mixed MNL models for discrete response, *Journal of Applied Econometrics* 15, 447–470.

McFadden, D., K. Train and W. Tye (1977b) An application of diagnostic tests for the independence from irrelevant alternatives property of the multinomial logit model, *Transportation Research Record* 637, 39–46.

McGillivray, R.G. (1970) Demand and choice models of mode split, *Journal of Transport Economics and Policy* 4, 192–207.

McGuire, C.B. (1952) Highway Capacity and Traffic Congestion: A Preliminary Study, Cowles Commission Discussion Paper: Economics No. 2048, Cowles Commission for Research in Economics, Chicago.

McIntosh, P.T. and D.A. Quarmby (1972) Generalised costs and the estimation of movement costs and benefits in transport planning, *Highway Research Record* 383, 11–26; first issued as Mathematical Advisory Unit Note 179, UK Department of the Environment, London (1970).

McLachlan, K.A. (1949) Coordinate method of origin and destination analysis, *Proceedings*, Highway Research Board, Washington, DC, 349–367.

McLynn, J.M., A.J. Goldman, P.R. Meyers and R.H. Watkins (1967) Analysis of a Market Split Model, Technical Paper No. 8, Northeast Corridor Transportation Project, US Department of Transportation, Washington, DC.

McNally, M.G. (1997) An activity-based micro-simulation model for travel demand forecasting, in *Activity Based Approaches to Travel Demand Analysis*, D.F. Ettema and H.J.P. Timmermans (eds), Pergamon, London, 37–54.

McNally, M.G. (2000a) The four-step model, Chapter 3 in *Handbook of Transport Modelling*, D.A. Hensher and K.J. Button (eds), Pergamon, Amsterdam, 35–52.

McNally, M.G. (2000b) The activity-based approach, Chapter 4 in *Handbook of Transport Modelling*, D.A. Hensher and K.J. Button (eds), Pergamon, Amsterdam, 53–69.

Meneguzzer, C. (1995) An equilibrium route choice model with explicit treatment of the effect of intersections, *Transportation Research Part B* 29 (5), 329–356.

Meneguzzer, C. (1997) Review of models combining traffic assignment and signal control, *ASCE Journal of Transportation Engineering*, 123 (2), 148–155.

Meng, Q. and Z. Liu (2012) Mathematical models and computational algorithms for probit-based asymmetric stochastic user equilibrium problem with elastic demand, *Transportmetrica* 8 (4), 261–290.

Merchant, D.K. and G.L. Nemhauser (1978) A model and an algorithm for the dynamic traffic assignment problems, *Transportation Science* 12 (3), 183–199.

Mertz, W.L. (1960a) The use of electronic computers, *Traffic Engineering* 30 (8), 23–27, 54–55.

Mertz, W.L. (1960b) Traffic assignment to street and freeway systems, *Traffic Engineering* 30 (10), 27–33, 53.

Mertz, W.L. (1961) Review and evaluation of electronic computer traffic assignment programs, *Highway Research Bulletin* 297, 94–105.

Metaxatos, P., D.E. Boyce, M. Florian and I. Constantin (1995) Introducing 'feedback' among the origin–destination, mode and route choice steps of the urban travel forecasting procedure in the EMME/2 system, *Proceedings, Fifth National Transportation Planning Methods Applications Conference*, Volume I, Transportation Research Board, Washington, DC, 11–17.

Metcalfe, R. and P. Dolan (2012) Behavioural economics and its implications for transport, *Journal of Transport Geography* 24, 503–511.

Metz, D. (2008) The myth of travel time saving, *Transport Reviews* 28, 321–336.

Meyburg, A.H. and P.R. Stopher (1974) A framework for the analysis of demand for urban goods movement, *Transportation Research Record* 496, 68–79.

Miller, E.J. (2003) Land use: transportation modeling, Chapter 5 in *Transportation Systems Planning*, K.G. Goulias (ed), CRC Press, Boca Raton, FL.

Miller, E.J., J.D. Hunt, J.E. Abraham and P.A. Savini (2004) Microsimulating urban systems, *Computers, Environment and Urban Systems* 28, 9–44.

Miller, E.J. and M.J. Roorda (2003) Prototype model of household activity-travel scheduling, *Transportation Research Record* 1831, 114–121.

Mills, E.S. (1972) Markets and efficient resource allocation in urban areas, *Swedish Journal of Economics* 74 (1), 100–113.

Mirchandani, P. and H. Soroush (1987) Generalized traffic equilibrium with probabilistic travel times and perceptions, *Transportation Science* 21 (3), 133–152.

Mitchell, R.B. (1959) Metropolitan Planning for Land Use and Transportation, Office of Public Works Planning, White House, Washington, DC.

Mitchell, R.B. and C. Rapkin (1954) *Urban Traffic*, Columbia University Press, New York.

Mogridge, M.J.H. (1990) *Travel in Towns*, Macmillan, London.

Mogridge, M.J.H. (1997) The self-defeating nature of urban road capacity policy: a review of theories, disputes and available evidence, *Transport Policy* 4, 5–23.

Mokhtarian, P.L. (1990) A typology of relationships between telecommunications and transportation, *Transportation Research Part A* 24, 231–242.

Mokhtarian, P.L. (1991) Telecommunications and travel behaviour, *Transportation* 18, 287–289.

Mokhtarian, P.L. (2002) Telecommunications and travel: the case for complementarity, *Journal of Industrial Ecology* 6, 43–57.

Mokhtarian, P.L. and C. Chen (2004) TTB or not TTB, that is the question: a review and analysis of the empirical literature on travel time (and money) budgets, *Transportation Research Part A* 38, 643–675.

Mokhtarian, P.L. and I. Salomon (2002) Emerging travel patterns: do tel-ecommunications make a difference?, Chapter 7 in *In Perpetual Motion*, H.S. Mahmassani (ed), Elsevier, Oxford, 143–182.

Moore, E.F. (1957) The shortest path through a maze, International Symposium on the Theory of Switching, Harvard University; *Proceedings*, Part II, Annals of the Computation Laboratory of Harvard University, Volumes 29–30, 1959, 285–292.

Morgeson, D. (1994) TRANSIMS presentation, Los Alamos National Laboratory, in *Travel Model Improvement Program Conference Proceedings*, G.A. Shunk and P.L. Bass (eds), Fort Worth, TX, 39–59, ntl.bts.gov/DOCS/443 (accessed 7 October 2013).

Morikawa, T. (1989) Incorporating Stated Preference Data in Travel Demand Analysis, Ph.D. thesis, Civil Engineering, Massachusetts Institute of Technology, Cambridge, MA.

Morikawa, T. and K. Sasaki (1998) Discrete choice models with latent variables using subjective data, in *Travel Behaviour Research*, J. de D. Ortúzar, D.A. Hensher and S.R. Jara-Diaz (eds), Pergamon, Oxford, 435–455.

Morrison, J. and V. Loose (1995) TRANSIMS Model Design Criteria as Derived from Federal Legislation, US Department of Transportation, Washington, DC.

Moser, G. and S. Bamberg (2008) The effectiveness of soft transport policy measures: a critical assessment and meta-analysis of empirical evidence, *Journal of Environmental Psychology* 28, 10–26.

Moses, L.N. and H.F. Williamson (1963) Value of time, choice of mode and the subsidy use in urban transportation, *Journal of Political Economy* 71, 247–264.

Mosher, W.W., Jr. (1963) A capacity-restraint algorithm for assigning flow to a transport network, *Highway Research Record* 6, 41–70.

Munizaga, M.A. and R. Alvarez-Daziano (2005) Testing mixed logit and probit models by simulation, *Transportation Research Record* 1991, 53–62.

Muranyi, T.C. (1963) Trip Distribution and Traffic Assignment, Traffic Assignment Conference, Report 66,552, Chicago Area Transportation Study, Chicago.

Murchland, J.D. (1966a) An Introductory Lecture on Traffic Assignment by Digital Computer, Transport Network Theory Unit, London Graduate School of Business Studies, London.

Murchland, J.D. (1966b) Some Remarks on the Gravity Model of Traffic Distribution, and an Equivalent Maximization Formulation, Transport Network Theory Unit, London Graduate School of Business Studies, London.

Murchland, J.D. (1967) Two Remarks on Congested Assignment, Transport Network Theory Unit, London Graduate School of Business Studies, London.

Murchland, J.D. (1969) Road network traffic distribution in equilibrium, Conference on Mathematical Models in the Economic Sciences, Mathematisches Forschungsinstitut, Oberwolfach, Germany.

Murchland, J.D. (1970a) Road network traffic distribution in equilibrium, in *Mathematical Models in the Social Sciences*, Volume 8, R. Henn, H.P. Kunzi and H. Schubert (eds), Anton Hain Verlag, Meisenheim am Glan, 145–183 (in German).

Murchland, J.D. (1970b) Braess's paradox of traffic flow, *Transportation Research* 4 (4), 391–394.

Murchland, J.D. (1970c) A Fixed Matrix Method for All Shortest Distances in a Directed Graph and for the Inverse Problem, Doctor of Economic Science thesis, Universität (TH) Fridericiana, Karlsruhe, Germany.

Murchland, J.D. (1977) Congested assignment: test problems with known solutions, *Urban Transportation Planning*, P. Bonsall, Q. Dalvi and P.J. Hills (eds), Abacus, Tunbridge Wells, Kent, 129–146.

MVA (1998) *Traffic Impact of Highway Capacity Reductions*, Landor Publishing, London.

MVA (2005) Multi-Modal Model Data Provision, report for the Denvil Coombe Practice on behalf of the Integrated Transport and Economic Appraisal Division, UK Department for Transport, London.

MVA and John Bates Services (2000) Improved Elasticities and Methods, UK Department of the Environment, Transport and the Regions, London.

MVA Consultancy, Institute for Transport Studies, University of Leeds, and Transport Studies Unit, University of Oxford (1987) *The Value of Travel Time Savings*, Policy Journals, Newbury, Berkshire.

Nagel, K., R.J. Beckman and C.L. Barrett (1999) TRANSIMS for urban planning, presented at the 6th International Conference on Computers in Urban Planning and Urban Management, Venice, Italy.

Nagel, K. and M. Schreckenberg (1992) A cellular automaton model for freeway traffic, *Journal de Physique* 2 (12), 2221–2229.

Nagurney, A. (1986) Computational comparisons of algorithms for general asymmetric traffic equilibrium problems with fixed and elastic demands, *Transportation Research Part B* 20 (1), 78–84.

Nagurney, A. (1991) Equilibrium modeling, analysis and computation: the contributions of Stella Dafermos, *Operations Research* 39 (1), 9–12.

Nagurney, A. (1993) *Network Economics*, 2nd edn 1999, Kluwer, Boston.

Nagurney, A. and D. Boyce (2005) Preface to 'On a paradox of traffic planning', *Transportation Science* 39 (4), 443–445.

Nagurney, A. and D. Zhang (1996) *Projected Dynamical Systems and Variational Inequalities with Applications*, Kluwer, Boston.

Nash, J. (1951) Non-cooperative games, *Annals of Mathematics* 54 (2), 286–298.

Neffendorf, H., M. Wigan, R. Donnelly, I. Williams and M. Collop (2001) The emerging form of freight modelling, European Transport Conference, Cambridge.

Neidercorn, J.A. and B.V. Bechdolt, Jr. (1969) An economic derivation of the gravity law of spatial interaction, *Journal of Regional Science* 9, 273–282.

Nemhauser, G.L. (1991) Mathematical programming at Cornell and CORE: the super seventies, in *History of Mathematical Programming*, J.K. Lenstra, A.H.G. Rinnooy Kan and A. Schrijver (eds), Elsevier, Amsterdam, 114–118.

Netherlands Economic Institute (1997) Relationship between Demand for Freight Transport and Industrial Effects, Rotterdam.

Netter, M. (1972a) Affectations de trafic et tarification au coût marginal social: critique de quelques idées admises, *Transportation Research* 6 (4), 411–429.

Netter, M. (1972b) Equilibrium and marginal cost pricing on a road network with several traffic flow types, in *Traffic Flow and Transportation*, G.F. Newell (ed), American Elsevier, New York, 155–163.

Netter, M. and J.G. Sender (1970) Equilibre Offre–Demande et Tarification sur un Réseau de Transport, Institut de Recherche des Transports, Arcueil, France.

Neuberger, H. (1971) User benefit in the evaluation of transport and land use plans, *Journal of Transport Economics and Policy* 5 (1), 52–75.

Newell, G.F. (1980) *Traffic Flow on Transportation Networks*, MIT Press, Cambridge, MA.

Nguyen, S. (1974a) Une approche unifiée des méthodes d'équilibre pour l'affectation du trafic, Ph.D. thesis, Recherche Opérationnelle, Université de Montréal, Montréal.

Nguyen, S. (1974b) An algorithm for the traffic assignment problem, *Transportation Science* 8 (3), 203–216.

Nguyen, S. (1976) A unified approach to equilibrium methods for traffic assignment, in *Traffic Equilibrium Methods*, M. Florian (ed), Springer, Berlin, 148–182.

Nguyen, S. and C. Dupuis (1984) An efficient method for computing traffic equilibria in networks with asymmetric transportation costs, *Transportation Science* 18 (2), 185–202.

Nguyen, S. and S. Pallottino (1988) Equilibrium traffic assignment for large scale transit networks, *European Journal of Operational Research* 37 (2), 176–186.

Nie, Y. (2010) A class of bush-based algorithms for the traffic assignment problem, *Transportation Research Part B* 44 (1), 73–89.

Nie, Y. (2012) A note on Bar-Gera's algorithm for the origin-based traffic assignment problem, *Transportation Science* 46 (1), 27–38.

Nielsen, O.A. (2000) A stochastic transit assignment model considering differences in passengers utility functions, *Transportation Research Part B* 34 (5), 377–402.

Nielsen, O.A. (2004) A large scale stochastic multi-class schedule-based transit model with random coefficients, *Schedule-Based Dynamic Transit Modeling*, N.H.M. Wilson and A. Nuzzolo (eds), Kluwer, Boston, 53–77.

Nökel, K. and S. Wekeck (2009) Boarding and alighting in frequency-based transit assignment, *Transportation Research Record* 2111, 60–67.

Noland, R.B. and L.L. Lam (2002) A review of the evidence for induced travel and changes in transportation and environmental policy in the US and the UK, *Transportation Research Part D* 7, 1–26.

Noland, R.B. and J.W. Polak (2002) Travel time variability: a review of theoretical and empirical issues, *Transport Reviews* 22, 39–54.

Noland, R.B. and K.A. Small (1995) Travel-time uncertainty, departure time choice, and the cost of morning commutes, *Transportation Research Record* 1493, 150–158.

Ogden, K.W. (1992) *Urban Goods Movement*, Ashgate, Brookfield, VT.

Oi, W.Y. and P.W. Shuldiner (1962) *An Analysis of Urban Travel Demands*, Northwestern University Press, Evanston, IL.

Oppenheim, N. (1993a) Equilibrium trip distribution/assignment with variable destination costs, *Transportation Research Part B* 27 (3), 207–217.

Oppenheim, N. (1993b) A combined, equilibrium model of urban personal travel and goods movements, *Transportation Science* 27 (2), 161–173.

Oppenheim, N. (1995) *Urban Travel Demand Modeling*, Wiley, New York.

Orcutt, G.H., S. Caldwell and R.F. Wertheimer (1976) Policy Exploration through Microanalytic Simulation, Urban Institute, Washington, DC.

Orcutt, G.H., M. Greenberger, J. Korbel and A. Rivlin (1961) *Microanalysis of Socioeconomic Systems*, Harper, New York.

Orden, A. and L. Goldstein (1952) Symposium on Linear Inequalities and Programming, Planning Research Division, Director of Management Analysis Service, Comptroller, Headquarters US Air Force, Washington, DC.

Ortúzar, J. de D. (1979) Testing the Theoretical Accuracy of Travel Choice Models with Monte Carlo Simulation, Working Paper 125, Institute for Transport Studies, University of Leeds, Leeds.

Ortúzar, J. de D. (1983) Nested logit models for mixed-mode travel in urban corridors, *Transportation Research Part A* 17 (4), 283–299.

Ortúzar, J. de D. (2001) On the development of the nested logit model, *Transportation Research Part B* 35 (2), 213–216.

Ortúzar, J. de D., J. Armoogum, J.-L. Madre and F. Potier (2011) Continuous mobility surveys: the state of practice, *Transport Reviews* 31, 293–312.

Ortúzar, J. de D., N. Eluru and K.K. Srinivasan (2012) Methodological developments in activity-travel behaviour analysis, Chapter 19 in *Travel Behaviour Research in an Evolving World*, R.M. Pendyala and C.R. Bhat (eds), www.Lulu.com, 357–365.

Ortúzar, J. de D. and L.I. Rizzi (2007) Valuation of transport externalities by stated choice methods, in *Essays on Transport Economics*, P. Coto-Millán and V. Inglada (eds), Physica, Heidelberg, 249–272.

Ortúzar, J. de D. and L.G. Willumsen (2011) *Modelling Transport*, 4th edn, Wiley, Chichester, West Sussex.

Oryani, K. and B. Harris (1997) Review of land use models: theory and application, *Proceedings, Sixth Transportation Planning Applications Conference*, R. Donnelly and J. Dunbar (eds), Transportation Research Board, Washington, DC, 80–91.

Overgaard, K.R. (1967) Testing a traffic assignment algorithm, in *Vehicular Traffic Science*, L.C. Edie, R. Herman and R. Rothery (eds), American Elsevier, New York, 215–221.

Owens, S. (1995) From 'predict and provide' to 'predict and prevent'? Pricing and planning in transport policy, *Transport Policy* 2, 43–49.

Owers, J. and M.H. Echenique (eds) (1994) Research into practice: the work of the Martin Centre in urban and regional modelling, *Environment and Planning B* 21, 513–650.

Pang, J.S. and D. Chan (1982) Iterative methods for variational and complementarity problems, *Mathematical Programming* 24 (1), 284–313.

Parkes, D.N. and N.J. Thrift (1975) Timing space and spacing time, *Environment and Planning A* 7, 551–570.

Parsons Brinckerhoff Quade & Douglas (2005) Transportation Model and Data Initiative, New York Best Practice Model, General Final Report to New York Metropolitan Transportation Council, New York, www.nymtc.org/project/BPM/model/bpm_finalrpt.pdf (accessed 8 October 2013).

Parthasarathi, P. and D. Levinson (2010) Post construction evaluation of traffic forecast accuracy, *Transport Policy* 17, 428–443.

Pas, E.I. (1984) The effect of selected socio-demographic characteristics on daily travel-activity behavior, *Environment and Planning A* 16, 571–581.

Pas, E.I. (1998) Time in travel choice modeling: from relative obscurity to center stage, Chapter 10 in *Theoretical Foundations of Travel Choice Modeling*, T. Gärling, T. Laitila and K. Westin (eds), Elsevier, Amsterdam, 231–250.

Pas, E.I. and A.S. Harvey (1997) Time use research and travel demand analysis and modelling, in *Understanding Travel Behaviour in an Era of Change*, P. Stopher and M. Lee-Gosselin (eds), Elsevier, Oxford, 315–338.

Patriksson, M. (1993) Partial linearization methods in nonlinear programming, *Journal of Optimization Theory and Applications* 78 (2), 227–246.

Patriksson, M. (1994) *The Traffic Assignment Problem*, VSP, Utrecht.

Patriksson, M. and M. Labbé (eds) (2002) *Transportation Planning*, Kluwer, Dordrecht.

Paulley, N. (2002) Recent studies on key issues in road pricing, *Transport Policy* 9, 175–177.

Paulley, N. and F.V. Webster (1991) Overview of an international study to compare models and evaluate land-use and transport policies, *Transport Reviews* 11, 197–222.

Pearmain, D. and E. Kroes (1990) Stated Preference Techniques: A Guide to Practice, Steer Davies and Gleave, London, and Hague Consulting Group, The Hague.

Peat, Marwick, Livingston & Co. (1967) Urban Planning System/360, Trip Distribution Programs, Federal Highway Administration, Washington, DC.

Peat, Marwick, Mitchell & Co. (1972) Implementation of the n-Dimensional Logit Model, Final Report to the Comprehensive Planning Organization, San Diego County, California.

Pendyala, R.M., K.G. Goulias and R. Kitamura (1991) Impact of telecommuting on spatial and temporal patterns of household travel, *Transportation* 18, 303–409.

Pendyala, R.M., R. Kitamura and D.V.G.P. Reddy (1998) Application of an activity-based travel demand model incorporating a rule-based algorithm, *Environment and Planning B* 25, 753–772.

Pendyala, R.M., R. Kitamura, A. Kikuchi, T. Yamamoto and S. Fujii (2005) Florida Activity Mobility Simulator: overview and preliminary validation results, *Transportation Research Record* 1921, 123–130.

Pendyala, R.M., K.C. Konduri, Y.-C. Chiu, M. Hickman, H. Noh, P. Waddell, L. Wang, D. You and B. Gardner (2012) Integrated land use-transport model system with dynamic time-dependent activity-travel microsimulation, *Transportation Research Record* 2303, 19–27.

Penn Jersey Transportation Study (1959) Prospectus, Philadelphia.

Pfaffenbichler, P., G. Emberger and S. Shepherd (2007) The integrated dynamic land use and transport model MARS, *Networks and Spatial Economics* 8, 183–200.

Pick, G.W. and J. Gill (1970) New developments in category analysis, Urban Traffic Model Research, Planning and Transport Research and Computation Co., London.

Pickrell, D. (1989) Urban Rail Transit Projects: Forecast versus Actual Ridership and Costs, Transportation Systems Center, US Department of Transportation, Washington, DC.

Pickrell, D.H. (1992) A desire named streetcar, *Journal of the American Planning Association* 58, 158–176.

Pickup, L. and S.W. Town (1983) The role of social science methodologies in transport planning, in *Recent Advances in Travel Demand Analysis*, S. Carpenter and P. Jones (eds), Gower, Aldershot, Hampshire.

Pigou, A.C. (1918) *The Economics of Welfare*, Macmillan, New York.

Pinjari, A.R. and C.R. Bhat (2011) Activity-based travel demand analysis, Chapter 10 in *Handbook of Transport Economics*, A. de Palma, R. Lindsey, E. Quinet and R. Vickerman (eds), Edward Elgar Publishing, Cheltenham, UK, and Northampton, MA, USA, 213–248.

Plourde, R.P. (1968) Consumer Preference and the Abstract Mode Model: Boston Metropolitan Area, Research Report R68–51, Massachusetts Institute of Technology, Cambridge, MA.

Popper, K.R. (1959) *The Logic of Scientific Discovery*, Hutchinson, New York.

Potts, R.B. and R.M. Oliver (1972) *Flows in Transportation Networks*, Academic Press, New York.

Powell, W.B. and Y. Sheffi (1982) The convergence of equilibrium algorithms with predetermined step sizes, *Transportation Science* 16 (1), 45–55.

Pradhan, A. and K.M. Kockelman (2002) Uncertainty propagation in an integrated land use – transportation modeling framework: output variation via UrbanSim, *Transportation Research Record* 1805, 128–135.

Prager, W. (1954) Problems of traffic and transportation, Proceedings, Symposium on Operations Research in Business and Industry, Midwest Research Institute, Kansas City, MO, 105–113.

Prager, W. (1955) On the role of congestion in transportation problems, *Zeitschrift für Angewandte Mathematik und Mechanik* 35, 264–268.

Prager, W. (1956–57) Book review of *Studies in the Economics of Transportation*, *Quarterly of Applied Mathematics* 14, 445.

Prais, S.J. and C.B. Winsten (1954) Trend Estimators and Serial Correlation, Cowles Commission Discussion Paper No. 383, Cowles Commission for Research in Economics, Chicago.

Pratt, R.H., K.F. Turnbull, J.E. Evans, IV, B.E. McCollom, F. Spielberg, E. Vaca and J.R. Kuzmyak (2000) *Traveler Response to Transportation System Changes: Interim Handbook*, Transit Cooperative Research Program, Transportation Research Board, Washington, DC.

Prekopa, A. (1980) On the development of optimization theory, *American Mathematical Monthly* 87 (7), 527–542.

Prestwood-Smith, P. (1977) The development of transport objectives, Chapter 2 in *Urban Transportation Planning*, P.W. Bonsall, Q.M. Dalvi and P.J. Hills (eds), Abacus, Tunbridge Wells, Kent, 7–20.

Putman, S.H. (1975) Urban land use and transportation models: a state-of-the-art summary, *Transportation Research* 9 (2–3), 187–202.

Putman, S.H. (1983) *Integrated Urban Models*, Pion, London.

Putman, S.H. (1991) *Integrated Urban Models* 2, Pion, London.

Putman, S.H. (1998) Results from implementation of integrated transportation and land use models in metropolitan regions, in *Network Infrastructure and the Urban Environment*, L. Lundqvist, L.-G. Mattsson and T.J. Kim (eds), Springer, Berlin, 268–287.

Putman, S.H. (2001) *Integrated Transportation and Land Use Forecasting: Sensitivity Tests of Alternative Model Systems Configuration*, Travel Model Improvement Program, US Department of Transportation and US Environmental Protection Agency, Washington, DC, ntl.bts.gov/lib/18000/18300/18370/PB2001108460.pdf (accessed 7 January 2013).

Pyers, C.E. (1966) Evaluation of intervening opportunities trip distribution model, *Highway Research Record* 114, 71–98.

Quandt, R.E. (1960) Models of transportation and optimal network construction, *Journal of Regional Science* 2 (1), 27–45.

Quandt, R.E. (1968) Estimation of modal splits, *Transportation Research* 2, 41–50.

Quandt, R.E. (ed) (1970) *The Demand for Travel*, Heath Lexington Books, Lexington, MA.

Quandt, R.E. and W.J. Baumol (1966) The demand for abstract modes: theory and measurement, *Journal of Regional Science* 6, 13–26.

Quarmby, D.A. (1967) Choice of travel mode for the journey to work, *Journal of Transport Economics and Policy* 1, 273–314.

Quigley, J.M. (1976) Housing demand in the short run: an analysis of polytomous choice, *Explorations in Economic Research* 3 (1), National Bureau of Economic Research, New York, 76–102.

Rasouli, S. and H. Timmermans (2012) Uncertainty in travel demand forecasting models: literature review and research agenda, *Transportation Letters* 4, 55–73.

Rassam, P., R. Ellis and J. Bennett (1971) The n-dimensional logit model: development and application, *Highway Research Record* 369, 135–147.

Ratrout, N.T. and S.M. Rahman (2009) A comparative analysis of currently used microscopic and macroscopic traffic simulation software, *Arabian Journal for Science and Engineering* 34, 123–132.

Raveau, S., R. Alvarez-Daziano, M.F. Yáñez, D. Bolduc and J. de D. Ortúzar (2010) Sequential and simultaneous estimation of hybrid discrete choice models: some new findings, *Transportation Research Record* 2156, 131–139.

Recker, W.W. (2001) A bridge between travel demand modeling and activity-based travel analysis, *Transportation Research Part B* 35, 481–506.

Recker, W.W., M.G. McNally and G.S. Root (1986) A model of complex travel behaviour: Part I, theoretical development; Part II, an operational model, *Transportation Research Part A* 20, 307–318, 319–330.

Reichman, S. and P.R. Stopher (1971) Disaggregate stochastic models of travel-mode choice, *Highway Research Record* 369, 91–103.

Resource Decision Consultants (1995) Activity-Based Modeling System for Travel Demand Forecasting, US Department of Transportation, Washington, DC, media.tmiponline.org/clearinghouse/amos/amos.pdf (accessed 8 October 2013).

Revelt, D. and K. Train (1998) Mixed logit with repeated choices: households' choices of appliance efficiency level, *Review of Economics and Statistics* 80, 647–657.

Rho, J.H. and T.J. Kim (1989) Solving a three-dimensional urban activity model of land use intensity and transport congestion, *Journal of Regional Science* 29 (4), 595–613.

Richards, M.G. (2006) *Congestion Charging in London*, Palgrave Macmillan, Basingstoke, Hampshire.

Richards, M.G. and M.E. Ben-Akiva (1975) *A Disaggregate Travel Demand Model*, Lexington Books, Lexington, MA.

Richardson, A.J., E.S. Ampt and A.H. Meyburg (1995) *Survey Methods for Transport Planning*, Eucalyptus, Melbourne.

Road Charging Options for London (ROCOL) Working Group (2000) *Road Charging Options for London: A Technical Assessment*, Her Majesty's Stationery Office, London.

Robbins, H. and S. Monroe (1951) A stochastic approximation method, *Annals of Mathematical Statistics* 22 (3), 400–407.

Roberts, M. and D.C. Simmonds (1997) A strategic modelling approach for urban transport policy development, *Traffic Engineering and Control* 38, 377–384.

Robertson, C.A. and D. Strauss (1981) A characterization theorem for random utility variables, *Journal of Mathematical Psychology* 23, 184–189.

Robertson, D.I. (1969) TRANSYT: a traffic network study tool, Report LR 253, Transport and Road Research Laboratory, Crowthorne, Berkshire.

Robillard, P. (1974) Calibration of Dial's assignment method, *Transportation Science* 8 (2), 117–125.

Rockafellar, R.T. (1967) Convex programming and systems of elementary monotonic relations, *Journal of Mathematical Analysis and Applications* 19 (3), 543–564.

Roden, D. (2009) Implementing DTA for the White House Area Transportation Study, Travel Model Improvement Program, Federal Highway Administration, Washington, DC.

Rogers, K.G., G.M. Townsend and A.E. Metcalfe (1970) Planning for the Work Journey – A Generalised Explanation of Modal Choice, Report C67, Local Government Operational Research Unit, Reading, Berkshire.

Rohr, C. (2005) The PRISM Model: Evidence on Model Hierarchy and Parameter Values, Report for the UK Department for Transport, RAND Europe, Cambridge.

Rohr, C., A. Daly, J. Fox, B. Patruni, T. van Vuren and G. Hyman (2012) Manchester Motorway Box: post survey research on induced traffic effects, *Planning Review* 48, 24–39.

Roorda, M.J., E.J. Miller and K.M.N. Habib (2008) Validation of TASHA: a 24-hr activity scheduling microsimulation model, *Transportation Research Part A* 42, 360–375.

Roos, D. (1966) *ICES System Design*, MIT Press, Cambridge, MA.

Rose, J.M. and M.C.J. Bliemer (2008) Stated preference experimental design strategies, Chapter 8 in *Handbook of Transport Modelling*, 2nd edn, D.A. Hensher and K.J. Button (eds), Elsevier, Amsterdam, 151–180.

Rose, J.M. and M.C.J. Bliemer (2009) Constructing efficient stated choice experimental designs, *Transport Reviews* 29, 587–617.

Rose, J.M. and M.C.J. Bliemer (2013) Stated Choice Experimental Design Theory: The Who, the What and the Why, Institute of Transport and Logistics Studies, University of Sydney, Australia.

Rose, J.M. and D.A. Hensher (2014) Toll roads are only part of the overall trip: the error of our ways in past willingness to pay studies, *Transportation* 41 (4), 819–837.

Rossi, T.F., S. McNeil and C. Hendrickson (1989) Entropy model for consistent impact fee assessment, *ASCE Journal of Urban Planning and Development*, 115 (2), 51–63.

Rossi, T. and Y. Shiftan (1997) Tour based travel demand modeling in the US, *Eighth Symposium on Transportation Systems*, Volume 1, Chania, Greece, 409–414.

Royal Swedish Academy of Sciences (2000) *The Scientific Contributions of James Heckman and Daniel McFadden*, Bank of Sweden Prize in Economic Sciences in Memory of Alfred Nobel, Stockholm.

RSG, AECOM, M. Bradley, J. Bowman, M. Hadi, R. Pendyala, C. Bhat, T. Waller, and North Florida Transportation Planning Organization (2014) Dynamic, Integrated Model System: Jacksonville-Area Application, SHRP 2 Report S2-C10A-RW-1, Transportation Research Board, Washington, DC.

Ruiter, E.R. (1967) Improvements in understanding, calibrating and applying the opportunity model, *Highway Research Record* 165, 1–21.

Ruiter, E.R. (1992) Development of an Urban Truck Travel Model for the Phoenix Metropolitan Area, Final Report to the Arizona Department of Transportation, Cambridge Systematics, Cambridge, MA.

Ruiter, E.R. and M.E. Ben-Akiva (1978) Disaggregate travel demand models for the San Francisco area: system structure, component models and application procedures, *Transportation Research Record* 673, 121–128.

Sacks, J., W.J. Welch, T.J. Mitchell and H.P. Wynn (1989) Design and analysis of computer experiments, *Statistical Science* 4 (4), 409–435.

Safwat, K.N.A. and T.L. Magnanti (1988) A combined trip generation, trip distribution, modal split, and trip assignment model, *Transportation Science* 22 (1), 14–30.

Salomon, I. (1986) Telecommunications and travel relationships: a review, *Transportation Research Part A* 20, 223–238.

Salvini, P.A. and E.J. Miller (2005) ILUTE: an operational prototype of a comprehensive microsimulation model of urban systems, *Networks and Spatial Economics* 5, 217–234.

Samuelson, P.A. (1970) *Economics*, 8th edn, McGraw-Hill, New York.

Sanko, N. (2014) Travel demand forecasts improved by using cross-sectional data from multiple time points, *Transportation* 41 (4), 673–695.

Sayer, R.A. (1976) A critique of urban modelling: from regional science to urban and regional political economy, *Progress in Planning* 6 (3), 187–254.

Schafer, A. and D.G. Victor (2000) The future mobility of the world population, *Transportation Research Part A* 34, 171–205.

Scheff, H. (1977) Fighting the Chicago Crosstown, Appendix B, *The End of the Road, A Citizen's Guide to Transportation Problemsolving*, National Wildlife Federation, Washington, DC.

Schittenhelm, H. (1990) On the integration of an effective assignment algorithm with path and path-flow management in a combined trip distribution and traffic assignment algorithm, Transportation Planning Methods, Summer Annual Meeting, Planning and Transport Research and Computation Co., Brighton.

Schneider, M. (1959) Gravity models and trip distribution theory, *Papers, Regional Science Association* 5, 51–56.

Schneider, M. (1960) Panel discussion on inter-area travel formulas, *Highway Research Bulletin* 253, 134–138.

Schneider, M. (1974) Probability maximization in networks, in *Proceedings, International Conference on Transportation Research*, Transportation Research Forum, Chicago, 738–755.

Schofer, R.E. and F.F. Goodyear (1967) Electronic computer applications in urban transportation planning, *Proceedings of the 22nd National Conference*, Association of Computing Machinery, 247–253.

Schwartz, D.M. (1962) Roads without end, Section Two, *Chicago Sunday Sun-Times*, Chicago, 16 September.

Scott Wilson Kirkpatrick & Partners (1969) Greater Glasgow Transportation Study, Glasgow.

Seidman, D.R. (1964) Report on the Activities Allocation Model, PJ Paper No. 22, Penn Jersey Transportation Study, Philadelphia.

Seidman, D.R. (1969) Construction of an Urban Growth Model, DVRPC Report No. 1, Technical Supplement, Volume A, Delaware Valley Regional Planning Commission, Philadelphia.

SELNEC Transportation Study (1971) The Mathematical Model, Technical Working Paper No. 5, Manchester.

SELNEC Transportation Study (1972) Calibration of the Mathematical Model, Technical Working Paper No. 7, Manchester.

Sen, A. and T.E. Smith (1995) *Gravity Models of Spatial Interaction Behavior*, Springer, Berlin.

Senior, M.L. and H.C.W.L. Williams (1977) Model based transport policy assessment, 1: the use of alternative forecasting models, *Traffic Engineering and Control* 18, 402–406.

Senior, M.L. and A.G. Wilson (1974) Explorations and syntheses of linear programming and spatial interaction models of residential location, *Geographical Analysis* 6, 209–238.

Ševčíková, H., A. Raftery and P. Waddell (2007) Assessing uncertainty in urban simulations using Bayesian melding, *Transportation Research Part B* 41 (6), 652–659.

Shahkarami, M. and N. Raha (2002) Urban freight modelling – the ways ahead, European Transport Conference, Cambridge.

Sheffi, Y. (1985) *Urban Transportation Networks*, Prentice Hall, Englewood Cliffs, NJ.

Sheffi, Y. and C.F. Daganzo (1978) Hypernetworks and supply–demand equilibrium obtained with disaggregate demand models, *Transportation Research Record* 673, 113–121.

Sheffi, Y. and W. Powell (1981) A comparison of stochastic and deterministic traffic assignment over congested networks, *Transportation Research Part B* 15 (1), 53–64.

Sheffi, Y. and W. Powell (1982) An algorithm for the equilibrium assignment problem with random link times, *Networks* 12 (2), 191–207.

Sheldon, R.J. and J.K. Steer (1982) The use of conjoint analysis in transport research, Summer Annual Meeting, Planning and Transport Research and Computation Co., Warwick.

Shepherd, S.P., J. Shires, A. Koh, N. Marler and A. Jopson (2006a) Review of Modelling Capabilities: Enhanced Analytical Decision Support Tools, Institute for Transport Studies, University of Leeds, Leeds.

Shepherd, S.P., P.M. Timms and A.D. May (2006b) Modelling requirements for local transport plans: an assessment of English experience, *Transport Policy* 13, 307–317.

Shepherd, S.P., X. Zhang, G. Emberger, M. Hudson, A.D. May and N. Paulley (2006c) Designing optimal urban transport strategies: the role of individual policy instruments and the impact of financial constraints, *Transport Policy* 13, 49–65.

Shrouds, J.M. (1995) Challenges and opportunities for transportation: implementation of the Clean Air Act Amendments of 1990 and the Intermodal Surface Transportation Efficiency Act of 1991, *Transportation* 22, 193–215.

Shuldiner, P.W. (1962) Trip generation and the home, *Highway Research Bulletin* 347, 40–59.

Simmonds, D.C. (1994) The 'Martin Centre Model' in practice: strengths and weaknesses, *Environment and Planning B* 21, 619–628.

Simmonds, D.C. (2001) The objectives and design of a new land-use modelling package: DELTA, Chapter 9 in *Regional Science in Business*, G. Clarke and M. Madden (eds), Springer, Berlin, 159–188.

Simmonds, D.C. and O. Feldman (2011) Alternative approaches to spatial modelling, *Research in Transportation Economics* 31, 2–11.

Simmonds, D.C. and B.G. Still (1998) DELTA/START: adding land use analysis to integrated transport models, World Conference on Transport Research, Antwerp.

Simmonds, D., P. Waddell and M. Wegener (2013) Equilibrium versus dynamics in urban modelling, *Environment and Planning B* 40, 1051–1070.

Simon, H.A. (1957) *Models of Man*, Wiley, New York.

Slavin, H.L. (1976) Demand for urban goods vehicle trips, *Transportation Research Record* 591, 32–37.

Slavin, H.L. (2004) The role of GIS in land use and transport planning, Chapter 19 in *Handbook of Transport Geography and Spatial Systems*, D.A. Hensher, K.J. Button, K.E. Haynes and P. Stopher (eds), Elsevier, Oxford, 329–356.

Slavin, H., Z. Tarem, E.A. Ziering and R. Brickman (1988) RailRider – a comprehensive commuter rail forecasting model, *Transportation Research Record* 1162, 8–15.

Sloman, L., S. Cairns, C. Newson, J. Anable, A. Pridmore and P. Goodwin (2010) The Effects of Smarter Choice Programmes in the Sustainable Travel Towns: Summary Report, UK Department for Transport, London.

Small, K.A. (1982) The scheduling of consumer activities: work trips, *American Economic Review* 72, 467–479.

Small, K.A. (1987) A discrete choice model for ordered alternatives, *Econometrica* 44, 409–424.

Small, K.A. (1992) *Urban Transport Economics*, Harwood, Chur, Switzerland.

Small, K.A. (2012) Valuation of travel time, *Economics of Transportation* 1, 2–14.

Small, K.A. and H.S. Rosen (1981) Applied welfare economics with discrete choice models, *Econometrica* 49, 104–130.

Small, K.A. and E.T. Verhoef (2007) *The Economics of Urban Transportation*, Routledge, Oxford.

Small, K.A., C. Winston and J. Yan (2005) Uncovering the distribution of motorists' preferences for travel time and reliability, *Econometrica* 73, 1367–1382.

Smeed, R.J. (1957) Book review of *Studies in the Economics of Transportation*, *Economic Journal* 67 (265), 116–118.

Smith, L., R. Beckman, K. Baggerly, D. Anson and M. Williams (1995) *TRANSIMS: TRansportation ANalysis and SIMulation System*, Project Summary and Status, report by the Los Alamos National Laboratory to US Department of Transportation and US Environmental Protection Agency, Washington, DC, ntl.bts.gov/DOCS/466.html (accessed 7 October 2013).

Smith, M.J. (1979) The existence, uniqueness and stability of traffic equilibria, *Transportation Research Part B* 13 (4), 295–304.

Smith, M.J. (1984) A descent algorithm for solving monotone variational inequalities and monotone complementarity problems, *Journal of Optimization Theory and Applications* 44 (3), 485–496.

Smith, T.E. (1978a) A cost-efficiency principle of spatial interaction behavior, *Regional Science and Urban Economics* 8 (4), 313–337.

Smith, T.E. (1978b) A general efficiency principle of spatial interaction, Chapter 4 in *Spatial Interaction Theory and Planning Models*, A. Karlqvist, L. Lundqvist, F. Snickars and J.W. Weibull (eds), North-Holland, Amsterdam, 97–118.

Smith, T.E. (1983) A cost-efficiency approach to the analysis of congested spatial interaction behavior, *Environment and Planning A* 15 (4), 435–464.

Smith, T.E. (1988) A cost-efficiency theory of dispersed network equilibria, *Environment and Planning A* 20 (2), 231–266.

Smock, R.B. (1962) An iterative assignment approach to capacity restraint on arterial networks, *Highway Research Bulletin* 347, 60–66.

Smock, R.B. (1963) A comparative description of a capacity-restrained traffic assignment, *Highway Research Record* 6, 12–40.

Snickars, F. and J.W. Weibull (1977) A minimum information principle: theory and practice, *Regional Science and Urban Economics* 7, 137–168.

Sobel, K.L. (1980) Travel demand forecasting by using the nested multinomial logit model, *Transportation Research Record* 775, 48–55.

Sosslau, A.B., A.B. Hassam, M.M. Carter and G.V. Wickstrom (1978) *Quick-Response Urban Travel Estimation Techniques and Transferable Parameters: User's Guide*, Report 187, National Cooperative Highway Research Program, Transportation Research Board, Washington, DC.

Southworth, F. (1982) An urban goods movement model: framework and some results, *Papers, Regional Science Association* 50, 165–184.

Southworth, F. (2003) Freight transportation planning: models and methods, Chapter 4 in *Transportation Systems Planning*, K.G. Goulias (ed), CRC Press, Boca Raton, FL.

Southworth, F. (2011) Modeling freight flows, Chapter 14 in *Intermodal Transportation, Moving Freight in a Global Economy*, L.A. Hoel, G. Giuliano and M.D. Meyer (eds), Eno Transportation Foundation, Washington, DC, 423–463.

Southworth, F., Y.J. Lee and D. Zavattero (1983a) A Motor Freight Planning Model for Chicago, Planning Working Paper No. 83–3, Chicago Area Transportation Study, Chicago.

Southworth, F., Y.J. Lee, C.S. Griffin and D. Zavattero (1983b) Strategic freight planning for Chicago in the year 2000, *Transportation Research Record* 920, 45–48.

Spear, B.D. (1976) Attitudinal modeling: its role in travel-demand forecasting, Chapter 4 in *Behavioral Travel-Demand Models*, P.R. Stopher and A.H. Meyburg (eds), Lexington Books, Lexington, MA, 89–98.

Spear, B.D. (1977) Applications of New Travel Demand Forecasting Techniques to Transportation Planning: A Study of Individual Choice Models, Federal Highway Administration, US Department of Transportation, Washington, DC.

Spear, B.D. (1996) New approaches to transportation forecasting models: a synthesis of four research proposals, *Transportation* 23, 215–240.

Spence, R. (1968) A critical assessment, *Transportation Engineering*, Conference Proceedings, Institution of Civil Engineers, London, 35–44.

Spiess, H. and M. Florian (1989) Optimal strategies: a new assignment model for transit networks, *Transportation Research Part B* 23 (2), 83–102.

Standing Advisory Committee on Trunk Road Assessment (1994) *Trunk Roads and the Generation of Traffic*, UK Department of Transport, London.

Standing Advisory Committee on Trunk Road Assessment (1999) *Transport and the Economy*, UK Department of the Environment, Transport and the Regions, London.

Starkie, D.N.M. (1973) Transportation planning and public policy, *Progress in Planning* 4, 313–389.

Steel, M.A. (1965) Capacity restraint – a new technique, *Traffic Engineering and Control* 7, 381–384.

Steenbrink, P.A. (1974a) Transport network optimization in the Dutch Integral Transportation Study, *Transportation Research* 8 (1), 11–27.

Steenbrink, P.A. (1974b) *Optimization of Transport Networks*, Wiley, London.

Stopher, P.R. (1969) A probability model of travel mode choice for the work journey, *Highway Research Record* 283, 57–65.

Stopher, P.R. and S.P. Greaves (2007) Household travel surveys: where are we going?, *Transportation Research Part A* 41, 367–381.

Stopher, P.R., Q. Jiang and C. FitzGerald (2005) Processing GPS data from travel surveys, Processus Second International Colloquium on the Behavioural Foundations of Integrated Land-Use and Transportation Models, University of Toronto, Ontario.

Stopher, P.R. and T.E. Lisco (1970) Modelling travel demand: a disaggregate behavioral approach – issues and applications, *Transportation Research Forum Proceedings* 11, 195–214.

Stopher, P.R. and A.H. Meyburg (1975) *Urban Transportation Modeling and Planning*, Lexington Books, Lexington, MA.

Stopher, P.R. and A.H. Meyburg (eds) (1976) *Behavioral Travel-Demand Models*, Lexington Books, Lexington, MA.

Stopher, P.R., A.H. Meyburg and W. Brög (eds) (1981) *New Horizons in Travel-Behaviour Research*, Lexington Books, Lexington, MA.

Stopher, P.R., B.D. Spear and P.O. Sucher (1974) Towards the development of measures of convenience for travel modes, *Transportation Research Record* 527, 16–32.

Stouffer, S.A. (1940) Intervening opportunities: a theory relating mobility and distance, *American Sociological Review* 5, 845–867.

Strauss, D. (1979) Some results for random utility models, *Journal of Mathematical Psychology* 20, 35–52.

Street, D.J. and L. Burgess (2007) *The Construction of Optimal Stated Choice Experiments: Theory and Methods*, Wiley, Hoboken, NJ.

Strohmaier, E., J.J. Dongarra, H.W. Meuer and H.D. Simon (2005) Recent trends in the marketplace of high performance computing, *Parallel Computing* 31 (3–4), 261–273.

Strotz, R.H. (1957) The empirical implications of a utility tree, *Econometrica* 25, 269–280.

Svenson, O. (1998) The perspective from behavioural decision theory on modeling travel choice, Chapter 7 in *Theoretical Foundations of Travel Choice Modeling*, T. Gärling, T. Laitila and K. Westin (eds), Elsevier, Amsterdam, 141–172.

Swait, J.D., J.J. Louviere and M. Williams (1994) A sequential approach to exploiting the combined strengths of SP and RP data: application to freight shipper choice, *Transportation* 21, 135–152.

Takayama, A. (1985) *Mathematical Economics*, 2nd edn, Cambridge University Press, Cambridge.

Talvitie, A. (1973) Aggregate travel demand analysis with disaggregate or aggregate travel demand models, *Transportation Research Forum Proceedings* 14, 583–603.

Tanner, J.C. (1961) Factors Affecting the Amount of Travel, Technical Paper No. 51, Road Research Laboratory, Crowthorne, Berkshire.

Tanner, J.C. (1965) Forecasts of future numbers of vehicles and cars in Great Britain, *Roads and Road Construction*, November and December.

Tanner, J.C. (1981) Expenditure of time and money on travel, *Transportation Research Part A* 15, 25–38.

Tatineni, M.R., M.R. Lupa, D.B. Englund and D.E. Boyce (1994) Transportation policy analysis using a combined model of travel choice, *Transportation Research Record* 1452, 10–17.

Taylor, N.B. (2003) The CONTRAM dynamic traffic assignment model, *Networks and Spatial Economics* 3, 297–322.

Thill, J.C. and I. Thomas (1987) Towards conceptualizing trip chaining behaviour: a review, *Geographical Analysis* 19, 1–18.

Thomas, T.C. and G.I. Thompson (1971) Value of time saved by trip purpose, *Highway Research Record* 369, 104–115.

Thompson, H. (1996) Akira Takayama: a memoir, *Review of International Economics* 4 (3), 371–381.

Thomson, J.M. (1970) Some aspects of evaluating road improvements in congested areas, *Econometrica* 38, 298–310.

Thomson, J.M. (1977) *Great Cities and Their Traffic*, Gollancz, London.

Thurstone, L. (1927) A law of comparative judgement, *Psychological Review* 34, 273–286.

Timmermans, H.J.P. (ed) (2005) *Progress in Activity-Based Analysis*, Elsevier, Amsterdam.

Timmermans, H.J.P. (2010) On the (ir)relevance of prospect theory in modelling uncertainty in travel decisions, *European Journal of Transport and Infrastructure Research* 10, 368–384.

Timmermans, H.J.P., T. Arentze and C.-H. Joh (2002) Analysing space-time behaviour: new approaches to old problems, *Progress in Human Geography* 26, 175–190.

Timmermans, H.J.P. and J. Zhang (2009) Modeling household activity behaviour: examples of state of the art modeling approaches and research agenda, *Transportation Research Part B* 43, 187–190.

Timms, P. (2008) Transport models, philosophy and language, *Transportation* 35, 395–410.

Tomazinis, A.R. (1962) A new method of trip distribution in an urban area, *Highway Research Bulletin* 347, 77–99.

Tomlin, J.A. (1966) Minimum-cost multicommodity network flows, *Operations Research* 14 (1), 45–51.

Tomlin, J.A. (1971) A mathematical programming model for the combined distribution–assignment of traffic, *Transportation Science* 5 (2), 122–140.

Traffic Research Corporation (1969a) Merseyside Area Land-Use/Transportation Study, Liverpool.

Traffic Research Corporation (1969b) West Yorkshire Transportation Study, Leeds.

Train, K. (1978) A validation test of a disaggregate mode choice model, *Transportation Research* 12, 167–174.

Train, K.E. (1980) A structured logit model of auto ownership and mode choice, *Review of Economic Studies* 47, 357–370.

Train, K. (1986) *Qualitative Choice Analysis*, MIT Press, Cambridge, MA.

Train, K.E. (1998) Recreation demand models with taste variation over people, *Land Economics* 74, 230–239.

Train, K.E. (2009) *Discrete Choice Methods with Simulation*, 2nd edn, Cambridge University Press, Cambridge.

Transport for London (2003) Micro-Simulation Modelling Guidance Note for TfL, Windsor House, London.

Transport Research Laboratory (2002) Strategic Transport Modelling Seminar, Crowthorne, Berkshire.

Transportation Research Board (1985) *Highway Capacity Manual*, 3rd edn, Special Report 209, Washington, DC.

Transportation Research Board (1995) *Expanding Metropolitan Highways*, Special Report 245, Washington, DC.

Transportation Research Board (2000) *Highway Capacity Manual 2000*, Washington, DC.

Transportation Research Board (2007) *Metropolitan Travel Forecasting*, Special Report 288, Washington, DC.

Transportation Research Board (2008) *Innovations in Travel Demand Modeling*, Volume 1, Session Summaries; Volume 2, Papers, Conference Proceedings 42, Washington, DC.

Travel Model Improvement Program (2005) Fiscal Year 2005 Annual Report, US Department of Transportation, Washington, DC.

Travel Model Improvement Program Online (1999) Early Deployment of TRANSIMS, issue paper, media.tmiponline.org/clearinghouse/issue_ paper/issue_paper.pdf (accessed 8 October 2013).

Travel Model Improvement Program Online (2009) Technical Synthesis – Feedback Loops, www.tmiponline.org/Clearinghouse/Items/Technical_ Synthesis_-_Feedback_Loops.aspx (accessed 7 October 2013).

Tressider, J.O., D.A. Meyers, J.E. Burrell and T.J. Powell (1968) The London Transportation Study: methods and techniques, *Proceedings of the Institution of Civil Engineers* 39, 433–464.

Tversky, A. (1967) Additivity, utility and subjective probability, *Journal of Mathematical Psychology* 4, 175–201.

Tversky, A. (1972) Elimination by aspects: a theory of choice, *Psychological Review* 79, 281–299.

Tversky, A. and D. Kahneman (1992) Advances in prospect theory: cumulative representation of uncertainty, *Journal of Risk and Uncertainty* 5, 297–323.

Tversky, A. and S. Sattath (1979) Preference trees, *Psychological Review* 86, 542–573.

UK Department for Transport (2003) Freight Modelling, Transport Analysis Guidance Unit 3.1.4, Integrated Transport Economics Appraisal, London (updated 2009).

UK Department for Transport (2004) Full Guidance on Local Transport Plans, 2nd edn, London.

UK Department for Transport (2005a) Introduction to Model Structures for Public Transport Schemes, Transport Analysis Guidance, Transport Analysis Guidance Unit 2.10.2, Integrated Transport Economics Appraisal, London (updated April 2009).

UK Department for Transport (2005b) Land-Use/Transport Interaction Models, Transport Analysis Guidance Unit 3.1.3, Integrated Transport Economic Appraisal, London (updated April 2009).

UK Department for Transport (2006a) Variable Demand Modelling: Key Processes, Transport Analysis Guidance Unit 3.10.3, Integrated Transport Economics Appraisal, London (updated April 2009).

UK Department for Transport (2006b) Road Traffic and Public Transport Assignment Modelling, Transport Analysis Guidance Unit 3.11.2, Integrated Transport Economics Appraisal, London (updated April 2009).

UK Department for Transport (2006c) Mode Choice Models: Bespoke and Transferred, Transport Analysis Guidance Unit 3.11.3, Integrated Transport Economics Appraisal, London (updated April 2009).

UK Department for Transport (2006d) Specification, Development and the Use of Models for Major Public Transport Schemes, Transport Analysis Guidance Unit 3.11, Integrated Transport Economics Appraisal, London (updated 2009).

UK Department for Transport (2006e) Expert Guidance on the Mixed Logit Model: Procedures and Documentation, Transport Analysis Guidance Unit 3.11.5, Integrated Transport Economics Appraisal, London.

UK Department for Transport (2007a) Model Structures and Traveller Responses for Public Transport Schemes, Transport Analysis Guidance Unit 3.11.1, Integrated Transport Economics Appraisal, London (updated April 2009).

UK Department for Transport (2007b) Modelling Road Pricing, Transport Analysis Guidance Unit 3.12.2, Integrated Transport Economics Appraisal, London.

UK Department for Transport (2009a) NATA Refresh: Appraisal for a Sustainable Transport System, Transport Appraisal and Strategic Modelling, London.

UK Department for Transport (2009b) The Economy Objective: The Reliability Sub-Objective, Transport Analysis Guidance Unit 3.5.7, Transport Appraisal and Strategic Modelling, London.

UK Department for Transport (2009c) The Treatment of Uncertainty in Model Forecasting, Transport Analysis Guidance Unit 3.15.5, Integrated Transport Economics Appraisal, London.

UK Department for Transport (2011a) Transport Analysis Guidance – webTAG, www.dft.gov.uk/webtag (accessed 30 June 2013).

UK Department for Transport (2011b) Parking and Park-and-Ride, Transport Analysis Guidance Unit 3.10.7, Consultation Document, Transport Appraisal and Strategic Modelling, London.

UK Department for Transport (2011c) Modelling Smarter Choices, Transport Analysis Guidance Unit 3.10.6, Consultation Document, Transport Appraisal and Strategic Modelling, London (in draft form).

UK Department for Transport (2011d) Variable Demand Modelling: Convergence, Realism and Sensitivity, Transport Analysis Guidance Unit 3.10.4, Integrated Transport Economics Appraisal, London.

UK Department for Transport (2011e) Variable Demand Modelling: Scope of the Model, Transport Analysis Guidance Unit 3.10.2, Integrated Transport Economics Appraisal, London.

UK Department for Transport (2011f) DIADEM User Manual, Version

5.0 (SATURN), www.gov.uk/government/uploads/system/uploads/ attachment_data/file/9136/diadem-user-manual-sat5.0.pdf (accessed 1 June 2014).

UK Department for Transport (2012) Transport Appraisal and Modelling Tools, www.gov.uk/transport-appraisal-and-modelling-tools#introduction (accessed 29 June 2013).

UK Department of the Environment (1971) Speed Flow Relationships To Be Used in Transportation Studies for the Department of the Environment, Advice Note 1A, London.

UK Department of the Environment, Transport and the Regions (2000) Guidance on the Methodology for Multi-Modal Studies, London.

UK Department of Transport (1989) National Road Traffic Forecasts, London.

UK Department of Transport (1997) *Traffic Appraisal of Road Schemes, Design Manual for Roads and Bridges*, Volume 12, Section 2, Traffic Appraisal Advice, Her Majesty's Stationery Office, London.

UK House of Commons (1972) *Urban Transport Planning*, Volume I, *Report and Appendix*, House of Commons Expenditure Committee, Her Majesty's Stationery Office, London.

US Department of Commerce (1950) Highway Capacity Manual, Bureau of Public Roads, Washington, DC.

US Department of Commerce (1954) Manual of Procedures for Home Interview Traffic Studies, Bureau of Public Roads, Washington, DC.

US Department of Commerce (1963a) Calibrating and Testing a Gravity Model for Any Size Urban Area, Bureau of Public Roads, Washington, DC.

US Department of Commerce (1963b) Instructional Memorandum 50-2-63, Urban Transportation Planning, Bureau of Public Roads, Washington, DC.

US Department of Commerce (1964) Traffic Assignment Manual, Bureau of Public Roads, Washington, DC.

US Department of Commerce (1966) Modal Split, prepared by M.J. Fertal, E. Weiner, A.J. Balek and A.F. Sevin, Bureau of Public Roads, Washington, DC.

US Department of Housing and Urban Development (1966, 1967, 1968) Factors Influencing Transit, Technical Report 1; Computer Program Specifications, Technical Report 2; Volume I, IBM 7090/94 Computer Programs Users' Reference Manual, Volume II, Technical Report 3; Modal Split Simulation Model, Technical Report 4; Recommendations for Urban Mass Transportation Research, Technical Report 5; IBM System/360 Computer Programs, General Information Manual, Volume I, Users' Manual, Volume II, Technical Report 6; Urban Mass

Transit Planning Project, Alan M. Voorhees and Associates, McLean, VA.

US Department of Transportation (1967) Guidelines for Trip Generation Analysis, Federal Highway Administration, Washington, DC.

US Department of Transportation (1969a) Urban Planning System 360, Trip Distribution and Peripheral Programs, Federal Highway Administration, Washington, DC.

US Department of Transportation (1969b) Urban Planning System 360, Traffic Assignment and Peripheral Programs, Federal Highway Administration, Washington, DC.

US Department of Transportation (1972a) Urban Transportation Planning, General Information, Federal Highway Administration, Washington, DC.

US Department of Transportation (1972b) U.M.T.A. Transportation Planning System, Reference Manual, Urban Mass Transportation Administration, Washington, DC.

US Department of Transportation (1973a) Traffic Assignment, prepared by Comsis Corporation, Federal Highway Administration, Washington, DC.

US Department of Transportation (1973b) Urban Origin–Destination Surveys, Federal Highway Administration, Washington, DC.

US Department of Transportation (1974) Computer Programs for Urban Transportation Planning, Federal Highway Administration, Washington, DC.

US Department of Transportation (1975) Trip Generation Analysis, Federal Highway Administration, Washington, DC.

US Department of Transportation (1976) Urban Transportation Planning System, Urban Mass Transportation Administration, Federal Highway Administration, Washington, DC.

US Department of Transportation (1977a) Computer Programs for Urban Transportation Planning, PLANPAC/BACKPAC General Information Manual, Federal Highway Administration, Washington, DC.

US Department of Transportation (1977b) User-Oriented Materials for UTPS, Federal Highway Administration, Urban Mass Transportation Administration, Washington, DC.

US Department of Transportation (1982) Microcomputers in Transportation, Urban Mass Transportation Administration, Washington, DC; updated annually to 1987.

US Department of Transportation (1995) CTPP Handbook, An Instructional Guide to the 1990 Census Transportation Planning Package, Federal Highway Administration, Washington, DC.

US Department of Transportation (2009) Reporting Instructions for the Section 5309 New Starts Criteria, Federal Transit Administration, Washington, DC.

US Department of Transportation (2010) Transportation Conformity: A Basic Guide for State and Local Officials, Federal Highway Administration, Washington, DC.

US Environmental Protection Agency (2000) Projecting Land-Use Change: A Summary of Models for Assessing the Effects of Community Growth and Change on Land-Use Patterns, Washington, DC.

van de Kaa, E.J. (2010) Applicability of an extended prospect theory to travel behaviour research: a meta-analysis, *Transport Reviews* 30, 771–804.

van der Hoorn, T. (1983) Experiments with an activity-based travel model, *Transportation* 12, 61–77.

Van Vliet, D. (1973) Road Assignment: Further Tests on Incremental Loading and Multipath Techniques, Note GLTS-54, Department of Planning and Transportation, Greater London Council, London.

Van Vliet, D. (1976) Road assignment – I, II, III, *Transportation Research* 10, 137–147.

Van Vliet, D. (1977) The application of mathematical programming to network assignment, Chapter 10 in *Urban Transportation Planning*, P.W. Bonsall, Q.M. Dalvi and P.J. Hills (eds), Abacus, Tunbridge Wells, Kent, 147–158.

Van Vliet, D. (1982) SATURN – a modern assignment model, *Traffic Engineering and Control* 23, 578–581.

Van Vliet, D., T. Bergman and W.H. Scheltes (1986) Equilibrium traffic assignment with multiple user classes, Summer Annual Meeting, Planning and Transport Research and Computation Co., Brighton.

Van Vliet, D. and P.D.C. Dow (1979) Capacity restrained road assignment, Parts I, II and III, *Traffic Engineering and Control* 20, 261–273.

Van Vliet, D., T. Van Vuren and M.J. Smith (1987) The interaction between signal setting optimisation and reassignment: background and preliminary results, *Transportation Research Record* 1142, 16–21.

Van Vuren, T. (2010) PRISM: an introductory guide, Mott MacDonald, Birmingham, with RAND Europe, Cambridge.

Van Vuren, T., A. Gordon, A. Daly, J. Fox and C. Rohr (2004) PRISM: modelling 21st century transport policies in the West Midlands region, Methods in Transport Planning, European Transport Conference, Strasbourg.

Van Vuren, T., H. Gunn and A. Daly (1995) Disaggregate travel demand models: their applicability for British transport planning practice, *Traffic Engineering and Control* 36, 336–337, 339–341, 343–344.

Van Wee, B., P. Rietveld and H. Meurs (2006) Is average daily travel time expenditure constant? In search of explanations of an increase in average travel time, *Journal of Transport Geography* 14, 109–122.

Van Zuylen, H.J. and L.G. Willumsen (1980) The most likely trip matrix estimated from traffic counts, *Transportation Research Part B* 14, 281–293.

Venables, A.J. and M. Gasiorek (1998) The Welfare Implications of Transport Improvements in the Presence of Market Failure, Report to the Standing Advisory Committee on Trunk Road Assessment, London.

VHB (2007) Determination of the State of the Practice in Metropolitan Travel Forecasting: Findings of the Surveys of Metropolitan Planning Organizations, Transportation Research Board, Washington, DC onlinepubs.trb.org/onlinepubs/reports/VHB-2007-Final.pdf (accessed 2 October 1013).

Von Falkenhausen, H. (1966) Traffic assignment by a stochastic model, in *Proceedings, 4th International Conference on Operational Science*, 415–421.

Voorhees, A.M. (1955) A general theory of traffic movement, *Proceedings*, Institute of Traffic Engineers, New Haven, CT, 46–56.

Voorhees, A.M. (1958) Forecasting peak hour of travel, *Highway Research Bulletin* 203, 37–46.

Voorhees, A.M. and R. Morris (1959) Estimating and forecasting travel for Baltimore by use of a mathematical model, *Highway Research Bulletin* 224, 105–114.

Vovsha, P. (1997) Cross-nested logit model: an application to mode choice in the Tel-Aviv metropolitan area, *Transportation Research Record* 1607, 6–15.

Vovsha, P. and M. Bradley (2006) Advanced activity-based models in context of planning decisions, *Transportation Research Record* 1981, 34–41.7

Vovsha, P., M. Bradley and J. Bowman (2005) Activity-based travel forecasting models in the United States: progress since 1995 and prospects for the future, Chapter 17 in *Progress in Activity-Based Analysis*, H.J.P. Timmermans (ed), Elsevier, Oxford, 389–414.

Wachs, M. (1973) Relating travel demand forecasting to social, economic, and environmental impacts, *Urban Travel Demand Forecasting*, Special Report 143, Highway Research Board, Washington, DC, 96–113.

Wachs, M. (1982) Ethical dilemmas in forecasting for public policy, *Public Administration Review* 42, 562–567.

Wachs, M. (1989) When planners lie with numbers, *Journal of the American Planning Association* 55 (4), 476–479.

Wachs, M. (1990) Ethics and advocacy in forecasting for public policy, *Business and Professional Ethics Journal* 9 (1–2), 141–157.

Wachs, M. (1996) A new generation of travel demand models, *Transportation* 23, 213–214.

Waddell, P. (2000) A behavioral simulation model for metropolitan policy analysis and planning: residential location and housing market components of UrbanSim, *Environment and Planning B* 27 (2), 247–264.

Waddell, P. (2002) UrbanSim: modeling urban development for land use, transportation and environmental planning, *Journal of the American Planning Association* 68 (3), 297–314.

Waddell, P. (2011) Integrating land use and transportation planning and modelling: addressing challenges in research and practice, *Transport Reviews* 31 (2), 209–229.

Waddell, P., A. Borning, M. Noth, N. Freier, M. Becke and G. Ulfarsson (2003) Microsimulation of urban development and location choices: design and implementation of UrbanSim, *Networks and Spatial Economics* 3, 43–67.

Waddell, P. and G. Ulfarsson (2004) Introduction to urban simulation: design and development of operational models, Chapter 13 in *Handbook of Transport Geography and Spatial Systems*, K.E. Haynes, P.R. Stopher, K.J. Button and D.A. Hensher (eds), Elsevier, Oxford, 203–236.

Waddell, P., G. Ulfarsson, J. Franklin and J. Lobb (2007) Incorporating land use in metropolitan transportation planning, *Transportation Research Part A* 41 (5), 382–410.

Walker, J.L. (2001) Extended Discrete Choice Models: Integrated Framework, Flexible Error Structures, and Latent Variables, Ph.D. thesis, Civil Engineering, Massachusetts Institute of Technology, Cambridge, MA.

Walker, J.L. (2002) Mixed logit (or logit kernel) model: dispelling misconceptions of identification, *Transportation Research Record* 1805, 86–98.

Walker, J.L. (2005) Making household micro-simulation of travel and activities accessible to planners, *Transportation Research Record* 1931, 38–48.

Walker, J.L. and M.E. Ben-Akiva (2002) Generalized random utility model, *Mathematical Social Sciences* 43, 303–343.

Walters, A.A. (1961) The theory and measurement of private and social cost of highway congestion, *Econometrica* 29 (4), 676–699.

Wang, Q. and J. Holguín-Veras (2008) Investigation of attributes determining trip chaining behavior in hybrid microsimulation urban freight models, *Transportation Research Record* 2066, 1–8.

Wardman, M.R. (1987) An Evaluation of the Use of Stated Preference and Transfer Price Data in Forecasting: The Demand for Travel, Ph.D. thesis, Transport Studies, University of Leeds, Leeds.

Wardman, M. (1988) A comparison of revealed preference and stated preference models of travel behaviour, *Journal of Transport Economics and Policy* 22, 71–91.

Wardman, M. (1998) The value of travel time: a review of British evidence, *Journal of Transport Economics and Policy* 32, 285–316.

Wardrop, J.G. (1952) Some theoretical aspects of road traffic research, *Proceedings of the Institution of Civil Engineers, Part II* 1 (2), 325–378.

Wardrop, J.G. (1961) The distribution of traffic on a road system, in *Theory of Traffic Flow*, R. Herman (ed), Elsevier, Amsterdam, 57–78.

Warner, S.L. (1962) *Stochastic Choice of Mode in Urban Travel*, Northwestern University Press, Evanston, IL.

Watanatada, T. and M. Ben-Akiva (1979) Forecasting urban travel demand for quick policy analysis with disaggregate choice models: a Monte Carlo simulation approach, *Transportation Research Part A* 13, 241–248.

Waters, W.G., II (1995) Values of travel time savings in road transport project evaluation, World Conference on Transport Research, Sydney.

Watson, P.L. (1972) An Annotated Bibliography on Urban Goods Movement, Transportation Center, Northwestern University, Evanston, IL.

Watson, P.L. (1975) *Urban Goods Movement*, Lexington Books, Lexington, MA.

Watson, S.M., J.P. Toner, A.S. Fowkes and M. Wardman (1996) Efficiency properties of orthogonal stated preference designs, European Transport Forum, Planning and Transport Research and Computation Co., London.

Webster, F.V., P.H. Bly and N.J. Paulley (eds) (1988) *Urban Land-Use and Transport Interaction*, Gower, Aldershot, Hampshire.

Webster, F.V. and N.J. Paulley (1990) An international study on land use and transport interaction, *Transport Reviews* 10, 287–308.

Wegener, M. (1985) The Dortmund housing market model: a Monte Carlo simulation of a regional housing market, in *Microeconomic Models of Housing Markets*, K. Stahl (ed), Lecture Notes in Economics and Mathematical Systems, Volume 239, Springer, Berlin.

Wegener, M. (1994) Operational urban models, *Journal of the American Planning Association* 60 (1), 17–29.

Wegener, M. (1998) Applied models of urban land use, transport and environment: state of the art and future developments, Chapter 14 in *Network Infrastructure and the Urban Environment*, L. Lundqvist, L.-G. Mattsson and T.J. Kim (eds), Springer, Berlin, 245–267.

Wegener, M. (2004) Overview of land use transport models, Chapter 9 in *Handbook of Transport Geography and Spatial Systems*, D.A. Hensher, K.J. Button, K.E. Haynes and P.R. Stopher (eds), Elsevier, Oxford, 127–146.

Wegener, M. (2011a) The IRPUD Model, Spiekermann & Wegener, Dortmund, Germany.

Wegener, M. (2011b) From macro to micro: how much micro is too much?, *Transport Reviews* 31, 161–177.

Weiner, E. (1969) Modal split revisited, *Traffic Quarterly* 23 (1), 5–28.

Weiner, E. (1997) *Urban Transportation Planning in the United States, An Historical Overview*, 5th edn, media.tmiponline.org/clearinghouse/utp/utp.pdf (accessed 22 August 2013).

Weiner, E. (2013) *Urban Transportation Planning in the United States*, 4th edn, Springer, New York.

Weiner, E. and F. Ducca (1996) Upgrading travel demand forecasting capabilities, *TR News*, No. 186, Transportation Research Board, Washington, DC; revised version published in *ITE Journal* 69 (7), 58–33.

Welch, M. and H.C.W.L. Williams (1997) The sensitivity of transport investment benefits to the evaluation of small travel-time savings, *Journal of Transport Economics and Policy* 31, 231–254.

Wen, C.H. and F.S. Koppelman (2000) A conceptual and methodological framework for the generation of activity-travel patterns, *Transportation* 27, 5–23.

Wen, C.H. and F.S. Koppelman (2001) The generalized nested logit model, *Transportation Research Part B* 35, 627–641.

Wheaton, W.C. (1974) Linear programming and locational equilibrium: the Herbert–Stevens model revisited, *Journal of Urban Economics* 1, 278–287.

Whelan, G.A. (2007) Modelling car ownership in Great Britain, *Transportation Research Part A* 41, 205–219.

Whiting, P.D. and J.A. Hillier (1960) A method for finding the shortest route through a road network, *Operational Research Quarterly* 11 (1/2), 37–40.

Wigan, M.R. (1977) Theory and implementation of demand–supply equilibrium analysis, Chapter 17 in *New Techniques for Transport Systems Analysis*, Special Report No. 10, M.R. Wigan (ed), Australian Road Research Board, Vermont, Victoria, 135–147.

Williams, H.C.W.L. (1976) Travel demand models, duality relations and user benefit analysis, *Journal of Regional Science* 16, 147–166.

Williams, H.C.W.L. (1977a) On the formation of travel demand models and economic evaluation measures of user benefit, *Environment and Planning A* 9, 284–344.

Williams, H.C.W.L. (1977b) The generation of consistent travel demand models and user-benefit measures, Chapter 11 in *Urban Transportation Planning*, P. Bonsall, Q.M. Dalvi and P.J. Hills (eds), Abacus, Tunbridge Wells, Kent, 161–175.

Williams, H.C.W.L. (1981) The use of micro-simulation in travel-activity analysis, International Conference on Travel Demand Analysis, St. Catherine's College, Oxford.

Williams, H.C.W.L. (1998) Congestion, traffic growth and transport investment: the influence of interactions and multiplier effects in related travel markets, *Journal of Transport Economics and Policy* 32, 141–163.

Williams, H.C.W.L., W.M. Lam, J. Austin and K.S. Kim (1991) Transport policy appraisal with equilibrium models, III: investment benefits in multi-modal systems, *Transportation Research Part B* 25, 293–316.

Williams, H.C.W.L. and L.A. Moore (1990) The appraisal of highway investments under fixed and variable demand, *Journal of Transport Economics and Policy* 24, 61–81.

Williams, H.C.W.L. and J. de D. Ortúzar (1982) Behavioural theories of dispersion and the mis-specification of travel demand models, *Transportation Research Part B* 16, 167–219.

Williams, H.C.W.L. and M.L. Senior (1977) Model based transport policy assessment, 2: removing fundamental inconsistencies from the models, *Traffic Engineering and Control* 18, 464–469.

Williams, H.C.W.L. and M.L. Senior (1978) Accessibility, spatial inter-action and the evaluation of land-use transportation plans, in *Spatial Interaction Theory and Planning Models*, A. Karlqvist, L. Lundqvist, F. Snickars and J.W. Weibull (eds), North-Holland, Amsterdam, 243–287.

Williams, H.C.W.L., D. Van Vliet, C. Parathira and K.S. Kim (2001a) Highway investment benefits under alternative pricing regimes, *Journal of Transport Economics and Policy* 35, 257–284.

Williams, H.C.W.L., D. Van Vliet and K.S. Kim (2001b) The contribution of suppressed and induced traffic in highway appraisal, Part 1: reference states; Part 2: policy tests, *Environment and Planning A* 33, 1057–1082, 1243–1264.

Williams, H.C.W.L. and Y. Yamashita (1992) Travel demand forecasts and the evaluation of highway schemes under congested conditions, *Journal of Transport Economics and Policy* 26, 261–282.

Williams, I.N. (1994) A model of London and the South East, *Environment and Planning B* 21, 535–553.

Williams, I.N. and J. Bates (1993) APRIL – a strategic model for road pricing in London, Summer Annual Meeting, Planning and Transport Research and Computation Co., Manchester.

Williams, I.N., Y. Jin, J. Pharoah, J. Bates and M. Shahkarami (2007) Guidance on Freight Modelling, WSP Policy and Research, Cambridge.

Willumsen, L.G. (1978) Estimation of an O-D Matrix from Traffic Counts: A Review, Working Paper 99, Institute for Transport Studies, University of Leeds, Leeds.

Willumsen, L.G. (1981) Simplified transport demand models based on traffic counts, *Transportation* 10, 257–278.

Willumsen, L.G., J. Bolland, Y. Arezki and M. Hall (1993) Multi-modal modelling in congested networks: SATURN + SATCHMO, *Traffic Engineering and Control* 34, 294–301.

Wilson, A.G. (1967) A statistical theory of spatial distribution models, *Transportation Research* 1 (3), 253–269.

Wilson, A.G. (1969) The use of entropy maximising models in the theory of trip distribution, modal split and route split, *Journal of Transport Economics and Policy* 3, 108–126.

Wilson, A.G. (1970) *Entropy in Urban and Regional Modelling*, Pion, London.

Wilson, A.G. (1971) Generalising the Lowry model, in *London Papers in Regional Science*, Volume 2, A.G. Wilson (ed), Pion, London, 121–133.

Wilson, A.G. (1973a) Travel demand forecasting: achievements and problems, *Urban Travel Demand Forecasting*, Special Report 143, Highway Research Board, 283–306.

Wilson, A.G. (1973b) Further developments of entropy maximising transport models, *Transport Planning and Technology* 1, 183–193.

Wilson, A.G. (1974) *Urban and Regional Models in Geography and Planning*, Wiley, London.

Wilson, A.G. (2000) *Complex Spatial Systems*, Pearson Education, Harlow, Essex.

Wilson, A.G. (2010) Entropy in urban and regional modelling: retrospect and prospect, *Geographical Analysis* 42, 364–394.

Wilson, A.G., J.D. Coelho, S.M. Macgill and H.C.W.L. Williams (1981) *Optimization in Locational and Transport Analysis*, Wiley, Chichester, West Sussex.

Wilson, A.G., A.F. Hawkins, G.J. Hill and D.J. Wagon (1969) Calibration and testing of the SELNEC transport model, *Regional Studies* 3, 337–350.

Wilson, A.G. and R. Kirwan (1969) Measures of Benefits in the Evaluation of Urban Transport Improvements, Working Paper 43, Centre for Environmental Studies, London.

Wilson, A.G. and C.E. Pownall (1976) A new representation of the urban system for modelling and for the study of micro-level interdependence, *Area* 8, 246–254.

Wohl, M. (1963) Demand, cost, price and capacity relationships applied to travel forecasting, *Highway Research Record* 38, 40–54.

Wong, S.C., C. Yang and H.K. Lo (2001) A path-based traffic assignment algorithm based on the TRANSYT traffic model, *Transportation Research Part B* 35 (2), 163–181.

Wood, R.T. (1967) Tri-State Transportation Commission's freight study program, *Highway Research Record* 165, 89–95.

Wood, R.T. and R.A. Leighton (1969) Truck freight in the Tri-State Region, *Traffic Quarterly* 23, 323–340.

Wootton, H.J. (1967) The analysis of public transport systems, British Computer Society Symposium, Edinburgh.

Wootton, H.J. (2004) Traffic forecasting and the appraisal of road schemes, Chapter 7 in *The Motorway Achievement*, Volume 1: *The British Motorway System: Visualisation, Policy and Administration*, P. Baldwin and R. Baldwin (eds), Thomas Telford, London, 265–303.

Wootton, H.J. and G.W. Pick (1967) A model for trips generated by households, *Journal of Transport Economics and Policy* 1, 137–153.

Worthy, J.C. (1995) Control Data Corporation: the Norris era, *Journal of the History of Computing* 17 (1), 47–53.

WSP (2005) EUNET2.0 Freight and Logistics Model, Final Report, Integrated Transport Economics Appraisal, UK Department for Transport, London.

WSP, University of Westminster, ITS, Leeds, RAND Europe, MDS-Transmodal, Katalysis, Oxford Systematics, Parsons Brinckerhoff and Imperial College (2002) Review of Freight Modelling, Final Report for Integrated Transport Economics Appraisal, UK Department for Transport, London.

WSP Development and Transportation (2010) Freight in London Model – FiLM, Final Report, Transport for London, Cambridge.

Wu, J.H. and M. Florian (1993) A simplicial decomposition method for the transit equilibrium assignment problem, *Annals of Operations Research* 44 (3), 245–260.

Wu, J.H., M. Florian and P. Marcotte (1994) Transit equilibrium assignment: a model and solution algorithms, *Transportation Science* 28 (3), 193–203.

Xie, J., Y. Nie and X. Yang (2013) Quadratic approximation and convergence of some bush-based algorithms for the traffic assignment problem, *Transportation Research Part B* 56, 15–30.

Yang, H. and H.-J. Huang (2005) *Mathematical and Economic Theory of Road Pricing*, Elsevier, Amsterdam.

Zachary, S. (1976) Some Results on Logit Models, Transportation

Working Note 10, Local Government Operational Research Unit, Reading, Berkshire.

Zahavi, Y. (1974) Travel Time Budgets and Mobility in Urban Areas, Final Report, Federal Highway Administration, US Department of Transportation, Washington, DC.

Zahavi, Y. (1978) Can transport policy decisions change travel and urban structure?, Summer Annual Meeting, Planning and Transport Research and Computation Co., Warwick.

Zahavi, Y., M.J. Beckmann and T.F. Golob (1981) The UMOT/Urban Interactions, Final Report to the Research and Special Programs Administration, US Department of Transportation, Washington, DC.

Zavattero, D.A. (1974) Urban Goods Movements and Transportation Planning, Paper No. 372.05, Chicago Area Transportation Study, Chicago.

Zhao, Y. and K.M. Kockelman (2002) The propagation of uncertainty through travel demand models: an exploratory analysis, *Annals of Regional Science* 36, 145–163.

Zipf, G.K. (1949) *Human Behavior and the Principle of Least Effort*, Addison-Wesley, Cambridge, MA.

Names index

Aashtiani, H.Z. 344–6, 530
Abdulaal, M. 344, 530, 575
Abraham, C. 131, 135, 141, 178–9, 325, 530
Abraham, J.E. 585
Abrahamsson, T. 334, 340–41, 530
Achim, C. 558
Adler, T. 161, 249, 254, 530, 571
AECOM 372, 376–9, 530, 596
Ahrens, G.-A.; Ahrens et al (2009) 341, 530
Akamatsu, T. 327, 531
Akçelik, R. 348, 467, 531
Alan M. Voorhees and Associates (AMV) 57, 455–62, 464, 466, 477
Albright, D. 371
Albright, R.L.; Albright et al (1977) 208–209, 531
Alex Anas & Associates 387, 531
Algers, S. 258–9, 262–6, 279, 287, 531
Algers et al (1995) 258–9, 262–5, 531
Algers et al (2005) 266, 279, 287, 531
Allaman, P.M., Allaman et al (1982) 253, 258, 531
Allsop, R.E. 330, 356, 531
Almendinger, V.V. 60–61, 531
Almond, J. 100, 314, 316 531–2
Alvarez-Daziano, R. 236, 239, 540, 586, 594
Amemiya, T. 143, 532
Ampt, E.S. 228, 532, 543, 570, 594
Ampt et al (1995) 228, 532
Anable, J. 545, 599
Anas, A. 66, 240–41, 243, 387, 532
Anderson, D.A. 578
Anderson, R. 557
Anderson, S.P., Anderson et al (1992) 240, 532
Anderstig, C. 340, 399, 532
Anowar, S.; Anowar et al (2014) 502, 532

Anson, D. 599
Antosiewicz, H.A. 298, 533
Apgar, W.C. 213, 570
Apple 449
Arentze, T.A. 285, 287, 533, 603
Arezki, Y. 413, 533, 614
Argonne National Laboratory 372, 379
Armoogum, J. 590
Arnott, R. 419, 533
Ash, A. 582
Ashley, D.A. 534
Asmuth, R.; Asmuth et al (1979) 344, 533
Association of Metropolitan Planning Organizations 381
Atherton, T. 149, 162, 210, 215–16, 218, 533, 536
Atkins Global (also known as WS Atkins) 106, 412, 462, 471
Aunet, B. 571
Austin, J. 613
Avineri, E. 514, 533
Axhausen, K.W. 212, 259, 266, 269, 284, 287, 380, 533, 534

Bachner, G. 577–8
Badoe, E.A. 556
Baggerly, K. 535, 599
Bain, R. 501, 514, 533
Balakrishna, R. 548
Balcombe, R. 430, 533
Balinski, M.L. 298, 534
Balmer, M.; Balmer et al (2008) 282, 286, 534
Bamberg, S. 432, 586
Banister, D.J. 257, 436, 446, 534, 581
Bar-Gera, H. 320–22, 325, 337, 338, 340, 476, 589, 534, 541–2
Bar-Gera et al (2012) 322, 534
Barnard, P.O. 566
Barrett, C. 371, 398, 587

Subject index